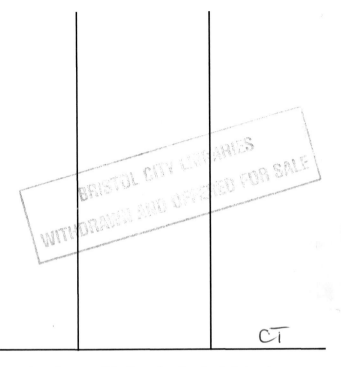
Please return/renew this item by the last date shown on this label, or on your self-service receipt.

To renew this item, visit **www.librarieswest.org.uk** or contact your library

Your borrower number and PIN are required.

THE ASSASSIN'S CLOAK

Alan Taylor has been a journalist for over thirty years. He was deputy editor of the *Scotsman*, managing editor of Scotsman Publications, and writer-at-large for the *Sunday Herald*. He has edited several acclaimed anthologies, most recently *Glasgow: The Autobiography*. He has been a Booker Prize judge. He is the author of *Appointment in Arezzo: A Friendship with Muriel Spark* and, in 2018, series editor of the centenary editions of Spark's novels. He is the co-founder and editor of the *Scottish Review of Books*.

Irene Taylor was born and brought up in Edinburgh. For many years she worked in public libraries. She has a degree in history from Edinburgh University and she now works for the National Trust for Scotland.

'A superb collection . . . Gossipy, funny, perceptive and vicious. Every dip-in is a sheer delight' *Observer*

'Utterly compulsive, thanks, in part, to the excellent editing and the way in which they have allowed the commonplace to co-exist with the sage, the hackneyed with the gnostic. Its cumulative effect is surprisingly moving' *The Times*

'For a delicious daily read, nothing can eclipse *The Assassin's Cloak*. This is the ultimate bedside book' *Daily Mail*

'Wonderful . . . The range of diarists and subjects is remarkable, and the anthology is one to which you will want to return again and again' *Sunday Times*

THE ASSASSIN'S CLOAK

An anthology of the World's Greatest Diarists

Edited by Irene & Alan Taylor

CANONGATE

This new edition first published in Great Britain, the USA and Canada in 2020 by
Canongate Books Ltd, 14 High Street, Edinburgh EH1 1TE

First published in Great Britain in 2000 by
Canongate Books Ltd

Distributed in the USA by Publishers Group West and in Canada by
Publishers Group Canada

canongate.co.uk

1

British Library Cataloguing-in-Publication Data
A catalogue record for this book is available on
request from the British Library

ISBN 978 1 78689 911 8

Book designed by Paddy Cramsie at etal-design.com

Typeset by Palimpsest Book Production Limited,
Falkirk, Stirlingshire

Printed and bound in Great Britain by Clays Ltd, Elcograf S.p.A.

Contents

Introduction

'A diary is like drink,' wrote the Scottish poet, William Soutar, 'we tend to indulge in it over often: it becomes a habit which would ever seduce us to say more than we ought to say and more than we have the experimental qualifications to state.' It must be said that Soutar, bedridden with a wasting illness, was a special case. Trapped from a young age in a small room in his parents' house in Perth, his view of the world circumscribed by the size of his window, he was, in effect, a prisoner. His diary was his constant companion, a visitor who never went away. Thus the temptation to over-indulge.

For many people, however, a diary is like a reproach, a perpetual reminder of our indiscipline, lack of application, weakness of resolve. How many diaries, started in the first flush of a new year, peter out even before the memory of the annual hangover? We open the pristine book with enthusiasm but after a few days what had been a torrent turns into a drip. Soon, whole weeks go by unremarked, blank page followed by blank page. Humdrum life intrudes and the compulsion to memorialise in print evaporates. There are few things quite as capable of inducing guilt as an empty diary.

Soutar, his life cruelly condensed, came to depend on his diary. It was his friend, crutch, confidant, shrink, father confessor, mirror of himself, for a diary is the most flexible and intimate of literary forms. As Thomas Mallon noted in his formative book on the subject, *A Book of One's Own: People and their Diaries*, diaries have been kept by everyone, from the barely literate to the leaders of men and women, from serial killers to conmen, kitchen maids to all-conquering heroes, children and nonagenarians, tinkers, tailors, soldiers and spies.

'Some,' wrote Mallon, 'are chroniclers of the everyday. Others have kept their books only in special times – over the course of a trip, or during a crisis. Some have used them to record journeys of the soul, plan the art of the future, confess the sins of the flesh, lecture the world from beyond the grave. And some of them, prisoners and invalids, have used them not so much to record lives as create them, their diaries being the only world in which they could fully live.'

Into the last category falls William Soutar, who but for his diary and a few verses in Scots for children – 'bairnrhymes' – would now be forgotten. Though he began keeping a diary in 1917, when he was nineteen years old and serving in the Atlantic with the Navy, it comprised little more than brief notes of appointments and books read. His diary took on a fresh complexion, however, after February 1929, when he fell ill with pneumonia. His right leg became increasingly disabled. In hindsight, the prescribed treatment seems medieval; weights were put on the leg to counteract muscle contraction. When this failed, the only hope was surgery. In May 1930, Soutar was operated on, paraphrasing Milton as he went to his fate:

> 'This is the day and this the happy morn.' At 9.30 got morphine and atropine injection. Off to theatre – *sine crepuscula toga* – at 10 a.m. Never saw actual theatre – elderly doctor chloroformed me in the 'green room'. Woke up again at 11.20 or so. Wasn't sick. Not an extra lot of reaction. Plaster of Paris troubling me more than the leg – nasty nobbly part at back – can't lie comfortably.

The operation was unsuccessful but the stoical, philosophical Soutar gives little indication of despair, of the hopelessness of his plight. As Alexander Scott, who edited his diaries, has observed, 'Soutar's main interest was not his own invalidism but the general human situation.' On occasion, he felt frustrated and sorry for himself but more often he managed to transcend his illness, setting himself goals – reading the *Encyclopaedia Britannica*, for example – and pursuing his ambitions. Due to his unusual circumstances, the world had to come to him, rather than the other way round. But unlike many other diarists who are consumed with themselves, egocentrics who seem to live only inside their own heads and are obsessed with their own troubles, Soutar managed to transcend the self, and enter an elevated state of being. Just a month before he died in October 1943, he wrote:

> The true diary is one, therefore, in which the diarist is, in the main, communing with himself, conversing openly and without pose, so that trifles will not be absent, nor the intimate and little confessions and resolutions which, if voiced at all, must be voiced in such a private confessional as this.

That is one definition of a diary but there are countless others that are equally valid. The elasticity of the form is a large part of its appeal, which is perhaps why it is so difficult to pin down. When, truly, is a diary a diary? What is the difference between a diary and journal or, for that matter, a log or a notebook? Dictionary definitions are not much help. *The New Shorter Oxford English Dictionary*, for example, says a diary is 'a daily record of events, transactions, thoughts, etc., esp. ones involving the writer'. A journal, on the other hand, is defined thus: 'A personal record of events or matters of interest, written up every day or as events occur, usu. in more detail than in a diary.'

It is a fine distinction and one which individual writers seem blithely to ignore. In his *Devil's Dictionary*, for instance, Ambrose Bierce wrote: 'Diary. A daily record of that part of one's life which he can relate to himself without blushing.' Oscar Wilde, however, went a step further. 'I never travel without my diary,' he had Gwendoline in *The Importance of Being Earnest* say. 'One should always have something sensational to read in the train.' For others, though, a diary serves more prosaic purposes. 'If a man has no constant lover who shares his soul as well as his body he must have a diary – a poor substitute, but better than nothing,' mused James Lees-Milne.

More often than not, writers question why they do or do not keep a diary. 'Why do I keep this voluminous journal?' asked the Rev. Francis Kilvert. 'I can hardly tell. Partly because life appears to me such a curious and wonderful thing that it almost seems a pity that even such a humble and uneventful life as mine should pass altogether away without some such record as this, and partly too because I think the record may amuse and interest some who come after me.' Sir Walter Scott deemed not keeping a regular diary one of the regrets of his life. But perhaps one of the most curious comments on diary-keeping came from A. A. Milne when he remarked in 1919, 'I suppose this is the reason why diaries are so rarely kept nowadays – that nothing ever happens to anybody.'

The idea that diaries are only worth keeping when great events are in train is barely worthy of examination. The human condition is such that there is always something happening somewhere, whether personally or politically, parochially or on the international stage. The most durable diarists have not always been those who mix in high society or are connected with the great and the good and have the opportunity to keek through the keyhole as momentous events unfold. The best diaries are those in which the voice of the individual comes through untainted by self-censorship or a desire to please. First, and foremost, the diarist must write for himself, those who do not, who are already looking towards publication and public recognition, invariably strike a phoney note. As Alan Clark, author of the most notorious twentieth-century *fin de siècle* diaries, said: 'Sometimes lacking in charity; often trivial; occasionally lewd; cloyingly sentimental, repetitious, whingeing and imperfectly formed. For some readers the entries may seem to be all of these things. But they are real diaries.'

The first real diarist was Samuel Pepys, who may not have patented the form but was certainly instrumental in its development. In the popular imagination a typical entry by Pepys opens with 'Up betimes' and closes 'And so to bed.' In fact, Pepys was much less formulaic than is supposed, though there is an admirable, unaffected directness to his approach, seizing the day with uncommon zest. Born in London on 23 February 1633, he was one of eleven children. His father was a tailor; his mother had been a domestic servant. From such humble beginnings Pepys rose precipitously in the world, which may account for his frequent compulsive and unabashed bouts of stocktaking. He was, even if he said so himself, 'a very rising man'.

Thus, typically, on 30 September, 1664, he reported: 'Up, and all day both morning and afternoon at my accounts, it being a great month both for profit and layings out, the last being £89 for kitchen and clothes for myself and wife, and a few extraordinaries for the house; and my profits, besides salary, £239; so that this weeke my balance come to £1,203, for which the Lord's name be praised!'

Pepys's naive enthusiasm for self-reckoning has been echoed by diarists down the decades, be they writers counting the words they have produced or monies they have made. Arnold Bennett, for example, made it a New Year's Eve ritual. Such record keeping is a valuable function of diaries but were they simply to consist of inventories they would be – as Robert Louis Stevenson said of books – 'a mighty bloodless substitute for life'. Life, unvarnished and uncensored, is what makes Pepys's diary such a constant source of wonder. In every entry, Pepys reveals something of his true self, from his disquiet at discovering that the food he had been served at a friend's house was rotten ('a damned venison pasty that stunk like a devil') to his views on Shakespeare ('the most insipid ridiculous play I ever saw in my life', he called *A Midsummer Night's Dream*) and his unalloyed and unequivocal delight at coming into a legacy.

Pepys, like Boswell in the eighteenth century and Alan Clark in the twentieth, was comically candid about the attractions of women, which he was not always able to resist. His diaries are perhaps at their most piquant when he describes close encounters of a sexual nature, not all of which were consummated. As Thomas Mallon observed, Pepys could forgive a woman almost anything – even spitting on him at the theatre – if she was pretty. At church, he risked groping a girl only to have her threaten to stick pins in him. Undeterred, he groped another. When he actually did succeed in satisfying his lust, he attempted to shroud it in a mongrel language, as he did on 31 March 1668, when he foisted himself on Deb, his servant girl: 'Yo did take her, the first time in my life, sobra mi genu and did poner mi mano sub her jupes and tocu su thigh.'

His delight in this adulterous act is as diverting as his disquiet at the vice at the royal court of 'drinking, swearing and loose amours'. Pepys was a mass of contradictions which serves only to endear him to us further. Nowhere is this more apparent than in his relationship with his wife, Elizabeth, who from her first appearance in his diary (when she burnt her hand dressing the remains of a turkey) to almost her last (when she was troubled with tooth-ache), was the perfect foil for his waywardness and vanity. They were married in 1655, when he was twenty-two and she was just fifteen. So hard up were they that he had to pawn his lute for forty shillings. The route out of penury came through Sir Edward Montagu, later created Earl of Sandwich, who married an aunt to Pepys's father. A close friend of Oliver Cromwell, Montagu was Pepys's mentor and secured his appointment in the Navy Office. From 'clerk of the King's ships', Pepys – a diligent bureaucrat and ardent in stamp-ing out corruption – rose to become secretary to the Admiralty.

In many ways, it was the ideal kind of post for a diarist. Though not hugely powerful himself he nevertheless had access to those charged with running the country. In that regard, Pepys is the predecessor of diarists like Harold Nicolson, whose career as a journalist and politician gave him a unique glimpse of Britain in the 1930s, including the rise of fascism, the influence of the Bloomsbury group and the Abdication crisis, and Sir Henry Channon, a charmer from Chicago who made a rapid rise in English society between the two world wars. Channon was well aware of the tradition in which he was following. 'Although I am not Clerk to the Council like Mr Greville nor Secretary to the Admiralty like Mr Pepys, nor yet "duc et pair" as was M. de St Simon, I have, nevertheless, had interesting opportunities of inti-macy with interesting people and have often been at the centre of things.'

Channon – or 'Chips', as he was nicknamed – was in no doubt that his diaries would one day be made available for public consumption. 'I some-times wonder,' he wrote in November 1936, 'why I keep a diary at all. Is it to relieve my feelings? Console my old age? or to dazzle my descendants?' Some fifteen years later he added, 'I feel that some day they may see the light of day and perhaps shock or divert posterity a little.' With that in mind he deposited his diaries in the British Museum with the initial instruction that they should not be consulted or published until fifty years after his death. But in the last year of his life he had a change of heart, and he began to edit them himself.

Chips's ambivalence is echoed by many other diarists, not least the great Pepys, who laboured over his diary in the wee small hours with the light weak and his eyesight failing. He began writing his diary on an auspicious date, the beginning of a new year and a new decade, 1 January 1660, and continued for almost ten years, bringing it to a reluctant close on 31 May 1669, believing that he was about to go blind. In the annals of diarists there has rarely been a more moving entry than that with which Pepys brought down the curtain on his work:

> And thus ends all that I doubt I shall ever be able to do with my own eyes in the keeping of my Journal, I being not able to do it any longer, having done now so long as to undo my eyes almost every time that I take a pen in my hand; and therefore whatever comes of it I must forbear: and therefore resolve from this time forward to have it kept by my people in long-hand, and must therefore be contented to set down no more than is fit for them and all the world to know; or if there be any thing (which cannot be much, now my amours to Deb are past, and my eyes hindering me in almost all other pleasures), I must endeavour to keep a margin in my book open, to add here and there a note in short-hand with my own hand.
>
> And so I betake myself to that course, which is almost as much as to see myself go into my grave: for which, and all the discomforts that will accompany my being blind, the good God prepare me!

Ironically, Pepys did not go blind and lived for another thirty-four years. His diary, his lasting memorial, which was written in shorthand, he had bound in leather in six volumes, not the act of a man who did not want to see them preserved. With the rest of his library, they were deposited at Magdalene College, Cambridge, where they lay undeciphered until 1825. In the opinion of O. F. Morshead, editor of a very popular but heavily censored edition of the diaries, the impetus to break the code may have been prompted by the publication in 1818 of the diaries of Pepys's contemporary John Evelyn. It is a tradition at Magdalene that Lord Grenville took one of the volumes to bed and by morning had worked out how to translate it. The entire diary was then handed over to John Smith, an undergraduate, who made a complete transcription. Working twelve hours a day, it took him more than three years to make a complete transcription of in excess of three thousand pages. It was, said Smith, 'very trying and injurious indeed to the visual organs'.

But however onerous the task it was justified by the finished work. Pepys was a fluent, engaging and observant chronicler, combining history, reportage and autobiography in a style reminiscent of a superior novelist who can describe a scene and catch the essence of a character in a few broad and eloquent brush strokes. From his own quirky, irksome and fascinating domestic arrangements to the Great Fire of London and the misery of the Plague, Pepys illuminated the essence of his age better than anyone before or since. His curiosity was boundless, his lack of self-consciousness intoxicating. His diaries show him warts and all, holding back nothing that is unflattering, of which there was much, particularly in regard to his wife, who, in her own 'diary', inspired by the feminist scholar, Dale Spender, describes his meanness, infidelity, heavy drinking and abuse. But despite his failings Pepys was a loving husband.

He had the true writer's ability to drop or raise his tempo as the situation demands. But more often than not he is most affecting when one anticipates it least, whether describing a chance encounter with a shepherd and his son whom he found reading the Bible to one another on Epsom Downs or relaying his disgust at the sycophancy shown to King Charles II when he plays tennis ('to see how the King's play was extolled without any cause at all was a loathsome sight').

In contrast to Pepys, John Evelyn was altogether more reserved and puritanical but while his diary pales in comparison with his more famous contemporary it has its own idiosyncratic appeal. Evelyn came from a family which had made its fortune in gunpowder and he was well enough off to live independently, travelling extensively around Europe, which he recorded colourfully. He made his name with *Sylva, a Discourse of Forest Trees*, a book on arboriculture, which proved very popular with landowners intent on improving their estates after the Civil Wars and Interregnum.

His diary begins, precociously, in 1620, during the reign of James I, when he was born and from the first he seemed to possess uncanny powers of description. His mother, he recalled, was 'of proper personage, well timber'd, of a browne complexion; her eyes and haire of a lovely black; of a constitution more inclyn'd to a religious Melancholy, or pious sadnesse; of a rare memory, and most exemplary life; for Oeconomiq pridence esteemed'd one of the most conspicuous in her Country.'

Its final entry ('The Raine and a taw upon a deepe Snow, hindred me from going to Church.') was made in January 1706 in the reign of Queen Anne and the year of Evelyn's death at the age of 85. A large part of it, however, was written in hindsight; only from 1684 onwards did it become a contemporary diary, with Evelyn's eye for the exotic immediately to the fore. 'I dined at Sir St: Foxes,' he recorded on 2 January 1684. 'After dinner came a felow that eate live charcoale glowing ignited, quenching them in his mouth, and then chanping and swallowing them downe: There was a dog also that seemd to do many rational actions.'

But assiduous though Evelyn was in keeping his diary, it was meant for his eyes only. No publication was ever intended and it only came to light through pure fluke in 1813 when Lady Evelyn, the widow of the diarist's great-great-grandson, was talking to William Upcott, a librarian and biblio-phile, at the family house in Surrey. Asked his hobbies, Upcott replied, 'Collecting manuscripts and autographs,' whereupon her ladyship opened a drawer and revealed a pile of manuscripts which had been used for cutting out patterns for a dress. Upcott instantly appreciated their significance and Lady Evelyn volunteered to show him more. 'Oh,' she declared, 'if you like papers like that, you shall have plenty, for *Sylva* Evelyn and those who succeeded him kept all their correspondence, which has furnished the kitchen with an abundance of waste paper.' And so the diaries – the *Kalendarium* – were discovered.

Lady Evelyn herself was unconvinced of their worth, and was reluctant to publish them. But shortly before her death she gave permission to a local antiquary to make the first selection, which appeared in 1818 with the title *Memoirs Illustrative of the Life and Writings of John Evelyn*, and while they sold well were soon eclipsed by Pepys's earthier and more appealing diaries. Interestingly, the two men knew each other and commemorated their meet-ings. For his part, Pepys found the bee-keeping Evelyn to be a merry dining companion, a cut above him intellectually: 'In fine, a most excellent person he is, and must be allowed a little for a little conceitedness.'

Evelyn, in turn, liked Pepys and visited him at the Tower, where he had been committed, unjustly in Evelyn's view, for misdemeanours in the Admiralty. On his death, Evelyn wrote generously of him, describing him as 'a very worthy, Industrious and curious person, none in England exceeding him in knowledge of the Navy'. Pepys had been his friend for almost forty years and requested that he be a pall-bearer at his funeral but Evelyn, himself incapacitated, was unable to attend.

The successful publication of these two diaries in the nineteenth century undoubtedly proved a spur to others to follow in their tracks. A diary, at least to begin with, is not a daunting prospect, like an epic poem, say, or a play or a novel. There is no imperative to publish or show anyone how it is progressing. You don't need to do any research or check facts. Entries can be long or short, factual or inaccurate, real or imagined. Though diarists, invariably, attempt to keep up a daily routine they just as invariably fail. Life has its insidious way of interrupting the flow. Some diarists take this in their stride while it throws others into a spin, as if they had forgotten to turn up for a dinner party or missed a job interview.

Time after time one comes across diarists chastising themselves for their laziness, their inconstancy, their lack of fidelity to a diary which they address as they might a lover. For communion with a diary is unlike any other literary activity. Once a diarist, always a diarist, it seems. A diary becomes part of a diarist's routine, an integral part of his or her household, a member of the family which needs to be nurtured like a baby or a pet kitten. Neglect is conspicuous but it need not be harmful, for silence has its own eloquence. While many diarists write entries daily, as if brushing their teeth, others let weeks and months go by without so much as writing a few lines.

Some diarists, such as Walter Scott, write during times of emotional and financial crisis, others when they are at their most happy and socially active. Evelyn Waugh, one of the greatest twentieth-century diarists, kept a diary for diverse reasons, wrote the editor of his diaries, Michael Davie, as an *aide-memoire* and as a source of material for his novels and autobiography. 'Fading memory and a senile itch to write to the *Times* on all topics have determined me to keep irregular notes of what passes through my mind,' he wrote in 1960, when he started his diary again after a break of some four years. Waugh, in common with most diarists, wrote with no intention of seeing his diary in the public domain and died before the decision was taken to publish it. He wrote privately and did not tell many of his friends that he kept a diary. Even his wife did not know. Though not by nature furtive, he seemed to want to keep his diaries to himself. Why, no one knows.

In contrast, the artist Andy Warhol, whose fame, among other things, comes from his saying that in future everyone in the world will be famous for fifteen minutes, liked to dictate his diary to an amanuensis, Pat Hackett. In her introduction to his diaries, she wrote:

I'd call Andy around 9 am, never later than 9:30. Sometimes I'd be waking him up, sometimes he'd say he'd been awake for hours. If I happened to oversleep he'd call *me* and say something like, 'Good morning, Miss Diary – what's wrong with *you*?' or 'Sweetheart! You're fired!' The calls were always conversations. We'd warm up while just chatting – he was always curious about everything, he'd ask a million questions: 'What are you having for breakfast? Do you have channel 7 on? How can I clean my can opener – should I do it with a toothbrush?' Then he'd give me his cash expenses and then he'd tell me all about the day and night before. Nothing was too insignificant for him to tell the Diary. These sessions – what he referred to as my 'five-minutes-a-day job' – would actually take anywhere from one to two hours. Every other week or so, I'd go over to the office with the typed pages of each day's entry and I'd staple to the back of every page all the loose cab and restaurant receipts he'd left for me in the interim – receipts that corresponded to the amounts he'd already told me over the phone. The pages were then stored in letter boxes from the stationery store.

Perhaps because of the way they were composed Warhol's diaries read like an extended gossip column. Names are dropped with insouciance reflecting the diarist's own celebrity. He moved in a world in which everyone was famous because they knew him. He was in the habit, says Pat Hackett, of referring to people as 'superstars', be they 'the most beautiful model in New York or the delivery boy who brought her a pack of cigarettes'.

Would one be so interested in Warhol's diaries if they did not contain the litany of rock stars, actors and artists, designers and writers? Perhaps not. But each diarist is an individual describing his or her life, for which they need make no excuses. As Kilvert indicated, curiosity is not the least of the attractions of reading a diary. Until the present age, when it is possible if one is so inclined to view every moment of complete strangers' lives via the Internet, a diary was the closest one could get to understanding the way people lived and thought. Reading Kilvert, for example, is to get inside the mind of a nineteenth-century English country parson. His diary runs from 1870 to 1879, almost the same span as Pepys's, but it came to light only in 1937 when the poet, novelist and critic William Plomer received 22 notebooks. His selection from them was published between 1938 and 1940.

So far, so straightforward. But Plomer, avowedly because he was pressed for space, destroyed the typed manuscript he had made of the notebooks, convinced that the originals would be preserved. They were not and out of the original 22 notebooks only two survive. We know, too, that Kilvert's wife, to whom he was married only a matter of months before he died, destroyed others of his diaries. It is a very odd case and raises more questions than can be answered. What is particularly controversial, however, is Plomer's assertion that he had retained everything of the diaries which was worth preserving. 'I can assure you,' he wrote in his selection, 'that the best and most essential parts of the Diary are in print. I left out what seemed to me commonplace and trivial.'

It is hard to see Plomer's action as other than arrogance. Without the commonplace and the trivial the best diaries would be bereft of much that makes them compelling and enduringly fascinating. Looking back over the diaries of the Rev. James Woodforde or Dorothy Wordsworth or even Josef Goebbels it is that which many people might not deem worth recording which sheds the most brilliant light on the diarist's character or illuminates the times in which they lived. Often, one is struck by the ability of great diarists to combine in a single entry news either momentous or terrifying, or both, with some minor observation or irritation of everyday life. It is in a diary that our private world imperceptibly merges with the cataclysmic events which make headlines in every language.

There are around 170 diarists in this anthology. Many of those represented are well known and many are not. There are diaries, of course, everyone wishes had been written. What wouldn't we give to read Shakespeare's diary, or that of Jesus or Mozart or Michelangelo? If everyone left behind a diary many unsolved mysteries could be cleared up. Would the conspiracy theorists still be in a job if Marilyn Monroe or JFK had written diaries of their relationship? Sometimes we almost wish diaries into being, so overwhelming is the desire to peep behind the arras of history. There is the unfortunate case of the Hitler diaries which fooled an eminent historian and a group of over-eager senior journalists who could scarcely believe their luck. Sadly, the diaries of him whose name is a byword for man's inhumanity to man proved to be fakes, causing exquisite embarrassment to all involved in their authentication and publication. That there have been many other spoof diaries did not sweeten the pill. At least in the case of the Holocaust there were many un-assailable witnesses to appalling actions of a state hell-bent on wiping out an entire race, many of whom are to be found in the pages that follow.

The idea of this anthology grew out of columns in two Scottish newspapers,

Scotland on Sunday and *The Scotsman*. Each week extracts from diaries for the corresponding period in the past were published, giving contemporary readers a flavour of what it was like in either the recent or the distant past. This book is an amplification of those columns. Entries are arranged day by day in chronological order throughout the year, an arrangement pioneered by Simon Brett in his diverting compilation *The Faber Book of Diaries*. Some days have more entries than others, depending on what our reading turned up. No day, unlike a real diary, has been left blank. The overriding principle of inclusion was enjoyment. Each of the 1800 or so entries was chosen because we believe it to be complete in itself, though some contribute to running stories which unfold as the year progresses. The book may be read continuously or dipped into as the days drift by. You pays your money and you takes your choice, but it's worth bearing in mind that pleasure delayed is pleasure doubly heightened.

All the diarists have been published commercially, whether or not that was their intention, but some are now out of print. Having sampled them, readers may like to seek them out in their original context. Every attempt has been made to keep the scope of the anthology as wide as possible. Diverse nationalities, ranging in date from the seventeenth century to the present day, are represented but not out of any sense of duty. Nor was there any thought of who made the ideal diarist. Here be cads and countrymen, wits and drones, neurotics, nymphomaniacs and narcissists.

All human life is here. But not every diarist. Some were excluded because they are dull (George Gissing and Søren Kierkegaard being notable examples) others because their diaries are not dated (John Cheever and Fyodor Dostoyevsky to name but two who are conspicuous by their absence) and therefore proved unsuitable for extraction. Still others, while diarists of a high order, such as Anne Frank, have fewer entries than might be expected because their diaries work as complete entities whose potency is diminished when quoted selectively. A few fictional diaries, including Adrian Mole and George and Weedon Grossmith's classic *Diary of a Nobody*, have been used, but sparingly.

The diary, as Thomas Mallon concluded, is a genre to which 'it is impossible to ascribe formulas and standards'. Ultimately, any attempt at definition is defeated by the diarists themselves, who are the most singular of species. More than any other branch of literature, diaries revel in otherness. Like a chameleon, a diary can change its colour to suit the mood of its keeper. It can be whatever the diarist wants it to be. Kafka used his to pour out his angst and limber up for his novels and short stories; Dorothy Wordsworth brought her botanical eye to the landscape of the Lake District, providing rich source material which her brother William mined for his poetry; Virginia Woolf spoke to hers as she might to an intimate friend, in so doing etching a portrait of the artist on the edge of the abyss.

All contributed to the mosaic that is life. But one keeps coming back to William Soutar, lying on his back in bed as his health evaporated. His diary is an inspiration; it may be the work of a dying man but he lived for the moment. Soutar sagely realised better than most the ambiguous potential of a diary, imbued as it inevitably is with secrecy, and all it implies. A diary may be like drink, but it is also only as reliable as the diarist, who may be honest or corrupt or deceitful or a self-delusionist. Not only can it persuade us to betray the self, wrote Soutar, 'it tempts us to betray our fellows also, becoming thereby an *alter ego* sharing with us the denigrations which we would be ashamed of voicing aloud; a diary is an assassin's cloak which we wear when we stab a comrade in the back with a pen. And here is this diary proving its culpability to its own harm – for how much on this page is true to the others?'

Alan Taylor
August 2000

Acknowledgements

Many people have contributed to this anthology, sometimes unsuspectingly. Throughout its long genesis countless suggestions have been made. Some bore fruit; others were added to the compost heap of rejection; all were very welcome. Two newspapers, *Scotland on Sunday* and *The Scotsman*, were enlightened enough to run diary columns for some years and their then editors deserve our thanks. In an enterprise such as this libraries play an essential role, none more so than Edinburgh City Libraries, principally the Central Lending Library whose long-suffering staff were unfailingly helpful. From the outset, our publisher, Canongate, provided enthusiasm, commitment and ideas, many of which have significantly improved the quality of the book. In particular, Jamie Byng and Judy Moir ferreted out diarists we had overlooked or never heard of and were a constant source of advice. Our biggest debt of gratitude, however, is to the diarists whose personal revelations and indiscreet observations made this anthology such fun to compile.

Irene and Alan Taylor
August 2000

JANUARY

*'The life of every man is a diary in which he
means to write one story, and writes another; and
his humblest hour is when he compares the volume
as it is with that he vowed to make it.'*

J. M. BARRIE

1 January

1662

Waking this morning out of my sleep on a sudden, I did with my elbow hit my wife a great blow over her face and nose, which waked her with pain, at which I was sorry, and to sleep again.

Samuel Pepys

1763

I went to Louisa at one. 'Madam, I have been thinking seriously.' 'Well, Sir, I hope you are of my way of thinking.' 'I hope, Madam, you are of mine. I have considered this matter most seriously. The week is now elapsed, and I hope you will not be so cruel as to keep me in misery.' (I then began to take some liberties.) 'Nay, Sir – now – but do consider–' 'Ah, Madam!' 'Nay, but you are an encroaching creature!' (Upon this I advanced to the greatest freedom by a sweet elevation of the charming petticoat.) 'Good heaven, Sir!' 'Madam, I cannot help it. I adore you. Do you like me?' (She answered me with a warm kiss, and pressing me to her bosom, sighed, 'O Mr Boswell!') 'But, my dear Madam! Permit me, I beseech you.' 'Lord, Sir, the people may come in.' 'How then can I be happy? What time? Do tell me.' 'Why, Sir, on Sunday afternoon my land-lady, of whom I am most afraid, goes to church, so you may come here a little after three.' 'Madam, I thank you a thousand times.'

James Boswell

1829

Having omitted to carry on my diary for two or three days, I lost heart to make it up, and left it unfilld for many a month and day. During this period nothing has happend worth particular notice. The same occupations, the same amusements, the same occasional alterations of spirits, gay or depressd, the same absence of all sensible or rational cause for the one or the other – I half grieve to take up my pen, and doubt if it is worth while to record such an infinite quantity of nothing. But hang it! I hate to be beat so here goes for better behaviour.

Sir Walter Scott

1866

Travelling in France, it is a misfortune to be a Frenchman. The wing of the chicken at a *table d'hôte* always goes to the Englishman. He is the only person the waiter serves. Why is this? Because the Englishman does not look upon the waiter as a man, and any servant who feels that he is being regarded as a human being despises the person considering him in that light.

The Brothers Goncourt

1902

What I have to write today is terribly sad. I called on Gustav – in the afternoon we were alone in his room. He gave me his body – & I let him touch me with his hand. Stiff and upright stood his vigour. He carried me to the sofa, laid me gently down and swung himself over me. Then – just as I felt him penetrate, he lost all strength. He laid his head on my breast, shattered – and almost wept for shame. Distraught as I was, I comforted him.

We drove home, dismayed and dejected. He grew a little more cheerful. Then I broke down, had to weep, weep on his breast. What if he were to lose – that! My poor, poor, husband!

I can scarcely say how irritating it all was. First his intimate caresses, so close – and then no satisfaction. Words cannot express what I today have undeservedly suffered, and then to observe his torment – his unbelievable torment!

My beloved!

Alma Mahler-Werfel

1914

What a vile little diary! But I am determined to keep it this year.

Katherine Mansfield

1915

We were kept awake last night by New Year Bells. At first I thought they were ringing for a victory.

Virginia Woolf

1970 [Ardnamurchan, Scotland]

As I was up long before the other members of the household I carried out the old ritual of going out by the back door, and bringing in a lump of coal by the front door. After that I did my usual daily stint of lighting the fire and making their morning tea for the sleepers! Some showers before daylight. Forenoon damp with intermittent smirr and hill fog. Wind Westerly, light to moderate, at first but veered Northwesterly in the evening. Showers from mid-day onwards. Afternoon and evening raw and cold. No sunshine. Apart from [his wife] Eliz's illness, the year just ended was a good one for us in every way. No post tonight.

Ian Maclean

1983

New Year's Day

These are my New Year resolutions:

1. I will revise for my 'O' levels at least two hours a night.
2. I will stop using my mother's Buff-Puff to clean the bath.
3. I will buy a suede brush for my coat.
4. I will stop thinking erotic thoughts during school hours.
5. I will oil my bike once a week.
6. I will try to like Bert Baxter again.
7. I will pay my library fines (88 pence) and rejoin the library.
8. I will get my mother and father together again.
9. I will cancel the *Beano*.

Adrian Mole

2 January

1763

I got dinner to be at two, and at three I hastened to my charmer.

Here a little speculation on the human mind may well come in. For here was I, a young man full of vigour and vivacity, the favourite lover of a handsome actress and going to enjoy the full possession of my warmest wishes. And yet melancholy threw a cloud over my mind. I could relish nothing. I felt dispirited and languid. I approached Louisa with a kind of an uneasy tremor. I sat down. I toyed with her. Yet I was not inspired by Venus. I felt rather a delicate sensation of love than a violent amorous inclination for her. I was very miserable. I thought myself feeble as a gallant, although I had experienced the reverse many a time. Louisa knew not my powers. She might imagine me impotent. I sweated with anxiety, which made me worse. She behaved extremely well; did not seem to remember the occasion of our meeting at all. I told her I was very dull. Said she, 'People cannot always command their spirits.' The time of church was almost elapsed when I began to feel that I was still a man. I fanned the flame by pressing her alabaster breasts and kissing her delicious lips. I then barred the door of her dining-room, led her all fluttering into her bedchamber, and was just making a triumphal entry when we heard her landlady coming up. 'O Fortune why did it happen thus?' would have been the exclamation of a Roman bard. We were stopped most suddenly and cruelly from the fruition of each other. She ran out and stopped the landlady from coming up. Then returned to me in the dining-room. We fell into each other's arms, sighing and panting, 'O dear, how hard this is.' 'O Madam see what you can contrive for me.' 'Lord, Sir, I am so frightened.'

Her brother then came in. I recollected that I had been at no place of worship today. I begged pardon for a little and went to Church . . . I heard a few prayers then returned and drank tea . . . I went home at seven. I was unhappy at being prevented from the completion of my wishes, and yet I thought that I had saved my credit for prowess, that I might through anxiety have not acted a vigorous part; and that we might contrive a meeting where I could love with ease and freedom.

James Boswell

1926

I went to tea at Sumner Place and we went on to dinner at a new restaurant called Favas which Richard has discovered which is very cheap indeed. I gave Richard the ties I had bought in Paris. I enjoyed the evening very much.

On Sunday I was bored.

On Monday I went to luncheon at Sumner Place and to a cinema in Shaftesbury Avenue to see the new Harold Lloyd film. Richard found an harlot who took us to drink at a club called John's in Gerard Street where there was a slot machine which gave me a lot of money and Alfred Duggan who gave me a lot of brandy. We went to dinner again at Favas with Anthony Russell. He brought me back and I made him drunk.

Evelyn Waugh

1926 [Paris]

Talk turned largely on mutual acquaintances: Diaghilev, Cocteau, Radiguet. When I spoke about the Russian Ballet's miraculous salvation and rejuvenation through war and revolution, Misia told us how badly off Diaghilev had been during the war. In Spain he nearly starved. It took months before the French Government granted him an entry permit, but at last Sert was able to fetch him from Barcelona. On the way to the frontier he asked Diaghilev whether he had anything compromising on him. No, nothing at all, he never carried anything compromising on him. Well, at any rate look whether you haven't anything in your pockets, Sert urged him. Only a few old letters. Yes, but what letters? Finally Diaghilev brought out a fat wad of papers, including two letters from Mata Hari. The French had just arrested her for espionage. There was barely time to destroy the correspondence before they reached the frontier.

Count Harry Kessler

1952

After tea I went to visit Khalid's surgery, where he treats the poor of Baghdad for free – a really horrifying experience which I could hardly bear to watch.

Half the men were suffering from stab wounds and broken heads, but there were also wretched women with ulcerous breasts and babies with rickets. Khalid was examining a woman who had some problem with her womb when her mother burst in screaming and shouting and dragged her out of the surgery. Apparently because the operation might mean she could bear no more sons, it was forbidden, so she will probably die in childbirth.

Maurice's students at the college are much more emancipated. They arrive shrouded in black abbas which they throw off to reveal tight-fitting skirts and sweaters with 'Wisconsin' printed on them. All the girls are in love with Mo because he is tall and blond. Unfortunately he has an awful habit of scratching his crotch when carried away by his own eloquence, and halfway through a lecture on Chaucer he'll notice fifty pairs of beady eyes glued to his trousers. Their work is excellent but erratic as they have a great desire to be colloquial – a splendid analysis of Hamlet's Act 1 will be followed by 'Well cheerio, so long, old sport – see you in Act 2!'

Joan Wyndham

1966

Went out and got the papers. The usual load of rubbish, apart from an interesting piece by Philip Toynbee on the boring pointlessness of the writing of Beckett and Burroughs. He should have cast his net wider, to include Osborne. He made the point that this kind of writing treats of despair despairingly. He rightly says that this is a fundamental misconception of Art.

Kenneth Williams

1978 [in Barlinnie Prison]

3.14am. I've been wakened for over an hour, am irritable and restless. The Radio Clyde disc jockey is speaking to people in their homes via telephone. I get the atmosphere of home parties from it. Pop music is blasting in my ears and I marvel at radio and how it must comfort lonely people. It's almost as though it's reassuring me I'm not alone. 3.55am. One of these days I won't be 'still here'. It's amazing how difficult I find it to think of myself being anywhere else.

Jimmy Boyle

1990

I seem to be the only Western playwright not personally acquainted with the new President of Czechoslovakia [Václav Havel]. I envy him though. What a relief to find oneself head of state and not have to write plays but just make history. And no Czechoslovak equivalent of Charles Osborne snapping at your ankles complaining that the history you're making falls between every possible stool, or some Prague Steven Berkoff snarling that it's not the kind of history that's worth making anyway. I wonder whether Havel has lots of uncompleted dissident plays. To put them on now would be somehow inappropriate. Still, he could write a play about it.

Alan Bennett

3 January

1853

I love Nature partly *because* she is not man, but a retreat from him. None of his institutions control or pervade her. There a different kind of right prevails. In her midst I can be glad with an entire gladness. If this world were all man, I could not stretch myself, I should lose all hope. He is constraint, she is freedom to me. He makes me wish for another world. She makes me content with this.

H. D. Thoreau

1870

I went to see old Isaac Giles. He lamented the loss of his famous old pear tree. He told me he was nearly 80 and remembered seeing the Scots Greys passing through Chippenham on their way to Waterloo. They looked very much down, he said, for they knew where they were going.

Rev. Francis Kilvert

1902

Bliss and rapture.

Alma Mahler-Werfel

1915

It is strange how old traditions, so long buried as one thinks, suddenly crop up again. At Hyde Park Gate we used to set apart Sunday morning for cleaning the table silver. Here I find myself keeping Sunday morning for odd jobs – typewriting it was today – and tidying the room – and doing accounts which are very complicated this week. I have three little bags of coppers, which each owe the other something. We went to a concert at the Queen's Hall, in the afternoon. Considering that my ears have been pure of music for some weeks, I think patriotism is a base emotion. By this I mean that they played a National Anthem and a hymn, and all I could feel was the entire absence of emotion in myself and everyone else. If the British spoke openly about WCs, and copulation, then they might be stirred by universal emotions. As it is, an appeal to feel together is hopelessly muddled by intervening greatcoats and fur coats. I begin to loathe my kind, principally from looking at their faces in the tube. Really, raw red beef and silver herrings give me more pleasure to look upon.

Virginia Woolf

1932

On my way back to Missouri I stopped in St Louis and I saw my first bread line – 200 starving men forming a gray line as they waited for food. The sight of them disturbed me.

Edward Robb Ellis

1940

James Thurber of the *New Yorker* is in Baltimore this week, revising a play. It is being performed at the Maryland theatre, and apparently needs considerable rewriting. Paul Patterson entertained Thurber at the *Sun* office yesterday, and I had a chance to talk with him. He was full of curious stuff about Ross, editor of the *New Yorker*. He said that Ross never reads anything except *New Yorker* manuscripts. His library consists of three books. One is Mark Twain's 'Life on the Mississippi'; the second is a book by a man named Spencer, falsely assumed by Ross to be Herbert Spencer, and the third is a treatise on the migration of eels. Despite this avoidance of reading Ross is a first-rate editor. More than once, standing out against the advice of all of his staff, he has proved ultimately that he was right. Thurber said that he is a philistine in all the other arts. He regards painting as a kind of lunacy, and music as almost immoral.

H. L. Mencken

1973

It has been nearly three weeks since I last wrote in this diary. At Christmas time the world goes dead and this now extends into the New Year. Ireland remains as violent as ever; we continue to offer the other cheek to Uganda and Iceland; labour relations have been relatively quiet over the holidays, the Vietnam war is on again, off again; Nixon begins his new term of office with an appalling world press; the newspapers, of course, are filled with our joining the European Community. I supported this cause in the *Daily Mirror*, long before other newspapers or Macmillan took it up. I still think it is not the best policy, but it is the only one, and the antics of Wilson and the Labour party are contemptible. But is it not mistimed? All European countries are faced with uncontrolled inflation and, as well, we have many problems unsolved from Ireland to labour relations, Italy is hanging on the edge of civil war and

France is not all that much better. May we not have signed the Treaty of Rome just before the collapse? Official comment is so widely optimistic on every subject that it is hard to judge what is really happening. We even have a new doctrine that optimism is a patriotic duty – criticism or even cautious comment are little better than sabotage. And in the meanwhile every problem is to be settled by negotiation and goodwill. No one must actually stand firm on anything – except in a demand for more money.

Cecil King

4 January

1664

To the Tennis Court and there saw the King play at Tennis, and others; but to see how the King's play was extolled without any cause at all was a loathsome sight, though sometimes indeed he did play very well and deserved to be commended; but such open flattery is beastly.

Samuel Pepys

1848

Such a beautiful day, that one felt quite confused how to make the most of it, and accordingly frittered it away.

Caroline Fox

1902

Rapture without end.

Alma Mahler-Werfel

1903 [*Discovery* expedition to Antarctica]

Epiphany Sunday. Good juicy brown beef dripping is one thing I long for, and a large jugful of fresh creamy milk in Crippetts dairy. Killed another dog today as he was too weak to walk. We turned out at 6 a.m., had breakfast and were on the march by 8.30 a.m. And though the surface was very heavy with ice crystals, soft and deep and smooth, there being no sun to glaze the surface, we did 4 and a half miles by lunch time, when the Captain [Scott] took a sight, but it was too overcast all over the land for me to sketch. We had an hour's rest and then made 3 and a half miles more in the afternoon. We have now only 8 dogs and they are good for no work at all. We camped at 4.30 p.m., when sky cleared over the land, but a cold breeze from the north made sketching impossible. We are all now pulling on foot in finnesko all day, heavy work for 7 hours or more, soft ice crystals with no crust. The sledges go very heavily when there is no sun, but run easily as soon as the sun comes out. I think much on the march of our return to the ship, when we shall I hope, find all our letters waiting for us. Le bon temps viendra.

Edward Wilson

1922

The snow is thicker, it clings to the branches like white new-born puppies.

Katherine Mansfield

1935

Now that I am growing older and can see young folks isolated from me by a number of years, I am sometimes halted by the thought, when looking on them: 'Is it a fact that my own youth ended at 24?' This, of course, is a time when the joys of physical freedom are emphasized, and the pleasures that gather around a home of one's own. And with this emphasis comes the thought that we are but human once, and that to be able to joy in action is a great privilege. The thought, of course, is but fleeting – for it is folly to brood: and has not one known the joy – which is enough; and are there not many who have never known it?

William Soutar

1953

I think that people who manifest their love for you, physically, when they know your lack of reciprocation, are abominably selfish. Sooner or later, the relationship *must* suffer, however noble its beginnings. I must be comparatively under sexed or something for I have never particularly wanted to make physical love to anybody. All this touching and kissing which seems so popular among others passes me by. Denis Goacher knows I'm virgin, and is always saying that I make up for it by flirting continually. He says I should *do* something. He can't believe I could be abnormal. To him, everyone must do something or die! Perhaps I am dead.

Kenneth Williams

1958

New year four days gone, along with resolutions of a page a day, describing mood, fatigue, orange peel or color of bathtub water after a week's scrub. Penalty, and escape, both: four pages to catch up. Air lifts, clears. The black yellow-streaked smother of October, November, December, gone and clear New Year's air come – so cold it turns bare shins, ears and cheeks to a bone of ice-ache. Yet sun, lying low on the fresh white paint of the storeroom

door, reflecting in the umber-ugly paint coating the floorboards, and shaft-
ing a slant on the mauve-rusty rosy lavender rug from the west gable window.
Changes: what breaks windows to thin air, blue views, in a smother-box? A
red twilly shirt for Christmas: Chinese red with black-line scrolls and oriental green ferns to wear every day against light blue walls. Ted's job chance at
teaching just as long and just as much as we need. $1000 or $2000 clear
savings for Europe. Vicarious joy at Ted's writing which opens promise for
me too: *New Yorker's* 3rd poem acceptance and a short story for *Jack and Jill*.
1958: the year I stop teaching and start writing. Ted's faith: don't expect: just
write: what? It will take months to get my inner world peopled, and the
people moving. How else to do it but plunge out of this safe scheduled time-
clock wage-check world into my own voids. Distant planets spin: I dream
too much of fame, posturings, a novel into print. But with no job, no money
worries, why, the black lid should lift. Look at life with humor: easy to say:
things open up: know people: horizons extend . . .

Sylvia Plath

5 January

1821 [Ravenna]
Rose late – dull and drooping – the weather dripping and dense. Snow on
the ground, and sirocco above in the sky, like yesterday. Roads up to the horse's
belly, so that riding (at least for pleasure) is not very feasible. Read the conclusion, for the fiftieth time (I have read all W. Scott's novels at least fifty times)
of the third series of 'Tales of my Landlord', – grand work – Scotch Fielding,
as well as great English poet – wonderful man! I long to get drunk with him.

Dined versus six o'the clock. Forgot that there was a plum-pudding, (I
have added, lately, *eating* to my 'family of vices,') and had dined before I knew
it. Drank half a bottle of some sort of spirits – probably spirits of wine; for
what they call brandy, rum, &c. &c., here is nothing but spirits of wine,
coloured accordingly. Did *not* eat two apples which were placed by way of
dessert. Fed the two cats, the hawk, and the tame, (but *not tamed*) crow. Read
Mitford's History of Greece – Xenophon's Retreat of the Ten Thousand. Up
to this present moment writing, 6 minutes before eight o' the clock – French
hours, not Italian.

Hear the carriage – order pistols and great coat, as usual – necessary articles. Weather cold – carriage open, and inhabitants somewhat savage – rather
treacherous and highly inflamed by politics. Fine fellows, though, – good
materials for a nation. Out of chaos God made a world, and out of high
passions comes a people.

Clock strikes – going out to make love. Somewhat perilous, but not disagreeable. Memorandum – a new screen put up to-day. It is rather antique, but will do with a little repair.

Lord Byron

1918

We went to Hampton Court. We walked across Bushby park, and along a raised bank beneath trees to the river. It was cold, but still. Then we took a tram to Kingston and had tea at Atkinsons, where one may have no more than a single bun. Everything is skimped now. Most of the butcher's shops are shut; the only open shop was besieged. You can't buy chocolates, or toffee; flowers cost so much I have to pick leaves instead. We have cards for most foods. The only abundant shop windows are the drapers. Other shops parade tins, or cardboard boxes, doubtless empty. (This is an attempt at the concise, historic style.) I suppose there must be some undisturbed pockets of luxury somewhere still; but the general table is pretty bare. Papers, however, flourish, and by spending sixpence we are supplied with enough to light a week's fires.

Virginia Woolf

1940

So far as politics and the war are concerned, everything is quiet as the grave. But Roosevelt has spoken to the House of Representatives. Covert but very malicious jibes against our regime and the Reich. He says he still hopes to keep America out of the war. That sounds anything but hopeful.

... The Russians are making absolutely no progress in Finland. The Red Army really does seem to be of very little military worth.

In London there is great outrage about our radio broadcasts in English. Our announcer has been given the nickname 'Lord Haw-Haw'. He is causing talk, and that is already half the battle. The aim in London is to create an equivalent figure for the German service. This would be the best thing that could happen. We should make mincemeat of him.

Josef Goebbels

1941

Lunch with the Chisholms. Bridget looked beautiful, pale and slim again, and somehow mysterious, like Mother Earth. We went in to see the baby. It was screaming desperately, in spasms, and plucking frantically at its mouth, as if fighting to express something – and it couldn't, it couldn't. The effort was almost as painful to watch as a death agony. Such a bitter struggle at the beginning of life. Such a superhuman effort: one can't believe that this little wrinkled crimson creature will survive it. But it forces its way, on and on, grimly, into time-consciousness – fighting and resting and fighting again. We stood awed and silent at the foot of the bed, unable to help – till the lady nurse bustled in, exclaiming, 'Isn't he cute? Isn't he? And doesn't he want his milk? I'll say he does!'

Then Hugh entered, fresh and dapper from his bath. He looked so ridiculous – the absurd little rooster who had graciously donated his valuable semen for this creative act. Bridget said she'd been told that male sperm and female ovaries can now be introduced into the body of another woman, who will then be able to bear the child. Under these circumstances, the child still inherits everything from its parents, not the foster mother. We imagined a society lady introducing 'Miss Jones – our carrier.' And Miss Jones would refer casually to her clientele: 'Last spring, when I was carrying for the Duchess of Devonshire . . .'

Christopher Isherwood

1978

When I got to Halston's the phone was ringing and it was [Ilie] Nastase, and Bianca [Jagger] told him to come over. He arrived with a boyfriend, just one of his friends, and he was intimidated by the place – Halston was dressing the Disco Queen in a coat he'd made for her that day, and she came down the stairs and Halston was saying, 'Come on Disco Queen.' He talks like baby talk. He didn't put any feathers in her hair this time. I told him he couldn't, that the newspapers wouldn't take her picture if she put one more feather in her hair.

And then Nastase's boyfriend decided not to come to Studio 54 with us, and when we got in the limo Halston was yelling at the driver because he couldn't find the black radio station, he said, 'What do you mean you don't know where the black station is – you're *black*, aren't you?' And then the driver said he couldn't see, meaning the radio dial, and Halston said, 'What do you mean you can't see, you're *driving*, aren't you?' and then he told me that you have to yell at the help or they don't respect you. He has over a hundred people working for him and they're all so terrified of him, they're always asking each other what kind of a mood he's in.

And I notice something – Bianca had two blemishes on her face! She's never had a blemish! I guess she's depressed about Mick, discoing the night away. She stays out until 6:00 then gets up for her 8:00 exercise class.

Andy Warhol

6 January

1662

This evening (according to costome) his Majestie opned the Revells of that night, by throwing the Dice himselfe, in the Privy Chamber, where was a table set on purpose, and lost his 100 pounds: the yeare before he won 150 pounds: The Ladys also plaied very deepe: I came away when the Duke of Ormond had won about 1000 pounds and left them still at passage, Cards etc: at other Tables, both there and at the Groome-porters, observing the wicked folly vanity and monstrous excesse of Passion amongst some loosers, and sorry I am that such a wretched Custome as play to that excesse should be countenanc'd in a Court, which ought to be an example of Virtue to the rest of the kingdome.

John Evelyn

1836

A brig called the *Agenoria* arrived from St. John's bringing 11 men, from the crew of a timber vessel, whom they had picked up in the most forlorn condition. They were capsized on the night of the 3rd [December] in a tremendous storm. Having cut the lanyards with much difficulty the vessel righted & the crew with the exception of 3 who were drowned, congregated on the quarter-deck. All their provisions were washed overboard & they continued till the 18th enduring the extremity of starvation and misery. On that day they came to the decision of drawing lots for who should die for his comrades & a young man of 19 was the victim. After prayers they cut his throat & drank the blood & devoured a considerable part of the body before it was cold. On the 20th another man being on the point of death, they cut his throat to save the blood & on the 24th another for the same reason. Having finished their horrible meal on that day a sail was discovered by the crew with tears of joy. This was the *Agenoria* which took them on board. They are now settled in the two Poor-Houses & where they are all likely to recover.

Barclay Fox

1915

I went to Adenkirke two days ago to establish a soup-kitchen there, as they say that Furnes station is too dangerous. We heard today that the station-master at Furnes has been signalling to the enemy, so that is why we have been shelled so punctually. His daughter is engaged to a German. Two of our hospital people noticed that before each bombardment a blue light appeared to flash on the sky. They reported the matter, with the result that the signals were discovered.

There has been a lot of shelling again today, and several houses are destroyed. A child of two years is in our hospital with one leg blown off and the other broken. One only hears people spoken of as, 'the man with the abdominal trouble', or 'the one shot through the lungs'.

Children know the different aeroplanes by sight, and one little girl, when I ask her for news, gives me a list of the 'obus' (shells) that have arrived, and which have 's'eclate' (burst), and which have not. One says 'Bon soir, pas de obus (Good evening, no shells),' as in English one says, 'Goodnight, sleep well.'

Sarah Macnaughtan

1917

I had one of my little dinners and went straight to bed. I am in best looks. Marie Bashkirtseff is always apologetic when she makes a similar entry in her diary, but why should one be? Today I could really pass a great deal of time very happily just looking at myself in the glass. It's extraordinary how one's whole outline seems to alter, as well as complexion and eyes.

Lady Cynthia Asquith

1932 [Rome]

Spend most of the day reading *fascisti* pamphlets. They certainly have turned the whole country into an army. From cradle to grave one is cast in the mould of *fascismo* and there can be no escape. I am much impressed by the efficiency of all this on paper. Yet I wonder how it works in individual lives and shall not feel certain about it until I have lived some time in Italy. It is certainly a socialist experiment in that it destroys individuality. It also destroys liberty. Once a person insists on how you are to think he immediately begins to insist on how you are to behave. I admit that under this system you can attain to a degree of energy and efficiency not reached in our own island. And yet, and yet . . . The whole thing is an inverted pyramid.

We meet Signora Sarfatti, a friend of Mussolini whom we met at the Embassy yesterday. A blonde questing woman, daughter of a Venetian Jew who married a Jew in Milan. She helped Mussolini on the *Popolo d'Italia*, right back in 1914. She is at present his *confidante* and must be used by him to bring the gossip of Rome to the Villa Torlonia. She says that Mussolini is the greatest worker ever known: he rides in the morning, then a little fencing, then work, and then after dinner he plays the violin to himself. Tom [Oswald Mosley] asks how much sleep he gets. She answers, 'Always nine hours.' I can see Tom doing sums in his head and concluding that on such a time-table Musso cannot be hard-worked at all. Especially as he spends hours on needless interviews.

Harold Nicolson

1942 [Jersey]

RAF dropped leaflets early this morning. Laurence found one and Joyce found one in our garden near the bee-hive! They were all written in French. They were not addressed specially to Channel Islanders. German officers were searching the countryside for them but our eyes are sharper than theirs! It is nice to think that our British friends were close to us today. We are not forgotten after all!

Nan Le Ruez

1944

My longing for someone to talk to has become so unbearable that I somehow took it into my head to select Peter for this role. On the few occasions when I have gone to Peter's room during the day, I've always thought it was nice and cosy. But Peter's too polite to show someone the door when they're bothering him, so I've never dared to stay long. I've always been afraid he'd think I was a pest. I've been looking for an excuse to linger in his room and get him talking without his noticing, and yesterday I got my chance. Peter, you see, is currently going through a crossword-puzzle craze, and he doesn't do anything else all day. I was helping him, and we soon ended up sitting across from each other at his table, Peter on the chair and me on the divan.

It gave me a wonderful feeling when I looked into his dark blue eyes and saw how bashful my unexpected visit made him. I could read his innermost thoughts, and in his face I saw a look of helplessness and uncertainty as to how to behave, and at the same time a flicker of awareness of his masculinity. I saw his shyness, and I melted. I wanted to say, 'Tell me about yourself. Look beneath my chatty exterior.' But I found that it was easier to think up questions than to ask them.

. . . That night I lay in bed and cried my eyes out, all the while making sure no one could hear me. The idea that I had to beg Peter for favours was simply revolting. But people will do almost anything to satisfy their longings; take me, for example, I've made up my mind to visit Peter more often, and, somehow, get him to talk to me.

You mustn't think I'm in love with Peter, because I'm not. If the van Daans had a daughter instead of a son, I'd have tried to make friends with her.

Anne Frank

1953

How impossible it is for me to make regular entries in the diary. I suddenly remember how I used to puzzle over the word at school. Always wondering why diary was so like Dairy and what the connection was. Never found out. Like that label on the bottle of Daddies Sauce – it never stopped. The man on the label was holding a bottle of Daddies Sauce and on the bottle was a label with a man holding a bottle of Daddies Sauce . . . ad infinitum ad nauseam for me at any rate.

Kenneth Williams

1973

A gathering at the Savoy after the National Theatre's *Twelfth Night* at the Old Vic. I had a giggle with Norman St John Stevas, an old acquaintance from television and radio panel games, and now Under-Secretary and spokesman for the Arts in the Commons. He is an extraordinary man: irreverent, very funny, very Catholic, and he can sometimes be delightfully indiscreet. I have always felt that his heart is in the right place. We were speaking of the energy of the Prime Minister [Edward Heath] in a very crowded week, which included Fanfare for Europe, Boat Shows, and battling with the TUC and CBI over a wage policy. Norman said that celibacy was a great aid to energy, didn't I find. I said I didn't. He remarked that since he had become a minister, all sexual desire had faded. Celibacy, he said, was the secret of Heath.

Peter Hall

7 January

1833

At half-past five, took coffee, and off to the theatre. The play was *Romeo and Juliet*; the house was extremely full: they are a delightful audience. My Romeo had gotten on a pair of trunk breeches, that looked as if he had borrowed them from some worthy Dutchman of a hundred years ago. Had he worn them in New York, I could have understood it as a compliment to the ancestry of that good city; but here, to adopt such a costume in *Romeo*, was really perfectly unaccountable. They were of a most unhappy choice of colours, too – dull, heavy-looking blue cloth, and offensive crimson satin, all be-puckered, and be-plaited, and be-puffed, till the young man looked like a magical figure growing out of a monstrous, strange-coloured melon, beneath which descended his unfortunate legs, thrust into a pair of red slippers, for all the world like Grimaldi's legs *en costume* for clown.

The play went off pretty smoothly, except that they broke one man's collar-bone, and nearly dislocated a woman's shoulder by flinging the scenery about. My bed was not made in time, and when the scene drew, half a dozen carpenters in patched trowsers and tattered shirt sleeves were discovered smoothing down my pillows and adjusting my draperies!

Fanny Kemble

1857

There has never been an age so full of humbug. Humbug everywhere, even in science. For years now the scientists have been promising us every morning a new miracle, a new element, a new metal, guaranteeing to warm us with copper discs immersed in water, to feed us with nothing, to kill us at no expense whatever and on a grand scale, to keep us alive indefinitely, to make iron out of heaven knows what. And all this fantastic scientific humbugging leads to membership of the Institut, to decorations, to influence, to stipends, to the respect of serious people. In the meantime the cost of living rises, doubles, trebles; there is a shortage of raw materials; even death makes no progress – as we saw at Sebastopol, where men cut each other to ribbons – and the cheapest goods are still the worst goods in the world.

The Brothers Goncourt

1936

Brian Lunn took me to lunch in the Inner Temple. It was like being back at Cambridge. I found him in a little wooden room, reading old divorce briefs. They were pencilled over with comment. The language was not at all bowdlerized. One contained a verbatim report of a telephone conversation a husband had overheard between his wife and her lover. He claimed that it proved adultery because, in this conversation, she used the same pet name for penis as with him.

Malcolm Muggeridge

1969

Dashed home to change hurriedly for the Buckingham Palace reception for the Commonwealth Prime Ministers. It was an awful nuisance having to dress but the only way I could see of meeting my old friends during my frantic week.

It was nice to see Indira Gandhi again: I warm to her. She is a pleasant, rather shy and unassuming woman and we exchanged notes about the fun of being at the top in politics. When I asked her whether it was hell being Prime Minister she smiled and said, 'It is a challenge.' Oddly enough, I always feel protective towards her.

Every group I spoke to greeted me as the first woman Prime Minister to be. I hate this talk. First I'm never going to be PM and, secondly, I don't think I'm clever enough. Only I know the depth of my limitations: it takes all I've got to survive my present job.

Barbara Castle

1975

I have received a letter from Martin Gilbert, who is engaged on vol. 5 of Winston Churchill's life. Among Sir Winston's archives he has come upon my name as a guest at Chartwell for four nights in January 1928. Can I give him any recollections of the visit? I have replied that I remember it fairly well. I was terrified of W. C., who would come into dinner late, eat his soup aggressively, growl in expostulation at Randolph's cheek, then melt so as to be gallant with the girls and tolerant of the boys: that one night we remained at the dinner table till midnight while W. C. gave us a demonstration of how the Battle of Jutland was fought, with decanters and wine glasses in place of ships, while puffing cigar smoke to represent gun smoke. He was like an enthusiastic schoolboy on that occasion. The rest of the visit he was in waders in the lake or building a wall, or pacing backwards and forwards in his upstairs room dictating a book to his secretaries. Thump, thump on the floorboards overhead.

James Lees-Milne

1994

Rugged is my favourite word.

If I had my way even workmen would wear velvet every day.

Ossie Clark

1995 [Brussels]

As I got up to leave the restaurant, the crêpe chef in the middle of the room gestured urgently to warn me of something. I assumed, 'Careful – this stuff is flambé', and waved to acknowledge. I moved between the tables around him. He cried out again. I realized he was saying 'Serviette!' and that I had it hanging neatly from below my now buttoned jacket – a large, white, triangular codpiece. Everyone looked at me with the patronizing admiration the Europeans show to the absent-minded and/or obsessed.

Brian Eno

8 January

1849 [Ireland]

I don't see that the misery of the country is at all increasing, it is only spreading. None of the lower orders need suffer for an hour, the Poor House is open. They bear a great deal before they will go there, hunger alone drives them into it, so that those who are out however wretched they may look are not as yet in want of food. The upper classes are now suffering, the farmer class a good deal, the landlord class a great deal. Every day we hear of the ruin of additional families, of themselves or their ancestors, yet who managed to live and let live till these unjust poor laws came to overwhelm them. That *we* have so far escaped is owing entirely to the Honourable East India Company's pay, small though it be, for the little property having but a debt of £1,000 upon it would yield but a bare £100 a year for the support of its owner after all the charges on it were paid unless we were to dismiss all the servants and labourers. We are tight enough as it is and must try and lessen our expenditure still.

Elizabeth Grant of Rothiemurchus

1934

At Marks and Spencer's I bought a peach-coloured vest and trollies to match with insertions of lace. Disgraceful I know but I can't help choosing my underwear with a view to it being seen.

Barbara Pym

1935

I arrived back at Elveden late, cold and hungry. Our guests were all still up but all the fifty servants had gone to bed, and I could get nothing to eat. In spite of that, of all the Iveagh houses I like Elveden. I love its calm, its luxurious Edwardian atmosphere. For a fortnight now I have slept in the King's bed, which both Edward VII and George V have used. And this morning, in the wee sma' hours, I had a humiliating accident – I somehow smashed the royal chamber pot. It seems a habit of mine, and one much to be discouraged. At Mentmore once, staying with the Roseberys, I broke Napoleon's pot in similar circumstance, a very grand affair covered with 'N's and Bees.

'Chips' Channon

1940 [Berlin]

Did a mike interview with General Ernst Udet tonight, but Göring, his boss, censored our script so badly that it wasn't very interesting. I spent most of the day coaching the general on his English, which is none too good. Udet, a likeable fellow, is something of a phenomenon. A professional pilot, who only a few years ago was so broke he toured America as a stunt flyer, performing often in a full-dress suit and a top hat, he is now responsible for the designing and production of Germany's war planes. Though he never had any business experience, he has proved a genius at his job. Next to Göring and General Milch, he is given credit in inner circles here for building up the German air force to what it is today. I could not help thinking tonight that a man like Udet would never be entrusted with such a job in America. He would be considered 'lacking in business experience.' Also, businessmen, if they knew of his somewhat Bohemian life, would hesitate to trust him with responsibility. And yet in this crazy Nazi system he has done a phenomenal job. Amusing: last night Udet put on a little party at his home, with three generals, napkins slung over their shoulders, presiding over his very considerable bar. There were pretty girls and a great deal of cutting up. Yet these are the men who have made the Luftwaffe the most terrible instrument of its kind in the world.

William L. Shirer

1943

Left flat early, bought sour apples and (at Fortnum & Mason's of all places) a head of celery – the last one left, price 1/-, *very* dirty & I could take it or leave it! Took it, as my object was to procure some vitamins for Stuart.

Lunched at the Westway Hotel with Howard Kershner (Director of Relief in Europe for the American Friends' Service Committee) who told me interesting facts about the food situation (including the fact that Churchill & Roosevelt are the persons really responsible & nothing but a large public agitation will move them). He also said that 6,000 Jews escaped to Spain from France, & are now in danger of being sent back to Germany by starving Spain, yet our Gvt. despite all its talk of atrocities will do nothing for them!!

Vera Brittain

1970

Cecil Beaton had sent me a card saying come to lunch and that it was to be just him and 'a load of old women.' The 'old women' turned out to be Loelia, formerly Duchess of Westminster, now Lady Lindsay, and Lady Hambleden. Cecil was in terrific form: 'I just flew in and went straight to the doctor for a couple of injections and slept for a week at Reddish.' Both *grandes dames* turned out to be highly engaging. Loelia Lindsay particularly so. She had a wonderful eye for changing social mores, recalling the blatant snobbery of the twenties when she was a deb when, if you had danced with a man the night before and had found that he was socially inferior, if you happened to see him the following day you would just look through him.

She recalled how once she went out to dinner, and returned explaining to her mother how wonderful the food had been, how delicious in particular the consommé with sherry had tasted. She was never allowed there again.

For her first weekend away, her mother insisted that she took gloves up to the elbow to wear in the evening. On descending the staircase with them on she found herself an anachronism, and, taking them swiftly off, tucked them behind a silver-framed portrait of Queen Ena of Spain.

Roy Strong

9 January

1821

The lapse of ages *changes* all things – time – language – the earth – the bounds of the sea – the stars of the sky, and every thing 'about, around, and underneath' man, *except man himself*, who has always been and always will be, an unlucky rascal. The infinite variety of lives conduct but to death, and the infinity of wishes lead but to disappointment. All the discoveries which have yet been made have multiplied little but existence.

Lord Byron

1836

I met Captain Gillard, master of the *Agenoria*, who confirmed all the statement of Capt. G. as far as he was competent. I saw the penknife belonging to Capt. G. with which the 3 men were butchered. I saw sticking to the blade – horrible, horrible! – a piece of human flesh, a relic of their cannibal meal!

Barclay Fox

1930

At the table directly opposite us was a rather attractive young couple. Probably a wedding-trip, for the table is covered with flowers. The young man was reading *Les Caves du Vatican*. This is the first time I have ever happened to meet someone actually reading *me*. Occasionally he turned toward me and when I was not looking at him, I felt him staring at me. Most likely he recognized me. Lacretelle kept telling me: 'Go ahead! Tell him who you are. Sign his book for him. . . .' In order to do this I should have had to be more certain that he liked the book, in which he remained absorbed even during the meal. But suddenly I saw him take a little knife out of his pocket. . . . Lacretelle was seized with uncontrollable laughter on seeing him slash *Les Caves du Vatican*. Was he doing so out of exasperation? For a moment I thought so. But no: carefully he cut the binding threads, took out the first few sheets, and handed a whole part of the book that he had already read to his young wife, who immediately plunged into her reading.

André Gide

1932

Read today that Corot, Degas, Manet, Cézanne were all 'paternal parasites' as regards money – if I can do my share in the Scottish Renaissance perhaps I'll justify my parasitism yet. Up to yourself, my boy, it's up to yourself.

William Soutar

1953

On Wednesday we lunched with the PM at Barnie Baruch's. Winston Churchill seems to have shrunk a lot and was very deaf in his left ear, which unfortunately was the side I was on, so conversation was a little difficult. But mentally he was extremely alert, and he had a charming old-world courtliness; he was dressed impeccably in a black suit. His skin is as pink and fresh and unwrinkled as a baby's and he poured some champagne from his glass over the Virginia ham, and dipped the end of his cigar in his brandy. He made a little speech to the Mayor of New York, a slippery ice-creamer from near Palermo called Impelliteri, making a pun which the Mayor failed to see.

Cynthia Gladwyn

1958

Jim Egan began at the *World Telegram* as a messenger boy and now works in our production department. Today he told me an amusing story. In 1940, when Franklin Roosevelt and Wendell Wilkie were vying for the presidency, Jim was sent on an errand to the *Herald Tribune*. He wore a huge Roosevelt button on his shirt. Going up in the elevator he was seen by Mrs. Helen Rogers Reid, who owned the *Trib*. Glaring at the Roosevelt button she snapped: 'Why are you wearing that thing?'

'Why not?'

'Well don't you know this is a Republican newspaper?'

'So what?'

'You're fired!'

'You can't fire me.'

'Why not?'

'Because I don't work here.'

Edward Robb Ellis

1977

It may be a little late in the day to start making New Year resolutions, but mine are none the less serious for that. I shall write them down to remind myself:

1. To make some money.

2. To think seriously about getting married – possibly to Jane, but ideally to someone with money.

3. To find somewhere else to live. I am getting too old for this type of flat life.

4. To move freely in society. I am always reading in the diaries of the famous how they dined here and lunched there; sat next to this person at table and met that one at the theatre. I see no reason why I should not do the same. My problem is that my life is too often taken up with domestic trivialities, and I allow my time to be wasted by people of little worth and influence. I shall take steps to break out of this little world in which I have become trapped in recent months, and give far freer rein to my personality and talents.

Christopher Matthew (Diary of a Somebody)

10 January

1824

Called on Miss Lamb. I looked over [Charles] Lamb's library in part. He has the finest collection of shabby books I ever saw. Such a number of first-rate works of genius, but filthy copies, which a delicate man would really hesitate touching, is, I think, nowhere to be found.

Henry Crabb Robinson

1872

This morning at prayers the pretty housemaid Elizabeth with the beautiful large soft eyes was reading aloud in Luke i how Zacharias saw a vision in the Temple, but for the word 'vision' she substituted 'venison'.

Rev. Francis Kilvert

1914

To one of these new night-clubs, Murray's in Bleak Street. Here were numerous people dancing the tango and the maxixe with jealous precision; the latter is rather a graceful dance, but, as to the former, the old lady in the current anecdote was not far wrong – 'I whip my dog when he does that.'

Not that these people seemed to get any physical fun out of the thing, as they were all grimly preoccupied with trying to tread it out according to the rules. It's an amusing place, though, and we sat there till three; there are an amazing lot of all-but-beautiful women in the London stage, and demi-monde, just now, and some who are quite – e.g., Sari Petrass, who is a lovely little creature, and looks like a duchess. Two years ago, I suppose, London was without any sort of place of this kind, and now there are about half a dozen flourishing like the greenest bay-trees; an excellent thing.

Sir Alan 'Tommy' Lascelles

1920 [Berlin]

To-day the Peace Treaty was ratified at Paris; the War is over. A terrible era begins for Europe, like the gathering of clouds before a storm, and it will end in an explosion probably still more terrible than that of the World War. In Germany there are all the signs of a continuing growth of nationalism.

Count Harry Kessler

1946

At the fashionable, carefree Carcano – Ednam wedding reception I remarked to Emerald [Cunard] how quickly London had recovered from the war and how quickly normal life had resumed. 'After all,' I said, pointing to the crowded room, 'this is what we have been fighting for.' 'What,' said Emerald, 'are they all Poles?'

'Chips' Channon

1953

[With] the young duke of Kent and his sisters, taken to see a famous illusionist in a London music hall. The number ends with some nudity, and the nanny doesn't know what to do. As they leave she ventures to ask, 'How did Your Highness enjoy the performance?' 'I'm scared.' 'Why, Your Highness?' 'Mama told me if I looked at naked women I'd turn to stone – and it's starting.'

Jean Cocteau

1979

Took off at 8.20 in a curious twin-engined, high-wing, old Russian plane which I viewed with apprehension and dismay, but which in fact proved to be extremely stable for the three-hour slow journey, diverting in order to see things like the Silingue Dam and to follow the course of the River Niger to Timbuctoo.

I was greeted at the airport by the military governor, mayor, etc, and then at the entrance to the main square, five miles away, by two Nubian maidens, one of whom presented me with some dates, which I ate, and the other with a bowl of camel's milk, which I put to my lips but refrained from drinking as it had the most nauseous smell. Then into the square where the whole population seemed to be lined up. Fortunately the population of Timbuctoo is now only about 8000 compared with 100,000 in 1500, so it was not quite as formidable a gathering as it might earlier have been. A lot of music and cheering, though quite whom or what they thought they were cheering I am not sure. Then I walked round the square and decided that the only thing to do was a Richard Nixon, plunge in, shake hands and then move on fifty yards and plunge again.

Roy Jenkins

1984

Two boxes arrived this morning, stuffed with PO cases and what officials call 'reading'. First thing, always, on top of all the folders are the grey sheets of diary pages. My heart sank as I looked at the stuffed days, the names of dreary and supercilious civil servants who will (never singly) be attending. I've got three months of this ahead of me without a break.

At dinner the other night Peter [Morrison], who is a workaholic (not so difficult if you're an unhappy bachelor living on whisky) showed Ian [Gow] and me, with great pride, his diary card for the day following. Every single minute, from 8.45 a.m. onwards, was filled with 'engagements'.

'Look,' he said. 'How's that for a diary?'

Ian, unexpectedly and greatly to his credit, said, 'If my Private Office produced a schedule like that I'd sack the whole lot, immediately.'

Alan Clark

1995

Peter Cook died yesterday and of course today is the funniest man who ever lived. He may almost have been. (Dud: 'So would you say you've learned from your mistakes?' Pete: 'Oh yes, I'm certain I could repeat them exactly.')

This morning, after dark thoughts about my life, I picked up *Whole Earth Review* and read the interview with Annie Nearing, now 94 years old. She said something that struck me right in the heart – though it seems very minor: 'People give so much attention to food.' This struck a chord because last night we left the Lacey meeting prematurely primarily so we could have a proper sit-down meal. A snack would have done me fine, and I was slightly discomfited that eating had come to occupy such a major position in our lives. Then I thought about all the evenings that evaporate in the long haze of preparing, eating, drinking, smoking. Lately, when cooking (unless I'm really in the mood) I find myself thinking, 'This is taking an absurdly long time.'

Generally my feeling is towards less: less shopping, less eating, less drinking, less wasting, less playing by the rules and recipes. All of that I want in favour of more thinking on the feet, more improvising, more surprises, more laughs.

Brian Eno

11 January

1857

There was wit and even poetry in the negro's answer to the man who tried to persuade him that the slaves would not be obliged to work in heaven. 'Oh, you g'way, Massa. I know better. If dere's no work for cullud folks up dar, dey'll *make* some fur 'em, and if dere's nuffin better to do, dey'll make em *shub de clouds along.* You can't fool this chile, Massa.'

H. D. Thoreau

1909

Madam Posfay was in the courtyard of the palace at the time of the murder of the King and Queen of Serbia, but knew nothing. 'What are they throwing bolsters out of the windows for?' she asked. It was the bodies.

Arnold Bennett

1920

Like every morning I have had my enema, in order to preserve a clear skin and sweet breath. It is a family habit, approved of by Dr Pinard. One of Maman's old great-aunts, the beautiful Madame Rhomès, died at the age of ninety and a half with a complexion of lilies and roses, skin like a child's. She took her little enema, it seems, at five o'clock every evening, so that she would sleep very well. She did it cheerfully in public. She would simply stand in front of the fireplace; her servant would come in discreetly, armed with the loaded syringe; Madame Rhomès would lean forward gracefully so that her full skirts lifted, one two there, and it was done! Conversation was not interrupted. After a minute or two my beautiful ancestress would disappear briefly, soon to return with the satisfaction of a duty performed.

Liane de Pougy

1912

Night. Height 10,530. Temp -16.3°. Minimum -25.8°. Another hard grind in the afternoon and five miles added. About 74 miles from the Pole – can we keep this up for seven days? It takes it out of us like anything. None of us ever had such hard work before. Cloud has been coming and going overhead all day, drifting from the S.E., but continually altering shape. Snow crystals falling all the time, a very light breeze at start soon dying away. The sun so bright and warm tonight that it is almost impossible to imagine a minus temperature. The snow seems to get softer as we advance; the sastrugi, though sometimes high and undercut, are not hard – no crusts, except yesterday the surface subsided once, as on the Barrier. Our chance still holds good if we can put the work in, but it's a terribly trying time.

Captain Robert Falcon Scott

1940 [Berlin]

Cold. Fifteen degrees below zero centigrade outside my window. Half the population freezing in their homes and offices and workshops because there's no coal. Pitiful to see in the streets yesterday people carrying a sack of coal home in a baby-carriage or on their shoulders. I'm surprised the Nazis are letting the situation become so serious. Everyone is grumbling. Nothing like continual cold to lower your morale. Learned today from a traveller back from Prague that producers of butter, flour, and other things in Slovakia and Bohemia are marking their goods destined for Germany as 'Made in Russia.' This on orders from Berlin, the idea being to show the German people how much 'help' is already coming from the Soviets.

William L. Shirer

1973

In the British Museum reading room I asked the superintendent if I might be allowed to visit the shelves in order to search for an article in an obscure Italian journal of the 1850s and 60s, the reference to which was evidently wrongly given in the bibliography I have consulted. He looked at me and said, 'We are not supposed to, but you seem all right.' 'I hope I am, but I don't know how you can tell,' I said. He called a black assistant, who took me miles and miles upstairs past shelves and shelves and shelves, all beautifully stacked. We arrived at a little office amidst this forest of books.

The charming assistant took me to the shelves where the *Rivista Europa* volumes were stacked – about forty of them. He had them all taken out on a trolley and put on a table for me. I found my article and read it; it was of no use to me, but I was struck by the kindness and helpfulness of everyone concerned. When I came to leave my friend was nowhere to be found. It was terrifying being left alone in this deserted forest, no sound, only endless speechless books. Depressing, and frightening. Enough to make a humble author feel a worm.

James Lees-Milne

12 January

1819

I sat up till two, as I did last night, to finish *Pride and Prejudice*. This novel I consider as one of the most excellent of the works of our female novelists.

Its merit lies in the characters, and in the perfectly colloquial style of the dialogue. Mrs Bennet, the foolish mother, who cannot conceal her projects to get rid of her daughters, is capitally drawn. There is a thick-headed servile parson, also a masterly sketch. His stupid letters and her ridiculous speeches are as delightful as wit. The two daughters are well contrasted – the gentle and candid Jane and the lively but prejudiced Elizabeth, are both good portraits, and the development of the passion between Elizabeth and the proud Darcy, who at first hate each other, is executed with skill and effect.

Henry Crabb Robinson

1840 [Ireland]

I have been thinking how best to encourage the school, and not being able to afford more help in money than it now costs, I have determined on giving fewer prizes – only one in each Division – instead I shall send ten children to school. I have also resolved on resuming my regular daily business as the only possible way of keeping things in order. Monday – The washing to be given out. Clothes mended. Stores for the week given to the servants. Tuesday – work for the week cut out and arranged, my own room tidied. Wednesday – accounts, letters, papers all put by. Thursday – housekeeping, closets, storeroom, etc. arranged, bottles put by, pastry made – in short every necessary job done for the week. Friday – gardening and poor people's wants. Saturday – put by clean clothes and school. Two hours generally does all, except on Thursday. Thus I am always ready and have plenty of time for other occupations. I also give an hour every evening to the little girls. Janey has a musick lesson every day – Annie every second day – twice a week French – twice a week English – twice a week dancing. Alas, when we see company all this happiness must be forborne, but we owe a duty to society as to other things and in its turn it must be paid and a little intercourse with our acquaintance is good both for ourselves and for our children. With friends it is delightful, and we have some even here I should be very sorry to have to part from. In the evening played some of Corelli's solos, read aloud Mrs Trollope's Domestic Manners of the Americans.

Elizabeth Grant of Rothiemurchus

1936

I realize now that I would marry if I could do so; but I am not wholly blind to the fact that my arrival at this nuptial mood has been accelerated by adventitious means. What woman – granting she overlook my disabilities – would expect that my affection was entirely unselfish. Yet – and this is perhaps a confession of my overweening self-regard rather than of my confidence in the magnanimity of women – I do believe that a woman would accept me for what I am and that our marriage should be one of mutual affection, and not a 'second-best' accommodation for security and comfort. No doubt to an outsider it must appear preposterous that at my age I should consider it not an impossibility to win the affection of such a woman as I might have reasonably hoped to have won when a whole man; but the hope is there and places me, I suppose, among the incorrigible.

William Soutar

1938 [Nanking]

A month ago today Nanking fell into the hands of the Japanese. The body of that Chinese soldier shot while tied to a bamboo sofa is still lying out in the street not 50 yards from my house.

John Rabe

13 January

1921

Rainy weather. Does the weather matter in a journal? Lunched alone; does *that* matter? (Grilled turbot and apple-pudding, if you want full details.) Talked to 'the Judge' about fox hunting for a few minutes. Then went to Cheyne Walk for tea with Gabriel. Bought yellow narcissi on the way. Buying flowers is refreshing, though I always give them away. Left at five, and played *The Beggar's Opera* for an hour: also refreshing. Dined at Arnold Bennett's and enjoyed it greatly. B. is always the same, and always nice. He showed me his manuscripts, which are very beautiful. That of *Old Wives' Tale* practically free from corrections. He had been to see George Moore, who said: 'Hardy is a villager; Conrad is a sailor; Henry James was a eunuch.'

Siegfried Sassoon

1945 [Bergen-Belsen]

Yesterday marked our first year here. It has been a terrible year, far from home, from the children, without news from them, a year of disappointment. The transport to Palestine, the peace that did not come, a year of hunger, cold, hounding, persecution and humiliation. Fortunately, though, apart from a few bouts of dysentery, we have not been seriously ill.

The food is getting worse and worse. At midday, swede soup, every day without a single potato. The 'extra' food is distributed centrally now. Every day there are genuine punch-ups over a ticket. From time to time there is no bread at all here – from time to time (tonight, for example) we are not allowed to use the toilet. Those who have diarrhoea must go outdoors. We have procured some buckets for ourselves, discarded jam buckets.

This morning, my neighbour had to resort to them.

This morning his bunkmate discovered to his horror that his shoes were full. The other had soiled himself twice during the night.

We are living amid the lice. For months I have not been able to change into clean underwear, nor had a shower. Naturally there is also no heating here, we suffer terribly from the cold in the huts, which are draughty and where the door is never shut.

Deaths, deaths, deaths.

For how long?

The persecution of the Jews continues. Nevertheless we are a year nearer to peace than on 13 January 1944.

Abel J. Herzberg

1953

Lunched with Jack Kennedy, the new Senator from Massachusetts. He has the making of a first-class Senator or a first-class fascist – probably depending on whether the right kind of people take the trouble to surround him. His brother is now counsel for McCarthy's committee and he himself has been appointed on McCarthy's committee, though Jack claims against his wishes. There was a time when I didn't quite understand why F.D.R. broke with Joe Kennedy. But the more I see of Jack, the more I can understand it.

Drew Pearson

1955 [Jamaica]

The Parachini [a neighbour] funeral was almost comical. It was also strident with local colour. The hearse and the funeral cortège were late and were unable to turn into the church gates and had to go straight on into Port Maria and then come back on the other side of the road. When the hearse finally drew up we observed that a common little Palmolive soap van had wormed its way into a position just behind it and directly in front of the relatives' car. On the side of the van in large letters was a slogan which read, 'A Lovelier Skin in Fourteen days'.

Noël Coward

1995

Took a long walk this morning – down 7th Avenue to 42nd Street. Such nostalgic air – cool but clear, straight up Manhattan fresh off the Atlantic, having crossed the Sargasso Sea, then accented with all those residual traces of faint fishiness, cinnamon muffins, subway urine, women's perfumes, bacon, coffee, newsprint.

Brian Eno

14 January

1833 [Washington]

We walked up to the Capitol and went first into the senate, or upper house, because [Daniel] Webster was speaking, whom I especially wished to hear. The room itself is neither large nor lofty; the senators sit in two semi-circular rows, turned towards the President, in comfortable arm-chairs. On the same ground, and literally sitting among the senators, were a whole regiment of ladies, whispering, talking, laughing, and fidgeting. A gallery, level with the floor, and only divided by a low partition from the main room, ran round the apartment: this, too, was filled with pink, and blue, and yellow bonnets; and every now and then, while the business of the house was going on, and Webster speaking, a tremendous bustle, and waving of feathers, and rustling of silks, would be heard, and in came streaming a reinforcement of political beauties, and then would commence a jumping up, a sitting down, a squeezing through, and a how-d'ye-doing, and a shaking of hands. The senators would turn round; even Webster would hesitate, as if bothered by the row, and in short, the whole thing was more irregular, and unbusiness-like than any one could have imagined . . .

Fanny Kemble

1935

Today I had a chance to explore the waterfront for the first time. New Orleans, a major world port, has ten miles of wharves and is used by scores of steamship lines and nine railroads. At the Thalia St wharf I watched as bananas from Central America were unloaded from a ship by sweating Negro longshoremen. They are paid 45 cents an hour and get work only about three days a week. As I sat watching the men, a hairy tarantula almost ran up my pant leg. Looking up, I began watching the sea gulls soaring over the river and ships and docks. Seldom have I seen such beauty. The sleek white birds have black-tipped wings and long necks, tuck their orange feet under them, and some glided so near that I saw their sparkling eyes. They are the essence of grace. I wish I were a poet because poetry is the best medium for describing these lovely lofty creatures. If I believed in reincarnation, I'd like to come back as a sea gull. I am curious about them, just as I am curious about everything. Life without curiosity wouldn't be worth living. Today I remembered the first two lines of a poem:

> What is this life if, full of care,
> We have no time to stand and stare.

Edward Robb Ellis

1938 [Corfu]

We climbed the dizzy barren razorback of Pantocratoras to the monastery from which the whole strait lay bare, lazy and dancing in the cold haze. Lines of dazzling water crept out from Butrinto, and southward, like a beetle on a plate, the Italian steamer jogged its six knots towards Ithaca. Clouds were massing over Albania, but the flat lands of Epirus were frosty bright. In the little cell of the warden monk, whose windows gave directly upon the distant sea, and the vague ruling of waves to the east, we sat at a deal table and accepted the most royal of hospitalities – fresh mountain walnuts and pure water from the highest spring; water that had been carried up on the backs of women in stone jars for several hundred feet.

Lawrence Durrell

1944

Anatole France, in his old age, intended to write a novel, of which the title was to be *Les Autels de la peur*. The Altars of Fear – could a better title be found for an account of our times?

Iris Origo

15 January

1912

It is wonderful to think that two long marches would land us at the Pole. We left our depôt today with nine days' provisions, so that it ought to be a certain thing now, and the only appalling possibility the sight of the Norwegian flag forestalling ours. Little Bowers continues his indefatigable efforts to get good sights, and it is wonderful how he works them up in his sleeping-bag in our congested tent. (Minimum for night -27.5°.) Only 27 miles from the Pole. We ought to do it now.

Captain Robert Falcon Scott

1941

Parsimony may be the end of this book. Also shame at my own verbosity, which comes over me when I see the – 20 it is – books shuffled together in my room. Who am I ashamed of? Myself reading them. Then Joyce is dead. Joyce about a fortnight younger than I am. I remember Miss Weaver, in wool gloves, bringing *Ulysses* in type-script to our tea-table at Hogarth House. Roger I think sent her. Would we devote our lives to printing it?

The indecent pages looked so incongruous: she was spinsterly, buttoned up. And the pages reeled with indecency. I put it in the drawer of the inlaid cabinet. One day Katherine Mansfield came, and I had it out. She began to read, ridiculing: then suddenly said, But there's something in this: a scene that should figure I suppose in the history of literature. He was about the place, but I never saw him. Then I remember Tom [T. S. Eliot] in Ottoline's [Lady Ottoline Morell] room at Garsington saying – it was published then – how could anyone write again after achieving the immense prodigy of the last chapter. He was, for the first time in my knowledge, rapt, enthusiastic. I bought the blue paper book, and read it here one summer I think with spasms of wonder, of discovery, and then again with long lapses of intense boredom. This goes back to a pre-historic world. And now all the gents are furbishing up their opinions, and the books, I suppose, take their place in the long procession.

Virginia Woolf

1943

A group of naughty little boys crept in [to the canteen] and started playing with the table-tennis gear. I went to chase them off, and collided with two little girls about twelve or fourteen. I said, 'Hallo, my dears, what do you want?' and got a very evasive answer. I noticed they were very bold-looking little things. It appears that they have haunted the canteen all week, and when Mrs. Diss came, I said, 'Do you know, I've never before seen girls or women hanging round the canteen' and she answered, 'No, but we have not had Scotties or Australians before. We were warned of the queer attractions they – and Americans too – have for young girls.' She had talked firmly and kindly to the two girls, and asked, 'Whatever would your mother think if she knew?' She had got a pert but pitiful reply, 'Oh *she* wouldn't say anything – but Dad would thrash me.' However, it appeared Dad was in the Middle East. The other said her mum was working, and she could not get in the house till seven o'clock when she came in.

When I told Mary, she said that, at Fulwood Barracks in Preston, it was really shocking to see such young girls 'seeking trouble'. We have seen little of it openly in Barrow, and it set me thinking again of the 'new world'. I wonder if the ones with such beautiful ideas, who blah so much about what will happen after the war, even dimly realise the stupendous tasks and problems awaiting them, the cosmic swing of change, the end of all things as we know them. I read in the paper of American school-teachers' problems with unruly adolescents who have never been disciplined.

Nella Last

16 January

1755

This morning about 1 o'clock I had the misfortune to lose my little boy Peter, aged 21 weeks, 3 days. Paid for flour and other small things. At home all day. In the even read the 11th and 12th books of *Paradise Regained*, which I think is much inferior for the sublimity of style to *Paradise Lost*.

Thomas Turner

1814

I have simplified my politics into an utter detestation of all existing governments; and, as it is the shortest and most agreeable and summary feeling imaginable, the first moment of an universal republic would convert me into an advocate for single and uncontradicted despotism. The fact is, riches are power, and poverty is slavery all over the earth, and one sort of establishment is no better, no worse, for a *people* than another.

Lord Byron

1854

I was struck today by the poetic beauty of the winter weather. In the sky a mist got up and the pale sun shone through it. On the roads the dung is beginning to thaw and there is a damp moisture in the air.

Leo Tolstoy

1912

Camp 68. Height 9,760. T. -23.5°. The worst has happened, or nearly the worst. We marched well in the morning and covered 7½ miles. Noon sight showed us in Lat. 89° 42' S., and we started off in high spirits in the afternoon, feeling that tomorrow would see us at our destination. About the second hour of the march Bowers' sharp eyes detected what he thought was a cairn; he was uneasy about it, but argued that it must be a sastrugus. Half an hour later he detected a black speck ahead. Soon we knew that this could not be a natural snow feature. We marched on, found that it was a black flag tied to a sledge bearer; near by the remains of a camp; sledge tracks and ski tracks going and coming and the clear trace of dogs; paws – many dogs. This told us the whole story. The Norwegians have forestalled us and are first at the Pole. It is a terrible disappointment, and I am very sorry for my loyal companions. Many thoughts come and much discussion have we had. Tomorrow we must march on to the Pole and then hasten home with all the speed we can compass. All the day-dreams must go; it will be a wearisome return. Certainly we are descending in altitude – certainly also the Norwegians found an easy way up.

Captain Robert Falcon Scott

1919

Liebknecht and Rosa Luxemburg have met with a dreadful and fantastic end. The midday editions of the newspapers have published the story. Last night Liebknecht was shot from behind while being taken in a truck through the Tiergarten and, so it is said, trying to escape. Rosa Luxemburg, having been interrogated by officers of the Guards Cavalry Division in the Eden Hotel, was first beaten unconscious by a crowd there and then, on the canal bridge, was dragged out of the car in which she was being removed. Allegedly she was killed. Her body has at any rate disappeared. But, according to what is known so far, she could have been rescued and brought to safety by party comrades. Through the civil war, which she and Liebknecht plotted, they had so many lives on their conscience that their violent end has, as it were, a certain inherent logic. The manner of their deaths, not the deaths themselves, is what causes consternation.

Count Harry Kessler

1979

Today I began a regime which will probably last for twenty-four hours. I jogged in the bedroom for about twenty-five minutes and did some exercises. Resolved not to eat any bread, potatoes or sugar, and to stop smoking. It's terrifying the extent to which one is dependent on drugs. If I tried to give up tea as well, I think I should go mad!

. . . It's 10.45 pm and I still haven't smoked.

Tony Benn

1995

Opening of *Interview with the Vampire* in Dublin. Tom Cruise comes over, bless his heart. He promised to do so months ago, and I had always thought circumstances would intervene. But here he is, causing a sensation in O'Connell Street. Police holding back crowds, as if the Beatles had returned. He makes his way through a quite terrifying line and finds time to talk to everybody. All I know is I couldn't do it.

A party afterwards in Dublin Castle. Liam Neeson turns up. And Michael D. Higgins and a group of British MPs who have come to see how the tax-breaks have worked for the Irish film industry, James Callaghan and a Labour spokesman for Defence among them. I talk to him for a while and get the impression they found the film quite loathsome. Maybe they don't want this kind of activity on their shores after all. When you have Shakespeare, why do you need movies?

Neil Jordan

17 January

1912

Camp 69. T. -22° at start. Night -21°. The Pole. Yes, but under very different circumstances from those expected. We have had a horrible day – and to add to our disappointment a head wind 4 to 5, with a temperature -22°, and companions labouring on with cold feet and hands.

Captain Robert Falcon Scott

1919

In the evening I went to a cabaret in the Bellevuestrasse. The sound of a shot cracked through the performance of a fiery Spanish dancer. Nobody took any notice. It underlined the slight impression that the [Russian] revolution has made on metropolitan life. I only began to appreciate the Babylonian, unfathomably deep, primordial and titanic quality of Berlin when I saw how this historic, colossal event has caused no more than local ripples on the even more colossally eddying movement of Berlin existence. An elephant stabbed with a penknife shakes itself and strides on as if nothing has happened.

Count Harry Kessler

1936

I read Kipling's verses all the afternoon (he died yesterday). It struck me how good the verses were, how full of genuine vitality, how full of contempt for what I despised – 'brittle intellectuals' – and of poetic genius; how, if he praised Empire, it was not at all because he had not counted the cost (who has expressed better the wrongs of the common soldier?) but because, men being what they are, he saw it as one of the less despicable manifestations of their urge to over-run and dominate their environment.

Malcolm Muggeridge

1962

Walter Shenson [film producer]. He said he'd been having a talk with Brian Epstein, the Beatles' manager. He was delighted that I'd like to do the film [script]. 'So,' W. Shenson said, 'you'll be hearing either from Brian or Paul MacCartney in the near future. So don't be surprised if a Beatle rings you up.' 'What an experience,' I said. 'I shall feel as nervous as I would if St Michael or God were on the line.' 'Oh, there's not any need to be worried, Joe,' Shenson said. 'I can say, from my heart, that the boys are very respectful of talent. I mean, most respectful of anyone they feel has talent. I can really say that, Joe.'

Joe Orton

1965

Winston Churchill, I fear, is dying at this very moment. I suppose it's just as well really. Ninety years is a long, long, time. Personally I would rather not wait until the faculties begin to go. However, that must be left in the hands of 'The One Above' and I hope he'll do something about it and not just sit there.

Noël Coward

18 January

1805

I've just been reflecting for two hours on my father's conduct toward me, being deplorably worn down by a strong attack of the slow fever I've had for more than seven months. I haven't been able to recover from it: first, because I didn't have the money to pay the doctor; in the second place, because, having my feet constantly in the water in this muddy city owing to lack of boots, and suffering in every way from the cold owing to lack of clothing and wood for the fire, it was useless and even harmful to wear down my body with remedies to get rid of an illness which poverty would have given me even if I hadn't had it already.

If you add to this all the *moral humiliations* and the worries of a life passed continually with twenty sous, twelve, two, and sometimes nothing in my pocket, you'll have a slight idea of the state in which that *virtuous* man has left me.

For two months I've been planning to put a description of my condition here; but, in order to describe it, you must regard it, and my only resource is to distract my attention from it.

Just calculate the effect of eight months of slow fever, fed by every possible misfortune, on a temperament which is already attacked by obstructions and weakness in the abdomen, and then come and tell me that my father isn't shortening my life!

Were it not for my studies, or rather the love of glory that has taken root in my breast in spite of him, I should have blown out my brains five or six times.

Stendhal

1824

I have been reading about an English judge who desired to live to a great age and accordingly proceeded to question every old man he met about his diet and the kind of life he led – whether his longevity had any connexion with food, alcoholic liquor, and so forth. It appears that the only thing they had in common was early rising and, above all, not dozing off once they were awake. *Most important.*

Eugène Delacroix

1940 [Amsterdam]

Ed [Murrow] and I are here for a few days to discuss our European coverage, or at least that's our excuse. Actually, intoxicated by the lights at night and the fine food and the change of atmosphere, we have been cutting up like a couple of youngsters suddenly escaped from a stern old aunt or a reform school. Last night in sheer joy, as we were coming home from an enormous dinner with a fresh snow drifting down like confetti, we stopped under a bright street-light and fought a mighty snow-ball battle. I lost my glasses and my hat and we limped back to the hotel exhausted but happy. This morning we have been ice-skating with Mary Marvin Breckinridge, who has forsaken the soft and dull life of American society to represent us here. The Dutch still lead the good life. The food they consume as to both quantity and quality (oysters, fowl, meats, vegetables, oranges, bananas, coffee – the things the warring peoples never see) is fantastic. They dine and dance and go to church and skate on canals and tend their business. And they are blind – oh, so blind – to the dangers that confront them. Ed and I have tried to do a little missionary work, but to no avail, I fear. The Dutch, like everyone else, want it both ways. They want peace and the comfortable life. But they won't make the sacrifices or even the hard decisions which might ensure their way of life in the long run. The Queen, they say, stubbornly refuses to allow staff talks with the Allies or even with the Belgians. In the meantime, as I could observe when I crossed the border, the Germans pile up their forces and supplies on the Dutch frontier.

William L. Shirer

1977

I worked until 2, then up at 6.30 to go off to begin my tour of European capitals as President of the Council of Energy Ministers.

I took my own mug and lots of tea bags. When we arrived in Paris we were met by the Ambassador, Nico Henderson, a tall, grey-haired, scruffy man, almost a caricature of an English public schoolboy who got to the top of the Foreign Office. I don't think I had ever met him before; he was rather superior and swooped me up in his Rolls Royce.

The end of a day of negotiations, and I enjoyed it very much. In a way it's very relaxing not to be a British Minister, just a European one.

But I must admit that the standard of living of, for example, the Ambassador – a Rolls Royce, luxurious house, marvellous furniture, silver plate at dinner – is indefensible. Ours is a sort of corporate society with a democratic safety valve. What a long time it will take to put it right. And how do you get measured steps in advance? Undoubtedly openness is one, and negotiations and discussions with the trade unions is another. Nobody should have power unless they are elected.

Tony Benn

19 January

1938 [Senegal]

Night of anguish. Went to bed early, very sleepy; but stifling. Stomach churning; never again take that frightful soft and sticky meat which is called 'fish' in this country.

At midnight I decide to have recourse to Dial. Badly closed tubes, which open and scatter the lozenges in my valise. In the bathroom, where I go to get some distilled water (but a mistake was made; the bottle contains syrup), I surprise cockroaches in the act of copulating. I thought they were wingless; but some (probably the males), without taking flight, unfold enormous trembling wings. When I am ready to go back to bed, I notice rising above the top of the wardrobe opposite my bed the erect head of a python, which soon becomes but an iron rod.

Got up at dawn. The main road, which passes our veranda, becomes active: a whole nation is going to market. Very 'road to India.'

André Gide

1959 [Paris]

The evening finished with a blonde lady (French) pounding the piano and everyone getting a trifle 'high'. Princess Sixte de Bourbon was definitely shocked when the Duke [of Windsor] and I danced a sailor's hornpipe and the Charleston, but there was no harm in it, perhaps a little sadness and nostalgia for him and for me a curious feeling of detached amusement, remembering how beastly he had been to me and about me in our earlier years when he was Prince of Wales and I was beginning. Had he danced the Charleston and hornpipe with me then it would have been an accolade to cherish. As it was, it looked only faintly ridiculous to see us skipping about with a will. The Princess needn't have been shocked, it was merely pleasantly ridiculous.

Noël Coward

1976

This morning there arrived by post from Switzerland a Xerox sent by Ali Forbes of a letter written to him by Stephen Spender, abusing me. In it Stephen says he has always loathed the sight of me, and disliked my very appearance, which is that of a sinister undertaker who with his spade thrusts moribund, not yet dead corpses into the grave. That he sees my soul as a brown fungus upon a coffin, etc. That he has never spoken more than a dozen sentences to me in his life. Now this is pretty mischievous of Ali Forbes, I consider. I am affected by Spender's letter. No, not gravely, because I do not like him and know that what he writes is pretentious tripe, yet affected by the knowledge that there is someone alive who can write such disagreeable things about me.

James Lees-Milne

1995

We fly to West Cork where Liam (Neeson) is waiting and go to meet the Collins family. Welcomed at the home of Liam Collins, Michael's nephew, and his wife, with old-fashioned rural courtesy. Visit the old farmhouse at Woodfield which has been landscaped quite beautifully into a fitting monument. No museums or interpretative centres here. Just a preserved old burnt-out farmhouse, with a lovely oak tree in the garden and a plaque or two. One gets the impression of quite severe intelligence here, and of a reticence that has accumulated over the years – a necessary reticence given that neighbours and families would have been divided by the events of the Civil War.

We go to the Four-Alls pub and hear stories of the various directors and actors who passed through here, researching the same film. Michael Cimino, Kevin Costner, even, apparently, John Huston. Kevin Costner we are told turned down the offer of a pint of Guinness for a cup of tea. Liam immediately orders four more pints. Then four more and more again until I'm almost footless.

Neil Jordan

20 January

1917 [Panshanger in Hertfordshire, home of Lord Desborough]
Instead of going to church, a party conducted by Lord Desborough went over to see the German prisoners. There are about a hundred of them in

the park and they work in the woods. I was not allowed to talk German to them. The specimens I saw were of the meek-and-mild type, not at all 'blond beasts'. They had rather ignominious identification marks in the form of a blue disc patched somewhere on to their backs: it looked as though its purpose was to afford a bull's eye to the marksman if they attempted to escape.

Lady Cynthia Asquith

1936

Eventually we get to Tain and go to the little inn where we are received by a man in a kilt and given a dram. We walk across to the Town Hall, where there are the Provost, two ex-Provosts, and the local dominie. A good platform. The hall is amazingly full for such a night. The gallery is packed. The Provost makes a speech, and then I talk for 45 minutes. It goes very well indeed. Then we take the old boys round to the inn and have more drams. And then off we go into the night. Twenty-five miles to Dingwall skidding and slithering. The sound of water in the mist. Then the lighted hotel and the journalists in the lounge and warmth and sandwiches.

'How is the King?' is our first question. 'The 11.45 bulletin was bad. It said that His Majesty's life was moving peacefully to its close.' How strange! That little hotel at Dingwall, the journalists, the heated room, beer, whisky, tobacco, and the snow whirling over the Highlands outside. And the passing of an epoch. I think back to that evening twenty-six years ago when I was having supper at the Carlton and the waiter came and turned out the lights: 'The King is dead.'

Harold Nicolson

1941 [Dresden]

A couple of weeks ago at the Jewish tea downstairs with the Katzes and Kreidles, Leipziger, an elderly medical officer and insurance doctor, garrulously and somewhat boastfully and conceitedly monopolized the conversation; recently Frau Voss comes back enchanted from one of her bridge parties: The medical officer had read so interestingly from a book about the doctor, it is his own life. So now all the Jews who have been thrown out are writing their autobiography, and I am one of twenty thousand . . . And yet: The book will be good, and it helps *me* pass the time. But then the old doubt also revived again, whether it would not have been better for me to learn English. Now on the one hand the new reduction in our money is in the offing, on the other the block on American visas has been lifted and it will soon be the turn of our quota number, and Sussmann . . . has passed on my documents by airmail to Georg. Wait and see . . .

It continues to be cold with snow (without interruption since December), apartment difficult to heat, bad chilblains on my chapped and swollen hands.

Victor Klemperer

1995

Travel back to Dublin. Do the *Late, Late Show* with Gay Byrne. For those who don't know, this is the Irish equivalent of Dave Letterman and Jay Leno rolled into one. And it has been running since they have had television in Ireland. I've avoided it for years, because it is the one thing that makes your face known here. As it is, I'm generally confused with Jim Sheridan and complimented for *My Left Foot*, which is fine by me. Actors and rock stars deserve that recognition since they're paid so much. Writers and directors are paid to be anonymous. And halfway through the show I realise that anonymity here for me is gone for ever. The interest in this Collins film is turning it into a national institution. My problem now is how to make a film that won't feel like a national institution.

Neil Jordan

21 January

1664

Up, and after sending my wife to my aunt Wight's to get a place to see Turner hanged, I to the office, where we sat all the morning. And at noon going to the 'Change, and seeing people flock in the City, I enquired and found that Turner was not yet hanged. And so I went among them to Leadenhall Street, and to St. Mary Axe, where he lived, and there I got for a shilling to stand upon the wheel of a cart, in great pain, above an houre before the execution was done; he delaying the time by long discourses and prayers one after another, in hopes of a reprieve; but none came, and at last was flung off the ladder in his cloake. A comely-looked man he was, and kept his countenance to the end: I was sorry to see him. It was believed there were at least 12 or 14,000 people in the street.

Samuel Pepys

1854

Here is a fact which needs to be remembered more often. Thackeray spent thirty years preparing to write his first novel, but Alexandre Dumas writes two a week.

Leo Tolstoy

1858 [New Orleans]

I am astonished more and more at the stupid extravagance of the women. Mrs H. (who gains her living by keeping a boarding house) has spent, she says, at least £60 on hair dyes in the last ten years. All the ladies, even little girls, wear white powder on their faces and many rouge. All wear silk dresses in the street and my carmelite [woollen material] and grey linen dresses are so singular here that many ladies would refuse to walk with me. Fashion rules so absolutely that to wear a hat requires great courage. Leather boots for ladies are considered monstrous. I never saw such utter astonishment as is depicted on the faces of the populace when I return from a sketching excursion. I do not like to come back alone so the Dr [her husband] always comes for me.

The people in the house would lend me any amount of flower garden bonnets if I would but go out in them. This is so like the Americans – they are generous and kind but will not let you go your own way in the world. My little plain bonnet and plaid ribbon is despised, all my wardrobe considered shabby and triste. I never saw people dress so much, and I must confess, too, with a certain taste which is caught from the French.

Barbara Leigh Smith Bodichon

1915

A stormy day. We walked back this morning. J. [John Middleton Murry; they married in 1918] told me a dream. We quarrelled all the way home more or less. It has rained and snowed and hailed and the wind blows. The dog at the inn howls. A man far away is playing the bugle. I have read and sewed to-day, but not written a word. I want to to-night. It is so funny to sit quietly sewing, while my heart is never for a moment still. I am dreadfully tired in head and body. This sad place is killing me. I live upon old made-up dreams; but they do not deceive either of us.

Later I am in the sitting-room downstairs. The wind howls outside, but here it is so warm and pleasant. It looks like a real room where real people have lived. My sewing-basket is on the table: under the bookcase are poked J.'s old house shoes. The black chair, half in shadow, looks as if a happy person had sprawled there. We had roast mutton and onion sauce and baked rice for dinner. It *sounds* right. I have run the ribbons through my underclothes with a hairpin in the good home way. But my anxious heart is eating up my body, eating up my nerves, eating up my brain, now slowly, now at a tremendous speed. I feel this poison slowly filling my veins – every particle becoming slowly tainted. Yes, love like this is a malady, a fever, a storm. It is almost like hate, one is so hot with it – and am never, never calm, never for an instant. I remember years ago saying I wished I were one of those happy people who can suffer so far and then collapse or become exhausted. But I am just the opposite. The more I suffer, the more of fiery energy I feel to bear it. Darling! Darling!

Katherine Mansfield

1918

[On Sunday] Lytton [Strachey] came to tea; stayed to dinner, and about 10 o'clock we both had that feeling of parched lips and used up vivacity which comes from hours of talk. But Lytton was most easy and agreeable. Among other things he gave us an amazing account of the British Sex Society which meets at Hampstead. They were surprisingly frank; and fifty people of both sexes and various ages discussed without shame such questions as the deformity of Dean Swift's penis; whether cats use the w.c., self abuse; incest – incest between parent and child when they are both unconscious of it, was their main theme, derived from Freud. I think of becoming a member. Lytton at different points exclaimed *Penis*: his contribution to the openness of the debate. We also discussed the future of the world; how we should like professions to exist no longer; Keats, old age, politics, Bloomsbury hypnotism – a great many subjects.

Virginia Woolf

1936

The King is dead – Long live the King. The eyes of the world are on the Prince of Wales, the new King Edward VIII. This morning everyone is in mourning, and the park is full of black crows. I went to the House of Commons at 6, which had been summoned by gun-fire – and unofficially, by radio. About 400 MPs out of 615 turned up, then the Speaker came in, and took his oath to Edward VIII, and we followed; the Prime Minister first . . . it took hours and I sat in the smoking room with A. P. Herbert and Duff Cooper waiting my turn. We talked of Royalty. Today is the anniversary of Lenin's death; tomorrow that of Louis XVI and Queen Victoria . . . Duff had just come on from St James's Palace where he attended the Privy Council to announce the accession of the King, and there they witnessed the King's Oath. 60 or 70 patriarchs, and grandees, in levee dress or uniform, presided over by Ramsay MacDonald as Lord President of the Council. They make an impressive picture, it seems, not unfunny and reminiscent of charades in a country-house; then they processed into yet another Long Gallery where they were received by the Princes . . . a few moments later the new King was sent for, and he entered . . . solemn, grave, sad and dignified in Admiral's uniform. Everyone was most impressed by his seeming youth and by his dignity. Much bowing, and he in turn swore his Oath.

When he left some of the Councillors were overcome by their emotions
. . . all this from Duff.

'Chips' Channon

1979

Had my first pipe for about five or six days. Somehow the pressure of not
smoking made me think of nothing but my pipe.

Tony Benn

22 January

1826

I feel neither dishonourd nor broken down by the bad – miserably bad news
I have received. I have walked my last on the domains I have planted, sate
the last time in the halls I have built. But death would have taken them from
me if misfortune had spared them. My poor people whom I loved so well!!
There is just another dye to turn up against me in this run of ill luck – i.e.
If I should break my magic wand in a fall from this elephant and lose my
popularity with my fortune. Then *Woodstock* and *Boney* may both go to the
papermaker and I may take to smoking cigars and drinking grog or turn
devotee and intoxicate the brain another way. In prospect of absolute ruin I
wonder if they would let me leave the Court of Session. I should like methinks
to go abroad

And lay my banes far from the Tweed.

But I find my eyes moistening and that will not do. I will not yield without
a fight for it. It is odd, when I set myself to work *doggedly* as Dr Johnson
would say, I am exactly the same man that I ever was – neither low spirited
nor *distrait*. In prosperous times I have sometimes felt my fancy and powers
of language flat – but adversity is to me at least a tonic and bracer – the
fountain is awakend from its inmost recesses as if the spirit of afliction had
troubled it in his passage.

Poor Mr Pole the harper sent to offer me £500 or £600, probably his
all. There is much good in the world after all. But I will involve no friend
either rich or poor – My own right hand shall do it – Else will I be *done*
in the slang language and *undone* in common parlance.

I am glad that beyond my own family, who are excepting L.[ady] S.[cott]
young and able to bear sorrow of which this is the first taste to some of
them, most of the hearts are past aching which would have been inconsolable

on this occasion. I do not mean that many will not seriously regret and some perhaps lament my misfortunes. But my dear mother, my almost sister Christy R[utherfor]d, – poor Will: Erskine – these would have been mourners indeed–

Well – exertion – exertion – O Invention rouze thyself. May man be kind – may God be propitious. The worst is I never quite know when I am right or wrong and Ballantyne, who does know in some degree will fear to tell me. Lockhart would be worth gold just now but he too would be too diffident to speak broad out. All my hope is in the continued indulgence of the public.

I have a funeral letter to the burial of the Chevalier Yelin, a foreigner of learning and talent, who has died at the Royal Hotel. He wishd to be introduced to me and was to have read a paper before the Royal Society when this introduction was to have taken place. I was not at the society that evening and the poor gentleman was taken ill in the meeting and unable to proceed. He went to his bed and never arose again – and now his funeral will be the first public place that I shall appear at – he dead and I ruind. This is what you call a meeting.

Sir Walter Scott

1848

Lady Beavale told me some anecdotes of the Royal children, which may one day have an interest when time has tested and developed their characters. The Princess Royal is very clever, strong in body and in mind; the Prince of Wales weaker and more timid, and the Queen says he is a stupid boy; but the hereditary and unfailing antipathy of our Sovereigns to their Heirs Apparent seems this early to be taking root, and the Queen does not much like the child. He seems to have an incipient propensity to that sort of romancing which distinguished his uncle, George IV. The child told Lady Beavale that during their cruise he was very nearly thrown overboard, and was proceeding to tell her how when the Queen overheard him, sent him off with a flea in his ear, and told her it was totally untrue.

Charles Greville

1864

Last night and tonight I have observed for the first time the noise of the new Charing Cross Railway. Even as I write the dull wearing hum of trains upon the Surrey side is going on: it goes on far into the night, with every now & then the bitter shriek of some accursed engine.

I almost welcome the loss, which I had been groaning over, of my view of the Thames; hoping that the new building when it rises may keep out these sounds. No one who has not tasted the pure & exquisite silence of the Temple at night can conceive the horror of the thought that it is gone for ever. Here at least was a respite from the roar of the streets by day: but now, silence and peace are fast going out of the world. It is not merely the torture of this new noise in a quiet place: but one knows that these are only the beginnings of such sorrows.

Our children will not know what it is to be free from sound of railways.

Arthur F. Munby

1935

Snow fell on roses today in New Orleans. These southern people couldn't have been more excited by the outbreak of another War between the States.

About 5 a.m. I walked downstairs and met a night watchman on a corner behind St. Louis Cathedral. In the glow of an antique street lamp he held the palm of his hand toward the white sky. A few flakes melted on his skin.

'Lookit that!' he exulted. 'Lookit that!' Pointing at himself, he said, 'Had a top-coat on when I began duty last night, but – gosh! I sure had to change into this overcoat, even if it does have moth holes in it!'

This is the first snowfall in New Orleans since 1899, according to old-timers. While they aren't all exactly sure of the date, they agree it has been 'some little spell' since the last time.

When I walked into the press room at the criminal court building, a reporter yelled: 'Eddie! Is this snow?'

'Why, sure.'

'Well,' he said slowly, 'I wasn't sure whether it was snow or ice.'

We got in his car to drive out to get a story and this southern boy exclaimed at almost every snowflake. Excitedly he pointed at what he called snowdrifts – none more than half an inch deep. When we returned he jumped out of his car, scooped up what little snow he could and sprinkled it on his hat and shoulders. Then he yelled to a telephone operator in the building and she threw on a coat and joined us outdoors. She shouted in amazement. We put her under a palm tree, then hammered at the trunk to shake some snow off the fronds and onto her. Proud as a queen in ermine, she ran back inside to show her white collar to her friends.

Later in the day a man on a streetcar told me: 'I got my wife and daughter out of bed and we all hurried into the yard. My little girl made a snowball and threw it at her mother. My wife said: "That's the first time I've ever been hit by a snowball!"'

Instead of working today, these people who never before had seen snow frolicked outdoors or hung around doors and windows to gawk at something they called a miracle. A burly Negro grinned and said: 'Man! Tom an'

Jerry sho catch hell today!' Eleven precincts reported snow.The twelfth precinct reported egg nogs.

Edward Robb Ellis

23 January

1662

By invitacon to my uncle Fenner's, where I found his new wife, a pitiful, old, ugly, ill-bred woman in a hatt, a midwife. Here were many of his, and as many of her relations, sorry, mean people; and after choosing our gloves, we all went over to the Three Crane Tavern, and though the best room in the house, in such a narrow dogg-hole we were crammed, and I believe we were near forty, that it made me loathe my company and victuals; and a sorry poor dinner it was too.

Samuel Pepys

1920

This day, the anniversary of the death of Louis XVI, brings back memories of my childhood in that corner of Brittany where all the old, right-minded families indicated their respectful mourning by keeping their shutters closed all day, going to mass dressed in black and doing penance to compensate for France's criminal gesture. My mother, my old aunts and their friends set the example. My youth and cheerfulness were put to a hard test. Faces had to be long. Only the humble folk were allowed the privilege of passing this day comfortably, but they were regarded with an indulgent and disdainful pity.

Liane de Pougy

1927

Vita [Sackville-West] took me over the 4 acres building, which she loves: too little conscious beauty for my taste: smallish rooms looking on to buildings: no views: yet one or two things remain: Vita stalking in her Turkish dress, attended by small boys, down the gallery, wafting them on like some tall sailing ship – a sort of covey of noble English life: dogs walloping, children crowding, all very free and stately: & [a] cart bringing wood in to be sawn by the great circular saw. How do you see that? I asked Vita. She said she saw it as something that had gone on for hundreds of years.They had brought wood in from the Park to replenish the great fires like this for centuries: & her ancestresses had walked so on the snow with their great dogs bounding beside them. All the centuries seemed lit up, the past expressive, articulate; not dumb & forgotten; but a crowd of people stood behind, not dead at all; not remarkable; fair face, long limbed, affable, & so we reach the days of

Elizabeth quite easily. After tea, looking for letters of Dryden's to show me, she tumbled out a love letter of Lord Dorset's (17th century) with a lock of his soft gold tinted hair which I held in my hand a moment. One had a sense of links fished up into the light which are usually submerged.

Virginia Woolf

1936

[Stanley] Baldwin spoke for 20 minutes about the late King. It is the sort of thing he does very well, and every word perfectly chosen, and perfectly balanced. He had a trying day as he was pall-bearer in the morning at the funeral of his first cousin Rudyard Kipling. Mr Baldwin's speech was 'The Question was—' that messages of condolence be sent to the King, and to Queen Mary. He was followed by Major Attlee for the Socialists. We on our side thought he would jar, and do badly, but on the contrary he was excellent . . . he, too, held the House. At 3.40 the Speaker left the Chair, preceded by the Serjeant-at-Arms and Mace, etc., and we followed in pairs. Harold Nicolson said 'Let's stick together', and we did. In solemn silent state we progressed into Westminster Hall, lining the East side. Harold and I were at the end of the queue, as befitted 'new boys', and thus were nearly on the steps and found ourselves next to the Royal Family; I could have touched the Queen of Spain, fat and smelling slightly of scent, and old Princess Beatrice. Opposite us, were the Peers led by the Lord Chancellor, who, unlike the Speaker, always seems a joke character. In the middle of the Great Hall stood the catafalque draped in purple.

We waited for 10 minutes . . . and I was rather embarrassed as my heavy fur-lined coat has a sable collar, a discordant note among all the black. I had been tempted to come into the hall without one, but that would certainly have meant pneumonia. I was sorry for the aged Princess next to me, shivering in her veil . . . After a little some younger women, heavily-draped, came in, and were escorted to the steps. I recognized the Royal Duchesses. Princess Marina, as ever, managed to look infinitely more elegant than the others; she wore violets under her veil and her stockings, if not flesh-coloured, were of black so thin that they seemed so.

The great door opened . . . the coffin was carried in and placed on the catafalque. It was followed by King Edward, boyish, sad and tired, and the Queen, erect and more magnificent than ever. Behind them were the Royal brothers. There was a short service . . . and all eyes looked first at the coffin, on which lay the Imperial Crown and a wreath from the Queen, and then we turned towards the boyish young King, so young and seemingly frail. Actually he is forty-two, but one can never believe it. After a few moments, the Queen and young King turned, and followed by the Royal Family, they left. The two Houses of Parliament then proceeded in pairs round the catafalque now guarded by four immobile officers and by Gentlemen-at-Arms . . . there was an atmosphere of hushed stillness, of something strangely sacred and awe-inspiring.

This King business is so emotional, it upsets and weakens me, and I am left with the feeling that nothing matters . . . almost an eve-of-war reaction. As we left, we were told that on the way to Westminster hall, the top bit of the Imperial Crown had fallen out during the procession, and had been picked up by a Serjeant-Major.

'Chips' Channon

1996

Today there is much fuss about Harriet Harman, of the Shadow Cabinet, sending her 11-year-old son to St Olave's School in what the media describe as 'leafy Orpington'. Presumably it is not very leafy at this time of year. Part of the trouble is that the boy has to take an exam and face an interview. Without such things I can't see how the school would know in what form to place him. Neither do I see why all the emphasis is put on Ms Harman's decision; presumably her husband should have at least 50 per cent say in the matter, and perhaps Master Joseph may have his views on education.

Alec Guinness

24 January

1684

The frost still continuing more and more severe, the Thames before London was planted with bothes in formal streetes, as in a Citty, or Continual faire, all sorts of Trades and shops furnished, and full of Commodities, even to a Printing presse, where the People and Ladys tooke a fansy to have their names Printed and the day and yeare set downe, when printed on the Thames: This humour tooke so universaly, that 'twas estimated the Printer gained five pound a day, for printing a line onely, at six-pence a Name, besides what he gott by Ballads etc: Coaches now plied from Westminster to the Temple, and from severall other staires too and froo, as in the streetes; also on sleds, sliding with skeetes; There was likewise, Bull-baiting, Horse and Coach races, Pupet-plays and interludes, Cookes and Tipling, and lewder places; so as it seem'd to be a bacchanalia, Triumph or Carnoval on the Water, whilest it was a severe Judgement upon the land: the Trees not only splitting as if lightning-strock, but Men and Cattell perishing in divers places, and the very seas so locked up with yce, that no vessells could stirr out, or come in.

John Evelyn

1856

A journal is a record of experiences and growth, not a preserve of things well done or said. I am occasionally reminded of a statement which I have made in conversation and immediately forgotten, which would read much better than what I put in my journal. It is a ripe, dry fruit of long-past experience which falls from me easily, without giving pain or pleasure. The charm of the journal must consist in a certain greenness, though fresh, and not in maturity. Here I cannot afford to be remembering what I said or did, my scurf cast off, but what I am and aspire to become.

H. D. Thoreau

1938 [Nanking]

We're all degenerating around here. We're becoming spineless, losing our respectability. In *Indiscreet Letters from Peking*, a book about the siege of Peking in 1900, Putnam Wheale reports how he and many other Europeans simply joined in the looting. I don't think we're all that far from it ourselves. My houseboy Chang bought an electric table fan worth 38 dollars for $1.20 today, and expects me to be pleased. A couple of genuine Ming vases, costing one dollar each, gaze at me with reproach from my fireplace mantel.

If I felt like it, I could fill the entire house with cheap curios – meaning stolen and then sold for a song on the black market. Only food is expensive these days: A chicken now costs two dollars, the exact same price as those two Ming vases.

John Rabe

1942 [Jersey]

Things are depressing all the time. Almost every night, the *Evening Post* reports sudden deaths. It is very strange – lack of proper nourishment must be the cause. Then there are lots of 'foreign' workmen in the island, brought by the Germans. These are half-starved, and half-clothed, and reported to have strange and dangerous diseases. However, we have all had a ration of a quarter pound of chocolate each this week. It was wonderful – chocolate!

Nan Le Ruez

1953

There are two kinds of men on tubes. Those who blow their noses and then examine the results in a handkerchief, and those who blow their noses without exhibiting any such curiosity, and simply replace the handkerchief in the pocket. I, generally, come under the first category.

Kenneth Williams

1996

The car taking me to Moorfields wriggled its way through tiny, twisted City streets which were almost deserted; a few thin clerks with blue noses hunched themselves against the bitter wind, walking stiffly and alone, like the black matchstick figures in a Lowry industrial townscape. The women to be seen were, for the most part, dressed as Paddington Bear. It is a pleasing hat but the face peeping from underneath it should be under thirty. The car slid past St Paul's Cathedral which somehow looked smaller than usual and rather drab. Elizabeth Frink's sheep, nearby, are being *driven* by their shepherd, as was pointed out to me a few years ago, and not *following* him as the Bible recommends. Things are out of joint.

Alec Guinness

25 January

1851

I've fallen in love or imagine that I have; went to a party and lost my head. Bought a horse which I don't need at all.

Leo Tolstoy

1885

Daudet spoke of the first years of his married life. He told me that his wife did not know that there was such a thing as a pawnshop; and once she had been enlightened, she would never refer to it by name but would ask him: 'Have you been *there?*' The delightful thing about it all is that this girl who had been brought up in such a middle-class way of life was not at all dismayed by this new existence among people scrounging dinners, cadging twenty-franc pieces, and borrowing pairs of trousers.

'You know,' said Daudet, 'the dear little thing spent nothing, absolutely nothing on herself. We have still got the little account books we kept at that time, in which, beside twenty francs taken by myself or someone else, the only entry for her, occurring here and there, now and then, is *Omnibus, 30 centimes.*' Mme Daudet interrupted him to say ingenuously: 'I don't think that I was really mature at that time: I didn't understand . . .' My own opinion is rather that she had the trustfulness of people who are happy and in love, the certainty that everything will turn out all right in the end.

The Brothers Goncourt

1936

My younger daughter managed to get through Downing Street and so had a very good view of the procession as it came down Whitehall from the station on its way to Westminster Hall for the Lying in State. She told me that she had never seen anyone look so ill or as unhappy as the Prince of Wales looked that day. He was evidently going through the most fearful mental and physical anguish. And I heard from someone else that in Trafalgar Square they were afraid he would not be able to go on to the very end.

Marie Belloc Lowndes

1940

Chaplin got on to the subject of the Duke of Windsor, whom he met several times during a trip to Europe. Windsor was then the Prince of Wales. His first question was, 'How old are you?' He wanted to know what Chaplin had done in the 1914 war – and when Chaplin told him, 'Nothing,' there was a frosty silence. Then Chaplin asked him how many uniforms he owned and how he knew which one to wear on any given occasion: did someone tell him?' 'No one,' Windsor replied coldly, 'ever tells me to do anything.'

Nevertheless, he seems to have taken a great fancy to Chaplin and often asked him down to Fort Belvedere. Chaplin nearly committed a serious breach of etiquette by going to the lavatory when Windsor was already there. This is strictly against the rules.

Although Windsor had at once begun calling Chaplin 'Charlie,' Chaplin had stuck rigidly to the formal 'Sir'. He imitated himself saying demurely: 'Oh, *no*, Sir! Oh, *yes*, Sir!' Behind all these anecdotes, there was the sparkle of guttersnipe impudence. One sees him in his classic role of debunker of official pomposity, always, everywhere. 'How can they possibly go on with all that nonsense?' he kept repeating.

Christopher Isherwood

1947

Embarked in the *America* full of cocaine, opium and brandy, feeble and low-spirited. One of the reasons for my putting myself under the surgeon's knife was to wish to be absolutely well and free from ointments for Laura's American treat. All the reasons for the operation [for piles] appeared ineffective immediately afterwards. The pain was excruciating and the humiliations constant. The hospital was reasonably comfortable and the nurses charming – the grace of God apparent everywhere. But I had ample time to reflect that I had undergone an operation, which others only endure after years of growing agony, when I had in fact suffered nothing worse than occasional discomfort. I took no advice, either from a physician or fellow sufferers, just went to the surgeon and ordered the operation as I would have ordered new shirts. In fact I had behaved wholly irrationally and was paying for it.

Evelyn Waugh

26 January

1837 [Paris]

Having seen all the high society the night before, I resolved to see all the low to-night, and went to Musard's Ball – a most curious scene; two large rooms in the Rue St Honoré almost thrown into one, a numerous and excellent orchestra, a prodigious crowd of people, most of them in costume, and all the women masked. There was every description of costume, but that which was the most general was the dress of a French post-boy, in which both males and females seemed to delight. It was well-regulated uproar and orderly confusion. When the music struck up they began dancing all over the rooms; the whole mass was in motion, but though with gestures the most vehement and grotesque, and a licence almost unbounded, the figure of the dance never seemed to be confused and the dancers were both expert in their capers and perfect in their evolutions. Nothing could be more licentious than the movements of the dancers, and they only seemed to be restrained within the limits of common decency by the cocked hats and burnished helmets of the police and gendarmes which towered in the midst of them. After quadrilling and waltzing away, at a signal given they began galloping round the room; then they rushed pell-mell, couple after couple like Bedlamites broke loose, but not the slightest accident occurred. I amused myself with this strange and grotesque sight for an hour or more and then came home.

Charles Greville

1847 [Paris]

Dined with M. Thiers. I never know what to say to the men I meet at his house. From time to time they turn round and talk art to me when they observe how profoundly bored I am with conversation about politics, the Chamber, etc.

How chilly and tiresome is this modern fashion for dinner parties! The flunkeys bear the brunt of the whole business and do everything but put the food into one's mouth. Dinner is the last thing to be considered, it is quickly polished off like some disagreeable duty. Nothing cordial or good-natured about it. The fragile glasses – an idiotic refinement! I cannot touch my glass without making it shake and spilling half the contents over the cloth. I get away as quickly as I can.

Eugène Delacroix

1930

When we made up our six months accounts, we found I had made about £3,020 last year – the salary of a civil servant; a surprise to me, who was content with £200 for so many years. But I shall drop very heavily I think. *The Waves* won't sell more than 2,000 copies.

Virginia Woolf

1938

For no reason at all I hated this day as if it was a person – it's wind, it's insecurity, it's flabbiness, it's hints of an insane universe.

Dawn Powell

1941

Sibyl [Lady Colefax] comes to stay. As usual she is full of gossip. She minds so much the complete destruction of London social life. Poor Sibyl, in the evenings she goes back to her house which is so cold since all the windows have been broken. And then at nine she creeps round to her shelter under the Institute for the Blind and goes to sleep on her palliasse. But all of this leaves her perfectly serene. We who have withstood the siege of London will emerge as Lucknow veterans and have annual dinners.

We have not yet taken Derna but we have invaded Italian Somaliland . . . Eritrea has been badly pierced, and we are within striking distance of Massawa. But all this is mere chicken-feed. We know that the Great Attack is impending. We know that . . . we may be exposed to the most terrible ordeal that we have ever endured. The Germans have refrained from attacking us much during the last ten days since they do not wish to waste aeroplanes and petrol on bad weather. But when the climate improves they may descend upon us with force such as they have never employed before. Most of our towns will be destroyed.

I sit here in my familiar brown room with my books and pictures round me, and once again the thought comes to me that I may never see them again. They may well land their parachute and airborne troops behind Sissinghurst and the battle may take place over our bodies. Well, if they try, let them try. We shall win in the end.

Harold Nicolson

1977

Sitting in a bus in London last week, it being a raw day I took out of my pocket my white lip salve and applied it to my chapped lips. An elderly woman sitting opposite put on a strongly disapproving face, and said, 'Well!' in a long-drawn-out tone. I paid not the slightest notice.

James Lees-Milne

1979

Got my pay cheque today. Thought I would celebrate by taking myself to a good restaurant. Walked home; thought about so many things. One of them was how some weeks ago in London I walked along Long Acre from Covent Garden where I had seen *Götterdämmerung* – alone as I thought, along the street I farted. It was much louder, after five hours of Wagner, than I had dreamed it could possibly be! Some boys and girls, rather charming, whom I had scarcely noticed, overheard me, or it, and started cheering. In the darkness I was more amused than embarrassed. Then a self-important thought came in my mind. Supposing they knew that this old man walking along Long Acre and farting was Stephen Spender? What would they think? Anyway, for some reason a bit difficult for me to analyse, it would be embarrassing. Then I saw how an incident like this divides people one knows into categories – those who would laugh and those who would be shocked (shocked anyway at me writing this down). I don't think F. R. Leavis would have been amused. But Forster, Auden, Isherwood, Connolly, Ackerley, and Matthew, my son, would be.

Stephen Spender

1988 [after a Hollywood film premiere]

We convertible down to the Hard Rock Café where Irv [his American agent] wedges me between big bellies and bozooms and the rhetoric of 'YOU'RE AN ACTOR? DO YOU DIRECT? WHO'S YOUR AGENT? PUBLICIST? MANAGER? GURU? SAW YOU IN WITHNAAALE AND AY. SO WHADDYA THINK OF THE MOVIE, HUH?'

Double-glazed eyes – either drunk, disappointed or dumb. Can there really be as many *stupid* people here as I think there are?

'Gotta remember this is not an A-list event, but kinda gives you a taster. Fun, huh?' Young women with piles of peroxided hair switch on like megawatt bulbs when an agent or director is radared. I meet an English agent who is trying to itemize it all with irony, but before I can mutter Davey Crockett, Irv is at my side and reacting like the Brit has lured me away.

'*Beware of the people poachers,*' he whispers in my ear.

I gasp for some fresh air outside, pocketing the traitorous card clipped me by the English agent, and am delivered back to the hotel by Irv. Get a room service sandwich that must have taken four grown men to prepare. I haven't yet asked *how* you're s'posed to get your jaw wide enough for a bite without double jointing.

It's impossible to imagine what this place does to your psyche and soul if you aren't working. The divide is *ruthless*. Every waiter seems to be an actor and they deliver the menu like an audition speech.

'HI, MY NAME'S WARREN AND I'LL BE YOUR WAITER FOR THE NIGHT. NOW THE SPECIALS GO LIKE THIS: TONIGHT WE HAVE CLAMS ON THE HALF SHELL, SHARK STEAK WITH A PIQUANT LIME AND DILL SAUCE, OR SAUTÉ OF LAMB'S BRAIN WITH A GUACAMOLE ACCOMPANIMENT AND I KNOW I SHOULDN'T BE SAYING THIS BUT THANKS FOR YOUR PERFOR- MANCE IN THAT MOVIE.'

Richard E. Grant

27 January

1658

After six fitts of a Quartan Ague it pleased God to visite my deare Child Dick with fitts so extreame, especiale one of his sides, that after the rigor was over and he in his hot fitt, he fell into so greate and intollerable a sweate, that being surpriz'd with the aboundance of vapours ascending to his head, he fell into such fatal Symptoms, as all the help at hand was not able to recover his spirits, so as after a long and painefull Conflict, falling to sleepe as we thought, and coverd too warme (though in midst of a severe frosty season) and by a greate fire in the roome; he plainely expird, to our un- expressable griefe and affliction. We sent for Physitians to Lond, whilst there was yet life in him; but the river was frozen up, and the Coach brake by the way ere it got a mile from the house; so as all artificial help failing, and his natural strength exhausted, we lost the prettiest, and dearest Child, that ever parents had, being but 5 yeares and 3 days old in years but even at that tender age, a prodigie for Witt, and understanding; for beauty of body a very Angel, and for endowments of mind, of incredible and rare hopes.

John Evelyn

1831

So fagd by my frozen vigils that I slept till after ten. When I lose the first two hours in the morning I can seldom catch them again during the whole day. A friendly visit from Ebenezer Clarkson of Selkirk, a medical gentleman in whose experience and ingenuity I have much confidence as well as his personal regard to myself. He is quite sensible of the hesitation of speech of which I complain, and thinks it arises from the stomach. Recommends the wild mustard as an aperient. But the brightest ray of hope is the chance that I may get some mechanical aid made by Fortune at Broughton Street which may enable me to mount a pony with ease, and to walk without torture. This would indeed be almost a restoration of my youth, at least of a green old age full of enjoyment – the shutting one out from the face of living nature is almost worse than sudden death.

Sir Walter Scott

1897

At a City branch of a certain bank yesterday morning two golden-haired girls, with large feathered hats, presented a piece of paper bearing a penny stamp and the words 'Please pay the bearer £2 10/- Henry T. Davies.' The cashier consulted his books and had to inform the ladies that Henry T. Davies had no account there. 'I don't know about that,' said one of them, 'but he slept with me last night, and he gave me this paper because he hadn't any cash. Didn't he, Clara?' 'Yes,' said Clara, 'that he did, and I went out this morning to buy the stamp for him.' The cashier commiserated with them, but they were not to be comforted.

Arnold Bennett

1933

I resent in a clipping, 'Father of the dead child.' Dead child – a waxen child stretched out. No – the child who died.

I resent, 'They lost a child too' – as though that were the same. It is never the same. Death to you is not death, not obituary notices and quiet and mourning, sermons and elegies and prayers, coffins and graves and worldly platitudes. It is not the most common experience in life – the only certainty. It is not the oldest thing we know. It is not what happened to Caesar and Dante and Milton and Mary Queen of Scots, to the soldiers in all the wars, to the sick in the plagues, to public men yesterday. It never happened before – what happened today to you. It has only happened to your little boy . . .

Anne Morrow Lindbergh

28 January

1661

To the Theatre, where I saw again 'The Lost Lady,' which do now please me better than before; and here I sitting behind in a dark place, a lady spit backward upon me by a mistake, not seeing me; but after seeing her to be a very pretty lady, I was not troubled at it at all.

Samuel Pepys

1780

We had for dinner a Calf's Head, boiled Fowl and Tongue, a Saddle of Mutton rosted on the Side Table, and a fine Swan rosted with Currant Jelly Sauce for the first Course. The Second Course a couple of Wild Fowl called Dun Fowls, Larks, Blamange, Tarts, etc., etc. and a good Desert of Fruit after amongst which was a Damson Cheese. I never eat a bit of Swan before, and I think it good eating with a sweet sauce. The swan was killed 3 weeks before it was eat and yet not the lest bad taste in it.

James Woodforde

1829

Burke the Murderer hangd this morning. The mob which was immense demanded Knox and Hare but though greedy for more victims received with shouts the solitary wretch who found his way to the gallows out of five or six who seem not less guilty than He. But the story begins to be stale insomuch that I believe a doggerel ballad upon it would be popular how brutal soever the wit.

Sir Walter Scott

1891

How surprised and shocked I am to hear that Ellie Emmet, whose heart, I had been led to suppose, was seared by sorrow, is contemplating marriage again, – Poor Temple's devotion, his tragic death, his fatherhood of her six children, all forgotten; not even his memory sacred, for she says she 'never loved before.' What ephemeræ we all are; to be sure, experience leaves no permanent furrow, but like writing on sand is washed out by every advancing ripple of changing circumstance. 'Twould seem to the inexperienced that one happy 'go' at marriage would have given the full measure of connubial bliss, and all the chords of maternity have vibrated under the manipulation of six progeny; but man lives not to assimilate knowledge of the eternal essence of things, and only craves a renewal of sensation.

Alice James

1920

I shall not remember what happened on this day. It is a blank. At the end of my life I may want it, may long to have it. There was a new moon: that I remember. But who came or what I did – all is lost. It's just a day missed, a day crossing the line.

Katherine Mansfield

1932 [France]

Alarming rumours are going about; country people are getting worried; tradesmen cannot get payment . . .

'Is it true what they say, that we are going to have war again?'

Three times in the last four days this question has been asked of Em. [his wife], who hastens to reassure as best she can.

'No country is in a state to make war today,' she replies.

'But then why have matches gone up two sous?'

André Gide

1975

Yesterday I had three letters from three friends, so different in every way that it was startling to find the same problem making for depression. One is a young married woman with two small children and a husband who is a company man. She feels shut out by his work, resents his cavalier way of bringing 'friends', meaning clients, home without warning, but especially their lack of communication because there is never time. He is also away a lot on business. The second is a friend whose husband retired recently; on his retirement they moved away from the town where they had always lived to be near the ocean. He is at a loose end and she feels caught, angry and depressed without being able to define why. The third is a woman professor, quite young, who lives happily with a woman colleague but speaks of her 'bone loneliness.'

'Loneliness' for me is associated with love relationships. We are lonely when there is not perfect communion. In solitude one can achieve a good relationship with oneself. It struck me forcibly that I could never speak of 'bone loneliness' now, though I have certainly experienced it when I was in love. And I feel sure that poignant phrase would have described my mother often.

May Sarton

1978

At Temple Meads Station in Bristol waiting for the late train back to London, I went to the buffet on the platform and bought a sandwich, a Fry's chocolate bar, some Wrigley's spearmint gum and an apple. I was about to pay when an old man in a raincoat pushed forward and thrust a pound note at the girl. I thought he was trying to get ahead of me and I was going to say, 'Excuse me', but it turned out that he was paying for my food, which came to 54 pence. He turned to me and said, 'I know you, I know who you are,' left the money and disappeared. I did not know what to do, but thought it was very touching.

Tony Benn

1986 [New York]

Friends of Alan's [Parker] invite us to dinner at an Italian restaurant called La Primavera, which they are trying out for the first time. More like La Prima Donnas. Hair in here is a real 'do', faces taut, diamonds sharp, toupées fixed and ties sapphire-pinned. New money, old flesh. Child-sized pasta portions clock in at thirty dollars. Talk is all deals and dollars and dumping money here to dough it up there. The artistic endeavour of making movies is relegated to a corner of minor irritation and inconvenience. *Yet* it seems *everyone* wants to know the stars. Meanwhile Alan is getting *major* attention from everyone in the place – maître d', waiters, other guests, and we cannot work out *why*. Until the owner 'compliments' him with 'You have lost so much weight Mr Kissinger.' We were taken aback long enough *not* to dispel the mistake and settled back for the five-star service, laughing all the way through complimentary dessert and liqueurs. *Must be these new glasses.*

Richard E. Grant

29 January

1660

Spent the afternoon in casting up my accounts, and do find myself to be worth £40 or more, which I did not think, but am afraid that I have forgot something.

Samuel Pepys

1837

Had a Lady to dinner here today. The Lady's maid is taken very sick today: I sopose she has been eating too much or something of the kind. But she is very subject to sickness. Last summer, when we were coming home from Canterbury, she actually spewed all the way, a distance of sixty miles and not less time than eight hours. The people stared as we passed through the towns and villages as she couldent stop even then. It amused me very much to see how the country people stood stareing with their mouthes half open and half shut to see her pumping over the side of the carriage and me sitting by, quite unconserned, gnawing a piece of cake or some sandwiches or something or other, as her sickness did not spoil my apatite. It was very bad for her but I couldent do her any good as it was the motion of the carriage that caused her illness. I gave her something to drink every time we changed horses but no sooner than it was down it came up again, and so the road from Canterbury to London was pretty well perfumed with Brandy, Rum, Shrub, wine and such stuff. She very soon recovered after she got home and was all the better for it after. It's eleven o'clock. My fire is out and I am off to bed.

William Tayler

1860

Saw Barriere who told us this striking anecdote. On the Place de Grève he had seen a condemned man whose hair had visibly stood on end when he had been turned to face the scaffold. Yet this was the man who, when Dr. Pariset had asked him what he wanted before he died, had answered: 'A leg of mutton and a woman.'

The Brothers Goncourt

1950

A lovely, remote time at Murphys'. They spoke of Elsa Maxwell and how she raised money for Russian Ambulance in World War 1, absconded with money, then returned to social success after three years. How a friend, Lily Havemeyer, had a caller who brought Miss Maxwell to lunch. Elsa looked over the place – marvelous for party – said to Lily (first meeting) 'You go shopping for the day and leave me your servants, your house and carte blanche and at night you will find yourself with a party all Paris will talk about.' 'No' was all Lily said.

Dawn Powell

1969

At Lindy Dufferin's party for Duncan Grant I'd chatted to David Hockney and suggested what a marvellous subject Fred Ashton would make for him. At the time Fred was perching on the arms of a sofa with his fingers exquis- itely arranged – the only word for it – around a cigarette. From afar *en profile* he looked like some exotic parakeet. David was clearly excited by the possi- bility. At the time he was drawing W. H. Auden so I thought that I ought to go and look.

Number 17 Powis Terrace is one of those late-Victorian stucco terraces in Notting Hill Gate with a vast columned portico and every sign that gentil- ity had long since fled. The houses were now tatty tenements and I climbed up what can only be described as a squalid staircase-well to be met by David. Original is the only word one could ever apply to him with his bleached blond hair and owl spectacles. But I couldn't help loving him and admiring his quick logic and unique perception. He's rather large and square, getting fat in fact, and somehow terribly conscious of it. The whole time I was there he kept on feeling beneath his shirt as though checking up on the expansion of the wodges. We sat down in his kitchen together with his slim blond American boy-friend Peter Schlesinger, and lunched off consommé, toast and pâté washed down with red wine. After it we went into the studio.

I don't think that I'd ever before encountered anyone so overtly homosexual. Against one wall rested two blown-up photographs of Peter, one in bikini underpants, the other in jeans with his flies left undone. All over the floor were scattered magazines with male nudes. David picked one up and complained how it had been seized by the Customs and then returned. On its cover was stamped 'Nudes – semi-erect'. He works from photographs but not when he draws people. He showed me some of Angus Wilson, one of which was very good although he didn't think so. He agreed to draw Fred Ashton for me, although I warned him about the Trustees [of the National Portrait Gallery]. The phone rang. It was a Spanish waiter who wanted to come round and strip for him to draw. The time had come to leave.

Roy Strong

30 January

1649

The Villanie of the Rebells proceeding now so far as to Trie, Condemne, and Murder our excellent King [Charles I], the 30 of this Moneth, struck me with such horror that I keep the day of his Martyrdom a fast, and would not be present, at that execrable wickednesse; receiving that sad [account] of it from my Bro: Geo: and also by Mr Owen, who came to Visit this afternoone, recounting to me all the Circumstances.

John Evelyn

1871

In a newspaper giving the news of the capitulation, I read the news of King William's enthronement as Emperor of Germany at Versailles, in the Hall of Mirrors, under the nose of the stone Louis XIV in the courtyard outside. That really marks the end of the greatness of France.

The Brothers Goncourt

1915

Preparations for my departure are well under way. I am breathlessly impatient to be off, but there is much to be done and the [Red Cross] Unit itself is not yet fully organised. My nurse's dresses, aprons and veils have been made already, and I have bought a flannel-lined, black leather jacket. An accessory to this jacket is a thick sheepskin waistcoat, for winter wear, whose Russian name, *dushegreychka*, means 'soul-warmer'. I hear that our unit will be stationed for a time on the Russo-Austrian Front in the Carpathian Mountains and that we will have to ride horseback, as direct communication can be established there only by riding; so high boots and black leather breeches have been added to my wardrobe. At the moment of my departure, Anna Ivanovna, my Russian 'mother', bade me kneel before her. Taking from her pocket a little chain, she fastened it round my neck. Then she blessed me, kissed me three times, 'In the name of the Father, of the Son and of the Holy Spirit', and wished me 'God speed'. I, too, was a soldier, going to war, for thus did all Russian mothers to their soldier sons. The little chain, with a small icon and cross attached to it, has already been blessed by a priest.

Florence Farmborough

1921

J. accused me of always bagging his books as soon as he had begun to read them. I said: 'It's like fishing. I see you've got a bite. I want your line. I want to pull it in.'

Katherine Mansfield

1938

I have advised the Duce not to let Biseo [Italian airman] continue his flight to Argentina, where some kind of hostile demonstration against our airmen was being prepared. There is really no point in exposing equipment and men to the not inconsiderable wear and tear of a three thousand kilometres' flight, in order to give the rabble of a second-class country like Argentina a chance to insult us. The Duce agrees – they will not go. Of all the countries in which I have lived Argentina is certainly the one I loved least – indeed I felt a profound contempt for it. A people without a soul and a land without colour – both failed to exercise any kind of charm on me. For several decades, when all sorts of human wrecks were making their way to South America, the worst of all used to stop at the first place they came to. That was the beginning of Buenos Aires, a city as monotonous and turbid as the river on whose banks it lies. In recent years there has been added to this unpleasant mixture a very plentiful Jewish element. I don't believe that can have improved things.

Count Ciano

1943

The first refugee children have arrived. They were due yesterday evening at seven – after a twelve hours' journey from Genoa – but it was not until nine p.m.

that at last the car drew up and seven very small sleepy bundles were lifted out. The eldest is six, the others four and five – all girls except one, a solemn little Sardinian called Dante Porcu. We carry them down into the play-room of the nursery-school (where the stove is burning, and supper waiting) and they stand blinking in the bright light, like small bewildered owls. White, pasty faces – several with boils and sores – and thin little sticks of arms and legs.

The Genoese district nurse who has brought them tells me that they have been chosen from families whose houses have been totally destroyed, and who, for the last two months, have been living in an underground tunnel beneath the city, without light or sufficient water, and in bitter cold. Their fathers are mostly dock-labourers; two of them have been killed.

The children eat their warm soup, still too bewildered fully to realize where they are – and then, as they gradually thaw and wake up, the first wail goes up – 'Mamma, Mamma, I want my Mamma!' We hastily produce the toys which we have prepared for just that moment; the little girls clutch their dolls, Dante winds up his motor, and for a few minutes tears are averted. Then we take them upstairs and tuck them up in their warm beds. Homesickness sets in again – and two of them, poor babies, cry themselves to sleep.

Iris Origo

1948

Gandhi has been assassinated. In my humble opinion, a bloody good thing but far too late.

Noël Coward

1969 [on the *Monte Anaga*, sailing to Las Palmas]

We were up to the sweet at lunch when the ship shuddered with an impact and the captain rushed from his table in the dining room and shot up to the bridge. A lot of passengers went running up to the deck, and practically emptied the room. I stayed for the coffee. Later it transpired that we'd hit a fishing boat amidships, cutting it in half & sinking it. We lowered a lifeboat and circled for survivors, and picked up four. There was one dead, and a further four missing. Another fishing boat hove to, and the crew shouted obscenities at our ship. Now, with the survivors on board, we have turned round and are making for Corunna, which is where the fishermen hail from. Obviously this will wreak havoc with our holiday plans. This fellow Bill on board organised a fund for the survivors of the disaster with the help of a priest and between 65 passengers we raised a measly 23 pounds which was quite shame-making. The radio officer said that you couldn't see the bows of the ship because we were sailing into the sun and it was blinding.

Kenneth Williams

1973

We were bidden to a dinner with Olive and Denis Hamilton given in honour of Harold Macmillan and turned out to be the only other guests and I'm still left wondering why they alighted upon us. . . . I suppose it was important and fascinating to meet the former Prime Minister, but I think that I would have to place him as one of the rudest men that I have ever met. He looks exactly like his own cartoons. Now about eighty, I would have thought, he's a bit geriatric with a runny nose, and his speech is a stream of consciousness interspersed with occasional lucid flashes. He was a pattern of memories, all of them political, and the Hamiltons kept on feeding him with memory questions. I was swatted down regularly if I ever attempted to open my mouth, never allowed to contribute one thing to the conversation, and if I even began a sentence he interrupted it. For most of the evening Julia and I sat in bored amazement. The only remarks tossed my way took the form of periodic incoherent denunciations of the Gallery's purchase of the Hill-Adamson albums: 'What do you want them for? Got drawer-loads of old photographs at home.' He really wasn't human and there was not a single comment he made which wasn't about himself. He was a caricature arch-reactionary, enough to make me want to vote Communist.

Roy Strong

1975

The sixties are marvelous years, because one has become fully oneself by then, but the erosions of old age, erosion of strength, of memory, of physical well-being have not yet begun to frustrate and needle. I am too heavy, but I refuse to worry too much about it. I battle the ethos here in the USA, where concern about being overweight has become a fetish. I sometimes think we are as cruel to old brother ass, the body, as the Chinese used to be who forced women's feet into tiny shoes as a sign of breeding and beauty. 'Middle-aged spread' is a very real phenomenon, and why pretend that it is not? I am not so interested in being a dazzling model as in being comfortable inside myself. And that I am.

May Sarton

31 January

1932

There is a dead and drowned mouse in the lily-pond. I feel like that mouse – static, obese and decaying. Vita [Sackville-West, his wife] is calm, comforting and considerate. And yet (for have I not been reading a batch of insulting press-cuttings?) life is a drab and dreary thing. I have missed it. I have made a fool of myself in every respect.

> *Surely there was a time I might have trod*
> *The sunlit heights, and from life's dissonance*
> *Struck one clear chord to reach the ears of God?*

Very glum. Discuss finance. Vita keeps on saying that we have got enough to go on with. But when one goes into it, that represents only two months. I must get a job. Yet all the jobs which pay humiliate. And the decent jobs do not pay. Come back to Long Barn. Arrange my books sadly. Weigh myself sadly. Have put on eight pounds. Feel ashamed of myself, my attainments, and my character. Am I a serious person at all? Vita thinks I should make £2,000 by writing a novel. I don't. The discrepancy between these two theories causes me some distress of mind.

Harold Nicolson

1938

As was to be expected, criticism of the parade step [the 'Roman step', similar to the German goose-step] has started up. The old soldiers are particularly against it, because they choose to regard it as a Prussian invention. The Duce is very angry – he has read me the speech he is going to make to-morrow, explaining and extolling the innovation. It seems that the King too has expressed himself unfavourably. The Duce's comment was: 'It is not my fault if the King is half size. Naturally he won't be able to do the parade step without making himself ridiculous. He will hate it for the same reason that he has always hated horses – he has to use a ladder to climb on to one. But a physical defect in a sovereign is not a good reason for stunting, as he has done, the army of a great nation. People say the goose-step is Prussian. Nonsense. The goose is a Roman animal – it saved the Capital. Its place is with the eagle and the she-wolf.'

Count Ciano

1947

What makes daily life so agreeable in America is the good humour and friendliness of Americans. Of course, this quality has its reverse side. I'm irritated by those imperious invitations to 'take life easy', repeated in words and images throughout the day. On advertisements for Quaker Oats, Coca-Cola, and Lucky Strike, what displays of white teeth – the smile seems like lockjaw. The constipated girl smiles a loving smile at the lemon juice that relieves her intestines. In the subway, in the streets, on magazine pages, these smiles pursue me like obsessions. I read on a sign in a drugstore, 'Not to grin is a sin.'

Everyone obeys the order, the system. 'Cheer up! Take it easy.' Optimism is necessary for the country's social peace and economic prosperity. If a banker has generously lent fifty dollars without guarantee to some Frenchman in financial straits, if the manager of my hotel takes a slight risk by cashing his customers' cheques, it's because this trust is required and implied by an economy based on credit and expenditure.

Simone de Beauvoir

1947 [New York]
I went to the drugstore and asked for Dial [sleeping pill]. I learned later that New York State has lately become alarmed at the suicides and has enforced a strict ban on the sale of barbiturates. The chemist said I must have a doctor's prescription.

'I am a foreigner here. I have no American prescription.'

'We have a doctor on the 17th floor.'

'I have to go out. I can't go and see him.'

'I'll fix it for you.'

He telephoned the doctor, 'Dere's a guy here says he can't sleep. OK to give him Dial, doc?' Was given a box of twenty tablets 'to the prescription of Dr Hart'. '$3 medical attention.' That was the best piece of service I have yet met in the USA.

Evelyn Waugh

1987
Eddie Brown [barber] and Mrs Wilson, manicurist, were amused in the morning when I told them a true story about Enoch Powell. There is a very chatty barber in the Commons who never stops telling MPs whose hair he cuts about politics and what his views are on the world. Enoch Powell went to have his hair cut by him one day, sat down and the barber said, 'How would you like your hair cut, sir?' 'In silence,' Enoch replied.

Woodrow Wyatt

FEBRUARY

*'I always say, keep a diary and someday it'll
keep you.'*

MAE WEST

1 February

1857 [New York]

An epidemic of crime this winter. 'Garotting' stories abound, some true, some no doubt fictitious, devised to explain the absence of one's watch and pocket-book after a secret visit to some disreputable place, or to put a good face on some tipsy street fracas. But a tradesman was attacked the other afternoon in broad daylight at his own shop door in the Third Avenue near Thirteenth Street by a couple of men, one of whom was caught, and will probably get his deserts in the State prison, for life – the doom of two of the fraternity already tried and sentenced. Most of my friends are investing in revolvers and carry them about at night, and if I expect to have to do a great deal of late street-walking off Broadway, I think I should make the like provision; though it's a very bad practice carrying concealed weapons. Moreover, there was an uncommonly shocking murder in Bond Street (No. 31) Friday night; one Burdell, a dentist, strangled and riddled with stabs in his own room by some person unknown who must have been concealed in the room. Motive unknown, evidently not plunder.

George Templeton Strong

1867

Tennyson is unhappy from his uncertainty regarding the condition and destiny of man. Is it dispiriting to find a great poet with no better grounds of comfort than a common person? At first it is. But how should the case be otherwise? The poet has only the same materials of sensation and thought as ordinary mortals; he uses them better; but to step outside the human limitations is not granted even to him. The secret is kept from one and all of us. We must turn eyes and thoughts to the finer and nobler aspects of things, and never let the scalpel of Science overbear pen, pencil and plectrum. A Poet's doubts and anxieties are more comforting than a scientist's certainties and equanimities.

William Allingham

1944 [Algiers]

We went to Hospital No.95. Incredible place, ex-boys' school, miles and miles of it, vaulted, monastic, cool in summer and cold right now. 2500 there. Far grimmer than 94. How lucky the boys were at Taplow – air, light, space, newness and even gaiety. In the first ward (we did all orthopaedics yesterday) there were two of the illest men I have ever seen, I think. Just skulls but with living wide, very clear eyes. It was a huge ward and difficult to know where to put the piano. We put it in the centre in the end which meant that I had to keep spinning round as I sang. I tried a monologue, but it was no good in there – too big, too decentralised. While I was walking around talking before we began I said to the illest of the two very ill ones that I hoped he'd excuse my back when I had to turn it on him and he said he would if I'd excuse him for not being shaved. Oh, gosh. [He died two days later.]

Joyce Grenfell

1952 [Egypt]

We were at the El Mansur race course by 7a.m. to watch the trials from Colonel 'Dickie' Bird's flat inside the grandstand. . . . 'The person we must find is Madame Paris,' Desmond said later as he shepherded us toward the betting hall: 'All the jockeys slept last night at her brothel and she knows which horses are being pulled or doped!' . . . We soon spotted Madame Paris, a short, fat woman with hennaed hair and puffy white cheeks, her red mouth a gash. She was shovelling money through the hatch with scarlet claws covered in rings. Desmond waylaid her and she whispered something in his ear. He came back beaming. 'Don't bet the favourite on the first race!' he announced. 'Madame P. says Mustapha is going to pull the horse!' Mustapha is one of the older jockeys, a great frequenter of Madame P.'s brothel and a drug addict. He is riding a horse belonging to Tariq, a senior government official's son, who doesn't want it to win – he is betting heavily on the second favourite.

There was a wild cry of 'Zerroff!' and the little horses disappeared in a cloud of dust, the jockeys hanging on to the britches of the one in front – except of course for the ones who had been paid to lose, and they were pulling on the reins like mad. Inexplicably Mustapha seemed to be winning. . . . 'Oh dear,' said Desmond, 'poor Mustapha *will* be in trouble! He wasn't pulling near hard enough, and Tariq will have lost a packet.'

Sure enough, just as we were about to go, there was a wild outcry from the bar, where Tariq was drowning his sorrows with drink. He had struck Mustapha and Mustapha had struck him back. As two soldiers dragged the jockey from the grandstand and manhandled him through the crowds, he shouted obscenities against the government, reserving his choicest language for Tariq, a well-known queer. 'OH FATHER OF PRICKS,' he yells, 'so many times has thine arse been breeched that . . .' The rest is so awful I really can't write it! . . . 'Not much like old Epsom, is it, dear?' Desmond said as we drove back in his car. 'No,' I said, 'but much more fun!'

Joan Wyndham

1971

Yesterday evening . . . Eardley and I spend some time goggling at the television – partly at yet another American moon shot, partly at a film about Anne of Cleves. The moon shots disgust me in some curious way; there seem such wide disparities involved – between the boredom of listening to a flat American voice reciting figures and distances, mixed with 'OKs' and 'ERs', and the horrifying human tensions and anxieties lying behind them – and between the courage and danger of the astronauts and the cowardly Eardley's enjoyment of that courage and danger. Perhaps I malign him or exaggerate the nature of his emotion, but I take his feelings as typical of many people's. So what is left but dismay and semi-disbelief as I loll back gazing with a sort of distaste at the infinitely brilliant mastery of space by men's minds.

Frances Partridge

2 February

1751

Having received a full answer from Mr P— [Vincent Perronet], I was clearly convinced that I ought to marry. For many years I remained single, because I believed I could be more useful in a single, than in a married state. And I praise God, who enabled me so to do. I now as fully believe, that in my present circumstances, I might be more useful in a married state; into which, upon this clear conviction, and by the advice of my friends, I entered a few days after.

John Wesley

1821

I have been considering what can be the reason why I always wake, at a certain hour in the morning, and always in very bad spirits – I may say, in actual despair and despondency, in all respects – even of that which pleased me over night. In about an hour or two, this goes off, and I compose either to sleep again, or, at least, to quiet. In England, five years ago, I had the same kind of hypochondria, but accompanied with so violent a thirst that I have drank as many as fifteen bottles of soda-water, in one night, after going to bed, and been still thirsty – calculating, however, some lost from the bursting out and effervescence and overflowing of the soda-water, in drawing the corks, or striking off the necks of the bottles from mere thirsty impatience. At present, I have *not* the thirst; but the depression of spirits is no less violent.

Lord Byron

3 February

1826

This is the first morning since my troubles that I felt at awaking

> I had drunken deep
> Of all the blessedness of sleep.*

I made not the slightest pause nor dreamd a single dream nor even changed my side. This is a blessing to be grateful for. There is to be a meeting of the Creditors to-day but I care not for the issue. If they drag me into the Court *obtorto collo* ['by the throat'] instead of going into this scheme of arrangement they will do themselves a great injury and perhaps eventually do me good though it would give me much pain.

Sir Walter Scott

1973

Still reading Walter Scott's journal. He, the least valetudinarian of men, recorded the incipient signs of his old age: 'Terrible how they increase the last year.' He clearly had little strokes, yet was not sure whether they were strokes or not. Found he could not marshal his words, and thought it was fear or nerves which caused this; that he must pull himself together and snap out of it. Reminders of mortality are indeed painful.

James Lees-Milne

1977 [Brussels]

Dinner at a very good fish restaurant enlivened, if that is the word, on the way out by sensing a slight feeling of embarrassment amongst the staff, which was indeed well founded, as we saw on the ground floor – we had been eating on the first floor – the upturned soles of a Japanese who seemed at least unconscious and possibly dead. When we got outside an ambulance drew up and a stretcher was rushed in. We asked Ron Argen, our inimitable driver, whether he knew what was happening. He said: 'Oh, yes, certainly, oyster poisoning. Quite often happens, but the restaurant is insured against it, so there is no need to worry.'

Roy Jenkins

1989 [Dungeness, Kent]

For two months after moving here I spent hours each day picking up fragments of countless smashed bottles, china plates, pieces of rusty metal. There

---

*Coleridge's 'Christabel', pt. 2, ll. 375–6.

was a bike, cooking pots, even an old bedstead. Rubbish had been scattered over the whole landscape. Each day I thought I had got to the end of the task only to find the shingle had thrown up another crop overnight.

Sunny days were the best for clearing up, as the glass and pottery glinted. I buried the lot on the site of an old bonfire at the bottom of the garden in a large mound, which I covered with the clumps of grass I dug out when I built the shingle garden.

I was describing the garden to Maggi Hambling at a gallery opening. And said I intended to write a book about it.

She said: 'Oh, you've finally discovered nature, Derek.'

'I don't think it's really quite like that,' I said, thinking of Constable and Samuel Palmer's Kent.

'Ah, I understand completely. You've discovered modern nature.'

Derek Jarman

4 February

1777

Dined at Lord Monboddo's with a good deal of company; drank rather too much. Called in on my way home at Mr. John Syme's to consult the cause, Cuttar against Rae. He followed the old method, and read over my paper from beginning to end. I was intoxicated to a certain degree. Met in the street with a coarse strumpet, went to the Castle Hill, was lascivious with her, but had prudence enough to prevent me from embarking. Was vexed that I had begun bad practices in 1777. Home and finished a paper.

James Boswell

1939

Vita and I go round to the Beales [tenant farmers on Nicolson estate] where there is a Television Set lent by the local radio-merchant. We see a Mickey Mouse, a play and a Gaumont British film. I had always been told that the television could not be received above 25 miles from Alexandra Palace. But the reception was every bit as good as at Selfridge's. Compared with a film, it is a bleary, flickering, dim, unfocused, interruptible thing, the size of a quarto sheet of paper as this on which I am typing. But as an invention it is tremendous and may alter the whole basis of democracy.

Harold Nicolson

1947

During the night, New York was covered with snow. Central Park is transformed. The children have cast aside their roller skates and taken up skis; they rush boldly down the tiny hillocks. Men remain bareheaded, but many of the young people stick fur puffs over their ears fixed to a half-circle of plastic that sits on their hair like a ribbon – it's hideous.

Simone de Beauvoir

1953

What could be funnier than the Goncourts' exclamation when they learned that the earth would not last more than a few thousand centuries: 'And what will become of our books?' Yet after all, it wasn't so stupid. Unless you write to eat, or to 'succeed' in the here and now, you wonder what impels you to exhaust yourself in the void and why you bother to seek distant friends, since you have them here at hand, the kind who read you like an open book without any need of paper and ink.

Jean Cocteau

1975

Thinking so much these days about what it is to be a woman, I wonder whether an ingrained sense of guilt is not a feminine characteristic. A man who has no children may feel personally deprived but he does not feel guilty, I suspect. A woman who has no children is always on the defensive.

May Sarton

1975

Late this afternoon in the House someone said to me, 'Have you heard the news? Margaret Thatcher has swept to the top in the leadership poll.' I fear that I felt a sneaking feminist pleasure. Damn it, that lass *deserves* to win. Her cool and competent handling of the cheaper mortgages issue in the last election campaign gave us our only moment of acute anxiety. All right, it was a dishonest nonsense as a policy, but she dealt with it like a professional.

Barbara Castle

5 *February*

1798

Walked to Stowey with Coleridge, returned by Woodlands; a very warm day. In the continued singing of birds distinguished the notes of a blackbird or thrush. The sea over-shadowed by a thick dark mist, the land in sunshine.

The sheltered oaks and beeches still retaining their own leaves. Observed some trees putting out red shoots. Query: What are they?

Dorothy Wordsworth

1809

At noon today, the 5th, I found Elisa in bed, I got in: fine thighs, but a face that looks stupid and lives up to its promise; twenty-four livres.

Stendhal

1882

Mr [John Everett] Millais is going to paint the portrait of one of the Duchess of Edinburgh's children. The Duchess is staying with Princess Mary, Kensington Palace. Mr Millais went to see her yesterday, doubtless very shy. She offended him greatly. She enquired where his 'rooms' were, evidently doubtful whether a Princess might condescend to come to them. 'My *rooms*, ma'am, are in Palace Gate [Kensington],' and he told papa afterwards, with great indignation, he daresay they were much better than hers. He is right proud of his house.

He says she speaks English without the slightest accent, the Russians are wonderful at languages. They say the late Czar prided himself on his good English, till he found when he came to England that, having learnt from a Scotchman, he spoke Scotch.

A pedestrian who had dropped half-a-crown before a blind person said, 'Why, you're not blind'! 'I, oh no sir, if the board says so, they've given me the wrong one, I'm deaf and dumb'! Queer thing how fast some blind folks can walk when no one is about!

Beatrix Potter

1884

Today, at the Brébant dinner, we talked about the crushing of the minds of children and young men under the huge volume of things taught them. We agreed that an experiment was being carried out on the present generation of which it was impossible to predict the consequences. And in the course of the discussion somebody advanced the ironical idea that our present-day system of universal education might well deprive society of the educated man and endow it with the educated woman: not a reassuring prospect for the husbands of the future.

The Brothers Goncourt

1931

The mother-in-law of Davidson (who is making a bust of me and at whose house I lunch today), a charming old lady of eighty-four, when – on the point of lighting a cigarette after the meal – I ask her if smoking bothers her, tells us that a similar question was put to her, before 1870, by Bismarck, in a train between Paris and Saint-Germain in which she happened to be alone with him. To which she replied at once:

'Sir, I do not know. No one has ever smoked in my presence.'

Bismarck immediately had the train stopped so that he could change to another compartment.

André Gide

1944 [Naples]

There have been newspaper accounts of urban buses seen careering away into the remote fastness of the Apennines, there to be reduced in comfort to their component parts. Trams, left where they had come to a standstill when the departing Germans wrecked the generating station, have been spirited away in the night. A railway engine, stranded in open country owing to the looting of rails and sleepers, was driven off when these rails and sleepers were quite incredibly relaid, to a place more discreetly located for its demolition.

No feat, according to the newspapers, and to public rumour, both of which dwell with great delight on such flamboyant acts of piracy, is too outrageous for this new breed of robber. In the region of Agropoli small ships left unguarded have been lifted out of the water and mysteriously transported away, and portions of their superstructures have later been discovered miles inland, hidden in orchards as if they had been carried there and left high and dry by some tidal wave. In revenge, said the newspaper reporting this case, a party of fishermen raided an isolated castle in the area and went off with tapestries which they used to repair their sails.

Nothing has been too large or too small – from telegraph poles to phials of penicillin – to escape the Neapolitan kleptomania. A week or two ago an orchestra playing at the San Carlo to an audience largely clothed in Allied hospital blankets, returned from a five-minute interval to find all its instruments missing. A theoretically priceless collection of Roman cameos was abstracted from the museum and replaced by modern imitations, the thief only learning – so the reports go – when he came to dispose of his booty that the originals themselves were counterfeit. Now the statues are disappearing from the public squares, and one cemetery has lost most of its tombstones. Even the manhole covers have been found to have marketable value, so that suddenly these too have all gone, and everywhere there are holes in the road.

Norman Lewis

6 February

I spent an hour with a venerable woman, near ninety years of age, who retains her health, her senses, her understanding, and even her memory, to a good degree. In the last century she belonged to my grandfather Annesley's congregation, at whose house her father and she used to dine every Thursday; and whom she remembers to have frequently seen in his study, at the top of the house, with his window open, and without any fire, winter or summer. He lived seventy-seven years, and would probably have lived longer, had he not begun water drinking at seventy.

John Wesley

1881

George Eshelby [local vicar] tells me that Mrs Travel's girl has been confined in her cottage of a stillborn child and that Williams [groom] has confessed that he is the father. Mrs Travel came with the same story. I blame her very much after the experience she had with her other girl that she permitted the daughter to come home from service without sending Williams away. The cottage is too small. Williams says it was no seeking of his. She laid on the top of him when he happened to drop asleep over his book. Even young Morris [footman] was found in equivocal positions with her. It appears to Williams she has tried to entrap him.

Dearman Birchall

1922 [Rome]

Today the Pope was at last elected: Cardinal Ratti, now Pius XI. It rained. Consequently the crowd was smaller than yesterday and armed with umbrellas. Fifteen minutes before noon a wisp of smoke could indistinctly be seen rising from the stove-pipe, becoming thicker, then stopping altogether. 'È nero!' 'È bianco! È fatto il Papa! È fatto il Papa!' Immediately there was a highly dangerous folding of umbrellas and a rush for the church doors. But they proved to have been suddenly closed and a file of soldiers was drawn up in front of them. As the pushing from behind continued, the crush amidst the re-opened umbrellas became almost intolerable. Excitement was at a peak. Everybody tried to keep an eye, between the spread umbrellas, on the loggia high up the façade of St Peter's from where the name of the elected Pontiff would be announced.

Almost three-quarters of an hour passed before there resounded abruptly cries of 'Ombrelli, ombrelli!' and, in a breathless tension, umbrellas (several thousand umbrellas) were snapped to. The glass door of the loggia was opened, attendants stepped forward and laid over the parapet a large velvet carpet embroidered with armorial bearings. Then there could be caught sight of a big golden crucifix and above the edge of the parapet the head and gesticulating hands of a cardinal. Deathly silence. The cardinal proclaimed: His Eminence – he paused – the Most Venerable Archbishop of Milan, Cardinal Ratti, had been elected Pope and had adopted the name Pius XI. An immense jubilation broke out, hats and handkerchiefs were flourished, and shouts of *E Viva!* re-echoed.

The cardinal and the *monsignori* made signs to the crowd to wait. There was still something to come. And after about ten minutes a big surprise occurred. For the first time since 1870 the Pope showed himself to the people of Rome assembled in the open square. Above the parapet of the loggia could be discerned a white arm moving in a gesture of blessing and rather full, not specially remarkable, scholar's features while at the same time there could be heard a deep, melodious, slightly unctuous voice very clearly pronouncing blessing upon the crowd. The latter, whenever the voice halted, answered with a resonant 'Amen'.

Count Harry Kessler

1941 [Holland]

Today I wasn't in the best of moods. A little disappointed in myself. I went to visit Miep, who didn't go to school because she wasn't well. A friend of theirs has been arrested. We're all supposed to register, we can't postpone it any longer, and I guess we'll get a 'J' stamped on our papers. Anyway. Whatever happens, happens. I don't want to think about it too much. Letter from Guus [her brother], dated December. He's so happy there, he's turning into a real American. Only he misses us, of course, but he says he thinks the country is even more beautiful and wonderful than our own lovely little country. Then it must be pretty special! He describes all sorts of domestic appliances, butter, tinned goods, advertisements, the bright lights, etc. and we meanwhile sitting here in the dark, simply drooling over his descriptions of the good life over there . . .

Edith Velmans

7 *February*

1682

I continu'd ill for 2 fitts after, and then bathing my leggs to the knees in Milk made as hott as I could endure it, and sitting so in it, in a deepe Churn or Vessell, covered with blanquets and drinking Carduus posset, then going to bed and sweating, I not onely missed that expected fit, but had no more.

John Evelyn

1856

Quarrelled with Turgenev, and had a wench at my place.

Leo Tolstoy

1943

Peter Blume – handsome, sweet, good, and, as a painter, the genius of our age – and his wife – also childishly good and devoted – had an enormous cocktail party. Two famous wits were present – James Thurber and S. J. Perelman – and this is the waggish dialogue that ensued, with me as a buffer.

(Enter Perelman.)

Perelman: Dawn, I hear your book is going like blazes. How many copies sold?

Me: (lying) Why, I imagine around fifteen thousand.

Perelman: Ah, here's Thurber. You know Dawn.

Thurber: Hello, Dawn, how many copies did your book sell? Fifty thousand?

Me: Well, more like twenty.

Thurber: Understand you got $15,000 from the movies. Shoulda got more. Would've if you'd held out.

Me: Well, it would still all be gone now no matter what I got.

Thurber: (glancing around, though almost blind) Big party. Musta set Peter back about fifty bucks. What'd he get for his picture?

Perelman: Do you realize that bastard Cerf takes 20 percent of my play rights, same as he did for 'Junior Miss'?

Thurber: Shouldn't do it. Harcourt never took a cent off me. Had it in the contract.

Perelman: I'd like to have lunch with you and discuss that, Jim. Jesus, Jim – 20 percent!

Thus does the wit flow from these two talented fellows.

Dawn Powell

1980

Just in time for Joyce Grenfell's Memorial Service. Westminster Abbey packed to the doors. What a well-loved lady she was; she had what the Zulus call 'shine'. How typical of her that she always referred to the side-duties of a celebrity – charity openings, bazaars and lunches – as 'fringe benefits' and worked as hard at them as her professional work. 'The lines', she used to say, quoting the Psalms, 'are fallen to me in pleasant places'. Bernard Levin and

I (we the undersized) crouch behind two of the largest men I have ever seen. Bach, Mozart – her favourite composers – modest, touching tribute from her local vicar, a reading – disappointing unmoving – from Paul Scofield and then the rush for the West Door, waspishly envying those who seem entitled to chauffeurs (eg Peter Hall and Permanent Secretaries). Heavy establishment top-dressing but lovely to see so many less famous faces. Memorial services may be disliked by those they honour, but to those left behind they serve as a sort of surrogate encounter with death.

Sir Hugh Casson

8 February

1841

My Journal is that of me which would else spill over and run to waste, gleanings from the field which in action I reap. I must not live for it, but in it for the gods.

They are my correspondents, to whom daily I send off this sheet post-paid. I am clerk in their counting-room, and at evening transfer the account from day-book to ledger. It is as a leaf which hangs over my head in the path. I bend the twig and write my prayers on it; then letting it go, the bough springs up and shows the scrawl to heaven. As if it were not kept shut in my desk, but were as public a leaf as any in nature. It is papyrus by the riverside; it is vellum in the pastures; it is parchment on the hills. I find it everywhere as free as the leaves which troop along the lanes in autumn. The crow, the goose, the eagle carry my quill, and the wind blows the leaves as far as I go. Or, if my imagination does not soar, but gropes in slime and mud, then I write with a reed.

H. D. Thoreau

1941 [Dresden]

Lissy Meyerhof sent six pairs of secondhand socks, presumably originally belonging to Erich's sons – a mercy, since I am running around with holes and sore, dirty feet. The package and the letter was accompanied by a note, translated from the Italian, from Hans Meyerhof, I was able to establish his concentration camp, on the Deserto . . .

Cohn, congenial Winter Aid man of the Jewish Community, whom I was this time unable to grant any additional donation, saw my completely torn carpet slippers and supported my application for a pair from the Jewish clothing store; I am to fetch them there on Monday. Yet another mercy.

On the evening of the fifth almost friendly contact with the corrupt and powerful Estreicher, with whom I clashed so violently in May because of the accommodation business. It was about reorganizing the billets, though we are spared. The Katzes on the ground floor are going to Berlin, in their place comes a homo novus, who appears to have given a very good bribe: He is not only to get two rooms just for himself, but a third one as well for his Aryan housekeeper . . .

On the fourth to Frau Kronheim for a touchingly nice short visit (real coffee, cake, a cigar) . . . A woman of about sixty, widow of a straw hat manufacturer, evidently once affluent, probably a little even now. Large room in Bautzener Strasse, of course bed and washstand y todo in the same room, most furniture in storage. Conversations naturally always the same: Affidavit – will America enter the war? – Recently: What is going to happen to Italy? – Here the English recovery is tremendous. Only yesterday I saw the December issue of *The Twentieth Century* at the dentist's . . . There the Italian offensive against and in (*in!*) Egypt was discussed and there was a big map, and today Benghazi has already been taken. Will England succeed in defeating Italy? Hitler's speech on January 30 ('I shall force a decision this year') had a different tone from all the previous ones. Nothing more about a seven years' war, nothing more about friendship with Russia and the Balkans – now only: We are prepared for *every* eventuality, and submarine threat against the USA. The speech is supposed to have sounded like a cry of rage, his voice breaking. True security or Despair? – Rumors everywhere of new levies and troops sent eastward and motorization.

Victor Klemperer

1945 [Bergen-Belsen]
I had hung my coat in a cupboard. Someone has stolen the buttons.

Abel J. Herzberg

1948
Looked in on Tony and Violet Powell, and laughed much over Duke of Windsor's Memoirs and Americanisms in them – for instance, 'Fatty' instead of 'Tubby'. Wondered if Royal Family had been given advance copy, or if they opened *Sunday Express* each week apprehensively.

Malcolm Muggeridge

1983 [Dundee]
A day off from filming *An Englishman Abroad* and I go to Edinburgh with Alan Bates. We climb the tower near the castle to see the camera obscura. The texture of the revolving bowl and the softness of the reflection convert the view into an eighteenth-century aquatint in which motor cars seem as

delicate and exotic as sedan chairs. The traffic is also rendered more sedate and unreal for being silent.

An element of voyeurism in it. The guide, a genteel Morningside lady, trains the mirror on some adjacent scaffolding where workmen are restoring a church. 'I often wonder,' she muses in the darkened room, 'if one were to catch them . . . well, unawares. I mean,' she adds hastily, 'taking a little *rest*.'

Alan Bennett

9 February

1826

Methinks I have been like Burns's poor labourer

> So constantly in Ruin's sight
> The view o't gives me little fright.*

Sir Walter Scott

1940

A letter came from Dan [her husband], dated January 29th: 'We have arrived and our official address is Notts Sherwood Rangers Yeomanry, Palestine. Letters by airmail take about a week.' I also had a letter from Whitaker [her husband's valet]. It was completely blacked out by a censor except for 'My Lady' at the top. I wonder what he wrote.

Countess of Ranfurly

1941 [POW Camp, Germany]

Last night's rumour of thousands of parcels was apparently true – except that they were all for Obermassfeld. But however disappointing it may be for us, I'm extremely glad this hospital is at last getting them, as they have had a rotten time. Wounds were taking twice as long to heal because the patients hadn't the food to build up on. Hunger must have cost hundreds of lives. However, tho' no food parcels, we hear there are 21 smokes ones – and smoke is half the battle. It is extraordinary, looking round the room during meals the number of backs which are now rounded. Anybody sitting with a straight back looks enormous. I suppose due to hard benches and stools. How odd it will seem to sit in an armchair again.

Captain John Mansel

---

*Burns's 'Twa Dogs', slightly adapted.

1991

'Iraqi morale wilts under allied onslaught'. Mine has rather wilted too. And the country has disappeared beneath a blanket of snow.

Gyles Brandreth

10 February

1661

(Lord's Day.) Took physique all day, and, God forgive me, did spend it in reading of some little French romances.

Samuel Pepys

1858 [New Orleans]

As all my paintings are finished and my easel packed up I seem to have unlimited hours in the day, so I went to a Slave Auction. I went alone (a quarter of an hour before the time) and asked the auctioneer to allow me to see everything. He was very smiling and polite, took me upstairs, showed me all the articles for sale – about thirty women and twenty men, twelve or fourteen babies. He took me round and told me what they could do: 'She can cook and iron, has worked also in the fields.' etc., 'This one a No. 1 cook and ironer –,' etc. He introduced me to the owner who wanted to sell them (being in debt) and he did not tell the owner what I had told him (that I was English and only came from curiosity), so the owner took a great deal of pains to make me admire a dull-looking mulatress and said she was an excellent servant and could just suit me. At twelve we all descended into a dirty hall adjoining the street big enough to hold a thousand people. There were three sales going on at the same time, and the room was crowded with rough-looking men, smoking and spitting, bad-looking set – a mêlée of all nations.

I noticed one mulatto girl who looked very sad and embarrassed. She was going to have a child and seemed frightened and wretched. I was very sorry I could not get near to her to speak to her. The others were not sad at all. Perhaps they were glad of a change. Some looked round anxiously at the different bearded faces below them, but there was no great emotion visible.

Before I went the young man of the house had said, 'Well, I don't think there is anything to see – they sell them just like so many rocking chairs. There's no difference.' And that is the truest word that can be said about the affair. When I see how Miss Murray speaks of sales and separations as regretted by the owners and as disagreeable (that is her tone if not her words), I feel inclined to condemn her to attend all the sales held in New Orleans in two months. How many that would be one may guess, as three were going on the morning I went down.

Barbara Leigh Smith Bodichon

1915

My neighbour talks for hours with the landlady. Both speak softly, the land-lady almost inaudibly, and therefore so much the worse. My writing, which has been coming along for the past two days, is interrupted, who knows for how long a time? Absolute despair. Is it like this in every house? Does such ridiculous and absolutely killing misery await me with every landlady in every city?

Franz Kafka

1922

Not many remarks about art have so gripped one as Meier-Graefe's comment on Delacroix: 'This is a case of a hot heart beating in a cold person.'

Bertolt Brecht

1947

In three days I'm leaving New York. I have a lot of shopping to do and business to take care of, and all morning long I stride along the muddy streets of the better neighborhoods. In their windows, candy stores display huge red hearts decorated with ribbons and stuffed with bonbons. Hearts are also ingeniously suspended in stationery stores and tie shops. It'll soon be Valentine's Day, the day when young girls give gifts to their boyfriends. There's always some holiday going on in America; it's distracting. Even private celebrations, especially birthdays, have the dignity of public ceremonies. It seems that the birth of every citizen is a national event. The other evening at a nightclub, the whole room began to sing, in chorus, 'Happy Birthday,' while a portly gentleman, flushed and flattered, squeezed his wife's fingers. The day before yesterday I had to make a telephone call; two college girls went into the booth before me. And while I was pacing impatiently in front of the door, they unhooked the receiver and intoned 'Happy Birthday.' They sang it through to the very end. In shops they sell birthday cards with congratulations all printed out, often in verse. And you can 'telegraph' flowers on one occasion or another. All the florists advertise in large letters, 'Wire Flowers.'

Simone de Beauvoir

11 February

1938

All the women in the region are excised. 'This,' we are told, 'is to calm their lust and ensure their conjugal fidelity.'

Immediately afterward we are told: 'You understand: since these women feel nothing, they give themselves to anyone whatever; nothing stops them . . . Oh, of course, they never give themselves for nothing!'

Obviously the two statements seem contradictory. One is forced to admit that if the aim were conjugal fidelity . . . But no (it seems); rather this: keep the wife from making love for pleasure. For money, it's all right! And the husband congratulates himself on having a (or more than one) wife who produces income.

This is one of the rare points on which all the Frenchmen, when questioned, agree. One among them, who has a great experience of the 'moussos' of Guinea, asserts that he has never met a native woman who sought pleasure in the sexual act; he even went so far as to say, not one who knew voluptuous pleasure.

André Gide

1941 [Holland]

'Seize the day,' says Mother. But I'm worried. At home everyone is so optimistic, but others are pessimistic. Many people are hanging around aimlessly in the streets, out of work. There are riots and demonstrations. It doesn't bode well for us. *Enfin* Let's hope that *'Alles sal reg kom'* – soon! Actually, I'm an idiot to grumble on like this. I'm still enjoying my life as much as I can.

Edith Velmans

1975

Everyone agog at the news that Margaret Thatcher has been elected Tory leader with a huge majority. Surely no working man or woman north of the Wash is ever going to vote for her? I fear a lurch to the right by the Tories and a corresponding lurch to the left by Labour.

To Buckingham Palace for the Queen's reception for the media, at least I suppose that's what we were. Newspaper editors; television controllers; journalists and commentators; Heath looking like a tanned waxwork; Wilson; Macmillan a revered side-show, an undoubted star; a few actors (Guinness, Ustinov, Finney); and all the chaps like me – John Tooley, George Christie, Trevor Nunn. And Morecambe and Wise.

It was two and a half hours of tramping round the great reception rooms, eating bits of Lyons pâté, drinking over-sweet warm white wine, everyone looking at everyone else, and that atmosphere of jocular ruthlessness which characterises the Establishment on its nights out. Wonderful paintings, of course, and I was shown the bullet that killed Nelson.

As we were presented, the Queen asked me when the National Theatre would open. I said I didn't know. The Duke asked me when the National Theatre would open. I said I didn't know. The Prince of Wales asked me when the National Theatre would open. I said I didn't know. At least they all knew I was running the National Theatre.

Home by 2 am with very aching feet. Who'd be a courtier?

Peter Hall

12 February

1927

But I am forgetting, after three days, the most important event in my life since marriage – so Clive [Bell, art critic] described it. Mr Cizec has bingled me. I am short haired for life. Having no longer, I think, any claims to beauty, the convenience of this alone makes it desirable. Every morning I go to take up [my] brush and twist that old coil round my finger and fix it with hairpins and then with a start of joy, no I needn't. In front there is no change; behind I'm like the rump of a partridge. This robs dining out of half its terrors.

Virginia Woolf

1938 [Nanking]

It really is high time for me to get out of here. At 7 o'clock this morning, Chang brought in Fung, a friend from Tientsin, who is watching the house of an American here and whose wife is expecting a baby, which for three days now has been struggling to see the light of this mournful world, and you really can't blame him. The mother's life is apparently in danger. Birth definitely needs to be induced. And they come to me of all people!

'I'm not a doctor, Chang. And I'm not a *kuei ma* [midwife], either. I'm the "mayor", and I don't bring other people's children into the world. Get the woman to Kulou Hospital at once!'

'Yes,' Chang says, 'that's all true; but you must come, otherwise won't work, otherwise woman not get into hospital, she die and baby, too. You must come, then everything good. Mother lives and baby, too!'

And that puts an end to that – 'Idiots, the whole lot of you!'

And so I had to go along, and who would believe it: As I enter the house, a baby boy is born, and the mother laughs, and the baby cries, and everyone is happy; and Chang, the monkey, has been proved right yet again. And the whole lark cost me ten dollars besides, because I had to bring the poor lad something. If this story gets around, I'm ruined. Just think, there are 250,000 refugees in this city!

John Rabe

1941

Early spring weather since yesterday. Grateful for every additional minute of daylight, for each degree of warmth, for each yard of ground that can be walked (this especially for Eva's sake). Eva has declined, lost weight, aged so very much – and yet, as my own body declines, I love her ever more ardently, d'amour say the French.

Hopeful, although threatened by catastrophe. Charge because room not blacked out. That can mean a fine of so many 100M that I am forced to sell the house; it can also be disposed of with 20M. There are examples of both; I assumed the worst for a whole day, I am calmer now.

It was truly a misfortune, liability through negligence, as can happen with a car. We are usually both extremely careful with regard to the blackout, on our evening walks we often grumble about illuminated windows, say the police should really do something. And now we ourselves are caught in the act. On the Monday (the tenth) all kinds of things came together, which made me lose the thread. During the day I usually return from shopping at about half past four. Unpacking, hauling coal, a glance at the newspaper, *blackout*, going out for supper. On Monday I found Frau Kreidl, whom both of us greatly dislike, here. She wanted to be consoled: The whole house had been inspected by the Gestapo – new tenants? Confiscation of the house? (Cupboards opened in our rooms also – there was rather too much tobacco in the house! But they saw only five packets, as a precaution four others are already with Frau Voss.) It grew late. So blackout after the meal. In the Monopol the food so bad that Eva didn't eat it. I wanted to get her something else at the station. Nothing there either. So I was very out of humor and distracted when we returned, immediately hurried into the kitchen to make tea. Against the night sky, once the light has been switched on, it is impossible to tell whether the shutters have been closed. When the policeman rang the doorbell at nine, we were quite unsuspecting, we led him to the window so that he could see for himself that it was blacked out. The man was courteous and sympathetic; he had to charge me because neighbours had reported the light. I had to state income and property: afterward 'the chief of police' will determine the level of the penalty. Until yesterday I was *only* expecting the worst; yesterday Frau Voss told me of a case in which someone had only paid 12M; admittedly the someone was the Aryan wife of a general, and I have a J on my identity card. Now I must wait, my mood going up and down.

Victor Klemperer

1951 [writing *East of Eden*]

Lincoln's Birthday. My first day of work in my new room. It is a very pleasant room and I have a drafting table to work on which I have always wanted – also a comfortable chair given me by Elaine [his wife]. In fact I have never had it so good and so comfortable. I have known such things to happen – the perfect pointed pencil – the paper persuasive – the fantastic chair and a good light and no writing. Surely a man is a most treacherous animal full of his treasured contradictions. He may not admit it but he loves his paradoxes.

Now that I have everything, we shall see whether I have anything. It is exactly that simple. Mark Twain used to write in bed – so did our greatest poet. But I wonder how often they wrote in bed – or whether they did it twice and the story took hold. Such things happen. Also I would like to know what things they wrote in bed and what things they wrote sitting up. All of this has to do with comfort in writing and what its value is. I should think that a comfortable body would let the mind go freely to its gathering. But such is the human that he might react in an opposite way. Remember my father's story about the man who did not dare be comfortable because he went to sleep. That might be true of me too. Now I am perfectly comfortable in body. I think my house is in order. Elaine, my beloved, is taking care of all the outside details to allow me the amount of free untroubled time every day to do my work. I can't think of anything else necessary to a writer except a story and the will and the ability to tell it.

John Steinbeck

1962

Had supper at the Savoy. Ted Heath was of the party. A complete bachelor, with great qualities. I wonder whether he could become Prime Minister one day – he is one of those mentioned. He has a funny schoolboyish habit of giggling and shaking his shoulders up and down when he laughs – rather endearing, but odd. Yet perhaps no odder than Rab's [Butler] strange hooting.

Cynthia Gladwin

13 February

1684

Dr. Tenison communicating to me his intention of Erecting a Library in St. Martines parish, for the publique use, desird my assistance with Sir Chr: Wren about the placing and structure thereof: a worthy and laudable designe: He told me there were 30 or 40 Young Men in Orders in his Parish, either, Governors to young Gent: or Chaplains to Noble-men, who being reprov'd by him upon occasion for frequenting Taverns or Coffè-houses, told him, they would study and employ their time better, if they had books: This put the pious Doctor upon this designe, which I could not but approve of, and indeede a greate reproach it is, that so great a Citty as Lond: should have never a publique Library becoming it: There ought to be one at St Paules, the West end of that Church, (if ever finish'd), would be a convenient place . . .

John Evelyn

1874

Yesterday I spent the whole day in the studio of a strange painter called Degas. After a great many essays and experiments and trial shots in all directions, he has fallen in love with modern life, and out of all the subjects in modern life he has chosen washerwomen and ballet-dancers. When you come to think of it, it is not a bad choice.

It is a world of pink and white, of female flesh in lawn and gauze, the most delightful of pretexts for using pale, soft tints.

He showed me, in their various poses and their graceful foreshortening, washerwomen and still more washerwomen . . . speaking their language and explaining the technicalities of the different movements in pressing and ironing.

Then it was the turn of the dancers. There was their green-room with, outlined against the light of a window, the curious silhouette of dancers' legs coming down a little staircase, with the bright red of a tartan in the midst of all those puffed-out white clouds, and a ridiculous ballet-master serving as a vulgar foil. And there before one, drawn from nature, was the graceful twisting and turning of the gestures of those little monkey-girls.

An original fellow, this Degas, sickly, neurotic, and so ophthalmic that he is afraid of losing his sight; but for this very reason an eminently receptive creature and sensitive to the character of things. Among all the artists I have met so far, he is the one who has best been able, in representing modern life, to catch the spirit of that life.

The Brothers Goncourt

1902

Before me on my table there are Christmas roses in a chased metal bowl. Although this clearly sounds a very stylish note and though I have always imagined it as something very pretty I feel nothing, nothing at all.

And it's the second day that the Christmas roses have stood before me.

Robert Musil

1926 [Berlin]

At one o'clock, just as my dinner-party guests were gone, a telephone call from Max Reinhardt. He was at [Karl Gustav] Vollmoeller's and they wanted me to come over because Josephine Baker was there and the fun was starting. So I drove to Vollmoeller's harem on the Pariser Platz. Reinhardt and Huldschinsky were surrounded by half a dozen naked girls, Miss Baker was also naked except for a pink muslin apron, and the little Landshoff girl was dressed up as a boy in a dinner-jacket. Miss Baker was dancing a solo with brilliant artistic mimicry and purity of style, like an ancient Egyptian or other archaic figure performing an intricate series of movements without ever losing the basic pattern. This is how their dancers must have danced for Solomon and Tutankhamen. Apparently she does this for hours on end, without tiring and continually inventing new figures like a child, a happy child, at play. She never even gets hot, her skin remains fresh, cool, dry. A bewitching creature, but almost quite unerotic. Watching her inspires as little sexual excitement as does the sight of a beautiful beast of prey.

Count Harry Kessler

1951

It must be told that my second work day is a bust as far as getting into the writing. I suffer as always from the fear of putting down the first line. It is amazing the terrors, the magics, the prayers, the straightening shyness that assails one. It is as though the words were not only indelible but that they spread out like dye in water and colour everything around them. A strange and mystic business, writing. Almost no progress has taken place since it was invented. The Book of the Dead is as good and as highly developed as anything in the 20th century and much better than most. And yet in spite of this lack of a continuing excellence, hundreds of thousands of people are in my shoes – praying feverishly for relief from their word pangs.

And one thing we have lost – the courage to make new words or combinations. Somewhere that old bravado has slipped off into a gangrened scholarship. Oh! you can make words if you enclose them in quotation marks. This indicates that it is dialect and cute.

John Steinbeck

1965 [Singapore]

At 2100 the whole of our party went to the fantastic home of Run Me Shaw, the brother of Run Run Shaw of Hong Kong. The story goes that the elder brother used to hang about for messages, saying 'Run run?', and when he had been sent on a message the younger brother would say 'Run me?' At all events they are both multi-millionaire magnates now.

The house is set in an elaborate garden with a large swimming pool, fountains, etc., with continually changing lighting systems. We were shown into an immense private cinema and then with evident pride he said to Patricia, Solly and me, 'Now I will show you my wonderful pink Toyland.'

Solly and I expected to see a display of toys, but in fact it was the most luxurious ladies' loo imaginable with two pink WCs at the far end, indeed a pink toilet.

Earl Mountbatten of Burma

14 February

1752

This being Valentine Day gave to 52 Children of this parish, as usual 1 penny each o. 4. 4. Gave Nancy this morning 1. 1. o.

The Rev. James Woodforde

1941 [POW camp, Germany]

How sick and tired I am of the nightly visitors' excited entry with 'What's the news?' As if we knew any. To make matters worse I heard somebody in the room talking defeatism – 'if we lose' and 'when we lose'. Slaving in salt mines in Silesia, etc. Hell, one tries to think of home, etc., to keep cheerful if possible, but it would drive one permanently mental if one had to contend with defeatism. Actually, I think half of us, if not the majority, are slowly going mental – tho' *we* think we're sane.

Captain John Mansel

1980 [Düsseldorf]

We had to take Hans Mayer's car and drive out to the country to a small town to photograph a German butcher. His company is called Herta, it's one of the biggest sausage companies in Germany. He was a cute guy. He had this interesting building. You could see all the employees. He had my Pig on the wall. Junk everywhere. A lot of toys. A lot of stuffed cows, stuffed pigs. Pigs, pigs, pigs all over the place. And there was art. There were funny things hanging from the ceiling. There were water-dripping paintings. He buys a lot of art, he said they sell more sausages that way because the people are very happy. Then he gave us a white smock and white hat. We went through and watched the ladies make the sausages. It was really fun. You could smell the sauerkraut cooking, but they didn't give us any hot dogs there. He had the whole portfolio of Picasso that I did the Picasso print of Paloma in. We looked at that, then we had to look at more pigs and more salamis and more hams and more ham art.

Then we took Polaroids for the portrait and had some tea. And his wife came by. They didn't offer us lunch. Then all of a sudden he asked us if we'd like to try one of his hot dogs. They cooked some up and we had two apiece. They were really good. He said he had to go have lunch back at the lunch room. We had to go off without lunch which we thought was really strange. We got in the car and drove to a restaurant in a place called Bottrop.

As soon as we came in they told us it was this crazy day where all the women chase the men. They cut off your ties. But since we knew that was happening – we saw these drunken ladies running round – we took our ties off and hid them in our pockets. But then they got my shirt tail and they cut it off and it was my good shirt and I was so mad. These women were really bullies. We got back in the car and drove back to Hans's gallery. I was so tired, and I was really upset about my shirt.

Andy Warhol

1983
ST VALENTINE'S DAY

Got four cards: one from Pandora [his girlfriend], one from Grandma, one from my mother and one from Rosie [his baby sister].

Big, big deal!

I got Pandora a Cupid card and a mini pack of 'After Eights'. My parents didn't bother this year, they are saving their money to pay for the solicitor's letter.

Adrian Mole

15 February

1869

I was in London. Saw Siamese twins. Born in Siam – visited England 1829. They are farmers in North Carolina, and are here to repair their loss of fortune by American war. All the surgeons concur in advising them not to attempt an operation. Chang has 6 girls and 3 boys. Hang has 6 boys and 3 girls. They have a melancholy cast of countenance but brighten up when spoken to. They walk with arms folded in what looks a painful position but is described as being 'perfectly comfortable'.

Dearman Birchall

1913

Tried to kiss her in a taxi-cab on the way home from the Savoy – the taxi-cab danger is very present with us – but she rejected me quietly, sombrely. I apologised on the steps of the Flats and said I feared I had greatly annoyed her. 'I'm not annoyed,' she said, 'only surprised' – in a thoughtful, chilly voice.

We had had supper in Soho, and I took some wine, and she looked so bewitching it sent me in a fever, thrumming my fingers on the seat of the cab while she sat beside me impassive. Her shoulders are exquisitely modelled and a beautiful head is carried poised on a tiny neck.

W. N. P. Barbellion

1915

We both went up to London this afternoon; L[eonard, her husband] to the Library, and I to ramble about the West End, picking up clothes. I am really in rags. It is very amusing. With age too one's less afraid of the superb shop women. These great shops are like fairies' palaces now. I swept about in Debenham's and Marshall's and so on, buying, as I thought, with great discretion. The shop women are often very charming, in spite of their serpentine coils of black hair. Then I had tea, and rambled down to Charing Cross in the dark, making up phrases and incidents to write about. Which is, I expect, the way one gets killed. I bought a ten and elevenpenny blue dress, in which I sit at this moment.

Virginia Woolf

1943

Hester the cook has a daughter, Elsie, who is the wife of a colored letter-carrier and the mother of two children. Some time ago I endorsed her application for a job at the Edgwood Arsenal, and she got it. She was graded as an unskilled laborer, and paid $3.60 a day. This morning Hester told me that she had been promoted to the rank of spray painter, and her pay lifted to $5.76 a day. It is amazing, with such opportunities open to colored women, that any of them go on working as domestic servants. Hester herself is probably too old for a government job; moreover she is lame. But Emma Ball, the maid, could get one easily, and be sure of rapid promotion, for she writes a good hand and is pretty intelligent. I am paying her $17 a week, which is considerably above the scale for housemaids in Baltimore. In addition, I give her a bonus of $150 a year, a present of $20 at Christmas and another of $20 when she begins her annual vacation of two weeks. Hester is paid $22 a week, with the same bonus and presents. Thus Emma receives $1,074 a year, besides her meals, and Hester $1,334. They have Thursday and Sunday afternoons and evenings off, and do not come to work until noon on Saturday. When I am out of town in August I often let them off all day. They eat precisely what I eat.

H. L. Mencken

16 February

1798

Went for eggs into the Coombe, and to the bakers; a hail shower; brought home large burthens of sticks, a starlight evening, the sky closed in, and the ground white with snow before we went to bed.

Dorothy Wordsworth

1912

12.5m. Lunch Temp. +6.1°; Supper Temp. +7°. A rather trying position. Evans has nearly broken down in the brain, we think. He is absolutely changed from his normal self-reliant self. This morning and this afternoon he stopped the march on some trivial excuse. We are on short rations, but not very short, food spins out till tomorrow night. We cannot be more than 10 or 12 miles from the depôt, but the weather is all against us. After lunch we were enveloped in a snow sheet, land just looming. Memory should hold the events of a very troublesome march with more troubles ahead. Perhaps all will be well if we can get to our depôt tomorrow fairly early, but it is anxious work with the sick man. But it's no use meeting troubles halfway, and our sleep is all too short to write more.

Captain Robert Falcon Scott

1932 [after the death of her partner, Lytton Strachey]

At last I am alone. At last there is nothing between us. I have been reading my letters to you in the library this evening. You are so engraved on my brain that I think of nothing else. Everything I look at is part of you. And there seems no point in life now you are gone. I used to say: 'I must eat my meals properly as Lytton wouldn't like me to behave badly when he was away.' But now there is no coming back. No point in 'improvements'. Nobody to write letters to. Only the interminable long days which never seem to end and the nights which end all too soon and turn to dawns. All gaiety has gone out of my life and I feel old and melancholy. All I can do is to plant snow drops and daffodils in my graveyard! Now there is nothing left. All your papers have been taken away. Your clothes have gone. Your room is bare. In a few months no traces will be left. Just a few book plates in some books and never again, however long I look out of the window, will I see your tall thin figure walking across the path past the dwarf pine past the stumps, and then climb the ha-ha and come across the lawn. Our jokes have gone for ever. There is nobody now to make 'disçerattas' with, to laugh over our particular words. To discuss the difficulties of love, to read Ibsen in the evening. And to play cards when we were too 'dim' for reading. These mouring sentinels that we arranged so carefully. The shiftings to get the new rose Corneille in the best position. They will go, and the beauty of our library 'will be over'. – I feel as if I was in a dream, almost unconscious, so much of me was in you.

★ ★ ★

And I thought as I threw the rubbish on the bonfire. 'So that's the end of his spectacles. Those spectacles that have been his companions all these years. Burnt in a heap of leaves.' And those vests the 'bodily companions' of his days now are worn by a carter in the fields. In a few years what will be left of him? A few books on some shelves, but the intimate things that I loved, all gone.

And soon even the people who knew his pale thin hands and the texture of his thick shiny hair, and grisly beard, they will be dead and all remembrance of him will vanish. I watched the gap close over others but for Lytton one couldn't have believed (because one did not believe it was ever possible) that the world would go on the same. [She shot herself on 11 March.]

Dora Carrington

1947 [staying in College accommodation while on a lecture tour]
Upon waking, I wonder just why I'm staying here in this sanatorium. The room is white and fluffy, like the one at Vassar. With nurselike attention, a woman has placed a breakfast platter beside me. Last evening, to spare me any fatigue, they brought my dinner to my room. Without leaving my bed, I drink the orange juice, eat the crusty rolls, and savor the charms of convalescence in the *café au lait*. Nothing is stranger to me than these restrained pleasures. Amid such attentive care I feel so fragile and precious I almost frighten myself. Perhaps I've undertaken a detox cure; no alcohol, no noise, no movies, no music, no fever. I draw an armchair up to the table. I've stayed here today to write an article before hurrying back to New York and going north. But I like to nurse the illusion that I'm restrained by force and working to distract myself. There's nothing more restful on a trip than to imagine you're in prison.

Simone de Beauvoir

17 February

1763

I dined at the Chaplain's table upon a roasted Tongue and Udder. N.B. I shall not dine on a roasted Tongue and Udder again very soon.

Rev. James Woodforde

1888

Today a dinner was given in Rodin's honour by his friends and admirers, a dinner at which I presided, with a draught in my back.

I found myself sitting next to Clemenceau with his round Kalmuck head, and he told me some anecdotes about the peasants in his province and how they would stop him out in the open during his tours of the department to consult him about their illnesses. He described one huge woman who, just as the horses of his brake were about to gallop away from some place or other, leaned on their cruppers and called out: 'Oh, Monsieur, I suffer from wind something awful!' To which the Radical deputy, giving his horses a crack of the whip which sent them on their way, replied: 'Then fart, my good woman, fart!'

The Brothers Goncourt

1912

A very terrible day. Evans looked a little better after a good sleep, and declared, as he always did, that he was quite well. He started in his place on the traces, but half an hour later worked his ski shoes adrift, and had to leave the sledge. The surface was awful, the soft recently fallen snow clogging the ski and runners at every step, the sledge groaning, the sky overcast, and the land hazy. We stopped after about one hour, and Evans came up again, but very slowly. Half an hour later he dropped out again on the same plea. He asked Bowers to lend him a piece of string. I cautioned him to come on as quickly as he could and he answered cheerfully as I thought. We had to push on, and the remainder of us were forced to pull very hard, sweating heavily. Abreast the Monument Rock we stopped, and seeing Evans a long way astern, I camped for lunch. There was no alarm at first, and we prepared tea and our own meal, consuming the latter. After lunch, and Evans still not appearing, we looked out, to see him still afar off. By this time we were alarmed, and all four started back on ski. I was first to reach the poor man and shocked at his appearance; he was on his knees with clothing disarranged, hands uncovered and frost-bitten, and a wild look in his eyes. Asked what was the matter, he replied with a slow speech that he didn't know, but thought he must have fainted. We got him on his feet, but after two or three steps he sank down again. He showed every sign of complete collapse. Wilson, Bowers, and I went back for the sledge, whilst Oates remained with him. When we returned he was practically unconscious, and when we got him into the tent quite comatose. He died quietly at 12.30 a.m. On discussing the symptoms we think he began to get weaker just before we reached the Pole, and that his downward path was accelerated first by the shock of his frost-bitten fingers, and later by falls during rough travelling on the glacier, further by his loss of all confidence in himself. Wilson thinks it certain he must have injured his brain by a fall. It is a terrible thing to lose a companion in this way, but calm reflection shows that there could not have been a better ending to the terrible anxieties of the past week. Discussion of the situation at lunch yesterday shows us what a desperate pass we were in with a sick man on our hands so far from home.

At 1 a.m. we packed up and came down over the pressure ridges, finding our depôt easily.

Captain Robert Falcon Scott

1931

Finished reading *The Intimate Journals of Paul Gauguin*. Very fresh mind – he at once joins the company of those whom we wish we could have met. Such a distinctive French book makes a Scot feel that he is rather a dog-collared dog. We cannot recall Mary Stuart without seeing the shadow of Knox at her back.

William Soutar

18 February

1814

Is there any thing beyond? – *who* knows? *He* that can't tell. Who tells that there *is*? He who don't know. And when shall he know? Perhaps, when he don't expect it, and, generally when he don't wish it. In this last respect, however, all are not alike; it depends a good deal upon education, – something upon nerves and habits – but most upon digestion.

Lord Byron

1852

I have a commonplace-book for facts and another for poetry, but I find it difficult always to preserve the vague distinction which I had in my mind, for the most interesting and beautiful facts are so much the more poetry and that is their success. They are *translated* from earth to heaven. I see that if my facts were sufficiently vital and significant, – perhaps transmuted more into the substance of the human mind, – I should need but one book of poetry to contain them all.

H. D. Thoreau

1867

Mist. Steamer to Yarmouth. Flags flying. The Queen expected from Osborne, coming to take a look at this part of the island. I say to Tennyson, 'Perhaps the Queen will visit you to-day.' He thinks it possible.

'Then I had better go?'

'No, stay by all means.'

Talking of the Queen, when Tennyson was at Osborne Her Majesty said to him, 'Cockneys don't annoy *us*,' to which Tennyson rejoined, 'If I could put a sentry at each of my gates I should be safe.'

'She was praising my poetry; I said, "Every one writes verses now. I daresay Your Majesty does." She smiled and said, "No! I never could bring two lines together!"'

The Queen, I find, has steamed past Yarmouth, landed at Alum Bay, and lunched there at the hotel.

William Allingham

1925 [while teaching at Arnold House school, Wales]

On Sunday I started on an awful thing called week's duty. It means that I have no time at all from dawn to dusk so much to read a postcard or visit a water-closet. Already – today is Tuesday, Shrove Tuesday – my nerves are distraught. Yesterday I beat a charming boy called Clegg and kicked a hideous boy called Cooper and sent Cooke to the proprietor. Yesterday afternoon I had my first riding lesson and enjoyed it greatly. It is not an easy sport or a cheap one but most agreeable. No letter from Olivia.

Yesterday in a history paper the boy Howarth wrote: 'In this year James II gave birth to a son but many people refused to believe it and said it had been brought to him in a hot water bottle.'

Evelyn Waugh

1947 [during miners' stoppages crisis]

Another arctic day, colder than ever. I went to shop in Harrods, knowing that they generate their own electricity. At the centre of Harrods is a large hall with rows of armchairs, in which a posse of weary elderly people had come to roost, to spend the hours in comparative warmth by a glimmering light. What were they thinking of in this twilight? I suppose of past comforts, of houses with servants who answered bells and put coals on the fire and drew the blinds and curtains when dusk fell, and brought tea, and polished silver. But now they were grateful for this refuge, where it was too dark even to read.

I returned home, put on my best hat, and armed with a bicycle lamp against the black-out, set out to see Sybil Colefax. Rose Macaulay was there today. She said it was monstrous that the BBC had cut the Third Programme because of the fuel crisis, as it is the one good thing we get, and only broadcasts from six to eleven in the evenings. We all urged her to take the matter up. [V. S.] Pritchett was there, at a loose end because the *New Statesman*, like other periodicals, has been suspended.

Cynthia Gladwyn

19 February

1665

At supper, hearing by accident of my mayds letting in a rogueing Scotch woman to helpe them to washe and scoure in our house, I fell mightily out, and made my wife, to the disturbance of the house and neighbours, to beat our little girle, and then we shut her down into the cellar, and there she lay all night.

Samuel Pepys

1860

Sitting by his fireside, Flaubert told us the story of his first love. He was on his way to Corsica. Till then he had done no more than lose his innocence with his mother's chambermaid. He happened on a little hotel in Marseilles where some women from Lima had arrived with sixteenth-century ebony furniture inlaid with mother-of-pearl at which everyone who saw it marvelled. Three women in silk dressing-gowns falling in a straight line from the back to the heels, together with a little Negro dressed in nankeen and wearing only Turkish slippers: for a young Norman who had hitherto travelled only from Normandy to Champagne and from Champagne to Normandy, all this was very tempting and exotic. It conjured up visions of a patio full of tropical flowers, with a fountain singing in the middle.

One day, coming back from a bathe in the Mediterranean and bringing with him all the life of that Fountain of Youth, he was invited into her bedroom by one of the women, a magnificent woman of thirty-five. He gave her one of those kisses into which one puts all one's soul. The woman came to his room that night and started making love with him straight away. There followed an orgy of delight, then tears, then silence.

He has gone back to Marseilles several times since then, but nobody has ever been able to tell him what became of these women. The last time he went through, on his way to Tunis to collect material for his Carthaginian novel, he went as usual to have a look at the house, but could not find it. He looked for it, hunted for it, and finally noticed that it had been turned into a toyshop, with a barber's on the first floor. He went upstairs, had himself shaved, and recognized the wallpaper of the bedroom.

The Brothers Goncourt

1932

Ellery Sedgwick, editor of the *Atlantic Monthly*, was here for dinner last night. Later in the evening Paul Patterson, Hamilton Owens, and John W. Owens dropped in. When Sedgwick left, along about midnight, Patterson and John Owens remained, and I finally got to bed a little after two o'clock.

Sedgwick was full of curious anecdotes. He told about being at a dinner party with the late Moorfield Storey. The name of Hearst came up, and Storey said: 'Hearst married a prostitute, and then gradually dragged her down to his own level.'

H. L. Mencken

1981

In the evening I distributed the prizes at the Prendergast School in Lewisham. The school, with nearly six hundred girls, is in the process of changing from grammar to comprehensive and has a high academic reputation, which the young, vital and very pretty headmistress has no intention of allowing to decline. I predict a brilliant career for her. She told me hair-raising stories of threats to the staff in her last school. The headmaster was pursued with a gun. She was visited by two thuggish-looking men, who said that they had come to 'do' her because of the way she had treated one of their relatives. She informed them coolly that there was a policeman in the next room (by some lucky chance, but perhaps not entirely by coincidence, there was). The two thugs took to their heels.

I distributed a number of prizes to black girls and asked the headmistress why they seemed to be specially applauded. Did the other girls feel sorry for them? No, I was told, it's because they are such good athletes. I am not an observant person, but I had noticed their long graceful limbs. 'The athletes and the naughty ones are always cheered the loudest.'

Lord Longford

20 February

When I am going out for an evening, I arrange the fire in my stove so that I do not fail to find a good one when I return though it would have engaged my frequent attention. So that, when I know I am to be at home, I sometimes make believe that I may go out, to save trouble. And this is the art of living, too, – to leave our life in a condition to go alone, and not to require a constant supervision. We will then sit down serenely to live, as by the side of a stove.

H. D. Thoreau

1890

K. told me these two tales when she was here. On her way North she overheard at the table a father and mother and two daughters talking. *Father* – 'It's delightful to be in a hotel where you can eat dinner without gloves on.' *Daughter* – 'Why, Father, I think it's quite rulable to do so when the family is alone.' *Father* – 'Your mother doesn't think so. I always have to eat my dinner and play whist with my gloves on.' This she actually heard, so there must exist a gloved and 'rulable' race somewhere in the broad land. Kath. also told me that she was on one of the big Mississippi steam-boats. In the evenings they used to have a hop in the saloon off which the state-rooms opened. At the doors of their rooms the Mammas sat matronizing their daughters; as they grew tired, they gradually 'retired,' put themselves in their berths, re-opened their doors and continued their duties from that vantage point!

Alice James

1898 [India]

Today we went to visit the Maharajah, for when he is well enough he likes to see his English guests. The palace is squalor itself and a labyrinth of narrow dark passages; I think nearly all royal palaces are that except those in the large cities. We were ushered into a room that was darker than any of them and in the centre, in the dim light, the Rajah sat, a tiny being, in the very middle of a plain *charpoy* [bedstead] with various nondescript people in attendance; round three sides of the room were small wooden cages of canaries whose voices made those of any other created being inaudible. The Maharajah is a dwarf, a cripple and paralysed in his legs, but his disabilities have not prevented him being a good ruler and loved by his subjects. He sat like some strange, half human creature with wholly human eyes, shaking hands with us all before we took our seats on the four chairs, two on either side of His Highness. Close to him sat the heir, a boy of perhaps eleven years old who is his nephew, very grandly dressed. It was rather trying, for the Maharajah said nothing after some mumbled civilities and we could not think what to say and some of us were not able to say it even if we could. Captain Stewart seemed nonplussed; the *Bankwallah's* sister knew no word of Hindustani, except perhaps how to ask for hot water, I, very little and that not of a sort to suit Maharajahs. The *Bankwallah* made some effort but His Highness' replies were hardly audible; I thought I ought to do something to try to relieve the strain, so, having carefully spread it out in my mind, I lifted up my voice and said, '*Ap ka misag kaisa hai, Maharajah Sahib?* [How is your health, Sir Maharajah?] There was a kind of murmur and silence fell again. By this time I was flattened out by embarrassment and the pathos of the sad little figure on the *charpoy* and the loneliness and gloom of it all. We felt at our wits' end and I think the feeling ran round us like hysteria. Then, without the smallest warning the youthful heir, who had not uttered, prompted I suppose by some satellite behind the Maharajah, raised a piercingly shrill voice and screamed (there is no other word for it) in one long, sustained breath 'Howdoyoudomadam!' It was as sudden as the stab of an assassin's knife and almost as fatal, and we could not imagine what this cryptic cry could mean till it dawned on us that it was a belated acknowledgement of my words to the lad's uncle.

After this we took our leave and, as we left, His Highness gave me and Miss K. each a couple of silver bangles and we were wreathed with jasmine and tinsel garlands. We were all rather shattered. We knew that the old man liked visits and took them as a compliment and we had meant to please him, and felt at the same time that such a possee of fools as we must have seemed could please nobody. It was Captain Stewart's fault for he knew the language well and was the responsible person among us. The Maharajah drives every day in the same direction along the road past the guest home but at a certain point he turns back because a few paces further on would bring him in sight of the cenotaphs of his forebears and he considers that unlucky.

Violet Jacob

1902

Four days ago a group of us went off sledding to Kiritein. Besides Herma, Hauer and Hannak were in my sledge. Return journey pretty. Fir branches against the bright night sky; singing in the telegraph wires. Because of the cold, drank a lot of schnapps and Herma got tired. Hauer recited all kinds of verse fragments. Herma and I were princess and prince. She lay in my arms with her eyes shut like a little child. A kiss – fleeting – secret – positively unnerving.

Robert Musil

1934

Am I wise to embrace a parliamentary career – can I face the continued strain? James Willoughby told me that he nearly gave up his parliamentary campaign in November, as he just could not stand the ordeal of speaking: when he confessed this to his agent, the man replied, 'Don't let not speaking well dishearten you: I have known candidates who could not even read.'

'Chips' Channon

1967

A party to meet our new Leader, Jeremy Thorpe. A huge crowd came and drank much champagne. Paul Hislop took Yehudi Menuhin for a Liberal candidate; David Frost kissed Violet Bonham Carter; Lord Gardiner, who looks so impressive when dressed in his Lord Chancellor's robes, came; but neither George Brown nor the Prime Minister did – just as well, I thought. Jeremy won't be as good as Jo [Grimond], whose wonderful looks, voice, and integrity, were a tremendous asset to the Party, especially on television. Jeremy is a bit of an actor; in fact, he would have made a marvellous actor. His imitations of Harold Macmillan, Harold Wilson, even Jo, are terrifyingly funny; and best of all is that of Ted Heath saying, 'Out of the House'. Admittedly Ted has behaved rudely to Jeremy, walking 'out of the House' when Jeremy took his place there as Liberal Leader.

Cynthia Gladwyn

21 February

1826

Corrected the proofs of *Malachi* this morning – it may fall dead and there will be a squib lost; it may chance to light on some ingredients of national feeling and set folk's beards in a blaze and so much the better if it does – I mean better for Scotland – not a whit for me—

Attended the hearing in P. House till near four o'clock so I shall do little to-night for I am tired and sleepy. One person talking for a long time, whether in pulpit or at the bar or anywhere else, unless the interest be great and the eloquence of the highest character, always sets me to sleep. I impudently lean my head on my hand in the Court and take my nap without shame – The Lords may keep awake and mind their own affairs – *Quae supra nos nihil ad nos* ['What is above us is nothing to do with us']. These Clerks' stools are certainly as easy seats as are in Scotland, those of the Barons of Exchequer always excepted.

Sir Walter Scott

1885

I saw a most extraordinary tricycle pass today. A bath chair made of wicker work in which reclined a smart lady, and behind, where one should push, a gentleman treadling, puffing and blowing and looking very sheepish. I wonder any one will make such an exhibition of themselves. How the bicycles swarm now, and yet a few years since, every one turned round to stare at a *velocipede*!

Beatrix Potter

1902

Went to the variety theater with Jacques and Hannak. Jacques – what a character – no one could beat him. One of the chanteuses wasn't bad-looking. Underwear all in grey. After the performance, however, we decided against inviting anybody. Flirted a little with the girl with grey underclothes who had her mother with her. If she had come to our table I'd certainly have behaved decently toward her. Because of that. While I was deep in conversation with Hannak, Jacques beckoned to her and went outside. In the garden he had his way with her – genius!

Robert Musil

1904 [Paris]

This afternoon, Lamoreax concert, to hear, chiefly, Richard Strauss's *Life of a Hero*. It came at the end of an exhausting programme, but I was much impressed by its beauty. I heard it under difficulties, for the audience grew restive, talked and protested. One old man insisted on going out. There is a rule about not entering or leaving during a piece, but this old man cried so loud and shook the doors so that the *pompiers* were obliged to let him through. Applause and hisses at the end, from a full audience. One more exhibition of the *bêtise* of an audience when confronted by something fresh, extravagant and powerful. It would be absurd to condemn this or any other particular audience, for all audiences are alike. The sarcastic and bitter opposition must be taken as a tribute to the power of the art. Was not *Tannhäuser* simply laughed off the stage at the first performance? I like the piece better than I thought I should – a great deal. The first thing of Richard Strauss that I have heard.

Twelve thousand five hundred words written this week.

Arnold Bennett

1970

Last night in Birmingham, giving a political speech to the local Monday Club. They were professional people, the chairman a very able young barrister of twenty-seven, one of the women a doctor, another a solicitor. The woman who sat on one side of me at dinner told me she busied herself collecting money for the Conservative Party and it was made clear to her that the businessmen of Birmingham looked to Powell more than to Heath. One man said she could have a cheque for £5 for the Conservatives but £1,000 if it was for Enoch. She said the racial feeling in Birmingham is very ugly. She had a small accident because she was driving while painting her nails! The car she ran into was driven by a coloured man and immediately about twenty people collected including a policeman and accused the coloured man of causing the accident. She had some difficulty in convincing them that she was entirely to blame.

Cecil King

1989

I finished Roy Jenkins's *European Diary*. An entertaining picture of the EEC world. There are some convincing portraits, notably Giscard [d'Estang], a somewhat unattractive figure, who, one feels, could well be accommodated in fiction. At first I was unable to put a finger on which novelist (for Giscard) when I wrote to Roy. Giscard's alleged affair with the Sorbonne student suggests perhaps a potential Stavrogin [character in Dostoevsky's *The Possessed*], tho' clearly he is without Stavrogin's (characteristically Russian) willingness to throw everything overboard according to mood. On reconsideration, Giscard is essentially a French figure, Stendhal or Balzac. Giscard's apparently phoney claims to *noblesse* is typical of characters in novels of either of the last. Proust less so. One certainly does not see Giscard in Proust's grand circles, nor Marcel's family, nor for that matter the Verdurins, where he would essentially have been regarded as a 'bore'. Perhaps M. de Norpois might have made some revealing comment on him as an ambitious young politician.

Roy's self-portrait is amusing, his taste for the arts, good living, smart society, appreciating such things as being given the Spanish Order of Charles III, because its blue-and-white riband often figures in Goya pictures of Spanish royalties and notabilities. That is absolutely the right reason for wanting the decoration. One recognizes that Roy was born into the purple of the Labour Party, even so his ease, unaffected pleasure in the *beau monde* is remarkable in its total lack of strain, to which I can think of no parallel on the Left; often missing in those of a higher bracket. At one point Roy's *Diary* records going to the loo with James Callaghan, then Prime Minister, after some dinner.

Callaghan 'made me a most fanciful offer'. I think Roy deliberately worded the entry so that one would think Callaghan suddenly gasped in a broken voice: 'Roy, have you never guessed after all these years what I feel for you?' It was, in fact, proffer of the Governorship of Hong Kong. Interesting that appointments are made in such circumstances.

Anthony Powell

22 February

1855

We saw 26 of the sick and wounded of the Coldstreams . . . There were some sad cases; – one man who had lost his right arm at Inkermann, was also at the Alma, and looked deadly pale – one or two others had lost their arms, others had been shot in the shoulders and legs, several, in the hip joint . . . A private, Lanesbury, with a patch over his eye, and his face tied up, had had his head traversed by a bullet, penetrating through the eye, which was gone, – through the nose, and coming out at the neck! He looked dreadfully pale, but was recovering well. There were 2 other very touching and distressing cases, 2 poor boys. I cannot say how touched and impressed I have been by the sight of these noble brave, and so sadly wounded men and how anxious I feel to be of use to them, and to try and get some employment for those who are maimed for life. Those who are discharged will receive very small pensions but not sufficient to live upon.

Queen Victoria

1944

Go for the day to Montepulciano and help to serve lunch at the communal kitchen started by Bracci, the Mayor, at which four hundred people are given lunch daily in two shifts. They usually get soup or macaroni, followed by vegetables or chestnuts, with a piece of bread of fifty grammes, and meat once or twice a week – all for half a lira – and a glass of wine for an extra half lira. To-day, being Shrove Tuesday, there was a slice (smallish) of roast beef in a plate of macaroni, followed by a small slab of chestnut-cake – and a glass of wine free. All this in addition to the usual scanty food ration, which thus remains available for the evening meal. The food was well cooked, and hot, the rooms clean and cheerful. Everyone who has applied – whether evacuees or the poor of the district – has been admitted. An admirable enterprise.

Iris Origo

1962 [San Francisco]

Coley [his secretary/manager] saw me off in Kingston on Tuesday, and I sped off through the bright skies at approximately the same moment that John Glenn Junior sped off in his capsule into outer space. He had been round the world three times before I landed at Miami airport. I did a little shopping and had my hair cut, and while this was going on I heard over the radio that Glenn had landed safely. It was a tremendously exciting moment, ruined for me by a blonde manicurist with a voice like a corncrake who made it almost impossible to hear what had happened.

Noël Coward

23 February

1938

I wonder every now and then, whether it is really worth it – this endless poverty, borrowing, uncertainty, frustration – all for the sake of a possibility that I may one day write something that will have value. Is my talent big enough to justify my leading this sort of life? If I were never to become a writer of very much importance, what would be the sensé of my making this attempt to live on nothing but what each day brings, to devote myself to nothing but trying to understand the sense of existence and to make words live on paper – this prolonged refusal to submit to everyone else's way of life? What small excuse, then, would there be for not coming to terms with the world, and gaining the security of an income earned in an ordinary way. How far more sensible it would be to work in a regular job, as everyone else has to who has no means of support and no other *raison d'être* – if I do not succeed, if I end by having nothing to show for all this struggle, the disgrace will be twofold, I shall be doubly *raté*, and the responsibility for a wasted life will be all my own.

David Gascoyne

1970 [Tangier]

On undressing, I discovered the infestation again! So I had to get dressed and procure the taxi and he knew where I wanted to go, and he waited for me! The all-night chemist in the Rue de Fez gave me the Benzyl Benzoate & I returned to the hotel. Put it all on and lay in bed with my balls on fire. Really it can't be an accident! This happened last time I was here! All these boys must be dirty. The only one who I've known with no mishap is Mohammed Halimi and he seems to have left Tangier. One thing is certain – it puts one off for years as far as I'm concerned! All the attraction flies out of the window and one just feels total revulsion.

Kenneth Williams

1977

I really had to pee. Fred [Hughes] came back from the bathroom and I asked him if there was anybody in there and he said no, that it was empty. I went in and was peeing and suddenly there was someone next to me saying, 'Oh my God, I can't believe I'm standing next to you, let me shake your hand,' and then he realized and said, 'No, I'll wash my hands and then we can shake.' I lost my concentration and had to stop peeing. And then more and more people started coming in and saying, 'Is it really you?' I got out.

Andy Warhol

24 February

1916 [Russia]

Yesterday I was commissioned to buy some coarse white cloth; accordingly, I walked to town and went into a small draper's shop. The Jewish owner was cleaning away the snow from the pavement, but seeing a customer, he put down his spade. Just as he was pulling down a roll of the material from the shelf, the shop-door opened and a fierce, bearded Russian face, with a fierce, thundering Russian voice, ordered him out into the street – 'immediately!' to continue sweeping the snow. I was annoyed at the Russian's rude inter-ference; so I, too, suddenly became loud and rude. Facing the infuriated soldier, I told him that I would not allow the Jew to leave the shop until my purchase was made. '*Durak* [fool!]' I cried. 'What right have you to interfere? I am carrying out an official commission. When I am ready, and *not before*, this man shall leave the shop.' It worked! The soldier turned and walked out into the street. Thinking it over afterwards, I was puzzled to decide what I should have done if it had *not* worked!

Florence Farmborough

1934

Tonight I danced in my room with the furniture pushed back, in my bathing suit. Jazz, Ravel, Mozart, Jazz. The compelling rhythms. You must dance. Abandon all else.

Elizabeth Smart

1981

The papers tell us that Prince Charles's engagement to Lady Diana Spencer will be announced today. [His wife] Elizabeth's book on the Queen Mother will be out in June; there will be just time to insert a statement that the engagement will give special pleasure to Prince Charles's grandmother. It all fits in very well with Elizabeth's conception of the Queen as a sublime exemplar of the family principle. We learn that Lady Diana's parents have a house next door to Sandringham and that her father was an equerry of King George VI. Elizabeth thinks of saying in her book that 'Lady Diana will fit into the royal family like a hand into a glove.' This, however, is too much of a cliché – can I think of another, better simile? I rack my brains hopelessly. She then comes up with this: 'She will fit in like a royal crest into its nest.' It is this which gives Elizabeth, in addition to all her academic qualities, the edge on other biographers.

Lord Longford

25 February

1808

Since the last entry I've killed three hares, the first quadrupeds in my life.

Stendhal

1942

Heart hurt for first time in years.

Dawn Powell

1942 [Holland]

It is now half-past seven in the morning. I have clipped my toenails, drunk a mug of genuine Van Houten's cocoa, and had some bread and honey, all with what you might call abandon. I opened the Bible at random, but it gave me no answers this morning. Just as well, because there were no questions, just enormous faith and gratitude that life should be so beautiful, and that makes this a historic moment, that and not the fact that we are on our way to the Gestapo this morning.

Etty Hillesum

1957

Ted's book of poems – *The Hawk in the Rain* – has won the first *Harper's* publication contest under the 3 judges: W. H. Auden, Stephen Spender & Marianne Moore! Even as I write this, I am incredulous. The little scared people reject. The big unscared practising poets accept. I knew there would be something like this to welcome us to New York! We will publish a bookshelf of books between us before we perish! And a batch of brilliant healthy children! I can hardly wait to see the letter of award (which has not yet come) & learn details of publication. To smell the print off the pages!

Sylvia Plath

1970

Today was Gladwyn's [Sir Gladwyn Jebb, her husband] motion in the Lords on the changes in the BBC's radio programmes, particularly in the Third Programme, which I urged him to table and so felt very responsible about the success of the debate. It went very well, there were seventeen speakers. G spoke very well, so I felt gratified. What a strange man Lord Annan is. Anxious to keep in with the government, he rose to his feet to state that he wondered why the BBC had bothered to announce the changes, since had they not done so they might have got away with it; a most deplorable argument, as orchestras might have been disbanded without anyone knowing. I could see the jaw of that philistine and uninspiring figure, Lord Hill, who had been responsible for it all, drop in astonishment.

Cynthia Gladwyn

1981

Norah [Baroness] Phillips joined us at lunch . . . She has a great deal to do with the Palace and hopes that her place is assured for the royal wedding [of Prince Charles and Princess Diana]. Elizabeth and I were (admittedly to my surprise) not asked to the wedding of Princess Anne. I being a Knight of the Garter to which order Prince Charles belongs, we might have a chance this time.

No doubt it all depends partly on whether it is a State occasion or a private wedding. Partly also on where it takes place. Most people seem to be assuming that it will be in Westminster Abbey. But Elizabeth sat next at dinner last night to the Dean of Westminster, Edward Carpenter. He said that they 'had heard nothing' which makes them fear that it will be in St Paul's. The latter holds an extra four hundred. Our chances of squeezing in would then be improved.

Lord Longford

26 February

1832

This day arrived, for the first time indeed, answer to last post end of December, arrived an epistle from Caddell full of good tidings. *Castl[e] Dangerous* and

Sir Robert of Paris, neither of whom I deemd sea worthy have performed 2 voyages, that is each sold off about £3400 and the same of the curr[e]nt year. It proves what I have thought almost impossible, that I might write myself [clear]. But as yet my spell holds fast. I have besides two or three good things in which I may advance with spirit. And with palmy hopes on the part of Caddell and myself. He thinks he will so[o]n cry victoria on the bet about the bet on his hat. He was to get a new one when I had paid off all my debts. And I, uncorrected by misfortune, supposed our who[le] plan had gone to the Devil and seriously thought of thinking [shrinking?] from the affair of my own exertions. Yet even when I was meditating all this I had sure enough to remark that it was a base cowardly think and that I should lose all the insurances which must come to £20,000 if I die without self Agency. I can hardly, now that I am assured that all is well again, form an idea to myself that I could think it was otherwise.

Sir Walter Scott

1985

I don't understand why Jackie O[nassis] thinks she's so grand that she doesn't owe it to the public to have another great marriage to somebody big. You'd think she'd want to scheme and connive to get into history again.

Andy Warhol

1989

1950 millibars, the lowest pressure recorded in the last 120 years. A long walk round the Ness to the power station; then up to the coastguard cottages, which I've never explored before. They are set in the middle of a moated mound which encloses a large area – once kitchen gardens.

It's difficult to find a good vegetable garden; even in the marshes I came across only one last autumn, as I travelled round with my camera filming the countryside for *War Requiem* – the supermarkets have wiped them out. Once all these little cottages grew their own, before the road was constructed during the war. Now no-one does.

Derek Jarman

27 February

1814

There is something to me very softening in the presence of a woman – some strange influence, even if one is not in love with them – which I cannot at all account for, having no very high opinion of the sex. But yet, – I always feel in better humour with myself and every thing else, if there is a woman within ken. Even Mrs. Mule, my firelighter, – the most ancient and withered of her kind, – and (except to myself) not the best-tempered – always makes me laugh, – no difficult task when I am 'i the vein'.

Lord Byron

1941

There is a rumour floating round today that we are going to a worse camp as a reprisal for the bad treatment of German prisoners at home – this from an officer. I can't really credit it. Granted we have been treated exceptionally well here, I own, but if the intention is reprisals – which I don't believe – this could equally well be made a Strafe Lager.

Scottie came into our room at 4.0 o'clock with news that we have to be packed by 9.0 a.m. tomorrow. Knowing Scottie, we took not the slightest notice – didn't even look up – but it proved shortly to be true.

Captain John Mansel

1942 [Holland]

How rash to assert that man shapes his own destiny. All he can do is determine his inner responses. You cannot know another's inner life from his circumstances. To know that you must know his dreams, his relationships, his moods, his sickness, and his death.

Very early on Wednesday morning a large group of us were crowded into the Gestapo hall, and at that moment the circumstances of all our lives were the same. All of us occupied the same space, the men behind the desk no less than those about to be questioned. What distinguished each one of us was only our inner attitudes. I noticed a young man with a sullen expression, who paced up and down looking driven and harassed and making no attempt to hide his irritation. He kept looking for pretexts to shout at the helpless Jews: 'Take your hands out of your pockets' and so on. I thought him more pitiable than those he shouted at, and those he shouted at I thought pitiable for being afraid of him. When it was my turn to stand in front of his desk, he bawled at me, 'What the hell's so funny?' I wanted to say, 'Nothing's funny here except you,' but refrained. 'You're still smirking,' he bawled again. And I, in all innocence, 'I didn't mean to, it's my usual expression.' And he, 'Don't give me that, get the hell out of here,' his face saying, 'I'll deal with you later.' And that was presumably meant to scare me to death, but the device was too transparent.

I am not easily frightened. Not because I am brave, but because I know that I am dealing with human beings and that I must try as hard as I can to understand everything that anyone ever does. And that was the real import of this morning: not that a disgruntled young Gestapo officer yelled at me, but that I felt no indignation, rather a real compassion, and would have liked to ask, 'Did you have a very unhappy childhood, has your girl-friend let you down?' Yes, he looked harassed and driven, sullen and weak. I should have liked to start treating him there and then, for I know that pitiful young men like that are dangerous as soon as they are let loose on mankind. But all the blame must be put on the system that uses such people. What needs eradicating is the evil in man, not man himself.

Something else about this morning: the perception, very strongly borne in, that despite all the suffering and injustice I cannot hate others. All the appalling things that happen are no mysterious threats from afar, but arise from fellow beings very close to us. That makes these happenings more familiar, then, and not so frightening. The terrifying thing is that systems grow too big for men and hold them in a satanic grip, the builders no less than the victims of the system, much as large edifices and spires, created by men's hands, tower high above us, dominate us, yet may collapse over our heads and bury us.

Etty Hillesum

1948

In Gide's Journal I have just read again how he does not wish to write its pages slowly as he would the pages of a novel. He wants to train himself to rapid writing in it. It is just what I have always felt about this journal of mine. Don't ponder, don't grope – just plunge something down, and perhaps more clearness and quickness will come with practice.

Denton Welch

28 February

1805

Yesterday and today, I saw the lovable Mélanie. My love increased amazingly. Tonight it was my whole life. I believe that M. Blanc, far from keeping her, is merely a man of letters who talks over her roles with her, but has exacted secrecy. In that case, what an angelic soul! She was far from even imagining my suspicions, and how far my coarse words are from interpreting her delicacy! She's in love with me and won't tell me so; tomorrow, I should let her see that I'm sad.

I'm going to bed at half-past nine tonight because I feel *che mi distruggo pensando a ella* [that I am wearing myself out thinking about her].

Stendhal

1935

How did she hurt me? Was it the day when she raised her arm to wave at someone across the street? The day when no one came to open the door to me, and then she appeared with her hair all ruffled? The day when she was whispering with him on the embankment? The thousands of times she made me hurry here and there?

But this has nothing to do with aesthetics; this is grief. I wanted to count my memories of happy moments, and all I can remember is the pangs I suffered.

Never mind, they serve the same purpose. My love story with her is not made up of dramatic scenes but of moments filled with the subtlest perceptions. So should a poem be. But it is agony.

Cesare Pavese

1956

This morning I went with Cressida [his daughter] to the H.M.V. place in Oxford Street to buy records and the following amusing incident occurred:-

It was terribly crowded, and we had great difficulty in getting anybody to attend to us. However eventually I managed to get some records to try – jazz records – and we found a young girl – I think she can't have been more than 17 – to shepherd us to a cubicle where one could play the records. She left me there to play the records while Cressida went off in search of other ones. As I was listening to the jazz, more or less dancing up and down to the rhythm, the door of the cubicle opened and who should put her head in but Elaine Burton, the Labour Member of Parliament for Coventry. Slightly embarrassed at being caught dancing on my own, I welcomed her. She said, 'I must tell you what the girl has just said to us. She said, "Do you know, I believe the Chancellor of the Exchequer is next door."' This is not the first time that, so long after I held the office, people have still regarded me as Chancellor. I suppose it is because I have so frequently broadcast and appeared on T.V. on financial questions.

Hugh Gaitskell

1958

Harry Cohn of Columbia Pictures died yesterday. I shall always remember him for having paid $750 for the title of 'Washington Merry-go-Round' [the title of one of Pearson's newspaper columns] in 1931 and made a million-dollar movie out of it. He used to laugh when he saw me in later years. My share was $375. Latterly he has been chiefly famous around Broadway for paying $25,000 to the Negro nightclub singer Davis [Sammy Davis, Jr] not to sleep with Kim Novak. Cohn claimed he discovered her first.

Drew Pearson

1983

Benjamin [Liu] picked me up and we tried to feed the big gingerbread house that little Berkeley Reinhold had given me for Christmas to the pigeons in the park. But they didn't like gingerbread and they didn't like candy. And I tried to get rid of some fruitcake, too, and they didn't like that, either, so I feel like just letting them starve. I mean, what do they *want*? They do like nuts, though, so maybe I'll bring them some peanuts sometime. Okay, so then we went downtown. (cab $6).

Andy Warhol

1989

My sense of confusion has come to a head, catalysed by my public announcement of the HIV infection. Now I no longer know where the focus is, for myself, or in the minds of my audience. Reaction to me has changed. There is an element of worship, which worries me. Perhaps I courted it.

Derek Jarman

29 February

1872

At half past four drove in open landau and four with Arthur, Leopold, and Jane C[hurchill], the Equerries riding. We drove round Hyde and Regent's Parks, returning by Constitution Hill, and when at the Garden Entrance a dreadful thing happened . . . It is difficult for me to describe, as my impression was a great fright, and all was over in a minute. How it all happened I knew nothing of. The Equerries had dismounted, [John] Brown had got down to let down the steps, and Jane C. was just getting out, when suddenly someone appeared at my side, whom I at first imagined was a footman, going to lift off the wrapper. Then I perceived that it was someone unknown, peering above the carriage door, with an uplifted hand and a strange voice, at the same time the boys calling out and moving forward. Involuntarily, in a terrible fright, I threw myself over Jane C., calling out, 'Save me,' and heard a scuffle and voices! I soon recovered myself sufficiently to stand up and turn round, when I saw Brown holding a young man tightly, who was struggling. They laid the man on the ground and Brown kept hold of him till several of the police came in. All turned and asked if I was hurt, and I said, 'Not at all.' Then Lord Charles [Fitzroy], General Hardinge, and Arthur came up, saying they thought the man had dropped something. We looked, but could find nothing, when Cannon, the postillion, called out, 'There it is,' and looking down I then did see shining on the ground a small pistol! This filled us with horror. All were as white as sheets, Jane C. almost crying, and Leopold looked as if he were going to faint.

It is to good Brown and to his wonderful presence of mind that I greatly owe my safety, for he alone saw the boy rush round and followed him! When I was standing in the hall, General Hardinge came in, bringing an extraordinary document which this boy had intended making me sign! It was in connection with the Fenian prisoners!

Queen Victoria

1920

Oh, to be a *writer*, a real writer given up to it and to it alone! Oh, I failed to-day; I turned back, looked over my shoulder, and immediately it happened, I felt as though I too were struck down. The day turned cold and dark on the instant. It seemed to belong to summer twilight in London, to the clang of the gates as they close the garden, to the deep light painting the high houses, to the smell of leaves and dust, to the lamp-light, to that stirring of the senses, to the langour of twilight, the breath of it on one's cheek, to all those things which (I feel to-day) are gone from me for ever . . . I feel to-day that I shall die soon and suddenly: but not of my lungs.

Katherine Mansfield

1928

Very much worn down, these last few days, by an absurd grippe that my petty daily occupations have not given me time to treat as I should have, by two days in bed. Cannot get myself to give up smoking. I had got out of the habit for two months, helped by Marc's example. Then both of us in Berlin allowed ourselves to be led into it again.

Despite this stultifying cold, I am not much aware of getting older, and have even rarely felt my mind more fit, my whole being more full of aspirations and desires. But I am constantly computing my age and telling myself that the ground may suddenly give way under my feet. I manage to get myself not to feel too melancholy over this.

André Gide

MARCH

'I have decided to keep a full journal, in the hope that my life will perhaps seem more interesting when it is written down.'

ADRIAN MOLE

1 March

1686

Came Sir Gilb: Gerrard to treate with me about his sonns marying my Daughter Susanna; The father being obnoxious, and in some suspicion and displeasure of the King, I would receive no proposal, 'til his Majestie had given me leave, which he was pleas'd to do: but after severall meetings, we brake off, upon his not being willing to secure any thing competant for my daughter['s] Children: besides that I found his estate to be most of it in the Coale-pits as far as N. Castle, and leases from the Bishop of Durrham, who had power to make concurrent Leases with other difficulties, so as we did not proceede to any conclusion.

John Evelyn

1851

Rule. In difficult circumstances always act on first impressions.

Leo Tolstoy

1871

After dinner last night Mr V. kindly anxious to cure my face ache made me drink four large glasses of port. The consequence was that all night and all today I have been groaning with a bursting raging splitting sick headache.

Rev. Francis Kilvert

1886

Rather heavy snow. There has been a most singular nuisance going on since Christmas about Manchester. A gang of young men called themselves *Spring-heeled Jacks* have been going about in the dusk frightening people. They wore india-rubbering dresses which would puff up at will to a great size, horns, a lantern and springs in their boots.

One jumped right over a cab in the Eccles Road, nearly frightening the gentleman inside out of his wits. One poor girl in Swinton Lane had a fit. They were cowardly bullies, also thieves for they took money. Some say they are Medical Students from Owens College, and it is not impossible I am afraid.

They were bad to catch, but the authorities sent some detectives. One of these met a *Jack* who demanded his money or his life. The detective pretended to be frightened and get out money, but instead he produced some handcuffs and caught him. Another was captured on a Sunday evening by some young men who beat him soundly, and then discovered he was an acquaintance. One was in the next garden to *Hopefield* a fortnight since.

The maids durst not stir out a step in the evening, which, my Aunt remarked, was just as well.

Beatrix Potter

1925 [Paris]

Yesterday afternoon we caught the Bois in one of its most unusual aspects. Just as we passed the gate, leaden clouds gathered over our heads and poured rain and hail on the startled promenaders. Mothers, children, nurses, lovers, old men and women, students and dogs, all suddenly disappeared. Automobiles rushed homeward and carriage drivers opened their umbrellas. Hugh [Guiler, her husband] and I did the same.

'I'm Scottish,' said Hugh. 'I love to walk in the rain.'

'So do I.'

'Well then, let's go.'

Suddenly the rain and hail stopped short, and gray-and-purple mist fell all around us and over the surface of the lake. We rented a boat, and Hugh rowed us to a little island, where we walked up a gravel hill to a chalet and sat on the porch before a white-top table and ordered chocolate and cakes. Behind us were a pair of lovers discreetly kissing. Before us stretched brilliant wet grass and mist-enveloped trees, from which came the cooing and twittering of birds. Beyond, the hill descended into the lake, and we would have thought ourselves miles away from Paris. We dreamed together on that quiet and soft afternoon, sipping chocolate and nibbling cakes and turning now and then to look at our little white boat rocking on its chain. When Hugh rowed us homeward, the rain started again. The leaden sky turned the lake's water black, and on this deep, black, undulating surface, swans languidly floated.

Anaïs Nin

1941

In the morning the milkmaid refused to come up. She is no longer allowed to deliver to Jews' Houses.

At midday at the bank only 178M had been transferred from the pension office instead of the 409M of previous months: the new 'social deduction' from Jews, 15 percent of income, deducted all at once for the three months January to March. – After that the butcher declared he would have to give less from now on because deliveries were so poor.

In the afternoon the news that Bulgaria had joined the Tripartite Pact. So Greece is lost, so Russia looks calmly on, so the route to Egypt through

Turkey-in-Asia is open, so Germany appears to be winning the war.

In the evening we wanted to eat something at the Pschorrbräu and found nothing edible without meat coupons, went to the Monopol and found only turnips, went to the station and found nothing at all, went back to the Monopol and ate the turnips. (All in spring weather and slush.) As soon as we were home there was a police check.

One day in my life in the Third Reich.

Victor Klemperer

1943

My husband has to do different work now – less 'large' work, and nearly all blitz repairs that take him into people's houses. He comes in *horrified* sometimes – really shocked – to tell of people with no coal, no sugar till they went downtown for their rations, meat for only two days a week, bread and jam for tea, women *ill* with standing for hours in queues. He stands and gazes on my gaily embroidered cloth, spread 'extravagantly with all *kinds* of food' – and never sees it's only cheese on toast, vegetable salads etc!

Nella Last

1963

Bunny's [David Garnett] remark about the convenience and simplicity of leaving one's body to a hospital has been rumbling in my mind and finally I took action on it. Two days ago I found myself staring in bewilderment at an envelope with 'INSPECTOR OF ANATOMY' written on it in large black letters. I thought for a moment I'd gone mad. But no, this is the gentleman who arranges for the hospitals' corpse-supply. I must admit it gave me a slight *frisson* as I saw myself laid out cold and stiff and pale, or kept on ice for two years, which seems possible. I shoved it away with a little burst of escapism. Then yesterday, 'This won't do,' I thought, and fished it out and dealt with it. I rang up H. M. Inspector. A delightful humorous Scotch voice answered, recommending me to leave myself to 'the nearest medical school' – because 'ye might die up in the north country or somewhere'. So it's done now and I feel another cupboard has been tidied.

Frances Partridge

2 March

1859 [New York]

Stopped at Barnum's on my way down town to see the much advertised nondescript, the 'What-is-it.' Some say it's an advanced chimpanzee, others that it's a cross between nigger and baboon. But it seems to me clearly an idiotic negro dwarf, raised, perhaps, in Alabama or Virginia. The showman's story of its capture (with three other specimens that died) by a party in pursuit of the gorilla on the western coast of Africa is probably bosh. The creature's look and action when playing with his keeper are those of a nigger boy. But his anatomical details are fearfully simian, and he's a great fact for Darwin.

George Templeton Strong

1940 [Palestine]

Probably because I had sat up all night on a hard seat being serenaded by the Austrialian soldiers singing 'Waltzing Matilda' and 'We're the boys from way down under' I found Palestine in the dawn rather disappointing – it was flat and less colourful than I expected. I ate breakfast on the train and reached Rehovoth at eleven. I climbed out on to sand, hardly daring to believe I was going to see Dan [her husband, serving in the Yeomanry].

I saw him a long way down the train looking up at the carriages. Tall, bronzed by the sun, wearing khaki shorts and tunic, marvellously good-looking . . . I stood and watched him, spellbound. I thought my heart would burst . . . Heaven is being together.

Countess of Ranfurly

1961 [Fiji]

There was a dinner party of thirty. Opposite me was seated Lieutenant-Colonel The Hon. Ratu Edward Cakobau, who has just been appointed a district commissioner. When the bandmaster came in for his glass of port, Ratu Edward leaned across and said to me, 'The bandmaster comes from the worst cannibal district in the island.'

I asked Ratu Edward if he were a great-grandson of King Thakimbau, and he replied, 'Yes.' I then asked him whether he knew that his great-grand-father had been to lunch with Queen Victoria in the late 1870s. He replied, 'Yes.' I then told him that the King had sat next to my mother, who, being a very cheeky young girl, had asked him if he regretted having given up cannibalism. She had always said that he had replied that all he missed was babies' toes.

Ratu Edward was highly amused and said, 'I don't think that can be right, for I always heard my great-grandfather particularly liked ladies' fingers.'

Edward Cakobau was shown the menu on board the ship bringing him back to Fiji recently, and said to the head waiter, 'This menu looks horrible, bring me the passenger list.'

Earl Mountbatten of Burma

1996

In the evening we watched an excellent TV interview with Dame Muriel Spark. She came over as wonderfully direct, honest, witty and charming. When she lived in Rome some years ago she invited us to drinks in her splendid apartment. At that time she wore her hair piled high; there were flashing jewels and chic clothes, and she was most affable. The last time I saw her was in June 1991, at the memorial service for Graham Greene. We sat next to each other; we were both required to get up and speak. She wore no make-up and was almost casually dressed. In her tribute to Graham she spoke of the financial help he gave her when she was a struggling writer. She said, 'It was typical of Graham that with the monthly cheques he often sent a few bottles of red wine to "take the edge off cold charity".' It says something very pleasing about both of them.

Alec Guinness

3 March

1886

Davis, the cowman, caught and killed a fine badger. It was sleeping in a corner under the manager at the stalls. He was feeding the cows and first stuck his foot into its rump, and beat it on the head. They are getting rare. I do not remember one being caught here before, though we have often found their holes in the wood. They are not in the least destructive of anything one wishes to preserve. We had it stuffed at a cost of 20/– and put into what the taxidermist called a menacing attitude.

Dearman Birchall

1928

Driving rain outside. Tremendous appetite for rest. Yet brain very active, at once receptive and creative. Ah, to be able to begin a new career; start out anew and under another name! How little satisfies those who are succeeding today! Launching a tone of voice, a gait, a bearing, is enough for them. No maturation of thought; no composition. (If ever, later on, someone reads these lines, he will wonder whom I am getting at . . . I am none too sure of it myself.)

André Gide

1943

When we got to Ambleside, I said to the conductress, 'Do you think if I got off the bus I could get on again?' She answered, 'Oh yes – leave your case on the seat'. I knew there should be a wait of fifteen minutes, so I hurried into a fish shop, where a pleasant old man apologised for the 'poor show' and said they had only cod and plaice. I got a tail-piece of cod, and he filleted it and gave me a handful of trimmings to cook for my little cat.

I rushed back to the car-park – to see my bus swing out, taking my case with it. I was at a loss till I saw a Windermere bus leaving, and ran to stop it. I said, 'Oh dear, the Barrow bus has left me behind – how will I get home?' The driver replied crossly, 'You had no right to leave your seat, madam. It was late in, and had only a nine-minute wait.' I smiled at him and said, 'No, I shouldn't have been tempted. But now, wouldn't your wife have been tempted if she had seen FISH – and got it for *your* tea?' He laughed and said, 'Aye, she would. Come on, jump in, and we'll overtake the Barrow bus for you.'

Nella Last

1983

I take a version of a script down to Settle to be photocopied. The man in charge of the machine watches the sheets come through. 'Glancing at this,' he says, 'I see you dabble in playwriting.' While this about sums it up, I find myself resenting him for noticing what goes through this machine at all. Photocopying is a job in which one is required to see and not see, the delicacy demanded not different from that in medicine. It's as if a nurse were to say, 'I see, watching you undress, that your legs are nothing to write home about.'

Alan Bennett

4 March

1656

This night I was invited by Mr Rog: L'Estrange to heare the incomperable Lubicer [Thomas Baltzar] on the Violin, his variety upon a few notes and plaine ground with that wonderful dexterity, as was admirable, and though a very young man, yet so perfect and skillfull as there was nothing so crosse and perplext, which being by our Artists, brough[t] to him, which he did not at first sight, with ravishing sweetness, and improvements, play off, to the astonishment of our best Masters: In Summ, he plaid on that single Instrument a full Consort, so as the rest, flung-downe their Instruments, as acknowl[e]dging a victory: As to my owne particular, I stand to this hour amaz'd that God should give so great perfection to so young a person.

John Evelyn

1968

Paid a visit to Mme Tussaud's to see my newly installed effigy. It is absolutely horrible. A raddled face under a red wig, with a mouth like Edith

Summerskill's [Physician and Labour MP]. Ted [her husband] assures me I really don't look like that. I had never been in the place before and was quite fascinated. One of the best likenesses is Harold Macmillan's and, when I pointed that out, Tussaud's man agreed. 'As Malcolm Muggeridge remarked, some people are naturally wax.' Apparently they had found me one of the most difficult likenesses to capture, so presumably I am not in that category.

Barbara Castle

1969 [at the premiere of *Isadora*]

The invitation bade those who came to wear 'gems and flowers'. I couldn't think what to do but my barber persuaded me to go wearing a false moustache which looked very fetching but kept falling off. The film, directed by Ken Russell, turned out to be pretty feeble but there was a great party afterwards at the Coliseum. The only drama of the evening occurred when the star of the film, Vanessa Redgrave, in a scarlet and gold sari, her hair encircled with flowers, fainted.

Roy Strong

1978 [Egypt]

I brought a couple of books from Barbara Cartland to give to Mrs Sadat who she understood read her books. However, the President said, 'No, no, I shall read them first, I am a great fan of Barbara Cartland myself.' He then suggested she might come out to Egypt and get some background information for writing one of her novels set in Egypt. I said I would pass on the invitation.

Earl Mountbatten of Burma

5 March

1858

Overheard at the next table at Broggi's:
'I've met his mistress.'
'But that's his wife!'
'He introduced her to me as his mistress, to rehabilitate her . . .'

The Brothers Goncourt

1935

If I had not been blessed, in youth, with an athletic fleetness, if I had not known the joy of leaping and dancing, if I had not known those moments of exhilaration when one's only expression of the knowledge that it is good to be alive is to strain the body to exhaustion – then I might have been tempted now to despise the pride of mere physical fitness, to sneer at the daily adulation of the boxer, or the football player, or the tennis star. But having known the same pride of youth – the sheer muscular exuberance which forces one to run against the wind or to lay hold of a friend and bear him to the ground – having known this, I am saved from jealousy and cannot betray the body by denying that it is a fine thing to feel the life is in flesh. Even yet I can feel it – as if a statue grown warm, not bitter, with the desire to run.

William Soutar

1945 [Bergen-Belsen]

Sleepless nights, filled, filled with the central problem: life or death, and when will it end? Filled, filled with the central national problems, the place of Judaism in the world. Religion, the concept of God. Constantly reaching back to the One eternal God – its meaning and how mankind deludes itself with having vanquished God. Will we manage with materialism? We cannot ignore what has happened, but what really matters is that we should stay alive! I have so much to say still.

The dying continues. One thing: the pessimists were right. Pessimists, optimists, they say nothing about the war. They all talk about themselves. For lack of facts, no one has insights. At most *Ahnung* [a notion] of the relative strengths. And I knew that Germany was powerful.

Everything is getting less, forty grams of butter a week instead of sixty. Half a piece of sausage, et cetera.

Starving, starving, Starving.

Abel J. Herzberg

1970

The celebration of two hundred years of Madame Tussaud's was the occasion for a vast fancy-dress dinner in their Hall of Fame to which a huge contingent of the diplomatic corps had been bidden, suitably festooned with sashes, ribbons and orders. The lead-up to this event was more than trying, as the press for some mysterious reason had got it into their heads that I was going either in drag as Madame Tussaud or as Dr Crippen. In the end I plumped for 'Sea-Green' Robespierre and decked myself in 1790s green satin with black frogging hired from Bermans. I resisted painting a thin red line around my neck as perhaps going a bit far, but it did cross my mind. However, on arriving at Baker Street I was assailed by a battery of photographers and as a consequence must be the first national museum director to figure on the front page of the *Daily Mail.* . . .

Too much drink flowed and I vaguely remember clambering into the tableau of Madame Tussaud modelling the severed head of Marie Antoinette, grabbing the head and being photographed nursing it by *Time*, something I later regretted. As an evening, however, it all fell curiously flat.

Roy Strong

6 March

1761

Went up into the Hall this afternoon after the Judge was in, and I could not get a tolerable Place some time, but at last I jumped from two men's shoulders and leaped upon the Heads of several men and then scrambled into the Prisoners Place where the Judge said I must not stay, so one of the Counsellors [i.e. Barristers] desired me not to make a noise, and he would let me have his Place, which was immediately under the Prisoners and opposite the Judge, where I sat and heard three or four tryalls, and likewise condemnation passed on Dumas, alias Darking, alias Hamilton, alias Harris. Was up there from 5 till 9, and then the Judge had finished everything. 1 condemned to die, 4 transported for seven years, 1 burnt in the hand and acquitted.

Rev. James Woodforde

1941

8.40 a.m. Posen (Poland). Our destination 100 km from here – by the map in the corridor. We seem well North. There are horse cabs in the station yard and a 1914–18 War Memorial. Two Party [Nazi] officers are strolling about on the platform looking very smart in their immaculate brown uniforms. Am rather amused to see a girl get into a waiting train near ours and pick up the Menu Card in the Dining Car. I can't think what it could have had on it bar Klippfisch and Sauerkraut. Also shaken to see some cold coffee thrown out of a window of that same train. I would have given anything for it. Crumbs from the rich man's table. We move out of Posen. 12. noon – Wreschen. We learn here that we haven't a hope of getting to our destination today. About another 200 miles to go. We are travelling very slowly and apparently 2 sides of a triangle. No more food – no more smokes. All stations have been taken over by the Reichsbahn. Is this Country our War Aim? Blimey! Miles upon miles of sweet F.A. except mud and more mud.

Captain John Mansel

1941

I was talking to the Masseys' chauffeur today about the bombings. 'What astonishes me,' he said, 'is the way those old houses fall down so easy. You take that big house on the corner of Berkeley Square – used to belong to

Lord T. My mother used to work there when I was a lad. It always seemed such a fine well-built old house and now it's just a pile of rubble. I would have thought that they would have stood up better – some of those big houses.' Although his tone was practical I thought I could catch an undernote of dismay queerly mixed with relief. That great gloomy house may have hung on in his memory since childhood. It must have seemed as permanent as a natural feature of the landscape and clothed in dim prestige. Now brutally it vanishes. This sudden destruction of the accustomed must shake people out of the grooves of their lives. This overnight disappearance of the brick and mortar framework of existence must send a shock deep into the imagination. These high explosions and incendiaries are like the falling stars and blazing comets – noted of old as foretelling great changes in the affairs of man.

Charles Ritchie

1946

An offensive letter from a female American Catholic. I returned it to her husband with the note: 'I shall be grateful if you will use whatever disciplinary means are customary in your country to restrain your wife from writing impertinent letters to men she does not know.'

Evelyn Waugh

7 March

1914

Have been feeling very 'down' of late, but yesterday I saw a fine Scots Fir by the roadside – tall, erect, as straight as a Parthenon pillar. The sight of it restored my courage. It had a tonic effect. Quite unconsciously I pulled my shoulders back and walked ahead with renewed vows never to flinch again. It is a noble tree. It has strength as a giant, and a giant's height, and yet kindly withal, the branches drooping down graciously towards you – like a kind giant extending its hands to a child.

W. N. P. Barbellion

1933

I walked along the Serpentine – not on the bank because there were too many people there. Why do people when they go for a walk look at each other? – but up on the other side of the road – and there was a breezy wind enough to blow your hair and make you feel a little like the mascots on motor cars – so I took my loose, loose hat off before the wind did. Before

I came to the end, I took a new path across – on my right were two lovers walking away – he bending over and around her with his arm and head. The sparrows were making so much spring noise that I took off my gloves and scarf in spite of the brick red dress showing, and stuffed them in my purse. And then just as I thought I was alone I saw two more lovers on my left who thought they were alone. They were sitting on a seat under a gigantic trunk of a tree.

I had to walk all across that long bare path trying to think of other directions to look in besides theirs. Even painful things pass and that did. It was not that they embarrassed me – I was afraid of embarrassing them and having them send unpleasant thought waves after me. 'Why did she have to come along then?' 'Why can't she get a lover of her own?' Very disconcerting.

Elizabeth Smart

1934

My 35th birthday. Actually I have lied so much about my age that I forget how old I really am. I think I look 28, and know I feel 19.

'Chips' Channon

1941 [Holland]

Tonight I asked Mother to repeat some of the wise old sayings that are good to know if you want to have a good life. E.g. from Schopenhauer, etc.: 'He who believes in goodness will gain goodness.'

And: 'Trouble is the scale on which the true worth of friendship is weighed.'

And I just found this one in my pocket diary: 'Look at the sun, then your shadow will fall behind you.'

Edith Velmans

1963

The 'lower classes' and death: Mrs Ringe's husband has been sufficiently ill lately for him to be taken into hospital. In talking to me she makes no bones about the trouble he is, how irritable and hard to please, how he 'won't pull himself together and try to do things', yet she's not blind to how ill he is. At the same time she refers often to the possibility of his death, pensions, and whether she should ever marry again. I'm sure she thinks constantly and simply about all that. She says nothing 'in bad taste' yet it gives me a shock that anyone should be able to contemplate their nearest and dearest as alive and dead at one and the same time. I almost beg her to be kinder to him and try to put herself in the state of mind of a sinking, dying man, and realize the horror of it for him. But I suppose she is being much more realistic than

I was for instance, who could only accept the possibility of death when it was forced on me and for short gasping stretches at a time, to build up as quickly as possible an optimistic ostrichism. Yet I consider myself a realist and my education ought to have trained me to face facts and control my thoughts, and not slide off into clichés like 'It's only the thought,' or 'We've all got it coming to us,' or 'It'll all come out in the wash.'

Frances Partridge

8 March

1852

N. P. Willis is stricken with deadly disease, epilepsy and consumption together. The idea of death and of the man who writes editorials for the *Home Journal* are an unnatural combination. Death seems too solemn a matter for him to have any business with it.

George Templeton Strong

1870

Yesterday there was an inquest at the Blue Boar, Hay, on the body of the barmaid of the Blue Boar who a day or two ago went out at night on an hour's leave, but went up the Wye to Glasbury and threw herself into the river. She was taken out at Llan Hennw. She was enceinte. Met the Morrell children returning from a walk with the first white violets and primroses.

Rev. Francis Kilvert

1918

Going up in the lift at Holborn the other day I stood next to a boy of four-teen or so, whose head only was visible among the crowd. I noticed that it was an extremely interesting, sensitive, clever, observant head; rather sharp, but independent looking. One couldn't tell from his cap whether he was well off or not. I came to the conclusion that he was the son of an officer with whom he stood. When we got into the street I looked at once at his legs. His trousers had holes in them. From that one could judge what a wretched affair his life will be.

Virginia Woolf

1919 [Paris]

Churchill arrived late last night from London, & breakfasted with the P. M. [Lloyd George] this morning. Full of his speech in the House on the Military Service Bill. He certainly does not lack self-confidence – in fact if he had a little less he might think a little more before he acts & speaks. One cannot help being fascinated by him, although I *cannot* bring myself to like him.

Frances Stevenson

9 March

1870

I saw Mr. Helps [Clerk of the Privy Council] this evening at half past six, who brought and introduced Mr. Dickens, the celebrated author. He is very agreeable, with a pleasant voice and manner. He talked of his latest works, of America, the strangeness of the people there, of the division of classes in England, which he hoped would get better in time. He felt sure that it would come gradually.

Queen Victoria

1874

Why am I such a coward! If I was going to have a leg cut off it could not be worse. Instead of which I am going to have a tooth stopped. Gracious goodness! Where's the world going to next! Coward, coward, coward, that's what I am, morally and physically.

Beatrice Webb

1914

I am too tired, I must try to rest and sleep, otherwise I am lost in every respect. What an effort to keep alive! Erecting a monument does not require the expenditure of so much strength.

Franz Kafka

1932

During the morning I went over to 52 Avenue Kléber where [Aristide] Briand died and has been laid out. Anyone can go in. A small, four-roomed apartment on the second floor. Petit bourgeois, almost seedy furnishings, an interior appropriate to a lower-middle-grade civil servant, few books, trivial prints on the walls. No sign of anything to satisfy intellectual or artistic needs, let alone a touch of luxury. Extraordinary! Did he really demand nothing over and above the average? I still see him sitting next to me, his eyes half closed as though he were dropping off to sleep, and listening while I tried to sound him out on what position he would concede Germany in the League of Nations. Suddenly he opened his eyes wide and gave an answer that clinched the matter: it would be ridiculous for Germany not to have a permanent seat on the Council, that is a foregone conclusion. The impression I had of him at that moment was of a highly intelligent, indeed crafty petit bourgeois. Perhaps it was this background which formed the bond of mutual understanding between Briand and [Gustav] Stresemann, innkeepers' sons, both of them.

Count Harry Kessler

1941 [POW camp, Poland]

The German doctor, fully endorsed by the Brigadier, orders that except for Naval personnel, all hair is to be cut short and beards removed. If this is not done within 3 or 4 days, the whole Camp will be subjected to convict crops. (Lice have been found and apparently before we arrived they were rampant.) Tunics and greatcoats to be smartened up and boots polished etc., on Appell [roll call]. In fact flat out militarism. The tricky part is how to effect this. When the Camp Officer appeared he greeted us all with a shouted 'Guten Morgen!' – to which we had to reply in unison 'good morning'. At 11 o'clock we had a service taken by Macintyre. The Chapel is worth sketching – another underground cul-de-sac – brickbuilt and from the austere point of view, thoroughly dramatic – in fact what I have always visualised as a prison chapel. Wooden rickety benches to sit on – extremely cold, but the driest room I have seen yet. It is a curious coincidence that we should have arrived here almost the 1st day of Lent – we have certainly given up enough! I personally look upon this as an extremely good experience for all of us – it will certainly make us appreciate the simplest things in life afterwards. I think we are all getting acclimatised now and have certainly not lost heart. It is just like a dream from which one is bound to wake up sometime.

Captain John Mansel

10 March

1853

As we turned the corner of a lane during our walk, a man and a bull came in sight; the former crying out, 'Ladies, save yourselves as you can!' the latter scudding onwards slowly but furiously. I jumped aside on a little hedge, but thought the depth below rather too great – about nine or ten feet; but the man cried 'Jump!' and I jumped. To the horror of all, the bull jumped after me. My fall stunned me, so that I knew nothing of my terrible neighbour, whose deep autograph may be now seen quite close to my little one. He thought me dead, and only gazed without any attempt at touching me, though pacing round, pawing and snorting, and thus we were for about twenty minutes.

The man, a kind soul but no hero, stood on the hedge above, charging me from time to time not to move. Indeed, my first recollection is of his friendly voice. And so I lay still, wondering how much was reality and how much dream; and when I tried to think of my situation, I pronounced it too dreadful to be true, and certainly a dream. Then I contemplated a drop of blood and a lump of mud, which looked very real indeed, and I thought it very imprudent in any man to make me lie in a pool – it would surely give me rheumatism. I longed to peep at the bull, but was afraid to venture on such a movement. Then I thought, I shall probably be killed in a few minutes, how is it that I am not taking it more solemnly? I tried to do so, seeking rather for preparation for death than restoration to life. Then I checked myself with the thought, It's only a dream, so it's really quite profane to treat it in this way; and so I went on oscillating, There was, however, a rest in the dear will of God which I love to remember; also a sense of the simplicity of my condition – nothing to do to involve others in suffering, only to endure what was laid upon me. To me the time did not seem nearly so long as they say it was: at length the drover, having found some bullocks, drove them into the field, and my bull, after a good deal of hesitation, went off to his own species. Then they had a laugh at me that I stayed to pick up some oranges I had dropped before taking the man's hand and being pulled up the hedge; but in all this I acted as a somnambulist, with only fitful gleams of consciousness and memory.

Caroline Fox

1919

P.M. [David Lloyd George] lunched at Mr Balfour's flat to meet with Queen of Rumania, & according to everybody, was in his best form. D. says she is very naughty, but a very clever woman, though on the whole he does not like her. She gave a lengthy description of her purchases in Paris, which included a pink silk chemise. She spoke of meeting President Wilson on his arrival. 'What shall I talk to him about?' she asked. 'The League of Nations or my pink chemise?' 'Begin with the League of Nations,' said Mr. Balfour, 'and finish up with the pink chemise. If you were talking to Mr. Lloyd George, you could begin with the pink chemise!'

Frances Stevenson

1936

What diarist has not, at some moment, become ashamed of the numerous entries which belittle a friend or slight an acquaintance? – and yet at the time the man or the woman appeared so, and had by words and gestures irritated the writer. And the nature of the entry is also a self-confession to the diarist's own moods and limitations; so that even if he return to these pages, which now accuse him, and efface their nay-saying, would the action not testify rather to a fear than to a generous impulse: would not the solicitude be primarily for the diarist's own good name? I shall leave all my entries, even such as may shame me – for I do not hate anyone; and I know that the moments of human sympathy are not rare. Mutual irritation, boredom, and actual antagonism are unavoidable; but at heart we all desire to like people and be liked.

William Soutar

11 March

1912

Titus Oates is very near the end, one feels. What we or he will do, God only knows. We discussed the matter after breakfast; he is a brave fine fellow and understands the situation, but he practically asked for advice. Nothing could be said but to urge him to march as long as he could. One satisfactory result to the discussion; I practically ordered Wilson to hand over the means of ending our troubles to us, so that any one of us may know how to do so. Wilson had no choice between doing so and our ransacking the medicine case. We have 30 opium tablets apiece and he is left with a tube of morphine. So far the tragical side of our story.

Captain Robert Falcon Scott

1956

I have been denying for years any basis in *A Time To Be Born* for the general idea that it is Clare Luce. I swear it is based on five or six girls, some known personally and some by talk, and often I changed the facts to avoid libel with resulting character a real person evidently and libelously Luce-ian. I insist it was a composite (or compost) but then I find a memo from 1939 – 'Why not do novel on Clare Luce?' Who can I believe – me or myself?

Dawn Powell

1967

Kenneth W[illiams] told a lot of stories during the evening . . . He told a story of how a woman had come up to him and said, 'You're on in that play at the Theatre Royal, aren't you?' and when he'd replied that he was, she said: 'Disgusting play. I walked out half-way through. What happened at the finish?' Kenneth said that Gordon Jackson who was with him said: 'By walking out madam, you forfeited your right to know.' 'Marvellous reply, wasn't it?' Kenneth said, his eyes shining.

Joe Orton

1978

I had a lot of dates but I decided to stay home and dye my eyebrows.

Andy Warhol

12 March

1780

Having gone to bed last night ruminating on my melancholy, I awaked
this morning with this text full in my mind: 'Howbeit this kind goeth not
out but by prayer and fasting.' This seemed to be a supernatural suggestion that piety alone could relieve me from the evil spirit. I was much
impressed with it, and my devotion was fervent today. Heard Dr. Blair in
the forenoon and I think Mr. Walker in the afternoon. Was a little at my
father's between sermons. Dined at Lord Monboddo's with Mr. David Rae,
Lady Duffus and one of her grand-daughters, a Miss Sinclair, and Mrs.
Hamilton and some of her boarders. The invitation was to see the rising
generation of females. We were very cheerful. But my Lord and I drank
too much claret. I stayed tea. Walked home a good deal inflamed; met an
old acquaintance in the street, and was in danger of being licentious with
her, so soon had wine overpowered my morning seriousness, which was
indeed 'like the morning cloud.' However, I got off. Sir Charles Preston
and Grange supped with us. Sandy said no divine lesson today, and Veronica
and Phemie said but little. I must never dine abroad on Sunday. My wife
was hurt by my being again on the confines of low debauchery. I was very
uneasy.

James Boswell

1915

Mr Liddell gave me a curious account of his duties as the Lord Chancellor's
secretary. He opens all the letters from lunatics. They have a right to send
unopened letters to the Lord Chancellor twice a month. He says some of
the letters that are coming in now are most pathetic, the burden of many
of them being, 'Only let me out, and I will at once enlist!' He said the
war had neither increased nor diminished the number of lunatics. I asked
him if he had ever discovered a sane man incarcerated unfairly. He said
no, but that they always looked out for such cases, and that he makes a
very special note when any new lunatic's letter arrives. He also makes very
particular enquiries when a lunatic writes a complaint of physical ill-
treatment. He says he believes the medical superintendents are always
humane, but that it is very difficult to get the right type of man to be a

male nurse, as the work is so depressing. I said it ought to be done by monks and nuns.

Marie Belloc Lowndes

1944

Hear the broadcast of the Pope's Benediction of the faithful in Piazza San Pietro – a crowd chiefly composed of the homeless and starving refugees who have now flocked into the city. It was a short address, without any political flavour: an admission of the Pope's inability to stop or mitigate the horrors of war even within his own city, a final appeal to the rulers on both sides – and, to the congregation before him, a repetition of the well-known words of Christian consolation: 'Come unto me, all ye that are weary and heavy-laden.' Perhaps never, in all the history of suffering humanity, have these words been spoken to so great an assembly of the homeless, the penniless and the bereft. And when, the address ended, the Pope paused a moment before the Benediction, from thousands of throats came a cry of supplication, unforgettable by anyone who heard it – a cry which sounded like an echo of all the suffering that is torturing the world: 'Give us peace; oh, give us peace.'

Iris Origo

13 March

1856

Out shopping, then to University hospital to ask John Marshall about a dead body. He got the one that will just do. It was in the vaults under the dissecting room. When I saw it first, what with the dim light, the brown & parchment-like appearance of it & the shaven head, I took it for a wooden imulation [imitation] of the thing. Often as I have seen horrors I really did not remember how hideous the shell of a poor creature may remain when the substance contained is fled. Yet we both in our joy at the obtainment of what we sought declared it to be lovely & a splendid corps[e]. Marshall evidently loves a thing of the kind. Home again by 5.

Ford Madox Brown

1887

At Swindon I went over Huntley & Palmer's biscuit factory. It is indeed a most gigantic enterprize. They take 500 sacks of flour a day turning out 100 tons of biscuits every working day. Their goods are appreciated in the interiors of both China and Africa. They use a vast quantity of coconuts, almonds, treacle, ginger, butter, eggs, lard, arrowroot, rice water, and isinglass.

I saw a large parcel of macaroons and coconut cakes come out of the ovens for a special order from Windsor Castle. They have over 3000 hands and there are many very interesting mechanical dodges invented by the Palmers. The income is immense but the two young ones work incessantly instead of spending their money and living in idleness.

Dearman Birchall

1921

[T. S.] Eliot dines here tonight, alone, since his wife is in a nursing home, not much to our regret. But what about Eliot? Will he become 'Tom'? What happens with friendships undertaken at the age of forty? Do they flourish and live long? I suppose a good mind endures, and one is drawn to it, owning to having a good mind myself. Not that Tom admires my writing, damn him.

Virginia Woolf

1941 [Linz]

To the meeting in the evening. Between huge crowds. The cheering never stops. Meeting overflowing. Fantastic atmosphere. I speak on the war situation. Each sentence is punctuated by storms of applause. I am on good form. Then the Gauleiter makes a short speech. And now, completely unexpected so far as the meeting is concerned, the Führer arrives. The storm of applause is quite indescribable. The Führer is lively and buoyant. He speaks for thirty minutes with the greatest élan. Total confidence in victory. The crowd goes wild.

Drive between endless crowds. At the hotel. Then I stand with the Führer on the balcony of his hotel room, and we look out over his home town. He loves this city very much, and this is understandable. He intends to establish a new centre of culture here. As a counterweight to Vienna, which will have to be gradually phased out of the picture. He does not like Vienna, basically for political reasons. I tell him a few things that I know about Vienna, aspects downright hostile to the Reich, which annoy him greatly. But Linz is his darling. I give him an account of my impressions, which he is very pleased with. A wonderful evening with the Führer. He expounds his views on the situation to me: everything is going well, both militarily and diplomatically. We can be very satisfied.

Josef Goebbels

1943

[J. Pierpont] Morgan the banker and [Stephen Vincent] Benet the poet died yesterday: B.B.Ç. had much to say of the former but little of the latter.

William Soutar

1949

It is a curious business certainly. Here are three doctors, three strangers to me and to Nancy [his sister], Drs Brodie, Glover and Walker, and I run to them for help in a matter which covers, includes and exposes the whole of our family life. In a few letters, half an hour's or an hour's conversation, I have to convey to them somehow our characters and history and personal relationships – everything that constitutes our half century of life and beyond. They make up a sort of tribunal to which I have to take my own and the family guilt, the family failure, and they are expected, on what I care or choose to tell them, not only to withdraw my sister from her self-imposed psychosis, but rearrange our shabby and unsuccessful personal relations, in such a way that we shall not destroy ourselves or each other again. What I am saying to these doctors, in effect, is 'Comfort me in my guilt. I have mismanaged my domestic affairs so badly that my sister preferred death to my care, in which she no longer believes. Can you somehow pull her out of it, so that I shall not feel responsible, for the rest of my days? Can you, without knowing any of us, or anything really about any of us, create an atmosphere in which we can all live?' No wonder Dr Brodie seems to me not to understand or give due importance to the dreadful subtleties which seem to me involved. Yet I expect him somehow to launder this half-century-old dirty washing.

J. R. Ackerley

1979

Just before the end of the council, Callaghan and I both went out and coincided in the loo, whereupon he made to me the most fanciful offer, saying, 'Would you like to be Governor of Hong Kong? I could possibly persuade Murray MacLehose to stay on until nearly the end of your time in Europe.' I said, 'Certainly not, Jim. I have never heard a more preposterous suggestion.' However, in a curious, rather heavy-footed way, he went on, saying, 'Oh, it's a very important job, you know. You would be good at it. What do you want to do when you come back to England? You'll go to the House of Lords, I presume.' I said, 'I am not at all sure, as I told you when you last suggested that to me. Not for the moment, certainly. I want to come back and look around and keep options open.' 'Well,' he said, 'you might find it quite difficult to get back into the House of Commons.' 'Certainly,' I said. 'And you might not like it when you got there,' he said. 'It has changed, it has deteriorated a lot.' I said, 'Yes, yes. All I intend to do is come back and look around at the political landscape, Jim, and certainly not become Governor of Hong Kong.'

Roy Jenkins

14 March

1802

William had slept badly – he got up at 9 o'clock, but before he rose he had finished the Beggar Boy – and while we were at Breakfast that is (for I had breakfasted) he, with his basin of broth before him untouched and a little plate of Bread and butter he wrote the Poem to a Butterfly! He ate not a morsel, nor put on his stockings but sate with his shirt neck unbuttoned, and his waistcoat open while he did it. The thought first came upon him as we were talking about the pleasure we both always feel at the sight of a butterfly. I told him that I used to chase them a little but I was afraid of brushing the dust off their wings, and did not catch them – He told me they used to kill all the white ones when he went to school because they were Frenchmen.

Dorothy Wordsworth

1856

To the University by 1/2 past 10. Draw the corps[e] till 1/2 past 2. Got on quite merrily & finished it 2 hours sooner than was obligate on me. As I was going met Marshall who could not keep away from the sweets of the charnel house.

Ford Madox Brown

1858

My dear [sister] Beth died at three this morning, after two years of patient pain. Last week she put her work away, saying the needle was 'too heavy,' and having given us her few possessions, made ready for the parting in her own simple, quiet way. For two days she suffered much, begging for ether, though its effect was gone. Tuesday she lay in Father's arms, and called us round her, smiling contentedly as she said, 'All here!' I think she bid us good-by then, as she held our hands and kissed us tenderly. Saturday she slept, and at midnight became unconscious, quietly breathing her life away till three, then, with one last look of the beautiful eyes, she was gone.

A curious thing happened, and I will tell it here, for Dr. G. said it was a fact. A few moments after the last breath came, as Mother and I sat silently watching the shadow fall on the dear little face, I saw a light mist rise from the body and float up and vanish in the air. Mother's eyes followed mine, and when I said, 'What did you see?' she described the same light mist. Dr. G. said it was the life departing visibly.

For the last time we dressed her in her usual cap and gown, and laid her on her bed, – at rest at last. What she had suffered was seen in the face, for at twenty-three she looked like a woman of forty, so worn was she, and all her pretty hair gone.

On Monday Dr. Huntington read the Chapel service, and we sang her favorite hymn. Mr Emerson, Henry Thoreau, Sanborn, and John Pratt, carried her out of the old home to the new one at Sleepy Hollow chosen by herself. So the first break comes, and I know what death means, – a liberator for her, a teacher for us.

Louisa May Alcott

1893 [hotel in Torquay]

I sniffed my bedroom on arrival, and for a few hours felt a certain grim satisfaction when my forebodings were maintained, but it is possible to have too much Natural History in a bed.

I did not undress after the first night, but I was obliged to lie on it because there were only two chairs and one of them was broken. It is very uncomfortable to sleep with Keating's powder in the hair. What is to be thought of people who recommend near relations to an hotel where there are bugs?

Beatrix Potter

1929

I became aware, around noon, that my gloominess this morning, despite a night of excellent sleep and such as I had not known for some time, came too, came especially, from the fact that I had not shaved, that my collar was dirty, my suit out of press from the last two nights when I had to go to bed dressed, my shoes not shined, etc. My eyes, my mind, could not fix on anything without finding something to scratch and make bleed . . . A ring from Montherlant came very appropriately, like a cock's crow, to drive away the twilight phantoms. I went back up to wash, shave, change linen, suit, and thoughts.

André Gide

1937

I am in such a twitter owing to two columns in the *Observer* praising *The Years* that I can't, as I foretold, go on with *Three Guineas*. Why I even sat back just now and thought with pleasure of people reading that review. And when I think of the agony I went through in this room, just over a year ago . . . when it dawned on me that the whole of three years' work was a complete failure: and then when I think of the mornings here when I used to stumble out and cut up those proofs and write three lines and then go back and lie on my bed – the worst summer in my life, but at the same time the most illuminating – it's no wonder my hand trembles.

Virginia Woolf

1941 [POW camp]

Everyone has his particular habits which in normal circumstances one would never think of taking offence at. I will illustrate a few in our room, without any mention of names. The fellow who always hums to himself very quietly when he is reading or you are talking to him. The man who persistently is stroking the long ends of his moustache with his tongue. The man who quietly spits out stray ends of tobacco from his cigarette; who eats abnormally slowly and endlessly chews a bit of nothing which I myself have swallowed in one. The man who dresses slowly and meticulously, looking no better for it, if anything rather a twirp. The man who you can rely on to produce an argument and who will always disagree with anything which is said. The man who is never present when he should be, who, being a bookworm, will pick up any book that comes into his line of vision, open it at the middle and page hop. The man who visits our room for this special purpose, who spends the whole day playing double pack Patience – and thereby taking up more than his fair share of room. And above all the man who *must* be first with the news or acknowledge with 'oh yes' news started by someone else, showing that he knew it already, and who likes to show that he is the origin of all communal benefits or news by the incessant use of the first personal singular. That will do for today.

Captain John Mansel

1957

With Val to see play *Look Back in Anger* by John Osborne. Play quite execrable – woman ironing, man yelling and snivelling, highbrow smut, 'daring' remarks (reading from Sunday paper; Bishop of . . . asks all to rally round and make hydrogen bomb). Endured play up to point where hero and heroine pretended to be squirrels.

Malcolm Muggeridge

15 March

1826

This morning I leave No 93 [in fact No 39] Castle Street for the last time. 'The cabbin was convenient' and habit made it agreeable to me. I never reckoned upon a change in this particular so long as I held an office in the Court of Session. In all my former changes of residence it was from good to better – this is retrograding. I leave the house for sale and cease to be an Edinburgh citizen in the sense of being a proprietor – which my father and I have been for sixty years at least. So farewell, poor 93, and may you never harbour worse people than those who now leave you.

Sir Walter Scott

1868

Fine and summer-like – With Stokes on the Quinton Road. Chervil and wood-sorrel out. Hawthorn sprays papered with young leaves. – Venus like an apple of light.

Gerard Manley Hopkins

1944

A bad raid last night with heavy civilian casualties, as usual, in the densely populated port areas. I was sent this morning to investigate the reports of panic, and frantic crowds running through the streets crying, 'Give us peace,' and 'Out with all the soldiers.' In Santa Lucia, home territory of the Neapolitan ballad, I saw a heart-rending scene. A number of tiny children had been dug out of the ruins of a bombed building and lay side by side in the street. Where presentable, their faces were uncovered, and in some cases brand-new dolls had been thrust into their arms to accompany them to the other world. Professional mourners, hired by the locality to reinforce the grief of the stricken families, were running up and down the street, tearing at their clothing and screaming horribly. One man climbed into the rubble and was calling into a hole where he believed his little boy was trapped under hundreds of tons of masonry, begging him not to die before he could be dug out. 'Hang on, son. Only a few minutes longer now. We'll have you out of there in a minute. Please don't die.' The Germans murder only the poor in these indiscriminate raids, just as we did.

Norman Lewis

1983

It was a beautiful day. Walked on the street and a little kid, she was six or seven, with another kid, yelled, 'Look at the guy with the wig,' and I was really embarrassed, I blew my cool and it ruined my afternoon. So I was depressed.

Andy Warhol

16 March

1883

What will be blown up next? Last night an attempt was made to blow up the Government Offices in Parliament Street. Not so much damage was done to the building, owing to its great strength, but the streets for some distance round were strewn with glass.

One thing struck me as showing the extraordinary power of dynamite, a brick was hurled 100 feet and then through a brick wall into some stables. Some one said the noise was like the 80 ton gun. I believe it was heard here.

An attempt was also made, but failed, on *The Times* office, which seems to prove it was the work of Irishmen, that paper having had a leading article in its last number in which it was stated the Irish had got enough and more than enough, and need ask for no more.

Papa says it is Mr Gladstone's fault. He takes the side of these rogues and then, if they think he is slackening, they frighten him on a bit – really we shall be as bad as France soon.

Beatrix Potter (aged 16)

1912

Lunched at 'Thirty' [luncheon club]. We all talked about the enduring power of love. Some of those present said that love goes in a man when the woman becomes middle-aged. I said that it often amazed me to see how love endured, though I admitted that in a certain class – the prosperous commercial class, no man, whatever his age, has any use for a woman, even for her company, after she is, say, forty. That is one of the things that strikes me in one circle I frequent. The moment you know a man at all well, he confides to you quite frankly what a bore he finds his wife's friends – that being a man of sixty talking of women between forty and forty-five.

Marie Belloc Lowndes

1945 [Bergen-Belsen]

Every day now transports of thousands of people are arriving from concentration camps. Men and women, including Dutch people, acquaintances, friends.

Twenty to twenty-five per cent are dead, sometimes more. On the way to our latrines there is a field full of corpses and more corpses. It is a gruesome sight. And no one knows about it or will believe it. It makes us profoundly dejected and pessimistic. The corpses are being thrown into lime now. The crematorium can no longer cope with the volume. The mortality rate in our camp is declining slightly. Except that we have had the first case of spotted fever.

T. [his wife] also has fever again, day after day. I am worn out and can hardly move. Almost the entire day I lie on the bed (if one can call it such). The filth is increasing. We are sick of it. For weeks I have been unable to make my bed.

Abel J. Herzberg

17 March

1798

I do not remember this day.

Dorothy Wordsworth

1806

I spent an hour with Mme. Tivollier, with whom I'm making great progress. I put my hand on her thigh without any objection on her part, I'd sleep with her with pleasure for a month.

Stendhal

1861

Flaubert said to us today: 'The story, the plot of a novel is of no interest to me. When I write a novel I aim at rendering a colour, a shade. For instance, in my Carthaginian novel, I want to do something purple. The rest, the characters and the plot, is a mere detail. In *Madame Bovary*, all I wanted to do was to render a grey colour, the mouldy colour of a wood-louse's existence. The story of the novel mattered so little to me that a few days before starting on it I still had in mind a very different Madame Bovary from the one I created: the setting and the overall tone were the same, but she was to have been a chaste and devout old maid. And then I realized that she would have been an impossible character.'

The Brothers Goncourt

1873

Old James Jones the sawyer of the Infant School told me that he remembers a reprobate drunken fellow named James Davies, but nicknamed 'Jim of the Dingle' being put in the stocks at Clyro by Archdeacon Venables and the parish constable. This Jim of the Dingle had a companion spirit as wicked as himself. And both of them belonged to the Herfordshire Militia. So when the Archdeacon and the Constable had gone away leaving Jim in the stocks, Jim's friend brought an axe and beat the stocks all to pieces and let the prisoner out. The two worthies fled away to Hereford to the militia and never returned to Clyro. But the Clyro people, seeing the stocks broken, demolished and burnt the stocks and the whipping post, and no one was ever confined or whipped at Clyro after that.

Rev. Francis Kilvert

1912

Friday March 16 or Saturday 17 – Lost track of dates, but think the last correct. Tragedy all along the line. At lunch, the day before yesterday, poor Titus Oates said he couldn't go on; he proposed we should leave him in his sleeping-bag. That we could not do, and we induced him to come on, on the afternoon march. In spite of its awful nature for him he struggled on and we made a few miles. At night he was worse and we knew the end had come.

Should this be found I want these facts recorded. Oates' last thoughts were of his Mother, but immediately before he took pride in thinking that his regiment would be pleased with the bold way in which he met his death. We can testify to his bravery. He has borne intense suffering for weeks without complaint, and to the very last was able and willing to discuss outside subjects. He did not − would not − give up hope till the very end. He was a brave soul. This was the end. He slept through the night before last, hoping not to wake; but he woke in the morning − yesterday. It was blowing a blizzard. He said, 'I am going outside and may be some time.' He went out into the blizzard and we have not seen him since.

Captain Robert Falcon Scott

1944

I can't think of anything except something horrible I have had to do, getting the warble fly maggots out of the cattle, oh god it was filthy. The chap came to licence Timo [the bull], said he'd pass him but he wasn't very good, he thought I'd best sell him locally, gave me a lot of good advice, . . . then said he had warble flies and pressed an awful maggot out of his back, I was nearly sick. Duncan [a neighbour] says not to worry too much, they all have them, but give them a dressing of sheep dip. He was very lousy too. I got in the two Ayrshires, we rubbed the dip into their backs, neither had any lice, but Linda had two warble maggots, I pressed them out, I couldn't make Joan do it. They pop out, it is a real nightmare. I couldn't bear one to touch me, nor could Joan. I tried to do Timo but he kicked like a sledgehammer, I expect all the Galloways have it. Oh dear, it is one of the many things I didn't know about . . .

Naomi Mitchison

1953

I was only thinking in the bath last night, that so many artists are *thin* that it must be significant. Aesthetic people usually seem to be thin. This must have something to do with nervous energy.

Kenneth Williams

1966

I turned up late at No. 10 today because I knew the P.M. had been at a monster meeting in Birmingham the night before with 10,000 people booing and jostling in the hall; I had seen it all on the I.T.N. News the night before. I found Harold [Wilson] lying in bed eating kippers, with one kipper skeleton thrown on the carpet for his Siamese cat to finish. Harold sleeps in a tiny little bedroom – I suppose it was the scullery-maid's bedroom in the old days – and there I had my breakfast with him. He looked a bit tired, having got back at three in the morning, but he was enormously elated by the Birmingham meeting and told me with great excitement the story of how Mary [his wife] had got a scratch on her neck when something had been thrown at her. Should we give that to the press, he pondered, and finally concluded that we should. When I asked him why, he said, 'Well, you see the Tories are deliberately leaving her out of the campaign because Heath has no wife. It's a positive advantage to us that I and Mary appear together and Heath has nothing. So I would like to see her brought back into the campaign.' I said that Mary must hate it. 'Oh no,' he said. 'She liked the meeting last night a great deal.' As I was going downstairs I ran into Mary and said, 'I hear you really enjoyed last night after all?' 'Enjoyed it!' she said, with agony on her face. 'Who told you that? That man?' Her relationship with Harold is fascinating. I am sure they are deeply together but they are now pretty separate in their togetherness. It is one of those marriages which holds despite itself because each side has evolved a self-containedness within the marriage.

Richard Crossman

18 March

1669

I went with my L[ord] Howard of Norfolk to visite Sir William Ducy at Charleton, where we dined: The servants made our Coach-men so drunk that they both fell-off their boxes upon the heath, where we were faine to leave them, and were driven to Lond: by two Gent: of my Lords: This barbarous Costome of making their Masters Wellcome by intoxicating the Servants had now the second time happn'd to my Coachman . . .

John Evelyn

1861

You can't read any genuine history – as that of Herodotus or the Venerable Bede – without perceiving that our interest depends not on the subject but on the man, – on the manner in which he treats the subject and the importance he gives it. A feeble writer and without genius must have what he thinks a great theme, which we are already interested in through the accounts of others, but a genius – a Shakespeare, for instance – would make the history of his parish more interesting than another's history of the world.

H. D. Thoreau

1938

In the bathroom of Kay's hotel apartment, washing my hands, struck by a sudden indescribable desolation while listening to her cross-channel telephone conversation, in the other room, with Freddie: 'Do you love me? Yes, but' (shouting) 'Do you LOVE ME? – SAME HERE!' Standing in one of the basins was an enormous bouquet of daffodils and narcissi that he had had sent to her. (I had never thought that I should one day reach the point when the spectacle of other people's happiness would arouse only bitterness in me. – And when they don't even realise their own happiness!)

David Gascoyne

1941 [POW camp]

The whole place seemed particularly cheerless this morning. When Appell [roll call] was sounded and the passages and stairs became filled with the mob going to parade, the scene struck me as being for all the world like a plague of rats and the only item missing a Pied Piper. The moat level passages are after all, in the dark, very like enormous sewers.

The talk in the room this morning started off with a discussion as to the way in which P.O.W.'s are now and will be after the war regarded at home. Peter Tunstall told us how in his aerodrome before he was captured, if any one was known to have been captured, they all said 'Oh well, he's all right for the rest of the war.' A popular opinion is that one will be greeted by 'You lucky devil having been a prisoner of war, you missed it all.'

Captain John Mansel

19 March

1931

The itch from which I have suffered for months (or, but with interruptions, for years) has recently become unbearable and, for the last few nights, has almost completely kept me from sleeping.

Besides, nothing appears on the outside; immediately under the skin, it is like a poison that wants to come out; an injection of extract of bedbugs. Can it get more intense? It doesn't seem so. But it can enlarge, spread to the whole body . . .

I think of Job looking for a piece of glass with which to scratch himself, and of Flaubert, whose correspondence, in the last part of his life, speaks of similar itchings. I tell myself that each of us has his sufferings, and that it would be most unwise to long to change them; but I believe that a real pain would take less of my attention and would after all be more bearable. And, in the scale of sufferings, a real pain is something nobler, more august; the itch is a mean, unconfessable, ridiculous malady; one can pity someone who is suffering; someone who wants to scratch himself makes one laugh.

André Gide

1941

Every year, the young girls come into flower on the beaches. They have only one season. The next year, they are replaced by other flower-like faces which, the previous season, still belonged to little girls. For the man who looks at them, they are yearly waves whose weight and splendour break into foam over the yellow beach.

Albert Camus

1946

Goering said under cross-examination at Nuremberg that he was sorry about the burning down of the Reichstag because he had to requisition the Kroll Opera House as alternative accommodation, and he regarded opera as in every respect a superior enterprise to the Reichstag.

Malcolm Muggeridge

20 March

1843

No news going. A hope of the Kirk of Scotland listening to reason – the refractory parsons are some of them giving in – Government has been quite firm, but very temperate and their exposition of the dispute [over the Disruption of the Church of Scotland] has much diminished the Kirk's supporters. On both sides the argument has been conducted with perfect temper, indeed the whole session has been remarkable for the gentlemanly tone of every debate. Would that such calmness could reach Ireland, where the violence of every feeling is displayed with the heat and the folly of lunaticks. All sides sinning alike, all parties, all creeds, and on all matters, publick, scientifick, religious, domestic. They will fight to frenzy about the placing of Jack Straws.

I am sure I wish they would *work* – the servants at least – we should all be a great deal more comfortable; their frightful idle habits are intolerable. I at any rate will not put up for another month with their dirt and their gossiping and their utter carelessness and indifference to our interests. The very moment I am better I'll put an end to our discomfort. There is no enjoyment of life while one has to act slave to one's own servants. Catharine Redmond, the child from school, the only one in the house who knew the meaning of *order* had to be sent away for a dirty habit never cured in her infancy; besides she nearly set fire to the house reading in bed – burned all the bed clothes, and in the morning never told.

Elizabeth Grant of Rothiemurchus

1871

Miserable news from Paris. Another Revolution, barricades, the troops of the line fraternizing with the insurgent National Guards, two Generals shot, two more in the hands and tender mercies of the beastly cowardly Paris mob. Those Parisians are the scum of the earth, and Paris is the crater of the volcano, France, and a bottomless pit of revolution and anarchy.

Rev. Francis Kilvert

1922 [Berlin]

Dined with the Einsteins. A quiet, attractive apartment in Berlin West (Haberlandstrasse). Rather too much food in a grand style to which this really loveable, almost still childlike couple lent an air of naïvety. An emanation of goodness and simplicity on the part of the host and hostess saved even such a typical Berlin dinner-party from being conventional and transfigured it with an almost patriarchal and fairy-tale quality.

I had not seen Einstein and his wife since their major excursion abroad. They admitted quite unaffectedly that their reception[s] in the United States and Britain were veritable triumphs. Einstein gave a slightly ironic, sceptical twist to their description by claiming that he cannot make out why people are so interested in his theories. His wife told me how he kept on saying to her that he felt like a cheat, a confidence trickster who was failing to give them whatever they hoped for.

Count Harry Kessler

1926

But what is to become of all these diaries, I asked myself yesterday. If I died, what would Leo make of them? He would be disinclined to burn them; he could not publish them. Well, he should make up a book from them, I think; and then burn the body. I daresay there is a little book in them; if the scraps and scratching were straightened out a little. God knows. This is dictated by a slight melancholia, which comes upon me sometimes now and makes me think I am old; I am ugly. I am repeating things. Yet, as far as I know, as a writer I am only now writing out my mind.

Virginia Woolf

1931

As if, beyond pains or itches, there were nothing to bother a man! The last few nights I was intrigued by strange moans coming from the next room. Kept awake myself by the itching, I noticed that they did not cease all night long. They did not exactly bother me, thanks to the wads I put in my ears at night, but I should have liked to know what it was.

And yesterday evening, coming back from dinner and on the point of entering my room, I am stopped by my neighbour, who was waiting at his door. He is a little man, perhaps no older than I, but so worn out, so worn down that it seems as if death has almost nothing to take from him.

He wants to beg my pardon for the disturbance his groans may have caused me. He is suffering from asthma and emphysema and cannot keep from moaning. All this said in English in the most courteous way. I protest at once that he does not disturb me at all and that he can moan all he wants; pity him cordially and leave him with the wish that he may have a somewhat better night.

Doubtless, compared with his anguish, my itch is nothing at all. Let us live with our sufferings and not want to change them. These wise reflections allowed me to sleep a bit better.

André Gide

1937

And this is what I daily take for granted: – Teeth-water at 6.45. Shaving gear thereafter. Fire lit; breakfast and newspaper: subscription to nature's 'pirlie-pig' collected: washing-water: feet dusted and bed made: my table, and all its accessories, lifted over: room dusted: fire kept going: dinner: 'water-works': fire kept going – odd job now and then. Tea: 'water-works': wireless put on for news: fire kept going: spot of supper: wireless: table, etc., lifted back: teeth-water and accessories: 'water-works': foot-pads shifted and bed clothes arranged; fire still burning brightly – and so to bed about 11 or 11.30. This the mere 'necessities' – but there are the many extras: personal extras such as leg-washing, hair-cutting, etc.: and the general extras such as entertaining friends, getting messages, and the cleaning of linen. A well-nigh endless list – and this is what I daily take for granted.

William Soutar

21 March

1762

After riding about two hours and an half from Evesham, we stopped at a little village. We easily perceived by the marks he had left, that the man of the house had been beating his wife. I took occasion from thence to speak strongly to her, concerning the hand of God, and his design in all afflictions. It seemed to be a word in season. She appeared to be not only thankful, but deeply affected.

John Wesley

1912

Got within 11 miles of depôt Monday night; had to lie up all yesterday in severe blizzard. Today forlorn hope, Wilson and Bowers going to depôt for fuel.

Captain Robert Falcon Scott

1944

Panicky with fear of burglars from childhood, I have ripened into someone afraid of everything – debtors, enemies, a knock at the door, a telephone call (these all represent demands on time and courtesy), teachers, doctors, admirers (these may be disappointed in me), my clothes, my work, editors, strange houses, familiar houses (I might get trapped in them), invitations, no invitations, businessmen, friends of friends, other races, dumb people, head waiters, elevator boys, mirrors, political thinkers, musicians, women and children. Nothing in my life has ever reassured me. My mind is as filled with terrors as my closet is with moths. I am not afraid of criticism or death or pain.

Dawn Powell

22 March

1922

Tens of thousands of people have encountered H. G. [Wells]: and thousands have written him up, or tried to write him down. Gossip about *him* is a fairly cheap commodity. I am grateful to (and full of admiration for) the bristling pugnacious little man for the way he succeeds in influencing (and creating) public opinion in the direction of sanity. But I always remember a remark he made 'at me' two or three years ago: 'Poetry has no particular importance; every man ought to compose his own poetry – in the morning, while he is shaving.'

Siegfried Sassoon

1945 [Bergen-Belsen]

The weather affects the mood of the camp most profoundly. Had it not been such a gloriously fine spring day today, we would all be feeling as dejected as on our worst days.

Last night a transport of two thousand people arrived from Buchenwald concentration camp. The shouting, abusing, crying, taunting, groaning, cracking of the whips and thuds of the beatings could be heard throughout the night.

This morning, behind hut 16 we saw hundreds of corpses being dragged onto a heap and stripped of their clothing. They also removed the gold teeth from their mouths. Never has it been as bad as this. All day, the heap of emaciated, naked bodies was left lying in the sun.

Their facial expressions are frightening. They seem to know what is being done to them.

Abel J. Herzberg

1953

I said to Bunny [his aunt] this morning, 'What a lot you have been coughing dear; I have heard you often in the night and all this morning.'

'Yes,' she said, 'I think it is a degenerative condition of the throat and chest,' and went on to say that she thought she would apply to Dr. S. for some more vitamin pills. 'Degenerative condition': admirable old lady, to have applied the phrase so detachedly to herself, even to have known it at all. The right words — her generation was better brought up than mine.

J. R. Ackerley

1963

There is a good deal of talk going on about Profumo, Minister of War, being involved in some form of sex scandal, arranged by Bill Astor [newspaper proprietor] and concerning a missing model. Profumo made a statement in the House of Commons today clearing himself of having seen the girl since December 1961. He is nice, but a poor creature to get himself embroiled in all this.

Cynthia Gladwyn

23 March

1778

I breakfasted, and slept again at home. Memorandum. In shaving my face this morning I happened to cut one of my moles which bled much, and happening also to kill a small moth that was flying about, I applied it to my mole and it instantly stopped the bleeding.

Rev. James Woodforde

1912

Blizzard bad as ever – Wilson and Bowers unable to start – tomorrow last chance – no fuel and only one or two [items] of food left – must be near the end. Have decided it shall be natural – we shall march for the depôt with or without our effects and die in our tracks.

Captain Robert Falcon Scott

1941 [POW camp]

We had the most wonderful surprise this evening. Eric had collected some spare biscuits and the cook made us 2 roly-poly cakes. They looked as if they had come out of Gunter's. Cocoa powder on the top looked like chocolate icing. Some sultanas had been included. At home one would probably have given it to the dog, but it tasted marvellous. The bits of biscuit looked like nuts. A bit of sugar on the top and the answer was no lemon.

The strafe is lessening again – the window boards are to come down tomorrow morning. We have a feeling we are going from here.

Captain John Mansel

1946

I had a poem in my head last night, flashing as only those unformed midnight poems can. It was all made up of unexpected burning words. I knew even in my half-sleep that it was nonsense, meaningless, but that forcing and hammering would clear its shape and form. Now not a word of it remains, not even a hint of its direction. What a pity one cannot sleepwrite on the ceiling with one's finger or lifted toe.

Denton Welch

24 March

1672

I din'd with Mr. Commissioner Cox having seene that morning my Chirurgeon cut off a poore creaturs Leg, a little under the knee, first cutting the living and untained flesh above the gangreene with a sharp knife, and then sawing off the bone in an instant; then with searing and stoopes stanching the blood, which issued aboundantly; the stout and gallant man, enduring it with incredible patience, and that without being bound to his chaire, as is usual in such painefull operations, or hardly making a face or crying oh: I had hardly the courage enough to be present, nor could I endure to see any more such cruel operations.

The leg was so rotten and gangreen'd that one might have run a straw through it; but neither did this the cure, for it not being amputated high-enough, the gangreene prevaild upon the knee, and so a second amputation of the Thigh, cost the poore Creature his life, to my very greate sorrow: I do not remember that ever in my life I smelt so intollerable a stink as what issu'd from the part was cut off, and which I ordered should immediately be buried in the Garden: Lord, what miseries are mortal men obnoxious to, and what confusion and mischiefe dos the avarice, anger, and ambition of Princes cause in the world, who might be happier with halfe they possesse: This stoute man, was but a common sailer.

John Evelyn

1919

D. [Lloyd George] told me a funny story about Clemenceau & Klotz [French minister of finance]. The latter is very unpopular, & a deputation of minis-ters waited upon C. asking that he should be removed as he was not playing the game. Clem. explained that he did not wish to dismiss him now, as it would unstabilise the Government. 'Very well, we must shut our eyes,' said they. 'Yes,' said Clemenceau, 'one always shuts one's eyes at the most delicious moment.' It was Clemenceau who also said that 'All the great pleasures of life are silent.'

Frances Stevenson

1940 [Berlin]

Easter Sunday, grey and cold, but the rain has held off. I cancelled my engage-ments with some German friends for lunch and tea. Couldn't face a German today, though they are no friends of Hitler. Wanted to be alone. Got up about noon and listened to a broadcast from Vienna. The Philharmonic, and a nice little thing from Haydn.

In the afternoon, a stroll. Surely the Germans must be the ugliest-looking people in Europe, individually. Not a decent-looking woman in the whole [Unter den] Linden. Their awful clothes probably contribute to one's impres-sion. Comparatively few soldiers in the streets. Few leaves granted? Meaning? Offensive soon?

I was surprised to notice how shabby the Kaiser's Palace at the end of the Linden is. The plaster falling off all over the place. Very dilapidated. The stone railing of the balcony on which Wilhelm II made his famous appearance in 1914 to announce to the delirious mob at the feet the coming of war appeared to be falling to pieces. Well, they were not delirious before Hitler's balcony when this war started.

I tried to read in the faces of the thousands what was in their minds this Easter day. But their faces looked blank. Obviously they do not like the war, but they will do what they're told. Die, for instance.

William L. Shirer

1956

Looking through the vast amount of luggage we seem to have brought with us on this trip, which was all stacked up in an adjoining dressing room, I came across two years' supply of loo-loo paper which staggered me. On enquiry I found that this was paper which had been delivered at Wilton Crescent the evening before we left and Pullen was under the impression that it was a special supply we got in for the trip!

Earl Mountbatten of Burma

25 March

1792

Day of [Mother's] funeral. I did not find myself much affected; the same thoughts as for some time past occupied my mind, but they had lost much of their effect. Should some thoughts which passed in my mind during the period spent in church, be the happy foundation of a system of belief, less liable to doubt and uncertainty than any that I have hitherto formed, I shall have reason to number this occasion among the happiest of my life, and to add this to what I already owe my mother for early habits of piety and devotions.

William Windham

1808

An efficacious remedy for love: eat peas. Tested today, March 25, after going for a very pleasant horseback ride and feeling a strong desire for the little girl who lives near the Bevern Palace.

Stendhal

1933

We drive to Hollywood. We are taken into the luncheon room where there is a table with flowers and four directors. They are quiet cultured people – not in the least the noisy boasting lot we had supposed. Gary Cooper comes to join us. The beginnings of a double chin and the hint of greying hair indicate that he may cease to be the *jeune premier*. Yet he is a nice shy quiet modest young man, devoid of any brains. They talk about the earthquake [in California] – how frightened they were. About Charlie Chaplin, his moodiness, his affectations, his genius for mimicry. About the life of a film – not more than three years; the film which they thought was an innovation in 1930 now seems to them as old-fashioned as 1886.

The stage-hands and property-men greet Gary Cooper with "'lo Gary, how's life?' He is very nice to them. He then leaves us to look for a house with a huge fence where he can live in peace.

Harold Nicolson

1944

Fear is expressed that the blood of San Gennaro may refuse to liquefy this year, and that such a failure might be exploited by secret anti-Allied factions and troublemakers to set off large-scale rioting of the kind that has frequently happened in Neapolitan history when the miracle has failed. Everywhere there is a craving for miracles and cures. The war has pushed the Neapolitans back into the Middle Ages. Churches are suddenly full of images that talk, bleed, sweat, nod their heads and exude health-giving liquors to be mopped up by handkerchiefs, or even collected in bottles, anxious, ecstatic crowds gather waiting for these marvels to happen. Every day the newspapers report new miracles. In the church of Santo Agnello, a speaking crucifix carries on a regular conversation with the image of Santa Maria d'Intercessione – a fact confirmed by reporters on the spot. The image of Santa Maria del Carmine, first recorded as having bowed its head to avoid a cannon-shot during the siege of Naples by Alfonso of Aragon, now does this as a matter of daily routine. This church used to be visited annually by the King and his court to watch the royal barber shave the hair that had miraculously grown on an ivory Christ during the preceding twelve months. The custom is likely to be renewed. And even if San Gennaro's blood doesn't liquefy they have a phial of the blood of St John in San Giovanni a Carbonara, which – say the papers – bubbles away every time the gospel is read to it.

Norman Lewis

1959

Flew up to Edinburgh today to make the film with Sir Compton Mackenzie at his house. We only wanted twenty-five seconds of him saying why he supports the Labour Party.

I arrived at 31 Drummond Place at 2.15. Sir Compton was still dressing and he appeared in a few minutes in a bright blue tweed suit looking twice as large as life. He remembered having met me before, and beckoned me into his room where he kept me talking until 4 o'clock, when the film unit was ready.

His testimonial was delivered so amusingly that the film crew began laughing and ruined the take. So we did it again. Afterwards we all shook hands again and they took photographs, got autographs, and hurried away.

Sir Compton took me round his house and showed me a huge empty room being redecorated in the basement. 'I am opening a ladies' hairdressing salon,' he said. I thought he was joking. But he wasn't. His secretary has a sister who is a hairdresser, and he said he thought it would be a nice idea if she could practise.

I knew he was a busy man, and kept trying to get away, but he insisted on my staying, and regaled me with stories and anecdotes until 7.30, when I had to catch my plane home.

It was a most amusing day. For him it was the beginning. He gets up after lunch, dresses, and starts work after tea at 4 o'clock. He works from then till 7, when he has dinner. He watches TV from 8 to 10, and works again from 10 to 2. He then goes to bed, reads and does crossword puzzles until 4 am, when he goes to sleep.

He was full of anecdotes.

Finally I left him and flew home to London in an hour and a half.

Tony Benn

26 March

1872

The New Barn meadows are fearfully cut by the timber carriages which are hauling away the fallen giants, ash and beech. The shouts of the timber haulers were ringing hollow and echoing through the wasted murdered dingle. My beautiful favourite Cwm is devastated and laid waste.

Rev. Francis Kilvert

1925

I was walking in Selfridge's basement yesterday afternoon, idling between two appointments, when I met Selfridge in rather old morning suit and silk hat. He at once seized hold of me and showed me over a lot of the new part of his store. Cold-storage for furs – finest in the world. Basement hall 550 feet long. Sub-basement with a very cheap restaurant where they serve 3,000 to 4,000 customers a day. He introduced me to the head of his baby-linen department: 'Here is a gentleman wants things for three of his children, one is three months, another ten months, and another a year old.' Then up his own private lift to the offices and his room, where I had to scratch my name with a diamond on the window – with lots of others. He showed me a lot of accounting. Then downstairs to book department. Fine bindings, etc. His first remark was, taking up a book: 'Human skin.' I had to hurry away. He kept on insisting that it was wonderfully interesting. And it *was*.

Arnold Bennett

1990 [rehearsing a production of *King Lear*]
At the start of the second week, the director, Deborah Warner, is late. Would Miss Warner like to say anything? Dear Diary, Miss Warner has no comment! The clocks went forward this weekend: there are twenty-six people in the room and one of them didn't realise that the clocks went forward. Thank you.

More parrot-phrasing. I'm beginning to feel like a naughty school-boy. It does take for ever, it's very boring, absolutely boring, but necessary, I suppose.

In the afternoon, the fruit game exercise: everyone chooses a fruit with not more than two syllables, we sit in a circle and one person walks round on the outside, telling a story trying to say the name of each fruit and repeat it a second time before the person whose fruit is mentioned can say it three times. For me these games reflect a bourgeois English childhood which means nothing to me and I'm not sure of their value here.

Brian Cox

27 March

1768
To have some account of my thoughts, manners, acquaintances and actions, when the hour arrives in which time is more nimble than memory, is the reason which induces me to keep a Journal. A Journal in which I must confess my *every* thought, must open up my whole heart! But a thing of this kind ought to be addressed to somebody – I must imagine myself talking – talking to the most intimate of friends – to one in whom I should take delight in confiding, and remorse in concealment: – but who must this friend be?

Fanny Burney

1851
Marya called for her passport. I feel I refrained from . . . only out of shame and the fact that she had pimples on her face. So I must note down *sensuality*.

Leo Tolstoy

1857
I would fain make two reports in my Journal, first the incidents and obser-vations of today; and by tomorrow I review the same and record what was

omitted before, which will often be the most significant and poetic part. I do not know at first what it is that charms me. The men and things of today are wont to lie fairer and truer in tomorrow's memory.

H. D. Thoreau

1935

Yesterday we went to the Tower, which is an impressive murderous bloody grey raven haunted military barrack prison dungeon place; like the prison of English splendour; the reformatory at the back of history; where we shot and tortured and imprisoned. Prisoners scratched their names, very beautifully, on the walls. And the crown jewels blazed, very tawdry. And we watched the Scots Guards drill; and an officer doing a kind of tiger pace up and down – a wax faced barber's block officer trained to a certain impassive balancing. The sergeant major barked and swore: the men stamped and wheeled like machines: then the officer also barked; all precise, inhuman, showing off – a degrading, stupefying sight, but in keeping with the grey wall, the cobbles, the executioner's block. People sitting on the river bank among old cannon. Ships &c. Very romantic; a dungeon like feeling.

Virginia Woolf

1939

I yearn for a beautiful woman with no sexual anxieties who will just take me! Have inhaled too much orgone radiation.

Wilhelm Reich

1961

Blackpool is the *end of the line*. It is the English Siberia. It is pure TORTURE. Hateful, tasteless, witless, bleak, boring, dirty, tat – IT HAS NOTHING. I loathe every disgusting minute of it.

Kenneth Williams

28 March

1667

To Lond: at Ar: house the [Royal] Society experimented the transfusion of blood, out of one animal into another; it was successfully don out of a sheep into a dog, 'til the sheep died, the dog well, and was ordered to be carefully looked to . . .

John Evelyn

1765

In the afternoon rode over to Chiddingly, to pay my charmer, or intended wife or sweetheart or whatever other name may be more proper, a visit at her father's where I drank tea, in company with their family and Miss Ann Thatcher. I supped there on some rasures of bacon. It being an excessive wet and windy night I had the opportunity, sure I should say the pleasure, or perhaps some might say the unspeakable happiness, to sit up with Molly Hicks, or my charmer, all night. I came home at forty minutes past five in the morning – I must not say fatigued; no, no, that could not be; it could be only a little sleepy for want of a rest. Well to be sure, she is a most clever girl; but however, to be serious in the affair, I certainly esteem the girl, and think she appears worthy of my esteem.

Thomas Turner

1931

Arnold Bennett died last night; which leaves me sadder than I should have supposed. A loveable genuine man; impeded, somehow a little awkward in life; well meaning; ponderous; kindly; coarse; knowing he was coarse; dimly floundering and feeling for something else; glutted with success; wounded in his feelings; avid; thicklipped; prosaic intolerably; rather dignified; set upon writing; yet always taken in; deluded by splendour and success; but naive; an old bore; an egotist; much at the mercy of life for all his competence; a shop-keeper's view of literature; yet with the rudiments, covered over with fat and prosperity and the desire for hideous Empire furniture, of sensibility. Some real understanding of power, as well as a gigantic absorbing power. These are the sort of things that I think by fits and starts this morning, as I sit jour-nalising; I remember his determination to write 1,000 words daily; and how he trotted off to do it that night, and feel some sorrow that now he will never sit down and begin methodically covering his regulation number of pages in his workmanlike beautiful but dull hand. Queer how one regrets the dispersal of anybody who seemed – as I say – genuine: who had direct contact with life – for he abused me; and I yet rather wished him to go on abusing me; and me abusing him. An element in life – even in mine that was so remote – taken away. This is what one minds.

Virginia Woolf

1973

I have lately been thinking that perhaps I shall never be able to cry again. Another emotion freezing up? But when this morning Schubert's Impromptu in G Flat was played on the wireless I was moved to tears. Glad of this.

James Lees-Milne

29 March

1652

Was that celebrated Eclipse of the Sun, so much threatned by the Astrologers, and had so exceedingly alarm'd the whole Nation, so as hardly any would worke, none stir out of their houses; so ridiculously were they abused by knavish and ignorant star-gazers.

John Evelyn

1912

Since the 21st we have had a continuous gale from W.S.W. and S.W. We had fuel to make two cups of tea apiece and bare food for two days on the 20th. Every day we have been ready to start for our depôt 11 *miles* away, but outside the door of the tent it remains a scene of whirling drift. I do not think we can hope for any better things now. We shall stick it out to the end, but we are getting weaker, of course, and the end cannot be far.

It seems a pity, but I do not think I can write more–
Last entry. For God's sake look after our people.

Captain Robert Falcon Scott

1943

Daily Herald this morning described burning Berlin on Saturday night as having looked 'like an oven'. I wonder who really gets satisfaction out of this terrible deterioration in human values.

Vera Brittain

1951 [while writing *East of Eden*]

It is amazing how many things there are to do in a house, new house or old house. And for some reason I love to make the little repairs and improvements myself. A curious penuriousness comes out in me about paying a man twenty-five dollars for doing badly what I do just as badly in less time. Besides I can improvise and most people can't. Give me a box of odds and ends of metal and wood and I can build damn near anything. But it isn't only penuriousness either. I love to do it. It gives me some kind of satisfaction. Now I have worked out a way of arranging plants on an old hat rack we bought. I think my method is wonderful but I had to invent it and I don't think anyone else would ever have thought of it. This gives me pleasure, believe it or not. And when that is finished I will have something else to work on. Now – I must stop thinking of my inventions and get back to my book.

John Steinbeck

1967

Peggy [Ramsay, his agent] rang about the Beatles' film script . . . The real trouble, she feels, is [Brian] Epstein [the Beatles manager]. An amateur and a fool. He isn't equipped to judge the quality of a script. Probably he will never say 'yes', equally hasn't the courage to say 'no'. A thoroughly weak, flaccid type. . . . Extraordinary the way someone like Epstein has absolutely no idea how valuable a property the Beatles are. Having commissioned a script he can waste time until it is taken from him. He'll then be back at square one with the original script (which was dull and of no interest), or faced with the job of commissioning another script from another author.

Joe Orton

30 March

1852

Slept well and got up late, at 10 o'clock. I am sometimes stupid enough to eat a lot of hot things with the purpose of testing whether my reproductive powers have been destroyed or not; I did this yesterday and so I had diarrhoea and was upset all day. *I must try to arouse sensuality as little as possible.*

Leo Tolstoy

1922

For me the loveliest moments of the evening were enclosed by the opening bars of [Schubert's] '*Du bist die Ruh*'. While I was wiping my eyes at the end of it, a man near me remarked: 'I always think that's a *most* over-rated song.'

Siegfried Sassoon

1943

The R.A.F. bombed Berlin again last night. Very windy to-day; dark evening. Daffodils all blown down; blossoms falling off trees. Magnolia in full bloom.

Vera Brittain

1944

We had a great day out. We went to the Nottingham Lace Market and ate whelks, ice cream and hot peas with mint out of tin cups. Felt rather sick. Then in the evening went to see wonderful Douggie Byng in a variety show. He wore lady's clothes with a huge bust and sang vulgar songs. He has a way of saying 'For King and country' with the emphasis on the wrong word. It makes it sound very rude indeed!

Joan Wyndham

1948

Started reading Goebbels' Diary. Interested to note that he, too, [was a] writer manqué who had begun by producing a bad novel and a play which no theatre would put on. Most men of action seem to be writers manqué, and correspondingly most writers, men of action manqué. Interesting theme.

Malcolm Muggeridge

1967

Kenneth [Halliwell] and I went to see Hermione Baddeley in *The Killing of Sister George*. Really, I suppose, it would've been better to see her at an evening performance, but the idea of traipsing all the way to Wimbledon to witness a performance of a play which I don't particularly fancy, and have seen once anyway, at eight o'clock at night and getting back about twelve didn't appeal to me. Yet I'd promised Hermione that I'd come. So the matinee it was. Actually it was fun. The place was full of Wimbledon matrons of the nastier sort and old people in various stages of mental and physical decay. The theatre was crumbling, the paintwork dirty, the carpets threadbare; the house had seen better days. Two or three usherettes in rusty, black dresses bustled about, taking orders for tea during the intervals.

Kenneth and I found our seats, on the aisle, row N. There was an elderly woman sitting in one of them. We showed her our tickets. 'The lady said I could sit anywhere,' she said. 'I've only got one eye.' This gave us pause for thought. 'Well, you can have the seat if you like,' I said. 'No, no! I'll go somewhere else. Only with my eye I have to be careful or I can't see.' I felt very guilty as she hurried away to another seat. The pianist began playing a selection of popular songs of the past fifty years. The audience brightened considerably. There was a buzz of anticipation in the air. A lot more women came in. 'I don't suppose they'll understand what the play is about,' I said to Kenneth. 'Don't you believe it,' he said. 'They'll know very well what it's about.' He was right. It became clear, from the opening scenes, that they understood and weren't amused. Hermione bounced around giving an absolutely outrageous performance. Everyone else in the play was repertory standard. There were hardly any laughs. The lesbianism seemed to stun them. Though I'd thought it was a second-rate play in the West End, light and offenceless, Wimbledon wasn't up to it. Glumly they sat. At the end of the first act the tea-trays were passed around and the piano began to play; this was the part the audience enjoyed. The second act began. There are two scenes in this act. When the curtain came down on the first scene half the audience thought it was the end of the act and the aisles of the theatre were suddenly crowded with old men and women hobbling out into the foyer. Suddenly the curtain shot up on the second scene and, to murmurs of irritation and surprise, the audience slunk back to its seat. During the third act, alarm grew at the (to them) uncontrolled sexual perversion and (to me) flat unimaginative dialogue. At the moment where Sister George orders her companion to drink the bath-water, a couple of old ladies rose and stumbled out. Kenneth and I went back to see Hermione, who looked very rouged and roguish. 'Oh, you naughty thing,' she said, 'you shouldn't've come at a matinee!' 'Why not?' I said. 'The audience gave an excellent performance.'

Joe Orton

31 March

1793

Employed a considerable time in endeavours to improve my hand, by trial of different methods of holding my pen; by one in particular, apparently very little promising, but which I saw lately used by Nepean. I cannot yet much boast of my success, yet the attempt must not be relinquished. After what I have remarked myself, confirmed by the remark which I once heard made by [Edmund] Burke, I am convinced that a good hand is not wholly without connection with a good style.

William Windham

1980

Last night, in a house in Kilchoan, I watched, willy-nilly, a 'Highland' programme on television. I was trapped and could not well make my escape. All present but me enjoyed the programme thoroughly; all were Highlanders; all believed themselves to be watching something authentically native. The room was crowded and I was the only scowler there. I was a small oasis of gloom in a desert of delight.

The star performer on this programme was the celebrated Mr X, a singer of popular songs in a pseudo-Gaelic vein and a man, I assure you, more admired in these parts than was the great Maighstir Alasdair in his prime, when he sheltered from the redcoats in the caves of Arisaig, in the desolation that followed Culloden, with his pockets empty and the poetry burning a hole in his mind. My solitary groan when he flashed into view was lost in a chorus of 'oohs' and 'ahs'. He was robed in the full Balmoral fig, the dress that never was on land or sea. He was Tailor-and-Cutter beautiful, an exquisite. O not a *sgian dhu* nor a grouse-foot brooch was out of place about him. His stockings were as unwrinkled as his brow. His hair reflected the studio lights as brightly as his toe-caps.

He sang and he glittered and he clutched his microphone to his mouth like a child with a lollipop. He swayed from the knees. He shimmered and he shimmied.

I thought of my grandfather, in the dungarees and the Burns-and-Laird Line guernsey, the seaboots and the flat cloth cap of all his days. I remember him standing in the peat-bog, in the true Highlands, heaving the newly-cut sods up on to the bank, his palms plated with callouses, an old-master network of ingrained dirt. And round about him the reality of his life sucked and squelched . . .

My stomach turns. Away with all this tartanry, this obscene and irrelevant clutter of sporrans and gewgaws! Whatever legitimacy it might have had – and it had precious little – has become so tainted a man must needs be lacking in pride and honour and a sense of the absurd to countenance it.

Alasdair Maclean

1984 [Oxford]

In the afternoon to a confirmation in the cathedral. Though it's not a large building, the bishop dons a mike in order to speak, but then, moving to the pulpit, forgets that he has done so and there is a terrible amplified slurring as he fouls the cable. However, the young, bearded priest who attends him (who is probably as much his sound man as his chaplain) disentangles his lordship so that he can get into the pulpit. Once there he unceremonially dons another mike, though presumably if this becomes a feature of the ordinary service it will end up being given ceremonial trappings and perhaps even a place in the liturgy.

The actual laying-on of hands has been personalized since that evening thirty-five years ago when H. H. Vully de Candole, the Bishop of Knaresborough, confirmed me in St Michael's, Headingley. Nowadays each candidate carries a card with his or her name on it in block letters, some, I imagine, with an aid to pronunciation in brackets. And there are Kims and Beckys and Mandys and Trevs, all blessed and admitted to communion by this miked-up bishop and with a casualness about it that nobody seems to find surprising and which I think myself a snob for even noticing. Few of the boys wear suits, and one of the older candidates goes up in almost doctrinaire Fabian undress in an anorak.

In the new form of service God is throughout referred to as You; only one Thou left in the world, and the fools have abolished it. Of course they can't do away with the vocative, which is every bit as archaic, so we still say 'O God'. It's a good job God doesn't have a name, or we'd probably be calling him Dave.

Alan Bennett

1991

The Duchess of York is having an affair with a young man, Wyatt, the rich son of a rich American family. He is the one who, with his mother, got into the Royal Box at Ascot because they thought they were inviting Verushka [Wyatt's wife] and myself.

The Duchess of York was there on that occasion and no doubt took the opportunity to get friendly with him.

Woodrow Wyatt

APRIL

'What is a diary as a rule? A document useful to the person who keeps it, dull to the contemporary who reads it, invaluable to the student, centuries afterwards, who treasures it!'

DAME ELLEN TERRY

1 April

1833

I think I acted Macbeth in a manner that would have gained me fame before any but an Edinburgh audience, which I look upon as one so like the vile pretender to superior wisdom described by Gratiano that I should as soon expect the standing pool to rise in waves, or become clear enough to reflect the images near it, as to observe one genuine display of sympathy from them. They seem to me grave cox-combs.

Charles Macready

1941

Sid and Mummy stayed over at the Grail House last night, so was alone in London for the first time since the blitz started. Went up to Sid's bedroom and read all her juicy books about psychopaths and sexual abnormalities and the symbolism of dreams. There was one by Kraft Ebbing that got me so excited that I remembered something Leonard had told me and took a candle from the little altar. Now I suppose I'm completely beyond the pale as far as the Church is concerned.

Joan Wyndham

1964

Had arranged to call for Idy Young and Alexis and bring them through for a day at the Zoo. We were coming down into Harthill at an easy 45 mph when a policeman stepped out and held up his hand, telling me that I had just passed through a radar speed check. The policemen were all very friendly. I thought it wise to describe myself as 'Sheriff', adding as if correcting myself that they had better put me down as 'Advocate', which would not sound so bad. They told me, after a short conference amongst themselves, that on this occasion they would give me a warning, so as to avoid any undesirable public-ity. I thanked them warmly, and resumed the journey. At the Zoo, we walked round the park and visited the aquarium. The keeper told me they fed the fish on nothing but horse flesh, and had much the best record of any aquarium for keeping fish.

Gordon Stott

1969 [Whitehall Court, London]

Today we entered a world so completely different to anywhere else that it was like an excursion into dreamland, nostalgic and unreal. The moment we drove into the courtyard of Buckingham Palace the ordinary life of London, the bursting crowds, the harassed faces, the bus queues in the cold wind, the dearth of taxis in the rain, all seemed extraordinarily remote. Smiling courtiers, Masters of the Household, eager equerries, charming ladies-in-waiting, all contributed to make the guests feel at ease in the grand setting. Upstairs in a beautiful room, the Music Room, overlooking the garden, we all gathered and were given drinks. We were altogether thirty-one for luncheon. Then in came the Queen, very pretty and smiling; the Duke of Edinburgh, handsome and smiling but with a hardness that cannot be concealed; the charming Prince of Wales with his desire to please, his tentative interest in everybody, his wild-rose colouring like his grandfather, his sensitivity contrasting with his father's lack of it; and finally Princess Anne, a thoroughly nice, almost handsome, English country girl, healthy and sensible and with no complications. It was tempting to wonder how these four human beings sort themselves out in private life.

Cynthia Gladwyn

1985

I have had five invitations to go on chat shows, because it's my sixtieth birthday on Wednesday. I suppose when you reach sixty the journalists think they can rehabilitate you as an eccentric, lovable old character. These shows would be entirely personal, nothing to do with politics, and I would be presented as an attractive person if I was prepared to go along with it on their terms. But people at home who know me as a fighter would say, 'God, he's sold out.'

Tony Benn

2 April

1947

Today, we're undertaking a long journey. The bus leaves at nine in the morning and will reach Jacksonville at two at night. This is an 'express' that makes only two or three stops. They sell sandwiches and Coca-Cola on board; the seats have movable backs, and at night everyone lights a little individual lamp, as in airplanes. And the steward encourages us, plotting our position from time to time, announcing the next stop and explaining the landscape. We're traveling through Louisiana, Mississippi, Alabama, and Florida. The branches of the delta are as vast as lakes; they glisten in the sun, and the Gulf of Mexico is as blue as a honeymoon dream. Palm trees, cacti, azaleas, flowering cities, tropical forests with thick vegetation, romantic houses emerging amid peaceful lawns, solitary, dilapidated shacks in the woods, the dazzling sea, languid lagoons, Spanish moss, luxurious and sordid – throughout the day the whole South reveals itself to us with its wrenching contrasts.

And throughout the day the great tragedy of the South pursues us like an obsession. Even the traveler confined to a bus and waiting rooms cannot escape it. From the time we entered Texas, everywhere we go there's the smell of hatred in the air – the arrogant hatred of whites, the silent hatred of blacks. At the stations the respectable, badly dressed lower-middle-class matrons stare with envious anger at the pretty black girls in bright dressed and joyful jewelry, and the men resent the nonchalant beauty of the young black men in light suits. American niceness has no place here. In the crowded line outside the bus, the blacks are jostled. 'You aren't going to let that Negress go in front of you,' a woman says to a man in a voice trembling with fury.

Simone de Beauvoir

1976 [during the filming of *Apocalypse Now* in the Philippines]

The helicopters used in the film are from the Philippine Air Force. Today, in the middle of the rehearsal for a complicated shot, they were called away to fight the rebels in a civil war about 150 miles to the south.

It is hard to know what is going on. There is no news of the war in the government-controlled press. I was talking to one of the Filipino crewmen. He said that a group of southern islands, which are predominantly Moslem, are fighting for independence. Francis has a government-supplied bodyguard at all times. There are guards at our house. The government seems to feel that if Francis were kidnapped by rebels, they might create an incident that could attract international attention.

Eleanor Coppola

1980

Fred [Hughes] and I had to leave for our private audience with the pope by 10:00 so we left Naples at 7:00. When we came to the outskirts of Rome the driver didn't know how to get into the city. We had to follow a cab to take us to Graziella's office to pick up two tickets to have a private audience with the pope.

We got our tickets and then the driver dropped us off at the Vatican. When we saw 5,000 other people standing around waiting for the pope too, I just knew that Graziella hadn't gotten us a private audience. But Fred put on airs and went to the guards and said that we had a private audience with the pope and they laughed.

They finally took us in to our seats with the rest of the 5,000 people and a nun screamed out, 'You're Andy Warhol! Can I have your autograph?' She looked like Valerie Solaris [woman who shot and nearly killed him in 1968] so I got scared she'd pull out a gun and shoot me. Then I had to sign five more autographs for other nuns. And I just get so nervous at church. And then the pope came out, he was on a gold car, he did the rounds, and then finally he got up and gave a speech against divorce in seven different languages. There was a bunch of cheerleaders saying, 'Rah-rah, the pope.' That took three hours. It was really boring, and then finally the pope was coming our way. He shook everybody's hand and Fred kissed his ring and got Suzie's cross blessed. He asked Fred where he was from and Fred said New York, and I was taking pictures – there were a lot of photographers around – and he shook my hand and I said I was from New York, too. I didn't kiss his hand. The people next to me were giving him a gold plate, they were from Belgium. The mobs behind us were jumping down from their seats, it was scary. Then Fred was going to take a Polaroid but I said they'd think it was a machine gun and shoot us, so we never got a Polaroid of the pope. As soon as Fred and I got blessed we ran out.

Andy Warhol

1996

At 13.00 went to the Equity office at the top of Upper St Martin's Lane to unveil a plaque in celebration of a hundred years of cinema. It has my name on it but I am only eighty-two – today. I pulled the cord which brought down half of its red veiling on my head and the other half on the president of Equity. I couldn't see what was written on the plaque so when a microphone was thrust at me I made an unprepared speech of a few ill-chosen words. Next time I'm in London I shall have a good look at it.

Alec Guinness

3 April

1661

Up among my workmen, my head akeing all day from last night's debauch. To the office all the morning and at noon dined with Sir W. Batten and [Sir William] Pen, who would needs have me drink two drafts of sack to-day to cure me of last night's disease, which I thought strange but I think find it true.

Samuel Pepys

1940

This morning I polished up an old box I found upstairs – it is of walnut with black and yellow inlay and a brass crest on the lid. It makes a beautiful box for relics – so in went all the letters, pressed flowers, Niersteiner corks, handkerchiefs, *Tilia platyphyllos* etc. It will still hold a few more letters, though it is quite nicely filled. I wonder what will happen to it. If I were to die tomorrow I should either have it sent back to him or buried with me (probably the latter) – but as it seems not very likely that I shall, I daresay it may be in my possession for years and years, until one day it becomes junk again and the box returns to the place where I found it – perhaps with the relics still in it. Dust to dust, ashes to ashes . . . What a great pleasure and delight there is in being really sentimental. I thought about this as I picked flowers in the garden this morning – violets – a great patch of them smelling lovely, sweeter than the lids of Juno's eyes, primroses plain and coloured, scyllas and wild celandines, so very much spring flowers. People who are not sentimental, who never keep relics, brood on anniversaries, kiss photographs goodnight and good morning, must miss a good deal. Of course it is all rather self-conscious and cultivated, but it comes so easily that at least a little of it must spring from the heart. I could write a lovely metaphysical poem about the relics of love in a box. Perhaps I will – for his seventieth birthday (in March 1989).

Barbara Pym

1941

Fear is the basis in love loyalty. Fear to break off for fear the next will not be as good or as permanent or that the old will do too well without you. Women don't leave a drunkard as often as is reported. The drunkard, being maverick, can always get other women and besides there is the maternal he arouses – also the sex interest since he is likely to be a different person every time.

Dawn Powell

1947

Between Jacksonville and Savannah this morning, N sat beside a young black man, since there was no other place. As soon as a seat among the whites became free, he pointed it out to her: 'I imagine you would rather not stay here,' he said dryly. She answered that she was quite comfortable where she was, and that she was French. Then he opened up and began to talk to her. He said that he'd entered the war as a volunteer in order to have the right, on his return, to the years of free study granted to veterans; now he's a scholarship student at a black university, where he's studying to become a lawyer. With bitter passion, he explained why he so ardently wants to earn the right to plead cases in court: this is one of the only concrete ways to fight for the black cause. Behind all these docile faces – through discouragement, fear, or, more rarely, hope – revolt is always imminent. And the whites know it.

Simone de Beauvoir

1951 [while writing *East of Eden*]
Waverly [his step-daughter] came home yesterday and we had a pleasant homecoming party. She was very tired so as usual Elaine and I stayed up for her. I guess we just have no sense. But in spite of that I am up early this morning. Feeling fine. Sometimes I get a little panicky – so many things I do not do now that I am writing. I put all the burdens on Elaine, of running the house and doing the many hundreds of things living entails. So far she hasn't complained. I help with what I can but I am very thoughtless – very. My mind goes mooning away. I never get very far from my book. And this must get pretty tiresome. I'm sure it does. I guess a writer is only half a man as far as a woman is concerned. And there is so much violence in me. Sometimes I am horrified at the amount of it. It isn't very well concealed either. It lies very close to the surface.

John Steinbeck

4 April

1835
I was told last night that the scene of noise and uproar which the House of Commons now exhibits is perfectly disgusting. This used not to be the case in better, or at least more gentlemanlike, times; no noises were permissible but the cheer and the cough, the former admitting every variety of intonation expressive of admiration, approbation, assent, denial, surprise, indignation, menace, sarcasm. Now all the musical skill of this instrument is lost and drowned in shouts, hootings, groans, noises of the most discordant that the human throat can emit, sticks and feet beating against the floor. Sir Hedworth Williamson, a violent Whig, told me that there were a set of fellows on his side of the House whose regular practice it was to make this uproar, and with the settled design to bellow Peel down. This is the *reformed* House of Commons.

Charles Greville

1870
In taking off my jersey of knitted wool in the dark with an accidental stroke of my finger down the stuff I drew a flash of electric light. This explains the crackling I had often heard.

Gerard Manley Hopkins

1903

There stood before me a little, pale, rather don-like man, quite bald, with a huge head and dome-like forehead, a ragged red beard in odd whisks, a small aquiline red nose. He looked supremely shy, but received me with a distinguished courtesy, drumming on the ground with his foot, and uttering strange little whistling noises. He seemed very deaf. The room was crammed with books: bookcases all about – a great sofa entirely filled with stacked books – books on the table. He bowed me to a chair – 'Will you sit?' On the fender was a pair of brown socks. Watts-Dunton said to me, 'He has just come in from one of his long walks' – and took up the socks and put them behind the coal-scuttle. 'Stay!' said Swinburne, and took them out carefully, holding them in his hand: 'They are drying.' Watts-Dunton murmured something about his fearing they would get scorched, and we sat down. Swinburne sat down, concealing his feet behind a chair, and proceeded with strange motions to put the socks on out of sight. 'He seems to be changing them,' said Watts-Dunton. Swinburne said nothing, but continued to whistle and drum. Then he rose and bowed me down to lunch, throwing the window open.

A. C. Benson

5 April

1664

Coming home I find my wife dressed as if she had been abroad, but I think she was not; but she answering me some way that I did not like I pulled her by the nose, indeed to offend her; though afterwards to appease her I denied it, but only it was done in haste. The poor wretch took it mightly ill, and I believe wringing her nose she did feel pain, and so cried a great while; but by and by I made her friends, and so after supper to my office a while, and then home to bed.

Samuel Pepys

1790

I met with one of the most extraordinary phenomena that I ever saw, or heard of: – Mr Sellers has in his yard a large Newfoundland dog, and an old raven. They have fallen deeply in love with each other, and never desire to to be apart. The bird has learned the bark of the dog, so that few can distinguish them. She is inconsolable when he goes out; and, if he stays out a day or two, she will get up all the bones and scraps she can, and hoard them up for him till he comes back.

John Wesley

1919 [Paris]

P.M. [Lloyd George] not feeling very well, & President Wilson is in bed, but the meeting went on just the same. Clemenceau was very pleased at Wilson's absence, & could not conceal his joy. 'He is *worse* today,' he said to D., & doubled up with laughter. 'Do you know his doctor? Couldn't you get round him & bribe him? . . .' The old man did not attempt to conceal his feelings on the subject.

Frances Stevenson

6 April

1890

The Emperor William seems to be a young man 'with whom it is always fourth of July,' – as some one said of old Coggswell, the postmaster in Newport. Mr. Hazard, at the expiration of the second Mrs. C., asked him if he wouldn't like to come to a *seance* at his house, when he could hear his wife and touch her hand, to which C. promptly replied, 'Oh, no, Mr. Hazard, thank you. I think it best to let bygones be bygones always!' A few months after, the third Mrs. C was being led to the altar.

Alice James

1981

I went off this morning to St Thomas's Hospital to have my swollen knee drained. My old friend, Dr Mac of Hurst Green, had called it housemaid's knee. The bright young doctor at St Thomas's said that strictly speaking it was clergyman's knee. Housemaids get their knee trouble from leaning forward, clergymen kneel in an upright position, so that their swelling is lower down. While awaiting my turn to be drained, I was accosted by a friendly drug addict with his young wife, admittedly 'stoned'. He sat down beside me and asked, 'What's your trouble, Lord Longford?' I pulled up my trouser leg and showed him my swollen knee. 'Ah!' he commented sagely. 'Myra Hindley has been kicking you! Give her my love; she must be a pleasant girl.'

Old labels die hard. The nurses recognised me as Lord Longford. There was a cry for Mr Pakenham; they assured me that it wasn't me. Of course it turned out to be.

Lord Longford

1982

The nation has been told that Britain and Argentina are not at war, we are at conflict.

I am reading *Scoop* by a woman called Evelyn Waugh.

Adrian Mole

7 April

1779

Johnson harangued upon the qualities of different liquors and spoke with great contempt of claret as so weak that 'a man would be drowned in it before he was made drunk.' He was persuaded to drink one glass of it, that he might judge not from recollection, which might be dim, but from immediate sensation. He shook his head, and said, 'Poor stuff! So, Sir. Claret is the liquor for boys; port for men; but he who aspires to be a hero must drink brandy. In the first place, the flavour of brandy is most grateful to the palate, and then brandy will do soonest for a man what drinking *can* do for him. There are indeed few who are able to drink brandy. That is a power rather wished for than attained. Yet, as in all pleasure, hope is a considerable part, I know not but fruition comes too quick by brandy. Florence wine I think the worst. It is wine only to the eye; it is wine neither when you are drinking it nor after you have drunk it. It neither pleases the taste nor exhilarates the spirits.' I put him in mind how jolly he and I used to drink wine together when we were first acquainted, and how I used to have a headache after sitting up with him. He did not like to have this recalled, or perhaps thought I boasted improperly; so would have a witty stroke at me: 'Nay, Sir; it was not the *wine* that made your head ache but the *sense* that I put into it.' BOSWELL. 'What, Sir, will sense make the head ache?' JOHNSON. 'Yes, Sir, when it is not used to it.' No man who has a true relish of pleasantry could be offended at this, especially if Johnson in a long intimacy had given him repeated proofs that he valued him.

James Boswell

1899

Yesterday I spoke to Karlweis [playwright and humorist] about keeping a diary. He said it was good to get into the habit of reckoning up with yourself, but that one never confronts oneself with the whole truth, there's always an element of coquetry about it. Sadly, I must admit that he's right. In these pages I have often lied and glossed over many of my faults. Forgive me, I'm only human . . .

Alma Mahler-Werfel

1922

Lord Carnarvon, the archaeologist, is dead. He was my love when I was eighteen. It was here at Nice, at the Restaurant Français, that I first saw him. He was twenty-five, I thought he was so fine, so distinguished, so thoroughbred, so chic that I adored him. Just to watch him and admire him was enough for my enthusiasm. He was introduced to me that same year at the clay-pigeon shooting at Monte Carlo. Tremendous heart-fluttering, I could have died at his feet. He left the next day! What a dear little silly I was. A few months later I saw him again in London, at Covent Garden. Lady Dudley had the measles and the key of her box was for sale according to custom, and I had bought it. Carnarvon walked in absent-mindedly during the interval: flutterings, smiles, excuses, compliments, confessions. He was vicious, an invert so they said. He loved me all the same . . . and was a delicious, agonizing lover, full of charm and cruel grace. So I became the rival of Lady de Grey – Gladys. I had the upper hand. He didn't make me very happy; he was fugitive, a traveller, always off to India, the Baltic, Scotland. I have kept a pearl in his memory, the most beautiful of all my pearls, the one valued today at a hundred thousand francs.

Liane de Pougy

1933

Since Germany seems bent upon getting rid of her brains, could not France offer to take in that 'gray matter' that our neighbours seem to scorn?

Could not the French government, above and beyond politics, offer Einstein, forced into exile by Germany, a chair in the Collège de France, as was done in the past for [the Polish poet Adam] Mickiewicz? A laboratory and the means of continuing his research . . . In order to create a sort of foreign annex to this Collège, which would perpetuate an ancient tradition of receptivity of which France would have reason to be proud, it would probably not be hard to gather together the necessary funds. Shall we have enough sense to make this gesture before another country gets ahead of us? And this time what a fine reason we should have for being glad to be French!

André Gide

1940

My days pass so pleasantly and uneventfully but really with nothing *accomplished*. I have done so little writing this year. But writing is not now quite the pleasure it used to be. I am no longer so certain of a glorious future as I used to be – though I still feel that I may ultimately succeed. Perhaps I need some shattering experience to awaken and inspire me, or at least to give me some emotion to recollect in tranquillity. But how to get it? Sit here and wait for it or go out and seek it? Join the ATS [Auxiliary Territorial Service] and get it peeling potatoes and scrubbing floors? I don't know. I expect it will be sit and wait. Even the idea of falling violently in love again (which is my idea of an experience!) doesn't seem to be much help in the way of writing. I seem to have decided already the sort of novels I want to write. Perhaps the war will give me something. Perhaps the Home Front novel I am dabbling with now will get published. Perhaps . . .

But women are so different from men in that they have so many small domestic things with which to occupy themselves. Dressmaking, washing and ironing, and everlasting tidying and sorting of reliques. I think I could spend my whole day doing such things, with just a little time for reading, and be quite happy. But it isn't *really* enough, soon I shall be discontented with myself, out will come the novel and after I've written a few pages I shall feel on top of the world again.

Barbara Pym

1940

Coby [Coburn Gilman, Powell's lover] said gloomily, 'All my life I've arrived at the station just after the Orient Express has left.'

Dawn Powell

1958

At dinner we agreed that one of the most significant pieces of news in yesterday's paper was in the society column, namely that Neil McElroy, the Secretary of Defense, had joined the Episcopalian Church. When a public figure joins the church at the age of fifty plus, it means one thing – he's planning to run for President of the United States.*

Drew Pearson

1968

The most important news since I wrote last has been the assassination of Martin Luther King at Memphis and the consequent rioting all over the United States, notably in Washington. The Negro problem was going to be a nightmare this summer anyway, but this murder makes a desperate situation even more so. Part of the attraction of the riots is the looting, which seems to be almost unrestrained. I always thought that when rioting breaks out, looters must be shot. Otherwise the situation will get entirely out of hand. [Lyndon] Johnson has made all the right gestures but it is exceedingly difficult to see any end to the tension, let alone the violence which seems to be in some way part of the American way of life.

Cecil King

---

* Contrary to Pearson's assertion, McElroy did not run for the Presidency.

8 April

1847 [6 am]

Hope is bad for *a happy man* and *good for an unhappy one*. Although I have gained a lot since I began to study myself, I am still very dissatisfied with myself. The more progress you make in self-improvement, the more you see the faults in yourself, and Socrates rightly said that the highest state of a man's perfection is the knowledge that he knows nothing.

Leo Tolstoy

1871

Still dreadful news from Paris. The Commune have everything their own way, and they go on quite as in the days of the old Revolution in the last century, though they have not yet proceeded to commit all the same horrors. They have however, thrown priests into prison, etc. They have burnt the guillotine and shoot people instead. I am so glad I saw Paris once more, though I should not care to do so again.

Queen Victoria

1941

With the Führer. He also admires the courage of the Greeks in particular. Perhaps there is still a touch of the old Hellenic strain in them. He forbids the bombing of Athens. This is right and noble of him. Rome and Athens are his Meccas. He greatly regrets having to fight the Greeks. If the English had not established themselves there, he would never have gone to the Italians' aid. It was their affair, and they should have been able to settle it alone.

The Führer is a man totally attuned to antiquity. He hates Christianity, because it has crippled all that is noble in humanity. According to Schopenhauer, Christianity and syphilis have made humanity unhappy and unfree. What a difference between the benevolent, smiling Zeus and the pain-wracked, crucified Christ. The ancient peoples' view of God was also much nobler and more humane than the Christians'. What a difference between a gloomy cathedral and a light, airy ancient temple. He describes life in ancient Rome: clarity, greatness, monumentality. The most wonderful republic in history. We would feel no disappointment, he believes, if we were now suddenly to be transported to this old, eternal city.

The Führer cannot relate to the Gothic mind. He hates gloom and brooding mysticism. He wants clarity, light, beauty. And these are the ideals of life in our time. In this respect, the Führer is a totally modern man.

Josef Goebbels

1976 [during the filming of *Apocalypse Now*]

Last night Francis had a birthday party on the beach across from the set. About three hundred people were invited, the cast, crew and the American and Vietnamese extras and some townspeople. Hundreds of pounds of hamburger and hot dogs were shipped from San Francisco. The band and food were flown in from Manila. They arrived at the beach in several trucks just as it was getting dark. The birthday cake was six feet by eight feet. It was made of twelve sheet cakes iced together. Two men decorated it in the light of the bandstand. They made mountains, a river, an ocean and waves of icing. They planted paper palm trees, little cardboard huts and a bridge to look like the set. They placed plastic helicopters, boats, soldiers, flags, flowers and candles, and letters that spelled 'Happy Birthday, Francis, Apocalypse Now.'

A thick smoke blew from the barbecues; someone had forgotten the spatulas and people were trying to turn their hamburgers with pieces of cardboard. A lot of meat fell through the grills and burned the coals. It was a warm night. There were no more cold drinks. Some people said not enough had been ordered. Others said guys were grabbing cases and running off down the beach in the dark.

A team of ladies with knives to serve the cake began removing the decorations and cuttings slices at the bottom while the decorators were still working on the top. I could hear two GI extras talking. They were standing on a bench behind me. One said, 'Wow, this is the most decadence I've ever seen.'

Eleanor Coppola

1990 [while rehearsing *King Lear*]

Went to the memorial service for Ian Charleson. Ian was one of my first students at LAMDA [drama school], the first group I ever taught. An extraordinarily talented boy. I hadn't seen him for two or three years and was driving down the street one day towards Shepherd's Bush when suddenly there he was. He had been ill for some time with Aids and I was utterly shocked at how changed he'd become. I met him again at Dreas Reyneke's body conditioning studio when he was debating whether to take over Daniel Day Lewis's Hamlet. He was angry because he hadn't been asked to do it in the first place. We had a long talk and I persuaded him to. I had seen his first Hamlet just after he left drama school which was quite remarkable for a young man. He had a purity of tone and was able to say a line as though you had never heard it before. Unfortunately I was not able to see his last Hamlet but those who did felt it was a most moving performance.

It was a sad afternoon, the church was filled to the brim and at the end of the service, hearing a recording of Ian singing 'Come unto these yellow sands' from *The Tempest*, there was a catch in all our breaths.

When Ian was playing Hamlet he knew he was dying, and with Hamlet's constant meditations on death the sense of that must have been all the more acute. The closeness of death is something of which I have to remind myself in *Lear*.

Brian Cox

9 April

1905

Cornillier called yesterday morning, and I was telling him about a good early picture by Tissot that Ullman had bought for 200 francs. He said that a long time ago Tissot had a mistress, with whom he had continued relations for a considerable period. He decided to break the *liaison*, and he wrote one letter to his mistress, giving her the gentlest possible hint that the affair must ultimately come to an end, and another to an intimate friend, saying brutally that he was sick of the thing and wanted to marry. He mixed the letters up, and the mistress received the wrong one. She committed suicide. Tissot was deeply affected, regarded himself as her murderer, and became *dévot*. This was really the origin of his journeys to Palestine, and the ruin of his art.

Arnold Bennett

1935

I met Morgan [E. M. Forster] in the London Library yesterday and flew into a passion. 'Virginia, my dear,' he said. I was pleased by that little affectionate familiar tag. 'Being a good boy and getting books on Bloomsbury?' I said. 'Yes. And Virginia, you know I'm on the Committee here,' said Morgan. 'And we've been discussing whether to allow ladies—'

It came over me that they were going to put me on: and I was then to refuse: 'Oh but they do—' I said, 'there was Mrs Green . . .' 'Yes, yes – there was Mrs Green. And Sir Leslie Stephen said, never again. She was so troublesome. And I said, haven't ladies improved? But they were all quite determined. No no no, ladies are quite impossible. They wouldn't hear of it.'

See how my hand trembles.

Virginia Woolf

1942

At tea-time went to Mayfair Hotel to see demonstration of 'Liberty cut' sponsored by Min[istry] of Health as an anti-typhus measure. New line of country for me; place crowded with hairdressers, representatives of the Press (mostly hard-working women plainly dressed), and fashionable ladies in mink coats looking as if they'd never heard of the war. Several leading hairdressers talked on importance of shorter hair for women in present crisis. Demonstrations of 'Liberty cut' on different girls followed, including a showing of the 'cut' itself. The number of men present interested me; it showed how much money there is to be made out of women's hair.

Vera Brittain

1976 [during the filming of *Apocalypse Now*]
Several hundred South Vietnamese people were recruited from a refugee camp near Manila to play North Vietnamese in the film. As I passed their rest area today they were rehearsing a little play while they waited for the next shot. They speak no English but one young man called out 'Stand by,' and everyone got quiet and ready. Then he clapped two sticks together and called 'Action' and the play began in Vietnamese. Later I noticed the group leader calling lunch in the same way. He said 'Stand by' and they all assembled; he clapped his sticks and called 'Action,' and they walked to lunch in a neat line.

Eleanor Coppola

1980
Left Vancouver 7 April. At Seattle Airport the man at the desk asked, when to pay the bill I produced my credit card, whether I was related to the poet Stephen Spender. So I said, 'That's me.' He looked pleased and said, 'Gee, a near-celebrity.'

Stephen Spender

10 April

1859
In the afternoon I walked up to Kilburn. On my way home, being importuned by a girl in the Strand to come home with her, I replied by way of excuse, 'But it's Sunday': on which she exclaimed, 'What, are you so *froom* as all that?' *Froom*, she explained, meant *religious*: but query the word, which is new to me.

Arthur F. Munby

1917
There has been a spate of very early marriages and I heard of a lady who was asked if she was happy about her youthful son's marriage. She replied, 'I don't know what I should feel if it were not wartime, for in that case he would still be at Harrow!'

Marie Belloc Lowndes

1966

Michael C. [Codron] told me this story about Lady Dorothy Macmillan saying to Mme. de Gaulle at the Elysée Palace, 'Now that your husband has achieved so much, is there any particular wish, any desire you have for the future?' and Madame replied, 'Yes – a penis.' Whereupon Gen. de Gaulle leaned over and said, 'No, my dear, in English it is pronounced Happiness.'

Kenneth Williams

11 April

1880 [London lodgings]

Settled at 56 Great Prescott St, to begin life as a working woman. With a very queer feeling I left the house in my old clothes and walked straight off to Princes Street and Wood Street, a nest of tailors. No bills up, except for 'good tailoress', and at these places I daren't apply, feeling myself rather an impostor. I wandered on, until my heart sank within me, my legs and back began to ache, and I felt all the feelings of 'out of work'. At last I summoned up courage and knocked at the door of a tailor wanting a 'good tailoress'. A fat and comfortable Jewess opened the door.

'Do you want a plain 'and?' said I, trying to effect a working-class accent.

'No,' was the reply.

'I can do everything except buttonholes,' I insisted.

'Where have you worked?'

'With my father, a master tailor. I've come from Manchester.'

'Rebecca,' shouted the fat Jewess to her daughter down the street, 'do you want a hand?'

'Suited,' shouted back Rebecca, to my mingled disappointment and relief. 'You will find plenty of bills in the next street,' she added in a kindly voice.

So I trudged on, asked at one or two other places, but all were 'suited'. Thought I, 'Is it because it's the middle of the week, or because they suspect I'm not genuine?' and looked sensitively into the next shop window at my reflection; certainly I looked shabby enough. I pass by a shop where a long list of 'hands wanted' is nailed up; but I have neither pencil nor paper and cannot in my dazed nervousness remember addresses and names – and how can I walk any longer? I feel quite strained. So in a fit of listless despair I take the top of the tram down Mile End Road. It is warm and balmy, and with a little rest from that weary trudge I pick up my pluck again. A large placard strikes my eye. 'Trouser and vest hands wanted immediately.' I descend quickly and am soon inside the shop. A large crowded room with a stout, clever-looking Jewess presiding at the top of the table, at which some thirty girls are working.

'Do you want trouser hands?'

'Yes, we do,' answers the Jewess.

'I'm a trouser finisher.'

The Jewess looks at me from top to toe; and somewhat superciliously glances at my draggled old dress.

'Call tomorrow at half-past eight.'

'What price do you pay?' say I with firmness.

'Why, according to the work; all prices,' answers she laconically.

'Then tomorrow, half-past eight,' and I leave the shop feeling triumphant to have secured a place, but a little doubtful of my powers of finishing trousers. So I hurry back to my little room, throw off my disguise, gulp down a cup of tea and rush off to a friendly Co-operative workroom to 'finish a pair of trousers' which I accomplished without difficulty in two hours. If they only expect 'finishing' I'm safe. Basting I have not really mastered.

Beatrice Webb

1929

Priceless story of Lenin and the death of his mother-in-law (Krupskaya's mother). Krupskaya tired of watching at the death-bed asked Lenin to sit by her mother while she slept. He was to call her if her mother wanted anything. Lenin took a book and began to read. Two hours later Krupskaya came back. Her mother was dead. Lenin was still reading. Krupskaya blamed him: 'Why did you not let me know?' Lenin replied: 'But your mother never called me!' Still, Lenin was not inhuman.

Sir Robert Bruce Lockhart

1933

This evening *L'éclaireur de Nice* informs us that Einstein accepts the chair that Spain has just offered him at Madrid. The event is announced in large capitals: *L'éclaireur* grasps its importance then.

I cannot admit that those qualified to make that offer in the name of France did not think of it . . . What reasons did they have for not doing so? . . . I am seeking, and for myself too, excuses.

As soon as the news of Einstein's exile appeared, I should have put forth the suggestion in *Marianne*. Still better: instead of barking with the others at that public meeting, have that suggestion to the French government voted by acclamation by the large audience. How I blame myself for not having thought of this then!

Every good Frenchman should be inconsolable that France did not have the sense to make this fine gesture, which would have been so natural to her and in which we should all have recognised ourselves.

André Gide

1945 [in transit from Bergen-Belsen camp]
The night is hell. We are sitting on our bench, folded double, rolled up, with pain in every muscle, and get in each other's way; aggression – bad as it is already – is mounting. The wagons are packed now. In our coach, which has seating for forty-eight people, sixty-two must live and sleep. Last night they gave us butter, one pound per four persons for four days. It is a lot, relatively, and we are not dissatisfied. The promised sausage – for which we are longing – has not arrived yet.

The night dragged by. First we experienced a heavy bombardment at Bergen station. Then suddenly a jerk and our journey had begun. Supposedly to Theresienstadt and Switzerland. The train crept forward. The sky was filled with bombardments and combat. It thundered and cracked. The night was cold and dark. I was constantly quarrelling with the woman facing me because of our feet. We were unable to sleep. From time to time someone would doze off and after a few minutes wake up with a sigh. That was the second night. How many more will there be? We are dreading it.

It is deathly quiet in Germany. We see nothing but soldiers and SS. It is dismal in Germany. Everyone expects the end any day now, the political catastrophe.

Abel J. Herzberg

12 April

1919
These ten minutes are stolen from *Moll Flanders*, which I failed to finish yesterday in accordance with my time sheet, yielding to a desire to stop reading and go up to London. But I saw London, in particular the view of white city churches and palaces from Hungerford Bridge, through the eyes of Defoe. I saw the old women selling matches through his eyes; and the draggled girl skirting round the pavement of St James's Square seemed to me out of *Roxana* or *Moll Flanders*. Yes, a great writer surely to be there imposing himself on me after 200 years. A great writer – and Forster has never read his books! I was beckoned by Forster from the Library as I approached. We shook hands very cordially; and yet I always feel him

shrinking sensitively from me, as a woman, a clever woman, an up to date woman. Feeling this I commanded him to read Defoe, and left him, and went and got some more Defoe, having bought one volume at Bickers on the way.

Virginia Woolf

1942

Often, I think how much later people marry. When I was a girl, it was considered very odd not be married at twenty-one or twenty-two, and my mother said seventeen or eighteen was the age most girls thought of marriage when she was young. Gran spoke of ploughmen with two and three children by the time they were twenty-one. I wonder if the war is going to cause a swing to earlier marriages. Looking around among friends' and acquaintances' boys and girls – sons of twenty-five to thirty with still no thoughts of marriage, and girls who are going off to the Services and saying, 'Oh, we will wait till after the war to get married.' If the country wants babies, I feel this conscription of women will be a backward step, for it is taking the best, most formative years from a girl's life, and giving her a taste of freedom from home drudgery that many crave for. Will they settle later to homes and children?

It's not very profitable to sit and think nowadays. So many problems, and they seem all to have such twists to them – *nothing* is straightforward.

Nella Last

1994

I invited John Gielgud to lunch to celebrate his ninetieth birthday. There were just the four of us: Sir John, Michèle [Brandreth], me and Glenda [Jackson]. (Glenda was Michèle's idea – and inspired. She looks so sour, but she was sweet and gossipy and exactly right for the occasion.) He arrived in central lobby at one, on the dot, twinkling and cherubic, and amazingly upright and steady.

'It's a great honour that you should join us, Sir John,' I said.

'Oh, I'm delighted to have been asked. All my real friends are dead, you know.'

The stories just poured out of him. 'Marlene [Dietrich] invited me to hear her new record. We were in New York. We all went and gathered round the gramophone, and when we were settled the record was put on. It was simply an audience applauding her! We sat through the entire first side and then we listened to the other side: more of the same!'

Gyles Brandreth

13 April

1872

The two old women Hannah Jones and Sarah Probert were both lying in bed and groaning horribly. I gave them some money and their cries and groans suddenly ceased.

Rev. Francis Kilvert

1926

Hugh [her husband] laughs at the womanly twist I give to great intellectual truths. Yet he agrees that it would be useful if we wrote down what it is we want and set aside what we cannot have. And then he adds, with characteristic cautiousness: 'But you must also have moderation in limitation.' With all this, we submit to one general ambition, for the sake of home and children. And we have agreed that in a year we must return to N.Y. and end our 'vacation in Europe.' In this I know we are wise. We are going to win money as Americans win money, but we shall be deeply different in the way we spend it.

Anaïs Nin

1945

It was announced at midnight that yesterday afternoon President Roosevelt died at Warm Springs, Georgia, from cerebral haemorrhage. Thought all day of my talk with him at the White House in December 1937 &, despite the altercations over bombing, felt I had lost a personal friend. Above all I was stunned with dismay, wondering what would happen to the future organisation. Sent a cable to Eleanor Roosevelt. Seems an ironic end – like Lincoln's – when the victory he worked for is almost here & both armies are approaching Berlin.

Vera Brittain

1967 [Bolivia]

A day of belching, farting, vomiting and diarrhea – a veritable organ concert. We remain absolutely immobilized, trying to digest the pig [cooked the previous day]. We have two cans of water. I was quite sick until I vomited, and then felt better. At night we ate fried corn and roasted calabash, plus the remnants of yesterday's feast – those who were able to.

Che Guevara

1991

Just before I left for Ascot Norman Lamont telephoned in a great state. He had found that the *News of the World* are running a story about him. The suggestion is that he has made £15,000 a year by letting his house out to some tenants, furnished. There is a clause which says he can get his house back when he requires it, which is perfectly normal and after all, they may lose the election and he may lose his job as Chancellor [of the Exchequer], etc.

We discussed whether he should ring Patsy Chapman [editor of the *News of the World*] but we thought on the whole to leave it alone. I said, 'If it is anything outrageous, I will answer it in the *News of the World* next week anyway.' He said it is getting absolutely impossible the way the press chase every minister in the government. The other day one of his ministerial colleagues had his house visited by a press man and when his wife opened the door he said, 'Oh we didn't know you were here. We thought you'd left your husband.'

He, Norman, had been told they had picture of him going into a brothel but he thought they may have got him confused with Lord Gowrie.

Woodrow Wyatt

14 April

1804

I talked with M. Salmon about his system concerning women; I urged him to publish it. He said no, but I believe he has made up his mind and the book is possibly already written. He holds that the Italian woman is the primitive woman; by modifying her in various ways, you get the French woman, the German woman, etc. He believes only in the virtues of temperament. He believes that woman's whole character consists of *an insatiable desire to please*, and that it's consequently impossible to overpraise them. He's seen miracles wrought by praise. A woman said of a man whose face was almost hideous, 'What a monster! He's an eyesore.' The monster praised her, succeeded in pleasing her and ended by sleeping with her.

Stendhal

1905

Didn't sleep at all last night. First hot, tormented, then, after I had opened the window, wonderfully calm. Birdsong from the garden – like the touch of soft, busy hands. Indescribably delicate morning tints over the objects in the room. The black of a mirror sucking up the darkness – simply beyond description. It is not black at all, cannot be captured with expressions for color; rather with ones for materials such as velvet, etc.

Robert Musil

1910

I've been reading through my books. I oughtn't to write any more. I think in this respect, I've done all I could. But I want to, I terribly want to.

Leo Tolstoy

1941

Back on day duty and getting up at six. No time to traipse up for breakfast so we collect things the night before. The result is often poisonous and bizarre, as for instance this morning – plum cake, cheese sandwiches, pork pie and chocolate biscuits, washed down with Eno's [liver salts]!

The bugs are much better now, but they still don't give us any Jeyes paper in the lavatory. I have worked my way steadily through a whole copy of Jung's *Psychology of the Unconscious* in the last few weeks with the result that there is hardly a WC in the house which is not 'hors de combat'.

Joan Wyndham

15 April

1778

Brewed a vessell of strong Beer today. My two large Piggs by drinking some Beer grounds taking out of one of my Barrels today, got so amazingly drunk by it, that they were not able to stand and appeared like dead things almost and so remained all night from dinner time today. I never saw Piggs so drunk in my life. I slit their ears for them without feeling.

Rev. James Woodforde

1802

I never saw daffodils so beautiful they grew among the mossy stones about and about them, some rested their heads upon these stones as on a pillow for weariness and the rest tossed and reeled and danced and seemed as if they verily laughed with the wind that blew upon them over the lake, they looked so gay, ever glancing ever changing. This wind blew directly over the lake to them. There was here and there a little knot and a few stragglers a few yards higher up but they were so few as not to disturb the simplicity and unity and life of that one busy highway.

Dorothy Wordsworth

1912

About noon the streets were full of posters announcing that the *Titanic* had struck an iceberg, half-way across the Atlantic on her maiden voyage. She got in touch with the mainland by means of her wireless installation, and hour by hour we were kept informed of her movements. There was something extraordinarily dramatic in the thought of this great overgrown monster wallowing about in mid-ocean, while we in Cornhill could almost watch her flounderings. Then suddenly the messages became blurred and ceased altogether; it was put about – no one yet knows by whom – that all the passengers were saved and that the ship was being towed into Halifax by one of the rescuing liners, and we all went to bed regarding it as a good joke.

Sir Alan 'Tommy' Lascelles

1917

I met General Sir John Cowans at dinner at Lord Haldane's. He was said to be the best Quartermaster-General since Moses. We made friends, and he asked if he could come and see me. This astonished Elizabeth Haldane, who murmured, speaking with more truth than civility, 'I was told that he only cared for young women!' I whispered back, 'Well, he apparently likes one of forty-nine!'

Marie Belloc Lowndes

1945

All the saloons and major restaurants of Baltimore were closed last night as a mark of respect to the dead Roosevelt, whose body passed through the city at midnight. It was silly, but it gave a lot of Dogberries a chance to annoy their betters, and so it was ordained. As a result the Saturday Night Club missed its usual post-music beer-party for the first time in forty years. All during Prohibition the club found accommodations in the homes of its members, but last night no member was prepared, so the usual programme had to be abandoned. August and I came home, had a couple of high-balls, and then went to bed.

Roosevelt, if he had lived, would probably have been unbeatable, despite the inevitable reaction against the war. He was so expert a demagogue that it would have been easy for him to divert the popular discontent to some other object. He could have been beaten only by a demagogue even worse than he was himself, and his opponents showed no sign of being able to flush such a marvel. The best they could produce was such timorous compromisers as [Wendell] Willkie and [Thomas] Dewey, who were as impotent before Roosevelt as sheep before Behemoth. When the call was for a headlong attack they backed and filled. It thus became impossible, at the close of their campaigns, to distinguish them from mild New Dealers – in other words, inferior Roosevelts. He was always a mile ahead of them, finding new victims to loot and new followers to reward, flouting common sense and boldly denying its existence, demonstrating by his anti-logic that two and two made five, promising larger and larger slices of the moon. His career will greatly engage historians, if any good ones ever appear in America, but it will be of even more interest to psychologists. He was the first American to penetrate to the real depths of vulgar stupidity. He never made the mistake of overestimating the intelligence of the American mob. He was its unparalleled professor.

H. L. Mencken

16 April

1912

But today came the news that she [the *Titanic*] had gone down with over a thousand souls on board within three hours of the collision, and very shortly after wireless messages broke off. Perhaps it is Nature's most effective *tour de force* since Sodom and Gomorrah; for she was the last word in ostentatious luxury, and the very embodiment of our insolent claims to have conquered the elements. Our civilisation has been very properly put in its place, as Roman civilisation was at Pompeii. I don't think even the San Francisco and Messina earthquakes made half such an impression on the world as this has. When they happened, we rather tended to say, 'What can you expect, with those Godless San Franciscans and those feckless Italians?' But this is essentially an international affair, and hits especially the two *soi-disant* most competent nations of two hemispheres.

Sir Alan 'Tommy' Lascelles

1926 [Florence]

This morning, after wandering for an hour, looking at the architecture and at the people, we turned our steps naturally to the Uffizi Gallery. We sought Botticelli first, because he always pleased us, and his frescoes in the Louvre are always in our minds.

We did not stay as long as we intended. The room was full of glossy-haired, smart young men from college, young women in sports suits with Baedekers, and old English couples. The young men were always interested in the same paintings which the young ladies studied, and the eyes of these ladies were always wandering off towards the glossy-haired and living works of art.

Anaïs Nin

1989

The ninety-eight Liverpool fans crushed to death at Sheffield bring back memories of a similar disaster at Bolton in 1946. We never took a Sunday paper at home but sometimes saw the *News of the World* when we went down to Grandma's on a Sunday night, and I think I knew at eleven years old that there was something wrong about the gusto with which the tragic story was written up, and something prurient about the way I gobbled up every word. Today I read very little, and because of being at the theatre see nothing of the live coverage on television. But already the process begins whereby terrible events are broken down and made palatable. They are first covered in a kind of gum: the personal reactions of bystanders, eyewitnesses giving their inadequate testimonials – 'It was terrible'; 'I'll never forget it'; 'Tragic. Bloody Tragic' – and then wreaths inscribed 'You'll never walk alone.' Then the event begins to be swallowed, broken up into digestible pieces, minced morsels: the reaction of the football authorities is gone into, then the comments of the police, the verdict of the Sports Minister and so on, day after day, until by the end of the week it will begin to get boring and the snake will have swallowed the pig. Then there are the customary components of the scene – the establishment of a memorial fund (always a dubious response) and the bedside visits by the Prime Minister. I find myself thinking, it would be Liverpool, that sentimental self-dramatising place, and am brought up short by seeing footage of a child brought out dead, women waiting blank-faced at Lime Street and a father meeting his two sons off the train, his relief turned to anger at the sight of their smiling faces, cuffing and hustling them away from the cameras.

Alan Bennett

17 April

1944 [Italy]

Spent the morning trying to alter the date of birth on the identity card of a young deserter who turned up this morning and firmly requested this service – with the same confidence with which others have asked for a clean shirt or some food. It is much more difficult to do than one would think, even though the type of my machine is fortunately of the same size as that used in his document, the difficulty being to put the new figure precisely in line with the others. And clumsiness is lent to one's fingers by the thought that the boy's life may hang on its being done well.

Iris Origo

1976 [Barlinnie Prison]

I thought of the beautiful cool evening, how I long to be walking in it outside this cell. All of this took place while I sat in the semi-dark reading a book. The thoughts on freedom were only momentary but so powerful that they seem to tear my soul apart. There is something about being alone in a cell, about the inability to rise from a chair, open the door and speak to someone. I would like to get up this minute and discuss this subject with someone. I would like to put these feelings into a piece of sculpture and although sitting typing out the feelings is important there is a tremendous amount of strain and frustration attached to it. During these periods I find it hard to read a book or watch TV, which I hardly do anyway. The only solution at such times is to tackle the mood and try to do something about it.

Jimmy Boyle

18 April

1912

Lunched at the 'Thirty' [luncheon club]. There was much talk of the *Titanic* tragedy. Lady Dorothy Nevill said that the wreck was a judgement from God on those idle rich people who want all earthly luxuries even on the water. She observed: 'I am told they even had a garden!'

Marie Belloc Lowndes

1934

A curious little fact. Instead of smoking six or seven cigarettes as I write of a morning, I now, for three mornings, make myself smoke only one. And rather enjoy doing without.

Virginia Woolf

1945 [in transit from Bergen-Belsen camp]

Yesterday we spent the night in a Berlin station. We went round the entire city and saw the terrible devastation. On the walls we could read 'Berlin kämpft, arbeitet und steht' [Berlin fights, works and stands] and other such resolute phrases. For the past two days there has been no food; last night we finally received one kilo of potatoes, seventy-five grams of soup vegetables, half a swede and a hundred grams of curd each. Today there would also be gherkins. The leadership is much taken with itself. We begged and partly plundered and have become fully fledged gypsies. For all that, we are eating much better than in the camp. The Hungarians are selling us their stolen goods.

In Berlin we also met the Hungarians again. They had sustained a heavy attack – fifty-six casualties, more than 250 wounded. A dangerous enterprise indeed! Yesterday I begged potato peelings from a soldier and cooked an excellent soup with them.

Abel J. Herzberg

1977

Then left at 11.25 in a cavalcade of cars for the one-minute drive to the White House . . . I was taken into the Oval Room for a private talk with [President Jimmy] Carter. He and I stood with our backs to the fireplace for photographs, while the following extraordinary exchange took place:

He said, 'I expect you know this room well. Have you been here often before?' I said, 'Yes, I think I have seen four of your predecessors here.' He very quickly said, 'That means you start with Kennedy, does it?' So I said, 'Yes, though I also met both Truman and Eisenhower, though neither when they were in office and therefore not in this room.' I then added, conversationally, 'But, to my great regret, I never set eyes upon Roosevelt. Did you, Mr President, by chance see him when you were a boy?'

'See him,' said Carter incredulously. 'I have never seen *any* Democratic President. I *never* saw Kennedy. I *never* saw Lyndon Johnson [astonishing]. I *saw* Nixon, and I both saw and talked to Ford, of course, and that's all. You see I am very new to this scene of Washington politics.' This he said without prickliness or chippiness or bitterness, simply as a matter of fact of which he was half but not excessively proud. It was quite different from the aggressive/defensive way in which Lyndon Johnson would have reacted had one got on to an analogous conversation with him about the Kennedy years.

Roy Jenkins

19 April

1939

Though the desire for women troubles the body and the mind, I am yet glad that desire is still so alive in me, for its death would be ominous of creative moribundity. The lesser desires of sense rarely disturb me now – as if the loveliness of earth had become quintessential in women; as if in them were now summated those other sensations which quicken the whole being as one enters a wood, or lies upon a hillside, or stares across the sea. We gather the world into the compass of our speculation; and when our sensuous scope is small, we can keep contact with the world only by quintessential symbol – so, in large measure unconsciously, the urge to retain living contact has intensified for me the significance of the commonplace. And since our contact with life has a trinal quality – natural, human, and metaphysical – there are for me three dominant images which are as doors into fuller life; and these are woman, tree and the unicorn.

William Soutar

1940 [Berlin]

Hitler's fifty-first birthday tomorrow, and the people have been asked to fly their flags. Said Dr. Goebbels in a broadcast tonight: 'The German people have found in the Führer the incarnation of their strength and the most brilliant exponent of their national aims.' When I passed the Chancellery tonight, I noticed some seventy-five people outside for a glimpse of the leader. In other years on the eve of his birthday, there were ten thousand.

William L. Shirer

1947

In the morning paper I come across two small events that together seem significant. The black singer Paul Robeson was supposed to give a recital in Peoria; at the last minute, the concert was canceled on the pretext that Robeson is a communist. The authorities insist that they didn't refuse to give him access to the hall because he's black but because he's a communist. Elsewhere, an amusing episode just reached its conclusion. Several weeks ago, a bus driver with a bus full of passengers traveling along some avenue got the bright idea to bypass all the stations and the terminal and to head out onto the highway amid his customers' panicked protests. He let them out in the end, then calmly continued on his way to Florida. When stopped and questioned, he cheerfully declared, 'That route was too monotonous. I've always wanted to see Florida. One fine morning, I said to myself, "Why not go to Florida?" So I went.' The driver has become a popular hero. Although he'd been fired, he went back to work yesterday amid ovations. He was interviewed, as well as photographed a hundred times, and in all the papers he's seen laughing through the windshield of the new bus he's just been given. Perhaps such a fantasy is conceivable only in New York; friends have told me that nothing similar could happen, for example, in Chicago. But even if they are incapable of doing it themselves, all Americans adore these uninhibited actions in which they see ready proof of their love of freedom. This driver is a 'character,' an original who has openly demonstrated that individualism America is so proud of. And certainly in France he would never have been reinstated in his job. It's true that America is much more indulgent of sudden whims and impulses that do not seriously challenge its authority. I knew a pious and capable mother whose children were envied by all their little friends because they were allowed to climb trees, fight with one another, and stick their tongues out at their old teachers. When they grew up, all the daughters docilely married the husbands chosen for them and the sons entered careers approved by their parents. The pleasure and pride they found in their independence had made them even more submissive prey in their parents' hands. The bus driver would certainly laugh in the face of anyone who might doubt the freedom of American citizens. Paul Robeson, however, didn't want to do anything eccentric; he just wanted to sing.

Simone de Beauvoir

1975

After a good night's sleep I feel fighting fit again. Anyway HCF [Hell's Corner Farm] always cures any neurosis or strain. And this morning one of the most comical incidents I have ever experienced left me laughing for hours. At 8.30am I went downstairs from our bedroom to the loo, opened the door and saw two bright eyes staring at me from the lavatory pan. It was a sweet little baby rabbit sitting at the bottom of the pan, with its nose and ears just above the water line. I was shaken to the core! I shut the door and went back upstairs to Ted [her husband], asking him seriously, 'Do you think I could possibly have DTs? There is a rabbit in the lavatory pan.' He was so scared at the very idea that he had to drink his tea before he went to have a look at it, saying, 'We'll set Printer [the dog] on it,' while I moaned, 'Oh, we couldn't do that. It wouldn't be fair after all it has gone through.' 'We're infested with the things,' said Ted angrily. When he peered into the loo he called out, 'It's drowned anyway.' I peered over his shoulder nervously. Its eyes were shut, its ears were flattened against its head, and it had gone limp. 'Well, it was alive when I looked at it,' I replied. 'If you want to kill it, why don't you get some more water and make sure it really is drowned?' But Ted would hear nothing of it: he *knew* it was dead. So he went and got his gardening gloves and a bucket and scooped out the limp rabbit, walking firmly down our long garden to throw the corpse over the hedge into the field. I was in the study working when I heard a roar of laughter from Eileen, watching through the kitchen window. At the hedge, calling on Printer to stand by, Ted tipped over the bucket. Out scuttled the rabbit, shook itself and was through the hedge before either Ted or Printer realized what was happening. 'It's pure *Watership Down,*' I chuckled. 'Once again, cunning rabbit outwits stupid man and dog.' It made our day. That rabbit *deserved* to escape, for Ted remembered that yesterday Printer had chased a baby rabbit through the garden and they thought it had escaped onto the road. Instead, it must have swerved into the house, through the dining room and into the downstairs loo. It must have been hiding in the corner all the time we were going to the loo last night and then somehow got into the pan. I shall never go to the lavatory again without remembering it sitting there. The dramas of the countryside are endless.

Barbara Castle

20 April

1874

Young elm leaves lash and lip the sprays. This has been a very beautiful day – fields about us deep green lighted underneath with white daisies, yellower fresh green of leaves above which bathes the skirts of the elms, and their tops are touched and worded with leaf too. Looked at the big limb of that elm that hangs over into the park at the swing-gate, further out than where the leaves were open and saw beautiful inscape, home-coiling wiry bushes of spray, touched with bud to point them. Blue shadows fell all up the meadow at sunset and then standing at the far Park corner my eye was struck by such a sense of green in the turfs and splashes of grass, with purple shadow thrown back on the dry, black mould behind them, as I do not remember ever to have been exceeded in looking at green grass. I marked this down on a slip of paper at the time, because the eye for colour, rather the zest in the mind, seems to weaken with years, but now the paper is mislaid.

Gerard Manley Hopkins

1919

What sort of diary should I like mine to be? Something loose knit and yet not slovenly, so elastic that it will embrace any thing, solemn, slight or beautiful that comes into my mind. I should like it to resemble some deep old desk, or capacious hold-all, in which one flings a mass of odds and ends without looking them through. I should like to come back, after a year or two, and find that the collection had sorted itself and refined itself and coalesced, as such deposits so mysteriously do, into a mould, transparent enough to reflect the light of our life, and yet steady, tranquil compounds with the aloofness of a work of art. The main requisite, I think on re-reading my old volumes, is not to play the part of censor, but to write as the mood comes or of anything whatever; since I was curious to find how I went for things put in haphazard, and found the significance to lie where I never saw it at the time.

Virginia Woolf

1934

After endless false starts, I have decided definitely to begin my diary again, and only hope I shall have the patience to continue. But as I am dictating it, it may be less scandalous and spontaneous than before.

'Chips' Channon

1938

The Duce has been made furiously angry, and with reason, by the bad behaviour of some farmers from Bari who were being entertained in the Party House in Munich – they even relieved themselves on the stairs. A disgusting incident, likely to lower us to an unbelievable extent in the opinion of the Germans. The Chief [Mussolini] said that our people must be imbued with a loftier national ideal, without which they cannot embark on the work of colonizing the Empire. He let fly at the 'sons of slaves', adding that if they had distinctive physical markings, he would exterminate them all, in the certainty of rendering a great service to Italy and to humanity.

Count Ciano

1941 [Holland]

It really gives you a sense of satisfaction, to know you can do it [a challenging 3-day, 236-kilometre bike trip], that you really achieved something. I'm sitting on my bed, with a sunburnt face and aching knees. Apart from that, everything is normal . . . except my state of mind. I need cheering up a little. You've got to admit it's a little upsetting when you enter a small village, and you see a sign: JEWS ARE NOT WELCOME HERE. There was a little café in Wilnis that we walked into on the first day. Nice people. They had a sign too but they kept it hidden in a cupboard. They showed it to us. It said JEWS NOT WELCOME. They'd refused to hang it up. We saw similar signs in other villages. Oh well.

Edith Velmans

21 April

1804

I'm still playing the lottery. I could have a room for 18 francs at my 51-franc boardinghouse, which makes 69 francs, with 11 francs for spending money, 80 francs. 12 x 80 = 960 + 240 francs for clothes. Consequently, it's possible to live in Paris, going to the theater once a month, for 1,200 francs [a year]. I know that there are rooms for 8 francs in the Rue Jacques. You can have dinner at Mme. Desbenet's for 28 sous, which makes, by the month, 50 fr. + 10 fr. expenses = 60 francs. 12 x 60 = 720 + 200 francs for clothes = 920 francs. You can live on 900 francs. If I had only 1,200 francs, I'd prefer not to be obliged to spend more that 60 francs a month so I could have 25 francs for entertainment each month. Thank heavens I haven't been pinched for money yet this year.

Stendhal

1904

I went down to Montparnasse and had tea with Mrs Stapley, who had hunted up an Empire secrétaire for me, in fact several. Afterwards we went to view them. The best one had a mirror at the back, above the small drawers. I said to the shopwoman that I objected to a mirror. 'Ah!' she said. 'But when Madame leans over your shoulder while you are writing—!' I bought the secrétaire and also a clock for 140 francs.

Arnold Bennett

1925

Setting out for my walk in the Park, I remembered my photograph in this month's *Vogue* (a journal which I ordinarily despise). Having purchased a copy and admired my physiognomy, I tucked it under my arm and sunned myself in Hyde Park. The bright flower-beds, and pale green froth of foliage, and the shadows of trees on prosperous greensward – these obvious things made a charming background for the people who sat or sauntered in the late afternoon light. But I was meditating, most of the time, not about eternal verities and austerities, but about my own photograph, in a fashion journal. What a conceited superficial ass the man must be, thinks my invisible reader. (For there *must* be one, or I shouldn't be writing these pages so punctiliously.) Worse still, I can remember wondering whether people will be impressed by the suffering aspect of the countenance. Lapsing a degree lower, I speculated as to the number of *Vogue* readers who might – after perusing the careworn countenance – order a copy of my *Selected Poems*. Vanity of vanities! But why should I feel ashamed to confess it? Such small episodes can help to stimulate me.

Siegfried Sassoon

1968

Ted [her husband] and I were sitting by the telly listening to the six o'clock news when there suddenly was Enoch Powell, white-faced and tight-lipped, delivering his Wolverhampton speech on immigration. As we listened to his relentless words – 'I see the Tiber running with blood' – intense depression gripped us. I knew he had taken the lid off Pandora's box and that race relations in Britain would never be the same again. This is certainly a historic turning point, but in which direction? I believe he has helped to make a race war, not only in Britain but perhaps in the world, inevitable.

Barbara Castle

22 April

1915

On Sunday, the violence of the thunderous detonations grew in length and strength. Then, suddenly, the terrible word *retreat* was heard. At first in a whisper; then, in loud forceful tone: 'The Russians are retreating!' And the first-line troops came into sight: a long procession of dirt-bespattered, weary, desperate men – in full retreat! We had received no marching-orders. The thunder of the guns came nearer and nearer. We were frightened and perplexed; they had forgotten us! But they came at last – urgent, decisive orders: we were to start without delay, leaving behind all the wounded and all the equipment that might hinder us. A dreadful feeling of dismay and bewilderment took possession of us; to go away, leaving the wounded and the Unit's equipment! It was impossible; there *must* be some mistake! But there was no mistake, we had to obey; we had to go. '*Skoro! Skoro!*' [Quickly] shouted familiar voices. '*Skoro! Skoro!*' echoed unfamiliar ones from the hastily passing infantry. 'The Germans are outside the town!'

Snatching up coats, knapsacks, any of our personal belongings which could be carried – we started off quickly down the rough road. And the wounded! They shouted to us when they saw us leaving; called out to us in piteous language to stop – to take them with us; not to forsake them, for the love of God; not to leave them – our brothers – to the enemy. Those who could walk got up and followed us; running, hopping, limping, by our sides. The badly crippled crawled after us; all begging, beseeching us not to abandon them in their need. And, on the road, there were others, many others; some of them lying down in the dust, exhausted. They, too, called after us. They held on to us; praying us to stop with them. We had to wrench our skirts from their clinging hands. Then their prayers were intermingled with curses; and, far behind them, we could hear the curses repeated by those of our brothers whom we had left to their fate. The gathering darkness accentuated the panic and misery. To the accompaniment of the thunder of the exploding shells, and of the curses and prayers of the wounded men around and behind us, we hurried on into the night.

Florence Farmborough

1925

The bus I got into at Piccadilly Circus was one of those which the London General Omnibus Company calls 'pirates'. These shabby buses are always slow starters, since they hope to pick up as many passengers as possible. At Trafalgar Square several people got in and then got out again, irritated by the dally-ing demeanour of the 'pirate'. I felt impatient myself, and was about to get out. Then I noticed the face of the conductor. He was a tired middle-aged man with a gentle diffident expression. I saw that he was sadly aware of his vehicle's lack of prestige. He stood – one hand on the bell-string – with a patient humble look which made me sympathetic. So I remained where I was, meditating on the humanising effect of the episode. And I was rewarded, for the old bus went down Whitehall at full gallop. I watched the grey-haired man gently collecting the pennies; he smiled charmingly at two poorly-dressed little boys, and I was glad to be healed by such simplicity. Strange that one can get a moral lesson from a motor omnibus.

Siegfried Sassoon

1952

At 4 p.m. I went to Slatters in Bond Street where Harold Nicolson was opening an exhibition of Dutch pictures in aid of a charity. Nicolson, who is two years older than me and has had a varied life in diplomacy and letters, is rather the man of affairs and club type of English gentleman in appearance than the scholar, artist or poet. He is, I imagine, a kind and human sort of man. His books are respectable, but perhaps none of them, except that about his experiences with Curzon, are of permanent interest. He had told me that he has long kept a daily journal, the contents of which could never be published in his life-time as it reveals too many secrets, and which he is leaving to Balliol. That might prove his memorial, as his experiences in diplomacy, journalism, literature, the B.B.C., Parliament, have provided wonderful material.

Maurice Collis

23 April

1858

Between the chocolate soufflé and the chartreuse Maria loosened her bodice and launched out on the story of her life.

It begins in a little village on the banks of the Marne, one of those cool shady places landscape painters love. She is a bargee's daughter, thirteen-and-a-half years old, with fair hair and white skin which the sun has not yet burned. A young man comes to see her, disguised as an architect. As in the storybooks, this young man is really the Comte de Saint-Maurice, the owner of one of the neighbourhood châteaux, a handsome, sophisticated young man of twenty-seven who entertains members of the Orléans family and is in the process of squandering his fortune.

Now the little village girl is installed in the château; and the young man loves her, for all that he locks her in her room whenever he brings down girls from Paris, whom he chases around his park, naked beneath gauze night-dresses with bows of ribbon which two little dogs from Havana tear with their teeth. And it all ends with the young man, completely ruined and hunted by the bailiffs, putting up the sort of resistance that belongs to more heroic times, and finally taking refuge in the roof of his château, where he blows out his brains. The girl is thrown out with her watch set in pearls and her diamond earrings. She is pregnant. She goes to a midwife to bear her child; the midwife sells her to a building contractor whom she hates at sight; and in order to earn a living she comes back to serve an apprenticeship to the midwife who delivered her child. And at that point Maria's story becomes the story of all women, with the difference that not many women learn how to be midwives.

The Brothers Goncourt

1861 [New York]

Everyone's future has changed in these six months last past. This is to be a terrible, ruinous war, and a war in which the nation cannot succeed. It can never subjugate these savage millions of the South. It must make peace at last with the barbarous communities off its Southern frontier. I was prosperous and well off last November. I believe my assets to be reduced fifty per cent, at least. But I hope I can still provide wholesome training for my three boys. With that patrimony they can fight out the battle of life for themselves. Their mother is plucky and can stand self-denial. I clearly see that this is a most severe personal calamity to me, but I welcome it cordially, for it has shown that I belong to a community that is brave and generous, and that the City of New York is not sordid and selfish.

George Templeton Strong

1929 [Berlin]

In the evening a concert by young Yehudi Menuhin. The boy is truly marvellous. His playing has the afflatus of genius and the purity of a child. His fantastic virtuosity remains a totally secondary factor, as though it were something to be taken for granted. A wonderful feeling for style, without the slightest suggestion of cheap effects or sentimentality. On the contrary, pure and profound sensibility. He played Beethoven's *Romance in F Major* (Opus 50) as I have only heard Joseph Joachim render it.

Count Harry Kessler

1945

In the late afternoon I dashed back and drove my car-load over to Campbeltown where we duly had our blood transfusion taken. Obviously the organisers were having difficulties as half the people who said they were going to come didn't while others did come who weren't expected. The only unpleasant thing was horrible cups of sweet tea that we were made to have . . .

My fellow blood transfusers talking about the prison camps. That really seems to have got under the skin of even Carradale [her farm in Scotland]. I keep on saying that when some of us talked about concentration camps three years before the war the people who talk about them now wouldn't listen. One just can't quite imagine the quality of the hell it must be in Berlin. I suppose Hitler and Goering will either get themselves killed or commit suicide. I hope they won't be martyrs anyhow!

Naomi Mitchison

1982

ST GEORGE'S DAY (ENGLAND). NEW MOON

Barry Kent came to school in a Union Jack tee-shirt today. Ms Fossington-Gore sent him home to change. Barry Kent shouted, 'I'm celebratin' our patron saint's birthday ain't I?'

Ms Fossington-Gore shouted back, 'You're wearing a symbol of fascism, you nasty NF lout.'

Today is also Shakespeare's birthday. One day I will be a great writer like him. I am well on the way: I have already had two rejection letters from the BBC.

Adrian Mole

24 April

1884

Why can't I talk to the children; to Tanya? Seryozha is impossibly obtuse. The same castrated mind that his mother has. If you two should ever read this, forgive me; it hurts me terribly.

Leo Tolstoy

1941

News of Churchill. He is said to be in a very depressed state, spending the entire day smoking and drinking. This is the kind of enemy we need.

I initiate a campaign against the widespread saying that 'The English are more stubborn than we are.' This must be eradicated.

New figures for box-office receipts. Another 30 million in profits. We are awash with money. Every film is a box-office hit.

A few shortages in Berlin, particularly tobacco and beer. I arrange for them to be alleviated. The public must be kept happy at the moment.

Josef Goebbels

1948

Four nights ago, with the moon pouring down and the nightingale singing and stopping, singing and stopping unaccountably, I suddenly heard another sound. I thought it was a laugh from some woman in the lane. I imagined her wandering round the fields with her lover after leaving the pub. I heard it again and then again. It was no laugh but extravagant sobbing. It rang out, drowning the nightingale, dirtying the night. I ran into Eric's room and told him. He came into my room and we sat by the open french door. The sobbing was a mechanical repetition of notes falling in a scale from high to low. The light was on in the bungalow through the apple trees. The weeping came from there, where a Hungarian lives with his English wife. They are young, newly married in September or October. There was no hint of comforting, reasoning from the husband, no word from the woman, just the hard boo-hoo crying, louder than any other crying I have ever heard, then a sudden ceasing, the light flicked off and nothing. The nightingale streamed on, the wind grew colder, and the moon milked itself into the grass's hair.

Denton Welch

1996

I'm glad I'm not having to undergo any surgery just now. Today's press is full of photographs of the Princess of Wales, in operating-theatre gear and pale make-up, sitting in on a serious operation. We are told she is doing the rounds of several hospitals. 'Pardon me, Your Royal Highness, but this is *my* hernia and I don't want anyone to stitch it up except the surgeon. Another whiff of gas, nurse, if you don't mind, and leave out the Calèche Parfum.'

Alec Guinness

25 April

1661

I went to the [Royal] Society where were divers Experiments in Mr. Boyls Pneumatique Engine. We put in a Snake but could not kill it, by exhausting the aire, onely made it extremly sick, but the chick died of Convulsions out right, in a short space.

John Evelyn

1829

Maxpopple [Scott's cousin, William Scott] dined and slept here with four of his family, much amused with what they heard and saw. By good fortune a ventriloquist and partial juggler came in and we had him in the library after dinner. He was a half-starved wretched-looking creature, who seemd to have eat more fire than bread. So I caused him to [be] well stuffd, and gave him a guinea rather to his poverty than to skill.

Sir Walter Scott

26 April

1890

Sidney Webb, the socialist, spent Sunday here.

I am not sure as to the nature of that man. His tiny tadpole body, unhealthy skin, lack of manner, Cockney pronunciation, poverty, are all against him. He has the conceit of a man who has raised himself out of the most insignificant surroundings into a position of power – how much power no one quite knows. This self-compliant egotism, this disproportionate view of his own position, is at once repulsive and ludicrous. On the other hand, looked at by the light of his personal history, it was inevitable. And he can learn; he is quick and sensitive and ready to adapt himself. This sensitiveness, combined as it undoubtedly is with great power, may carry him far. If the opportunity comes, I think the man will appear. In the meantime he is an interesting study. A London retail tradesman with the aims of a Napoleon! A queer monstrosity to be justified only by success. And above all a loop-hole into the socialist party; one of the small body of men with whom I may sooner or later throw in my lot for good and all.

Beatrice Webb

1917

Moira told me an amusing story of Lady Wolverton. The latter, thinking the time had come to economise, got into a bus. She sat beside a woman who kept loudly sniffing and she asked her aggressively if she hadn't got a handkerchief. The woman replied: 'Yes, but I never lends it in a bus.'

Lady Cynthia Asquith

1942 [Holland]

Just a small red, faded anemone. But I like the idea that in years to come, I shall chance upon it again between these pages. By then I shall be a matron, and I shall hold this dried flower in my hands and say with a touch of sadness:

'Look, this is the anemone I wore in my hair on the fifty-fifth birthday of the man who was the greatest and most unforgettable friend of my youth. It was during the third year of World War II, we ate under-the-counter macaroni and drank real coffee, on which Liesl got "drunk", we were all in such high spirits, wondering if the war would be over soon, and I wore the red anemone in my hair and somebody said, "You look a mixture of Russian and Spanish," and somebody else, the blond Swiss with the heavy eyebrows, said, "A Russian Carmen," and I asked him to recite a poem about William Tell for us in his funny Swiss burr.'

Etty Hillesum

1945 [in transit from Bergen-Belsen camp]

Night fell, it got misty. A pale moon shone. The sleepless hours dragged by. Silence, silence, except for the intermittent popping of anti-aircraft fire and the sound of explosions. Occasionally the crackle of gunfire. We were waiting to come under attack. Nothing happened.

And early in the morning, very early – Russian sentries stood farther along the road. Liberty!

Tovarishchi Svoboda. Comrades, liberty!

They gave us cigarettes.

Up till now, though, 26 April, they have not bothered about us.

They show no concern for us, apart from leaving us the local inhabitants to plunder. And this plundering was carried out thoroughly and without mercy.

We have nothing. We are ill. We were billeted on farmers. The train is empty. Me legs are swollen and inflamed. T. [his wife] has bronchitis, diarrhoea and fever. Nothing is happening.

Nine of us are living in one house. We are ill. Tired. How is it in Holland? Outside, the birds are chirping.

I lie awake at night and count the strokes of the clock. Is this freedom?

Abel J. Herzberg

27 April

1657

I tooke preventing Physick.

John Evelyn

1859 [New York]

Walked to 109th Street Sunday afternoon. The cutting on Fourth Avenue at Fiftieth Street through the old Potters Field is a disgrace and scandal. It exposes a fossiliferous stratum some three feet thick of close-packed coffins or shells, and debris of dead paupers. Ribs, clavicles, and vertebrae abound all along the railway tracks, and one might easily construct a perfect skeleton from these stray fragments without resorting to the remains *in situ*, were not many of the specimens imperfect, having been gnawed and crunched by the gaunt swine that are co-tenants with Hibernian humanity of the adjoining shanties. This is within a hundred yards of a dense population.

George Templeton Strong

1934

A diary is like drink; we tend to indulge in it over often: it becomes a habit which would ever seduce us to say more than we ought to say and more than we have the experiental qualifications to state. It is a kind of private paper which demands its quota of news every day, and not rarely becomes a mere recorder of spiritual journalese. But not only can it persuade us to betray the self – it tempts us to betray our fellows also, becoming thereby an *alter ego* sharing with us the denigrations which we would be ashamed of voicing aloud; a diary is an assassin's cloak which we wear when we stab a comrade in the back with a pen. And here is this diary proving its culpability even to its own harm – for how much on this page is true to the others?

William Soutar

28 April

1941 [Cairo]

I slept tormented by sandflies after a torpid khamsin day. Bonner Fellers [American Attaché] fetched me for lunch. He said, 'We reckon this is one of your worse emergencies – the whole Mediterranean is threatened. America must declare war soon.' Then he talked about the German 88-millimetre gun which he says is excellent. He grumbled because the US War Department and our War Office turned the gun down before the war as it has only a small shield to protect the crew and both thought it would prove too costly in men. As it outranges most other weapons and is very mobile, Bonner thinks this was a grave mistake. 'Anyway,' he said, 'the Germans now have it in the Desert where it is deadly.' The Germans also have a very good Fifth Column.

The Desert war continues. We have bombed Barce. This evening I took Whitaker [her husband's valet] and his friend McCall to a movie – we saw *Congo Maisie*, 'a tropical love tangle with allure and alligators'. I got home in time to hear Mr Churchill's broadcast. He made a long and very honest statement.

Countess of Ranfurly

1943

Amy came late & tearful to announce that her sister Lily's husband was killed in N. Africa on April 6th and the news came by letter from the War Office yesterday. Her fellow-workers at the factory collected abt. £10 for her so that she could have a few days away from work. She asked if I would draft a letter of thanks for her which I did. She & the young man only had abt. 3 weeks together all told after they were married – & never a home of their own at all. Such is war for the 'little people' whom the politicians indifferently sacrifice to satisfy their own swollen egos.

Vera Brittain

1980

Invalid Children's Exhibition by Norman St J. Stevas. A moving and desperate occasion. One of the prize-winners, sitting in his chair like a piece of crumpled-up paper thrown into a wastepaper basket, emits regular whoops of (I hope) pleasure. The pride of the parents, teachers and helpers in the achievement of their charges brings tears to the eyes.

Sir Hugh Casson

29 April

1836

[Programme changes by theatre manager had robbed Macready of some of his best scenes in the last act of Richard III]

Went to the theatre; was tetchy and unhappy, but pushed through the part in a sort of desperate way as well as I could. It is not easy to describe the state of pent-up feeling of anger, shame, and desperate passion that I endured. As I came off the stage, ending the third act of *Richard*, in passing by [theatre manager] Bunn's door I opened it, and unfortunately he was there. I could not contain myself; I exclaimed: 'You damned scoundrel! How dare you use me in this manner?' And going up to him as he sat on the other side of the table, I struck him as he rose a back-handed slap across the face. I did not hear what he said, but I dug my fist into him as effectively as I could; he caught hold of me, and got at one time the little finger of my left hand in his mouth, and bit it. I exclaimed: 'You rascal! Would you bite?' He shouted out: 'Murder! Murder!' and, after some little time, several persons came into the room. I was then upon the sofa, the struggle having brought us right round the table. Willmott, the prompter, said to me: 'Sir, you had better go to your room, you had better go to your room.' I got up accordingly and walked away, whilst he, I believe – for I did not distinctly hear him – was speaking in abuse of me. Dow came into my room, then Forster and young Longman. Wallace soon after, evidently deeply grieved at the occurrence. They talked and I dressed, and we left the theatre together. Wallace and Forster, on Dow leaving us, went home with me, and taking tea, discussed the probable consequences of this most indiscreet, most imprudent, most blameable action. Forster was strongly for attempting to throw Mr Bunn overboard on the score of character, but Wallace manifestly felt, as I felt, that I had descended to his level by raising my hand against him, and that I was personally responsible for so doing. I feel that I am; and, serious and painful as it is, I will do my duty. As I read the above lines, I am still more struck with my own intemperate and unfortunate rashness. I would have gone through my engagement in forbearance and peace, still enduring wrong on wrong, as for six years I have been doing, but my passions mastered me, and I sought to wreak them. No one can more severely condemn my precipitation than myself. No enemy can censure me more harshily, no friend lament more deeply my forgetfulness of all I ought to have thought upon. My character will suffer for descending so low, and the newspapers will make themselves profit of my folly. Words cannot express the contrition I feel, the shame I endure . . .

[In the lawsuit that followed, Bunn was awarded damages of £150]

Charles Macready

1937 [Corfu]

It is April and we have taken an old fisherman's house in the extreme north of the island – Kalamai. Ten sea-miles from the town, and some thirty kilometres by road, it offers all the charms of seclusion. A white house set like a dice on a rock already venerable with the scars of wind and water. The hill runs clear up into the sky behind it, so that the cypresses and olives overhang this room in which I sit and write. We are upon a bare promontory with its beautiful clean surface of metamorphic stone covered in olive and ilex: in the shape of a *mons pubis*. This is become our unregretted home. A world. Corcyra.

Lawrence Durrell

1942 [Holland]

I am so glad that he is a Jew and I am a Jewess. And I shall do what I can to remain with him so that we get through these times together. And I shall tell him this evening: I am not really frightened of anything, I feel so strong; it matters little whether you have to sleep on a hard floor, or whether you are only allowed to walk through certain specified streets, and so on – these are all minor vexations, so insignificant compared with the infinite riches and possibilities we carry within us. We must guard these and remain true to them and keep faith with them.

I once quietly bemoaned the fact that there is so little space for our physical love in your two small rooms, and no chance of going elsewhere because of all those notices and prohibitions. And now it seems a veritable paradise of promise and freedom; your little rooms, your small table lamps, my lilac soap, and your gentle caressing hands. God knows how much that means to our relationship, to all that may lie in store for us. Not that I worry unduly about the future. You can't tell how things will turn out in the long run, and so I don't bother too much about it. But if things are to be harder for us, I am quite ready to bear it.

Etty Hillesum

1980

Letter today from a Friend of the [Royal] Academy:

'Dear President, Are your chandeliers by any chance made of soup?
Yours sincerely, . . .'

Stung, I go on to the landing and look. He's right and we arrange to remove them for cleaning. Amazing for how long one can fail to notice sluttery in one's own house. Usually it comes to the surface when you are trying to sell it. 'Is this your *living* room,' potential buyers ask incredulously, as they gaze at the chipped paint, torn paper and book-laden window-sills.

Sir Hugh Casson

30 April

1841

Where shall we look for standard English but to the words of any man who has a depth of feeling in him? Not in any smooth and leisurely essay. From the gentlemanly windows of the country-seat no sincere eyes are directed upon nature, but from the peasant's horn windows a true glance and greeting occasionally. 'For summer being ended, all things,' said the Pilgrim, 'stood in appearance with a weather-beaten face, and the whole country full of woods and thickets represented a wild and savage hue.' Compare this with the agricultural report.

H. D. Thoreau

1870

This evening being May Eve I ought to have put some birch and wittan (mountain ash) over the door to keep out the 'old witch'. But I was too lazy to go out and get it. Let us hope the old witch will not come in during the night. The young witches are welcome.

Rev. Francis Kilvert

1925

Talking (or being talked to) by Clifford Sharp after my club dinner, I put out one of my modest antennae in search of reassurance about the art of keeping a journal. But the editor of the *New Statesman* pooh-poohed the idea of any modern diary being important as literature. 'Pepys is the only existing masterpiece; there *are* no other diaries. And Pepys is great because he was that rarest thing, a man who could write and was at the same time a simple-minded man.' This rather dashed me, though he doesn't know that I am a diarist, and is probably unaware that I am somewhat simple-minded. I'd merely suggested that a modern diary might be more interesting to posterity than most modern novels.

Siegfried Sassoon

1945 [San Francisco]

Miss Smithson, my secretary, says that agencies – the hotel authorities? or F.B.I.? – have put up a small photograph of me in the women's washroom with printed underneath, 'Avoid contact with the above person who is suffering from a contagious disease.' This will cramp my style in personal and diplomatic contacts.

Charles Ritchie

MAY

*'Why has my motley diary no jokes? Because it is
a soliloquy and every man is grave alone.'*

RALPH WALDO EMERSON

1 May

1939

Bobby Lewis said [William] Saroyan's egotism came from his grandmother. An Armenian, she settled in Fresno, California and remained thoroughly Armenian all her days. Commenting on her next-door neighbour she said, 'She is so stupid. Think of it. She has lived next door to me for 28 years and still can't speak a word of Armenian.'

He wrote a play about two people which he hoped the Group [Theatre] would produce. Saroyan, his hero, is in bed onstage with a woman, in darkness. On screen behind them are pictures of waves breaking.

'You're the best lay I ever had,' said the prostitute.

'Not only that,' he answers, 'but I'm the best writer you ever had.'

After a silence, one enormous wave sweeps all the others and the screen blacks out. Lights go on as woman gets up naked and crosses stage to bathroom. 'The greatest play ever written,' says Saroyan.

Dawn Powell

1944 [Cairo]

If only we could leave this place. I'm having far too much fun here. All my days to myself and far too much time to indulge. Everything is out of proportion in this climate and conditions warp all views. I despise myself to my depths. I suppose it's because I'm quite unused to attention that when it comes it takes me breath away a bit. Most girls have their whirls at eighteen or so. I never did and now I don't quite get it. Bad at doing things lightly and I'm muddled and unhappy and long to get away home. Still no planes coming in or out to Cairo. It looked as if we would get off tonight but a khamsin blew all yesterday and nothing was able to land.

On Friday dined with large party including Joan and Aly Khan. I did some monologues and sang, and later we turned on the gramophone and danced on the balcony. It was cool out there and starry. Long session with the follower [Aly Khan] in which I tried to make myself clear. Can't deny I'm not enjoying it. Whirls are fun and the ego swells visibly. But it's all out of proportion and as such wrong. *It* thinks this is *the* great thing; even took *it*self to really believe it. Suppose *it* never had the chance with that upbringing and limitless resources. Entirely despise character and cruelty and goings-on, but I *like* the creature and can see there has been something there that might once have amounted to something. But swamped with self and indulgence and piracy. Hasn't any idea about reality. Can't fathom me but intrigued by what *it* can't understand. Lives entirely in the minute, completely selfishly without a thought for anyone else. Or am I wrong? Next morning dozens of heavenly roses. Can't deny I don't enjoy the whole thing. Must tell Reggie [her husband]. But it is all wrong even so and I'm surprised at myself for getting so swep' up. Things seem to matter so little out here. Vision gets blurred by the sun and it is all so easy and wallowing and far, far away and I feel adrift and very odd.

Joyce Grenfell

1945

This morning's papers contained horrible photographs of Mussolini and his young mistress hanging upside down from the top of a garage in a Milan Square.

Churchill in House said he would announce end of war when it came. But at 10.30 Mrs Burdett rang me to say programme had been interrupted to announce death of Hitler & appointment of Admiral Doenitz as his successor. Heard this at midnight. Three world-figures gone in 3 weeks is too much to take in.

Vera Brittain

1958

It is hard to imagine, considering the inherent silliness, cruelty and superstition of the human race, how it has contrived to last as long as it has. The witch-hunting, the torturing, the gullibility, the massacres, the intolerance, the wild futility of human behaviour over the centuries is hardly credible. And the laws, as they stand today, are almost inconceivably stupid. With all this brilliant scientific knowledge of atom splitting and nuclear physics, etc., we are *still* worshipping at different shrines, imprisoning homosexuals, imposing unnecessary and completely irrelevant restrictions on each other. Hearts can be withdrawn from human breasts, dead hearts, and, after a little neat manipulation, popped back again as good as new. The skies can be conquered. Sputniks can whizz round and round the globe and be controlled and guided. People are still genuflecting before crucifixes and Virgin Marys, still persecuting other people for being coloured or Jewish or in some way different from what they apparently should be. There are wars being waged at this very moment in Indonesia, Algeria, the Middle East, Cyprus, etc. The Pope still makes pronouncements against birth control. The Ku-Klux-Klan is still, if permitted, ready to dash out and do some light lynching. God, for millions of people, is still secure in his heaven, and *My Fair Lady* opened in London last night.

Noël Coward

2 May

1933

When one can no longer give free play to one's limbs the actions of others are followed with a more than normal intensity – so that one may enjoy movement vicariously, so to speak. Being a man, it is the movements of women which have gained in attractiveness – so that to watch either Bella or Gladys hanging out clothes becomes an entertainment not without its so-called sex-appeal. It is but natural that an unnatural mode of life tends to proliferate through all one's being – and there is the grave danger of becoming sensually unbalanced. I know this danger only too well, for I am blessed – or cursed – with a full-blooded virility which is incompatible with my stagnant bodily state.

William Soutar

1945

They've announced on Hamburg radio that Hitler is dead! Berlin has surrendered to the Russians.

As soon as we came off watch we all piled into cars and set out for the nearest pub, with Oscar, Pandora and I crammed into Dizzy's car.

When we had drunk so many toasts that we could hardly stand, someone took over the piano and we sang till closing time. The whole pub turned out to shout goodbye. The ride home was a nightmare – we went tearing through the night, whooping and singing, with screeching brakes and screaming horns. Then three times round the WAAF Mess, howling like wolves – according to custom – and when we reached the RAF Mess we found it practically ablaze.

Some types had got hold of 'Fodo', the stuff they use to clear fog, and had lit it all over the bars. They were dancing round it, wearing huge negro masks from the Xmas pantomime, and waving broomsticks – a fantastic sight!

We spotted Gussy and Vlady sitting entwined in the dark of the Ladies' Room with a bottle of vodka between them listening to the Warsaw Concerto – all very romantic. Dizzy put on the most hideous mask he could find and jumped on them from behind – terrible screams!

Then the rest of the drunken horde rushed in, somebody got the piano and we did all sorts of crazy dances. Dizzy is a wizard dancer, he leaps all over the floor like a cat. At midnight we all went over to the WAAF Mess for sausages and tea in the kitchen.

Joan Wyndham

1945

One feels Hitler's death is just rather pointless now. He should have died some time ago. I wonder how many people comfort themselves with thinking he's frizzling. The Italian news is grand, I wonder if they'll go on over the Brenner. I know this part of Austria where the fighting is, pretty well, the Voralberg pass, the Innthal, all so magic and lovely. I wonder what's happening in Denmark.

Naomi Mitchison

1997

I wake up to a different world. I very rarely watch TV over breakfast, but this morning I feel obliged to turn it on to catch the pictures of last night's events – the ones I slept through. I am amazed, stunned by the cheering crowds who lined the streets in the middle of the night. It doesn't resemble an election victory so much as a liberation, and Tony and Cherie Blair greet the crowd like conquering heroes. Whichever way you lean politically, there is no ignoring the strength of feeling which lies behind this. The people have spoken, and they've opted for change.

I spend longer than usual getting up and making my tea, and then it dawns on me that I'm inventing delays because I don't want to go out. I feel as if the landscape will have shifted in some way, and when a friend calls, I ask if it's safe to leave the house. It seems that where there is so much passion and strength of feeling in the air, there must surely be some physical manifestation to demonstrate it. Perhaps the speed limits will have altered, or Tony Blair's head will be on the currency. Something radical must have changed. I brave it, and go out to buy the papers, intrigued to read the detailed dissection of the election results. And nothing out there has changed, except the weather. It's glorious and will undoubtedly be taken by those who believe in such things as a good omen. People are smiling a bit more than usual, I find. But when the newsagent asks one of his regulars what she thinks about the new government, she simply replies, 'I don't like politicians.'

Deborah Bull

3 May

1787

Dined at home: and though I ate only some minced veal, some spinach, and eggs, in moderate quantity, felt myself greatly oppressed, so as to afford a strong instance in confirmation of the opinion, that a solitary dinner, for whatever reason, does not so soon pass away as one ate in company. The reason first occurring would be, that for a dinner ate in company some time was taken; but the fact does not seem to correspond; or I have made, if I am not mistaken, as many intervals in dining alone, and have yet found that digestion does not take place so quickly. Besides the effect that company may have on the mind, much, I apprehend, is to be ascribed to the action given to the lungs and stomach by talking.

William Windham

1943

The prisoners of war have arrived – fifty of them, all from the camp at Laterina, near Arezzo. As far as public feeling is concerned, they could hardly have come at a worse moment. The memory of [the bombing by Allied aircraft of] Grosseto is still fresh, and the keepers' wives who live in the same building (an old castle half a mile from us) are prepared to barricade themselves in.

Very quickly, however, these fears were dispelled. Antonio met the men at Chianciano station, helped them to get their kit loaded into our ox-carts, and started them on their twenty-mile tramp to the castle. He soon discovered that the Italian officer who is in charge of them is himself married to an Englishwomen, and is a bank-clerk who used to work in Threadneedle Street – and one of the prisoners, a Guardsman, has a Maltese wife. By the time they reached the castle the most cordial relations were established, and on arrival the men were delighted with their quarters: two large rooms on the ground floor of the castle, giving on the court, another big room (once the stables), a dining-room, a kitchen and a wash-room, with twelve basins and two showers – all freshly whitewashed and perfectly clean, if primitive. The thick walls of the castle, with high, barred windows, are a sufficient safeguard against any attempts to escape – and indeed, one of the prisoners, as he saw Antonio testing one of the bars, with the carpenter, remarked humorously, 'If you're doing that for me, sir, don't bother!' Beds for the prisoners (double-tiered bunks, with straw-filled sacks for mattresses) are provided by the Italian Army – also the cooking utensils, and the prisoners' food. An Italian lieutenant is in charge, with a guard of ten men (mostly very small Sicilians), and the prisoners are represented by their corporal – a stolid Yorkshireman named Trott, gardener, we soon discovered, to the Earl of Durham!

Iris Origo

1975

I have bought for fifty pence a rubber stamp, and having arranged the letters I put on the backs of envelopes 'Down with the Marxists'. The stamp looks just like those tiresome advertisement scrawls with which the Post Office disfigures postcards sent to one, so that one cannot read the text.

James Lees-Milne

4 May

1913 [Prague]

Always the image of a pork butcher's broad knife that quickly and with mechanical regularity chops into me from the side and cuts off very thin slices which fly off almost like shavings because of the speed of the action.

Franz Kafka

1926

To-day was the first day of the general strike. Many more motors about. I walked round to Victoria, which was shut up (both stations) one small entrance guarded by policemen. I heard someone say that a train had gone somewhere during the morning. Yet in the vast empty station Smith's bookstalls were open. So were (outside) the cafés. The populace excited and cheery, on this 1st day of the strike. No evening paper. News from the Wireless at very short intervals, 1/2 hour intervals at night up to midnight. I should think that nearly all theatres would soon be closed. Already to-day there has been a noticeably increasing gravity in the general demeanour.

Arnold Bennett

1938

I shall not record a chronicle of the Führer's stay, as it is amply reported in the press. I shall confine myself to a few unpublished incidents and conversations and impressions.

The first thing is of a domestic nature. The Court [of King Victor Emmanuel III] has absolutely declined to retire into the background and has shown itself to be a useless encumbrance.

When the Führer arrived, the populace was greatly disappointed to see that the founder of Italy's political power was not by his side in the triumphal progress through the imperial streets, which owe their conception and their realization to him. The Germans probably felt it as much a we did. At Naples too there was some sort of unpleasant incident, due to the incompetence of those in charge of the ceremony. The whole atmosphere is moth-eaten – a dynasty a thousand years old does not like the manner of self-expression of a revolutionary régime. To a Hitler, who to them is nothing but a *parvenu*, they prefer any paltry little king, of Greece or Denmark even, with a crown on his head and some indeterminate number of quarterings.

When Ribbentrop told me of the incidents, I made him speak to the Duce. The Duce said: 'Tell the Führer to exercise patience. I have been exercising patience for sixteen years . . .' Ribbentrop replied that the one good thing the Social Democrats did in Germany was to liquidate the monarchy for ever.

The military parades have been magnificent. The Germans, who may have been a little sceptical on this point, will leave with a very different impression.

Count Ciano

1939

Drafted telegram to [Sir Charles] Hambro giving assurance that we should hang on to Northern Norway. To Foreign Office at 5.30. Found 20 boxes [of documents]! Got through as much as I could. Home by 8. Dined and worked. Planning conquest of Iceland for next week. Shall probably be too late! Saw several broods of ducklings.

Sir Alexander Cadogan

1942 [Holland]

We're all wearing our stars. I can't stop laughing – I can't help it. It's such a hoot, this star business. You hear the most ridiculous stories, and the jokes are making the rounds faster than the rumours. The people wearing stars are greeted warmly by strangers, people take their hats off to you in the street, make all sorts of comments like 'Keep your chin up' – it's wonderful. Today apparently even a German soldier greeted Father. I had sewn mine on my scarf, you are not supposed to, but I'll just wait until someone says something about it. Everybody was incredibly nice at the Distribution Office. Someone said to me, 'Why don't you take that silly thing off! Throw it away!' It really is a hoot.

Edith Velmans

1955

I give blood in the crypt of St Martin in the Fields. The donors are all rather ordinary-looking people – the women burdened by shopping baskets. I can imagine (for a novel) a little, frail laden woman saying 'Oh I have given blood' and putting others to shame. My right arm aches so that I can hardly write – is there any connection, I wonder?

Barbara Pym

5 May

1863

Aubryet told us the other day that a little girl in the street had offered him her sister, a child of fourteen. Her job was to breathe on the windows of the carriage so that the police could not see inside.

The Brothers Goncourt

1922

We talked over old times: then of Barfield's fortnight in Italy last vac. He told of how in a restaurant he had a call of nature and after peevishly hunting his phrase book found that the Italian (literally) was 'Where can she make a little water, please?' In answer to this the garçon replied, 'Wherever she likes.'

C. S. Lewis

1937 [Corfu]

The books have arrived by water. Confusion, adjectives, smoke, and the deafening pumping of the wheezy Diesel engine. Then the caique staggered off in the direction of St. Stephano and the Forty Saints, where the crew will gorge themselves on melons and fall asleep in their coarse woollen vests, one on top of the other, like a litter of cats, under the ikon of St. Spiridion of Holy Memory. We are depending upon this daily caique for our provisions.

Lawrence Durrell

1945

I can't recall ever falling asleep in fifty years, save on a few occasions when I was ill or much in my cups, without reading at least half an hour. The theory that the practise is damaging to the eyes seems to me to be buncombe. My eyes, despite some sclerotic changes, are perfectly good at 65. I not only read in bed every night; I also do nearly all my daylight reading lying down. I believe fully in the Chinese maxim that it is foolish to do anything standing up that can be done sitting, or anything sitting that can be done stretched out.

H. L. Mencken

1963

How to invent names for fictitious characters without fear of prosecution? This morning's *Times* has births to Clague, Fimbel, Futty and Prescott-Pickup.

Evelyn Waugh

1991

The treat I had been looking forward to. Lunch with Paul Channon, the son of Chips Channon the great diarist.

Paul told me that his father never read again the pages he had written in his diary, they were just left in manuscript, unedited, untouched, ungone over, even the elementary mistakes once they had been written. They had all been typed since his death. There were stacks of them held in a secure place, millions of words. Often he didn't write them for months at a time and sometimes for years at a time.

Woodrow Wyatt

6 May

1914

My parents seem to have found a beautiful apartment for F[elice Bauer] and me; I ran around for nothing one entire beautiful afternoon. I wonder whether they will lay me in my grave too, after a life made happy by their solicitude.

Franz Kafka

1915

Papers full of *Lusitania*. They think 1,500 have been drowned. It shows vividly how one's standards have altered − in fact, how out of drawing everything is. Very nearly as big a disaster as the *Titanic*, which loomed so large in one's life for months and this is merely an incident, so full has one 'supped of horrors'. It will, however, arouse great rage, and one wonders how America will take it.

Lady Cynthia Asquith

1933 [on the ground after a flight with her husband, Charles Lindbergh]
Clear. 'Look out and see if you can see a house.'

'No, but I can see a telephone line and a road!'

'There's a house − way off there − and there.'

'All right, you can drink all you want now.'

My fingers are splitting with dryness. I comb my hair (how silly the curls seem matted in my neck!) and clean off with cold cream. C. takes the cowl off, finds nuts slipped.

A car comes up – two weathered ranchers and a little boy.

'Have a forced landing?'

'Lindbergh's my name.'

'Well, I swear! My wife has cried over you folks – cried and cried . . . How is the new baby? . . . Oh, this is a pitiful country round here – just desert.'

Ann Morrow Lindbergh

1935 [George V's Silver Jubilee]

I couldn't sleep for excitement and got up at 7.15. I dressed, woke Honor [his wife] and we walked through Green Park to St James's Palace to the Ponsonby's house where a group of friends had collected to watch the procession. The usual people fainting in the heat (Royal weather) . . . guards lining the street, bunting and after a long wait the first procession, and the Speaker (Honor's cousin, Fitzroy) passed at a walking pace in a gorgeous coach. Then came the Prime Ministers of the Dominions, led by Ramsay MacDonald, seated with his daughter, Ishbel. He looked grim and she dowdy. No applause. Then the Lord Chancellor, wig and all; then the minor Royalties – a few cheers. Then masses of troops, magnificent and virile, resplendent in grand uniforms with the sun glistening on their helmets. Then thunderous applause for the royal carriages. The Yorks in a large landau with the two tiny pink children. The Duchess of York was charming and gracious, the baby princesses much interested in the proceedings, and waving. The next landau carried the Kents, that dazzling pair; Princess Marina wore an enormous platter hat, chic, but slightly unsuitable. She was much cheered . . . So it passed. Finally the Prince of Wales smiling his dentist smile and waving to his friends, but he still has his old spell for the crowd. The Norway aunt who was with him looked comic, and then more troops, and suddenly the coach with Their Majesties. All eyes were on the Queen in her white. and silvery splendour. Never has she looked so serene, so regally majestic, even so attractive. She completely eclipsed the King. Suddenly she has become the best-dressed woman in the world.

'Chips' Channon

1939

Vernon and I left New York by Greyhound bus at 7:45 in the morning. The buses are built like streamlined Martian projectiles; they seem designed to destroy everything else on the road. When a new driver comes on board, he brings his nameplate with him, and hangs it up in view of the passengers. 'N. Strauser. Safe. Reliable. Courteous.'

Out through the Holland Tunnel, Jersey City, Newark. The Pulaski Skyway lifts you across the flat brown marshes and drops you into a country of factories, pylons, transformers, gas stations, hot-dog stands, tourist cabins, used tire dumps, milk bars, cemeteries for automobiles or men. The stream of traffic is so swift that it is dangerous to swerve or stop. The road has eaten the landscape. Travel has defeated itself. You can drive at eighty miles an hour and never get anywhere. Any part of the road is like all other parts.

'Folks,' says the driver, 'the next comfort stop is Wilmington. You'll have fifteen minutes.' Everybody must get out while we take in gas. The first rush is to the toilets, where an old man tells me indignantly that the rear seats are hard on the kidneys. Then we line the counter for hot dogs, milk, Coca-Cola.

We cross the Maryland state line. The country begins to come alive. A little town with a leafy street of frame houses. The Minister sitting on his porch under a sign which says 'Marriage Licences,' waiting, like the other tradesmen, for business. The war memorial has two separate columns of names – the white and the colored dead.

We get to Washington at 4:30. We shall stay here several days.

Christopher Isherwood

1945

Last week I would not go to see the Belsen horror-camp pictures. I felt the ones in the paper quite dreadful enough. They were shown again tonight, as 'requested' by someone. I looked in such pity, marvelling how human beings could have clung so to life: the poor survivors must have had both a good constitution and a great will to live. What kept them alive so long before they dropped as pitiful skeletons? Did their minds go first, I wonder, their reasoning, leaving nothing but the shell to perish slowly, like a house left untenanted? Did their pitiful cries and prayers rise into the night to a God who seemed as deaf and pitiless as their cruel jailers?

I've a deep aversion to interference, having suffered from it all my life till recent years. I've always said, 'Let every country govern itself, according to its own ways of thought and living. Let them develop their own way and not have standards forced on them, standards so often governed by commercial or political considerations, rather than their own good. Let them reach out in friendly neighbourliness, rather than "by order" or treaties or pacts.' Now I see it would not do. Germany had that creed, developed to a degree of isolationism. People knew about concentration camps, but nothing could seemingly be done about it. This horror is not just one of war. No power can be left so alone that, behind a veil of secrecy, *anything* can happen.

Nella Last

1974

The Old Vic's Lilian Baylis celebration, *Tribute to the Lady*. The world and his wife were there, and the Queen Mum. I had to play the courtier. But she is very funny, and well informed about the theatre.

I reminded her of an occasion in 1959 or 1960 but not in much detail. The story is this. She came to open the new BBC Television Centre at Shepherd's Bush and, as part of the programme that was being televised in her presence, Ralph Richardson, Arnold Wesker, and I had a discussion on whether or not we should have a National Theatre. Before we began Ralph had produced an ageing newsclip from his pocket and told me it was 'the speech that Her Majesty had made' when she had laid the foundation stone in the early fifties for the National Theatre. He asked me if I, as chairman of the discussion, would give him the cue that he could read it out. I said I would, making a mental note to do no such thing. It was rather purple palace-ese.

We had our discussion. I wound up speedily, giving Ralph no chance to read the Queen Mum's speech. We then lined up to be presented. While we were waiting he told me how disappointed he was that I had not given him his cue. I muttered that it had not seemed appropriate.

When, though, the Queen Mum talked to Ralph, she mused, 'I wonder if we shall ever have a National Theatre?' 'Ah, Ma'am,' said he, 'I still remember with pleasure that fine speech you made when you laid the foundation stone. I remember every word of it.'

'Do you really?' said the Queen Mum. 'Can you say some of it for me now?'

Ralph made noises like an expiring fish. He could hardly pull his newsclip out of his pocket. Then, superb actor that he is, he began to make it up. It was much better than the original. He rolled out fine phrases about the National being a sounding-board of English drama for generations to come etc. The Queen Mum looked pleased. 'Ah yes,' she said, 'it's coming back to me.'

Ralph looked at me sheepishly afterwards. 'That was a close one, cocky,' he said.

Peter Hall

7 May

1919

P.M. [Lloyd George] went down to Versailles to present the Peace terms to the German delegates – a most beautiful spring day. I do not think D. realised before he went what an exciting event it would be, but he came back quite exhausted with emotion – ill, in fact, & it was some time before he became himself again. The Germans were very arrogant & insolent, & [the German foreign minister, the Graf von] Brockdorff-Rantzau did not even stand up to make his speech [it was later explained that when he was suffering from emotion his legs became powerless]. This infuriated the allied delegates, & Hughes got up in a passion & came to the P.M. & said: 'Is Clemenceau going to allow this fellow to go on like this?' D. said that he felt he could get up & hit him, & he had the greatest difficulty in sitting still. He says it has made him more angry than any incident of the war, & if the Germans do not sign, he will have no mercy on them. He says for the first time he has felt the same hatred for them that the French feel. I am rather glad that they have stirred him up, so that he may keep stern with them to the very end. If they had been submissive & cowed he might have been sorry for them.

Frances Stevenson

1931

I might as well be a hypochondriac, although I'd never be a good enough one to even think up all the things the matter with me – teeth, sinus trouble, tonsils, rheumatism, tumour, ovarian cysts, and dandruff. I want to get away. I *have* to get away if any pieces are to be saved.

Dawn Powell

1938

The Führer has had a greater personal success than I had expected. Considering that he arrived in the midst of general hostility and was only imposed by the will of Mussolini, he has succeeded pretty well in melting the ice around him. His speech of last night helped a lot. His personal contacts too have won him sympathy. Particularly among women.

The King [Victor Emmanuel III] remains as hostile towards him as ever and tries to make out that he is some kind of psycho-physiological degenerate. He told the Duce and me that the first night of his stay at the Palace, at about one in the morning, Hitler asked for a woman. This caused a great commotion. Then it was explained – apparently he can't get to sleep, unless with his own eyes he sees a woman remake his bed. It was difficult to find one, but at last a hotel chambermaid arrived and the problem was solved. Supposing it to be true, it would be interesting and mysterious. But is it true? Or is it rather malice on the part of the King, who also insinuated that Hitler injects himself with stimulants and narcotics?

Count Ciano

8 May

1938

Mussolini believes that Hitler puts rouge on his cheeks in order to hide his pallor.

Count Ciano

1945

When you long with all your heart for someone to love you, a madness grows there that shakes all sense from the trees and the water and the earth. And nothing lives for you, except the long deep bitter want. And this is what everyone feels from birth to death.

Denton Welch

1945 [VE Day]

Later that evening we decided to brave the West End. Mummy and Sid, who both remembered scenes of rape and wild debauchery from World War I, put on the most unseductive clothes they could find, with heavy, man-proof trousers – everything in fact bar a couple of chastity belts.

There was wild excitement in Trafalgar Square, half London seemed to be floodlit – so much unexpected light was quite unreal. There were people dancing like crazy, jumping in the fountains and climbing lamp-posts, and a dull red glow in the sky from bonfires which reminded us of the Blitz.

Most of the pubs seemed to be running out of booze, so I took them both to the York Minster where red wine was flowing in torrents. Behind the bar was Monsieur Berlemont, his magnificent moustache practically standing on end with excitement. We sat at the little round corner table, the same table where I first got drunk with Rupert – it seems like a hundred years ago. A French sailor kissed Mummy and changed hats with her, taking her little brown velvet cap and giving her his with a pom-pom on top. Very embarrassed, she hastily rearranged her hair, pulling it over her ears. She never could stand people seeing her ears, although they are perfectly nice ones.

Sid got squiffy on one pernod – it reminds her of absinthe and her art student days in Paris.

We were all fairly unsteady by the time we left Soho and headed for Piccadilly, fighting our way slowly through the crowds towards Whitehall, where we had heard Churchill was appearing. Everyone was singing the old songs, 'Roll Out the Barrel', 'Bless 'em All', and 'Tipperary', and dancing in circles. At one point I got whirled away into the dance by a group of Polish airmen and I thought I was lost for ever, but managed to keep one eye on the beacon of Sid's bright red hair. As I fought my way back, one of my shoes came off and had to be abandoned.

We linked arms and slowly made our way towards Whitehall – when we got there we were packed like sardines. Everybody was singing 'Why are we waiting?' and 'We want Winnie' – a few people fainted but suddenly all the floodlights came on, sirens wailed and there he was on the balcony making the V sign, just like on *Pathé Gazette*.

He made a wonderful speech but I don't remember very much of it except for the bit where he said, 'Were we downhearted?' and we all yelled, 'No!' Then we sang 'Land of Hope and Glory' and I think we all cried – I certainly did. It was one of the most exciting moments of my life.

Limped home with my stockings in ribbons, the whole sky ringed with searchlights.

Joan Wyndham

1975 [Moscow]

At the Naval Headquarters. The Chief of Naval Staff Admiral Sergeyeef gave me a great welcome and was very cheery; we talked a lot about our respective Navies.

In glancing up at a shelf in his office I saw a model of the POLARIS SUB-MARINE which I recognized immediately as one I had given to the Russian Naval Attaché. I drew his attention to this and told him I had sent it to his predecessor, the Chief of the Naval Staff, in 1958 through the Russian Naval Attaché, as I understood they were keen to know what a POLARIS submarine looked like inside. He also again expressed his great gratitude for this, and the trust I had shown in them by sending it over long before there were any plans available. I suggested he should put a little plaque up indicating that I had given it and he said he would. In fact I am thinking I am going to have a little plaque made and send it to him, as it is historically interesting.

The real truth of the story is really quite interesting. Round about 1958 I was visiting the American Chief of Naval Operations, Admiral Burke, and found he had on his desk quite a good little model of the POLARIS submarine, the side of which could be opened to see all the details of the lay-out. He was very angry and said that it had just been sent to him by a friend who had bought it in the open market at Schwarz's toy shop in New York. He complained bitterly that after all the trouble to keep all the plans absolutely Top Secret, the details had leaked to a toy maker who had the nerve to put a model on sale where everybody could buy it. I asked him if I could have the model, and he said certainly and gave it to me.

When I came back I put it up on my mantelpiece in the First Sea Lord's office. A week later, by chance, the Russian Naval Attaché called, saw the model and asked whether it was that of the POLARIS submarine. I replied it was; would he like to see the inside? He could hardly believe his ears when I offered this, and then I opened the side and he saw the full Top Secret details of the POLARIS submarine lay-out revealed. I asked him if he was interested, and he said he was absolutely thrilled at my showing so much confidence in him to show him this Top Secret model. I asked if he would like to keep it. Again he could hardly believe his ears, but I said it was on condition that he gave it to the Russian Chief of the Naval Staff with my compliments. This he did. Little did the Russian CNS realize that it had been bought in a toy shop, and it still is an object of the greatest interest in the present CNS's office.

Earl Mountbatten of Burma

1976

Henry, my great-nephew, told me that a contemporary of his was travelling in a London bus. A girl got in, so he politely offered her his seat. She slapped his face for his politeness, being Women's Lib. I asked Henry what he would have done in the circumstances. He said, 'Slapped back, to same tune'.

James Lees-Milne

9 May

1872

This morning I conceived the idea of a poem in the style of Tam o'Shanter – the scene to be laid in the ruined Church of Llanbedr Painscastle. Two lovers who had made an assignation in the church-yard to be terrified by seeing through the windows an assembly of devils, ghosts, lawless lovers and murdered children.

Rev. Francis Kilvert

1938

When Goebbels was going through the rooms of the Quirinal, he said, as he passed the throne: 'Keep that gold and velvet object. But put the Duce on it. That chap' – indicating the King – 'is too small . . .'

Count Ciano

1945

So yesterday was Victory Day . . .

Far into the night there was the noise of singing and shouting at the pub and fireworks going off, and in the sky the glimmer of some huge bonfire, or was it the illuminations of London?

Neither of us could sleep, and there were awful thoughts and anxieties in the air − the breaking of something − the splitting apart of an atmosphere that had surrounded us for six years.

Denton Welch

1972

The big news today is of the blockade of North Vietnamese ports by American mines, together with continued bombing by American aircraft of targets in North and South Vietnam. This is obviously a highly dangerous escalation of the war, and is only understandable if regarded from [President Richard] Nixon's personal point of view. American vital interests have little part in the decision. It seems to be assumed that the Russians will not retaliate. Is this a reasonable assumption?

Cecil King

10 May

1671

To Lond: din'd at Mr. Treasurers where dined Monsieur de Gramont and severall French noblemen: and one Bloud [Colonel Blood] that impudent bold fellow, who had not long before attempted to steale the Imperial Crowne it selfe out of the Tower, pretending onely curiositie of seeing the Regalia there, when stabbing (though not mortaly) the keeper of them, he boldly went away with it, thro all the guards, taken onely by the accident of his horses falling. How he came to be pardoned, and even received to favour, not only after this, but severall other exploits almost as daring, both in Ireland and here, I could never come to understand: some believed he became a spie of severall Parties, being well with the Sectaries and Enthusiasts, and did his Majestie services that way, which none alive could so well as he: But it was certainely as the boldest attempt, so the only Treason of this nature that was ever pardon'd: The Man had not onely a daring but a vilanous un-mercifull looke, a false Countenance, but very well spoken, and dangerously insinuating.

John Evelyn

1864

Near Covent Garden this afternoon I met Charles Dickens, walking along alone and unnoticed. A man of middle height, of somewhat slight frame, of light step and jaunty air; clad in spruce frockcoat, buttoned to show his good and still youthful figure; and with brand new hat airily cocked on one side, and stick poised in his hand. A man of sanguine complexion, deeply lined &

scantly bearded face, and countenance alert and observant, scornful somewhat and sour; with a look of fretfulness, vanity; which might however be due to the gait and the costume.

Thus he passed before me, and thus, in superficial casual view, I judged of him. Anyhow, how unlike the tall massive frame, the slow gentle ways, the grave sad self-absorbed look, of Thackeray!

Arthur F. Munby

1939

Lunched at the Ritz in the Edwardian Louis Quinze dining-room. The women in feathered and flowered straw hats seem pre-last-war. It was like the opening chapter of an old-fashioned society novel. The London season seems unrealistic in the face of anti-gas precautions and evacuation orders. Snobbery must indeed be a lusty plant that grows even on the edge of the precipice.

Charles Ritchie

1940

Today Germany invaded Holland and Belgium. It may be a good thing to put down how one felt before one forgets it. Of course the first feeling was the usual horror and disgust and the impossibility of finding words to describe this latest *Schweinerei* by the Germans. Then came the realisation that the war was coming a lot nearer to us – air bases in Holland and Belgium would make raids on England a certainty. People one met were either gloomy (Mr Beauclerk, the electrician, and Mr Cobb, the wireless shop), slightly hysterical (Miss Bloomer) or just plainly calm like Steele. I think I was rather frightened, but hope I didn't show it, and anyway one still has the 'it couldn't happen to us' feeling. Then there is the very real, but impotent, feeling of sympathy for these poor wretches who are the latest victims. In the news the Dutch and Belgian Ministers spoke and the Dutch Minister sent a greeting to his wife and children and grandchildren. Then it was the most difficult thing to control oneself, and I know that if I had been alone I couldn't have done. Later came the news of Mr Chamberlain's resignations and his speech, in that voice which brings back so many memories mostly of crisis. But even if he has failed, and we can't be sure yet that he has, there is no more courageous man in the government or indeed anywhere, I'm sure of that. But Winston Churchill will be better for this war – as Hilary [her sister] said, he is such an old beast! The Germans loathe and fear him and I believe he can do it.

It was odd to remember that this day used to be a great anniversary for me. Seven years ago, on May 10th 1933, I first went out with Henry. Imagine a lovely summer evening at the Trout with the wisteria out and the soft murmuring of the water. And my heart so full of everything. And now, emotion recollected in tranquillity . . . dust and ashes, dry bones. Or are they not so dry as all that? I don't suppose I shall ever know.

Barbara Pym

1942 [Jersey]

Tonight, we all listened to Mr Churchill's speech – it was one of the most encouraging he has made and we felt cheered and began to hope that the war and this Occupation might end this year. There were 16 of us in the breakfast-room listening-in. I wonder what the Germans would have said if they had seen us, smiling at our Prime Minister's remarks!

Nan Le Ruez

11 May

1654

I now observed how the Women began to paint themselves, formerly a most ignominious thing, and used only by prostitutes.

John Evelyn

1761

I took my leave of Edinburgh for the present. The situation of the city, on a hill shelving down on both sides, as well as to the east, with the stately castle upon a craggy rock on the west is inexpressibly fine. And the main street, so broad and finely paved, with the lofty houses on either hand (many of them seven or eight storeys high), is far beyond any in Great Britain. But how can it be suffered, that all manner of filth should still be thrown even into this street continually? Where are the Magistracy, the Gentry, the Nobility of the land? Have they no concern for the honour of their nation? How long shall the capital city of Scotland, yea, and the chief street of it, stink worse than a common sewer? Will no lover of his country, or of decency and common sense, find a remedy for this?

John Wesley

1940

I'll probably never execute my old plan to do a model funeral service for agnostics, admittedly damned. I am now too near my own need for it to give it the proper lightness of touch. Some day somebody else will do one. It is really amazing that none has ever been drawn up. An agnostic's funeral, as things stand, consists mainly of idiotic speeches – that is, when there is any ceremony at all.

H. L. Mencken

1989

The People has a lurid article: *Movie Boss With AIDS – Glad to die in a shack!* What people do to sell newspapers! I don't know how they can live with their consciences – though, of course, out of use so long, they have shrivelled to the size of an appendix.

Derek Jarman

1995

I have to travel to New York for the Ireland America Award. The Irish American Foundation have set up a marquee in Central Park where one of those large charity dinners is held. Tony O'Reilly hosts it, all sorts of Irish-American billionaires there. This is the other side of the coin to Noraid I suppose. They go to opera rather than movies, breed horses, know the country through its stud farms. I sit with Mr O'Reilly and his charming wife throughout dinner and can't bring myself to mention the fact that I am suing his newspaper, the *Sunday Independent*, for libel.

Neil Jordan

12 May

1663

After dinner Pembleton [dancing-master] came, and I practised.

Samuel Pepys

1849 [New York]

Last night passed off intolerably quietly, owing to the measures taken by the magistrates and police. But it is consolatory to know that law and order have thus far prevailed. The city authorities have acted nobly. The whole military force was under arms all night, and a detachment of United States troops was also held in reserve. All the approaches to the Opera House were strictly guarded, and no transit permitted. The police force, with the addition of a thousand special constables, were employed in every post of danger; and although the lesson had been dearly bought, it is of great value, inasmuch as the fact has been established that law and order can be maintained under a Republican form of government.

Philip Hone

1932 [Berlin]

[Theodor] Plievier and [Wieland] Herzfelde, talking about the distress prevailing in the working quarters of Berlin, mentioned a fact of which I was unaware. Some twenty to thirty thousand waifs, aged between eleven and fifteen, live there in packs of fully organised small gangs to which admission is possible only after very complicated induction ceremonies, in part of a sadistic sort. The head of the gang is called 'The Bull', if he is a boy, or 'The Cow', if a girl. They are utterly amoral, prepared to commit any crime whatever, and are to a considerable extent syphilitic and cocaine addicts.

Count Harry Kessler

1935 [Bombay]

In the afternoon I went with Hydari to the cinema to see *Chu Chin Chow*. Films reflect national characteristics. Hydari represents just about the Chu Chin Chow stage in English life – that is, the latter part of the war. His humour is of that period. Going to England for their education has the same effect on most Indians as Oxford and Cambridge on most Englishmen – it arrests their development, they are so exhilarated at finding themselves fellow citizens with the race that has conquered them that they stabilize their lives then and there. Hydari is the sort of man who says: 'I like a joke but that was going too far,' or: 'If a man can get his greens without hurting anyone – I bar home-breakers – good luck to him. I've nothing to say against it . . .' a sort of censorious tolerance.

Malcolm Muggeridge

1937

The Coronation [of George VI]. I go to see Ramsay MacDonald for a moment and find him sitting in his room punching a hole in his sword-belt and looking very distinguished in a Trinity House uniform. I tell him how well he looks. 'Yes,' he answers, 'when I was a visitor to a lunatic asylum I always noticed how well the worst lunatics looked.'

Harold Nicolson

13 May

1941

Appalling news comes in the evening. [Rudolf] Hess, against the Führer's orders, has taken off in a plane and has been missing since Saturday. We must presume him dead. His adjutants, who were the only ones aware of his intentions, have been arrested on the Führer's orders. The Führer's statement gives delusions as the reason for his action, some madness to do with illusionary peace-feelers. The entire affair is thoroughly confused at the moment. We are forced to issue the statement immediately. A hard, almost unbearable blow. At the moment it is impossible to see where the affair will lead.

I receive a telephone call from the Berghof [Hitler's chalet at Berchtergaden]. The Führer is quite shattered. What a sight for the world's eyes: the Führer's deputy a mentally disturbed man. Dreadful and unthinkable. Now we shall have to grit our teeth.

And above all we shall have to try to shed some light on this totally mysterious affair. At the moment I can think of no way out. But one will be found. I instruct the press and radio to merely report it, without comment. And then wait for the reaction. London will soon have her say. And we shall not be short of a reply.

Hess toyed with the idea of a possible peace. It seems that he had become too remote from the day-to-day struggle and had turned soft. This business is going to be hard to see through. I immediately have shots of him removed from the latest newsreel. Reuter is still quiet. But the storm will, of course, break during the next few hours. I am besieged by telephone calls from all sides, Gauleiters, Reichsleiters, etc. No one wants to believe this madness. It sounds so absurd that it is hard not to dismiss it as a fabrication. The Führer orders that Hess's work in the Party Chancellery be continued as normal. I must go the Obersalzberg. There I shall hear more details. Nothing can be said on the telephone.

Josef Goebbels

1941

The milkman says that Hess has come down in Glasgow with a sprained ankle by parachute! He says it was in the midnight news. . .

And after all it was! We all yelled with surprise when it really was true, and what a lovely story, the hay fork and the cup of tea and everything. Wonder what they'll do with him and how useful he can be made.

Naomi Mitchison

1945

When all seems rubbish that you wrote, in this and all your other books – when you have nothing good to show yourself, to give yourself a feeling of delight. What can you do but plough on through thick mud?

Denton Welch

1997

Darcey Bussell [ballerina] was on her way this afternoon to Madame Tussaud's for another session with the scuptor whose job it is to recreate her in wax.

She told me she had asked at the last session how long waxworks remain on display, and was told that it generally depends on how long the subject remains in the limelight. So presumably they've already moved John Major into storage. We had to laugh. Not only do you see yourself replaced on the cast sheet by someone younger, better, more glamorous, but you are melted down, only to be recast in their image. That must be the ultimate indignity.

Deborah Bull

14 May

1929

I was waiting with Dorothy Bussy, on the edge of the road, for the train that was to take us up to Menton. Not far away three strangers, a man and two women, were also waiting. (Foreigners, certainly, and tourists.) The man with already white hair, the women noticeably younger; all three of them thick, meaty, with a hoarse, loud way of talking. I should probably not have been able to recognize right away that they were Dutch. 'What vulgarity!' Mme Bussy said to me. 'And to think that you took them for English! Just see them eat!' And in fact from a huge shopping-basket they take out food that they begin gluttonously to stuff themselves with. – 'And, to begin with, nothing is so unpleasant to me as to see other people eating when I am not eating myself.' Since we have just got up from the table, I offer her a stick of chewing gum, which she refuses. Ah! now they have reached the effusions; one of the two women has embraced the man, who seems to be fainting and whom she covers with kisses; her clucking made me turn round; 'Gustave! . . . Gustave . . . Oh! . . .' But, to our great surprise, we see the man decrease, melt, slip slowly from the arms of his wife, who goes on stammering ever more frantically; 'Gustave! Gustave!'

And now the man is on the ground, having probably suffered a stroke, his eyeballs turned in their sockets, and his mouth gaping. We hasten to help him up, to seat him on the wall of the road, or better on a chair, which the tavern-keeper's wife brings on the run. The tavern-keeper is following her, offering cognac, vinegar, and spirits of mint; my companion holds out a glass of water. And at first I am angry to see the Dutch wife, while she is caring for her husband, not give up a half-eaten strawberry or cherry tart that she was doubtless in the act of eating, when suddenly, seeing the object more closely, I realise that it is a set of false teeth that slipped out of her husband's mouth at the moment of his fall, which she is now trying to put back in place without being noticed, turning her back to the public through a sense of decency, sheltering herself and sheltering him as best she can. Poor good people who now seem to me so pitiable! How could I have been so mistaken about them at first! Let us be careful of such unsympathetic judgements: one runs the risk of taking dental plates for tarts . . .

André Gide

1941

Yesterday: Another crazy day. The wild alarums and rumours start at first thing in the morning. Total chaos. Everything from high treason to peace-offers. Meanwhile, clarity at last: Hess has landed by parachute in Scotland. Let his plane crash and sprained his ankle in the fall. Then he was found by a farmer and later arrested by the Home Guard. A tragi-comedy. One doesn't know whether to laugh or cry.

Josef Goebbels

1945 [Berlin]

Something dreadful – or eerie is going on all around us. Every house door is locked. You can't visit your friends because no one opens to a knock. If you're lucky you run into someone you want to visit on his way home, and after a brief exchange he quickly slips behind the door, which is instantly locked behind him. Why? Because everyone is afraid of Russian soldiers, who try to force their way into homes at every opportunity. Granted, many of them are harmless, but many aren't, and those that just rob you aren't the worst. Above all people are afraid, and rightly so, that they'll rape the girls and women in the house. I wish I could prove that the people who tell stories about these sorts of rapes are liars. But I can't!

John Rabe

1952

A little stirring of sex today. Not much. It occurs to me that, of all the sensual pleasures, sex is the only one which depends partly on reciprocation. That's its power. Imagine if an orange said: 'Darling, I was just longing for *you* to eat me. I was so afraid that horrible old man would. He's not at *all* my type.'

Christopher Isherwood

1968

Tonight to the Italian plays at the Aldwych. I sat immediately behind Tony Snowdon, dressed in his white polo-neck jersey, his now auburn-coloured hair dressed in two handsome waves, the perfection of which seemed to preoccupy him very much. After the supper at the Italian Embassy, even though the crowds thinned out, Princess Margaret would not leave. She kept on approaching the door, and just as we were encouraged to think she really was about to take her departure, she suddenly went back into the centre of the room and became engaged in animated conversation – all just to tease and annoy. [Lady] Diana [Cooper] said she remembered staying at Hatfield when Princess Margaret (then unmarried) was there; and how, after dinner, she was adamant in refusing to play or sing, until eventually a move to bed was made, at which she went and sat down at the piano till four o'clock.

Cynthia Gladwyn

1989

I find it difficult to write each day, but if I don't I'm swamped with guilt. Where does the compunction come from?

Perhaps I inherited it from Dad – he could never keep still for a moment; even when reading a newspaper he would tap his foot keeping time to silence. Back and forth I go into the garden, like the boy with anorexia who weighed himself every five minutes. At rest, a nervous pit quickly develops in my stomach and overwhelms me, forcing my mind to change direction.

I'm sleeping better, even have nights when I do not wake. But awake, I have the concentration of a grasshopper. Only the pressure of a film set keeps me focused for a day.

Derek Jarman

15 May

1824

What moves men of genius, or rather, what inspires their work, is not new ideas, but their obsession with the idea that what has already been said is still not enough.

Eugène Delacroix

1925

Two unfavourable reviews of *Mrs. D.* (*Western Mail* and *Scotsman*); unintelligible, not art etc. and a letter from a young man in Earls Court. 'This time you have done it – you have caught life and put it in a book . . .' Please forgive this outburst, but further quotation is unnecessary; and I don't think I should bother to write this if I weren't jangled. What by? The sudden heat, I think, and the racket of life. It is bad for me to see my own photograph.

Virginia Woolf

1939 [on a Greyhound Bus]

Cattle country, undulating, deserted. The cowboys in overalls and half-boots with queerly sinister crooked heels. As it grew dark, lightning flickered along the horizon. A boy and girl got on the bus – both deeply sunburnt and about fifteen years old, going through to California. The boy seemed utterly exhausted and rather lost, but his sister was lively. She flirted precociously with an unpleasant man in a straw hat. There was also a baby, apparently travelling alone. Everybody wanted to take charge of it. In a curious way, the atmosphere of the covered wagon survives. We were all pioneers, on this adventure together.

Christopher Isherwood

1981

A cousin of Elizabeth's, who is happy to style herself a lesbian, had asked me to address her group, a flourishing affair, with at least three hundred members. My subject was 'Outcasts', on which I have spoken and indeed preached to general audiences. I myself have been described as 'the outcasts' outcast', so I suppose that I have a certain standing in the discussion. I told them that when writing a book on St Francis of Assisi I had selected homosexuals, male and female, as an important category of outcasts. I knew more about male homosexuals than lesbian. I was told by my best friend in my house at Eton that 75 per cent of the boys had had homosexual experience. I said I hadn't noticed it, to which he replied, 'That's because you are somewhat unobservant and also rather repressed.'

Lord Longford

16 May

1917

Max [Beaverbrook] told the following last night. He had bought the story from a divorce detective for £50 but dare not use it. A woman consulted a divorce detective about her husband's apparent infidelity, and the 'tec said that before doing anything she had better cease to live with him, as if she lived in the same house she might 'condone' his offence and so endanger a divorce. She said she didn't want a divorce, she was very much in love with her husband, and she only wanted to know who the other woman was.

The 'tec at first refused the case, then took it on. The woman then told the 'tec that her husband was in the habit of going away for week-ends, never saying in advance that he was going to stay away, but always telegraphing that he was detained. One night while he was asleep (after return from a week-end) she went through his pockets and found a letter from a house agent by the seaside to say that he could have possession of a certain house; also a cloak-room ticket, Victoria Station. The ticket was for a smallish bag. The 'tec and the lady went together to Victoria, and got the bag, which was locked. The 'tec pulled apart one side of it, and bloodstained stuff was disclosed. They left the bag at the cloakroom. 'What can this be?' the 'tec in effect asked. 'Nothing,' said the lady. 'My husband goes fishing and he's probably put a wounded fish into an old shirt or something.' And she went on: 'Now, you're in *my* service? You're in nobody else's?' The 'tec agreed and she reiterated the fact and he positively agreed.

Sometime later she rang up the 'tec and said: 'My husband has just left for Victoria in a taxi. You had better watch him there and if necessary follow him.' The 'tec replied: 'Something grave has occurred, and I must ask you to come here to my office at once, and bring a woman friend with you. Most important.' He insisted. She arrived at his office at 6.30. The 'tec said: 'I'm sorry to inform you that your husband was arrested for murder at 5.55 at Victoria.' The lady said: 'You villain. You scoundrel. It is you who have sold him to the police. Yet you swore you were in my service only.' The husband was now of course in prison.

Arnold Bennett

1932

Max Jacob [French poet] came to see us the other evening with a handsome set of false teeth 'which cost eleven thousand francs', said he with pride. They made him look younger, and also more diabolic than ever. He is busy trying to sell some paintings and place an article and some poems. He is very pleased with himself and is still living at the Hôtel Nollet – on credit, so he says, while he waits for the result of the case he brought against the insurance company after his bad motor accident three years ago. The Nollet is expensive; they like artists there, and exploit them. Max paid for his teeth with seven thousand francs, one painting and two drawings. He is seeing a lot of Nathalie Barney and told us in a heavily meaningful way that she had forced 1,700 francs into his hands saying: 'I have heard that you are in want, take this, you can pay me back later.' He had sent her a parcel of his manuscripts.

Liane de Pougy

1944

This afternoon as I went down to the river I saw three children with their hands in a ditch and they were chanting on and on like church-intoning, 'Keep right on to the end of the war, keep right on to the end of the war!' They sang it with such delight. It seemed to be a sort of charm to them.

When they heard me pass, they all looked up and began to giggle guiltily. Then the day before yesterday I found two small boys trying to push an enormous cart up an incline. And I helped them and at last we got it going. The boys had taken their football boots off and were paddling along the road in their socks. They thanked me between sweating groans and smiles and deep breaths.

Yesterday I went to Tunbridge Wells to be X-rayed. Quite an ordeal of lying about with nothing on for over an hour. And the peculiar injection in the arm made my head spin and alarm grow in me. They took many plates of my spine and lower down. All the room was blue, with baby-blue blankets and horrible little glass fishes and china rabbits and bronze dogs and clay horses and woolly birds on the mantelpiece. Also pictures of darling children and little wife. Why *do* doctors always go in for this sort of thing? It was as if they would obtrude their private life on you against your will. One could not miss so many toys and photographs, however blind.

I was so delighted that it was all over that I bought a little old print of 'Pomona, Goddess of Fruit' and a little cut-glass dish. One shilling.

Denton Welch

1952

At rehearsals of [*School for*] *Scandal* today, Guy Verney terribly rude to me on stage, in front of company. 'You may ruin everyone's performance in *Candlelight* but you're not to do it in my production.' Of course I had to reply from the stage, couldn't let it go at that – 'You may criticise my work in your own production,' I said, 'but don't indulge in cheap contumely about my work in *Candlelight*' – I was white with rage. In the evening he apologised and insisted on buying me a drink etc. O! I loathe and abhor the man.

Kenneth Williams

1968

More dressing up, this time to make history. I am the first woman apart from royalty to dine as the Treasurer's guest at the Honourable Society of Gray's Inn. Dingle, my host, has told me I have got to put on my full dibs. Guests are introduced into the dining-hall with almost as much ceremonial as at the Guildhall banquet. Everyone else was in white tie and decorations, the students in the hall in subfusc. So I made quite a stir as I swept in in my green bouffant and my topazes, the successor in guest terms, they tell me, to Queen Elizabeth I and Queen Elizabeth II, and trying to look the role. Having all been lined up at the high table, we were then taken through the centuries-old ceremony of sipping from a goblet of mead and eating a small piece of cake. And of course we had to finish up by circulating the loving cup. What tickles me is how much men adore this kind of ceremonial. They are far more play actors at heart than women are.

Barbara Castle

17 May

1826

Last night Anne [his daughter] after conversing with apparent ease dropd suddenly down as she rose from the supper table and lay six or seven minutes as if dead. [Dr.] Clarkson has no fear of the result of these affects.

Sir Walter Scott

1976

I went to Claridges, where a large Supper Ball was given by EMI to celebrate their Première [of *Aces High*]. I sat between Diana Wellington and Marianna Monckton. Diana said how much they had appreciated my being kind to their daughter, Jane Wellesley, after the papers had been hounding her because Charles [Prince of Wales] had been seen a lot with her.

She was very bitter about the way the press had treated not only Jane but Valerian [Jane's father] and herself about the whole affair. If they had committed some ghastly crime the newspapers could not have persecuted them more. She said the media could kill Charles's chance of having a happy marriage because what young girl could possibly put up with this appalling persecution. Any girl who would accept a proposal in the face of such prospects would surely not be the right one for Charles to marry in any case. So what was he going to do? She thought he was absolutely charming and it certainly wasn't his fault. She wished him luck in finding the right wife, but unless he could in fact meet her quite secretly, without the media knowing about it, she thought the chances of a marriage coming off with the right person would be rather slim.

Earl Mountbatten of Burma

1990

I'm writing this on the train to Truro. We're off for three days' civilised filming. Trewithian, Glendurgan, Mount Edgcumbe. There's a hilarious picture of John Selwyn Gummer [Minister of Agriculture] on the front page of *The Times*: 'Where's the beef? Mr John Gummer pressing a burger on his reluctant daughter Cordelia, aged four, at Ipswich yesterday to underline his message that beef is safe.' Jim Henson and Sammy Davis Jr have died. The joy of a train journey like this is it gives you the time and space to read the obituaries with a clear conscience. Jim Henson is one of my heroes: a true innovator. He gave us the original Fozzie Bear to put on show at the Teddy Bear Museum.

Gyles Brandreth

18 May

1839

On the 4th of April I broke a blood-vessel, and am now dying of consumption, in great suffering, and may not live many weeks. God be merciful to me a sinner.

God be praised for giving me such excellent parents. They are more than any wishes could desire, or than any words can sufficiently praise. Their presence is like sunshine to my illlness.

Emily Shore

1938

What worries me is my lack of elegance. I go to the best hosiers, the best tailors, the best haircutters: I have the most perfect valet in London: I am always washing and scrubbing: my hairwash comes from Floris. Yet, when I mix with the elegant, I feel scrubby. My shirt pops, my tie becomes crooked, my waistcoat bulges, my hair gets deranged, and I look like Lord Aberconway drunk. I suppose it is all a question of shape. If I were concave all these things would fall into, and remain in, place. As it is, they slip off.

These reflections are prompted by the fact that I went to a First Night. Mr Gordon Selfridge was in front of me – how patrician he appeared! Mr Noel Coward was beside me – how young and distinguished he looked! Mr Ernest Thesiger, Mr Charles Graves – all of them looked as if they belonged. I looked like a hippo in Piccadilly. Incongruous I looked, and ill at ease. But it was a well acted play, and I took Sibyl [Colefax] on to the Savoy for supper. There was I and my girl-friend (a peeress, for all they knew) supping at the Savoy. And yet when I said 'Waiter!' it was of no avail. The waiter just fetched a chafing dish and brewed delicious sauces for someone else, while I chafed.

Harold Nicolson

1939

The man who avoids having children because he does not want to support them, will have to support other men's children.

Cesare Pavese

1942 [Holland]

The threat grows ever greater, and terror increases from day to day. I draw prayer round me like a dark protective wall, withdraw inside it as one might into a convent cell and then step outside again, calmer and stronger and more collected again. I can imagine times to come when I shall stay on my knees for days on end waiting until the protective walls are strong enough to prevent my going to pieces altogether, my being lost and utterly devastated.

Etty Hillesum

1943

To-day we learn that the planes dropped some bombs on the airport at Ostia, but not on the town, and flew over Rome (of which every stone must have been distinguishable in the clear moonlight) on their way there and back, dropping numerous leaflets. These are adorned on one side with a large skull and cross-bones, on the other by a map of Italy, showing how easily all the principal Italian cities can be reached by the Allies by air – with an appeal to the Italian people to throw off the Fascist and German yoke before it is too late.

Meanwhile each day and night continue to be of an unequalled indescribable beauty. Never have I seen a more lovely Roman May. The flower stalls are piled high with irises and roses and madonna lilies, the fountains play, the cafés on the side-walk are thronged with pretty young women in summer hats ogling the tight-waisted young men who still, in astonishing numbers, walk up and down the pavements. In the *Giardino del Lago* the children sail their boats and watch the Punch and Judy shows and feed the swans, while an occasional plane swoops overhead. And yet the sense of menace is there. At night the streets, lit only by moonlight or starlight, are of an uncanny beauty – silent and deserted, with no eye to see.

Iris Origo

19 May

1860 [New York]

Thy Nose, O W. H. Seward, is out of joint! The Chicago Convention nominates Lincoln and Hamlin [as Republican presidential candidates]. They will be beat, unless the South perpetrate some special act of idiocy, arrogance, or brutality before next fall.

Lincoln will be strong in the Western states. He is unknown here. The *Tribune* and other papers commend him to popular favor as having had but six months' schooling in his whole life; and because he cut a great many

rails, and worked on a flatboat in early youth; all which is somehow presump-
tive evidence of his statesmanship. The watchword of the campaign is already
indicated. It is to be 'Honest Abe' (our candidate being a namesake of the
Father of the Faithful). Mass-meetings and conventions and committees are
to become enthusiastic and vociferous whenever an orator says Abe. But that
monosyllable does not seem to me likely to prove a word of power. 'Honest
Abe' sounds less efficient than 'Frémont and Jessie,' and that failed four years
ago.

George Templeton Strong

1941

. . . walked up Bond St. to do small amount of shopping & found huge smash
of last Saturday had brought down whole corner of Bond St. & Bruton St.
where Speight's was. Even pedestrians couldn't get through so I turned off
into Savile Row & found most of that gone too. Back into Bond St. via
Conduit St. wh. is also now mostly rubble. Even the most familiar streets are
ceasing to be recognisable; I kept saying to myself: 'What *was* this?' & forgetting what was there. Struck again by the usual incongruity of Western Front
ruin & almost next door beautiful flowers & smart hats in the still standing
Bond St. shops. I thought nothing could be worse than the *acres* of ruin wh.
I passed in the taxi & on the top of the bus coming back from Bow yesterday, but this bit of the West End rivals them. Finally arrived at Spiller's in
Wigmore St. to have my glasses re-screwed, & found that their premises too
had been wrecked at the back by incendiaries & high explosives, & my usual
man & his typist were carrying on behind boarded up doors in a shop wh.
looked as though it were only held together with string. But they took my
glasses for repair. Query: What is the effect on one's mind of constantly
walking about amid the utter ruins of lovely or familiar things?

Vera Brittain

1944

Today as I passed a cottage on my bike a little girl came out of the door
dressed in an old chiffon ball-dress that reached to the ground all round her.
The V of the neck came to her navel almost. She looked at me and gave a
self-conscious touch with her hand to the waist of her dress. Then she touched
her hair at the back, and looked at the other two ordinarily dressed children
that had come out with her, contemptuously.

Further on, by Hartlake Bridge, where my favourite haystack for picnick-
ing is, I found soldiers and lorries. The soldiers were dressing and washing
and changing behind the lorries. One could see pink chests and brown arms
and necks showing from the rings of white singlets. They were laughing and

swearing and shouting, the whole scene extravagantly noisy and male. And one understood so well what was meant by the tradition of the Army. It was something that exaggerated or completely changed the ordinary behaviour of ordinary civilian men.

Denton Welch

1947

At a party I meet several writers and say goodbye to most of my friends. At La Fayette, a restaurant where the marble tables make a sad effort to evoke a French café, I have a brief interview with Dos Passos, whom I knew in Paris. He rarely comes to New York; he lives very quietly in Provincetown in New England, where he is writing a book on the Jeffersonian period. He doesn't think war is imminent. 'I think they will be successful in keeping the conflict localized,' he tells me. 'Perhaps they'll fight in China – China is local, too.'

I go to declare the money I've earned these past four months and to pay the required taxes. In France this operation would have taken days of coming and going. Here, the business is transacted one-on-one, as always, and it's settled in half an hour. The official sitting across from me examines the sheet of paper I've submitted and asks me for my word of honor as verification – nothing more. Then he helps me deduct my expenses: transportation, secretarial help, receptions, hotels, laundry? He's the one who makes all these suggestions with touching enthusiasm. He deplores the fact that the total is not more substantial and that I still have to pay some taxes. Two imprints from the rubber stamp and I'm free to leave America.

Simone de Beauvoir

20 May

1933

Excellent speech by Hitler in the Reichstag. If Hitlerism had never made itself known otherwise, it would be more than merely acceptable. But it remains to be seen where the real face ends and the grimace begins.

André Gide

1934

Church at 8 and 11.30. All my worst thoughts seem to be brought up to the surface on such occasions – like a poultice drawing the poison out of a boil perhaps–!

Barbara Pym

1939

I do not keep a diary for the same reasons an adolescent girl does but because these notes on my remarkable existence may someday be of use.

Wilhelm Reich

1940 [Karkur, Palestine]

Winston Churchill, now Prime Minister, has made another broadcast. It gave us a clear understanding of the gravity of the hour and of his absolute belief in the British people – that we will never surrender. His news was petrifying but I felt braver for his words. Whitaker came up to the bungalow. He, too, had taken courage from Mr Churchill. We had a chat before his bath and he looked over the top of his spectacles and said, 'My Lady, the likes of me believe we will win this war, somehow, someday. I think it would help all our "hesprits du corpses" if you and His Lordship gave a ball in this bungalow – just like they did before Waterloo.' I agreed. When he'd gone back to camp I locked the doors, pulled the curtains and wept till I fell asleep.

Countess of Ranfurly

1940 [Aachen]

This has been a day in my life. To have seen the destruction of war, what guns and bombs do to houses and people in them, to towns, cities, bridges, railroad stations and tracks and trains, to universities and ancient noble buildings, to enemy soldiers, trucks, tanks, and horses caught along the way.

It is not pretty. No, it is not beautiful. Take Louvain, that lovely old university town, burned in 1914 by the Germans in their fury and rebuilt – partly by American aid. A good part of it is a shambles. The great library of the university, rebuilt by the donations of hundreds of American schools and colleges, is completely gutted. I asked a German officer what happened to the books. 'Burned,' he said.

I must have looked a little shocked as I watched the desolation and contemplated this one little blow to learning and culture and much that is decent in European life. The officer added: 'Too bad. A pity. But, my friend, that's war. Look at it.' I did. But it hurt.

William L. Shirer

1983

In the evening I often bike round Regent's Park. Tonight I am mooning along the Inner Circle past Bedford College when a distraught woman dashes out into the road and nearly fetches me off. She and her friend have found themselves locked in and have had to climb over the gate. Her friend, Marie, hasn't made it. And there, laid along the top of one of the five-barred gates, is a plump sixty-year-old lady, one leg either side of the gate, bawling to her friend to hurry up. I climb over and try to assess the situation. 'Good,' says Marie, her cheek pressed against the gate, 'I can see you're of a scientific turn of mind.' Her faith in science rapidly evaporates when I try moving her leg, and she yells with pain. It's at this point that we become aware of an audience. Three Chinese in the regulation rig-out of embassy officials are watching the pantomime, smiling politely and clearly not sure if this is a pastime or a predicament. Eventually they are persuaded to line up on the other side of the gate. I hoist Marie over and she rolls comfortably down into their outstretched arms. Much smiling and bowing.

Marie's friend says, 'All's well that ends well.' Marie says she's laddered both her stockings and I cycle on my way.

Alan Bennett

21 May

1829

This is only the 23 on which I write yet I have forgotten any thing that has passd on the 21st. worthy of [note]. I wrote a good deal I know and dined at home. The step of time is noiseless as it passes over an old man. The *non est tanti* [the feeling that all is worthless] mingles itself with every thing.

Sir Walter Scott

1925

For some reason I am fresh and alert, although today has been exacting, and I slept atrociously last night. I had two vivid 'surface dreams' in which I was in a state of poetic afflatus and quite confident that I was really doing 'the big stuff' at last. The second afflatus concerned a poem about driving a motor-car in a snowstorm, and the only extant line is 'And there the ship lay with her funnel'. Freud would assert that this signified something sexual. But he would be wrong, I think. The line arose from my needing to rhyme 'tunnel'. But perhaps 'tunnel' is sexual too!

Siegfried Sassoon

1941

At Annemarie's [an Aryan friend] in Pirna [near Dresden] for money. With heavy heart – she has not come to see us for two years. Fear? Disloyalty? – But she was completely unaffected, warm, passionately anti . . . She really cannot get away, Dressel is standing in as head of the Heidenau Hospital, all the work of the clinic is on her shoulders, also she has serious heart problems.

(She has an unnaturally thick, swollen head, a constant dry cough.) A number of her remarks encouraged me. 'What are you going to do with the American affidavit? You cannot use it while the war is on, and afterward you won't need it anymore.' – 'I always knew that the war is going to be lost, this absurd underestimation of England!' – 'In the last few weeks ten thousand people have been called up here in Pirna district alone. Everything is being sent east. Russia! And America will come too.' 'Why does the Führer not say a word about the Hess affair? He really *ought* to say something. What excuse will he use – Hess has been sick for years? But then he shouldn't be Hitler's deputy. He flew in a Messerschmitt plane, so high that the anti-aircraft guns could not reach him.' – 'Sonnenstein has long ceased to be the regional mental asylum. The SS is in charge. They have built a special crematorium. Those who are not wanted are taken up in a kind of police van. People here all call it "the whispering coach." Afterward the relatives receive the urn. Recently one family here received two urns at once. – We now have pure Communism. But Communism murders more honestly.'

Victor Klemperer

22 May

1847 [Ireland]

A meeting yesterday which did not end well. The relief now afforded at a great expense is but a mockery – one pound of dry meal a day to adults, half a pound to children without any sort of kitchen; it may keep them alive a few weeks, but in the end a pestilence must ensue; the quantity is not sufficient and the quality is defective. The recipients do nothing for it; it is a present we make to the idle. At present a ton and a half of Indian meal is the consumption, £24 per week.

The people are in a deplorable condition; the willing horses must help them, and 'fear not but trust in providence.' I have a difficulty in supplying ourselves with meat at present, let alone the poor; the meat is up to tenpence and a shilling in the markets; beef not to be had; mutton very scarce. We are to buy another cow and give milk instead of broth in future, except to the sick whom we must nourish with a share of what we have. If an epidemick break out the Colonel [her husband] says he will pack us all off out of the country in a moment. But I must write, write for bread and not for my amusement, so good-bye journal, and let me turn with resolution to my tale.

Elizabeth Grant of Rothiemurchus

1937 [Corfu]

At evening the blue waters of the lagoon invent moonlight and play it back in fountains of crystal on the white rocks and the deep balcony; into the high-ceilinged room where N.'s lazy pleasant paintings stare down from the walls. And invisibly the air (cool as the breath from the heart of a melon) pours over the window-sills and mingles with the scent of the exhausted lamps. It is so still that the voice of a man up there in the dusk under the olives disturbs and quickens one like the voice of conscience itself. Under the glacid surface of the sea fishes are moving like the suggestion of fishes – influences of curiosity and terror. And now the stars are shining down frostblown and taut upon this pure Euclidian surface. It is so still that we have dinner under the cypress tree to the light of a candle. And after it, while we are drinking coffee and eating grapes on the edge of the mirror a wind comes: and the whole of heaven stirs and trembles – a great branch of blossoms melting and swaying. Then as the candle draws breath and steadies everything hardens slowly back into the image of a world in water, so that Theodore can point into the water at our feet and show us the Pleiades burning.

Lawrence Durrell

1962

Lunched with folks and sat in their garden. Heard me on radio doing 'Desert Island Discs'. Not bad, really. Voice came over a bit common and pouffy.

Kenneth Williams

23 May

1652

The morning growing excessively hot, I sent my footman some hours before, and so rod negligently, under favour of the shade, 'til being now come to within three miles of Bromley, at a place called the procession Oake, started out two Cutt-throates, and striking with their long staves at the horse, taking hold of the reignes, threw me downe, and immediately tooke my sword, and haled me into a deepe Thickett, some quarter of a mile from the high-way, where they might securely rob me, as they soone did; what they got of mony was not considerable, but they tooke two rings, the one an emrald with diamonds, an [Onyx], and a pair of boucles set with rubies and diamonds which were of value, and after all, barbarously bound my hands behind me, and my feete, having before pull'd off my bootes: and then set up against an Oake, with most bloudy threatnings to cutt my throat, if I offred to crie out, or make any noise, for that they should be within hearing, I not being the person they looked for: I told them, if they had not basely surpriz'd me, they should not have made so easy a prize, and that it should teach me hereafter never to ride neere an hedge; since had I ben in the mid way, they durst not have adventur'd on me, at which they cock'd their pistols, and told me they had long guns too, and were 14 companions, which all were lies: I begg'd for my Onyx and told them it being engraven with my armes, would betray them, but nothing prevaild: My horse bridle they slipt, and search'd the saddle which they likewise pull'd off, but let the horse alone to graze, and then turning againe bridld him, and tied him to a Tree, yet so as he might graze, and so left so bound: The reason they tooke not my horse, was I suppose, because he was mark'd, and cropt on both Eares, and well known on that roade, and these rogues were lusty foote padders, as they are cald: Well, being left in this manner, grievously was I tormented with the flies, the ants, and the sunn, so as I sweate intollerably, nor little was my anxiety how I should get loose in that solitary place, where I could neither heare or see any creature but my poore horse and a few sheepe stragling in the Coppse; til after neere two houres attempting I got my hands to turne paulme to paulme, whereas before they were tied back to back, and then I stuck a greate while ere' I could slip the cord over my wrist to my thumb, which at last I did, and then being quite loose soone unbound my feete, and so sadling my horse, and roaming a while about, I at last perceiv'd a dust to rise, and soone after heard the rattling of a Cart, towards which I made, and by the help of two Country fellows that were driving it, got downe a steepe bank, into the highway againe; but could heare nothing of the Villians: So I rod to Colonel Blounts a greate justiciarie of the times, who sent out hugh and Crie immediately.

John Evelyn

1912

Yesterday I went to the *Titanic* enquiry. I found it intensely interesting. I am longing to hear the passengers' evidence for it is quite clear that every officer was trying to shield first the captain, second the company, and third, himself. One of the younger officers went so far as to say that he did not know for certain that any women or children were drowned, and when he was pressed about this he admitted that he knew 1,600 souls had gone down but, declaring that as he never looked at newspapers, he had no idea as to the proportion of women and children.

Marie Belloc Lowndes

1929

Dined with a merchant captain who told me a curious fishing story about Japan. There the fishermen train young cormorants to fish for them. They take them out at night, tie a string to their legs, put a ring round their necks to prevent them swallowing the fish and then with lanterns to attract the fish set them free from the boat. The queer thing is that the fisherman seems to know by the feel of the string whether the bird has its fill of fish or not. In this way they can fill a boat with fish in a night.

Sir Robert Bruce Lockhart

1938

A Cinderella evening. Tonight there were two grand balls – and we were invited to neither. But what is sinister is that Lady Astor either forgot us, or deliberately omitted us from her ball tonight in honour of the King and Queen. I thought that such social humiliations were over: that I was too secure, or too indifferent to mind them: but I find I do, which is ill-bred of me.

'Chips' Channon

24 May

1685

We had hitherto not any raine for many monethes, insomuch as the Caterpillar had already devoured all the Winter fruite through the whole land, and even killed severall greate and old trees; such two Winters, and Summers I had never known.

John Evelyn

1902

At the moment my attitude to all kinds of sensuality is frivolous in the extreme – I accept and enjoy every kind of sensual experience without any form of restraint.

There was a time when the opposite was true. A certain mistrust of banal sexuality, etc.; not wanting to enjoy, etc. In those days I would have treated with suspicion, and rejected, much of what I now surrender to without thinking and which I am occasionally tempted to see as that alone which is firm, unambiguous, whereas understanding is eternally erratic, eternally insubstantial.

The conflict between understanding and the senses that I traversed in earlier years has now been turned on its head without having yet led to any tangible results. So take care!

Robert Musil

1958 [Tokyo]

Went to dinner with the Professors, a Miss S. from Pittsburgh and others. For some reason we got on to the subject of Beethoven and I told them about the recently published biography which portrays Beethoven as the brutal persecutor of his sister-in-law from whom after the death of his brother he successfully stole his nephew Karl, in whose life he tried to enact the role of a mother. Miss S. was quite dismayed; 'You do disappoint me, Mr Spender. Until now I had always thought his music so beautiful. In fact one of the things I used to look forward to after I was dead was meeting Beethoven to tell him how very much I had appreciated his music on earth.'

Stephen Spender

25 May

1889

Began my early-morning readings. This is my day: tea at 6 o'clock, study from 6 to 8 o'clock. Notes and chat till 11; Father till lunch. Cigarettes and bask in the sun, and a siesta after lunch. 3.30 to 5.30 study. Then a delightful walk or ride: supper, cigarette with Father; saunter in the moonlight or starlight; to bed at 10 o'clock. An alternation of vigorous study and dreamy restfulness – of sleep, exercise, food (including in food the delicious and well-beloved cigarettes!) and the enjoyment of natural beauty, the whole softened and humanized by devotion to that loving gentle nature with its gradually decaying power of body and mind. But the one inspiring influence is Faith – faith in the worthwhile of individual effort for the common good.

Beatrice Webb

1929

[Lord] Beaverbrook's birthday – he gave a large party to all his old friends of fifteen years' standing and a cheque for £250 to each guest. There was also a lottery with numerous prizes amounting to £500 for the servants.

Sir Robert Bruce Lockhart

1953

Nijinsky's journal. I had always imagined that Nijinsky's scowling silence concealed hatred for the milieu of the Ballets Russes. His journal is like what Chaplin's would be if he were overcome, in Switzerland, by some form of madness. For Nijinsky is not mad. He is the victim of a rather childish mysticism, a humanitarianism which divinizes him. He is God. He will save the world. He will have 'pity on the hearts of men.' He suffers from Diaghilev's coldheartedness, and Stravinsky's – that's what disgusts him. Marriage has upset him. He was doomed to solitude – a marriage to himself. The quite terrible journal poorly documents this because of his idée fixe: the terror of being shut up, being put in a lunatic asylum.

Jean Cocteau

1964

I had resolved that while Caroline [his wife] was in America I would do some repairs around the house. I started work at 4pm and it was an absolute disaster. The first job I attempted was to replace the old lavatory seat, but I couldn't get the old fittings off, so I banged with the hammer and bust the lavatory bowl, and now the water comes out the back when you flush. The cost of that intervention will be £70 or £80. Then I tried to repair a faulty switch outside the bedroom, but I wasn't sure what to connect to what, so ended up putting the old broken switch back on. Then I replaced bulbs around the house.

Tony Benn

26 May

1703

This [day] dyed Mr. Sam: Pepys, a very worthy, Industrious and curious person, none in England exceeding him in the Knowledge of the Navy, in which he had passed thro all the most Considerable Offices, Clerk of the Acts, and Secretary to the Admiralty, all which he performed with great Integrity: when K: James the 2d went out of England he layed down his Office, and would serve no more: But withdrawing himself from all publique Affairs, lived at Clapham with his partner (formerly his Cleark) Mr. Hewer, in a very noble House and sweete place, where he injoyed the fruit of his labours in g[r]eate prosperity, was universaly beloved, Hospitable, Generous, Learned in many things; skill'd in Musick, a very greate Cherisher of Learned men, of whom he had the Conversation. His Library and other Collections of Curiositys was one of the most Considerable; The models of Ships especialy etc. Beside what he boldly published of an Account of the Navy, as he found and left it, He had for divers years under his hand the History of the Navy, or *Navalia* (as he call'd it) but how far advanced and what will follow of his, is left I suppose to his sister's son Mr. Jackson, a young Gent: whom his Unkle had educated with extraordinary Accomplishments, and worth to be his Heire: Mr. Pepys had ben for neere 40 years, so my particular Friend, that he now sent me Compleat Mourning: desiring me to be one to hold up the pall, at his magnificent Obsequies; but my present Indisposition, hindred me from doing him this last Office.

John Evelyn

1920

In the middle of the night of May 23–24 some unhappy railway-track watchman had a horrible time. He met an old gentleman wearing white pyjamas who stopped him and said: 'I know this sounds very odd, but I am the President of the Republic and I have fallen out of my train.'

Malesherbes, with its lunatic asylum, was quite near, so there was our good man scratching his head and wondering what on earth to do. To his great relief the gentleman, having spoken, fainted. Our railwayman summoned whoever was available at that time of night and in such a place – his wife among them – and Monsieur Deschanel, for it *was* him, woke up reposing comfortably under respectful surveillance in the level-crossing keeper's house. The wife, quicker on the uptake, had recognized him from his portrait which has already been much reproduced all over the place.

As my learned friend remarked yesterday, we will be the laughing stock of Europe! We are all sniffing the air for mystery, crime, assassination attempts . . . Moral: a President of the Republic in the twentieth century must not sleep or indulge himself in the comfort of pyjamas.

Liane de Pougy

1924

London is enchanting. I step out upon a tawny coloured magic carpet, it seems, and get carried into beauty without raising a finger. The nights are amazing, with all the white porticos and broad silent avenues. And people pop in and out, lightly, divertingly like rabbits; and I look down Southampton Row, wet as a seal's back or red and yellow with sunshine, and watch the omnibuses going and coming and hear the old crazy organs. One of these days I will write about London, and how it takes up the private life and carries it on, without any effort.

Virginia Woolf

1937

Marie [housemaid] came in very happy today, knuckles scraped. Just beat up a man on the subway, she explained; boy, did she feel fine! Old man about 50 sitting opposite her exposing himself. She called a colored man over and he said lady, there's nothing I can do. Oh no? she said, well I can. So she sailed in socking the old boy, let her bundles and purse fly, everyone tried to stop her – men came up. 'Let me handle this,' she told them and socko, while passengers gathered round and said 'Look at the little lady giving it to him.

That old boy's getting the beating of his life. Let her be!' Conductor expostulated – she said 'The law's on my side.' A lady said 'Something might happen.' 'Never mind that,' cried Marie happily, 'I can always offend myself!'

Dawn Powell

1942 [Holland]

We walked along the quay in a balmy and refreshing breeze. We passed lilac trees and small rosebushes and German soldiers on patrol. We spoke about our future and how we would so like to stay together. Then I walked back home in the evening, through the soft night, feeling light and languid from the white Chianti, and I was suddenly absolutely certain of what I now again doubt: that I shall be a writer one day. Those long nights through which I would write and write would be the most beautiful nights of all.

Etty Hillesum

1955

Bunny [his aunt]: 'Nancy called me a half-wit the other day. I said, "Well, half a loaf is better than no bread." '

J. R. Ackerley

1995

Almost daily we read of the outside interests of Members of Parliament – declared or undeclared. Today I was reminded of going to the House of Commons in 1950 to seek information about the etiquette of points of order (such as putting on a hat) in mid-Victorian times. I was about to play Disraeli in a film (*The Mudlark*) and wished to bone up on my part. I asked Benn Levy, an MP and friend, if he could help. He said, 'Come with me and we'll ask the Father of the House [Nicholas Winterton]. He is sure to know.' Winterton, when found, stooped from his immense height to listen to my query. Then he asked, 'For which company are you making the film?' I told him it was for 20th Century-Fox. 'I have an interest in the Rank organization,' he said, 'and I couldn't possibly give information to a rival company.' With that he cranked himself upright again and stalked away, his interest very much declared.

Alec Guinness

27 May

1922

After tea bathed (water 68 degrees). Some pups there, who, even naked, I divined to be either Sandhurst cadets or very young officers. They conducted

before morning. And neither of them had spoken a single word! I don't think that anything which I had ever seen touched me so keenly.

Florence Farmborough

1947

The Duchess of Windsor comes in. She is much improved. That taut, predatory look has gone; she has softened. She says that they do not know where to live. They would like to live in England, but that is difficult. He retains his old love for Fort Belvedere. 'We are tired of wandering,' she says. 'We are not as young as we were. We want to settle down and grow our own trees. He likes gardening, but it is no fun gardening in other people's gardens' . . . He wants a job to do. 'You see,' she says, 'he was born to be a salesman. He would be an admirable representative of Rolls Royce. But an ex-King cannot start selling motor-cars.' I feel really sorry for them. She was so simple and sincere.

Harold Nicolson

29 May

1935

Sometimes when I think of my poor mother, lonely, abandoned, half-mad, I have fits of remorse – am I a young Nero, heartless and selfish? But what else can I do? She has never been able to keep a friend or be with anyone for long, she is so eccentric . . .

'Chips' Channon

1976

I have just read Bob Dylan's name in *Time* magazine. It made me think of the night he came to our house in San Francisco. I got this actual pang of embarrassment sitting here, halfway around the world, a year later. He came with Marlon Brando and some people after Bill Graham's concert. Francis made a huge pot of spaghetti with olive oil, garlic and broccoli. I was in the kitchen getting things and everyone sat down at the table. Bob was hanging up his jacket or something. When he got to the dining room all the chairs were filled except one next to the children down at the end, so he sat down there, not near his wife or Marlon or Francis. He sat there looking real glum and about halfway through he got up and left. I tried to tell myself he was tired from the concert and probably wasn't hungry. But I kicked myself for not being a smooth hostess. I am never comfortable with groups of people that I don't know, and yet I am constantly in the midst of spontaneous dinners of ten or fifteen people, many of whom are strangers. I suppose if I ever really learn to relax and enjoy it, Francis will decide to become a hermit.

There used to be a woman who called me once in a while and said, 'Ellie, tell me, who was at your house for dinner last week?'

A famous person I don't know is like an unfamous person I don't know; I feel shy and uncomfortable, maybe more so.

Eleanor Coppola

30 May

1800

Day of Divorce Bill. Up late. Unusually languid and incapable of exertion. So perplexed between the two things I had to do, viz. the business of the Divorce Bill and motion about Soldiers' Children, that in the state of bodily languor in which I was I could do nothing.

William Windham

1800

In the morning went to Ambleside, forgetting that the post does not come till the evening. How was I grieved when I was so informed. I walked back resolving to go again in the evening. It rained very mildly and sweetly in the morning as I came home, but came on a wet afternoon and evening – but chilly. I caught Mr Olliff's Lad as he was going for letters, he brought me one from Wm and 2 papers. I planted London pride upon the wall and many things on the Borders. John sodded the wall. As I came past Rydale in the morning I saw a Heron swimming with only its neck out of water – it beat and struggled amongst the water when it flew away and was long in getting loose.

Dorothy Wordsworth

1835

The father and mother both occupied with their daughter's [actress Fanny Kemble] book, which Kemble told me he had 'never read till it appeared in print, and was full of sublime things and vulgarities,' and the mother 'was divided between admiration and disgust, threw it down six times, and as often picked it up.'

Charles Greville

1905

With the regularity of some law at work the following process runs full circle within me:

I am arrogant, dismissive, reticent, refined, happy. Some or other sense of power takes territorial hold. I have taken too much pleasure in my muscles while I was rowing or I am working at philosophy with an intensity that blunts the senses. I feel first that my arrogance, with its conciliatory frontage on the outside world, is deserting me. I am no longer so friendly; I am less witty. I feel empty and work out of sheer desperation. My behavior in company deteriorates. I suffer a defeat. I feel that, by comparison with some other person, I am stupid. I behave with spectacular ineptitude, I cannot find an appropriate rejoinder to some insult. A few hours later I am, once again, arrogant, dismissive, reticent, refined, happy.

Robert Musil

31 May

1661

I went to my father's, but to my great grief I found my father and mother in a great deal of discontent one with another, and indeed my mother is grown now so pettish that I know not how my father is able to bear with it. I did talk to her so as did not indeed become me, but I could not help it, she being so unsufferably foolish and simple, so that my father, poor man, is become a very unhappy man.

Samuel Pepys

1824

To hear the *Barber of Seville* at the Odeon – very satisfying. I sat next to an old gentleman who had seen Grétry, Voltaire, Diderot, Rousseau, and so on. He once saw Voltaire paying his celebrated compliments to the ladies, in one of the salons. As he left, this old gentleman heard him remark: 'In you, I see the beginning of a century, in myself, one that is ending – the century of Voltaire.' The modest philosopher was evidently taking pains to name his century in advance, for the benefit of posterity! This gentleman was also taken by one of his friends to breakfast with Jean-Jacques in the rue Plâtrière. They left together and walked through the Tuileries, where they came upon some children playing ball: 'There,' said Rousseau, 'that is how I should like Emile to take exercise,' and other similar remarks. But a ball belonging to one of the children happening to strike the philosopher on the leg, he flew into a violent passion, and abruptly leaving his friends, ran after the child with his cane.

Eugène Delacroix

1834

We sallied forth at 9, sight-seeing. We first adjourned to the National Gallery of Arts & Inventions. Many very interesting things there, amongst others a canvas tube for a man to slip through from any height in case of fire. A man descended by it to the Square for our edification. From this place we adjourned to the Fleas [exhibition of performing fleas] taking a pastry cook's & sundry other shops in the way. Messrs. Flea & Co. gave great satisfaction dancing, driving, riding, duelling &c. From the fleas we went to a very good oxy-hydrogen micro-scopic exhibition. After staying there an hour we walked to the new Bazaar which was extremely splendid. We made numerous purchases. We got home to dinner at 3 middlingly fagged.

Barclay Fox

1915

Sitting at tea in the farm house today E—— cried suddenly, pointing to a sandy cat in the garden:

'There, – he's the father of the little kittens in the barn, I'll tell you how we know: P—— noticed the kittens had big feet and later on saw that old Tom stalking across the garden with big feet exactly the same kind.'

'So you impute the paternity of the kittens to the gentleman under the laurel bushes?'

I looked at the kittens to-night and found they had extra toes. 'Mr Sixtoes', as W—— calls him, also possess six toes, so the circumstantial evidence looks black against him.

W. N. P. Barbellion

1932 [Berlin]

Street rioting. Several thousand Nazis, singing their songs and yelling *Heil* tried to escort the Marine Guard on its way through the streets to the Presidential Palace. Goebbels made a speech from a lorry in the Wilhemstrasse. When the police tried to hold back the crowd and shut off the Bendlerstrasse, a shower of stones was flung at them. They then used their rubber truncheons and eventually employed their fire-arms. A woman received a shot in the shoulder and was carried away. People ran past my window. My man-servant Friedrich was downstairs and came back very excited because the concierge, a fanatical Nazi, said that the Nazis will 'deal' with the policeman who shot the woman.

Count Harry Kessler

1938

A great hullabaloo is being made in Germany over the people's car – seven million are to be built and almost every family will have its own little car. Mussolini's comment, on reading a report on the subject, was that this will promote the spirit of hedonism already innate in the Germans and make the people less warlike. If you turn your people into bourgeois, you also turn them into pacifists.

Count Ciano

1940

Sara is dead five years today – a longer time than the time of our marriage, which lasted but four years and nine months. It is amazing what a deep mark she left upon my life – and yet, after all, it is not amazing at all, for a happy marriage throws out numerous and powerful tentacles. They may loosen with years and habit, but when a marriage ends at the height of its success they endure. It is a literal fact that I still think of Sara every day of my life and almost every hour of the day. Whenever I see anything that she would have liked I find myself saying that I'll buy it and take it to her, and I am always thinking of things to tell her. There was a tremendous variety in her, and yet she was always steadfast. I can recall no single moment during our years together when I ever had the slightest doubt of our marriage, or wished that it had never been. I believe that she was equally content.

H. L. Mencken

1945 [Berlin]

If, as has happened on occasion, I were to be asked today why I remained in the party, I can only reply that those of us overseas never came into contact with the kind of people who were eyewitnesses to the atrocities that are said to have been committed by members of the SS, etc. We were 'idealists of the first water' and it was our impression that any ugly stories were just rumors, nothing more than enemy propaganda, especially since, as I've mentioned, no one could say that he had seen the atrocities he was describing with his own eyes.

John Rabe

1973

By this morning's post I receive a letter from Nancy [Mitford], still in her firm hand, but misspelt and shaky, and piteous. It begins, 'It's very curious dying and would have many a drole amusing & charming side were it not for the pain. We had screams over the Will. The Dame's [Alvilde Lees-Milne] share. "But she'll be furious if she only gets *that*."' Then she says the doctors are tiresome they will not give her a date for her death. They merely say 'Have you everything you want?', meaning as much morphia. I have been haunted by this letter all day. Extraordinary that someone on the threshold of death can write like this, and still make jokes.

James Lees-Milne

JUNE

'I got out this diary and read, as one always reads one's own writing, with a kind of guilty intensity.'

VIRGINIA WOOLF

1 June

1837

I awakened feeling dull. The weather is neither cheerful nor depressing. It makes me restless. The trees are tossed by gusty, fantastic wind. The sun is hidden. If I put on my dressing-gown I am too hot, if I take it off I am cold. Leaden day in which I shall accomplish nothing worth while. Tired and apathetic brain! I have been drinking tea in the hope that it would carry this mood to a climax and so put an end to it.

George Sand

1912

Wrote nothing.

Franz Kafka

1917

We discuss post mortem affairs quite genially and without restraint. It is the contempt bred of familiarity, I suppose. E—— says widows' weeds have been so vulgarised by the war widows that she won't go into deep mourning. 'But you'll wear just one weed or two for me?' I plead, and then we laugh. She has promised me that should a suitable chance arise, she will marry again. Personally, I wish I could place my hand on the young fellow at once, so as to put him thro' his paces – shew him where the water mains runs and where the gas meter is, and so on.

You will observe what a relish I have for my own *macabre*, and how keenly I appreciate the present situation [he was terminally ill]. Nobody can say I am not making the best of it. One might call it pulling the hangman's beard. Yet I ought, I fancy, to be bewailing my poor wife and fatherless child.

W. N. P. Barbellion

1923

Rink asked me if I should like a free seat for the Folk Dancing tomorrow. I replied that I really did not understand that sort of thing: I could be said to like dancing only as a girl who picnicked in a ruin could be said to like architecture.

C. S. Lewis

1940

I returned from a happy day at Alton to find that one of the men in my company had shot himself. He left a note for the CSM apologizing for causing trouble and saying he is too sensitive to be a corporal – a promotion I had encouraged him to expect. He was at pains to see that his bullet injured no one else. Two stretcher bearers confronted with blood for the first time resigned their posts. The consequences of this man's death took up most of the week. There was an inquest and later a funeral with military honours. The sergeants entertained his relatives. The funeral went off very smoothly. The men in the suicide's tent had no objection to remaining there. He had kept the ammunition by him since his training at Chatham.

Evelyn Waugh

1941

The big news this morning is clothes rationing. Oliver Lyttleton is only going to allow us 66 coupons per annum. A suit takes 26. Luckily I have 40 or more. Socks will be the shortage. Apart from these, if I am not bombed, I have enough clothes to last me for years. . . .

The evacuation of Crete is announced and we are told that over 15,000 men got away in our ships. I doubt whether the defence of the island was even worthwhile. It may have delayed the attacking forces in their downward march but it means also a further decline in our prestige. British Expeditionary Forces are now known as 'Back Every Friday'!

'Chips' Channon

1970 [croft in Ardnamurchan, Scotland]

Wind Southerly to Westerly light to moderate. Heavy rain around 6 a.m. Dry during the day with quite a lot of sunshine. Evening cloudy. This was an eventful day. As we were completely out of coal Jessie [his daughter] and I decided to motor to the Ferry Stores for some, after breakfast. We went to the Post Office for Old Age pensions as well. On the way back, on the brae above the falls, we noticed steam coming from the bonnet of the banger. The bottom radiator hose had burst so we had no option but to abandon the car and walk home over the hill. It was quite warm and, as we were carrying our stores and two stone of coal, we were pretty tired. We sat at the top of Bealach Faotidh and ate some biscuits, where Liz [his wife] and I had done the same thing half a century ago. Truly, history repeating itself.

Ian Maclean

2 June

1916

What a muddle I've been in with girls, in spite of all my headaches, insomnia, grey hair, despair. Let me count them: there have been at least six since the summer. I can't resist, my tongue is fairly torn from my mouth if I don't give in and admire anyone who is admirable and love her until admiration is exhausted. With all six my guilt is almost wholly inward, though one of the six did complain of me to someone.

Franz Kafka

1930 [Paris]

Em. [his wife] and Mlle Zaglad are speaking of hospitals and the scandalous abuses committed in them, of the bad food served to the invalids, of the injustices, the favours, and the easy blackmail that nurses and orderlies exercise over the unfortunate patients. But whoever denounced these abuses would play into the hands of the political left; and this is why people are so often silent. Meanwhile that fear of the hospital which is so often encountered in the masses, alas, is only too justified.

Recently, on my way to see my poor niece shortly before her end, I took a taxi.

'To the hospital [a small private one] in rue Boileau,' I say to the driver. He asks me:

'What number?'

'I don't know. But you must know it . . . After all! – the hospital . . .'

Then, turning round and in a tone of voice that mingled hatred, scorn, irony, and rancour:

'*For us*, it's Lariboisière [large public hospital].'

And these innocent syllables, pronounced with the drawl of the Paris street-urchin, took on the ring of a death-knell.

'Go on!' I told him. 'People die in private hospitals just the same as in the wards.'

But his remark had sent a cold shiver down my back.

André Gide

1941 [POW camp]

Rumours running riot now about move.

Having a shower and feeling hearty, I started singing loudly. Bill E. suddenly said, 'The old John I haven't seen for many months.' So you see one starts on the depression grid without ever knowing it.

Captain John Mansel

1942 [Holland]

I feel the end is near. Not my end, but the end of the war. I can't sleep. For the past hour squadrons of aeroplanes have been flying overhead. English planes. On their way to Germany. They have been coming for the past three nights. Cologne and Essen have been bombed. I wonder which city is going to get it tonight! It's a loud, constant drone. Some bombs have been dropped over The Hague as well. Even so, it's a comfort, to me.

Edith Velmans

1943

Dr. F. E. Townsend, the old age pension man, dropped off in Baltimore yesterday and I took him to lunch at the Belvedere.

The doctor told me a long tale about his cousin, a man of his own age, who lately came down with cancer of the prostate. He said that at his advice the cousin submitted to castration and that the effects were magnificent. The cancer vanished and the patient put on 40 pounds of flesh. This seems plausible enough. Castration for cancer of the prostate is now widely practised. Apparently the testicular hormones encourage the development of the cancer and when the supply of them is cut off it tends to wither. Townsend told me that his cousin is now strong enough to operate a three-acre chicken farm and is otherwise in prime condition. He said that he was thinking seriously of getting castrated himself. His prostate is normal, but he believes that he is underweight and that adding 30 or 40 pounds would improve his general health. He said somewhat primly: 'My reproductive stage is now over, and I see no reason why I shouldn't sacrifice a couple of useless glands.'

H. L. Mencken

1953

From nine this morning to six this evening, we haven't turned off the broadcast of the coronation of Queen Elizabeth. The radio seemed to come out of the night of time. It must have been an incredible spectacle to see – but it was fabulous to hear. It was related to those great bards, those troubadours who recount and embellish. The difference, in our day and age, is that in each house, the troubadour-reporter doesn't invent and doesn't try to embellish. He observes and holds his microphone toward the music, the bells, the tides of the crowd.

Jean Cocteau

3 June

1658

A large Whale taken, twixt my Land butting on the Thames and Greenewich, which drew an infinite Concourse to see it, by water, horse, coach, on foote from Lond, and all parts: It appeared first below Greenewich at low-water, for at high water, it would have destroyed all the boates: but lying now in shallow water, incompassd with boates, after a long Conflict it was killed with the harping yrons, and struck in the head, out of which spouted blood and water, by two tunnells like Smoake, from a chimny: and after an horrid grone it ran quite on shore and died. The length was 58 foote: 16 in heights, black skin'd like Coach-leather, very small eyes, greate taile, small finns and but 2: a piked snout, a mouth so wide and divers men might have stood upright in it: No teeth at all but sucked the slime onely as thro a grate made of that bone which we call Whale bone: The throate [yet] so narrow, as would not have admitted the least of fishes . . .

John Evelyn

1802

Yesterday morning William walked as far as the Swan with Aggy Fisher. She was going to attend Goan's dying Infant. She said 'There are many heavier crosses than the death of an Infant', and went on, 'There was a woman in this vale who buried 4 grown-up children in one year, and I have heard her say when many years were gone by that she had more pleasure in thinking of those 4 than of her living Children, for as Children get up and have families of their own their duty to their parents "wears out and weakens". She could trip lightly by the graves of those who died when they were young, with a light step, as she went to Church on a Sunday.'

Dorothy Wordsworth

1858

The lady artists of Boston are going to give me a soirée next Saturday. Oh, that reminds me of the best joke of all: A gentleman who had heard of Barbara Smith as an artist went to see her pictures, not knowing I was married, did not understand the (Bodichon) which they had put, as well as BLS. 'Oh,' said a friend, 'it's the name of a style like P. R. B. [Pre-Raphaelite Brotherhood], you know, etc.' 'Oh, yes! ah!' So the gentleman goes to the clerk, and he wanting to be thought wise says, 'Oh, yes, sir!' So the gentleman goes about saying, 'Barbara L. Smith is a fine artist, in the Bodichon style you know.' Miss Clarke hears of it and is in fits of laughter at the Bodichonite.

Barbara Leigh Smith Bodichon

1871

Mrs Griffiths told me that a few days ago a man named Evans kicked his wife to death at Rhulen. He kicked her bosom black and her breasts mortified.

Rev. Francis Kilvert

1930

Astounding and enchanting change in the weather, which becomes warm. I carry chair, writing-materials, rug, and cushion into the garden, but am called in to have a look at the Pantry Sink, please, as it seems to have blocked itself up. Attempted return to garden frustrated by arrival of note from the village concerning Garden Fête arrangements, which requires immediate answer, necessity for speaking to the butcher on the telephone, and sudden realisation that Laundry List hasn't yet been made out, and the Van will be here at eleven. When it does come, I have to speak about the tablecloths, which leads – do not know how – to long conversation about the Derby, the Van speaking highly of an outsider – *Trews* – whilst I uphold the chances of *Silver Flare* – (mainly because I like the name).

Shortly after this, Mrs. S. arrives from the village, to collect jumble for Garden Fête, which takes time. After lunch, sky clouds over, and Mademoiselle and Vicky kindly help me to carry chair, writing-materials, rug, and cushion into the house again.

Robert receives letter by second post announcing death of his godfather, aged ninety-seven, and decides to go to the funeral on 5th June. (Mem.: Curious, but authenticated fact, that a funeral is the only gathering to which the majority of men ever go willingly. Should like to think out why this should be so, but must instead unearth top-hat and other accoutrements of woe and [see] if open air will remove smell of naphthaline.)

E. M. Delafield

1937

The Windsor wedding has taken place in a foreign country amid a blaze of publicity and rather cracked trumpets, and the photographs of him and Wallis show an animated ecstatic pair. Reaction here, however, is setting in and people are angrily demanding why he should be so snubbed? And the House of Commons is embarrassed and feels guilty . . .

The present King and Queen are popular, very, and increasingly so, but they have no message for the Labour Party who believe them, and rightly I fear, to be but the puppets of a Palace clique. Certainly, they are too hemmed in by the territorial aristocracy, and have all the faults and virtues which Edward VIII lacked in this particular field. Still, it is the aristocracy which still rules England although nobody seems to believe it.

When I got home I found a telegram from the Duke of Windsor saying 'Many thanks for your good wishes. We shall write when we get the present. Edward'. It must have been sent directly after the Service as it arrived at 4 o'clock.

'Chips' Channon

1940

My guess is that in the long run the newspapers will lose their more moronic customers to the radio. Thus their future lies with the relative intelligent minority. That minority holds nearly all of the money of the country. The newspapers, however, neglect it progressively. The Baltimore *Sun* has gradually lopped off every feature that appeals to intelligence, and supplanted it with something aimed directly at idiots. The whole magazine section has disappeared completely, and in place of it there is now a series of comic sections almost as large as the whole remainder of the paper. Meanwhile, the editorial policy has steadily deteriorated. There was a time following the last war when a serious effort was made to lift it to an enlightened level, but now it has got down to a point where it actually marches ahead of the boobs themselves in maudlin imbecility. One hears better talk in smoking cars and barber shops than one can get from the editorial page of what is, in theory, supposed to be a rich, intelligent and honest newspaper. My guess is that this is bad medicine. Nothing is going to be accomplished by trying to out-demagogue the radio crooners. The function of a newspaper in a democracy is to stand as a sort of chronic opposition to the reigning quacks. The minute it begins to out-whoop them it forfeits its character and becomes ridiculous. I believe that many people already notice this deterioration, and that it is responsible to some extent for the movement toward the radio.

H. L. Mencken

4 June

1831

I wonder if I shall burn this sheet of paper like most others I have begun in the same way. To write a diary, I have thought of very often at far & near distances of time: but how could I write a diary without throwing upon paper my thoughts, all my thoughts – the thoughts of my heart as well as of my head? – and then how could I bear to look on *them* after they were written? Adam made fig leaves necessary for the mind, as well as for the body. And such a mind as I have! So very exacting & exclusive & eager & head long – & strong & so very very often *wrong!* Well! But I will write: I must write – & the oftener wrong I know myself to be, the less wrong I shall be in one thing – the less *vain* I shall be!—

Elizabeth Barrett Browning

1857

Marie came this morning dressed in mourning, her eyes swollen, her voice choking, to read us a black-edged letter: her sister was dead. Women, garrulous by nature, become eloquent under the stress of passion or emotion. All of them, whether illiterate or well educated, prostitutes or marchionesses, find words and phrases and gestures which are ideal, the envy, and the despair, of those who try to write works of true-to-life emotion. There is an overwhelming case against tragedy contained in those unrehearsed sorrows, those spontaneous tears and words, and that speech springing straight from grief.

Marie told us what she was doing about mourning clothes. I doubt if there is any woman's grief, and I am speaking of the most sincere and poignant grief, into which there does not enter, right at the beginning, a preoccupation with her mourning clothes. There are very few cases of bereavement in which the woman does not say to you: 'It's a good thing I didn't buy a summer dress.'

The Brothers Goncourt

1899

Yesterday evening at 8:00 Johann Strauss died. In my opinion an absolute classic and the greatest musical genius to have lived. I genuinely mourn him. Such effervescence, such grace and elegance – words cannot define the essence of his waltzes. For me he stands beside Schubert and Brahms, he was a classic. a.m. completed a song: 'Hinaus'.

p.m. cycled to Steeg. A farm-worker, who didn't know that you should give way to the left, rode straight into me. We both came crashing to the ground. Nothing happened to him, and I survived with a few grazes. I started cursing and swearing, and the poor fellow kept repeating:

I beg yer pardon, lady.

In the evening I was feeling cheerful, so I played one waltz after another.

Alma Mahler-Werfel

1956

Cedars of Lebanon Hospital. I came here last Friday after Dr. Sellars suddenly informed me that I had hepatitis – from Don, I suppose. The time of incubation was just right. Actually, I've been feeling lousy ever since May 17, when I started what Sellars thought was flu. Now that the jaundice is visibly 'out,' I'm better.

The unpleasant part of this illness is the feeling of utter fatigue. Also a tendency to grey thoughts of old age, weakness, death. These somewhat stimulated by reading Arnold Bennett's *Journals* – a very sympathetic man, but such a pitiful blind workhorse, self-driven until he dropped. At the end of it all, he could say: 'I made a plan and stuck to it.' Well, that's something, certainly. But the note of obstinacy is tragic, too. It's the obstinacy of an insect.

Christopher Isherwood

1982

We (we!) drop leaflets on the Argentine troops besieged in Port Stanley [during the Falklands War], urging them to lay down their arms. Were such leaflets dropped on our troops we would consider them contemptible and ludicrous; our leaflets are represented as a great humanitarian gesture.

Alan Bennett

1989

Drove from Tucson to Gila Bend a couple hours before dusk and stopped at the crest of some mountain watching the light fade over the curve of the earth with silhouettes of goofy cactus and desert scrub and occasional cars or trucks slicing through the silence and one flippy bat tiny wobbling through the wind under a roadside lamp getting knocked around trying to catch insects gathering from the shadows and a bunch of honeybees trying to drink from the steel rim of the flooded water fountain some of them stupid and drowning and a sixteen-wheel rig pulled in just as it got dark and a young guy with no shirt covered in sweat and dirt and wearing cowboy boots jumped out: What's up? and kicked each tire on his truck while I held my breath and then he climbed back in and drove away and I wondered what it'd be like if it were a perfect world.

David Wojnarowicz

5 June

1660

A-bed late. In the morning my Lord [Admiral Sir Edward Montagu] went on shore with the Vice-Admiral a-fishing, and at dinner returned. In the afternoon I played at ninepins with my Lord, and after supper my Lord called for the lieutenant's cittern, and with two candlesticks with money in them for symballs, we made barber's music, with which my Lord was well pleased. So to bed.

Samuel Pepys

1913

The motion of a woman on a horse has – seen from beneath, from a bench – an immense sensuality about it. As if, with each step, she were being seized from below by a wave and lifted upward.

Robert Musil

1938

Saw today in an English paper a notice of somebody's journal, recently published, containing a sort of daily account of the year's events described from a personal angle: which led me to reflect that, considering the extraordinary and momentous nature of 'the times', (apart from the fact that this is a quite different type of journal in its intention), these pages contain singularly little reflection of contemporary history. Demonstrations in London, Spain, and Anschluss, do appear, but only in passing. It's true that I've lost most of my former interests in politics during the last year, but I've never been at all unaware of, or indifferent to, the things that are going on; and I have a very strong general sense of the present state of the world. I've never altogether been able to decide whether or not I wanted this book to be published some day. I suppose it's not uninteresting to read, but quite what its interest is I find it difficult to say: a record of the late 1930's; or a 'mon cœur mis à nu' sort of confessions? Perhaps not quite either one or the other: there's not enough general contemporary detail on the one hand, and it's not really sufficiently intimate on the other. I've given most of my most 'hidden' self away, I think, but have confessed to singularly little of my factual life, so that the self-portrait, insofar as this is one, tends to be rather too flattering. I ought to force myself to be much more painful about money and love, for instance – In the end, perhaps, the real reason for keeping a journal is vanity or narcissism, unless one is absolutely determined that no one shall read it: which I am not.

David Gascoyne

1941 [POW camp]

Riot Act read before we leave – entrain. Red X parcels had been issued on Thorn station – 1 per head. Had filled 2 beer bottles with cold tea for our journey, will use one for washing with. 2 important events at Guesen – 1st sight for 2 years of young girls in bathing suits – caused a great sensation; 2nd – 1st *cold* water drink for over 3 months.

Posen 6.0–11.0. When pulling into Posen in urgent need of shit – but not allowed. We all get a wash and plenty of drinking water; then coffee – a different sort of journey from the going to Thorn. Guards all full of fun and laughter – like idea of returning to Germany. Some haven't been back for years, having been in Poland, Norway, Holland, France, Belgium etc. Endless rolling stock full of vehicles, punts etc. Blackout everywhere.

Captain John Mansel

1943

Yesterday at 11.30, while I was yet dressing after my Sabbath ablutions, D. B. Low came in to sound my chest – now a corrugated wheeze-box. After roaming all regions, he came back to a spot at the top of my right lung. It must have been a slightly ludicrous scene as I lay with my shirt collarless and my head encased in a blue beret set at an acute angle while David invited me to whisper one, one, one, one. The whispering definitely certified a cavity – and I suppose David realized, as surely as myself, that he was listening-in to a grave. I had a fleeting impulse to ask: 'How long do you think I may live?' but refrained as I considered it was rather premature, and also because I was not quite certain that I wished to know just yet.

William Soutar

1968

The whole day made unreal and horrible by the shooting of Robert Kennedy. The senseless mad awful act has resulted in him being operated on, for a removal of a bullet from the brain. Everyone seems utterly stunned by it.

Kenneth Williams

1982

Up early. I went into one of those Korean produce stores and there were about 15 people in there, it was mobbed, and I listened to this guy rave about a pineapple for ten minutes and by the time he was through, I was dying to get one, too.

He was saying, 'I want it ripe and ready! Juicy! Luscious! Ready to eat, right off the bat!' And then I turned around and it was [Richard] Nixon. And one of his daughters was with him, but looking older – maybe Julie, I think. And he looked pudgy, like a Dickens character, fat with a belly. And they had him sign for the bill. There were secret service with him. And the girl at the cash register said he was 'Number One Charge'.

Andy Warhol

6 June

1837

Superb weather. Hideous sore throat and black melancholy for thirty-six hours.

After the desolation of winter, when spring is bringing new life, man, of all animate beings, wearies most quickly and most completely of the delights of outside nature. He attributes his inner perturbations to changes in the atmosphere, and so excuses the unevenness of his moods, the susceptibility of his miserable nerves. But when the sun is shining in a sapphire sky, when a happy wind is singing among the leaves and softly rocking the branches, when the whole world is intoxicated with perfume, fresh air, light, and love, why does this shabby creature still continue his disconsolate wail? Why is his capacity for happiness so short-lived that it cannot last through one week of pleasant weather?

George Sand

1842

To the Carlyles', where we were received with great cordiality in the library, which looks well suited to the work performed there. Thomas Carlyle came in in his blouse, and we presently got, I know not how, to Swedenborgianism. Swedenborg was a thoroughly practical, mechanical man, and was in England learning shipbuilding. He went into a little inn in Bishopsgate Street, and was eating his dinner very fast, when he thought he saw in the corner of the room a vision of Jesus Christ, who said to him, 'Eat slower.' This was the beginning of all his visions and mysterious communications, of which he had enough in his day.

Caroline Fox

1843

Religious feuds are rife. The Church and the Puseyites are at loggerheads here, and the Church and the Seceders in Scotland; and everybody says it is all very alarming, and God knows what will happen, and everybody goes on just the same, and nobody cares except those who can't get bread to eat.

Charles Greville

1920 [Berlin]

A crucial date for Germany. The German Republic's first Reichstag elections. Fears of a putsch have proved unfounded. Indeed the streets are quieter and emptier than on ordinary Sundays, perhaps because it rains now and again. At eleven in the morning I was the sole voter at my polling centre, whereas on the occasion of the National Assembly elections eighteen months ago I had to queue.

Count Harry Kessler

7 June

1852

Feel proud, I don't know what about. But I'm satisfied with myself morally. I've still got a rash, but I'm sure it's venereal disease, the mercury or the gold, despite the fact that the doctor says it's nettle rash.

Leo Tolstoy

1918

L[eonard] was told the other day that the raids are carried out by women. Women's bodies were found in the wrecked aeroplanes. They are smaller and lighter, and thus leave more room for bombs. Perhaps it is sentimental, but the thought seems to me to add a particular touch of horror.

Virginia Woolf

1946 [Berlin]

On 3 June, I was finally denazified by the Denazification Commission for the British Sector in Charlottenburg (District Office, Witzleben Strasse 3–4). The decision reads: 'Despite your having been the deputy local leader in Nanking and although you did not resign from the NSDAP on your return to Germany, the commission has nevertheless decided to grant your appeal on the basis of your successful humanitarian work in China, etc.' And with that, the nerve-racking torture is over! Thank God! I've received congratulations from many friends and the directors at Siemens and been given a few days vacation by the firm to recover from the ordeal.

John Rabe

1953

Last year, I dined at the Anchorenas with the Windsors. After dinner the duke had lost his cigarette holder. We were all of us down on all fours. 'He loses everything,' the duchess murmured, 'and I'm always the one who finds it for him again.' I was thinking: 'Not his crown.'

Jean Cocteau

8 June

1978

The dinner was for thirty-two or thirty-six, with a curious mixture of strands: Mrs Onassis, Sam Spiegel . . . I sat between Pamela Harlech and Jackie, about which I could not complain. Jackie was at her best. I have never had a better conversation with her, not only very friendly, but also interesting, with a lot of talk about White House life, mostly when Jack was President, but also her return visits there and her relations with LBJ, towards whom she was surprisingly friendly and favourable, and with Nixon, to whom she was much less so.

Jack, she said, except occasionally, did not much like formally arranged dinner parties, because he could not decide in advance whom he wanted to see. But he would often ring up at 5 or 6 o'clock and say, 'Get somebody for dinner.' He did not greatly like having Ethel and Bobby [Kennedy], not because he didn't like Ethel, he did rather, and certainly not because he didn't like Bobby, but because Bobby was too much on his conscience and kept demanding to know what he had done, what he had decided about this or that, telling him what he ought to do in the future. [The] Bradlees (*Washington Post*), who turned out to be snakes-in-the-grass, were there a lot. But David and Sissie Gore came more than anybody else, she said, so much so that it became difficult because David would always chuck everything else, which in my view was probably his duty (the main duty of ambassadors is to have close contact with the heads of the government to which they are accredited) but which led to his breaking long-arranged dinner engagements at which he was to be the guest of honour and created some Washington ill-feeling.

Roy Jenkins

1979

The marriage [Marianne Faithfull to Ben Brierly] – we were late. Marianne looking radiant, nervous, wonderful – her voice carried better than his and when she was told Nicholas [her son] was too young to sign as a witness she said, 'Never mind, darling, next time I get married.' I wish them luck.

Ossie Clark

1992

Our nineteenth wedding anniversary. It began with me declining to comment on the state of the marriage of the Prince and Princess of Wales. All the papers (here and, apparently, right round the world) are full of backwash from the serialisation of Andrew Morton's revelations about Diana – how she's suffered from bulimia, has attempted suicide, is locked in a loveless marriage. I had nothing to offer, but others were less reticent. Lord St John of Fawsley (who now looks like a Tenniel drawing of himself – the Fish Footman meets the Red Queen) was Olympian: 'A warning needs to be uttered that our institutions are fragile.' Peter Mandelson, Labour MP for Hartlepool, declared that the scurrilous book proves there are no longer any boundaries between fact and fiction when it comes to royal reporting. I said, 'I'm taking my wife to lunch at the Royal Oak at Yatterden.' – which I did, and it was good, but I wasn't relaxed because all the time I was half-thinking that I ought to get back to Westminster.

Gyles Brandreth

9 June

1800

In the morning W. cut down the winter cherry tree. I sowed French Beans and weeded. A coronetted Landau went by when we were sitting upon the sodded wall. The ladies (evidently Tourists) turned an eye of interest upon our little garden and cottage. We went to R. Newton's for pike-floats and went round to Mr Gell's Boat and on to the Lake to fish. We caught nothing – it was extremely cold. The Reeds and Bulrushes or Bullpipes of a tender soft green, making a plain whose surface moved with the wind. The reeds not yet tall. The lake clear to the Bottom, but saw no fish. In the evening I stuck peas, watered the garden and planted Brocoli. Did not walk for it was very cold. A poor Girl called to beg who had no work at home and was going in search of it to Kendal. She slept in Mr Benson's Lathe [barn], and went off after Breakfast in the morning with 7d and a letter to the Mayor of Kendal.

Dorothy Wordsworth

1872

I went to see Mrs. Prosser at the Swan, a young pretty woman dying I fear of consumption which she caught off her sister, Mrs. Hope of the Rose and Crown in Hay. It was a sad beautiful story. She was warned not to sleep with her sister who was dying of decline and told that if she did she herself would probably be infected with the disease. But her sister begged her so hard not to leave her and to go on sleeping with her that she gave way. 'What could I do?' she said. 'She was my only sister and we loved each other so. I have been married seven years,' she said, 'and now my first child has just come, a little girl, and it does seem so hard to go away and leave her. But if it is the

Lord's will to take me I must be content to go. My left lung is quite gone,' she said looking at me with her lip trembling and her beautiful eyes full of tears.

Rev. Francis Kilvert

1917

Siegfried Sassoon lunched with me at the Reform yesterday. He expected some decoration for admittedly fine bombing work. Colonel had applied for it three times, but was finally told that as that particular push was a failure it could not be granted. Sassoon was uncertain about accepting a home billet if he got the offer of one. I advised him to accept it. He is evidently one of the reckless ones. He said his pals said he always gave the Germans every chance to pot him. He said he would like to go out once more and give them another chance to get him, and come home unscathed. He seemed jealous of the military reputation of poets. He said most of war was a tedious nuisance, but there were great moments and he would like them again.

Arnold Bennett

1930

It requires a great effort to convince myself that I am now as old as those who seemed to me so old when I was young.

André Gide

1943

At four a.m., in the Clinica Quisisana, my second daughter, Donata, is born. During the long night before her birth I heard from the next room, through my own pain, the groans for morphia of a young airman whose leg had been amputated.

Iris Origo

1943

Mrs. Vass in the kindness of her ample bosom brought me a bottle of concentrated orange-juice to pep up the vitamins. I find on the label that the quantity suitable for me is that for an expectant mother. Well, I suppose I may claim to be both father and mother of such bairns as I produce; and certainly I am ever expectant that they have the breath of life in them.

William Soutar

1956 [Saturday]

On Thursday . . . Edward and I drove to Rocquebrune to lunch with Emery Reves [Churchill's overseas literary agent], Wendy Russell, the most fascinating lady, Winston Churchill, Sarah [Churchill's daughter], and Winston's secretary. The lunch was a great success, particularly from my point of view, for it seems, from later reports, that I was charming, witty, brilliant, etc. What I really was was profoundly interested. There was this great man, historically one of the greatest our country has produced, domestically one of the silliest, absolutely obsessed with a senile passion for Wendy Russell. He followed her about the room with his brimming eyes and wobbled after her across the terrace, staggering like a vast baby of two who is just learning to walk. He was extremely affable to me and, standing back to allow me to go into a room before him, he pointed to a Toulouse-Lautrec painting of a shabby prostitute exposing cruelly and cynically a naked bottom, flaccid and creased, and said in a voice dripping with senile prurience, 'Very appetizing!'

This really startled me. To begin with I doubt if Lautrec had ever for an instant intended it to be alluring, and the idea of the saviour of our country calling it appetizing once more demonstrated his extraordinary flair for choosing the right word. I am convinced that 'appetizing' was what he really thought it. I reflected, on the way home, how dangerous an enemy repressed sex can be. I doubt if, during the whole of his married life, Winston Churchill has ever been physically unfaithful to Lady Churchill, but, oh, what has gone on inside that dynamic mind? This impotent passion for Wendy Russell is, I suppose, the pay-off. Sex heading its ugly rear at the age of eighty-three, waiting so long, so long, too long. It was disturbing, laughable, pitiable and, to me, most definitely shocking. I forgave the old man his resolute enmity of years, then and there. He, the most triumphant man alive, after all has lived much less than I.

Noël Coward

10 June

1669

I went that evening to Lond: to carry Mr. Pepys to my Bro: (now exceedingly afflicted with the Stone in the bladder) who himselfe had ben successfully cut; and carried the Stone (which was as big as a tenis-ball) to shew him, and encourage his resolution to go thro the operation. 12 home: 16 To Lond: and tooke leave of my Bro: going out of towne: 17: home . . .

John Evelyn

1802

I wrote to Mrs Clarkson and Luff – went with Ellen to Rydale. Coleridge came in with a sack-full of Books etc. and a Branch of mountain ash. He had been attacked by a cow. He came over by Grisdale. A furious wind. Mr Simpson drank tea. William very poorly – we went to bed latish. I slept in sitting room.

Dorothy Wordsworth

1804

I'm so worn out by my thoughts that I can't write them down, in spite of a bottle of beer I went out to buy at Blancheron's.

Stendhal

1919

I have discovered that I cannot burn the candle at one end and write a book with the other.

Katherine Mansfield

1981

To one of those luncheons at George Weidenfeld's where one is lucky even to be introduced to the guest of honour one has been invited to meet. This time it was Franklin Murphy . . . president of a lot of banks. I sat next to his wife and worked rather hard at being polite. After a bit, she said: 'I didn't hear your name, I am afraid. Are you a professor?' I said I had been a professor and my name was Spender. She said, 'I'm afraid I've only heard of one Spender – Stephen Spender – and he's dead I believe.' 'Well, I'm Stephen Spender.' She took this in good part, repeated it to everyone at the end of the meal, with relish, so we won't forget each other.

Stephen Spender

1997 [on tour in Japan]

Performance days are always a bit tense, but the stress of the day was relieved for me by a comment, downstairs at breakfast, from a dancer who will remain anonymous. The more conventional elements of breakfast, toast, cereal and so on, were served alongside a tiny green salad with a very dubious-looking dressing, a slick of pale-coloured, viscous-textured fluid. I didn't say a word, merely looked aghast, and a porcelain-perfect ballerina piped up, 'Yeah, there's a man out the back with a magazine.' The incongruity of the source of the comment has kept me laughing all day. Face like an angel, mind like a sewer.

Deborah Bull

11 June

1897 [in India]

A bad night of heat but woke at 5.30 to find a blazing golden sunrise and the row of young *goldmohur* trees outside, emerald green. I never saw such colour. Oh, the freshness of that dripping green, after the night! A shower had come. Got up and rode to Harsola where the hedges are full of green *Hoya viridiflora* which I want to paint. Its long winding shoots were so tough that I was almost dragged out of my saddle in pulling a stray out, for the mare mistrusted it and insisted on backing. I kicked her furiously and hung on but the thing was like an india rubber rope and I could get no purchase on it. But a piece broke at last, just as a bullock cart was coming along to get in my way, and I had time to whip round with my treasure and make for home before the sun should wilt the blossom. When I got there it had closed up and was hanging in a miserable rag but as a last resource I threw it into a *chatti* [earthen vessel] of water in the bathroom and put on the lid, and when I came back after breakfast and lifted the thing off, there the *Hoya* lay, perfectly fresh and beautiful, and exquisite clusters of sea-green blossom lying spread on the water. Spent the rest of the morning on its portrait.

Violet Jacob

1922

Yesterday afternoon I dropped down Hay Hill for a cup of tea at Gunter's. There I encountered [art historian, Tancred] Borenius, who was eating a pink ice with Oscar Wilde's niece. Borenius talked of nothing but the Sitwells (who returned from Italy two days ago). Osbert [Sitwell] is a nuisance. I cannot dismiss him from my life. But I intend to keep him at more than arm's length for several more months. He is a case where one must assert one's independence. Borenius is a nice man, and he stood me a large pink ice. After that I sat in Hyde Park while the band played *Bohème* to a Saturday evening sunset-effect and a horde of anonymous Londoners.

After dinner (mollified by a demi-bottle of Sauterne) I read Freud's new book for two hours. Freud can't see straight about sex, but he has discovered a lot about the mechanism of the human mind.

This afternoon I enjoyed myself in Brompton Road. First I went to the International Theatre Exhibition at the Victoria and Albert Museum. But I was more inclined to look at the human exhibits than the art exhibits.

Then I popped into Brompton Oratory; the choral Mass seemed *the last word in dope*. (I noticed the drugged look in the faces of the audience as they came out.) The choir sang a bit of Elgar's *Apostles* very finely. It was a pleasant and interesting intermezzo, that Catholic celebration. I sat next to a red-haired youth whose beauty added to the interest of the proceedings.

My next diversion was ten minutes in Tattersall's Yard. The place discreetly thronged with top-hatted sportsmen, among whom I noted several familiar faces. The smell of stable evoked more sensuous images than all the incense at the Oratory, and I came away secretly gloating over the fact that I own two horses myself. I would rather win a point-to-point than hob-nob with ten cardinals.

Siegfried Sassoon

1940

I had a talk to Ian MacLaren, the plumber, who said there had been bad anti-Italian riots in Campbeltown; the three Italian shops had been broken up. The old man had been rather rash, saying that England needed a totalitarian govt and so on, but the younger ones were all decent, good citizens who gave money in charity and paid their taxes; one had contributed £50 to the Provost's fund; one of the youngest generation was in a mine sweeper. Ian had passed there early in the evening, and had seen a crowd hanging about and laughing, and wondered what was going to happen; people were beginning to get drunk; but he went home, then heard crashes and came out again and found the shops being broken up. If the tide had been in they would have put the old man into the harbour; the worst were the Polish sailors. But mostly they were like 'grown-up boys', out for a bit of fun, and could easily be made to go the other way. Half of them were no good, on public assistance and so on. Someone had said it was a shame, and had promptly been knocked down. He, Ian, had stood by; you couldn't help thinking it was funny. But he would be as friendly as he could to the Italians next time he saw them.

Naomi Mitchison

1942

B.B.C. Board. We discuss whether the clergy should use the microphone to preach forgiveness to our enemies. I say I prefer that to the clergy who seek to pretend that the bombing of Cologne was a Christian act. I wish the clergy would keep their mouths shut about the war. It is none of their business.

Harold Nicolson

12 June

1840

On Wednesday afternoon, as the Queen and Prince Albert were driving in a low carriage up Constitution Hill, about four or five in the afternoon, they were shot at by a lad of eighteen years old, who fired two pistols at them successively, neither shot taking effect. He was in the Green Park without the rails, and as he was only a few yards from the carriage, and, moreover, very cool and collected, it is marvellous he should have missed his aim. In a few moments the young man was seized, without any attempt on his part to escape or to deny the deed, and was carried off to prison. The Queen, who appeared perfectly cool, and not the least alarmed, instantly drove to the Duchess of Kent's, to anticipate any report that might reach her mother, and having done so, she continued her drive and went to the park. By this time the attempt upon her life had become generally known, and she was received with the utmost enthusiasm by the immense crowd that was congregated in carriages, on horseback, and on foot. All the equestrians formed themselves into an escort and attended her back to the Palace, cheering vehemently, while she acknowledged, with great appearance of feeling, these loyal manifestations.

Charles Greville

1874

Bathing yesterday and to-day. Yesterday the sea was very calm, but the wind has changed to the East and this morning a rough and troublesome [sea] came tumbling into the bay and plunging in foam upon the shore. The bay was full of white horses. At Shanklin one has to adopt the detestable custom of bathing in drawers. If ladies don't like to see men naked why don't they keep away from the sight? To-day I had a pair of drawers given me which I could not keep on. The rough waves stripped them off and tore them down round my ankles. While thus fettered I was seized and flung down by a heavy sea which retreating suddenly left me lying naked on the sharp shingle from which I rose streaming with blood. After this I took the wretched and dangerous rag off and of course there were some ladies looking on as I came up out of the water.

Rev. Francis Kilvert

1934

The case of F. Scott Fitzgerald becomes more distressing. He is boozing in a wild manner, and has become a nuisance. His wife, Zelda, who has been insane for years, is now confined at the Sheppard-Pratt Hospital, and he is living in Park Avenue with his little daughter, Scotty, aged 12. Some time ago he appeared at the apartment of the Duffys with Scotty, and horrified Anne Duffy by his performance. What he did she refuses to say, but obviously it was very shocking. Several years ago, visiting Joe Hergesheimer at West Chester, Pa., he caused a town sensation by arising at the dinner table and taking down his pantaloons, exposing his gospel pipe. Joe has refused to have anything to do with him since. He was lately laid up at the John Hopkins, suffering with a liver complaint. The young doctors of Baltimore avoid him as much as possible, for he has a playful habit of calling up those he knows at 3 a.m. and demanding treatment, *i.e.,* something to drink. How he manages to get any work done I can't imagine. His liver trouble is reported to be cirrhosis. He calls up the house now and then, usually proposing that Sara [Mencken's wife] and I go automobiling with him, but he is always plainly tight, and Sara always puts him off. His automobile driving is fearful and wonderful.

H. L. Mencken

13 June

1848

The expected Chartist demonstration yesterday ended in smoke, both here and in the provinces; nevertheless, great preparations were made of military, police and special constables. It rained torrents the whole day, which probably would have been enough to prevent any assemblages of people; but the determined attitude of the Government and the arrests that have taken place intimidated the leaders. Everybody had got bored and provoked to death with these continued alarms, but it is now thought that we shall not have any more of them. The Chartists themselves must get tired of meeting and walking about for nothing, and they can hardly fail to lose confidence in their leaders, whose actions so ill correspond with their promises and professions. A man of the name of MacDougal, who appears to be the chief of the London Chartists, harangued his rabble a few days ago, declared the meeting should take place in spite of Government, and announced the most heroic intentions. He went to the ground (at one of the *rendezvous*), and finding a magistrate there, asked him if the meeting was illegal, and if the Government really intended to prevent it. The magistrate referred him to the printed placard, by which he would see that it was illegal, and that the Government did intend to prevent it; on which he made a bow, said he did not intend to oppose the law, would go away, and advise his friends to do the same; and off he went. The failures have been complete everywhere and nobody feels any alarm.

Charles Greville

1932 [Oxford]

I had a note from Rupert and Miles asking me to go to the flicks. I dashed to Carfax at 7.30 and we went to *Goodnight Vienna* at the Queener. It was lovely, and somehow appropriate. We sat at the back in the corner and I had two arms around me for the first time in my history. The flick was over at 10, so we stopped at the coffee stall by Cowley Place on our way back. We drank to each other in chocolate Horlicks.

Barbara Pym

1967

I had been asked by the Central Office of Information to write a sketch on [L.S.] Lowry and so went to the Lefevre. On entering the gallery, I saw Lowry sitting on a sofa giving an interview to a journalist. I told him of this commission to write an article on him. He seemed very happy that I should do so. The next day there was a picture in *The Times* of Lowry talking to the Postmaster General in the Lefevre Gallery. It is a good likeness, with the curious stare and smiling look that he has. He complained to me of his poverty, as usual, which is a kind of fiction. The walls contained thousands of pounds of Lowry on sale (many of them already sold). He had invented an ingenious way of making a little money, he told me. The G.P.O. next month are bringing out a 1s. 6d. stamp on which will be one of Lowry's pictures, a very signal recognition that I had never heard of before for an artist. Lowry's idea is now to have 500 postcard sized reproductions of the picture on the stamp, and to sell them himself from his house at 2s. 6d. a time with his autograph, to persons who come bothering him. If he sells his 500 that would net him about £60 minus costs, a modest sum one might think for a man who commands £3,000 even for a small picture. However he is like that, as indeed he has always been.

Maurice Collis

14 June

1850

Once again I have taken up my diary, and once again with new fervour and a new purpose. How many times is that? I can't remember. Never mind, perhaps I'll drop it again; but it's a pleasant occupation and it will be pleasant to re-read it, just as it was pleasant to re-read my old ones. There are lots of thoughts in one's head, and some of them seem very remarkable, but when you examine them they turn out to be nonsense; others on the other hand seem sensible – and that's what a diary is needed for. On the basis of one's diary it's very convenient to judge oneself.

Leo Tolstoy

1916

Lunched at Downing Street. While I remember, I must record two 'Margots' [Margot Asquith, wife of PM] – Talking of Mr Balfour's neglect of distributing medals, 'Shall I tell you what's the matter with Arthur? He's got no womb . . . no womb!' And when Violet asked her if she was going to wear her hat with ostrich feathers for Kitchener's memorial service, 'How can you ask me? Dear Kitchener saw me in that hat twice!'

Lady Cynthia Asquith

1919 [Paris]

D. [Lloyd George] and the President [Wilson] have had some rather warm passages on the League of Nations. D. contended that the annexation of Silesia was not in accordance with the principles of the League. 'But Mr Lord [R. H. Lord, American historian] says so-&-so,' said the President in defence. 'Mr Lord!' exclaimed D., 'Mr Lord! When I agreed to the 14 points I did so because I thought they expressed the wishes of the American people, & not because Mr Lord wanted them!'

Frances Stevenson

1962

Went to park. Full of girls who sit up, bending over their male companions who are lying down, receiving their kissings & caressings. It is disgusting to watch. No wonder Billy Graham thought our parks so foul. But I'm sure Hyde is the worst. There is so much riff-raff living near.

Kenneth Williams

1981

The big news yesterday was the firing of six blank shots at the Queen on her way to the Trooping of the Colour. I note the matter-of-fact acceptance by everyone of the Queen's coolness during and after the incident. It is assumed by now that this middle-aged woman will always behave calmly and if required heroically, which is no doubt a correct assumption. As a monarchist, I am loyal but not sentimental. Elizabeth [his wife] is far more easily moved by royal occasions, about which she writes so beautifully. But of the Queen herself I am a passionate admirer.

Lord Longford

15 June

1933

Sold my play 'Jig-Saw' to Theatre Guild and received $500 for option – also sold short thing to *New Yorker* for $70. Went to tea for Bernard Sobel at Pierre's: Ogden Nash and I got tight and pigged all the cocktails we could find. I paid Francis $100 of the $650 I owe him, paid Louise $100, Marie $50, Dr. Hornbeck $20, Mr. David $20, Joe $60, Ten Eyck $39.50 Funny how little you can do with $500 – barely stave off lawsuits here and there.

Dawn Powell

1940

I have been too rushed this historic week to write my diary in any detail. The events crowd thick and fast and each one seems worse than the other. Yet a curious psychological effect is produced. Fear and sorrow seem to give way to anger and pride. It may be because I know that I shall kill myself and Vita will kill herself if the worst comes. Thus there comes a point where Hitler will cease to trouble either of us, and meanwhile by every means in our power we will continue to worry him.

Then there is another state of mind which I notice. I am able almost entirely to dismiss from my thoughts any consideration of the future. I do not even have such pangs about the past as I had when the situation was less catastrophic. My reason tells me that it will now be almost impossible to beat the Germans, and that the probability is that France will surrender and that we shall be bombed and invaded. I am quite lucidly aware that in three weeks from now Sissinghurst may be a waste and Vita and I both dead. Yet these probabilities do not fill me with despair. I seem to be impervious both to pleasure and pain. For the moment we are all anaesthetised.

Harold Nicolson

1940

Cabinet at 10. French army seems to have disintegrated. After, Neville [Chamberlain] brought up proposal – which he didn't think much of (nor I) – for fusion of British and French Governments – I had meanwhile drafted telegram to Bordeaux, suggesting French Government should come here. That is the most practical step. Draft approved. I broke away at lunchtime – I've had 10 weeks non-stop and it's too much, almost, even for me! Went out in a deluge of rain and picked peas and dug potatoes for our dinner, which was excellent. Did some writing after, but won't look at work! Everything *awful*, but 'Come the three corners of the world and we will shock them'. We'll all fight like cats – or die rather than submit to Hitler. U. S. look pretty useless. Well, we must die without them.

Sir Alexander Cadogan

1969

That Beatle who is married to an Asiatic lady was on the Frost Programme. The man is long-haired & unprepossessing, with tin spectacles and this curious nasal Liverpudlian delivery: the appearance is either grotesque or quaint & the overall impression is one of great foolishness. He and his wife are often 'interviewed' from inside *bags* in order to achieve 'objectivity' and they have 'lie-ins' whereby they stay in bed for long periods & allow a certain number of people into the room. I think this man's name is Ringo Star or something (No – it's John Lennon) but he began as a 'singer' and instrumentalist with this group called The Beatles and one searches in vain for any valid reason for his being interviewed *at all*. What this ex-pop-singer is doing pontificating about the state of humanity, I cannot imagine. It's mind-bending to listen to.

Kenneth Williams

1981 [lunching at Windsor]

To my surprise and gratification I was put next to Lady Diana Spencer, the heroine of the hour. Her beautiful face, lovely complexion and eyes are set off by a chin which is pronounced in profile. Her striking independence of mind will always remain a keen memory. Curiously enough Elizabeth [his wife], who had not met her, finished a recent article by referring to this 'independence'.

In the same spirit Diana told me that Norman Hartnell and the other top dressmakers had implored her to allow them to make her wedding dress, but she had chosen the Emmanuels. She had liked something of theirs that she had seen. I asked whether they were well known. She replied, 'They are now.' Her manners are excellent towards elderly gentlemen and, I should judge, everyone else.

There was a lot to drink at lunch, white wine, red wine, champagne, port, brandy. Not to mention gin and tonic, sherry, whisky and soda previously. Diana never touches alcohol, nor, she told me, do her friends.

I look back on today's proceedings through rose-tinted glasses after my meeting with Lady Diana. Prince Charles was very gracious to me and Elizabeth about the books we had sent him, which we ourselves had written. But I cannot quite put out of mind the thought of the fourteen hundred guests on 29 July (including some like Ken Livingstone who have treated the invitation with contempt), among whom we are not included. Relationships with royalty are not, and never have been, quite like those with other people.

Lord Longford

1982

Mrs Thatcher announces the surrender [by the Argentine forces] of Port Stanley in well-modulated tones. Film follows of the funeral of the commandos killed at Goose Green, the simple service and the youth of the wounded unbearable. A pilot of one of the Harriers talks about the effectiveness of the Sidewinder missiles. 'A bit of an eye-opener,' is how he puts it. A bit of an eye-closer too. Not English I feel now. This is just where I happen to have been put down. No country. No party. No Church. No voice.

And now they are singing 'Britannia Rules the Waves' outside Downing Street. It's the Last Night of the Proms erected into a policy.

Alan Bennett

1982

There has been an Argentinian surrender, and the reaction now is of tremendous enthusiasm and support for Mrs Thatcher. However, this is not the moment to unbend but the time to reaffirm everything that we've said. It won't be popular, but if you've taken a principled position you don't withdraw from it.

I went to the house to hear the Prime Minister announcing the surrender. Michael Foot [leader of the Labour Party] congratulated her and her forces; somehow it was odious and excessive. I was called, and I asked if the PM would publish all the documents and the costs in terms of life, equipment and money of a tragic unnecessary war. The Tories erupted in anger because this was Jingo Day.

I said the world knew very well that the war would not solve the problem of the future of the Falklands Islands. 'Does she agree that in the end there must be negotiations, and will she say with whom and when she will be ready to enter into such negotiations?' She said she couldn't publish the documents, she saw no reason to negotiate with Argentina, she thought the war tragic but not unnecessary, because the freedom of speech which the Right Honourable Gentleman made such excellent use of had been won for him by people fighting for it. Rubbish, but the Tories loved it.

Tony Benn

1983

Jenny Easterbrook has a very pale skin and large violet eyes. Her blonde hair is *gamine* short, her sexuality tightly controlled. She makes plain her feelings on several counts (without expressing them): one, that I am an uncouth chauvinist lout; two, that it is a complete mystery why I have been made a Minister; three, that my tenure in this post is likely to be a matter of weeks rather than months.

I did, though, get a reaction when I asked, in all innocence, if she would take dictation. She had, after all, described herself to me only yesterday as 'a secretary'. And I wanted to clear my head by writing my own summary memo. 'Can't you do shorthand?'

'I'm an official, not a typist.'

Alan Clark

16 June

1670

I was forc'd to accompanie some friends to the Bear-garden etc: Where was Cock fighting, Beare, Dog-fighting, Beare and Bull baiting, it being a famous day for all these butchery Sports, or rather barbarous cruelties: The Bulls did exceedingly well but the Irish Wolfe dog exceeded, which was a tall Grayhound a stately creature in deede, who beate a cruell Mastife: One of the Bulls tossed a Dog full into a Ladys lap, as she sate in one of the boxes at a Considerable height from the Arena: There were two poore dogs killed; and so all ended with the Ape on horse-back, and I most heartily weary, of rude and dirty passetime, which I had not seene I think in twenty yeares before.

John Evelyn

1889

What ghastly lives some people lead. The Bradleys, who make baskets, have a hen who in a polite manner lays *two!* eggs for my breakfast every morn. The daughter told Nurse the other day that her father had not been sober since Christmas. It seems he has drunk all his life, that there are 15 children and that [the] eldest son, a lad of nineteen who is a pattern of virtue looks after everything and that his father maltreats him horribly. This girl is so pretty, and what is better has grace, which you see so rarely here. One of them is married and I suppose the remaining 14 are ready at any moment to plunge into matrimony. How overwhelming is the virtue of the poor! This doesn't include their fondness for the conjugal state.

Alice James

1940

G[ladwyn] J[ebb] rang up – as he always does – to say awful things were happening which he couldn't tell me on the telephone. Just to 'warn' me. Fat lot of good *that* does. Telephone call 4.45 – could I return to London at once: I should be wanted to leave 'on a sea trip tonight'. So packed and had hurried tea and started 5.20. Car behaved splendidly and we got home 7.50.

Orders are to leave with Winston and others from Waterloo 9.40. Embark in 'Galatea' midnight for Concarneau, or some point on coast of Brittany, to meet [French prime minister Paul] Reynaud. Packed and dined. But at 8.50 Foreign Office rang up to say trip off. 9.30 rang up to say trip on again. (I had kept my bag ready packed!) Jumped into taxi and got to Waterloo at 9.55. Found Winston had just gone back again to No. 10. So came home. Cabinet offices warn me to be ready at a moment's notice. Life rather like that of a fireman. (Only with no hope of putting out the fire!) Got into bed and at about 11.45 Cabinet Offices rang up to say Reynaud had resigned and Pétain formed a Government. There might be a Cabinet meeting – would I stand by. I said I would 'lie by', in bed – turned out the light and went to sleep!

Sir Alexander Cadogan

17 June

1812

At four o'clock dined in the hall with [Thomas] de Quincey, who was very civil to me, and invited me cordially to visit his cottage in Cumberland. De Quincey is, like myself, an enthusiast for Wordsworth; his person is small, his complexion fair, and his air and manner those of a sickly, enfeebled man. From which circumstances his sensibility, which I have no doubt is genuine, is in danger of being mistaken for a puling and womanly weakness. At least, coarser and more robustly healthful persons will think so. His conversation is sensible, and I *suppose* him to be a man of information on general subjects. His views in studying the law will never, I think, be realized. He has a small independent fortune, and the only thing he wants is a magnificent library; this he is willing to purchase by giving for a few years' close attention to the law. But he is resolved on no account to put himself under a special pleader, nor will he live more than six months during the year in London. I represented to him that I feared *nothing* could be expected from the law *so* studied. A man must be altogether or not at all a lawyer . . .

Henry Crabb Robinson

1929

Tommy [Countess of Rosslyn] told me two good stories: one about Juliet Duff and one about Lady Theo Acheson. Former who is very tall had a tremendous success with all the young people in Berlin. All the young men pursued her. No one could understand her *succès* until it was discovered that the Berlin *jeunesse dorée* thought she was a man masquerading as a woman.

Lady Theo Acheson had wonderful hair of which she was very proud. In her passport form under the sub-heading 'any peculiarities' she put in 'hair below the knees'. In the passport this was abbreviated by the passport officer to 'hairy legs'!

Sir Robert Bruce Lockhart

1942

Elsie and I went to town to see if we could get any fish. There were about 100–150 people in the fish-market, and not one fish to be seen! All the counters were empty. However, there were a few mackerel hidden underneath, and Elsie got three for themselves and three for Mrs Howells. She was lucky; many people were disappointed. Fancy no fish to be had in Jersey; to think that the Germans deprive us even of that! Went on beach and paddled – sea-air does one good and is a pleasant change.

Nan Le Ruez

1978

Went to *Saturday Night Fever* this evening. It's a computer picture, expertly made, beautifully shot, and with a blazing star performance from a new young man – John Travolta. I think the computer was asked, 'If you wanted to remake in the late seventies an Astaire/Rogers film, with all its appeal, and particularly its appeal to the young, what would you do?' This movie is the answer. A feeling of manipulation pervades the whole affair – and of course it works on the audience. I think what depresses me is that up to quite recently I have always believed popular art in all its manifestations in history was popular because it had merit – in some sense it was good. The public's own vitality saw to that. But now this isn't so any more. Market research provides the right product, the public is manipulated: 1984 has come.

Peter Hall

1990

This morning I killed the heron.

He has been raiding the moat, starting in the early hours, then getting bolder and bolder, taking eight or nine fish, carp, nishikoi, exotica, every day.

I had risen very early, before five, with the intention of getting a magpie who has been pillaging all the nests along the beech hedge. But returned empty-handed. They are clever birds, and sense one's presence.

Suddenly Jane [his wife] spotted the heron from the casement window in my bathroom.

I ran down and took the 4.10 off the slab, cocked the hammer. He was just opposite the steps, took off clumsily and I fired, being sickened to see him fall back in the water, struggle vainly to get up the bank, one wing useless.

I reloaded, went round to the opposite bank. Tom beat me to it and gamely made at him, but the great bird, head feathers bristling and eyes aglare, made a curious high-pitched menacing sound, his great beak jabbing fiercely at the Jack Russell.

'Get Tom out of the way,' I screamed.

I closed the range to about twenty feet and took aim. I did not want to mutilate that beautiful head, so drew a bead on his shoulder.

The execution. For a split second he seemed simply to have absorbed the shot; then very slowly his head arched round and took refuge inside his wing, half under water. He was motionless, dead.

I was already sobbing as I went back up the steps: 'Sodding fish, why should I kill that beautiful creature just for the sodding fish . . .'

I cursed and blubbed up in my bedroom, as I changed into jeans and a T-shirt. I was near a nervous breakdown. Yet if it had been a burglar or a vandal I wouldn't have given a toss. It's human beings that are the vermin.

Alan Clark

18 June

1657

I saw at Greenwich a sort of Catt brought from the East Indies, shaped and snouted much like the Egyptian Ratoone, in the body like a Monkey, and so footed: the eares and taile like a Catt, onely the taile much longer, and the Skin curiously ringed, with black and white: With this taile, it wound up its body like a Serpent, and so got up into trees, and with it, would also wrap its whole body round: It was of a wolly haire as a lamb, exceedingly nimble, and yet gentle, and purr'd as dos the cat.

John Evelyn

1920

How this Germany bores me! It's a good middling country, with lovely pale colours and wide landscapes; but what inhabitants! A degraded peasantry whose crudeness however doesn't give birth to any fabulous monsters, just a quiet decline into the animal kingdom; a middle class run to fat; and drab intellectuals. The answer: America . . .

Bertolt Brecht

1932

Now that the year is walking in all her glory – I sometimes drop into a bitter mood. It is a season in which the body should rejoice. The women are able to display themselves thro brilliant colours, and sometimes the sight of a fresh young girl with the sun in her hair seems to awaken, more strongly this year, a sense of frustration. But this is little enough – the bitterest moments are yet to come; tho' I do not feel they will grow to be more than moments. There are many different planes of battle – and many camouflages to disguise cowardice. If I believed in a guardian angel – what ought I to pray? 'Protect me from appealing to anybody's pity.'

William Soutar

1943

This morning I got a most unexpected phone call from Veronica inviting me to a cocktail party given by old Lady Lovat at the castle.

All the local lairds were invited, and tottered forth from their castles in kilt and sporran.

I was cornered by a quite fantastic roaring old Highland pansy called Major Monroe-Ferguson, the Oscar Wilde of the Highlands. He appeared to know my relations, and talked for ages about family trees. Apparently he is so mean that if you visit him at Novar Castle you have to bring your own sandwiches.

All the women seem to affect the same kind of headgear, an inverted felt porridge-bowl, with a moulting eagle's feather secured to it by the clan badge. I escaped the Major and stayed firmly by the food.

Joan Wyndham

1947

I suddenly heard my own name in a book talk on the wireless. I had only heard it once before, when my first book was published. The man, Woodrow Wyatt, only mentioned it with those of a few other writers he thought interesting, but it gave me great pleasure – perhaps especially since I was all alone in the house. I hugged it to me, as if my own name were a Christmas or a birthday surprise.

Denton Welch

19 June

1837

Went to rehearsal, having previously looked at the newspaper for the King's health. Went to theatre; when half dressed a person passed by door saying the

King 'was off'. Upon inquiry I heard that notices of the event – his death – had been fixed up at the offices of the *Courier* and *Observer*, and it was said that it had been up at the Mansion House more than two hours since. The state of suspense in which I was kept to the very moment of the beginning of the play so agitated me that when I went on the stage I was weaker than I often am when I finish a character. I laboured through Richard, but it was labour, and most ineffectual. I was very bad, very bad.

Charles Macready

1938

The 'Sunday Express' today published a most extraordinary paragraph to the effect that I am really 41 instead of 39, and hinted that I had faked my age in the reference books. The awful thing is that it is true. Now I feel apprehensive and shy, as one does when one is in disgrace. Honor is being very sweet and loyal about it . . . I told her she would be a widow two years earlier.

'Chips' Channon

1938

The sum total of eighteen years of difficult scientific work – after twenty-five years of homelessness and transience.
  1. I am without a home or a passport.
  2. Am an émigré Jewish sexologist, scientist, socialist.
  3. Have lost my children.
  4. Lack the support of a scientific organisation.
  5. Have been ostracized as a charlatan, swindler, and con man.
  6. Have been deserted by the second woman I loved.
  7. Deserted by dozens of pupils.
  8. Thrown out of two large organizations.
  9. Must appear in court to prove my identity.
  10. Am penniless.
  11. Have no hope for success during my lifetime – or for children.

Wilhelm Reich

20 June

1937

Three days in New York almost knocked me out. I had to eat three heavy dinners, and to drink more than was good for me. I was certainly not tight, but nevertheless I developed a most uncomfortable gastritis. Today I have subsisted on four eggs, two glasses of milk and an ice cream soda. The ice cream soda was the first that I had drunk for at least thirty years.

H. L. Mencken

1940 [Paris]

The men who went down to Orléans and Blois yesterday tell a horrible tale. Along the road they saw what they estimated to be 200,000 refugees – people of all classes, rich and poor, lying along the roadside or by the edge of the forests, starving – without food, without water, no shelter, nothing.

They are just a few of the millions who fled Paris and the other cities and towns before the German invaders. They fled, tearing in fright along the roads with their belongings on their backs or on bikes or in baby-carriages, and their children atop them. Soon the roads were clogged. Troops were also trying to use them. Soon the Germans came over, bombing the roads. Soon there were dead and dying. And no food, no water, no shelter, no care. It is estimated there were seven million refugees between here and Bordeaux. Almost all face starvation unless something is done at once. The German army is helping a little, but not much. It has had to carry most of its own food into France from Germany. The Red Cross is doing what it can, but is wholly inadequate.

A human catastrophe, such as even China has not experienced. (And how many Frenchmen or other Europeans softened their hearts when a flood or a famine or a war snuffed out a million Chinese?)

William L. Shirer

1942 [Holland]

Soon you'll have grease spots all over your books and ink spots all over your sandwiches, said Pa. The others are still at lunch, I have pushed my plate to one side and am copying out bits of Rilke between the extremely good strawberries and the odd kind of rabbit food we are eating . . . And now the room is empty, and I am writing amid crumbs on the tablecloth, a lonely radish, and dirty napkins. Käthe is already washing up in the kitchen. It is half past one. I shall take a nap for an hour. At five o'clock Becker is sending me a man who wants to take Russian lessons. Tonight I must read Pushkin for one hour. I don't have to stand in queues and have few worries about the housekeeping. I don't think there's another person in all Holland who has it as easy, at least that's how it seems to me. I feel a very strong obligation to make full use of all this time I have to myself, not to waste one minute of it. And yet I still don't work with enough concentration and energy. I really have obligations, moral obligations.

Etty Hillesum

1942

This is a black day, for we have had to give up our wireless. Herbert packed it, and took it to the parish hall. Everyone feels it very much as it is our only link with England. One feels so mad against the Germans (wrong as it is to feel so) for we have done nothing to deserve this. However, let us be thankful that it is only our wireless sets that have been taken and not our young men. We shall never be at rest until the Germans have gone – may they depart soon! Then, another disturbing thing: today on the *Evening Post* there is an Order from the German Commandant. He has arrested ten persons in Jersey, as hostages, because of leaflets with inciting contents, which have been printed and distributed; also for sabotage in connection with the telephone. If the perpetrators don't give themselves up, these ten persons are to be interned on the Continent. One has heard of this sort of thing in European countries under occupation and now it has come to this little island. Some girls had shown me one of these leaflets, trying to persuade people not to give up their wireless. I wish people would keep quiet, and not put us all into trouble. It is no use going against the Germans unless it is a matter of conscience.

Well, we do feel depressed about everything tonight.

Nan Le Ruez

21 June

1933 [sailing in Sweden]

In the afternoon we had to stop for one and one half hours while the boat climbed seven locks. Mrs Watt [her travelling companion] stayed on the ship, but most of the people went in a taxi to see the watermen work. I walked along the road a little way and then climbed right up into the woods, up the rocks, through the wet moss and small blueberry plants. I usurped the crows' kingdom. They screamed at me and cawed and were very unpleasant. They circled above me above the pines. The country was lovely – I understood it in a jiffy. Through the trees the water was branching off in two directions – and forests as far as the eye could see. Real forests. Birch and evergreen and underbrush. I went through the wet woods and the drops fell on my hair. The scent of those woods was divine: little yellow scutellarias, wild false lily of the valley and real lily of the valley. The hill I was on hung over the locks. I could see the boat being raised. There was cliff between it and me and another cliff on the other side with fir trees on its top.

I took off my shoes and tried to bunch up my tweed skirt. It was tight and bulky. Fat black slugs like walruses lay about on the ground. They had two little removable horns and creased leather backs. They lay about with a careless nonchalant air. Oh! that was a heavenly hour. My woods, my rocks, my smells.

Elizabeth Smart

1974

This morning I endeavoured to get a Bath number for three-quarters of an hour. Three times I rang the exchange, three times the supervisor. Finally, I was driven so mad with rage that I shouted abuse down the mouthpiece and smashed the telephone to smithereens on the hearthstone. Pieces of it flew across the room to the windows. Instead of feeling ashamed I felt greatly relieved. And if it cost me £50 to repair it was worth it. I only wish the telephonist who was so obstructive and impertinent to me had been the hearthstone. [Lady] Caroline [Somerset] reminded me yesterday that wrath was one of the seven deadly sins.

James Lees-Milne

22 June

1837

I have often observed that most people grow bold and hard when they are treated with gentleness and consideration. But as soon as they meet harshness and violence, they lose all self-assertion and become conciliatory and soft. This trait of human nature is almost always apparent in love, and unhappily it often appears in the personal conflicts between friends.

It has always seemed to me contemptible that people should be dominated by fear rather than by love. But, strange to say, this dominance is inevitable. It is necessary to the maintenance of society, and is as essential to the most democratic government as to one of absolute power.

George Sand

1866

Very fine. Train to Lyndhurst Road and walk into [New] Forest – beeches cut down – warm – pretty country towards Dibden and Southhampton. Tents, with folk like gypsies (but they say *no*) peeling rushes for rushlights: you leave a strip of green on the pith for backbone. Beaulieu, the Duke's park, old church and ruins. Village, tide in. Cottage hung with roses, man in front garden tells me he has lived there fifty-three years. I praise the beauty and quiet, but he often thinks he 'ought to a' pushed out into the world –

gone to London or some large place.' Boys fishing for bass. The miller's, a piano going inside ('It is the miller's daughter', no doubt). Rasher and ale at the inn. The young lady at the bar with short curls and towny air finds it 'very dull here'. I walk away at 20 to 9, sunset light over heath and forest, long road. The night-jar whirring.

William Allingham

1919 [Berlin]

Scheidemann and Rantzau have resigned [rather than assent to the Versailles Treaty]. The new [Gustav] Bauer Cabinet proposes to sign the peace treaty under protest and with reservations. These relate to acknowledgement of Germany's sole war-guilt and extradition of the Emperor as well as other so-called criminals.

The German Navy, interned at Scapa Flow, has scuttled its ships.

This evening I have been indescribably depressed, as though the entire sap of life has dried up inside me.

Count Harry Kessler

1931

Did three pages on the novel. Tired to death but work out of sheer nervous desperation, weight of responsibility, necessity for making plans about Jojo [her son] this fall, making money for these plans. I can't see or think about anything else; Joe's concern over me, to the neglect of his child, makes me doubly responsible. What other fate need I have expected after my first 21 years' training in work, worry, insecurity and frustration? One has to be born and raised fortunately in order to be forever fortunate.

Thinking it over, no great woman writers ever raised kids, did they (except Sigrid Undset)? All the 'charming' lady literati have had charming children but then they write magazine trash. Women seem to me the greatest opportunists, the most unscrupulous artists in the world – they turn any genius they have into money without a pang – whereas the man artist, supporting his family by distortions of his genius, never ceases to bemoan his lost ideal.

Dawn Powell

1977

Yesterday I went to London for two funny little ceremonies. The first was the presentation of a red rose to the Lord Mayor in the Mansion House at 11.30 a.m. on behalf of Lady Knollys, in permanent rent, or rather contrition, for having built in 1381 a bridge across Seething Lane connecting her house to a garden the other side, this without first obtaining the Lord Mayor's permission. We were lined up on either side of the Egyptian Hall. The Lord Mayor walked in, wearing a badge (no chains) of office and a tail-coat. Followed by a Master of the Watermen in long sable and ermine gown. On either side stood a row of Doggett's Watermen, wearing scarlet uniform and caps, holding an oar each. The Master read aloud an explanation of the purpose of the ceremony. A clerk presented to the Lord Mayor a freshly picked red rose on a golden embroidered cushion. During the address the Lord Mayor stood, with dignity and aplomb, only his eyes smiling. A nice man. Ceremony over, we moved to the next room and were given sherry, and a red rose each.

London Library, shopping and Sotheby's in afternoon. Consider making a bid for a lock of Dickens's hair on 6th July. Then at 6.30 to 24 Chester Square to attend the unveiling of a plaque to Mary Shelley who lived in this house towards the end of her life. A Mrs Hass organized the whole thing, and put up and paid for the plaque. She made a speech just like Joyce Grenfell and called upon an earnest young lady with scooped-back hair, *pince-nez* and a green cloak to read a poem of Shelley's to Mary. This she did on the pavement in the most affected, genteel and emotional manner, so that I could hardly contain myself. Refrained from catching Sheila Birkenhead's eye for fear I should explode. Traffic roaring past and passers-by on foot were amazed at the spectacle. Motored home, eating *en route* at the first motorway station – filth. Arrived home at 11 p.m.

James Lees-Milne

23 June

1761

About 1.50 it pleased Almighty God to take from me my beloved wife, who, poor creature, has laboured under a severe though lingering illness for these 38 weeks past, which she bore with the greatest resignation to the Divine Will [she was aged 27H]. In her I have lost a sincere friend and virtuous wife, a prudent and good economist in her family and a very valuable companion (and one endued with more than a common share of good sense). I will once more say she was virtuous even in the most strictest sense of the word virtue; she was always decent in her apparel and remarkably sweet and cleanly in her person, and had by nature a cheerful though religious turn of mind. Therefore I have lost an invaluable blessing, a wife who, had it pleased God to have given her health, would have been of more real excellence to me than the greatest fortune this world can give. Oh, may her agonizing pains and dying groans have such a constant impression on my mind that (through the assistance [of] God's Grace) I may ever have the thought of death in my mind, and that by a truly religious course of life may be prepared to meet that King of Terrors; may the memory of her virtues always excite in me a love of that which is good and virtuous, and may I endeavour to copy the many excellencies she was undoubtedly possessed of; therefore I may justly say with the incomparable Mr. Young: 'Let them who have ever lost an angel pity me.'

We dined on the remains of yesterday's dinner.

Thomas Turner

1894

Very soon after I got to my room, I received the joyful news that dear May had been safely delivered of a son [the future Duke of Windsor], a fine strong child! What joy! What a blessing! How relieved and thankful to God I feel for this great mercy!

Queen Victoria

1924

As soon as I was up I went to an exhibition of Lovat Fraser's printed work at the First Edition Club. I was again strengthened in my conviction of his bewildering charm and my contempt for those who abuse him as a 1920 fashion! I went abroad to Kensington where I stole Alec's [Waugh's older brother] large paper copy of Max's [Beerbohm] *Works*. I gave luncheon to Tony [Bushell] at the Previtali and returned home. By far the most important event of the morning was my ordering of a new stick. I tried to get one as like as possible to the old one but found nothing so beautiful – and indeed I think it would have seemed to me rather indecent had I done so. The one I have chosen is of English oak but lighter and a little longer than my other one. I am having a small golden plate about the size of a shilling let into the top, engraved with my name and crest. I think it will be a success. I arrived home to find a wire from Alastair [Graham] asking me to meet him for dinner at the Previtali. We had a quiet and pleasant dinner and wandered down by the way of many pubs to the Embankment and back in the same manner to the Café Royal. There we found a sweet drunk man called Wilkinson who had been at Radley. Soon we were joined by the foul Tasha Gielgud and in her company a pert young woman dressed almost wholly as a man. They had many drinks with us and attracted a great deal of attention. We managed in the end to get rid of them only by leaving the restaurant ourselves and putting them to lesbianize in a taxi. And so home.

Evelyn Waugh

1930

Tennis-party at wealthy and elaborate house, to which Robert and I now bidden for the first time. (Also, probably, the last.) Immense opulence of host and hostess at once discernible in fabulous display of deck-chairs, all of complete stability and miraculous cleanliness. Am introduced to youngish lady in yellow, and serious young man with horn-rimmed spectacles. Lady in yellow says at once that she is sure I have a lovely garden. (Why?)

Elderly, but efficient-looking, partner is assigned to me, and we play against the horn-rimmed spectacles and agile young creature in expensive crêpe-de-chine. Realise at once that all three play very much better than I do. Still worse, realise that *they* realise this. Just as we begin, my partner observes gravely that he ought to tell me he is a left-handed player. Cannot imagine what he expects me to do about it, lose my head, and reply madly that That is Splendid.

Game proceeds, I serve several double-faults, and elderly partner becomes graver and graver. At beginning of each game he looks at me and repeats score with fearful distinctness, which, as it is never in our favour, entirely unnerves me. At 'Six–*one*' we leave the court and silently seek chairs as far removed from one another as possible.

E. M. Delafield

1947

On my instructions Laura [his second wife] purchased a wireless set. Sir Max Beerbohm had made me think that the Third Programme might interest us, particularly when we are in Ireland. I have listened attentively to all programmes and nothing will confirm me more in my resolution to emigrate.

Evelyn Waugh

1965

There has been another high-flown debate in the House of Lords about suggested (idiotic) amendments to the Homosexual Bill, in the course of which Lord Montgomery announced that homosexuality between men was the most abominable and bestial act that any human being could commit! It, in his mind, apparently compares unfavourably with disembowelling, torturing, gas chambers and brutal murder. It is inconceivable that a man of his eminence and achievements could make such a statement. The poor old sod must be gaga.

The Beatles have all four been awarded MBEs, which has caused considerable outcry. Furious war heroes are sending back their bravely-won medals by the bushel. It is, of course, a tactless and major blunder on the part of the Prime Minister [Harold Wilson], and also I don't think the Queen should have agreed. Some other decoration should have been selected to reward them for their talentless but considerable contributions to the Exchequer.

Noël Coward

1967 [Tangier]

Larbi [local male prostitute] turned up at five. We took him to Frank's [Professor Frank Holroyd] flat to watch my mask being made. An unnerving experience for me. Under the influence of drugs the plaster being put over my face didn't bother me much – though I had an overwhelming desire to laugh at the ridiculousness of it all – but when the time came to fill in my ear thus taking my *sound* as well as my vision by half, I found the whole thing got very frightening and sinister. Suddenly I wasn't in control any more. I didn't know what was my invention and what was real. I had to insist on my ear not being blocked with plaster. Left Frank pottering around with the finished mould. Though, as Kenneth [Halliwell] said, 'All the masks he ever does look the same, so what is the point of taking an impression of somebody's face?'

Joe Orton

1973

I have decided that the reason why one keeps a diary is the compulsion to write something, anything. Secondly, all intending writers are well advised to keep diaries, for practice, like doing scales. Mine are absolutely unstudied. I never pause an instant to consider whether I write grammatically, or not. No doubt diary-keeping is also a kind of vanity. One has the sauce to believe that every thought which comes into one's head merits recording.

James Lees-Milne

1983

It's not yet eight o'clock and already I've been in my office half an hour. I like to get here early, before anyone else arrives, then I can scowl at them through the communicating doorway as they take their places around the outer office. I am still so ignorant of the basic material that this is one of the few ways I can start to assert an ascendancy.

It is (naturally and heartbreakingly) a glorious summer morning, and I have drawn back to their maximum extent the sliding windows, thus buggering or – I trust – partially buggering the air-conditioning system. There is a tiny *balcon*, a gutter really, with a very low parapet, below knee height. Certain death on the Victoria Street pavement eight floors below. Sometimes I get a wild urge to relieve my bladder over it, splattingly on the ant-like crowds. Would this get one the sack? Probably not. It would *have* to be hushed up.

Alan Clark

24 June

1690

Dined with and visited me Mr. Pepys, Mr. Stuart and other friends. Mr. P sent the next day to the Gate-house, and severall greate persons to the Towre, on suspicion of being affected to K James: amongst which was my Lord Earle of Clarendon, unkle to the Queene.

Mr. Pepys was the next morning imprisoned etc.

John Evelyn

1940

I was called at 7, dressed and ate nervously; at 8.15 we set out for Euston. Honor and I had the child [son Paul, aged 5, about to be evacuated to the USA] between us; he was gay and interested. At the station there was a queue of Rolls-Royces and liveried servants and mountains of trunks. It seemed that everyone we knew was there.

We led our child to his compartment, and clung hungrily to him until the whistle blew and then after a feverish hug and kiss, we left him. I care more for Paul than for all of France, and mind his departure dreadfully. For the first time in my life I felt a surge of remorse for my own appallingly callous treatment of my parents, who perhaps once loved me as I love Paul.

As the Cease Fire between France and Germany came into effect at 12.25 this morning, we can now be prepared for the Battle of Britain – or rather on Britain.

'Chips' Channon

1942

All week I've missed Alfred [her fiancé, 'stranded' in England, due to occupation of Jersey] terribly and have had a lot of wicked thoughts, such as anger, disappointment – don't know really how to express it all, because Alfred and I are having to wait so long for marriage. We are getting old, and it is over four years since we got engaged. It seems to spoil things to wait so long.

Nan Le Ruez

1981

The only conversation which sticks in my mind from last night was one with Prue Windlesham, fashion editor until recently of *The Times* and a tower of strength as a judge of the Catherine Pakenham Award. I told Prue that in my opinion normal men didn't dress with a view to appearing attractive. She disagreed totally. She assured me that men dressed either to create an impression of power (e.g. Kissinger, 'Power is the supreme aphrodisiac') or for servitude. I insisted that men of seventy-five and upwards dressed for impotence. I must have been reading too much *King Lear*.

Lord Longford

25 June

1920 [Berlin]

Stresemann, Berger and Rheinbaben lunched with me at Hiller's. (A nice little bill, by the way. Thousand marks for four, just a simple lunch.) Stresemann, with a party meeting timed for two, stayed until a quarter to three, regardless of Rheinbaben's vehement entreaties. Far better, he declared, to let the members blow off steam first and then, fifteen minutes before the Reichstag session and election of the Reichstag President, put in an appearance and take matters in hand. A sovereign display of contempt for his party vassals.

Count Harry Kessler

1942

From a letter from my father with his inimitable sense of humor: 'Today we have entered the cycleless age. I have delivered up Mischas's bicycle personally. In Amsterdam, I see from the paper, the Jews may still cycle about. What a privilege! At least we need fear no longer that our bicycles will be stolen. That is some balm for the nerves. In the wilderness we also had to do without bicycles, for forty long years.'

Etty Hillesum

1967 [Tangier]

It is half past nine and the Fatima [maid] hasn't arrived yet. Perhaps she isn't coming today. I hope not. Women are a terrible drag to have around. It's like a holiday when she isn't here. Although the last two months have been very enjoyable and a great success, neither Kenneth [Halliwell] nor I will be sorry to leave on Friday. I feel the need to do something fresh. Not work – though undoubtedly I shall finish *What the Butler Saw* – just a change of scene. Even sex with a teenage boy becomes monotonous. Ecstasy is as liable to bore as boredom. I need the atmosphere of London for a month or two in order to stir me from the lethargy into which I am in danger of falling.

Joe Orton

26 June

1910

Lev Nik [Tolstoy] accused me today of disagreeing with him about *everything*. About what? I asked. The land question, the religious question, everything . . . But this is not true. It's simply that I don't understand Henry George's ideas on the land question; and I consider it utterly unjust to give away land and deprive my children. It's the same with the religious question. We both believe in God, in goodness, and in submitting to God's will. We both hate war and capital punishment. We both love and live in the country. We both dislike luxury. The only thing that I don't like is Chertkov [Tolstoy's friend and publisher], and I love Lev Nik. And he does not love me, but loves his idol.

Sofia Tolstoy

1976 [Barlinnie Prison]

I've had a bellyful of pussyfooting with you stinking shits and your cowardly ways. I want to destroy your system. I want to live. I want to walk for a spell without having some great fucking wall stopping me taking another step. I just want to be free. I want to see the stars without seeing bars. I want to be caught in a busy shopping crowd. I want to see children playing nonsense games. I want to see a dog pissing against a lamp post. I want to take my girlfriend for a walk. I want to sleep a whole night beside her. I want to see all of you suffer less. I want away from institutions.

Jimmy Boyle

1976

When Francis talked to [Marlon] Brando, he said he asked about me and the kids. I've actually only met the man briefly twice. The six weeks he was working on *The Godfather*, I didn't go to the set because I was pregnant. I had Sofia during those weeks. I went to the party the last day he worked. We were introduced; I had the baby with me. She must have been about two weeks old. He picked her up and marveled at her little toes and examined her long fingers. I felt that he was completely comfortable with her. There were no expectations, no pretensions, no bullshit, he just was. Francis is like that. He likes little kids. He'll talk to any little kids and get them to play with him. They have no preconceptions about him and movies. It's a relief.

I even notice it myself. When I am cashing a check or using a credit card, people often ask me if I am related to Francis Ford Coppola. Sometimes I say I am married to him. People change before my very eyes. They start smiling nervously and forget to give me my package or change. I think I look fairly normal. I wear sweaters and skirts and boots. Maybe they are expecting a Playboy bunny. I don't know. Last year I was buying a Honda car and the salesman was all bored, business pleasantries. When he wrote up the contract and found out what my name was, he got totally flustered. Finally he asked if he could ask me a personal question. I said yes. He asked, with real concern, why I wasn't buying a Porsche or a Mercedes. I told him that I drive almost exclusively in San Francisco and I thought that the Honda was the best car for that. I could see my answer didn't satisfy him.

Eleanor Coppola

27 June

1913

At the foot of the cliffs met an old man gathering sticks. As he ambled along dropping sticks into a long sack he called out casually, 'Do you believe in Jesus Christ?' in a tone of voice in which one would say, 'I think we shall have some rain before night.' 'Aye, aye,' came the answer without hesitation from a boy lying on his back in the sands a few yards distant, 'and that He died to save me.'

Life is full of surprises like this. The only other sounds I have heard to-day were the Herring Gull's cackle. Your own gardener will one day look over his rake and give the correct chemical formula for carbonic acid gas. I met a postman once reading Shelley as he walked his rounds.

W. N. P. Barbellion

1926

The local people arranged a pilgrimage to Lourdes. All Brittany went on it. The sister of my cook, Marie, took part. She prayed for me and asked that what I wished for should be accomplished. She came back yesterday, and no later than that same evening I had a telegram from an agency saying: 'Have found firm purchaser [of the family house] who sees solicitor tomorrow, drop all negotiations.' A little miracle! Coincidence, a sceptic would say, but I prefer to believe in miracles. Is not every person's existence a miracle in itself?

Liane de Pougy

1945 [Bermuda]

Every morning at about noon a crowded ferry boat passes and the gentleman in charge announces places of interest through a loudspeaker. His voice echoes across the still water, and whenever the boat passes Spithead Lodge I hear him explaining that whereas the house was originally the home of Eugene O'Neill, the celebrated American playwright, it is now the new home of none other than Noël Coward. The first time I heard this I was swimming along doing a stately Margate breast-stroke with my head high out of the water. I looked up in dismay, saw about twenty nuns peering at me through binoculars, and sank like a stone. I don't really mind this daily publicity but unfortunately it does encourage the boat's passengers to spring into taxis the moment they land and come belting out to stare at me over the wall and take photographs. The other morning I was caught, practically naked, covered in dust and sweat and carrying a frying-pan in one hand and a slop-pail in the other. I paused graciously while they took their bloody snapshots, and pressed on with my tasks and occupations. Noël Coward is *so* sophisticated.

Noël Coward

1967

Went to Larbi's [local male prostitute] house by taxi. The house was outside Tangier. In a sprawling suburb of Moorish houses.

The house was lit by oil lamps – the cooking was done on an oil stove, yet on the wall there was a telephone and in the second bedroom was an extension. 'My brother, he *travail* on the *telegraphie*,' Larbi said by way of explanation. There were framed photos of him on the wall. Larbi suddenly produced a gun and pointed it at me. I held up my hands. 'I kill you,' Larbi shouted wildly. We all laughed as he pulled the trigger. I had the feeling that no writer with an eye for the ironic could resist having the gun loaded and the playwright of promise falling dead beside the telephone extension. 'An Evelyn Waugh touch,' Kenneth [Halliwell] said as I told him after the gun had clicked harmlessly.

Joe Orton

28 June

1662

This day a genteel woman came to me, claiming kindred of me, as she had once done before, and borrowed 10s. of me, promising to repay it at night, but I hear nothing of her. I shall trust her no more.

Samuel Pepys

1774

This being my birth-day, the first day of my seventy-second year, I was considering, How is this, that I find just the same strength as I did thirty years ago? That my sight is considerably better now, and my nerves firmer, than they were then? That I have none of the infirmities of old age, and have lost several I had in my youth? The grand cause is, the good pleasure of God, who doeth whatsoever pleaseth Him. The chief means are, 1. My constantly rising at four, for about fifty years. 2. My generally preaching at five in the morning; one of the most healthy exercises in the world. 3. My never travelling less, by sea or land, than four thousand five hundred miles in a year.

John Wesley

1871

[Thomas] Carlyle told me of an ignorant old Scots wife who, speaking of some family, said, 'There's twa sons, baith doin' weel in Glasgie; tane's an Imposter, and t'ither's a Malefactor'; it was found that she meant 'Upholsterer' and 'Manufacturer'.

William Allingham

1919

Went to Versailles for the signature of the Peace. Though I am glad I was there, yet the thing as a whole was rather disappointing. It was very badly stage-managed by the French, the peace delegates (including D.) [Lloyd George] having to push their way into the Salle des Glaces, along with the visitors. Almost half the room was taken up with representatives of the Press. The Press is reducing everything that is noblest and impressive in modern life into terms of Press photographs and Press interviews. In fact they try to dominate everything. How can you concentrate on the solemnity of a scene when you have men with cameras in every direction, whose sole object is to get as near as they can to the central figures? How can you be impressed as much as you would like to be by what is said, when you know that all round you are people taking notes, and that the people who are speaking *know* that they are taking notes. One or two reporters, for the sake of preserving a record, would not be so bad. But they have to be dealt with in armies nowadays. The Press is destroying all romance, all solemnity, all majesty. They are as unscrupulous as they are vulgar.

Frances Stevenson

1932

Just realized to-day that it was round about this time, 10 years ago, when I was Mercer's [Soutar's cousin] age (24), that the pains and stiffness in my back began. We were on holiday at Montrose. When I look at Mercer I can scarcely accept the fact that my youth was actually dying then. Seeing him walking about in my clothes – I sometimes wonder what strange necessity brought about the humiliation of my body. Man must look for a reason, and when he has lost his old gods must peer into himself. It is not a self-compliment to surmise that one had to sacrifice one's body to make a self.

William Soutar

1940 [Berlin]

Today was the twenty-first anniversary of the signing of the Treaty of Versailles. And the world it created appeared to be gasping its swan-song today as German troops reached the Spanish border, and Soviet troops marched into Bessarabia and Bukovina. In Paris last week I learned on good authority that Hitler planned a further humiliation of France by holding a victory parade before the Palace of Versailles on this twenty-first anniversary. He would make a speech from the Hall of Mirrors, where it was signed, proclaiming its official end. For some reason it was called off. It is to be held, instead, in Berlin, I hear.

Official comment of Russia's grabbing Bessarabia and Bukovina from Rumania today was: 'Rumania has chosen the reasonable way.'

William L. Shirer

1959

In the evening – an abortive dinner party at Hugh Paddick's. There was a Canadian there. Every time you ask them why they like this country they say things like 'So cultural over here . . . so tolerant and cosmopolitan – not bigoted . . .' etc., all *so* untrue. This is a country where Art has never been taken seriously, where bigotry flourishes, and where 'tolerance' is a device to cover a multitude of sins – most of which are based on laziness & stupidity. What these people really mean is that they find more sympathetic queens in London than they did in provincial Canadian cities. What the hell has this to do with culture?

Kenneth Williams

1983

Today is the sixty-ninth anniversary of the assassination of the Archduke Franz Ferdinand at Sarajevo, the date from which the world changed. At the time no one realised what it meant, though I often think of that prize-winning spoof headline in the *New York Daily News* in 1920: 'Archduke found alive, World War a Mistake.'

Alan Clark

29 June

1791

The three Eldest Master Custance made us a long morning Visit, eat some Gooseberry Fool &c. My hay Stack thatched this Day – No Rain on it. Dinner to day Beans and Bacon, and a green Goose rosted. There was a Tempest this Evening about 9 o'clock – we had not much of it thank God. The News of to day, is, that the French King and Queen &c. are retaken and carried back to Paris. I hope that it is not true, tho' on Lloyds Paper.

Rev. James Woodforde

1838

The Coronation [of Queen Victoria] (which, thank God, is over) went off very well. The day was fine, without heat or rain – the innumerable multitude which thronged the streets orderly and satisfied. The appearance of the Abbey was beautiful, particularly the benches of the peeresses, who were blazing with diamonds. The Queen looked very diminutive, and the effect of the procession itself was spoilt by being too crowded; there was not interval enough between the Queen and the Lords and others going before her. The different actors in the ceremonial were very imperfect in their parts, and had neglected to rehearse them. Lord John Thynne, who officiated for the Dean of Westminster, told me that nobody knew what was to be done except the Archbishop [of Canterbury] and himself (who had rehearsed), Lord Willoughby (who is experienced in these matters), and the Duke of Wellington, and consequently there was a continual difficulty and embarrassment, and the Queen never knew what she was to do next. They made her leave her chair and enter into St Edward's Chapel before the prayers were concluded, much to the discomfiture of the Archbishop. She said to John Thynne, 'Pray tell me what I am to do, for they don't know'; and at the end, when the orb was put into her hand, she said to him, 'What am I to do with it?' 'Your Majesty is to carry it, if you please, in your hand.' 'Am I?' she said, 'it is very heavy.' The ruby ring was made for her little finger instead of the fourth, on which the rubric prescribes it should be put. When the Archbishop was to put it on, she extended the former, but he said it must be on the latter. She said it was too small, and she could not get it on. He said it was right to put it there, and, as he insisted, she yielded, but had first to take off her other rings, and then this was forced on, but it hurt her very much, and as soon as the ceremony was over she was obliged to bathe her finger in iced water in order to get it off.

Charles Greville

1919

D[avid Lloyd George] had a wonderful reception at the station. I think he had an idea that his reception would be rather a wash-out, as he knew that Winston had turned down the idea of getting troops to line the streets. But the welcome he had was far more spontaneous than any organisation could have made it, & to crown all, the King [George V] himself, with the Prince of Wales, came to the station to meet him. The people at the court tried to dissuade him from doing so, saying that there was 'no precedent for it'. 'Very well,' replied the King, 'I will make a precedent.' And everyone seems to have appreciated his action. Everyone threw flowers at D. & a laurel wreath was thrown into the Royal carriage. It fell on the King's lap but he handed it to D. 'This is for you,' he said. D. has given it to me, & though it will fade, I will keep it all my life [she did].

Frances Stevenson

1937

It has been predicted that when I have reached a certain age, I shall receive power. A sudden influx of force, 241/4 days before 29th birthday (4 p.m., Sept. 15th 1945!) I believe nothing of it! *But*, in spite of almost totally clouded outward aspect at present, – débris, exhaustion, – I cannot deny the possibility that after long and incessant struggling and painful development, one might reach a state of this kind: force to enable one to make *coherence* of oneself; to *see*, – not the answer to any Sphinx's riddle, or Solomon's Key, – but something like a finally convincing image of the significance of one's life, an *assurance of destiny*. Coherence: a gathering-together of the dispersed powers of one's personality. Such a state could not be lasting, but might, nevertheless, permanently alter the *level* of one's life. Attainment to a lasting deliverance from the trivial and the unmeaning: from the quicksands.

David Gascoyne

1940 [Palestine]

The Germans are attacking Britain with massive daylight raids. An almighty struggle [the Battle of Britain] is going on in the air. As radio news reaches us, day after day, we are amazed at the courage of our fighter pilots and the damage they are doing to enemy planes. But we are fearful of this onslaught – for all our people. Meanwhile it is vital we get the French Fleet to join us or destroy it. The Vichy Government has broken off relations with Britain.

A Frenchman called de Gaulle is trying to rally the French in England. No letters are reaching us. We are all trying not to show our deep anxiety – we dress well, make up our faces carefully and talk cheerfully. But really we are terrified.

Countess of Ranfurly

30 June

1908

The day before yesterday a blind man came and abused me. Yesterday I went to see him at Nikolayev's and told him I loved him (1) because he was seeking God's truth, (2) because he – as a man who hated and gave offence – ought to be loved and (3) because he might perhaps need me, and as I said goodbye I shook his hand. Before he left he wanted to see me. I was glad. He said: 'I didn't mean to shake your hand, I can't shake hands with a scoundrel, a villain, a pharisee, a hypocrite.'

Leo Tolstoy

1941

Yesterday: Day of special announcements. Twelve in all, and we begin broadcasting them on the radio at 11 a.m. The entire world is glued to its radio sets. We have won complete dominance in the air, have taken Grodno, Brest-Litovsk, Kovno and . . . Two Red armies trapped east of Bialystok. No chance of a breakout. Minsk in our hands. The Russians have lost 2233 tanks and 5107 aircraft. This is what we tell the public. It is too much all at once. By the end, one can sense a slight numbness in the way they receive the news. The effect is not what we had hoped for. The listeners can see through our manipulation of the news too clearly. It is all laid on too thickly, in their opinion. I had warned of this at the time, but in vain. Nevertheless, the effect is still tremendous. Particularly abroad. In the USA, the sole reaction is boundless astonishment. We are back at the pinnacle of triumph.

No English raids during the night. We attack Hull.

We are now operating three clandestine transmitters aimed at Russian tendencies; first Trotskyist, the second separatist, and the third nationalist. All hard against the Stalin regime. We are pulling out all the stops and working with the techniques we perfected during the Western campaign. In official broadcasts we are taking a hard line against Moscow, using techniques totally suited to the Bolshevik mentality. The Russian military communiqués are becoming more stupid by the day. They must be drafted by Jews. Trivial, moronic and simple-minded, like an editorial in the *Rote Fahne* ['Red Flag', newspaper of the German Communist Party 1919–33]. We can deal with them easily.

The new song for Russia is ready. The musical arrangement by Schulze is better than Niel's. And so we choose the former. Anacker and Tiessler are arguing about the authorship of the text. I enforce a compromise. At 2.30 p.m. it is broadcast for the first time on the radio and arouses the greatest enthusiasm all over the country. The nation spends the entire Sunday in a state of huge excitement. Within a few hours, we have succeeded in making good the slight damage to morale caused by the unwise scheduling of the special announcements, and then resentment is replaced by pride and enthusiasm. The press completes the job by some well-rounded editorials. A wonderful Sunday, a rainy day brightened by the light of victory.

Josef Goebbels

1943

The other day, the thought came to me that I no longer whistle or sing; but this is no indication of depression, its cause is poor respiration: the singing often comes up in the silence. However, we have here yet another proof of how dependent is the spirit upon the expressiveness of the flesh.

William Soutar

1955

The television people came at 10 and stayed until 6.30. An excruciating day. They did not want a dialogue but a monologue. The whole thing is to be cut to five minutes in New York and shown at breakfast-time. They filmed everything including the poultry. The impresario kept producing notes from his pocket: 'Mr Waugh, it is said that you are irascible and reactionary. Will you please say something offensive?' So I said: 'The man who has brought this apparatus to my house asks me to be offensive. I am sorry to disappoint him.' 'Oh, Mr Waugh, please, that will never do. I have a reputation. You must alter that.' I said later, not into the machine: 'You expect a lot for $100.' 'Oh, I don't think there is any question of payment.'

Evelyn Waugh

1967

No difficulty with the customs, I simply chose the customs officer that, in an emergency, I wouldn't mind sleeping with, and got through without having even to open my case. London hot, very little difference in actual temperature from Tangier. 'How dead everyone looks,' Kenneth [Halliwell] remarked as we arrived at Gloucester Road. We took a taxi home. Kenneth went for some milk. But the supermarket had closed down during our absence and we had to borrow a bottle of milk from the people next door. A great many letters. And press cuttings. Invitations to parties which I shall not accept. Mick Jagger has been arrested on a drugs charge. All a put-up job I should think.

Joe Orton

1985

It was Gay Day parade day. Got a cab and the driver was a happy faggot, he said, 'Hi! Did you go to the parade?' and I just said, '*What* parade?' and he dropped the subject, talked about the weather (cab $5). And on the news the hostages from TWA 847 [hijacked to Beirut by Shi'ite terrorists] were free, and then they weren't free and then they were free.

Stephen Sprouse called and we made plans to meet, I said I'd pick him up at 9:00 and we'd go down to Odeon for dinner (cab $7). It was sort of empty (dinner $70). Then we walked over to the Area. Then I remembered there was a Gay Day party at the Palladium. We started to walk up. Saw some cops by the stable where they keep their horses on Varick Street. They were just back from the parade, laughing. One of them had his nightstick pointing out from his basket and they were laughing about their experiences of the day. A cute one said hi to me (cab $7).

Andy Warhol

1995

At Innsbruck airport – one of the nicest in Europe. A flat valley between impressive mountains and an outdoor café from which to watch. Gliders drifting up just below the tops of the mountains. The planes roll in just a few yards away. I sat there thinking I'd rarely been so happy in my whole life. Combination of 'legal' (i.e. non-guilt-making) time off and being near transport – realise I've always liked docks, stations, airports.

Then home to Irial's [daughter] sports day. Faintly irritating, being surrounded by all those really awful parents of other kids, offering each other novels and TV documentaries and executive directorships in between screaming at their kids to 'WIN, WIN, WIN!'

Brian Eno

JULY

'For the first time in forty years I have failed to keep this journal with any care. I am sick. That seems to be my only message.'

JOHN CHEEVER

1 July

1828

On going to the Glebe I found nine haymakers, including Moses Heal, White and George, in the four-acre field which was cut, part of it on Saturday, and five mowers in the twelve-acre field. There ought to have been the whole of that ground down, as it is only about ten acres, although computed at twelve, and nearly three-quarters of an acre is in barley. I spoke to the haymakers about being idle; they said they only stopped to take a lunch at eleven, and had not been idle. White, who was the spokesman and had brought a clan of his relations into the field, said that they had been working very hard. I said I could not perceive it by what had been done in the field.

I went up into the Glebe field after tea. The haymakers had complained of the beer which was brewed by Feare, and some of which I drank at dinner and thought it very good. The mowers said they thought it excellent. I told them if they were dissatisfied I would not employ them. I went to White, who is a sly fellow and the secret instigator of this mutiny, and paid him off.

A little after all the women went, and were paid by my daughter at the Parsonage. As it seemed to threaten rain, and the grass was left about in the four-acre field, I desired the mowers to put it up in great cock. Moses Heal was inclined to be insolent when I spoke to him about permitting the haymakers to leave the field till the hay was put in cock, and said, instead of the beer being bad, it is actually too strong to be drunk in great quantities.

On my return home I spoke to Betty and her fellow servant whom I had seen standing before the door to gape at everyone passing by, saying it was a discredit to any modest woman to do so. Betty then said that the month's warning I had given them was more than up, and that she and Goold wished to leave me to-morrow. I told them they certainly should do so.

John Skinner

1942 [Holland]

New measures again. Not only are we not allowed to cycle any more, we are not allowed to ride the trams either. We have to be off the streets by eight, and we are not allowed inside non-Jewish homes. Shopping is restricted for us to the hours between three and five p.m. It's a mess. I've moved back home; I couldn't stay at the Fernandes' [non-Jewish friends] any more. I did have a wonderful time there. At my last meal with them last night, I read them a poem of thanks I had written. We were all so moved and depressed because of the new measures, and crying so hard about everything, that we ended up sobbing with laughter. It was a comical tragedy, really.

Edith Velmans

1974

For whom do I compose? For the listener within me. Sure, I hope other listeners may find a sympathetic point of contact, and I need those listeners. But I don't know who they are. There may be as many audiences as there are pieces, and the audiences don't necessarily overlap. 'The' audience is neither vast nor wee. Mick Jagger's audience is not *La Traviata's*, and hers isn't Billie Holiday's, and hers isn't Mélisande's, and hers isn't Berg's, and his isn't Webern's, and Balanchine's isn't Martha's [Graham], and hers isn't Twyla's [Tharp], and Twyla's isn't mine. Does art soothe death, or the death of love? Not much. The cause of art is never enough. Art is usually about love and death, but death and love are not art, nor even about art, not even [Yukio] Mishima's. Priority: anyone can die of love, but only I can pen my tunes.

Ned Rorem

1986

Arnold Schwarzenegger was having a party for the Statue of Liberty at Café Seiyoken and I wasn't even invited. And I wasn't invited to Caroline Kennedy's wedding either.

Andy Warhol

2 July

1930

Finished a very interesting and convincing study on *J.-J. Rousseau's Malady* that I had sent for. The author reduces everything to the fact that he did not pass his urine, whence slow poisoning of the blood, etc.

I recall that after the birth of R.P. the nurse came to tell the father that the baby 'pissed awry.'

'I don't give a damn, if only he thinks straight,' exclaimed the father with perhaps more humor than wisdom.

André Gide

1956

Tonight we had our annual dinner with the Windsors. The party was chiefly American and included Mrs Donahue, the colossally rich Woolworth woman who pays for a great deal in the Windsors' life. She is the mother of the homosexual Donahue for whom the Duchess conceived such a notorious passion two or three years ago, and during which she became rude, odious and strange. One had the impression that she was either drugged or drunk. She spent all her time with the effeminate young man, staying in night clubs till dawn and sending the Duke home early: 'Buzz off, mosquito' – what a way to address the once King of England! Finally Donahue's boy-friend is alleged to have told him 'It's either her or me', and so he chucked the Duchess.

Cynthia Gladwyn

1973

Had to do an interview for American TV on the lawns of Shepperton [Studios] to promote *The Homecoming* film. 'Who would you like to be if you weren't Peter Hall?' said the interviewer. I have never considered this before. I had to be honest and say that I had no desire to be anybody else at all. I'd like to be a better me, a cleverer me, a more organised me. And wouldn't mind being a me of twenty-eight knowing what I knew at forty. But the thought of being somebody else is inconceivable. Not because I'm particularly pleased with myself – I just can't imagine *being* somebody else. Perhaps you only want to be somebody else when you are very much in love. You want to become the other person.

Peter Hall

1980

Drinks at a St James's Street club. Usual problem in finding the right one. Clubs pride themselves on having no nameplate up for some silly reason – the Americans would call it 'preppy'. Intimidation of non-members perhaps? It continues inside. Can I wait by the fireplace? Am I allowed upstairs? Where is the gents? Is that alcove restricted to members over 60? The whole business gives me the creeps. I can't believe I am alone in disliking clubs. I feel so insecure, dreading equally the deference of the staff and the bonhomie of the bar. It may be a relic of school: that flight of steps forbidden to new boys, the exclusive jargon or apparel of prefects, the tedious rituals and traditions in which the male sex seems so incurably embedded. Nevertheless the party is agreeable, the pictures nice and the architecture splendid.

Sir Hugh Casson

1981

[John] McEnroe behaves badly at Wimbledon and in one particularly ludicrous moment shouts at a linesman, 'You're a disgrace to the human race.'

Some group captain on the high chair then docks him a point and an argument ensues as to whether McEnroe was, as he insists, talking to himself and, if he was, whether it was in order to talk to oneself on court (or even breathe).

Of course, now that Wimbledon is all about money, behaving badly is exactly what is required, certainly of McEnroe, and all the claptrap about decency and fair play is just the English at their usual game of trying to have it both ways. Wimbledon is now a spectacle, just as a wrestling match, say, is a spectacle, and a spectacle needs a Hero and a Villain. It's a contest between Right and Wrong, not because McEnroe is particularly badly behaved but because the Wimbledon authorities have sold out to television and this kind of drama is just what viewers enjoy. So McEnroe doesn't really have a choice, only a role.

Many of McEnroe's critics point out how [Jimmy] Connors has 'reformed': how three or four years ago he was the rogue, disputing calls, not attending the line-up, and how much better behaved he is now. This misses the point. Connors has to be better behaved, not because his character has changed or his tennis manners have improved but because he has no part in the spectacle. Or if he had (if he had beaten [Björn] Borg in the semi-final for instance) he would have had to be cast in the Hero's role.

All this is written at five in the morning, I seem to get these impulses to argue first thing – another bout a few days ago being on English philosophy, a subject of which I know and care as little as I do about tennis. But it isn't just in the early morning. They go on all the time, these disputes with myself, and particularly when I'm cycling around. I catch passers-by looking at me, and it's not out of recognition; seeing my frowning face and my jaw working away, they are thinking, 'This is a lunatic.'

Alan Bennett

1981

Rather an amusing flare-up at our S & J [Sidgwick & Jackson, publishers] management committee today. William told us that Billie Jean King was short of funds because her sponsors had dropped out after the revelations of her lesbian affair. Her memoirs, to be suitably ghosted, were on offer. There was an immediate outcry among the five women present about the atrocious behaviour of the sponsors and general sympathy for Billie Jean. I disingenuously asked whether Sir Charles Forte was likely to approve of a book in which Billie Jean 'told all'. William held his peace but our zestful young feminists literally shrieked when I suggested that there ought to be more sympathy for her discarded girl-friend, now in a wheelchair, than for her. They accused this unfortunate girl-friend of blackmailing their heroine. Spirited young women seem to feel challenged when any man makes the mildest comment on the private life of any member of their sex. I might have defended myself on the grounds that I was probably one of the few men in London who had addressed three different groups of lesbians, but I felt that I had caused enough annoyance for one morning.

Lord Longford

3 July

1890

Went downstairs to sleep. Got up late. Depressed and bored; idleness, luxurious living, useless talk. It's as if cog wheels are swimming in grease, get clogged and won't engage. Sometimes the wheels don't go for lack of oil, sometimes because they are full of slush. Should one write for people like that? Why? I've a strange reluctance to write. Yesterday I thought vividly about women. A woman holiday-maker came to question me when I was mowing. The main feature about women is their lack of respect for thought, lack of trust in what it – thought – will lead to. Hence falsehood, distortion of the truth, making play with ideas and spiritual gifts generally. If men were not so bound to women by sexual feeling and the indulgence which results from it, they would see clearly that women (for the most part) don't understand them, and they wouldn't talk to them. Except for virgins. You begin to get to know women from your wife, and you get to know them completely from your daughters. These are the women whom you can look at quite freely.

Mowed a lot. Still the same melancholy.

Leo Tolstoy

1962

Set to, and cleaned the flat, which left me feeling virtuous. Went to the butcher for steak for my lunch. He said to me, 'I think you're a bit of prime meself, there you are – four & sixpence my angel . . .' I giggled & felt like a high school girl. It was nice.

Kenneth Williams

1980

Lunch at Macmillan [publishers] over this diary. Their enthusiasm for it is warming but I have to do the work and it begins to weigh. Keeping notes is not that difficult – it's the translation of those notes into something faintly readable that is so alarming – no inside stories of rows in the Cabinet . . . no back-stage gossip . . . no gripping yarns of hazardous travel adventures . . . no Lady Cunard.

Sir Hugh Casson

4 July

1664

Find my wife this day of her own accord to have lain out 25s. upon a pair of pendantes for her eares, which did vex me and brought both me and her to very high and very foule words from her to me, such as trouble me to think she should have in her mouth; and reflecting upon our old differences, which I hate to have remembered. I vowed to breake them, or that she should go and get what she could for them again. I went with that resolution out of doors; the poor wretch afterwards in a little did send out to change them for her money again. I followed Besse her messenger at the 'Change, and there did consult and send her back; I would not have them changed, being satisfied that she yielded.

Samuel Pepys

1832 [New York]

It is a lovely day, but very different from all the previous anniversaries of independence. The alarm about the cholera has prevented all the usual jollification under the public authority. There are no booths in Broadway, the parade which was ordered here has been countermanded, no corporation dinner, and no ringing of bells. Some troops are marching about the street, 'upon their own hook,' I suppose. Most of the stores are closed, and there is a pretty smart cannonade of crackers by the boys, but it is not a regular Fourth of July. The Board of Health reports to-day twenty new cases and eleven deaths since noon yesterday. The disease is here in all its violence and will increase. God grant that its ravages may be confined, and its visit short! I wrote to-day for the girls to return from Hyde Park forthwith. They are all going to Rockaway. Catherine [his wife] is greatly alarmed, and we are to ascertain whether the seashore is a place of safety.

Philip Hone

1871

Hannah Jones told me about the madwoman of Cwmgwanon. They keep her locked up in a bedroom alone, for she will come down amongst them stark naked. She has broken the window and all the crockery in the room, amuses herself by dancing naked round the room and threatens to wring her daughter-in-law's neck. Then she will set to and roar till they can hear her down the dingle at John Williams's house, nearly half a mile.

Rev. Francis Kilvert

1937 [Corfu]

We breakfast at sunrise after a bathe. Grapes and Hymettos honey, black coffee, eggs, and the light clear-tasting Papastratos cigarette. Unconscious transition from the balcony to the rock outside. Lazily we unhook the rowboat and make for the point where the still blue sea is twisted in a single fold – like a curtain caught by a passing hand. A shale beach, eaten out of the cliff-point, falling to a row of sunken rocks. A huge squat fig-tree poised like a crocodile on the edge of the water. Five fathoms directly off the point so that sitting here on this spit we can see the dolphins and the streamers passing within hail almost. We bathe naked, and the sun and water make our skins feel old and rough, like precious lace. Yesterday we found the foetus of an octopus, colourless ball of gelatine, which throbbed invisibly in the palm of the hand; to-day the fisherboys have found our beach. They have written 'Angli' in charcoal on one of the rocks, we have responded with 'Hellenes' which is fair enough. We have never seen them. N. draws a little head in a straw hat with a great nose and moustache.

Lawrence Durrell

1940 [Geneva]

Everyone here is full of talk about the 'new Europe,' a theme that brings shudders to most people. The Swiss, who mobilized more men per capita than any other country in the world, are demobilizing partially. They see their situation as pretty hopeless, surrounded as they are by the victorious totalitarians, from whom henceforth they must beg facilities for bringing their food and other supplies. None have any illusions about the kind of treatment they will get from the dictators. The papers are full of advice: Prepare for a hard life. Gone the high living standard. The freedom of the individual. Decency in public life.

William L. Shirer

1965

On Sunday night I went to see the Beatles. I had never seen them in the flesh before. The noise was deafening throughout and I couldn't hear a word they sang or a note they played, just one long, ear-splitting din. Apparently they were not a success. The notices were bad the next day. I went backstage to see them and was met by Brian Epstein [the Beatles manager], who told me they had gone back to the hotel and would I go there. So off I went, and, after being received by Brian Epstein and Wendy Hanson [their publicist] and given a drink, I was told that the Beatles refused to see me because that ass David Lewin [*Daily Mail* columnist] had quoted my saying unflattering things about them months ago. I thought this graceless in the extreme, but decided to play it with firmness and dignity. I asked Wendy to go and fetch one of them and she finally reappeared with Paul McCartney and I explained gently but firmly that one did *not* pay much attention to the statements of newspaper reporters. The poor boy was quite amiable and I sent messages of congratulations to his colleagues, although the message I would have liked to send them was that they were bad-mannered little shits. In any case, it is still impossible to judge from their public performance whether they have talent or not. They were professional, had a certain guileless charm, and stayed on mercifully for not too long.

I was truly horrified and shocked by the audience. It was like a mass masturbation orgy, although apparently mild compared with what it usually is. The whole thing is to me an unpleasant phenomenon. Mob hysteria when commercially promoted, or in whatever way promoted, always sickens me. To realize that the majority of the modern adolescent world goes ritualistically mad over those four innocuous, rather silly-looking men is a disturbing thought. Perhaps we are whirling more swiftly into extinction than we know. Personally I should have liked to take some of those squealing young maniacs and cracked their heads together. I am all for audiences going mad with enthusiasm after a performance, but *not* incessantly *during* the performance so that there ceases to be a performance.

Noël Coward

1991

Independence Day. [Robert] Altman party in Malibu. Dress code: red, white and blue. Buy US Flag stickers and plaster my clothes, hair and face with them, and trek up the coast looking like a stamped parcel for just about the best party I have ever been to. Why? Well, I will try . . . EASE. In every sense. Their condo is on the Pacific Ocean. I don't mean NEAR but ON the beach. The living room is dominated by the sound and sight of the pounding surf immediately beyond the wall-to-wall windows. Katherine is the coolest, keenest hostess I know, makes everyone feel hugely welcome, every detailed arrangement seem effortless, unfussed.

She has been married to Bob for thirty years, and they kind of 'top 'n' tail' one another with an outward show of EASE. Like hand-hewn spoons. They are somewhere in their sixties chronologically, but are indeterminately ageless and inquisitive, yet without any vestige of that certain strain that develops like a virus – 'middle-aged trendism' – whereby desperadoes attempt to be-bop themselves into frillier fashions, tighter pants and nightshade red or black hairdyes, the haunted look of 'last call at the singles bar' furrowing up a pack of brows. Please, God, when my turn swifts up, do NOT let me fit a rug to my balding cranium or wrench some designer jeans around my saggy 'cheeks'. Remember this wisdom. EASE . . .

Richard E. Grant

5 July

1852

Have been at home all day writing. Tonight went on the roof awhile. It's a beautiful sight the city presents. In every direction one incessant sparkle of fire balls, rockets, roman candles, and stars of all colors shooting thick into the air and disappearing for miles around, with now and then a glare of colored light coming out in some neighborhood where fireworks on a large scale are going off. A foreigner would put it in his book of travels as one of the marvels of New York, and compare it to a swarm of tropical fireflies gleaming in and out through a Brazilian forest.

George Templeton Strong

1938

With no rules that I put faith in, no instinct to guide me except the instinct of self-preservation, a soft heart, a calculating head and a divided mind, is it any wonder that I cause confusion when what I want is so simple – a woman who will love me and who will sleep with me sometimes, who will amuse me and listen to me and not flood me with love.

Charles Ritchie

1943

Leaving the Café Royal we linked arms and charged up the narrow staircase leading to the Arts Theatre Club. We were instantly spotted by reception and it was a right turn, down the stairs, and out into St Martin's Lane in five minutes flat. It seems that it is not 'Ah, here comes Dylan [Thomas], that promising young poet!' but 'Watch out, here comes that crashing old bore Dylan, let's get him out of here quick.'

Just then the air-raid siren went off. We hailed a taxi and persuaded the driver to take us to Ruthven's [Todd] studio. As soon as I'd sunk into my seat Dylan smothered me in wet beery kisses, his blubbery tongue forcing my lips apart. It was rather like being embraced by an intoxicated octopus. I tried to tell myself that I was being kissed by a great poet but it was a relief when the taxi finally stopped.

Joan Wyndham

1949 [sailing to South America]

At noon we pass the Tropic of Cancer beneath a vertical sun that kills every shadow. However, it's not excessively hot. But the sky is full of a nasty haze and the sun looks like a sickness. The sea looks like an enormous swelling with the metallic brilliance of decay. In the afternoon, a great event: we pass a ship that's following the same route we are. The greeting that the two ships give each other with three grand prehistoric animal roars, the waving of the passengers lost at sea and alert to the presence of other human beings, the irrevocable separation on the green, malevolent waters – all that weighs on the heart a little. Afterwards I remain staring at the sea for a long time, full of a strange and good exaltation. After dinner I go to the bow. The emigrants play the accordion and dance in the night, where the heat seems to mount as if it were day.

Albert Camus

1974

We had decided on Nantucket for three negative reasons: no mosquitoes, no need for a car, no social temptations. The positive virtues are those of many a New England area: clean air, swimmable sea, homegrown tomatoes. The house, rented from a Miss Melva Chesrown, charming and comfortable, two floors quaintly furnished, and a geranium garden.

Community is 101 percent heterosexual WASP, non-intellectual well-off Republicans with too many children of whom the females are prettier than the males. The food (like the paintings in the clever wharf galleries) is blandly costly, and the movies are safe, chic revivals: *Million Dollar Legs*, which is surrealism for the unwashed – or rather, for the overwashed – and *To Have and Have Not*, which holds up neatly, Bacall being that contradiction: a human star. Bogart–Bacall has nothing to do with acting, everything to do with presence.

In the Unitarian Church there is a conventional concert series run by cultured behatted matrons who do not know my name. In the charming bookstore there are shelf upon shelf of best-sellers dusted daily by macrobiotic thirty-year-olds who do not know my name. So much for a life's work.

Ned Rorem

6 July

1661

Waked this morning with news, brought me by a messenger on purpose, that my uncle Robert is dead, and died yesterday; so I rose sorry in some respect, glad in my expectations in another respect. So I made myself ready, went and told my uncle Wight, my Lady, and some others thereof, and bought me a pair of boots in St. Martin's and got myself ready; and then to the Post House and set out about eleven and twelve o'clock, taking the messenger with me that came to me. And so we rode and got well by nine o'clock to Brampton, where I found my father well. My uncle's corps in a coffin standing upon joynt stools in the chimney in the hall; but it begun to smell, and so I caused it to be set forth in the yard all night, and watched by two men. My aunt I found in bed in a most nasty ugly pickle, made me sick to see it. My father and I lay together to-night, I greedy to see the will, but did not ask to see it till tomorrow.

Samuel Pepys

1745

After talking largely with both the men and women Leaders, we agreed it would prevent great expense, as well of health as of time and of money, if the poor people of our society could be persuaded to leave off drinking of tea. We resolved ourselves to begin and set the example. I expected some difficulty in breaking off a custom of six-and-twenty years' standing. And, accordingly, the three first days, my head ached, more or less, all day long, and I was half asleep from morning to night. The third day, on *Wednesday*, in the afternoon, my memory failed, almost entirely. In the evening I sought my remedy in prayer. On *Thursday* morning my head-ache was gone. My memory was as strong as ever. And I have found no inconvenience, but a sensible benefit in several respects, from that very day to this . . .

John Wesley

1874

Nothing is lost in this world. If we leave off loving one person, we immediately transfer our affections to somebody else, even without knowing it, and if we fancy we care for nobody we are mistaken. If it isn't a man then it's a dog or a piece of furniture, and we love it with the same passion, only in another way. If I loved I should like my love to be returned with equal strength; I should not even tolerate a word from any one else; but such love is not to be found. Therefore I shall never love any one, for no one will ever love as I could love.

Marie Bashkirtseff

1936

There is something classical in Mussolini's seaplane flying to Rome being struck by lightning. It would seem as if the Gods themselves were jealous of this dynamic man. Only once have I met him. It was in 1926. [Viscount George] Gage and I were motoring through Europe and turned up at Perugia. The whole town was en fête with garlands and bands and photographers and we were told that Il Duce was arriving the next morning. At 4 a.m. next day the streets were crowded with singing, black-shirted boys and George and I leant out of our window watching them. I got tickets for a lecture Mussolini was going to give at the University, and we duly arrived and found ourselves in a small room along with 40–50 other people, the cream of Perugian society. Suddenly the door opened . . . a little man, Napoleonic in stature, in a black coat, raised his right hand in a Fascist salute and advanced down the room as the audience stood up. He mounted the rostrum and spoke for an hour, very fast in flowing Italian, about Hannibal and the Punic Wars. My Italian was never very good, nevertheless I understood almost every word he said. He held the audience spellbound, and made cold chills run down my spine. It gave me more of a thrill than my interview with the Pope.

When it was over we were led up, because we were English, and introduced to him and I shook his warm big hand.

This is my only personal contact with Mussolini. Now all our Roman friends meet him often, as during the past few years he has deigned to go out into society.

'Chips' Channon

1943

I noticed a very funny note in the kitchen from old Kate who 'does' for my mother. 'Madam,' it said, 'had one [bomb] at the top of our street. I was shot out of my bed. It was gastley, all night digging. Today I am nearly a cripple, I can hardly walk. I think it must be rumatism. I am breaking up. The butcher has run out of sausages.' My mother's note for today simply said, 'Dear Kate, so glad you are still alive. I think we will have Welsh Rarebit tonight.'

Joan Wyndham

1971

Tonight Gerry [her husband] and I went to *Hair*. It was ghastly. To begin with, the noise was deafening, as Gerry would sit in the front row, thinking he would not hear otherwise and wanting to see all the nudity. Then it was altogether so squalid and filthy, everybody in the cast looking unwashed and drugged, wearing grubby trendy clothes. The very first thing that happened was when one of the men on the stage made a beeline for me, removed his dirty blue jeans and said, 'Lady, hold these for me.' I refused to put out my hand, so he dropped them on my feet, later returning for them, when again I did not move, so Gerry had to pick them up. But the worst was when tiny white paper pellets, supposed to be snow, were showered down on to the stage and the first row of the stalls, so that we were covered with confetti which stuck in our hair and went down our necks. We arrived at the Savoy, to the acute embarrassment of Gerry, looking as though we had just been married.

Cynthia Gladwyn

1975

Found such a good word by chance in the dictionary – opsimath. I am an opsimath, one who develops slowly.

James Lees-Milne

7 July

1851

I have been tonight with Anthony Wright to look through Perez Blood's tele-scope a second time. A dozen of Blood's neighbors were swept along in the stream of our curiosity. One who lived half a mile this side said that Blood had been down that way within a day or two with his terrestrial, or day, glass, looking into the eastern horizon [at] the hills of Billerica, Burlington, and Woburn. I was amused to see what sort of respect this man with a telescope had obtained from his neighbors, something akin to that which savages award to civilized men, though in this case the interval between the parties was very slight. Mr. Blood did not invite us into his house this cool evening, – men nor women, – nor did he ever before to my knowledge. I am still contented to see the stars with my naked eye. Mr. Wright asked him what his instrument cost. He answered, 'Well, that is something I don't like to tell.' (Stuttering or hesitating in his speech a little as usual.) 'It is a very proper question, however.' 'Yes,' said I, 'and you think that you have given a very proper answer . . .'

H. D. Thoreau

1854

I lack modesty! That's my great defect. What am I? One of four sons of a retired lieutenant-colonel, left an orphan at seven years of age in the care of women and strangers, having received neither a social nor an academic educa-tion and becoming my own master at the age of seventeen, without a large fortune, without any social position, and, above all, without any principles; a man who mismanaged his affairs to the last degree, who spent the best years of his life without purpose or pleasure, and who finally banished himself to the Caucasus to escape from his debts and above all his habits, and from there, by seizing on to connections which had existed between his father and the Commander-in-Chief of the army, was transferred to the army of the Danube at the age of twenty-six as an ensign, almost without means except his pay (because what means he has he must use to pay his outstanding debts), without patrons, without the ability to live in society, without knowledge of the service, without practical talents – but with enormous self-love! Yes, that is my social position. Let us see what sort of person I am.

I am ugly, awkward, untidy and socially uneducated. I am irritable, boring to other people, immodest, intolerant (*intolérant*) and bashful as a child. I am almost an ignoramus. What I know I have somehow learned myself in snatches, piecemeal, unsystematically, and it amounts to very little. I am intemperate, irresolute, inconstant, stupidly vain and passionate like all people who lack character. I am not brave. I am unmethodical in life, and so lazy that idleness has become for me almost an insuperable habit. I am intelligent, but my intelligence has never yet been thoroughly tested by anything. I have neither practical, social nor business intelligence. I am honest, i.e. I love goodness and have made a habit of loving it; and when I deviate from it I am dissatisfied with myself and return to it with pleasure; but there are things which I love more than goodness – for example, fame. I am so ambitious, and this feeling has been so little satisfied, that as between fame and virtue, I fear I might often choose the former if I had to make a choice.

Yes, I am not modest; and that is why I am proud at heart, but bashful and shy in society.

Leo Tolstoy

1910

Lev Nik [Tolstoy] went to see his idol [his publisher Chertkov] today, despite the weather. I realise today that although his last diaries are very interesting, they have all been *composed* for Chertkov and those whom it pleases Mr Chertkov to show them! And now Lev Nikol. never *dares* to write a word of love for me in them, for they all go straight to Chertkov and he would not like this.

Sofia Tolstoy

1948

Last week there was a wireless programme on Marie Bashkirtseff [Russian artist and diarist]. As I listened again to some of her preposterous boasts and aspirations, Eric suddenly turned to me and said in one of his comic, assumed voices, 'I think this little girl is rather like you.' What was it? A condemnation? A compliment? Both? Why did it please since she was, after all, rather contemptible? I think it pleased me because I like to be likened to someone so conscious, so striving, so unresigned. She had the horrible one-track-mindedness of a successful businessman or a devout missionary. She wasted nothing, or if she wasted, she knew all about it, and was violent with herself afterwards. It is strange why egoists of Marie's sort are not more hated – laughed at they often are, for their antics or vanity; but some people come to love them just because of their belief in themselves.

Denton Welch

8 July

1930

Got a note from [Thomas] Moult asking if he might include 'The Thoughts of God' among *the Best Poems of 1930*. Well! Well – and who's going to be the first to come along and say – so-and-so is still to be amongst the best poems of 2030? That's more to the point.

William Soutar

1938

'He has found a purpose in life in his children'. So that they in turn may find the same in theirs? But what point is there in this endless procreation? We care so little about other people that even Christianity urges us to do good *for the love of God*. Man prefers to punch his fellow man in the mouth, and is such a fool that to give himself an object in life he has to produce a son.

Cesare Pavese

1941

The enemy has made a 'V' (Victoire) into his propaganda symbol in the occupied territories. Without any more ado, I have the symbol commandeered by us. Now we are using this 'V' ourselves and saying that it means a German victory. End of problem! I had given the matter a lot of thought, but I would never have dreamed that the solution would be so simple. In other respects the position in the occupied territories remains very unclear. Our fight against Bolshevism has brought us many friends. But the effect of hunger is too strong. Even in the Balkans there is real starvation. Particularly in Greece. A lot of grumbling in Italy. Mussolini is not taking a firm enough line. Sympathy with us has also declined slightly in Rumania. Worries, wherever one looks.

Josef Goebbels

9 July

1940 [Karkur, Palestine]

Dan [her husband] told me the Sherwood Rangers are moving north to Haifa and broke it to me gently that the horses are not coming. They are being sent to a Remount Depot where Mouse Townsend, who really cares for horses, will be in charge. The Sherwood Rangers are to man coast guns and eventually become mechanised cavalry.

For a long time we've known that horse cavalry has no place in modern warfare, but now the horses are going away we feel frightful – so many of them are old friends, hunters and part of our families. It is so sad that these lovely animals will never again graze in England's green fields or enjoy a good stable. We feel like traitors to have brought them here and now must leave them behind, and I'm remembering what my father told me about the British horses which were left in Palestine after the First World War and how, through ignorance, they were neglected and ill treated.

This afternoon Dan's little groom came up from camp to see me – in floods of tears. Together we went down to the horse lines so I could say goodbye to Horse Number Nine and Dan's beautiful chestnut mare . . . I stroked all the velvet noses as I walked back along the lines, and I felt sick with sadness. Whitaker [her husband's valet] returned to the bungalow with me and he was crying too. Wives are not allowed in the camp, but no one scolded me. Whitaker said, 'I've grown to like horses. They are so much better than bicycles.'

Countess of Ranfurly

1982

I was invited to a surprise birthday lunch party at a restaurant on 48th Street for Phyllis Diller's sixty-fifth birthday. So I decided to stay uptown until that at 1.30.

When I walked in a lady with glasses said that she still had my mother's book, and I was trying to think of which lady in my advertising days would I have given one to, and I just couldn't place who this grandmother-looking woman was, and then someone said, 'Kaye!' and it dawned on me – Kaye Ballard. And so I went running back and had to pretend as if I'd just been out of it. And she was fun, she's in *The Pirates of Penzance*. It's funny, these people were such big TV stars, and then when you lose your ratings, you're just like a normal person.

And at 2:00 Phyllis Diller arrived. She said that they told her it was a *New York Times* Interview and that they wanted her to wear a bright-colored dress because it would photograph better, but she hadn't known why, since the *Times* was black and white.

The press was there and they took photographs. And it was embarrassing because I'd brought Phyllis a Cow print wrapped in an *Interview* [Warhol's magazine] and she thought the wrapping was the art and she was being so careful with it, and she said, 'Faaabulous.'

Andy Warhol

10th July

1660

This day I put on first my new silk suit, the first that ever I wore in my life. Took my wife to Dr. Clodius's to a great wedding of Nan Hartlib to Mynheer Roder, which was kept at Goring House with very great state, cost, and noble company. But among all the beauties there my wife was thought the greatest. After dinner I left the company and carried my wife to Mrs. Turner's, not returning, as I said I would, to see the bride put to bed.

Samuel Pepys

1834 [New York]

There has been of late great excitement in consequence of the proceedings of a set of fanatics who are determined to emancipate all the slaves by a *coup de main*, and have held meetings in which black men and women have been introduced. These meetings have been attended with tumult and violence, especially one which was held on Friday evening at the Chatham Street Chapel. Arthur Tappan and his brother Lewis have been conspicuous in these proceedings, and the mob last night, after exhausting their rage at the Bowery Theater, went down in a body to the house of the latter gentleman in Rose Street, broke into the house, destroyed the windows and made a bonfire of the furniture in the street. The police at length interfered, rather tardily, I should think; but the diabolical spirit which prompted this outrage is not quenched, and I apprehend we shall see more of it.

The conduct of the Abolitionists has been very indiscreet, but their number has been too small to give reasonable ground of alarm; and this attack upon one of their leaders will add to their strength by enabling them to raise the cry of persecution.

Philip Hone

1975

Yesterday in London I was waiting for a bus at Tottenham Court Road, in my place in a queue. Behind me a woman under thirty was pushing her way forward. I deliberately elbowed her back to the rear where she belonged and was myself the last person allowed on the bus. I had to stand inside. The conductress politely asked the woman to get off the platform where she had placed herself, saying, 'There is no more room for standing.' The woman, who was foreign, almost coffee-coloured, shouted abusively, 'The English always say No to one.' Irked by this remark, and also by the woman's presence preventing the bus from moving on, it being excessively hot, I said to her tartly: 'Perhaps they only say No to you.' She spat in my face, I wiped my face and spat in hers. She spat back. Quick as lightning I slapped her face as hard as I dared. Enraged, I said, 'Get off this bus immediately, you odious woman,' and she did. Awkward silence. In that typically British way no one said a word. At the next stop I got off, having I suppose behaved badly.

James Lees-Milne

1980 [New York]

Why American is a foreign language: we lunch in a café near Gramercy Park, sitting out on a heavy, overcast day. I order a screwdriver and drink it quickly and ask for another.

'I guess it's kind of hot,' the waiter says.

'Yes,' says Lynn, 'and the glasses are kind of small.'

'Yes,' says the waiter. 'That's true also.'

No Englishman would say 'That's true also' (although it's a perfectly grammatical sentence), because it's written not spoken English. Only Ivy Compton-Burnett would write it as dialogue.

Alan Bennett

11 July

1863

I walked up to Kilburn by six to see Hannah [Cullwick the servant who became his wife]: but though she was out, in her old bonnet & working dress, expecting me, it was impossible even to exchange a quiet word with her. All down the side roads, & among the unfinished houses, I sought in vain for some place for talk; she following, and I half beside myself with the thought that she could only follow. Everywhere there were prying eyes and folks who might know her as Mr. So & So's servant, and who at any rate would stare if they saw us together. And in the end we had to return; she walking off the path and somewhat behind, that she might not seem to be with me, and I talking to her hurriedly over my shoulder! The increase of pity and tenderness that all this begat in me, is certainly bought dear with such a bitter experience. Without one kiss or one touch of the hand, the servant goes back to her kitchen, and I to whence I came . . .

Arthur F. Munby

1924

Chris [Hollis] turned up in the morning and told me a good story. Mr Justice Phillimore was trying a sodomy case and brooded greatly whether his judgement had been right. He went to consult [former Lord Chancellor]

Birkenhead. 'Excuse me, my lord, but could you tell me – What do you think one ought to give a man who allows himself to be buggered?' 'Oh, 30s or £2 – anything you happen to have on you.'

Evelyn Waugh

1941

When I came to the end of the page proofs on 'Newspaper Days' I discovered to my consternation that the last page was 313, which reads 13 both ways. My long-standing suspicion about 13 suggested that I either cut the book to 312 pages or expand it to 314. In the midst of my cogitation on the subject, I took a look at 'Happy Days' to see how many pages it had made. They ran to 313 precisely! I therefore decided to let 'Newspaper Days' stand. Making it run precisely the same length as 'Happy Days' was really an extraordinary feat of copyreading. I shall boast of it when my real autobiography comes to be written.

H. L. Mencken

1943 [Val D'Greia]

Donata's [her daughter] christening – a day of strange contrasts. We wake at five a.m. to a dull booming sound – a naval bombardment, we presume, from enemy ships on the Tuscan coasts, or perhaps the bombing of Grosseto or Livorno, perhaps a preface to invasion. All day we listen in eagerly for an explanation of this sound, which is never forthcoming. The bulletins, both from Rome and London, tell of further landings in Sicily. Meanwhile Donata's little festa takes place. Baskets of flowers and small presents are brought to her by the children of the place. The guests are gathered, and at eleven Mons. B. celebrates Mass in Gianni's chapel. The introit is appropriate: 'The Lord is the light of my life: whom shall I fear? The Lord is the protector of my life: of whom shall I be afraid? . . . If arms in camp should stand together against me my heart shall not fear.' At five-thirty we all go to the Castelluccio church for the christening: at the church door are gathered a large crowd of peasants and of children, who afterwards come back to the garden with us.

When all is over, and the children are gone, we turn on the radio: the landings in Sicily continue.

Iris Origo

1951 [while writing *East of Eden*]

Last night an evil came on me. I planned, laughing behind my hand, to play hooky today and go fishing and pick up my work on Saturday. My course was set and my criminal path taken. And then this morning was an overcast and windy sky. The very forces of nature conspired to keep me pure. But being pressured into virtue, I am having a very hard time getting started today. I wish I had been allowed to be the sinner I wanted to be. Maybe I need some sin.

John Steinbeck

12 July

1804

According to the *Journal de Paris*, it's possible for a man to give birth to a child and for both of them to live afterward. The thing happened in Holland.

Stendhal

1920 [Berlin]

As my barber was shaving me this morning, he whispered that in three months' time the Bolsheviks would be in Warsaw and then we would turn, hand in hand with them, on France. He would join up a second time for that. I only mention this because it is precisely among ordinary people that feeling against France and in favour of a new war has recently spread more and more. The most improbable individuals come out with it.

Count Harry Kessler

1955

High summer continues. I shall not go to London until it breaks. This is a pleasant house in the heat. For the first time since I planted it the honey-suckle outside my bedroom window scents the room at night. I don't sleep naturally. I have tried everything – exercise, cold baths, fasting, feasting, solitude, society. Always I have to take paraldehyde and sodium amytal. My life is really too empty for a diarist. The morning post, the newspaper, the crossword, gin.

Evelyn Waugh

13 July

1910

Let us assume that I have gone mad, and my 'fixation' is that Lev Nik [Tolstoy] should get his diaries back and not allow Chertkov [his publisher] to keep them. Two families have been thrown into confusion, there have been painful arguments – not to mention the fact that I have suffered to the very limits of my endurance. (I have not eaten a thing all day). Everyone is depressed, and my tortured appearance annoys everyone like a bothersome fly.

What can be done to make everyone happy again, and put an end to my sufferings?

Get the diaries back from Chertkov, all those little black oilcloth notebooks, and put them back on the desk, letting him have them, one at a time, to make excerpts. That's all!

Sofia Tolstoy

1923

When I'm thinking about this past spring I keep seeing the Cochon d'or, a restaurant at La Villette almost opposite the slaughter-house. All the snobbiest people were mad about it. One day my sultana, Madame Fabre-Luce, let fall: 'I never go anywhere, but I do, do, *do* so want to see this famous *Cochon d'or* everyone's talking about.' We went into action at once. Georges telephoned the handsome Italian *patron* and a menu was planned. The Duchess came disguised as a rake – little brown suit, hat over one ear, scarf flung carelessly round her neck – her dear little face alert and amused. Nathalie – Grey – was the foreigner who is eager to see everything. As for my sultana, she was borne along in her sumptuous car – after a detour to pick us up – her usual self: rich pastel finery from the rue de la Paix, pearls, rings, gleaming jewels, Cartier handbag with coral, ivory, onyx and diamonds . . . She descended from her chariot with a little amused look as though she were playing a practical joke on someone. 'Oh my God,' I thought, 'they are going to jeer at us! Whatever will happen?' I tried to shelter and surround my sultana. The *patron* conducted us to a little back room where our table was reserved. It was a Wednesday, market day. We were surrounded by huge, sweaty, red-faced men finishing their lunch, not very reassuring. They stared, but not unkindly. My friends' charm got to work. Voices became less loud. No one lit a pipe, no one spat on the floor, no one swore. It was as though we were providing them with a charming little performance. The commonest of the lot kept on winking at me. We ate like ogres. The pâté was really excellent, the chicken exquisite. As for the steak, we cried our admiration aloud. You don't know what red meat is if you haven't had it there: firm and melting, with an unbelievable flavour; you put it on your tongue and it evaporates – a marvel! We exclaimed with delight, our confidence quite restored, enchanted to be there. We felt that all those men were our brothers!

Certainly the Ritz, where we went five or six times, is good fun like a big liner packed with smart strangers; but the food there is horrible.

Liane de Pougy

1932

Have had so much trouble getting my left leg up and down that I kept it flat to-day. Spent a rotten day with it – not sharp pains; but a slow ache so that I couldn't find a position in which I could sit comfortably . . . Often, I believe, the troubles of the mind are not so distracting to an artist as the aches of the body. Anyhow to-day, for example, I could not settle to do anything. Christopher Smart and [John] Clare could write poetry from a mad-house – but who can write at all when suffering from influenza, say, or severe toothache?

William Soutar

1937

I have stopped writing poetry since more than a year, I tell my friends, because the writing of poetry seems to me to be a dishonest occupation (*viz.* Pascal), a compromise, a deception; or at best a pleasant pastime or hobby for those with nothing better to do. It would be better for everyone, I argue, if nine out of ten poets at present writing became silent. – Whereupon they reply: Oh! it's all very well for a *Rimbaud* to talk like that; at least *he* had written superlative poetry before he decided to dismiss the Muse. But if one has written only mediocre verse, and is capable perhaps of writing only a little better, then *one has no right* to treat what one has not yet shown oneself capable of doing as not worth the effort. And so on.

What! because I have never written poems as good as X's, which make me impatient, am I therefore to persevere, knowing all the time that no matter how fine the phrases, the ecstasy, the spell, it would always be *something else* that I wanted to say?

David Gascoyne

1942 [Holland]

I crammed until the last possible moment. Hannie and I set off for school together. It was raining. Seeing us walking along in the rain, with our stars on, an out-of-service bus stopped for us. The bus driver said he'd take us wherever we were going. It was really nice of him, but we thought it safer not to accept. We said we couldn't because then we might land in jail, and he said, 'Well, then we'll all go to jail together, that will be a blast.' 'O.K,' we said, 'but not right now, thanks: we are on our way to our finals . . .' We decided we had better get going. 'Next time perhaps, after the war,' we told him and continued on our way.

Edith Velmans

1985

Watched the Live Aid thing on TV. Bobby Zarem's office had been calling, wanting me to go down there, but when you're with that many big celebrities you never get any publicity. Later on that night Jack Nicholson introduced Bob Dylan and called him 'transcendental'. But to me, Bob Dylan was never really real – he was just mimicking real people and the amphetamine made it come out magic. With amphetamine he could copy the right words and make it all sound right. But that boy never felt a thing – *(laughs)* I just never bought it.

Andy Warhol

14 July

1860

Opened the shutters & lighted the kitchen fire. Shook my sooty things in the dusthole & emptied the soot there. Swept & dusted the rooms & the hall. Laid the hearth & got breakfast up. Clean'd 2 pairs of boots. Made the bed & emptied the slops. Clean'd & wash'd the breakfast things up. Clean'd the plates; clean'd the knives & got dinner up. Clean'd away. Clean'd the kitchen up; unpack'd a hamper. Took two chickens to Mrs Brewer's & brought the message back. Made a tart & pick'd & gutted two ducks & roasted them. Clean'd the steps & flags on my knees. Blackleaded the scraper in front of the house; clean'd the street flags too on my knees. Wash'd up in the scullery. Clean'd the pantry on my knees & scour'd the tables. Scrubbed the flags around the house & clean'd the window sills. Got tea at 9 for the master & Mrs Warwick in my dirt, but Ann carried it up. Clean'd the privy & passage & scullery floor on my knees. Wash'd the dog & clean'd the sinks down. Put the supper ready for Ann to take up, for I was too dirty to go upstairs. Wash'd in a bath & to bed without feeling any the worse for yesterday [when she had climbed up the chimney to sweep it clean].

Hannah Cullwick

1910

I have not slept all night and was within a hair's-breadth of suicide. These expressions of my suffering, however extreme, could not possibly do them justice. Lev Nik. [Tolstoy] came in, and I told him in a terrible state of agitation that everything lay in the balance: it was either the diaries or my life, he could choose. And he did choose, I am thankful to say, and he got the diaries back from Chertkov [his publisher].

Sasha drove over to Chertkov's to fetch the diaries and give him a letter from Lev Nikolaevich. But my soul is still grieving, and the thought of suicide, clear and firm, will always be with me the moment they open the wounds in my heart again.

So this is the end of my long and once happy marriage . . .! But it is not quite the end yet: Lev Nik's letter to me today is a scrap of the old happiness, although such a small and shabby scrap!

My daughter Tanya has sealed up the diaries, and tomorrow she and her husband will take them to the bank in Tula. They will fill out a receipt for them in the name of Lev Nik. and his heirs, and will give this receipt to L. N. I hope to God they do not deceive me, and that Jesuit Chertkov doesn't wheedle the diaries out of Lev Nik on the sly!

Not a thing has passed my lips for three days now, and this has worried everyone terribly for some reason. But this is the least of it . . . it's all a matter of passion and the force of grief.

Sofia Tolstoy

1941 [Dresden]

The dreaded Sunday special announcement came and exceeded all expectations. Stalin Line taken, in the south considerable forward advance from Romania (from Romania, away from the oil centre, which was supposed to be under threat). Emphasis, and rightly so, evidently, that the war against Russia has been decided, that Hitler can carry on the war for years, that he is invincible master of the whole continent. Asia will be added to Europe. For us in a personal sense that means slavery until the end of our lives. Very depressed evening. On top of the catastrophic news there was the most extreme sultriness and, as usual on a Sunday, the food was especially gruesome and miserable. Nothing edible at Pschorr, other restaurants shut, finally the Neustadt railway station packed and suffocatingly hot.

Victor Klemperer

1948

I was married – and how debonair and confident I was – 15 years ago today. I rose early, dressed slowly, went to Delhez, the fashionable Figaro, to be shaved and coiffed, and there my best man, Freddie Birkenhead, met me: I then entertained 15 ushers to luncheon at Buck's Club – I remember every detail. Today was different.

'Chips' Channon

15 July

1675

This was a journey of Adventure and knight errantry, one of the Ladys servants being as desperatly in love with Mrs. Howards Woman, who riding on horseback behind his Rival, the amorous and jealous Youth, having a little drink in his pate, had certainly here killed himselfe, had he not ben prevented for alighting from his horse and drawing his sword, he endeavored to fall upon it twise or thrice, but was interrupted; [by] our Coach-man and a stranger that passed by, after which running to his rival and snatching another sword from his side (for we had beaten his owne out of his hand) and on the suddaine pulling downe his Mistriss, would have run both of them through; but we parted them, though not without some blood: This miserable Creature Poyson'd himselfe for her not many daies after they came to Lond.

John Evelyn

1866

Breakfast at 9.30. A. T. [Alfred Tennyson] out at 12. Swan Green forest path, Haliday's Hall, we *swim* through tall bracken. T. pauses midway, turns to me, and says solemnly, 'I believe *this* place is quite full of vipers!' After going a little further, he stopped again and said, 'I am told that a viper-bite may make a woman silly for life, or deprive a man of his virility.'

We entered Mark Ash, a wood of huge solemn Beech trees, the floor thick-matted with dead leaves; a few trees were broken or fallen; some towered to a great height before branching. We sat on the roots of a mighty Beech. T. smoked. We shared sandwiches and brandy. Then he produced a little pocket *As You Like It*, and read some parts aloud.

William Allingham

1935

Anniversary of the day on which I got married and on which, with one thrust which quite deprived me of breath, I lost my virginity.

Liane de Pougy

1940

What can the future hold for us, personally, now? What can one look for? Only to save from the wreckage one's hopes, one's possessions, and some part of one's fortune. What a mess! I have little heart to go on – à quoi bon? All I want is an oval library with doors leading into a rose garden, by the sea.

'Chips' Channon

1969

The journalist Godfrey Winn had come my way as a result of the Annigoni portrait [of the Queen], having been asked to write it up. He's a perfectly nice man but everything was said when, as I took him round the Gallery, he stood in front of a Lawrence portrait of a strikingly handsome young man and with a grotesque grimace exclaimed, 'Why can't I look like that?'

Roy Strong

1995

A and I watching Live Aid (ten years old today [actually, ten years old on 13 July]) on TV tonight. I sort of finally got the point. It wrapped the world. Christo's Reichstag is quite minor by comparison – the Reichstag took 20 years to organize, Band Aid 10 weeks. The achievement, for me, is not the money that was raised but the idea that it might be possible to (temporarily) bind a large part of the globe together around one issue. I'm surprised I feel so strongly about this – and thrilled (as often) to find myself to have been wrong. Are pop musicians the only people who can address the world as though it is one place? Or was that the last gasp of unrealistic, pre-post-modern idealism? Contrast it with the indifference about Bosnia (Serbs in Srebrnica, rape, starvation, ethnic cleansing – it's all 'over there').

The failure of Band Aid is that poor Geldof ('Good old Bob,' said Anthea after the programme) was expected – by me too – to know what to do with all the money. It's so obvious that the momentum he created should have been harnessed by people who already knew that, who were good at that. Why don't people do what they're good at and get others to do the rest?

Brian Eno

16 July

1870

War declared against Prussia by France. All grades of opinion in the English newspapers. Concur in calling it an unprovoked aggression. *The Times* says [it's] the greatest national sin which has occurred since Napoleon 1st.

Dearman Birchall

1870

After tea Mrs Bridge took us round into the garden to show us her hives. One bee instantly flew straight at me and stung me between the eyes, as I was poking about the hives in my blind way. I did not say anything about it and Mrs Bridge congratulated me on my narrow escape from being stung.

All the while the miserable bee was buzzing about entangled in my beard, having left its sting between my eyes. Consequently I suppose he was in his dying agony.

Rev. Francis Kilvert

1879

I am singularly weary; I have heard that the typhoid fever begins in that way.

I have had bad dreams. If I were to die? I am quite astonished that I do not tremble at the thought of death. If there is another life it must certainly be better than the life I lead here on earth. And if there should be nothing after death? That would be all the more reason for not being terrified, and for desiring the end of troubles without greatness, and torments without glory. I must make my will.

I begin to work at eight o'clock in the morning and at about five I am so tired that my evening is wasted; in fact, I must make my will.

Marie Bashkirtseff

1919

One of Cocteau's jokes. Talking of a chameleon, he said: 'Its master put it down on a tartan rug and it died of over-exertion.'

Liane de Pougy

1931

Mr. Maconachie called. Wonderful old man. You can note his secret pleasure now when he comes away with the phrase, 'I remember – 80 years ago when I was a boy . . .' He *must* enjoy the sound of that, for one can feel shop-soiled enough even when one can merely say 'I remember 20 years ago . . .'

William Soutar

1953

During the last week a journalistic orgy has been taking place over poor Princess Margaret and Peter Townsend. He has been posted to Brussels and she is in South Africa with the Queen Mother. She is returning tomorrow, poor child, to face the *Daily Mirror* poll which is to decide, in the readers' opinion, whether she is to marry a divorced man or not! It is all so incredibly vulgar and, to me, it is inconceivable that nothing could be done to stop these tasteless, illiterate minds from smearing our Royal Family with their sanctimonious rubbish. Obviously the wretched Peter Townsend should have been discreetly transferred ages ago. Now it is too late and everyone is clacking about it from John O'Groats to Land's End. One can only assume that the 'advisers' in Buckingham Palace and the Lord Chamberlain's office are a poor lot. A welter of pseudo-religious claptrap is now swirling around the feet of the poor Princess and the unfortunate young man. He was the innocent party in his divorce, but the Church is adamantly squeaking its archaic views. I suspect that she is probably in love with him but, whether she is or not, it should never have been allowed to reach the serious stage. I feel sorry for all concerned but even more contemptuous than usual of the Press.

Noël Coward

1980

There's so much in the papers about Ronald Reagan and it looks like he's on his way to become president, it does look scary. I voted once. In the fifties, I don't remember which election. I pulled the wrong lever because I was confused, I couldn't figure out how to work the thing. There was no practice model outside, it was a church on 35th Street between Park and Lex. This was when I was living at 242 Lexington. And then I got called for jury duty and I wrote back: 'Moved.' I've never voted again.

Andy Warhol

17 July

1739

I rode to Bradford, five miles from Bath, whither I had been long invited to come. I waited on the Minister, and desired leave to preach in his church. He said, it was not usual to preach on the week-days; but if I could come thither on a Sunday, he should be glad of my assistance. Thence I went to a gentleman in the town, who had been present when I preached at Bath, and, with the strongest marks of sincerity and affections, wished me good luck in the name of the Lord. But it was past. I found him now quite cold. He began disputing on several heads; and at last told me plainly, one of our own College had informed him they always took me to be a little crack-brained at Oxford . . .

John Wesley

1768

Alas, alas! my poor Journal! how dull unentertaining, uninteresting thou art! – oh what I would give for some Adventure worth reciting – for something which would surprise – astonish you!

Fanny Burney

1833

Went to Drury Lane to see Paganini. His power over his instrument is surprising; the tones he draws from it might be thought those of the sweetest flageolet and hautboy, and sometimes of the human voice; the expression he gives to a common air is quite charming. His playing 'Patrick's Day' was the sweetest piece of instrumental music I ever heard; but he is a quack.

Charles Macready

1849 [Ireland]

We are not to grace the royal festivities. The Colonel was undecided for some time, but on calculating the cost, he thinks it would be not only inconvenient but wrong in these times to incur such expense. I don't agree with him, I think our duty to our daughters requires this effort from us, and that we keep them beneath their proper position by not presenting them among the society they ought to belong to. For it is not only the court they lose but every entertainment made for her majesty, at none of which they can appear. Perhaps he is right, at any rate he is the master, so there is no more about it. I may be too vain or too ambitious, former recollections interfering with the poor Officer's wife; while he may err on the other side, having never mixed with the world in his early youth and going out to India before he was capable of understanding the fitness of forms at home. He is also extremely shy, I am not pushing, both too proud and too indolent, but I know my own place and I should like if possible to keep my girls in it. But it is not to be. They had set their young hearts on it, having now a large dancing acquaintance among really nice people and they had been settling their dresses with the Lady Leesons, who are full of it too. It is a good trial – and so Adieu.

Elizabeth Grant of Rothiemurchus

1931

Have been in bed a year now – can't say that I worry much about it – too well looked after.

William Soutar

1949 [Rio de Janeiro]

I return to the hotel to wait for the faithful Abdias [Brazilian actor] who's supposed to take me to dance the samba after dinner. Disappointing evening. In an outlying neighborhood, a kind of working class dance hall lit, of course, by neon. For the most part there are only blacks, but in Brazil this means a great variety of skin colors. Surprised to see how slowly these blacks dance, as if underwater. Perhaps it's the climate. The Harlem madmen would probably calm down here. Except for the color of the skin, nothing distinguishes this dance hall from a thousand others throughout the world. Speaking of this, I notice that I have to conquer in myself a reverse prejudice. I like blacks *à priori*, and I'm tempted to see in them qualities that they don't really have. I want these people to be beautiful, but if I imagine them with white skin, I find a rather pretty collection of clerks and dyspeptic employees. Abdias agrees. The race is ugly. However, of the mulatto women who immediately come to drink at our table, not because it's ours but because we're drinking there, one or two are pretty. I'm even attracted to one who's lost her voice, dances a lax samba with another woman, taps me on the side to awaken my appetite, and then suddenly informs me that I'm bored. Taxi. I return to the hotel.

Albert Camus

18 July

1831

I heard Paganini today – he is divine – he had the effect of giving me hysterics – yet I could pass my life listening to him – Nothing was ever so sublime.

Mary Shelley

1859 [Boulogne]

. . . dined at a restaurant, and along the quay at dusk . . . I walked down the deserted pier, & saw the moon rise from dark clouds over the town. Coming back, a fishwoman walking alone in the shadow came up to me, & to my astonishment proposed a walk and 'pleasure' on the beach. Was she married? 'Oh yes: but he is away, & and will never know – que voulez vous?' Whereupon I gave vent to certain appropriate remarks, and the fishwoman vanished quickly. This is the only case of the kind I met with: & I daresay it too is due to us English . . .

Arthur F. Munby

1932 [Berlin]

Yesterday there were again fifteen dead and numerous wounded all over the country, twelve of the fatalities occurring in Altona alone. The Nazis, several thousand strong and doubtless meaning to provoke an incident, marched in their spick and span uniforms through the poorest quarters of Altona. The predictable result occurred. The unemployed and the loafers, probably criminal elements too, attacked them. But the guilt rests upon those who provided the provocation. There is great and general distress about this fresh Sunday bloodshed.

At one o'clock the Government announced over the radio a general veto on demonstrations throughout the country. But it took good care not to deal with the real cause of the bloodshed, the provocative Nazi uniform.

Count Harry Kessler

1954

At lunch today we were told by the Duchesse de Talleyrand about a most unfortunate gaffe made by the Duke of Windsor at the supper party following her son's wedding. He had spilt coffee over the dress of his next-door neighbour by making too hasty a gesture, and had been much comforted by the fact she was a Rothschild who could well afford another dress. After apologies had been made, and to start the conversation going again, he brightly remarked to her, 'Since you are a Rothschild, can you tell me which is the Rothschild with whom Pamela Churchill is having an affair?' To which she replied, 'Sir, that's worse than the coffee; that's my husband!'

Cynthia Gladwyn

19 July

1821 [Coronation of George IV]

I only got my ticket on Wednesday at two and dearest Mary [his wife] and I drove about to get all that was wanted. Sir George Beaumont lent me ruffles and frill, another friend a blue velvet coat, a third a sword; I bought buckles, and the rest I had. I went to bed at ten and arose at twelve, not having slept a wink. I dressed, breakfasted, and was at the Hall-door at half-past one. Three ladies were before me. The doors opened about four, and I got a front place in the Chamberlain's box, between the door and the throne, and saw the whole room distinctly. Many of the doorkeepers were tipsy; quarrels took place. The sun began to light up the old Gothic windows, the peers to stroll in, and other company of all descriptions to crowd to their places. Some took seats they had not any right to occupy; and were obliged to leave them after sturdy disputes. Others lost their tickets. The hall occasionally echoes with the hollow roar of voices at the great door, till at last the galleries were filled; the Hall began to get crowded below. Every movement, as the time approached for the King's appearance, was pregnant with interest. The appearance of a Monarch has something in it like the rising of the sun. There are indications which announce the luminary's approach; a streak of light – the tipping of a cloud – the singing of the lark – the brilliance of the sky, till the cloud edges get brighter and brighter, and he rises majestically into the heavens. So with a king's advance. A whisper of mystery turns all eyes to the throne. Suddenly two or three rise;

others fall back; some talk, direct, hurry, stand still, or disappear. Then three or four of high rank appear from behind the throne; an interval is left; the crowds scarce breathe. Something rustles, and a being buried in satin, feathers, and diamonds rolls gracefully into his seat. The room rises with a sort of feathered, silken thunder. Plumes wave, eyes sparkle, glasses are out, mouths smile, and one man becomes the prime object of attraction to thousands. The way in which the king bowed was really royal. As he looked towards the peeresses and foreign ambassadors he showed like some gorgeous bird of the East.

B. R. Haydon

1920 [Munich]

In mid-week wrote 'Ballad on many Ships', followed by a fourth act to *Drums in the Night*, a final one. On Saturday morning again entirely revised the fourth act, this time not at all like Baal which I now realised I completely messed up. Baal has turned to paper, gone academic, smooth, well-shaped, wearing bathing trunks and all that. Instead of becoming more earthy, care-free, outrageous, simple . . . In future I shall produce nothing but flaming mud pies made of shit.

Bertolt Brecht

1940

The Hitler we saw in the Reichstag tonight was the conqueror, and conscious of it, and yet so wonderful an actor, so magnificent a handler of the German mind, that he mixed superbly the full confidence of the conqueror with the humbleness which always goes down so well with the masses when they know a man is on top. His voice was lower tonight; he rarely shouted as he usually does; and he did not once cry out hysterically as I've seen him do so often from this rostrum. His oratorical form was at its best. I've often sat in the gallery of the Kroll Opera House at these Reichstag sessions watch-ing the man as he spoke and considered what a superb actor he was, as indeed are all good orators. I've often admired the way he uses his hands, which are somewhat feminine and quite artistic. Tonight he used those hands beauti-fully, seemed to express himself almost as much with his hands – and the sway of his body – as he did with his words and the use of his voice. I noticed too his gift for using his face and eyes (cocking his eyes) and the turn of his head for irony, of which there was considerable in tonight's speech, especially when he referred to Mr. Churchill.

I noticed again, too, that he can tell a lie with as straight a face as any man. Probably some of the lies are not lies to him because he believes fanat-ically the words he is saying, as for instance his false recapitulation of the last twenty-two years and his constant reiteration that Germany was never really defeated in the last war, only betrayed. But tonight he could also say with the ring of utter sincerity that all the night bombings of the British in recent weeks had caused no military damage whatsoever. One wonders what is in his mind when he tells a tall one like that. Joe [Harsch], watching him speak for the first time, was impressed. He said he couldn't keep his eyes off his hands; thought the hand-work brilliant.

William L. Shirer

1967

I went to listen to the Abortion Bill in the Lords, which our excellent young Scottish member, David Steel, presented in the Commons. A crowded house, swarming with bishops and large-familied Roman Catholic peers who gave impassioned vent to their feelings about the sanctity of human life. Far the best speaker, I thought, was Lord Soper. As in the Homosexual Bill last week, he spoke excellent good sense, standing out in contrast to the awful Lord Dilhorne, who seems to me to be so prejudiced and retrograde that I feel quite angry when I see his unattractive bulky figure rise up.

Cynthia Gladwyn

20 July

1944

An attack on Hitler's life, but unfortunately the bastard wasn't killed.

Joan Wyndham

1971

To BBC. The discussion of Wilde, Corvo & Solzhenitsyn was chaired by Derek Parker & was with Marie Rambert, Jennie Lee & me. I agreed with J. L. on Wilde, but disagreed with both of them on Solzhenitsyn. I said that I thought *One Day in the Life of Ivan Denisovich* was rotten. I think it is. It may be excellent as a report on conditions in a political prison etc. but as a realistic novel, it is rotten.

Kenneth Williams

21 July

1851

There is no glory so bright but the veil of business can hide it effectually. With most men life is postponed to some trivial business, and so therefore is heaven. Men think foolishly they may abuse and misspend life as they please and when they get to heaven turn over a new leaf.

I see the track of a bare human foot in the dusty road, the toes and muscles all faithfully imprinted. Such a sight is so rare that it affects me with surprise, as the footprint on the shore of Juan Fernandez did Crusoe. It is equally rare here. I am affected as if some Indian or South-Sea-Islander had been along, some man who had a foot. I am slow to be convinced that any of my neighbors – the judge on the bench, the parson in the pulpit – might have made that or something like it, however irregular. It is pleasant as it is to see the tracks of cows and deer and birds. I am brought so much nearer to the tracker – when again I think of the sole of my own foot – that when I behold that of his shoe merely, or am introduced to him and converse with him in the usual way, I am disposed to say to the judge whom I meet, 'Make tracks.'

H. D. Thoreau

1943

All today, whatever I've been thinking about, a girl's face has haunted me. I sat by her in the bus last evening. I always like to sit in a bus or train – to watch people, and wonder what they are, where they are going etc. I felt such cold despair radiate from this girl that I turned to look at her. She was only about fourteen or fifteen, poorly dressed, and she had made no attempt to make the best of what looks she had: her hair was untidy, she had a loose coat on, and her ungloved hands twisted and folded and unfolded on her lap – her only movement. I thought, 'Poor child, someone has been cross with her, and she is of an age to make mountains out of molehills.' The bleakness and despair of her little ashen face, the stony look of her blue eyes, as she stared straight in front of her. Then she rose, and I could have cried out in pity as I saw she was going to have a baby. She walked down the sidewalk to the station, but she had no luggage, not even a handbag. I've wondered and wondered all day about her, and her pitiful story. I hope she has a mother, a kind one.

Nella Last

1970

A preview of Kenneth Tynan's much heralded *Oh! Calcutta!* at the Round House in Chalk Farm turned out to be an occasion notable for the boredom of it all. I have never been so aware how anti-erotic nudity could be, or, when it came to the nude *pas de deux*, of the accuracy of Fred Ashton's observation that there were some parts of the anatomy over whose movements the choreographer had no control. There it was, a vast pile-up of sketches on wife-swapping, masturbation, knickers, lesbianism, *et al.* Joe Orton's sketch on country-house perversions was the only jewel in this tarnished crown, but even that needed cutting.

Roy Strong

22 July

1873

To-day the heat was excessive and as I sat reading under the lime I pitied the poor haymakers toiling on the burning Common where it seemed to be raining fire.

Rev. Francis Kilvert

1910

How I hate the man who talks about the 'brute creation', with an ugly emphasis on *brute*. Only Christians are capable of it. As for me, I am proud of my close kinship with other animals. I take a jealous pride in my Simian ancestry. I like to think that I was once a magnificent hairy fellow living in the trees and that my frame has come down through geological times *via* sea jelly and worms and Amphioxus, Fish, Dinosaurs, and Apes. Who would exchange these for the pallid couple in the Garden of Eden?

W. N. P. Barbellion

1934 [Karlsbad]

For more than a week I have been going about bareheaded, according to the very pleasant custom of Karlovy Vary [Czech name for Karlsbad], favoured by the shady trees hereabout; very exactly since the day when I bought myself a marvellous and irresistible Anglo-Tyrolian headdress I didn't need at all, which remains in my cupboard. I wore a hat only one evening, to go into a synagogue to hear a very beautiful concert; I had to borrow a hat at the entrance, a rather filthy one that stuck to my head. '*Vergessen sie nicht es wiederzubringen*' [Do not forget to bring it back], I was told. Never fear!

André Gide

1940 [Berlin]

Hitler has given Mussolini a birthday present. It's an anti-aircraft armoured train.

William L. Shirer

1965 [Addis Ababa]

To the City Hall . . . the Lord Mayor, a cheerful fat man, apologized for the lift being so new that it was not yet working. We climbed up four flights of stairs, at the end of which it was clear that his object was to show me the TV studio.

I explained to him I had been there the night before, and then he suggested as an alternative we should climb the remaining flights to the roof garden to which he had taken Lilibet [Queen Elizabeth] to see the unrivalled view of Addis Ababa. When we got to the door of the roof garden it was locked. He then sent for the key. It didn't arrive. Other messengers were sent; panic stations ensued, but no key could be found.

I noticed that the bottom right-hand panel of the door was missing, and although it was a fairly small opening, I knelt down and put my head through and found that by twisting my body I could just get my shoulders through and crawl through the empty panel. I shouted back suggesting that nobody would follow me, but I maliciously hoped that they would and they did. Next came the Ambassador, who was fairly agile, followed by my ADC General, then Peter Lithgow crawled through and finally with much struggle and pushing they got the Lord Mayor through the hole.

While we were looking at the view, the latter was in a frenzy to get the door open because he didn't fancy having to crawl back through the hole. Carpenters arrived, they tried to unscrew the door and then to get it off its hinges. Finally, the Lord Mayor came up himself and rattled the door and bashed it and very nearly broke it down. While he was doing that, I quietly crawled back through the hole and the whole party had to crawl back again on their hands and knees. It was all most entertaining.

Earl Mountbatten of Burma

1986

I've been watching this stuff on Fergie [Duchess of York] and I wonder why doesn't the Queen Mother get married again.

Andy Warhol

1990

On the return journey I cut across to the old A20, passing the sign for Hothfield where in the nurses' quarters on a summer's evening in 1955 I experienced the most perfect physical sensation, never before or since, with Marye. Jealous and inquisitive colleagues tried and rattled her door, departing in the end to get Matron. She, stout woman, portentously interrogated Marye through the keyhole, but the sweet girl (who looked, now I come to think about it, not unlike a bustier version of Jenny [Easterbrook, his secretary] on HRT) kept her superior at bay for some precious minutes while I got dressed and climbed out of the window to stumble across unlit lawns and rose bushes.

Alan Clark

23 July

1861

Home to the Temple at 6, and to Mudie's. Coming thence along Oxford Street, I saw before me, striding along in company with an Italian organ-grinder, a tall young man in full Highland costume; wearing a Glengarry bonnet, a scarlet jacket, a sporran and a tartan kilt & stockings, his legs bare from the knee to the calf. It was not a man – it was Madeleine Sinclair the street dancer, whom I used to see in a similar dress a year ago. She and her companion turned into a quiet street, and she danced a Highland fling to his music, in the midst of a curious crowd.

For no one could make out whether she was man or woman. Her hair and the set of her hips indeed were feminine; but her hard weatherstained face, her large bony hands, and her tall strong figure, became her male dress so well that opinions were about equally divided as to her sex. 'It's a man!' said one, confidently. 'I believe it's a woman,' another doubtfully replied. One man boldy exclaimed, 'Of course it's a man; anybody can see that!' I gave her a sixpence when she came round with her tambourine; and she told me she had been in Paris five months for pleasure, and was now living on Saffron Hill, and dancing in the streets every day, always wearing her male clothes . . .

Arthur F. Munby

1880

Who will give me back my wasted spoiled, and lost youth? I am not yet twenty, and the other day I found three grey hairs. I boast of it, it is a fearful proof that I exaggerate nothing. Were it not for my childish face I should look old. Is it natural at my age?

Oh! but there arises at the bottom of my heart such a storm, that it is better to cut all this short by telling myself that I shall always have the resource of blowing my brains out before they begin to pity me.

Marie Bashkirtseff

1930

Edith Sitwell has grown very fat, powders herself thickly, gilds her nails with silver paint, wears a turban and looks like an ivory elephant, like the Emperor

Heliogabalus. I have never seen such a change. She is mature, majestic. Her fingers are crusted with white coral. She is altogether composed. A great many people were there – and she presided. But though thus composed, her eyes are sidelong and humorous. The old Empress remembers her scallywag days. We all sat at her feet – cased in slender black slippers, the only remnants of her slipperiness and slenderness. We hardly talked together, and I felt myself gone there rather mistakenly, had she not asked me very affectionately if she might come and see me alone. Her room is crowded with odds and ends of foreigners.

Virginia Woolf

1935

Last night I went to the Golden Dragon, a Negro nightclub on South Rampart St., to listen to Louie Armstrong.

Not long ago he came back to New Orleans where he was born, came back in triumph because in England he had played a command performance for King George VI. This is his homecoming, so Louie lifted up his golden trumpet and blew glad notes.

Yowls of joy soared from hundreds of throats: '. . . Lissen-a-that! . . . Lissen-a-that! . . . His old theme song, sure nuff!'

Louie was ladling out *When It's Sleepytime Down South*.

South Rampart St. was the place to be last night. One of its own had made good – and made good and made good! Now he was back with them again, grinning his infectious grin, braying the lyrics in his brassy voice, same old Louie. He gave his trumpet one last loving kiss, and then there was Satchelmouth at the microphone. He wore no tie, his shirtsleeves were rolled up, and around his neck he wore a towel, like every other champion. On the fourth finger of his left land he wore a ring with diamonds that glittered and glinted and vied with one another to shine the best.

Pale moon shinin' on the fields below / Darkies singin' sweet an' low . . .

The rasping and gurgling of his voice made my spine feel like a xylophone. He slid from one note to a lower one and then careened down to a guttural bass note lower than my worst sin. As he sang he mopped his face and weaved back and forth, but he kept his black eyes on the mike under his nose, like a serpent hypnotizing a bird. Not until he reached the end of the ballad did he free the mike from his spell, but when he did so he let out one final boom that could have frightened the poor thing to death.

With his towel he swabbed the sweat from his squat face, and grinned and laughed, and the dancers crowded around him, holding up hands to be shaken and things to be autographed. One cinnamon-colored woman begged for his autograph: 'Please, Louie baby! Aw, please, Louie baby! C'mon an' write on this here card, woan you?'

Louie signed and sweated and talked with me about his childhood. He was born in a poor part of New Orleans on July 4 1890, and as a child he was a street singer. When he was twelve he shot off his father's gun on New Year's Eve and was sent to the Colored Waifs' Home for Boys. There he was taught to read music and play the drums, bugle and cornet. Later he learned more from Joe (King) Oliver, the greatest cornetist in New Orleans before the war. Louie switched from the cornet to the trumpet, and the gold one he used tonight was given to him in England. After charming the British monarch, Louie crossed over to Europe, where his reputation became phenomenal. Now everybody knows he is the world's greatest jazz musician. He has worn out four trumpets and no welcomes.

Edward Robb Ellis

1990

I saw [Michael] Heseltine in the post office of the Commons today, and said to him, 'I noticed when you were interviewed not long ago on television that one of my books was on the shelf behind you. I presume it was there to impress people!'

'I'll remove it at once,' he replied.

Tony Benn

24 July

1860

Office 10.23 to 5.21 . . . Went to the newsroom, and home 8.45. Found my housekeeper Miss Mitchell and a policeman in anxious talk: my rooms, at 4 p.m., had been broken open and robbed.

It is curious to observe one's own behaviour under such a new sensation. My first impulse was to laugh; and I accompanied the friendly peeler upstairs with a cheerful calmness which was perfectly heroic. The sight of the empty plate basket, cupboard standing open, housekeeper aghast, and real policeman, struck me as really 'good fun' – the realization of a drama which hitherto one had only read of. My loss was only seven spoons, four forks, sugar tongs, a coral pin, and a favourite coat: had it been greater, perhaps I should not have felt so jolly: as it was, I felt a sort of grotesque admiration for the ingenious protestant who wrought the deed of darkness.

Arthur F. Munby

1871

Robert says the first grass from the scythe is the *swathe*, then comes the *strow* (tedding), then *rowing*, then the footcocks, then *breaking*, then the *hubrows*, which are gathered into *hubs*, then sometimes another break and *turning*, then *rickles*, the biggest of all the cocks, which are run together into *placks*, the shapeless heaps from which the hay is carted.

Gerard Manley Hopkins

1944

Last week a nobleman in our street was lifted by his servants from his deathbed, dressed in his evening clothes, then carried to be propped up at the head of the staircase over the courtyard of his palazzo. Here with a bouquet of roses thrust into his arms he stood for a moment to take leave of his friends and neighbours gathered in the courtyard below, before being carried back to receive the last rites. Where else but in Naples could a sense of occasion be carried to such lengths?

Norman Lewis

1980

We go to the Royal Garden party. I always enjoy this – the centre courtyard and the tweaked curtains in the upper floors, the glimpse of that lovely low-ceilinged oval drawing room, the sudden burst of green grass, brass bands, striped tents, multi-coloured hats. Spot my old friend John W (he's clearly on the same rota as me) – carrying, as usual, his plastic shopping bag into which he pops the occasional cupcake to take back to his village children . . . 'straight from the Queen's tea table', he tells them. He circumnavigates the garden at high speed, returned to me at HQ with snippets of information. 'The Ambassadress has lost her left heel' . . . 'the Bishop of —— has ice-cream on his apron' . . . 'A flamingo seems to have fainted.' Tea in the Royal Tent, standing in its own circus ring guarded by Yeomen of the Guard. A red ticket, a permissive wave from a gloved hand, a table on which stand twenty toppers, upturned as if waiting to be filled up from a teapot, royal footmen, helpful ushers, introductions. Royalty in close proximity always charges the air and causes behaviour to go into a different gear. Preoccupations with falling crumbs, top heavy tea-spoons, the tendency of high heels to sink inexorably and anchor-like into the turf. Beyond the ropes, the guests sit on chairs or stand gazing with frank curiosity at the Queen and us downing éclairs. We behave under such scrutiny like extras in the background of a Drury Lane musical . . . feigned conversation interest . . . tiny forced laughs . . . exaggerated courtesies . . . wariness in the face of *mille-feuilles*.

Sir Hugh Casson

25 July

The only thing I have heard worth recording is a strange enough matter regarding the Duke of Wellington. He has got himself (at eighty-two years of age) into, if not a scrape, an embarrassment with Lady Georgiana Fane, who is half cracked. It seems that he has for some years past carried on a sort of flirtation with her, and a constant correspondence, writing her what might be called love letters, and woefully committing himself. He has now broken with her, and she persecutes him to death. She is troublesome, and he is brutal. He will not see her, or have anything to do with her. She tries to get at him, which it seems she can only do as he comes out of church (early service) at St. James's and she made a scene there not long ago. She says all she wants is that he should behave *kindly* to her, which is just what he will not do. Meanwhile she has placed his letters in the hands of her solicitor, Mr. Frere (an outrageous thing), who tells her they are sufficient to establish a case against him for a breach of promise of marriage. Nothing of this queer but lamentable affair seems to have got out, and for the credit of the Duke it is to be hoped it may not. It would be painful to see him an object of ridicule and contempt in the last days of his illustrious life. He has always had one or more women whom he likes to talk to and got to be intimate with, and often very odd women too, but the strangest of all his fancies was this tiresome, troublesome, crazy old maid.

Charles Greville

1917

Went to dine to Barrie's [J. M. Barrie] with Thomas Hardy and wife. Barrie has an ugly little manservant, and the finest view of London I ever saw. Mrs Hardy a very nice woman, with a vibrating attractive voice. Hardy was very lively; talked like anything. Apropos of Tchekoff he started a theory that some of Tchekoff's tales were not justifiable because they told nothing unusual. He said a tale must be unusual and the people interesting. Of course he soon got involved in the meshes of applications and instances; but he kept his head and showed elasticity and common sense, and came out on the whole well. He has all his faculties, unimpaired. Quite modest and without the slightest pose.

Later in the evening Barrie brought along both Shaw and the Wellses by phone. Barrie was consistently very quiet, but told a few A1 stories. At dusk we viewed the view and the searchlights. Hardy, standing outside one of the windows, had to put a handkerchief on his head. I sneezed. Soon after Shaw and the Wellses came Hardy seemed to curl up. He had travelled to town that day and was evidently fatigued. He became quite silent. I then departed and told Barrie that Hardy ought to go to bed. He agreed. The spectacle of Wells and G.B.S. talking firmly and strongly about the war, in their comparative youth, in front of this aged, fatigued and silent man – incomparably their superior as a creative artist – was very striking.

Arnold Bennett

1926

At first I thought it was [Thomas] Hardy, and it was the parlour-maid, a small thin girl, wearing a proper cap. She came in with silver cake stands and so on. Mrs. Hardy talked to us about her dog. How long ought we to stay? Can Mr. Hardy walk much etc. I asked, making conversation, as I knew one would have to. She has the large sad lacklustre eyes of a childless woman; great docility and readiness, as if she had learnt her part; not great alacrity, but resignation, in welcoming more visitors; wears a sprigged voile dress, black shoes and a necklace. We can't go far now, she said, though we do walk every day, because our dog isn't able to walk far. He bites, she told us. She became more natural and animated about the dog, who is evidently the real centre of her thoughts – then the maid came in. Then again the door opened, more sprucely, and in trotted a little puffy-cheeked cheerful old man, with an atmosphere cheerful and business-like in addressing us, rather like an old doctor's or solicitor's, saying 'Well now—' or words like that as he shook hands. He was dressed in rough grey with a striped tie. His nose has a joint in it and the end curves down. A round whitish face, the eyes now faded and rather watery, but the whole aspect cheerful and vigorous. He sat on a three-cornered chair (I am too jaded with all this coming and going to do more than gather facts) at a round table, where there were the cake stands and so on; a chocolate roll; what is called a good tea; but he only drank one cup, sitting on his three-cornered chair. He was extremely affable and aware of his duties. He did not let the talk stop or disdain making talk. He talked of father: said he had seen me, or it might have been my sister, but he thought it was me, in my cradle. He had been to Hyde Park Place – oh Gate was it. A very quiet street. That was why my father liked it. Odd to think that in all these years he had never been down there again. He went there often. Your father took my novel – *Far From the Madding Crowd*. We stood shoulder to shoulder against the British public about certain matters dealt with in that novel. You may have heard. Then he said how some other novel had fallen through that was to appear – the parcel had been lost coming from France – not a very likely thing to happen, as your father said – a big parcel of manuscript; and he asked me to send my story. I think he broke all the Cornhill laws – not to see the whole book; so I sent it in chapter by chapter and was never late. Wonderful what youth is! I had it in my head doubtless, but I never thought twice about it. It came out every month. They were nervous, because of Miss Thackeray I think. She said she became paralysed and could not write a word directly she heard the press begin. I daresay it was bad for a novel to appear like that. One begins to think what is good for the magazine, not what is good for the novel.

Virginia Woolf

1976 [during the filming of *Apocalypse Now*]

On the plane, I started reading *The Diary of Anaïs Nin, 1947–1955*. A number of women I respect have told me how terrific the diaries are. I almost never read. I have stopped being embarrassed about it only recently. I hardly ever watch television. I am not sure exactly how I get my information. It seems to come into my life in other ways. Someone else may be at home in their living room, watching a TV program about emerging nations. I am here [Philippines]. I don't see it as better or worse. One of the things that fascinated me in the part of Anaïs Nin's diary that I read was her description of some events in 1948 that perfectly fit my experience years later. Odd little things, like her description of meeting Kenneth Anger, or the chickens outside her window in Acapulco. She says of Mexico, 'Freedom from the past comes from associating with unfamiliar objects; none of them possesses any evocative power.' I feel that freedom here.

Eleanor Coppola

26 July

1800

Still hotter. I sate with W[illiam] in the orchard all the morning and made my shoes. In the afternoon from excessive heat I was ill in the headach[e] and toothach[e] and went to bed – I was refreshed with washing myself after I got up, but it was too hot to walk till near dark, and then I sate upon the wall finishing my shoes.

Dorothy Wordsworth

1933

Diaries – I am getting sick of this one – I am too lazy. Read six and a half hours of *Lady Chatterley's Lover*. Read till 1 o'clock. Good. Very good. The last letter from Oliver Mellors, the gamekeeper, is great. And pure. And strangely, it was infinitely comforting. At lunch:

'What's that you're reading?'

'*Lady Chatterley's Lover* by DH Lawrence.'

'Isn't that book banned in England?'

'Yes, I think it is.' I read her extracts from Frieda Lawrence's letters.

'Is it on moral grounds?'

'Yes. I think it's because he goes into detail so much.'

'It must be pretty disgusting if England won't allow it. They're really awfully lenient about literature.' Pause.

'I certainly don't want to read it.'

'I think it's perfectly disgusting to want to read a book my country won't allow.'

Well! I did not reply. I could not. Why tell her I did not even know it was banned. That several 'Oxford people' had been a bit scornful because I had not read it. That I bought it because I thought it was something I should read? That anyway I didn't care one way or any other what my country read? That it was good. Great. I did say, before her last remark, that 'Oxford people' had asked me if I had read it. And also, I said, 'Goodness! Can't you form your own opinion?' She looked glum and aggrieved. I hurried back to read it after lunch.

Elizabeth Smart

1934

I feel caddish, even treacherous sometimes keeping this diary from the eyes of my wife – yet it is our only secret. She knows I keep it, but if she were to read it, and I knew she were, it would lose much spontaneity, and cease to be a record of my private thoughts. Once or twice in the past I have dictated a few harmless paragraphs to a Secretary – and they have never been the same, becoming impersonal and discreet immediately. And what is more dull than a discreet diary? One might just as well have a discreet soul.

'Chips' Channon

1943

Fall of Mussolini!

Dear Josiah Wedgwood died – just too soon to know that the dictators were beginning to fall.

Vera Brittain

1943

The long-expected news has come at last: Mussolini has fallen. The news was given by radio last night, but we did not hear it until this morning. Mussolini has resigned, the King has appointed Marshal Badoglio in his place and has himself taken over the command of the Army. A proclamation of Badoglio's announces: 'Italy will keep her pledge; the war continues.'

As the broadcast closes E. burst into my room: 'Have you heard? After twenty years – after twenty years . . .' We all have a lump in our throat. Hope – perplexity – anxiety – doubt – then hope again – infinite relief. A weight has been lifted, a door opened; but where does it lead? We spend the day in speculation, fed by driblets of news. First a proclamation of martial law, with the institution of a curfew at sunset and a prohibition of any public meetings: moreover, it is forbidden to carry firearms or to circulate in any private vehicle; a few hours later we hear with delight of the disbanding of the Fascist militia: its members are to be incorporated in the regular Army. In the evening comes the list of the new Cabinet; mostly permanent officials or under-secretaries. It is clearly to be a moderate, traditional government of administrators, not of 'great men'. Italy has had enough of heroes. But still innumerable questions are unanswered. What has happened to Mussolini and his satellites? And above all – increasingly with every hour – what about Germany?

Iris Origo

27 July

1892

Reached Perth about seven o'clock in the morning, and washed in uncommonly cold water. Got the *Scotsman* and also copy of the preceding day's issue with caustic comments on Carnegie's strike.

Scotch papers are refreshingly acrimonious and spiteful provided you agree with them. I sometimes wonder, considering the metaphysical abstruse turn of Scotch intellect, that the articles provided by their political journalists should be brilliant rather than profound. They make *The Times* leaders appear ponderous in comparison. Exceedingly well written and doubtless well informed, or they could not be so versatile in argument, but they concern themselves more with the cut and thrust arguments of party politics than with fundamental principles and the evolution of politics. They reserve their powers of metaphysical dissection for philosophy and the Kirk, wherein perhaps they are wise, certainly practical, but it leaves the Scotch open to the accusation of being politicians first and patriots afterwards.

Beatrix Potter

1911

Percy and I decided to bicycle. We started about 11.0: went slowly to Barton, and so to Haslingfield: then between Haslingfield and Harston we lay long on the grass, near ricks, listening to owls and the snorting of some beast that drew nigh, to far-off dogs barking, and cocks crowing. The stars were like the points of pendants in the irregular roof of a cave – not an even carpet or set in a concave. We went on about 1.0, and then made a long halt near the G.N.R. bridge on the way to Newton; but no trains passed, so we went on about 1.45 to Shelford; and this was very sweet, so fragrant and shadowed by dark trees, while Algol and Aldebaran and other great shining stars slowly wheeled above us.

We got to the G.E.R. bridge at Shelford – I was anxious to see trains – and a half-a-dozen great luggers jangled through with a cloud of steam and coloured lights. There was one that halted, and the guard walked about with a lantern; a melancholy policeman was here, in the shadow. The owls again hooted and screamed and the cocks roared hoarsely.

Suddenly we became aware it was the dawn! The sky was whitening, there was a green tinge to the east, with rusty stains of cloud, and the stars went out. We went on about 2.30 to Grantchester, where the mill with lighted windows was rumbling, and the water ran oily-smooth into the inky pool among the trees. Then it was day; and by the time we rode into Cambridge, getting in at 3.30, it was the white morning light – while all the places so mysteriously different at night had become the places one knew. We found some bread-and-butter, and smoked till 4.0, when we went out round the garden, the day now brightening up: after which I went to bed, but P. walked until 5.0. The mystery, the coolness, the scent, the quiet of it all were wonderful, and the thought that this strange transformation passes over the world thus night by night seemed very amazing.

A. C. Benson

1949 [staying with Siegfried Sassoon]
Our last evening we were speaking of his post-1920 diaries – I was trying to think of something he could do to beguile the coming winter evenings. We discussed them. He said, after a muffled preamble to excuse the remark, 'I do think I'm a man in whom posterity will be interested.' He then gave a resumé of the peculiarities of his character, life and work which, taken together and with his unpublished diaries, would probably have this far-reaching effect.

J. R. Ackerley

28 July

1871
Gipsy Lizzie was at the School. Again I am under the influence of that child's extraordinary beauty. When she is reading and her eyes are bent down upon her book her loveliness is indescribable.

Rev. Francis Kilvert

1941

There is a rude article about me in *Truth* saying that I have 'the mincing manner of a French *salon*', that I lack virility and should retire from public life and bury myself in books. All rather true, I suppose. But I happen to enjoy public life. I could never be merely an observer.

Harold Nicolson

1942 [Holland]

7.30 a.m. I shall allow the chain of this day to unwind link by link. I shall not intervene but shall simply have faith. 'I shall let You make Your own decisions, oh God.' This morning I found a buff envelope in my letter box. I could see there was a white paper inside. I was quite calm and thought, 'My call-up notice, what a pity, now I won't have time to try repacking my rucksack.' Later I noticed that my knees were shaking. It was simply a form to be filled in by the staff of the Jewish Council. They haven't even issued me with an identity number yet. I shall take the few steps I have to. My turn may not come for a long time. Jung and Rilke will go with me in any case. And if my mind should be unable to retain very much later on, nevertheless these last two years will shine at the edge of my memory like a glorious landscape in which I was once at home and which will always remain part of me. I feel that I am still tied by a thousand threads to everything I treasure here. I will have to tear myself away bit by bit and store everything inside me, so that when I have to leave I shall not abandon anything but carry it all with me.

Etty Hillesum

29 July

1837

Walked to Oxford Street, took cab home. The cabman insisted on two shillings, which I resisted; and, on his persisting, I made him drive me to the police office, where a deposit was made for the measurement of the ground. I walked home.

Charles Macready

1873

[Thomas] Carlyle tells me of his 'sitting' to Whistler. If he makes signs of changing his position, Whistler screams out in an agonised tone, 'For God's sake, don't move!'

Carlyle said that all Whistler's anxiety seemed to be to get the *coat* painted to ideal perfection; the face went for little. He had begun by asking two or three sittings, but managed to get a great many.

At last Carlyle flatly rebelled. He used to define Whistler as the most absurd creature on the face of the earth.

William Allingham

1966

Down to the cottage, housekeeperless, to a weekend of hard domestic work and cooking. No one has any idea of the problems of a woman Minister!

Barbara Castle

1981

Prince Charles's Wedding. A day which has brought much happiness and I feel sure lasting benefit to the nation in a renewed sense of unity. Having prowled about among the crowds early on, I watched the wedding itself on television with Elizabeth; then went to lunch with Kevin and Ruth [son and daughter-in-law]. Three of their most attractive friends were present. Janet Hobhouse, half American, beautiful but rather sad highbrow writer; Sophie Baker, also beautiful by no means sad, photographer, long-time friend of all the children; a broad-shouldered, dynamic architect, recent escort of Princess Margaret, though some years younger. We watched the second part of the programme covering the royal appearances on the balcony and an earlier interview with Charles and Diana. Janet summed up our sophisticated feelings: 'The country is in good hands.'

Lord Longford

1981

Sat and watched the royal wedding on TV. There were perhaps two million people out in London, and this tremendous ceremonial display was watched throughout the world by 750 million people – without doubt the biggest television audience that had ever seen anything. The image presented to the rest of the world was of a Britain about as socially advanced as France before the French Revolution! We are slipping back to eighteenth-century politics. We've got to fight like anything to recover the position that we had even in 1945. I had that feeling most strongly. It was feudal propaganda, turning citizens into subjects.

Tony Benn

30 July

1924

They have let me know that I have been granted the Military Medal in memory of my son who had the right to it because of his two citations. The address proclaimed 'Widow Pourpe'. I am absolutely *not* the Widow Pourpe, nor have I ever been, having been divorced. In law I then reverted to being Madame Chassaigne. So the Widow Pourpe is informed that she will be given the Military Medal for her son Marc Pourpe, killed by the enemy; that if she wants the ceremony of handing over she must travel to Longvic, and that she will not be reimbursed for any expenses she incurs! If she prefers, she can have it brought to her by the commandant of her local police station. I feel shocked, bruised, wounded, ruffled and indignant. To be threatened with the police! The neighbourhood will think that they are coming to arrest me.

Liane de Pougy

1951

People always talk about climate, about good air. It's what's underground that counts, that influences us. Paris had good foundations: sand. New York has metal underpinnings. Pagnol says Americans try to get off the ground – they invent crepe soles and jump up on tables; they build skyscrapers. I work much more easily out at sea. In our villages, disease and madness come from underground. There are villages in the east of France (iron mines) where cases of insanity are past counting. In Milly, the subsoil is sand and water. It is important to be aware of the foundations where you live.

Jean Cocteau

1955

No one gets up in the morning. When they do they immediately sprawl on sun mattresses on the strip of rank grass which only a low brick parapet separates from the shingle beach covered with similarly supine proletarians. As there was no cook we were obliged to lunch at a dreary hotel at Sandwich, but I had a keen appetite and ate two helpings of boiled beef. There was a helicopter advertising Hennessy's brandy on the lawn. I paid for luncheon. Afterwards Diana [Lady Cooper] and I drove through the streets of Sandwich looking at antique shops empty of anything desirable. Daphne Straight came to supper of cold lobster and brawn.

Evelyn Waugh

31 July

1900

A terrible day! When I had hardly finished dressing Lenchen and Beatrice knocked at the door and came in. I at once asked whether there were any news, and Lenchen replied, 'Yes, bad news, very bad news; he has slept away!' Oh, God! My poor darling Alfie gone too! My third grown-up child, besides three very dear sons-in-law. It is hard at eighty-one! It is so merciful that dearest Alfie died in his sleep without any struggle, but it is heartrending.

It is a horrible year, nothing but sadness and horrors of one kind and another. I think they should never have withheld the truth from me, as long as they did. It has come [as] such an awful shock. I pray God to help me to be patient and have trust in Him, who has never failed me! Everyone is quite stunned . . . Felt terribly shaken and broken, and could not realise the dreadful fact. Recollections of dear Alfie's childhood and youth crowded in upon me. People are so dreadfully shocked, and the Navy feels it deeply, for he was much beloved in the service, and greatly admired, having been such an excellent officer . . .

Quantities of telegrams kept pouring in, and the day was spent in answering them. We dined again alone, and later Beatrice read to me in my room out of some of my favourite religious books, which was soothing.

Queen Victoria

1933

After lunch I took some Yeastvite tablets and continued to take them after tea and supper. A slightly unromantic way of curing lovesickness I admit, but certainly I feel a lot better now. (Hilary [her sister] is playing 'Stormy Weather' incessantly – my theme song I think!) After lunch I read Richard Aldington's new book, *All Men are Enemies* – it was rather interesting but intensely depressing. After tea I turned to Burton's *Anatomy of Melancholy* and began to read about Love Melancholy – but I haven't yet got to the part where he deals with the cure. Perhaps I'm suffering from the spleen too – in that case I may be completely cured by taking a course of our English poets – which all points to drowning my sorrows in work. I think I shall try to develop a 'Whatever is, is right' attitude of mind – and quite honestly I suppose all this *is* rather good for me – and an affair with Lorenzo probably wouldn't be!

Barbara Pym

AUGUST

'Only good girls keep diaries. Bad girls don't have the time.'

TALLULAH BANKHEAD

1 August

1897

Watson, the late registrar of the Royal College of Music, went to get shaved in a provincial town. 'How easy it would be for me to cut your throat, sir!' said the barber as he was stropping the razor. Watson considered a moment and fled. The next day the barber did cut a customer's throat. He had become a homicidal maniac.

Arnold Bennett

1914

All Europe is mobilising.

W. N. P. Barbellion

1939

The Regent was reminiscent at luncheon, for our blue rococo dining room always makes him think of our famous Edward VIII dinner party a few days before the Abdication trouble began. He re-told the story today, of how the then King had sent for his brother, the Duke of Kent, on that famous Thursday, having himself only just come back from his triumphant tour in Wales; he began by saying that he wanted his brothers to know, before they met that evening at 'Chips' Dinner Party' that he was going to marry Wallis. The Duke of Kent gasped, 'What will she call herself?' 'Call herself?' the King echoed, 'What do you think – Queen of England of course.' 'She is going to be Queen?' 'Yes and Empress of India, the whole bag of tricks.' The King was cock-a-hoop, gay, happy and confident. The Duke, flabbergasted, rushed home to dress and tell his wife and Princess Olga. Looking back upon it, no wonder Princess Olga was late. Honor [his wife] and I were sublimely unconscious of the hidden drama lying behind our dinner party. The Duke of Kent had not known whether to congratulate Wallis when he saw her, or not.

'Chips' Channon

1943

I suddenly thought tonight, 'I know why a lot of women have gone into pants – it's a sign that they are asserting themselves in some way.' I feel pants are more of a sign of the times than I realised. A growing contempt for man in general creeps over me. For a craftsman, whether a sweep or Prime Minister – 'hats off'. But why this 'Lords of Creation' attitude on men's part? I'm beginning to see I'm a really clever woman in my own line, and not the 'odd' or 'uneducated' woman that I've had dinned into me. Not that in-laws have bothered me for some time now. I got on my top note, and swept all clean, after one sticky bit of interference and bother. I feel that, in the world of tomorrow, marriage will be – will *have* to be – more of a partnership, less of this '*I* have spoken' attitude. They will talk things over – talking *does* do good, if only to clear the air. I run my house like a business: I have had to, to get all done properly, everything fitted in. Why, then, should women not be looked on as partners, as 'business women'? I feel thoroughly out of time, I'm not as patient as I used to be, and when one gets to fifty-three, and after thirty-two years of married life, there are few illusions to cloud issues.

Nella Last

1948

Brian Easdale's daughter Josephine was here . . . Josie came round to us and danced on the lawn in her bare feet. They were narrow and smooth and bread-coloured. When she came nearer I saw that she was quite ugly with the ugliness of eight. Her remarks held surprises. When Eric asked her what she wanted to be, she said, 'A teacher.' 'Why?' he continued, rather taken aback by her unromantic choice. 'Because Mummy's going to have a baby and that hurts, so I want to be something that doesn't have to have a baby.'

Did she feel that it was impossible for a schoolmistress to have a baby? Or just that she was exempt from the unpleasant task?

Denton Welch

1950

It is hot, steamy and wet. It is raining. I am tempted to write a poem. But I remember what it said on one rejection slip: After a heavy rainfall, poems titled 'Rain' pour in from across the nation.

Sylvia Plath

2 August

1914
Will England join in?

W. N. P. Barbellion

1914

Germany has declared war on Russia. – Swimming in the afternoon.

Franz Kafka

1915

House pride in newly-wed folk, for example, H. and D. today at Golders Green or the Teignmouth folk, is very trying to the bachelor visitor. They will carry a chair across the room as tenderly as tho' it were a child, and until its safe transit is assured, all conversation goes by the board. Or the wife suddenly makes a remark to the husband *sotto voce*, both thereupon start up simultaneously (leaving the fate of Warsaw undecided) while you, silenced by this unexpected manoeuvre, wilt away in your chair, the pregnant phrase still-born on your lips. Presently they re-enter the room with the kitten that was heard in the scullery or with a big stick used to flourish at a little Tomtit on the rose tree. *She* apologises and both settle down again, recompose their countenances into a listening aspect and with a devastating politeness, pick up the poor, little, frayed-out thread of the conversation where it left off with: 'Europe? You were saying . . .' I mobilise my scattered units of ideas but it is all a little chilly for the lady of the house if she listens with her face and speaks with her lips – her heart is far from me: she fixes a glassy eye on the tip of my cigarette, waiting to see if the ash will fall on her carpet.

W. N. P. Barbellion

1920

Yesterday a messed-up day if ever there was one. My bad nerves had to endure a rude assault, the arrival of these three sooth-sayers: Cocteau, Max Jacob and young Raymond Radiguet, a poet who is making a name for himself and who is only seventeen. (Max's explanation: 'My dear, infant prodigies stay seventeen until they are twenty-five.') Oh what a procession – starved-looking and dingy – led by Cocteau with his sharp, ravaged look like some vicious and anxious spinster, then shy, writhing Radiguet with shut eyes and open mouth, or vice versa, as though his skin were too tight. Max, always a bit of a carnival mask – Max has decided to live or die by every word which fell from the lips of Cocteau – of Cocteau patron of the arts, of Cocteau who puts on performances, organizes tours far from the theatres, who helps people even as he uses them as ladders.

Slovenly, incongruous and noisy, first they rumpled the rugs, smothered Georges's lavatory with tar, laid claim to our washbasins, our soap – and to other things as well. At table it was even worse and nearly ended in tears. Cocteau – and it's not as though he didn't know how to behave because he comes from a perfectly decent family of scriveners – Cocteau began without ceremony to pick at a dish of fruit standing by him, and this during the first course! I signalled to Georges who smiled and said to the indignant Fatoum 'Take away that dish', which she did. First coldness.

At the centre of my table there was a rich and magnificent vase of dahlias. 'I can't see Max because of the flowers' – 'I can't see Jean because of the flowers' – 'Well, what of it? You don't have to see each other' – 'Yes, we do' – 'Yes we do' – 'Too bad, there's no solution' – 'Take away the flowers' – 'Liane, they must go . . .' and Cocteau reached out for them. Outraged, I rose threateningly to my feet and said sharply: 'Listen, I am going and you can have my place, then you can give what orders you like.' Second coldness. Cocteau let go of the vase. Max was green, I was disagreeable, Georges was embarrassed and Radiguet was scared. . . .

Afterwards, the reek of tobacco, and abandon. The gentlemen threw their ash on the ground, their fag-ends into the fireplace, their matches on the carpet, rumpled the cushions, knocked my books about, rummaged through our papers, etc. What a session! . . . The day dragged. I made them take a walk in the park; I took them to visit a neighbouring estate, I gave them the traditional chocolate and cakes at four o'clock. They left at seven o'clock. Not one witty or amusing word or thought.

Liane de Pougy

1973 [Nantucket]

9 p.m. After twenty minutes of *Blazing Saddles* we leave the theater, discouraged. There's still enough calm afterglow on South Water Street for our stroll toward the wharves to watch the sunset, balanced this evening by the moon, which has become a perfect lavender globe. This cheers us up. Then we stop by the Hub to buy ten postcards.

'That's fifty-two cents,' announces the salesgirl, one of the prettyish Vassar types who swarm the island in summer to learn about life by getting a job.

'Why fifty-two? How much is one card?'

'A nickel.'

'Then if I buy each card as a separate purchase, they'd only come to fifty cents.'

'You'd be ripping us off by avoiding the tax.'

'On the contrary, you're ripping me off by manipulating the tax.'

'Are you speaking to me, personally?'

'I'm saying the policy is unfair. Usually to sell an item in quantity is to lower the price. Here the more I buy, the more you charge, yet you say I'm ripping you off. The customer as usual is wrong, and I resent it.'

Yet I paid what she asked, and went off feeling awful. Returning to the safety of the house I finish the peach cobbler made this afternoon and begin the penultimate piece of my Cincinnati opus – a scurrying toccata called *Apples*, for three oboes and three violas.

(That loathsome new verb – *to rip off*!)

Ned Rorem

3 August

1800

I made pies and stuff the pike – baked a loaf. Headach after dinner – I lay down. A letter from Wm rouzed me, desiring us to go to Keswick. After writing to Wm we walked as far as Mr Simpson's and ate black cherries. A Heavenly warm evening with scattered clouds upon the hills. There was a vernal greenness upon the grass from the rains of the morning and afternoon. Peas for dinner.

Dorothy Wordsworth

1832 [sailing to America]

Breakfasted at eight; got up, and dressed, and came upon deck. The day was lovely, the sea one deep dark sapphire, the sky bright and cloudless, the wind mild and soft, too mild to fill our sails, which hung lazily against the masts, – but enough to refresh the warm summer's sky, and temper the bright sun of August that shone above us.

Walked upon deck with Miss Hodgkinson [fellow passenger] and Captain Whaite: the latter is a very intelligent, good-natured person; rough and bluff, and only seven and twenty; which makes his having the command of a ship rather an awful consideration.

At half-past eleven got my German, and worked at it till half-past one, then got my work; and presently we were summoned on deck by sound of bell, and oyes! oyes! oyes! – and a society was established for the good demeanour and sociability of the passengers. My father was in the chair . . . A badge was established, rules and regulations laid down, a code framed, and much laughing and merriment thence ensued.

Fanny Kemble

1937

A woman, unless she is an idiot, sooner or later meets a piece of human wreckage and tries to rescue him. She sometimes succeeds. But a woman, unless she is an idiot, sooner or later finds a sane, healthy man and makes a wreck of him. She always succeeds.

Cesare Pavese

1940

Jennie [housemaid] in emancipated mood this morning, dashing about at her window-cleaning with no stockings on: sometimes the glimpse of a free, young body gives me a sudden, hollow feeling in the pit of my stomach.

William Soutar

1944

I dined with the [Harold] Macmillans at the villa in Naples. They told me that when our King was staying at Villa Emma he saw some police in a patrol launch having a fierce argument with a couple in a fishing boat. Later he enquired what it was all about and was informed that when the security police ordered the little old man and his large lady to fish further afield the couple refused to budge. After protesting vehemently in Italian the lady pulled out of her pocket an immense visiting card on which was written 'The King and Queen of Italy'. After that they were left to fish in peace.

Countess of Ranfurly

1951

Women growing old – many traces of age. The fact is, many middle-aged ladies who look twenty years younger than their age show it. A stranger – marveling at the clear, smooth skin, unlined throat – is shocked at the age revealed by her thinking. There are things, like a bald head, that can't be helped but can at least be hidden. The end of sex finds women resenting older men, who are invariably childish, demanding, selfish and catty. Men as they age seem to go home to Mama, after leaving her on her own for 30 years. Suddenly their men friends are unsatisfactory; they want Mama's cookies and warming pan. This is just the time Mama finds the company of her own sex most rewarding. Don't be sorry for elderly ladies on sprees – they're usually having the time of their life without having to do what the Man says.

Dawn Powell

4 August

1922

Letter from Max Jacob. Crafty – this is how he does it: 'Jacques Emile Blanche (painter and writer) is waiting for me in Normandy, the Lazarus family has asked me to Hacqueville, the Daudets want me in their country house – but, my dears, it is you I choose!' Thanks a lot! We are not going to answer. If he turns up we will accept him as a gift (!) from God, Whose will it is that His creatures should be put to the test.

Liane de Pougy

1949 [on lecture tour in South America]

Press conference in the morning. Lunch standing up at Andrade's. I don't really know why, but at 3 o'clock, I'm taken to the city [São Paulo] penitentiary, 'the most beautiful one in Brazil.' In fact, it is beautiful, like a penitentiary in an American film. Except for the odor, the hideous odor of man that lingers in every prison. Iron bars, doors, bars, doors, etc. And the signs. 'Be good' and above all 'Optimism.' I feel ashamed in front of one or two of the prisoners – and these are ones with special privileges – who have service jobs in the prison. Then the doctor-psychiatrist treats me to an interminable dissertation on the classification of perverse mentalities. And as I leave, someone repeats the ritualistic, 'Make yourself at home here' to me.

Albert Camus

1973

To bed early. Began reading Mrs Gaskell's *North and South*. I have never read it before. I began with a great feeling of relief; I was reading something which had nothing to do with work. Within four chapters, I caught myself thinking of it as a film . . .

Peter Hall

5 August

1880

Haslemere – very fine: Helen and I started about 3.30 to walk to Tennyson's, as invited. In the shady lane the carriage overtook us. T. had kindly called for us. He was in the carriage with his little grandson, Alfred, in his nurse's lap, and Mr Fields, an American guest. Little Alfred, aged three, had on the great Alfred's black sombrero, and the child's straw hat with a blue ribbon was stuck on the top of the poet's huge head, and so they drove gravely along.

William Allingham

1932 [Berlin]

Assaults, bomb-throwings, and murders continue in East Prussia, Bavaria, and Holstein. It has now been officially established that the cases of arson and bomb-throwing at Königsberg were committed by Nazis. The Government held a Cabinet meeting on the subject yesterday, but confined itself to threatening vigorous action. It obviously hesitates about getting on the wrong side of the Nazis.

Count Harry Kessler

1937 [Sorrento]

The buildings, the walls along the roads, are covered with inscriptions in huge characters; appeals to the Duce and quotations from him, perfect slogans, wonderfully chosen and likely to galvanize youth, to *enroll* it. Among all such, these three words: *Believe. Obey. Fight*, return most frequently as if conscious of summing up the very spirit of the Fascist doctrine. This allows a certain sharpness of ideas and at the same time points out to me the 'positions' of anti-Fascism. And nothing leads to greater confusion than the adoption of this slogan by Communism itself, which claims to be still anti-Fascist, but is so only politically, for it too asks the party members to *believe, obey*, and *fight*, without inquiry, without criticism, with blind submission. Three-quarters of the Italian inscriptions would be just as suitable to the walls of Moscow. I am told that an adversary can be overcome only on the same ground, only by his very arms, that it is appropriate to fight the sword with the sword (something of which I am, moreover, in no wise convinced). It is appropriate first of all and above all to fight the spirit with the spirit, and this is what is scarcely ever done any more. Historians of the future will examine how and why, the end disappearing behind the means, the Communist spirit ceased to be opposed to the Fascist spirit, and even to be differentiated from it.

André Gide

1981

Elizabeth [his wife] went off this morning to stay with Harold [Pinter] and Antonia [Fraser] in Ischia. I must somehow survive in her absence. Harold Nicolson and his wife operated what was ultimately a beautiful marriage based quite largely on letter writing. It seemed natural to him to spend Monday to Friday away from his wife. Personally if I am away from Elizabeth for a short while I feel diminished and I have never understood the philosophy of taking a holiday.

Lord Longford

6 August

1915

The most intimate and extensive journal can only give each day a relatively small sifting of the almost infinite number of things that flow thro' the consciousness. However vigilant and artful a diarist may be, plenty of things escape him and in any event re-collection is not re-creation . . .

To keep a journal is to have a secret liaison of a very sentimental kind. A *journal intime* is a super-confidante to whom everything is told and confessed. For an engaged or married man to have a secret super-confidante who knows things which are concealed from his lady seems to me to be deliberate infidelity. I am as it were engaged to two women and one of them is being deceived. The word 'Deceit' comes up against me in this double life I lead, and insists I shall name a plain thing bluntly. There is something very like sheer moral obliquity in these entries behind her back . . . Is this journal habit slowly corrupting my character? Can an engaged or married man conscientiously continue to write his *journal intime*?

W. N. P. Barbellion

1945

It was a sunny evening and a whole gang of us, including Oscar, Pandora, Gussy and myself, were hanging around the wooden gate at the end of the field waiting for some transport to pick us up for the late watch. I remember I was studying some caterpillars, striped in brilliant black and yellow, that were devouring a yellow-petalled ragwort. I was thinking how much I would have appreciated these creatures when I was a child, and how I would have kept them in a cardboard box with holes punched in the top, when I noticed Flight Sergeant Kelly hurrying across the field. First she walked a bit, then she broke into a run and walked again. It seemed odd because she wasn't late for the transport.

When she came up to us she said, 'There's a terrible bomb been dropped on Japan – the worst ever! It's to do with re-directing the energy from the sun, or something. Everybody thinks the Japs will surrender any minute!'

She probably expected a barrage of questions – or even cries of 'Good show!' – but there was nothing, only a shocked silence.

She went on to tell us that it was called an atomic bomb and the whole of Hiroshima had been wiped out and the Japs would certainly sue for peace within the next few days.

I think I was stunned, not so much because of the bomb as at the thought of the war ending. Later, when the meaning finally sank in, I felt the strangest mixture of elation and terror. It was as if my whole world had suddenly come to an end. Five years of security and happy comradeship, the feeling of being needed – and ahead a kind of uncharted wilderness, lonely and frightening.

At the same time there was a small but undeniable feeling of excitement, like the end of school term, the hols looming ahead. I was vividly aware of everything about me, the dusty golden ragwort, the blue sky, even the knots in the wooden gate under my hand.

Joan Wyndham

1962

Marilyn Monroe committed suicide yesterday. The usual overdose. Poor silly creature. I am convinced that what brought her to that final foolish gesture was a steady diet of intellectual pretentiousness pumped into her over the years by Arthur Miller, and 'The Method'. She was, to begin with, a fairly normal little sexpot with exploitable curves, and a certain natural talent. I am sure that all the idiocies of her last few years, always being late on the set, etc., plus over-publicity and too many theoretical discussions about acting, were the result of all this constant analysis of every line in every part she had to play, and a desperate longing to be 'intellectual' without the brain to achieve it. It is a sad comment on contemporary values that a beautiful, famous and wealthy young woman of thirty-six should capriciously kill herself for want of a little self-discipline and horse-sense. Judy [Garland] and Vivien [Leigh] in their different ways are in the same plight. Too much too soon and too little often.

Noël Coward

7 August

1915

On a bus the other day a woman with a baby sat opposite, the baby bawled, and the woman at once began to unlace herself, exposing a large, red udder, which she swung into the baby's face. The infant, however, continued to cry and the woman said,—

'Come on, there's a good boy – if you don't, I shall give it to the gentleman opposite.'

Do I look ill-nourished?

W. N. P. Barbellion

1974

JH returned from New York Sunday with a headache. By last night the ache had turned to what he felt was a cerebral hemorrage after three days of high fever and near-constant delirium. I waited in the emergency ward of Nantucket's Cottage Hospital while JH was being inspected this morning at dawn. And I inspected the flow of the very young in other emergencies – mostly long-haired children with ticks in their ears or gashes in their poison-ivied toes. One young couple brought in their son Brian, age two, who since yesterday had refused to open his eyes. There he was in his mother's arms, silky skinned, unsmiling and unprecedented, shrieking when prodded, the parents more innocent than he in his sophisticated visual autism. What became of Brian I do not know. JH emerged, after sinus X rays (negative), diagnosed as a flu carrier and told to take two aspirins and rest. He's sleeping now, thank God, silently.

Ned Rorem

8 August

1835

'Oh! I have passed a miserable night', I may well say, as a greater man said before me. The Irish Flea Association were so occupied in holding a section on human Physiology upon my devoted body that it was out of the question to think of sleeping while transactions of such interest were going forward. Early in the morning I assassinated 4 of the committee together with their President, Mr. Bug.

Barclay Fox

1945

The papers are full of the atomic bomb [Hiroshima] which is going to revolutionize everything and blow us all to buggery. Not a bad idea.

Noël Coward

9 August

1818

The Green Devils have haunted me all the way and all the while I have been out. If any one wishes to know what sort of things they are, I can only say they are not quite so bad as Blue Devils, being no other than green peas a month too old to be eaten by me who am very fond of them when young. I have heard Mr Wharton, the member for Beverley, says all women ought to be hung out of the way at forty; peas are like them and should never be brought to anything but pigs after the pods are full.

Rev. Benjamin Newton

1838 [New York]

I saw in one of the papers the death announced at New Haven of Henry Bedlow, aged 71 years, an old beau who at one time made a great noise in

New York. This man, then about 24 years old, was tried for a rape on a Miss Sawyer, step-daughter of Callahan, a pilot, who lived in Gold Street, near my father's. He was acquitted, as I dare say he ought to have been; but her father being well known amongst the seafaring people, and the case, if not a rape, being an aggravated one of seduction, the popular indignation was excited to the highest pitch. A mob collected and pulled down the house to which the libertine had decoyed his victim, a famous brothel kept by a Mother Carey in Beckman Street at the corner of Theater Alley, on the very spot where I built the Clinton Hotel. Well do I remember, although the occurrence took place nearly fifty years ago, sitting in the branches of one of the large buttonwood trees in the burial ground of the Brick Presbyterian Church, opposite the scene of action, and enjoying the dispersion of 'Mother Carey's chickens,' the destruction of mahogany tables and looking-glasses. These excesses did not stop here, for the mob, once excited, continued their riotous proceedings several successive nights, and many houses of ill-fame in other parts of the city were demolished and their miserable inmates driven naked and houseless into the streets.

Philip Hone

1873

Mackerel fishing but not much sport. Besides I was in pain and could not look at things much. When the fresh-caught fish flounced in the bottom of the boat they made scrapes of motion, quite as strings do, nodes and all, silver bellies upwards. Their key markings do not correspond on the two sides of the backbone. They changed colour as they lay. There was sun and wind. I saw the waves to seaward frosted with light silver surf but did not find out much, afterwards from the cliffs I saw the sea paved with wind – clothed and purpled all over with ribbons of wind.

Gerard Manley Hopkins

1915

An officer we knew from the Bakhchisarary Regiment spoke of the pitiable plight of the men in the trenches. Their clothes were torn and filthy, many were without boots; water and food were scarce. He related an incident he'd seen: A party of wounded soldiers was walking along the highroad when a general in a car drew up and began a scathing interrogation. Most of the men were dreadful to look upon – dirty, unkempt, with blood on their hands and faces. '*Merzavets!* [Villain!]' he shouted at one man. 'Where are thy boots?' The soldier, with green, grey face and blood-stains on his shirt, made answer in a weak, scarcely audible voice; the general, suddenly enraged, rose from his seat and struck the man full in the face with his gloved fist. Not a sound from the soldiers. The car sped on and the tired feet, booted and bootless, trudged on their way.

He went on: 'Our soldiers are simply heroes. Look how they are fighting. The trenches are badly made – they're quite unworthy of the name of trench, for they are just burrows, some of them not even an *arshin* [28 inches] in depth. The sappers hadn't time to finish them was the excuse and we have to pass on this abominable lie to our men.'

Florence Farmborough

1972

Lunch at the Café Royal with the Wrightsmans and Jackie Kennedy Onassis. She's in her early forties with a cute, slightly lined, sixties face, dipped hair and the hands of an old woman, the flesh withered and with enormous knuckles, today covered with sticking-plaster. She was dressed with under-played chic in trousers and a Hermès raincoat. Nervous, with eyes popping, she moved with almost teenage animation. The impression was of an intelligent, rich woman, bored with life marooned on a Greek island, envious of the Wrightsmans' London lifestyle and longing for New York. In conversation she was a receiver rather than a giver.

Roy Strong

10 August

1661

This morning came the maid that my wife hath lately hired for a chamber maid. She is very ugly, so that I cannot care for her, but otherwise she seems very good.

Samuel Pepys

1941

There are certain peculiarities about staying in a country house in wartime. One is the problem of the black-out. When you retire to your room for the night you find that it has been most thoroughly blacked out in several layers. First the extremely tall heavy windows have been securely closed and fastened (these can only be opened by pulling on two long cords with white bobbles attached to the ends of them). Then the shutters have been closed and fastened with mighty crossbars fitting into grooves. The black-out curtain hangs the whole length of the window and then come the long heavy curtains which also can only be made to come apart by pulling the correct pulleys, so that one gazes in dismay at the number of possible cords all twined around knobs.

If you pull the wrong combination of pulleys (i.e. one of the curtain cords and one of the cords that open the window) you are involved in a breathless struggle which yields no results save frustration. It must be remembered that the business of opening the windows has to be done in the pitch dark as the light must be turned out before you begin playing about with curtains. One night staying at Stansted I was completely defeated by the combination of obstacles and panting with exhaustion after wrenching at shutters and pulling at cords I took to my bed and tossed all night in breathless confinement. But at Waddesdon I triumphed, and what a relief to hear the wind sighing in the trees and to feel the soft night air! Then, of course, fumbling your way by the light of a small hand-torch along black corridors filled with unfamiliar furniture to the W. C. (which one had failed to mark by daylight) or alternatively to the bedroom of your girl-friend is another country-house hazard. At Waddesdon the valet asked me what I would like for breakfast. 'Coffee,' he suggested, 'toast or anything cooked, sir?' What a question in any English country house! But I stood out for an egg – felt the Rothschilds should be able to manage it – somehow!

Charles Ritchie

1945

All the time one keeps on thinking of this bomb, and what it may make the future look like. A perpetual menace over everything but may be as salutary as hell fire was in its time. . . . Probably the world is in for a period of communism. It will be unpleasant in some ways but it won't destroy other values nearly as badly as Nazi-ism. I intend that my children shall survive.

. . . We wonder if this really is VJ day or whether the mikado business will hold things up. One hopes they won't go dropping another bomb. We all read all we can in the papers and discuss it fruitlessly.

Naomi Mitchison

1946

It was the *New Yorker* yesterday that asked me for a story. Now today I am sent the *Sun Bathing Review* and told that Bernard Shaw, Laurence Housman, Naomi Mitchison, Vera Brittain, A. E. Coppard, J. C. Flugel, Robert Gibbings and C. E. M. Joad have written for it and will I write too – a likely theme, the value of nudity in schools 'as a means of countering the unhealthy practices with which anyone who has been educated at a boarding school is familiar'.

I think the only thing I can truthfully say in reply is that I feel that nudity would increase the 'unhealthy practices', whatever they may be, perhaps set a fashion through the whole school for them – that is, 'nudity' of this magaziny-shiny-photograph sort. The booklet is uncomfortable. I know that if someone came into this room at this moment, I would hurriedly explain that it had been sent to me, and that I had not bought it for my own delight. Why do other people's fetishes seem ugly and improper? I am fond of naked people, but not of a great to-do and business of nakedness. To read this magazine is to be half told that if everyone would suddenly strip off their clothes the world might be made quite wonderful.

The articles are very like the tracts Evie's sister brought me from the Bible and Tract Society. God and Jesus are replaced by Sun and the Naked Body.

Yet, just because I have had my thoughts drawn to nakedness, I think of this high wind battering the house, making it shake and creak, and I am more aware of the air playing on my body as I laze on the bed only in my cotton kimono, the sort that Japanese men wear when they go for their steam baths.

Denton Welch

11 August

1782 [Edinburgh]

Went to the New English Chapel in the forenoon. Felt an unpleasing indifference, and thought that if I were to become a constant attendant there, I should experience insipidity and perhaps disgust. Mr. Nairne and I were engaged to dine with the Solicitor at Murrayfield. We first visited Dr. Beattie, and were well with him; then Lady Colville, and walked with her in her garden. Then went on to Murrayfield by a very pretty walk along the Water of Leith, and over walls, so as to have a straight road. The Solicitor first entertained us by giving us full freedom to pull cherries off six trees richly loaded. Then there was old brandy, then a good hearty dinner, and then abundance of wine. Mr. Menzies of the Customs, Mr. Andrew Stewart, Junior, Mr. Carnegie the advocate, and a Mr. Anderson from London were there. We were exceedingly jovial. The two last went away earlier than the rest of us. We drank till between nine and ten. I was much intoxicated, and having insisted to walk to town, fell and hurt my hands; after which Mr. Menzies took me into his chaise, in which he had Mr. Nairne. I came out at the foot of the West Bow. Mr. Nairne walked with me to the head of James's Court. I then wandered about an hour in the street, but most fortunately met with no strong temptation, so got home clear. Mr. Kentish obligingly endeavoured to see me home. But I cunningly evaded. I was quite unhappy to find myself again in such a brutal state, after a full Session of sobriety. I was vexed that I had employed Sunday so ill, and that my children had not said divine lessons. I resolved to be more strictly upon my guard. I was very sick. I went to my own bed.

James Boswell

1835

At dinner the conversation led to the alleged cause of Lord Byron's parting with Lady Byron, and some observations were made which occasioned me disagreeable sensations; being evidently perceived, it made me quite embarrassed, and I did not in consequence recover the tone of my mind all day, uncomfortable as to the impression my want of self-possession might have caused, for which there was no actual reason. In the same way I always became embarrassed and confused before I had children, when the want of them was alluded to. I am very weak in this respect.

Charles Macready

1929

Hugh [her husband] was obliged to go to Nice for three days, and he was unhappy because I couldn't go. I sent him away just loaded down with tenderness and love and thoughtfulness. My love for him is my religion. I love him with words; as I look at him I say to myself: Look how fine his head is, how tall he is, how sensitive his furry hands, how high his forehead. I love him with my senses. I love him with re-creations of our life together, of past love. I love him with my mind, admire him. I love him gratefully for his wide understanding, his love of me. I *want* to love him, because he *ought* to be loved. I hate myself for whatever I make him suffer for. I have moments when I know that no multiple lives or loves can be worth his love, when I desire desperately to be able to control the overflow of my excessive nature and imagination. I love, *really*, only him.

Anaïs Nin

1943

Visit to Jane Austen's house . . . I put my hand down on Jane's desk and bring it up covered with dust. Oh that some of her genius might rub off on me! One would have imagined the devoted female custodian going round with her duster at least every other day.

Barbara Pym

12 August

1914

We all await the result of a battle between two millions of men. The tension makes me feel physically sick.

W. N. P. Barbellion

1935

Have been reading some odd little childish songs – our poets go in for them at times. There was this by Cocteau: 'Amstram-gram-bouret-bour-et-ratatam', and readers roared with delight. Between each couplet of one of his songs, Max Jacob had the line: 'I-want-to-make-pipi-and-I'm-going-to-make-it-here.' I don't really understand the artistic value of this kind of thing, or what is funny about it.

Liane de Pougy

1940

Came over to Wemyss Bay in the very crowded boat. All the mouth of the Clyde filled with mixed shipping. Submarines and things. On the line up the small, sad and nameless stations; one slept for a moment and tried to guess where one was on waking, but no clues. . . . Somewhere a new works with buried and isolated shops, presumably for explosive of some kind. . . . The only nice things the strips of stuff on the windows of the waiting rooms at Paisley (?) making clean patterns. A bit unnecessary to take off the names at Glasgow Central?

In the streets, strange uniform, Polish mostly, and camouflaged cars and lorries. Odd and dizzy being in a crowd again. Few people take their gas-masks. We go to a flick and see half a Marx brothers: great fun. The news-reel with the horrible commentator making frightful jokes and encouraging morale I suppose: Pathé. How I hate it all. How I should like to see united effort for construction, for peace (but would the same man still do the newsreel propaganda?); how I should like to look out of a train some day, spotting new constructive things instead of new war things.

Naomi Mitchison

13 August

1653

I first began a Course of yearely washing my head with Warme Water, mingld with a decoction of Sweet herbs, and immediately, with cold Spring water, which much refreshd me, and succeeded very well with me divers yeares.

John Evelyn

1944

Today a begrimed and bedraggled waif calling herself Giuseppina appeared at the office. This alert 12-year-old would tell me nothing about herself other than her age, that her parents had been killed in the great bombing, and that she lived 'under a house' down by the river. There are boy-orphans by the hundred like her, barefooted, ragged and hungry, but somehow managing to survive and fill the gaunt streets with their laughter, but this was the first abandoned girl I had seen. Giuseppina told me she had come for her blanket as usual.

I was astonished. Blankets are one form of currency in this Italy in ruins – but currency of a fairly high denomination, good Australian or Canadian spec- imens fetching the equivalent of a low-grade factory-worker's weekly wage. I told her I had no blankets to give away, and offered her a packet of army biscuits, which she gracefully refused. 'Isn't this still the police station?' she asked. I agreed that it was, and she told me that the man who had been here before – clearly my Canadian predecessor – had given her a blanket once a week.

Only at this point did I realize the tragic significance of the request, and that this skinny, undeveloped little girl was a child prostitute. The *scugnizzi* of Naples and Benevento are intelligent, charming and above all philosoph- ical – notably more so than children from protected homes – and this female version of the breed was in no way different from her male counterparts. Much as she may have been disappointed by my rejection of her services, nothing but good humour showed in her face. She bobbed something like a curtsy. 'Perhaps I'll take the biscuits after all,' she said. Then, with a wave, she was off.

Norman Lewis

1977

In a London self-photographic box by the Passport Office I had two snaps taken. They were so gruesome, I looking like a sinister undertaker, only plus, that A. [Alvilde, his wife] insisted I have others taken in Bath. She said she could not live with one of these every time she looked into my passport during the next ten years. I went to Woolworths in Bath today, and tried again. Result just as bad, although am rendered smirking like a sinister footpad, instead of snarling like a confidence trickster. My God, how absolutely hideous I have become. Sad really, when you think. As long as I keep clean. I suppose all I *can* do is to maintain that one standard.

James Lees-Milne

1979

Returned to London, and was diverted to read on the plane, in the New York *Herald Tribune*, that Miss Piggy [in *The Muppets*] has been banned from Iranian television during Ramadan because 'Moslems do not eat pork and consider pigs unclean.'

Peter Hall

14 August

1846 [Ireland]

The newspapers tell us that flogging in the army is virtually abolished – restricted to fifty lashes and only to be employed in the most flagrant cases, subject, too, to medical control and regulated by weather and other causes. It was disgraceful to the service that such barbarian customs should have prevailed so long – in such a refining age. We have begun, keep the schoolmaster going, let him teach not reading only, but the doctrines of the new testament practically – where then would be the corner poutings, the scolding, flogging, prisons, hangings of the ignorant and therefore vicious adult. We have begun, slowly, yet surely, and by geometrical progression we must proceed. Did ever anyone utter an angry word that did not raise an angry feeling? Having sermonised I may dress and walk to call on the Duchess who sent us three brace of grouse last night.

Elizabeth Grant of Rothiemurchus

1920

Little doing. In the afternoon I went to the baths but found the water dirty and full of the most dreadful greasy-haired cads.

Evelyn Waugh

1932

In the morning at Marseilles read the news that Hindenburg, during yesterday afternoon's interview with Hitler, declined to make him Chancellor and that thereupon the negotiations between the Nazis and the Government were broken off. The crucial talk between Hindenburg and Hitler lasted only thirteen minutes. What now? Civil war or the inglorious crumbling of the Nazi movement? The one thing certain is that we are heading for darkest reaction. It is difficult to say which of the two competing parties, the Nazis or the [Kurt von] Schleicher clique, is the more reactionary. The only hope is for these two lots of bigots to exterminate each other, now that they have fallen out.

Count Harry Kessler

15 August

1913

Agonies in bed toward morning. Saw only solution in jumping out of the window. My mother came to my bedside and asked whether I had sent off the letter [to the parents of his fiancée, Felice Bauer, regarding their marriage] and whether it was my original text. I said it was the original text, but made even sharper. She said she does not understand me. I answered, she most certainly does not understand me, and by no means only in this matter. Later she asked me if I were going to write to Uncle Alfred, he deserved it. I asked why he deserved it. He has telegraphed, he has written, he has your welfare so much at heart. 'These are simply formalities,' I said, 'he is a complete stranger to me, he misunderstands me entirely, he does not know what I want and need, I have nothing common with him.'

'So no one understands you,' my mother said. 'I suppose I am a stranger to you too, and your father as well. So we all want only what is bad for you.'

'Certainly, you are all strangers to me, we are related only by blood, but that never shows itself. Of course you don't want what is bad for me.'

Through this and several other observations of myself I have come to believe that there are possibilities in my ever-increasing inner decisiveness and conviction which may enable me to pass the test of marriage in spite of everything, and even to steer it in a direction favorable to my development. Of course, to a certain extent this is a belief that I grasp at when I am already on the window sill.

Franz Kafka

1924

By the way, why is poetry wholly an elderly taste? When I was twenty I could not for the life of me read Shakespeare for pleasure; now it lights me as I walk to think I have two acts of *King John* tonight, and shall next read *Richard the Second*. It is poetry that I want now – long poems. I want the concentration and the romance, and the words all glued together, fused, glowing; have no time to waste any more on prose. When I was twenty I liked Eighteenth Century prose; now it's poetry I want, so I repeat like a tipsy sailor in the front of a public house.

I don't often trouble now to describe cornfields and groups of harvesting women in loose blues and reds and little staring yellow frocked girls. But that's not my eyes' fault; coming back the other evening from Charleston, again all my nerves stood upright, flushed, electrified (what's the word?) with the sheer beauty – beauty abounding and superabounding, so that one almost resents it, not being capable of catching it all, and holding it all at the moment.

Virginia Woolf

1932

The reason I write is because there is no one to talk to and I might as well build up a completely private life.

Dawn Powell

1938 [Corfu]

Theodore says that in the mountains, where shepherds must pasture their flocks half the year round in the fastnesses far from any village, it is customary to have a ewe instead of a wife. Far from betraying any unusual sensitivity to a practice so well known, each shepherd has his own favourite ewe, which he tricks out with bells and tassels according to his fancy. This ewe is known as the favourite one.

He records a conversation with one of the shepherds in Epirus which carried the authentic Holborn Empire note of cynicism. 'What point is there,' asked Theodore in his academic manner, 'in having this ridiculous practice?' (He was referring to the trinkets which adorned one of the chosen ewes.)

The shepherd thought for a moment and then replied, as one who offers an opinion verified by long personal experience: 'From every point of view they are superior to our wives. But above all they do not talk.'

Lawrence Durrell

1940

The thing I'll never forget about these coastal towns in Belgium and France is the way the Belgians and French pray every night for the British bombers to come over, though often when their prayers are answered it means their death and often they cheer the bomb which kills them. It is three a.m. now and the German *flak* has been firing at top speed since eleven thirty p.m. when we heard the first thud of a British bomb tonight down by the harbour. Fortunately the British seem to be aiming accurately at the harbour and nothing has fallen near enough to us here in the town to cause much worry. There is no air-raid alarm. The sound of the anti-aircraft and the bursting of the bombs is your only signal. No one goes to the cellar. When the Germans have cleared out, we sit in the back room with the French proprietor, his family, and two waiters and drink vin rouge to each new British bomb that crashes. To bed now, and fear there are bugs in this room.

William L. Shirer

1943

In the evening went into the Queen's with Margaret [Earp] to have a drink and listen to the band – orchestra I should say. It was nice in a way but I couldn't help feeling sad. It would have been better if we'd had some male company of course. There was a full moon when we got out. I went doggedly to bed and read a novel by Stephen McKenna. On how many evenings, when one is older, does one just go 'Doggedly to bed'. (Obviously the title of something.)

Barbara Pym

1945

When the end of the war was announced last night I was in my office, working on my record of my magazine days. My first news of it came with the blowing of factory whistles and ringing of church bells. Even the nuns of the House of [the] Good Shepherd clanged their bell, though only briefly. This was at 7.05 p.m. The uproar went on intermittently for two hours, with morons dashing by in their automobiles, blowing their horns. At 8.50 I went to Baltimore and Gilmor streets to mail letters. A few dozen of the neighbourhood oakies, lintheads and other such vermin were gathered there in ragged groups, but they were making no noise. At 9.10 the celebration in West Baltimore ceased abruptly, and after that there was only an occasional toot of an automobile horn. I heard a couple of shots about midnight: they seemed to come from the linthead barracks in the 1500 block of Baltimore Street.

The *Sun* of this morning reports that the crowd in Baltimore Street, from Eutaw to the Fallsway, ran to 200,000. For 200,000 read 50,000: such estimates are always grossly exaggerated, especially when made by the police. In my reportorial days I often counted a crowd, and then asked the cops to estimate it. They always at least doubled it, and usually tripled or quadrupled it. Any number above 1,000 staggers the police.

H. L. Mencken

1990

Began serious work on my Government of Britain Bill. It's extremely difficult writing a completely new constitution from scratch on your own. On the other hand, having a blank piece of paper and knowing how power works and is abused is helpful as a starting point. The problem will be devising a constitution for Scotland and Wales. I think I shall make provision for national parliaments for Scotland and Wales, and they must decide on their own constitutions. So I am left with the English Assembly and how it should work. There is a difficulty about proportional representation and a second chamber. I've been talking about this for two years, and now everyone else is moving on it, and I shall be left behind if I don't make some progress soon.

Tony Benn

16 August

1875

I was at an adjourned Petty Session and we convicted two boys under the Juvenile Offenders Act of stealing two rabbits value 1/-. We sentenced one to receive eight and the other ten strokes of a birch rod.

Dearman Birchall

1912

This evening the whimpering of my poor mother because I don't eat.

Franz Kafka

1922

I should be reading *Ulysses*, and fabricating my case for and against. I have read 200 pages so far – not a third; and have been amused, stimulated, charmed, interested, by the first 2 or 3 chapters – to the end of the cemetery scene; and then puzzled, bored, irritated and disillusioned by a queasy undergraduate scratching his pimples. And Tom [T. S. Eliot], great Tom, thinks this on a par with *War and Peace*! An illiterate, underbred book it seems to me; the book of a self taught working man, and we all know how distressing they are, how egotistic, insistent; raw, striking; and ultimately nauseating. When one can have the cooked flesh, why have the raw? But I think if you are anaemic, as Tom is, there is a glory in blood. Being fairly normal myself I am soon ready for the classics again. I may revise this later. I do not compromise my critical sagacity. I plant a stick in the ground to mark page 200.

Virginia Woolf

1940 [Boulogne]

Our officers and officials have been careful to see that we do not talk with any returning German pilots. But I talked to a number of navy and army men in charge of the coastal guns yesterday and this morning and was surprised that they all thought the war would be over in a few weeks. One naval captain in charge of a big gun at Cap Blanc-Nez, half-way between Calais and Cap Gris-Nez, took me this morning into his little dug-out, scooped out of the side of the slope, to show me how he had fixed it up. It was very cozy. He had slung a hammock between the two walls and had a little table crowded with German books and magazines. He was a straw-blond, clean-cut young man from near Hamburg, and extremely intelligent.

'You've got a nice little place here,' I said. 'Only—'

'Only what?' he laughed.

'Well, I know Normandy in winter, and from the end of October until

April it's damned cold here and it rains every day. Your dug-out is all right now, captain, but it won't be so comfortable over the winter.'

He looked at me in complete amazement.

'Why, I haven't the slightest intention of spending the winter here,' he said, deadly serious now. 'Why, the war will be over long before then. You were kidding, I think, isn't it?'

'No, I wasn't kidding,' I said, a little taken back by his dead certainty. 'Do you mean you think the invasion will be completed and England conquered before Christmas, captain?'

'I shall be at home with my family this Christmas,' he said.

William L. Shirer

1942 [Jersey]

The Germans have now got to our field making their railway, and today they have Russians working on it. Hundreds have arrived, even women. It is said that people in town wept to see them pass. One Russian, at work today, asked John if he were English: 'I Soviet, you English,' and he clapped his hands joyfully! It is a strange thing that we should be allied with Russia. One does not know what to think about these things. Yet we feel so sorry for these Russians – far from home, half-starved and half-naked. Then, the fact of us all being under the Germans is a link. One feels friendly towards all who are suffering in the same way as oneself.

Nan Le Ruez

1953

If you are reading this diary after my death, you are probably wondering why the paragraphs inexplicably jump from one subject to the next. It is because I am gossiping to myself here; between any two paragraphs I may receive a visit which changes my ideas and orients them in an unexpected direction. Moreover, I advise those who edit these diaries to cut what I jot down for reference and the repetitions which occur, because I don't remember if I've already described the things I've described.

Jean Cocteau

1975

Yesterday I had a letter from a young woman who is living alone, a film maker of some reputation. She wants to do a film on people who live alone, and will come next week to talk about her plans. I gather she has some doubts about the solitary life. I told her that I feel it is not for the young (she is only thirty-three). I did not begin to live alone till I was forty-five, and had 'lived' in the sense of passionate friendships and love affairs very richly for twenty-five years. I had a huge amount of life to think about and to digest, and, above all, I was a *person* by then and knew what I wanted of my life. The people we love are built into us. Every day I am suddenly aware of something someone taught me long ago – or just yesterday – of some certainty and self-awareness that grew out of conflict with someone I loved enough to try to encompass, however painful that effort may have been.

May Sarton

17 August

1860

In Oxford Street a fashionable prostitute accosted me who once before had begged me to go home with her; & she now explained her importunity by saying 'All my gentlemen have left town, and I really am so hard up – I shall have to give up my lodgings!' 'Then why not go out of town too?' 'I've nowhere to go to!' This, spoken by a girl who though not interesting was elegant & well-dressed, gives one a sad sense of the loneliness of such a life – and a glimpse also of the embarrassment which besets these London butter-flies when the season is over. She was a farmer's daughter from near Chesterfield; & came to town, nominally to be a draper's assistant, but really to become of her own accord what she is. N.B. *After nine months*, her family still think she is at the shop.

Arthur F. Munby

1949 [France]

I went to the [National] Assembly this afternoon and heard Churchill speak. Tonight we dined with the Eccleses and they talked freely about him, as they had been with him the previous night. He lives at a villa put at his disposal by the City of Strasbourg, where everything is provided for him, though he refused to accept the wine, saying, 'I have my own resources'. His private plane, a Dove, awaits him in its hangar. He sent a wire for Mrs Churchill to come: 'It's no good, Clemmy, you must come.' She had been bathing in France and thus arrived with two bathing-dresses, a bathing wrap, and rope sandals, ill equipped for entertainments in Strasbourg. David has the impression that Churchill is by no means dependent on his family, but likes them to be around. Sybil said that Winston held forth for a long time on Napoleon, and gave a moving description of the Hundred Days; wonder-ful language flowed from him and there were tears in his eyes. Churchill was also very funny about whether Attlee would go to America about the financial crisis: he thought not, because 'when the mouse is away the cats might play.'

Cynthia Gladwyn

1989 [Eriboll]

This morning I bathed, before breakfast, in the loch just opposite the targets. I don't know what the temperature is; a tiny trace of Gulf Stream perhaps, but not much. One feels incredible afterwards – like an instant double whisky, but clear-headed. Perhaps a 'line' of coke does this also. Lithe, vigorous, energetic. Anything seems possible.

Alan Clark

18 August

1965

Churchill's funeral at St Paul's was most impressive. From where we sat, nearly under the dome, we saw beautifully. The splendid heralds in their brilliantly-coloured tabards, carrying Churchill's emblems draped in black crepe, were a wonderful sight. Most moving of all were the body-bearers, who carried the enormously heavy coffin with perfect timing, their heads leaning almost tenderly against the great swaying burden on their shoulders. But the television lighting takes away much of the mystery of such an occasion. At the Duke of Wellington's funeral gas lighting was first introduced, and must have been far more impressive. Even better would have been the torches and candles of Nelson's funeral, leaving so much of the great cathedral in darkness.

Cynthia Gladwyn

1969

In the Post Office at 10.45 a woman said, 'I have seen you on television & I didn't think you were so good'. I replied, 'When I ask you about your profession you can talk to me about mine, until then, be quiet' and walked out.

Kenneth Williams

1970

Georgia [Tennant] took me to Ken Tynan's pornographic revue *Oh! Calcutta!* at the Round House. I got there early and stood watching the mixed crowds coming in – self-conscious, demure, hearty and 'beat'. The show presented no surprise except perhaps that beautiful naked bodies are more beautiful when fully displayed and the bush is an adornment. There were some lovely girls, particularly a negress; two muscular Michael-Angelesque young men and two others that were flabby and unattractive. There was something inevitably phoney in the assumed lustfulness of their movement and dancing, when no male had the ghost of an erection. And the little sketches were despicably feeble, their prep-school humour sprinkled with defiantly uttered four-letter words. Could anything have been made of such a performance? Yes, if it had been (a) really funny and (b) really pornographic.

I got a fearful tickle in my throat and nearly expired of trying to stop coughing. Georgia thought I was upset by the performance, and said she was, and 'had no idea it would be all about SEX'. I'm not sure if I managed to convince her that I was not in the faintest degree embarrassed, but I've had a brute of a summer cold for a fortnight and can't get rid of it.

Frances Partridge

1995

All out to the lovely big Atlantic beach, where we stayed all afternoon. Seeing the variety of humankind (undisguised by their clothes) gives you a warm, sympathetic feeling for people. One of the tremendous shocks of going to a nudist colony must be meeting people nude and then seeing them put on clothes and become what they choose to project themselves as – 'I had no idea that's who you thought you were.' It's like when you meet someone you've only ever seen in uniform.

Brian Eno

19 August

1870

Ben Lloyd of the Cwm Bryngwyn reeling up the steep fields above Jacob's Ladder carrying a horse collar and butter tub. Just as I came up the drunken man fell sprawling on his back. He got up looking foolish and astonished, and I gave him some good advice which he took in good part at first. I asked if he were married. Oh, yes, and had great-grandchildren. A nice example to set them, I thought. When I said how his wife would be vexed and grieved to see him come rolling home, I found I had touched a tender point. He became savage at once, cursed and swore and threatened violence. Then he began to roar after me, but he could only stagger very slowly so I left him behind reeling and roaring, cursing parsons and shouting what he would do if he were younger, and that if a man did not get drunk he wasn't a man and of no good to himself or the public houses, an argument so exquisite that I left it to answer itself.

Rev. Francis Kilvert

1901 [*Discovery* Expedition to Antarctica]

Soon after prayers this morning we had a consultation over [James] Skelton. He has had bad toothache and a swollen face for nearly a week. He will not undergo any treatment at all – simply will not stand the pain of having his gum lanced or a stump drawn. So today we had a sail rigged up on deck to make a small room. In it we put the carpenter's bench, a mattress and pillow and then in [George] Murray's presence I gave him ether, and [Reginald] Koettlitz drew a tooth and we made a job of it. He was under nearly 25 minutes and the whole thing was very successful. He knew absolutely nothing of what had been done, went off almost immediately. There was much amusement on deck over his loud and amusing songs and unparliamentary remarks as he was recovering from the effects of the ether. He was only sick once, and had practically no after effects. I gave it him on the practical experience I had gained by receiving it myself last year.

Edward Wilson

1952

1 A.M. Face it kid, you've had a hell of a lot of good breaks. No Elizabeth Taylor, maybe. No child Hemingway, but god, you are growing up. In other words, you've come a long way from the ugly introvert you were only five years ago. Pats on the back in order? O.K., tan, tall, blondish, not half bad. And brains, 'intuitiveness' in one direction at least. You get along with a great many different kinds of people. Under the same roof, close living, even. You have no real worries about snobbishness, pride, or a swelled head. You are willing to work. Hard, too. You have willpower and are getting to be practical about living – and also you are getting published. So you got a good right to write all you want. Four acceptances in three months – $500 *Mille*, $25, $10 *Seventeen*, $4.50 *Christian Science Monitor* (from caviar to peanuts, I like it all the way).

Sylvia Plath

1989

Drove down to Dungeness with Sandy Powell and Paul Treacy.

Paul is dying, has lost nearly three stone. He says people treat him with the most extraordinary insensitivity. They collide with him on the street. They can't believe someone so young is walking with a stick. Others are so curious they are speechless when he talks to them. One ghastly inquisitive at a cocktail party badgered him with questions. How did it feel to be dying? It so distressed him he had to escape and cry in the corridor, as he had only been diagnosed the day before with Karposi's Sarcoma, on top of all his other problems.

A homeopathic doctor quizzed him about his sex life: 'You've never been to bed with a woman?!' he asked incredulously; then 'How long do they give you to live?' – before banging him a bill for £68 for some pills he had made up. And a further bill for the consultation. For this he had waited in the heat for over an hour. I'm glad to say he threw the pills back in the quack's face.

Derek Jarman

20 August

1667

There was now a very gallant horse to be baited to death with doggs, but he fought them all, so as the fiercest of them, could not fasten on him, till they run him thro with their swords. This wiccked and barbarous sport, deserv'd to have ben published in the cruel Contrivers, to get mony, under pretence the horse had killed a man, which was false: I would not be perswaded to be a Spectator.

John Evelyn

1879

I do not think I shall ever have a sensation which is not mixed with ambition. I despise people who are nobodies.

Marie Bashkirtseff

1922

I had just got to Honfleur when Lewis telephoned me about Balthy's death. I had heard nothing. I was overcome and telephoned her sister Justine, a twitchy, bony little old woman of seventy-one. 'Justine, it's Liane, I'm appalled. Is there anything I can do to help?' – 'Yes,' replied Justine crisply, 'there is something you can do to help. You can send me some chocolates.' I almost dropped the telephone. I ordered 'la Marquise de Sévigné' to send her a bag of chocolates and enclosed a card with our condolences. That's Basques for you, a race apart!

Liane de Pougy

1953

A great lesson from Kafka's diary. He wrote it during the First World War, which he never mentions. Not a single line refers to it.

Jean Cocteau

21 August

1940

To sit on a seat with a man, except in a café, is taboo for a virgin.

Whatever people say, the fastidious, formal manner of the upper classes is preferable to the slovenly easy-going behaviour of the common street lout. In moments of crisis the first know how to act, the second becomes an uncouth brute.

Cesare Pavese

22 August

1743

After a few of us had joined in prayer, about four I set out, and rode softly to Snow-Hill; where, the saddle slipping quite upon my mare's neck, I fell over her head, and she ran back into Smithfield. Some boys caught her, and brought her to me again, cursing and swearing all the way. I spoke plainly to them, and they promised to amend. I was setting forward, when a man cried, 'Sir, you have lost your saddlecloth.' Two or three more would needs help me to put it on; but these too swore at almost every word. I turned to one and another, and spoke in love. They all took it well, and thanked me much. I gave them two or three little books, which they promised to read over carefully.

John Wesley

1854

As soon as dinner was over we started on foot for Colney Hatch station. The rail only goes to Hatfield we found, but then got a ride on the top of the bus here in the most lovely weather. We should have thought more of the fields no doubt were we not so much used to them of late. However one field of turnips against the afternoon sky did surprise us into exclamation with its wonderful emerald tints. And then we passed a strange sight; two tall chimneys standing separately in a small space of ground about a rod I suppose, the rest covered with black looking rubbish, some of it smoking, some children looking at it. This the day before had been a house the home of a young couple married some three months, the man a wheel right. Fire surprised them in bed the previous night it would seem and they had to escape as they were in their bed clothes. And here lay all that they possessed flattened down in to black ashes. I broke a tooth a day or two ago and the gap seemed for some days hard to reconcile with my impressions of what forms sought to surround my tongue. If so it is with the remains of a decayed tooth, the gap caused by the loss of all one has must be harder still to realise at first. However they are young and no life was lost and as the man is not an artist there is yet hope of prosperity in store for them.

Ford Madox Brown

1919

I have to admit that I'm up to my neck in frivolity, buried in dresses to the point of ruin! Fifteen different garments! My wardrobe jam-packed! My girl, this is not the way for an old woman to behave – particularly since you never wear anything but black and white, or a little grey, so that you always look as though you were in the same dress. Why fritter away your money so absurdly?

Liane de Pougy

1931

My last day at the *Evening Standard*. I have learnt much in this place. I have learnt that shallowness is the supreme evil. I have learnt that rapidity, hustle and rush are the allies of superficiality. My fastidiousness has been increased and with it a loathing of the uneducated. I have come to believe that the gulf between the educated and the uneducated is wider than that between the classes and the more galling to the opposite side. I have not been popular in the office. I make perfunctory farewells. As I leave the building I shake my shoes symbolically.

Harold Nicolson

1979

A long weekend at the Edinburgh festival. It was strange moving so quickly from the glossy prosperity of Salzburg to this hard Scottish city. Yet in some ways I prefer Edinburgh – it has a freedom, a lack of constraint, which seems good.

Peter Hall

23 August

1915 [on the Russian Front]

Finger and hand cases came to the fore again; many of them had walked in themselves, despite the fact that they had been warned to apply for aid only at the divisional Unit, where the medical staff had its own harsh methods of treatment for self-inflicted wounds. One old soldier, with grey threads in his beard and pathetic brown eyes, held out a trembling, blood-stained hand; I washed it and, under the thick blood-coating, there was revealed the dark tell-tale stain of a wound received at close quarters. I looked at him and he knew that I *knew*, but nothing even akin to cowardice could be read in that haggard face; I saw in it only despair and a great exhaustion of mind and body. I painted the wound quickly with iodine; the dark stain faded somewhat under the yellow tincture. He was trembling all over now; I bandaged him; the necessary details of name and regiment were written down and he was despatched, together with other walking cases, to the Base. A man with a self-inflicted wound is a difficult person to deal with; one could not hastily condemn him, for so many conflicting influences would first have to be taken into consideration and we became sensitive to the signs from which we could detect those cases which were the outcome of cowardice. On the other hand, it was not difficult to distinguish the soldiers whose excitable nature and raw-edged nerves could induce them, in a weak, desperate moment, to seek this outlet as a definite means of deliverance from the scene of their physical suffering and mental anguish.

Florence Farmborough

1932 [France]
According to the newspapers here, the death sentence passed on five Nazi murderers by a court at Beuthen has caused terrific excitement throughout the Nazi Party. It evidently thought itself above the law while committing the vilest crimes. Hitler has sent the murderers a personally signed telegram, assuring them of his sympathy and declaring it 'a point of honour' that they shall be pardoned. And these are the sort of people who are now to enter the Government!

Count Harry Kessler

1956
A motto: Do it tomorrow; you've made enough mistakes today.

Dawn Powell

1975 [Barlinnie prison]
It's 8.45pm and the night has a long way ahead. I want to get up and pace the floor and not think about anything. I want to run away from what's inside me. The walls stand firm and the locked door becomes an intimidating enemy. I am locked in with myself. I see me – too much. I hate to be confronted with the fact that I AM NOT BAD! The fantasy of taking them inside my soul to show them all is well will remain a dream.

Jimmy Boyle

24 August

1854

As I was coming back from Le Pollet before dinner yesterday I came upon a poor old horse lying upon the ground, as I thought dead. In fact it was dying, and I began to quarrel with a great lout who was trying to beat it on to its legs again. To my great surprise the wretched animal managed to take a few steps when it got up although it was clearly in great pain. I saw it again today and at about the same time; it was then standing, with flies covering its scars and eyes, sucking what little blood remained in it. I resolutely sat down in the middle of the road and made several drawings. All this, occurring in the carriage-drive along the river Arques, created great astonishment among the elegant passers-by, who wondered what interest there could possibly be in the poor old screw which they saw me drawing.

Eugène Delacroix

1895

Went to see Ginnet's Circus at Ambleside and had a good laugh. I would go any distance to see a Caravan (barring lion-taming), it is the only species of entertainment I care for.

Mr. Ginnet himself hath gone-off in appearance since I saw him last on the same spot ten years since, when he rode a young red-roan bull. Doubtless since converted. He has subsided into a most disastrous long frock-coat and long, tight trousers with about a foot of damp at the bottom of them, and cracked a whip feebly. Were I inclined to weave a romance I might suspect that he had had reverses not unconnected with the bottle.

The Circus has fallen-off in the way of horses which represent capital, and stronger in the variety line. Probably a boisterous element introduced by growing lads. The neat little jockey had developed into a big, loutish, rough, rider, very gentle however with the little child Millie Ginnet. She was exceedingly pretty and nice-mannered in her clothes, and indeed seemed too well clothed under her bathing-drawers, a marvellous little bundle, by no means painfully proficient.

The scornful Madam Ansonia was arrayed in blue and silver, and, alighting from her piebald, put on goloshes publicly in the ring, The fair-haired enchantress did not appear unless indeed she had shrivelled into Madame Fontainebleau, who displayed her remarkable dogs in an anxious cockney accent, and twinkled about in high-heeled French boots and chilly apparel. Tights do not shock me in a tent associated with damp grass, they suggest nothing less prosaic than rheumatics and a painfully drudging life.

Beatrix Potter

1920

The rain rinses the last thoughts from one's head. Thoughts are impurities. That's why they start up in winter. Paper has lost its power to stimulate me. I hang like a bat in a turret of idleness: mouth downwards.

Bertolt Brecht

1949 [Rio de Janeiro]

At 1:30 Pedrosa and his wife come to take me to see paintings by the insane, in a suburban hospital of modern lines and ancient filth. My heart contracts seeing faces behind the tall, barred windows. Two interesting painters. Without a doubt the others have what it takes to send progressive Parisian minds into ecstasy. But, in fact, it's ugliness. Even more striking in the ugly and vulgar sculptures. I'm appalled when I recognize a psychiatrist from the hospital as the young man who, in the beginning, asked me the most idiotic question I was asked in all of South America. He's the one who decides the fate of these unfortunate people. Moreover, he's in the advanced stages of illness himself. But I'm even more appalled when he tells me that he's going to make the trip to Paris with me on Saturday. Enclosed with him in a metal cabin for 36 hours – this is the final ordeal.

Albert Camus

1952

There is nothing more abject, more harmful than this exploitation of heroism in the weeklies and in the press in general. [*Paris*] *Match* this week, devotes fourteen pages to an underground expedition on which one explorer met his death. His comrade decided to photograph him dying at the bottom of a hole. A full page shows his last glance. The article speaks of this *sublime hero* (whom no one asked to do anything – who made this expedition on his own – whereas miners die in the mines several times a day. Besides, the expedition had no scientific purposes whatever). The Carbuccia boy has publicized Alain Bombard's experiments concerning survival at sea; he was filmed as he set out. *They should have filmed his return* – or else filmed his death. A journalist's eye is on him: enormous publicity of the void. Naturally – as though on the brink of the prehistoric crevice – we shall see his wife waiting, his father in front of the microphones and the cameras . . .

Jean Cocteau

25 August

1818

Heard of a famous dandy at Harrowgate of the name of Stewart, a relative of Lord Castlereagh, who being asked by the Master of Ceremonies to dance enquired of him if the lady he meant to introduce him to was handsome, and being told she was he enquired if she was rich, and being told she had a good fortune asked if she danced well, and being answered in the affirmative said, 'Trot her out.' When he came to her he took out his quizzing glass and having eyed the lady some time through it says to the M.C., 'Trot her back again.'

Benjamin Newton

1940

The newspapers and the fish were both late in arriving as a bomb fell on the Epping–Ongar road last night, and there are tales of raids everywhere, particularly in Kent, and two over the London area. I am burying another tin box, containing my diaries for the first year of the war; Mortimer the gardener is again my accomplice.

'Chips' Channon

1947

Left Stockholm by the morning aeroplane and arrived at Oslo at 1 o'clock. Everything very shabby, the town airless and dusty in unusual heat, the inhabitants straggling about the streets in their shirt-sleeves eating ice-cream. The Grand Hotel in the builders' hands; constant hammering. But they have the agreeable Scandinavian habit of serving constant meals. Dinner lasts from 12 till 6; at 6 supper begins, lasts till 12. A midget female socialist came to introduce herself as my agent and took me to see my publisher, who hasn't published anything yet. A press conference was arranged for 6.30 that evening. Half a dozen journalists came, of whom two or three knew no English. A girl was quite drunk. The press attaché from the British Embassy did all the talking. Dined with agent and publisher.

Evelyn Waugh

26 August

1661

This morning before I went out I made even with my maid Jane, who has this day been my maid three years, and is this day to go into the country to her mother. The poor girl cried, and I could hardly forbear weeping to think of her going, for though she be grown lazy and spoilt by Pall's coming, yet I shall never have one to please us better in all things, and so harmless, while I live. So I paid her wages and gave her 2s. 6d. over, and bade her adieu, with my mind full of trouble at her going.

Samuel Pepys

1868

Proof of the whole book [*Little Women*] came. It reads better than I expected. Not a bit sensational, but simple and true, for we really lived most of it, and if it succeeds that will be the reason of it. Mr. Niles, [her publisher] likes it better now, and says some girls who have read the manuscript say it is 'splendid!' As it is for them, they are the best critics, so I should be satisfied.

Louisa May Alcott

1922

I dislike *Ulysses* more and more – that is think it more and more unimportant; and don't even trouble conscientiously to make out its meanings. Thank God, I need not write about it.

Virginia Woolf

1995

Pissed into an empty wine bottle so I could continue watching *Monty Python*, and suddenly thought, 'I've never tasted my own piss,' so I drank a little. It looked just like Orvieto Classico and tasted of nearly nothing.

Brian Eno

27 August

1854

They are going to launch a large vessel called a clipper at noon today. Another of these American inventions to make people go faster and faster. When they have managed to get travellers comfortably seated inside a cannon so that they can be shot off like bullets in any given direction civilisation will doubtless have taken a great step forward. We are making rapid strides towards that happy time when space will have been abolished; but they will never abolish boredom, especially when you consider the ever increasing need for some occupation to fill in our time, part of which, at least, used to be spent in travelling.

Eugène Delacroix

1905

It is characteristic of a particular social stratum of girls that, the first time, they do not give away their innocence but are robbed of it. They cry and beg one not to do anything to them; but then they give in, partly out of respect, partly because they are disarmed by the charm of the higher caste, partly from the sweet shock of awakened sensuality.

The way in which they are 'taken' at the inception of their love life is something that draws into their life the consequences of a stigma.

Robert Musil

1933

I was reading the diaries I kept when I was 15 and 18, and profoundly depressed by them – I'm glad time goes on. But I mustn't forget 'Soir de Paris' perfume reminds me of John Mott – that 'Pêche Marie Rose' was the nicest sweet we ever had – and I shall never be able to smell the fascinating sweet smell of Cyclax Special Lotion without being carried back to last term. As I write this I have a Boncilla beauty mask on my face – tightening my skin – nice if uncomfortable feeling.

Barbara Pym

1942

My grandfather, I believe, made a mistake when he came to this country. He was an unhappy man himself and his descendants have had many troubles. I believe, in truth, that immigration is always unwise – that is, when it is not enforced. I believe my chances in Germany would have been at least as good as they have been in America, and maybe a great deal better. I was born here and so were my father and mother, and I have spent all of my 62 years here, but I still find it impossible to fit myself into the accepted patterns of American life and thought. After all these years, I remain a foreigner.

H. L. Mencken

1976 [during the filming of *Apocalypse Now*]

Francis is feeling the pressure of being at the financial limit, having all the chips on the table. His deal is such that, as the film goes over budget, he has to guarantee the overages personally. If the film is a blockbuster it will be okay, but if the film is pretty good but has gone far over budget, he could end up being wiped out financially and owe millions. I think about that sometimes. Perhaps there is a part of me that wants him to fail. Be back in some simple life-style and all that. At one point in the past, it was really strong, as if returning to a 'simple' life would take me out of where I was and I would be happier. At least I know now that it doesn't change things that much. You can be rich and unhappy, or poor and unhappy. I guess women have a hard time as the man grows more successful, powerful, and wish for a time when the balance was more equal. It comes from the fact that the relationship changes. The successful man is usually good at what he does, and likes it, and spends a lot of time doing it – and less and less time with his wife and family. When I stopped feeling like a victim, I started having a lot of fun with Francis. We have odd moments of really interesting time together, rather than more usual amounts of time half tuned out.

Eleanor Coppola

1979

Edinburgh: To the Degas exhibition. I loved that. It is small enough to enjoy and so many masterpieces. Yet it's strange how the over-reproduced painting becomes such an artefact that when you see it in reality it seems impossible, unreal, and a bit disappointing. Then, in the evening, to [Maurizio] Pollini playing Schubert and Schumann. I think I have never heard such a superb musician: clear, disciplined, passionate, without being careful. A master. He thinks with his fingers. He turns music from a sensual experience into a metaphysical one.

Dreadful news today. The IRA have murdered Lord Mountbatten, his grandson, and, it is suspected, some of his family. They were all on holiday off Ireland in a fishing boat which was blown up. The papers speak of radio-controlled lobster pots. I feel sick.

Peter Hall

1979

Bess [Church] gave me the shattering news of Mountbatten's assassination in Ireland. I had last seen him at the Euro Gala at Drury Lane in May, after fifteen years quite close official association with him, not only over the prison inquiry in 1966, but also over various aviation matters before that; and indeed there had been a certain continuing relationship with him in Brussels. Dreadful though it is, I suppose that from his point of view it is not too bad as he had begun to give the impression of not knowing what to do with the rest of his life and might even have welcomed a dramatic death, although not one with these side-effects. He was a pretty remarkable man on the whole, not a great intellect but with exceptional drive and power to pull or push people along with him. He was also good at grandeur without pompousness. We watched this evening [a] television tribute to him which was very well done by Ludo Kennedy.

Roy Jenkins

28 August

1660

At home look over my papers and books and house as to the fitting of it to my mind till two in the afternoon. Some time I spent this morning beginning to teach my wife some scale in music, and found her apt beyond imagination. To the Privy Seal, where great store of work to-day. This day I heard my poor mother had then two days been very ill, and I fear she will not last long. To bed, a little troubled that I fear my boy [servant Will Waynman] is a thief and has stole some money of mine.

Samuel Pepys

1905

On the theme of the advisability of building a marriage on infidelity. Canaletto. White wigs and these skirts with twin humps give every woman the option of a love life. Wearing these it is permissible to be ugly. The woman becomes pure sexuality and pure wit, there is no thing called 'beauty' to serve as the mean. Canaletto's women are pug-faced and thin as rakes. But their clothing makes of them something quite unnatural over which the spirit can range freely. And when one practises another form of intercourse with them one snuffs out the candles.

Robert Musil

1940

Christopher Hobhouse's widow comes. She tells me that he left her on Monday evening at 4.30 in their little bungalow at Hayling Island. He went down to the Fort [at Portsmouth] and half-an-hour later there was a bombing attack and Christopher and three fellow officers were blown to pieces. They would not let her even attend the funeral since there was so little left. Poor girl. She is to have a baby in March and wants me to be godfather. She is left without a bean. I feel so sad about it.

Harold Nicolson

1940 [Berlin]

We had our first big air-raid of the war last night. The sirens sounded at twelve twenty a.m. and the all-clear came at three twenty three a.m. For the first time British bombers came directly over the city, and they dropped bombs. The concentration of anti-aircraft fire was the greatest I've ever witnessed. It provided a magnificent, a terrible sight. And it was strangely ineffective. Not a plane was brought down; not one was even picked up by the searchlights, which flashed back and forth frantically across the skies throughout the night.

The Berliners are stunned. They did not think it could happen. When this war began, Göring assured them it couldn't. He boasted that no enemy planes could ever break through the outer and inner rings of the capital's anti-aircraft defence. The Berliners are a naïve and simple people. They believed him. Their disillusionment today therefore is all the greater. You have to see their faces to measure it. Göring made matters worse by informing the population only three days ago that they need not go to their cellars when the sirens sounded, but only when they heard the *flak* going off near by. The implication was that it would never go off. That made people sure that the British bombers, though they might penetrate to the suburbs, would never be able to get over the city proper. And then last night the guns all over the city began pounding and you could hear the British motors humming directly overhead, and from all reports there was a pell-mell, frightened rush to the cellars by the five million people who live in this town.

William L. Shirer

1941

We are in the Belleville Hotel right on Lake Windermere, sleeping in bunks. Every morning at crack of dawn we have to hit the parade ground and all day long there are lectures in the Nissen huts on how to be an administration officer.

Here is a typical day's programme – parade (and at least four things found wrong with my appearance – 'Ropy do, Wyndham, your collar is filthy!'). Then a lecture on VD and scabies, followed by compulsory hockey in a thunderstorm – then another lecture on pregnant WAAFs. As if this wasn't enough we have a compulsory cello concert after dinner – can you imagine, after all that a *cello* concert?

Joan Wyndham

29 August

1660

Office day. Before I went to the office, my wife and I examined my boy Will about his stealing of things, as we doubted yesterday; but he denied all with the greatest subtility and confidence in the world. To the office; and after office, then to the church, where we took another view of the place where we had resolved to build a gallery; and have set men about doing it. Home to dinner; and there I find that my wife hath discovered my boy's theft and a great deal more than we imagined. At which I was vexed and intend to put him away.

Samuel Pepys

1847 [Ireland]

Delightful weather. Mild and the crops so fine. Every able-bodied person employed about here, or might be, did they choose to work; there are however a few who prefer receiving alms, actually sit still doing nothing, trusting to the compassion of anyone inclined to feed them. The new poor law practice will soon set all this to rights.

Very little stir about politicks in these days. Dislike of the ministry seems to be the only feeling very much alive in the public mind, a dislike of some individuals and a want of confidence in the whole. No wonder after the deficiences of last session, foreign troubles and home distresses. The Queen of Spain and her husband don't get on. In France there has been the most horrid murder: the Duke of Praslin has murdered his wife, and in the most barbarous manner in the middle of the night. These wretched great! The aristocracy has indeed need of a reformation. The Duc was not a faithful husband; he was not even decent in his gallantries, choosing as his mistresses the governesses of his children. These French manners are very distressing. All their habits are at variance with virtue. Amongst our own aristocracy it is very much the same. They are all much to be pitied, for true happiness they know nothing of.

Elizabeth Grant of Rothiemurchus

1940 [Berlin]

I had my own troubles at the radio [station] last night. First, the censors announced that we could no longer mention a raid while it was on. (In London Ed Murrow not only mentions it, but describes it.) Secondly, I got into somewhat of a row with the German radio officials. As soon as I had finished my broadcast, they ordered me to the cellar. I tried to explain that I had come here as a war correspondent and that in ordering me to the cellar they were preventing me from exercising my profession. We exchanged some rather sharp words. Lord Haw-Haw, I notice, is the only other person around here, except the very plucky girl secretaries, who does not rush to the shelter after the sirens sound. I have avoided him for a year, but have been thinking lately it might be wise to get acquainted with the traitor. In the air-raids he has shown guts.

William L. Shirer

30 August

1660

We found all well in the morning below stairs, but the boy [servant] in a sad plight of seeming sorrow; but he is the most cunning rogue that ever I met with of his age.

Samuel Pepys

1755

Oh, what a happiness must there be in a married state when there is sincere regard on both sides and each party truly satisfied with each other's merit; but it is impossible for tongue or pen to express the uneasiness that attends the contrary.

Thomas Turner

1939

The long answer from the German Government has come today and is thought to be unsatisfactory by most. The Cabinet met to consider it. Meanwhile we are still urging Germany and Poland to negotiate, though the Germans seem determined to have their way, and are as unaccommodating as possible. All day we were on a seesaw Peace – War – Peace. The Italian news however I thought distinctly encouraging and [Foreign Minister, Count] Ciano has now definitely promised that Italy will be neutral and suggested that she was veering round to us. But Leger of the French Foreign Office sent me a telegram warning us not to believe these tales and his gloomy report corroborated [Prince] Paul of Yugoslavia's impression, who warned me by telephone not to trust 'The Macaronis'.

Tentative evacuation has been ordered for tomorrow. Peace is in the balance.

'Chips' Channon

1985

I'm not sure if it was last night, but, anyway, whenever it was it was pretty humiliating: I picked a guy up – not young or handsome – and he asked if I had a place. We were on our way home when he caught sight of me – full-face under a street lamp. 'I don't think I'll bother,' he said.

Ossie Clark

31 August

1790

William Kingston, the man born without arms, came to see me of his own accord. Some time since he received a clear sense of favour of God; but after some months he was persuaded by some of his old companions to join in a favourite diversion, whereby he lost sight of God, and gave up all he had gained: But God now touched his heart again, and he is once more in earnest to save his soul. He is of a middling height and size, has a pleasing look and voice, and an easy, agreeable behaviour. At breakfast he shook off his shoes, which are made on purpose, took the tea-cup between his toes, and the toast with his other foot. He likewise writes a fair hand, and does most things with his feet which we do with our hands.

John Wesley

1842

It is fully twenty years since I was on the Clyde. I thought the scenery more beautiful now than then; probably some of the young woods are stately timber now, besides a few more houses built and grounds generally better kept. No Scotchman need talk of the misery of Ireland till Greenock, Paisley etc improve, the *country* is improving certainly, but I was struck with the stunted look of the vegetation, shorter shoots, smaller leaves, less vigorous trees, and the stature of the people, that again surprised me. I took all the workmen for boys, so much shorter are they than our handsome Irish.

We had to wait above an hour at Greenock so got the luxury of washing, combing etc., also a little refreshment for on board the eating was disgusting, not to be touched by a poor half sickly body like me. One train took us in little more than another hour to Glasgow, another in rather better than two to Edinburgh, these many changes are disagreeable enough particularly as there is very little time for them, but the expedition and the cheapness are wonderful. Within a few miles of Edinburgh we heard the Queen had not come the wind being quite against her. Yet bonfires were blazing on the Pentlands all along the shores of Fife and a splendid one on Arthur's seat.

Elizabeth Grant of Rothiemurchus

1939

It has been decided to evacuate three million mothers and children tomorrow from the menaced areas. It is rather grim. Historic names such as Rochester, Chatham, Southwark, come over at us in the calm cultured voice of the announcer. I read *Nicholas Nickleby* to cheer me up. How unreal Dickens is! Jazz-band sentimentality. The 6 o'clock news is very glum. It has been a grey day but the sun comes out in the evening and we have a calm twilight under which the garden stretches itself at ease. The flag hangs limply on its flag-staff. It is odd to feel that the world as I knew it has only a few hours more to run.

Harold Nicolson

1945

The Allies march on to victory, more triumphs everywhere. What a fortnight it has been. 'Key towns', of which one has never heard, fall daily, and Paris has been liberated twice in three days. Coats are turning inside out in the Balkans, and old Hindenburg must be turning, too, in his grotesque tomb at Tannenburg.

'Chips' Channon

1997

I was woken at about 4 a.m. by the telephone. It was Torje [her partner], in Toronto. He had just returned from dinner and turned on CNN. 'I thought you'd want to know; there's been a car crash in Paris. They're saying that Dodi Al Fayed is dead, and Princess Diana is injured.' In my semi-conscious state, I turned on the television. For about half an hour I watched the coverage, saw the wreckage of the Mercedes in that Paris tunnel, and wondered at Diana's luck, to have survived what must have been an enormous impact. My God! Eventually I dozed back to sleep and the television turned itself off.

About five hours later the phone woke me again. It was my friend David. We agreed that it was all dreadful, and asked how it could have happened. I didn't know that we were talking at cross-purposes. After he hung up, I turned on the TV to see newscaster Peter Sissons alongside a portrait of Diana, with the fateful legend '1961–1997'. The earlier reports weren't true. It wasn't just a broken arm, slashed thigh and concussion. She's dead. Like the rest of the nation, I can't quite take it in. It's not just the loss, both to her family and to the country, although that goes without saying. There's something more, something deeper, something harder to define. We always think that those things 'won't happen to us'. Yet if they can happen to a member of the Royal Family, a family which should be cocooned in the cotton wool of invincibility, safe and untouchable, it most certainly *can* happen to any of us. Her life hasn't quite been the fairytale she was promised – it's been closer to a movie script, with its outrageous extremes of tragedy, melodrama and glamour. Until now, I've never seen her as real, just a face on the news-stands. But in her horrific and pointless death, she's at last become vulnerable and real to me and to everyone else. How sadly ironic that it's only when she's robbed of her life that I can finally think of her as human.

Deborah Bull

SEPTEMBER

*'To write a diary every day is like returning to
one's own vomit.'*

ENOCH POWELL

1 September

1841

I was surprised by seeing that brutal obelisk still standing near Invergarry Castle, which the late Glengarry erected about 1812 to commemorate what his inscription styles *'the swift course of feudal justice'*, which means the murder by one of his ancestors of seven men. It was defaced for many years by passengers and the people, and when I saw it, with Thomas Telford, engineer, very soon after its erection, he could scarcely keep his hand off it . . .

The great Highland estate of Glengarry, consisting of a magnificent country, was sold last year to Lord Ward, by the son of him of the obelisk, to pay his father's debts; and this son, the existing Glengarry, a respectable young man, I am told, is trying what he can do in Australia. His father was famous in his day, and by flattery and the affectation of Highland usages, had the good fortune to get Sir Walter Scott to immortalise him in several of his works, as a fine specimen of the chieftain. But none knew better than Scott that he was a paltry and odious fellow, with all the vices of the bad chieftain and none of the virtues of the good one; with the selfishness, cruelty, fraud, arrogant pretension and base meanness of the one, without the fidelity to superiors, and the generosity to vassals, the hospitality, or the courage of the other.

Scott used to account for his enduring these sort of people by saying that they were 'savage and picturesque, both of which is in my way'.

The only fearlessness he ever displayed was in an act of madness which Telford and I saw, and to which, as to his duel, he was driven by insolent fury. A boat, in which he wished to cross Loch Oich, or Loch Lochy, left the shore without him, and a laugh showed that it had done so on purpose to avoid him, on which he plunged, with the pony he was on, into the water to swim after it. The people pretended not to see, and rowed as hard as they decently could. Telford and others were in ecstasy with the hope that they were at last to be relieved of him. And certainly he ought to have drowned. But after being carried very nearly across (a mile I should suppose), by the vigour of a creature more meritorious than its rider, he got on board and was praised for what he had done.

Lord Cockburn

1899

At Grundlsee, the day before yesterday, I pulled out one of my molars. First I loosened it with a finger, then I pressed it inwards with a nail-file, causing the gum to turn blue. Finally I took a piece of thick twine and pulled at it until it fell into my hand. I should add that it took frequent pauses, during which I considered calling the whole thing off. Only the fear of a swollen jaw and even greater pain persuaded me to keep at it. It hurt like mad, and blood flowed profusely. But it gave me the inner satisfaction of prevailing over myself. It's not easy to pull out one of your own teeth, especially if it's scarcely loose.

Alma Mahler-Werfel

1903 [*Discovery* expedition to Antarctica]

We have finished all our mutton, having had it every Sunday all through the winter. As it was all tainted, I think it's a good thing there was no more. The beef also is decidedly tainted, and a large percentage of the condensed milk is quite bad.

Every Tuesday for dinner we have skua, half a bird to a man, enough for a meal and very good indeed. One day in the week we have stuffed seal's heart, another seal steak and kidney pie, another seal steak and onions, and so on.

For breakfast we have the best dish of all – seal's liver, twice a week, other days stewed seal meat or curried. Thursday is known to everyone as 'Scurvy Day', being the only day in the week on which we have tinned meat. No one likes it so much as the seal, but it gives a day off to the cooks, who otherwise never get a holiday. On the whole we live very wholesomely – plenty of porridge, and good butter and good bread and jams, plenty of seal meat, fresh, palatable and well cooked. Skua gull, and cheese. Tea, coffee and cocoa. Lime juice every day and claret once or twice a week. Only our vegetables are a hopeless failure. The potatoes are eatable, but none of the others are.

Edward Wilson

1924

Most of the day writing this diary. In the afternoon to a cinema. *Resolved* to go to no more cinemas promiscuously.

Evelyn Waugh

1927 [Grenoble]

Up further, finally we reached in the very crest of the peaks a community of mighty buildings, staunch and gray and with peaked roofs – impressive.

'La Grande Chartreuse.' It was cool evening, and no sound. Into the court – massive, evenly cut buildings. The roof was slated blue, a hard gray blue like the sheer rocks of the mountain cliffs just above. It was austere, deserted, magnificent. We walked through mighty halls of these Carthusian monks, down cloisters. It was cold and shadowed.

We saw a monk's 'cell', or apartment. Each monk had *two* rooms and a chapel *and a garden*! A bookcase, a desk, windows out into his garden where an apple tree was brushing against the window. He was by himself for five days and on the sixth with the thirty-five other monks. What a heavenly life! All your books, quiet, your own garden, an apple tree, no interruptions, air. We leaned out of the window and there was no sound except the quiet tinkle of cows coming in somewhere. And in the distance the two fountains splashed in the great court. What austere peace.

Anne Morrow Lindbergh

1932 [Paris]

Guest of the American copper-king Guggenheim at Hiller's.

Next to me sat Wanda Prittwitz. She told me, with great delight, that all her relations are Nazis and what a good thing it is about the 'Movement' that all these young people, whatever their social status, feel themselves to be comrades. The spirit of *camaraderie* among them is wonderful. She herself is not a Nazi, but, though remaining a Nationalist, she is of course an anti-Semite. So, presumably, am I? No, I retorted, else I would not tonight be the guest of a Jew. She is so dotty that she did not even feel the thrust, but went gushing calmly on. Baroness Rebay (a painter, responsible for arranging the party), whose father was a general during the war, lived in Strasbourg until 1918 and still feels herself to be an Alsatian. She too has strong Nazi leanings, though holding it against them that they have closed the Bauhaus at Dessau. The splendid thing about the 'Movement' is, according to her, that it is teaching ordinary folk that they too must make sacrifices, whereas during the war it was only 'our sort' who did that. All the same, I remarked, several million ordinary folk were killed and several hundred thousand starved to death; none of my acquaintances died of hunger.

Count Harry Kessler

1939

Jenny had just started to clean my window when the 10.30 a.m. news-bulletin began intimating that Germany had invaded Poland. Mother passed on the news to Jenny who, on returning to her window-cleaning, exhibited such an increased acceleration that she was done in less than half her normal time. With a like exuberance she tackled the summer-house windows; dashing up and down the steps, and now and then sticking out her chest like a belligerent bantam. Evelyn remarked in the evening that the public-houses were crowded with young fellows, and numerous militia-men rolling along the streets. My own recollection of a personal reaction prompted by a similar mood takes me back to June, 1916. On the afternoon when the report of Kitchener's death was made public, I was crossing from the Academy to the North Inch [Perth] where, on a strip of grass bordering the path to the left of the old cannon, a number of senior boys were practising putting the weight in preparation for the approaching sports. Before I had joined them, somebody informed me that Kitchener had been drowned. This bit of news immediately galvanized me into a mindless exuberance, and I instantly set off towards the potential athletes, 'Hurrah! Kitchener's dead!' then, on joining the staring party, I picked up the weight and gave it a mighty heave, outdistancing the previous throws. I suppose the unconscious thought expressing itself in such a display of animal boisterousness is: 'Look, Death, look; here is somebody alive and very much alive.'

William Soutar

1945

A German journalist on the set today told me that Germany was recovering by leaps and bounds, that the Nazis were numerous and that the Germans worked twelve hours a day without cups of tea every hour or so. As he said this, he cast a contemptuous glance round our stage. Everybody in sight was standing about drinking tea. We have a five-day week; two of those days are early days; it is impossible really to put our backs into it and finish the picture. The British Film Industry is on the verge of dissolution. I wonder why?

Noël Coward

1997

The public clamour after Diana's death is increasing. Newspapers have devoted whole issues, the television last Sunday was devoted to her entirely, and Kensington Palace and its surrounding park have become a sea of flowers as never-ending waves of devotees turn it into a shrine in her honour. The lighted candles, photographs, and messages pinned to the trees take me back to Kyoto and its Shinto shrines, but the open emotions are more South Asian and belie the Englishness of Kensington Gardens. It seems that we live in a topsy-turvy world; a woman who was often mocked and belittled in her life is now praised and beatified in her death. Most of the papers, particularly the tabloids, managed to sanitise their Sunday editions before they hit newsstands, but one or two of the old-style items slipped through the net, reminding us that until a few days ago, Diana was a woman in the midst of a headline-grabbing love affair, and not the saintly icon she has now become. Alone amongst the papers, the street-vendored *Big Issue*, run, as it presumably is, on a shoestring, could not afford to scrap its print run and remove a tongue in cheek, sniping article, written before Sunday morning's tragedy. Instead, they were obliged to insert an apology slip and cross their fingers in the hope that their readers wouldn't take offence. It would be too sadly ironic if a charity devoted to one of her 'causes', the homeless, were to suffer deficits through her death.

Deborah Bull

2 September

1666

(Lord's Day) Some of our mayds sitting up late last night to get things ready against our feast to-day, Jane [maid] called us up about three in the morning to tell us of a great fire they saw in the City. So I rose and slipped on my night-gowne and went to her window, and thought it might be on the back-side of Marke-lane at the farthest; but, being unused to such fires as followed, I thought it far enough off; and so went to bed again and to sleep. About seven rose again to dress myself, and there looked out of the window and saw the fire not so much as it was, and further off. So to my closett to set things to rights after yesterday's cleaning. By and by Jane comes and tells me she hears that above 300 houses have been burned down to-night by the fire we saw and that it is now burning down all Fish-street, by London Bridge. So I made myself ready presently and walked to the Tower, and there got up upon one of the high places, Sir J[ohn] Robinson's little son going up with me; and there I did see the houses at that end of the bridge all on fire, and an infinite great fire on this and the other side of the bridge. So with my heart full of trouble, I down to the water-side, and there got a boat and through bridge, and there saw a lamentable fire. Poor Michell's house, as far as the Old Swan, already burned that way, and the fire running further. Every body endeavouring to remove their goods, and flinging into the river or bringing them into lighters that lay off; poor people staying in their houses as long as till the very fire touched them, and then running into boats, or clambering from one pair of stairs by the water-side to another. Among other things the poor pigeons, I perceive, were loth to leave their houses, but hovered about the windows and balconys till they were, some of them burned, their wings, and fell down.

Samuel Pepys

1847

Travelled in the omnibus with two nuns; their habit made a deep impression on me as I thought of the general corruption of morals and the abandonment of all good principles. I like to see this habit which enjoins, at any rate on those who wear it, an absolute respect for the virtues – for devotion, self-respect and regard for others, even if only on the surface.

Eugène Delacroix

1927

Considering I only slept 2 hours last night I was in astonishing creative form to-day.

Arnold Bennett

1937

A week or so ago, received a letter from Kay Hime. 'My precious D. – quite mad, but I'm going to be married. He's rather like you (of course!) and you'll like him I think. I like him *very* much.' (Extraordinarily, charmingly naive, and so Kayish, the last sentence). This evening arrived an official invitation to the reception, with the scrawled note: 'Please come and stand by me—' How is one to understand such an orientation of mind?

Curious, it was here, in Paris, very nearly four years ago, that we first met, and here I am again, now to learn of her marriage, and we were so very nearly married, then. I shall always regard those days, I think, as the happiest of my life. By this time, something in me has become so estranged from her (her innocence, candour and naiveté), that the strongest emotion I feel on learning of her marriage to someone else (in spite of the fact that at one time we seemed to be *the* couple, and everyone thought of us being together), is above all that of a 'man of letters': an egotistical curiosity as to how I am reacting to the circumstance. (If I were like that through and through, as the genuine professional is supposed to be, I should indeed be dead!)

David Gascoyne

1950 [Château de la Garoupe]

A day of sun-bathing and water-skiing. We went out in the 'small' yacht, and bathed blissfully, then had cocktails at the famous Eden Roc. Lunched at 3.30 p.m. As we came home in the speedboat we saw a dark female figure silently fishing from the shores of the adjacent villa, the Château de la Cröe (where the Windsors lived for some summers): it was the old Queen of Italy, a famous fisher-woman. As she casts her lonely line, does she think of her daughter, Princess Mafalda, dying in a prison-camp? of

Mussolini? Of all her lost Quirinalian splendour? Or just whether the fish will bite?

'Chips' Channon

1961

Reminiscence. When Ducker of the Turl died I told Catherine Walston that I must find a new bootmaker. She took me to Thrusal of Cambridge (with whom I have dealt ever since). On my first visit he was measuring me for my last when Catherine suddenly drew attention to Thrusal's own boot which was almost circular, like the boots ponies wore on their hooves when drawing lawn mowers. 'That's exactly the kind of shoe I have been looking for all my life.' 'I regret to say, madam, that I am obliged to wear it because of a defor-mity of the foot.'

Evelyn Waugh

1979

Listened to a wonderful radio programme of people recalling the day war was declared, exactly forty years ago. I remember it vividly. Neville Chamberlain broke the news on the radio as I shredded beans for my mother on the doorstep of 121 Blinco Grove, Cambridge. We all expected immedi-ate air raids, and she and I were rather frightened. Father was on relief Sunday duty at some country station, we weren't sure where, so we went down to Cambridge station to ask, and they didn't know either. Then he came home, as he came home every day throughout the war. Most families, of course, had hideous separations, or worse. We had none. I suppose I must also count myself lucky to have lived through so many years of relative peace, whatever the horrors, the Vietnams, the terrorists.

Peter Hall

3 September

1658

Died that archrebell Oliver Cromewell, cal'd Protector . . .

John Evelyn

1666

The Fire having continued all this night (if I may call that night, which was as light as day for 10 miles round about after a dreadfull manner) when consp[ir]ing with a fierce Eastern wind, in a very drie season, I went on foote to the same place, when I saw the whole South part of the Citty

431

burning from Cheape side to the Thames . . . The Conflagration was so universal, and the people so astonish'd that from the beginning (I know not by what desponding or fate), they hardly stirr'd to quench it, so there was nothing heard or seene but crying out and lamentation, and running about like distracted creatures, without at all attempting to save even their goods; such a strange consternation there was upon them, so as it burned both in breadth and in length. The Churches, Publique halls, Exchange, Hospitals, Monuments, the ornaments, leaping after a prodigious manner from house to house and streete to streete, at great distance from the other, for the heate (with a long set of faire and warm weather) had even ignited the aire, and prepared the materials to conceive the fire, which devoured after a[n] incredible manner, houses, furniture and everything: Here we saw the Thames coverd with goods floating, all the barges and boates laden with what some had time and courage to save, as on the other, the Carts etc carrying out to the fields, which for many miles were strewed with moveables of all sorts, and Tents erecting to shelter both people and what goods they could get away: ô the miserable and calamitous spectacle, such as happly the whole world had not sense the like since the foundation of it, nor to be out don, 'til the universal Conflagration of it, all the skie were of a fiery aspect, like the top of a burning Oven, and the light seene above 40 miles round for many nights: God grant mine eyes may never behold the like, who now saw above ten thousand houses all in one flame, the noise and crakling and thunder of impetuous flames, the shreeking of Women and children, the hurry of people, the fall of towers, houses and churches was like an hideous storme, and the aire all about so hot and inflam'd that at the last one was not able to approch it, so as they were force'd [to] stand still, and let the flames consume on which they did for neere to whole mile[s] in length and one in bredth: The Clowds also of Smoke were dismall, and reached upon computation neere 50 miles in length: Thus I left it this afternoone burning, a resemblance of Sodome, or the last day: It call'd to mind that of 4 Heb: '*non enim hic habemus stabilem Civitatem*': the ruines resembling the picture of Troy: London was, but it is no more: Thus I return'd.

John Evelyn

1922

I notice one characteristic symptom in myself – in the matter of money. When I was travelling with Turner and staying in Munich, I never thought about expense at all, but flung the marks about and ordered the expensive wine etc. with perfect freedom. But as soon as I am alone I positively enjoy parsimony, and find myself carefully limiting my daily expenditure on food to a decent minimum – about 750 marks. By this method I shall have lived for over a fortnight on £5 when I return to Munich. It is a recurrence to habits formed before the war, when I had to think about every pound I spent. Luckily it is a habit which only functions when I am alone.

Siegfried Sassoon

1939 [Carradale, Kintyre]

As we listened to Chamberlain speaking, sounding like a very old man, I kept wondering what the old Kaiser was thinking, whether he was old enough to see it all fully. At the end Joan said How could he ask God to bless us? . . . As God Save the King started Denny [her son] turned it off and someone said Thank you.

The maids hadn't wanted to come through; I told Annie, who was wonderfully cheerful and said she remembered the Boer War, and Bella who said Isn't that heartbreaking. After a bit she began to cry, a saucepan in her hands, said Think of all our men going, then to me Of course you've got boys too. Dick said Think of the women in Germany all saying that too, but there was no response. Then she asked When will they send our men over? But none of us had much idea.

Naomi Mitchison

1939

Two days ago we left Torridon. It seems an age. As we stacked our guns, golf-clubs and fishing rods into the back of our Buick, fear pinched my heart: those are the toys of yesterday I thought; they belong to another world . . . Questions teemed through my mind: where will Dan's Yeomanry, the Notts Sherwood Rangers, go? Will I be able to see him? Mummy, ill in hospital in Switzerland – should I fetch her back to England? And Whitaker – our cook-butler – perhaps he is too old to be a soldier? It was raining. The windscreen wipers ticked to and fro' and it seemed as if each swipe brought a new and more horrifying thought to me. We had started on a journey – but to where? And for how long? . . .

This morning we piled camp beds, saddle and saddle bags into the back of the Buick and started: Dan in uniform, Whitaker in his best navy pinstripe suit and myself in a fuss. We listened to Mr Chamberlain broadcasting that 'a state of war exists' as we sped up the Great North Road.

Dan left me with his Mother. She offered him her beautiful chestnut mare to be his second charger and he accepted gratefully. In twenty minutes, he and Whitaker were gone . . .

Thousands of children are being evacuated from London to the country. They, and their parents, must feel as desolate as me.

Countess of Ranfurly

1945

Six years ago today war was declared. Now we are starting again with officially declared peace and the world in physical and spiritual chaos. History
in the making can be most exhausting.

Noël Coward

1963

Re-reading Robert Byron. It was fun thirty-five years ago to travel far and
in great discomfort to meet people whose entire conception of life and
manner of expression were alien. Now one has only to leave one's gates.

Evelyn Waugh

1977

Joan Hewitt staying here last weekend watched me winding up the grandfather clock in the kitchen. She told me how during the last war Aunt
Dorothy had a visit from some evacuee youths from Glasgow. One of them
said to Aunt Dorothy, 'I want to go to the toilet.' So she said, 'Go down the
passage and you will find it the first door on the right.' Within a flash the
youth was back, saying, 'The door's too small. I couldn't get through it' –
referring to the door of this clock. Mercifully he didn't pee through it.

James Lees-Milne

4 September

1864

At dinner was a sensible and cultivated General Smith. He left the navy, for
which he still retains a preference, and went into an infantry regiment. When
the Waterloo campaign began, the headquarters with three companies were
on their way from the West Indies. The battalion was made up at home, and
was sent up from Brussels to the field, arriving at 11 o'clock – 702 men;
fifteen officers, of whom seven were wounded. They were under General
Lambert. They remained stationary until 6 p.m., when Smith was cut over
in the leg, and had to hobble to the rear. He got upon a return tumbril; was
helped up by an officer of the Light Division, who had an arm in a sling,
and was very civil. They went very slowly through the forest of Soignes; the
sides of the road were deep mud, pavement in the middle. A staff-officer rode
up and asked the man with the arm in sling whether he really was so badly
wounded as not to be able to return to duty: he said he was; the staff officer
said he was sorry to hear it. Smith ascertained after they got to Brussels that
it was a sham. I asked him these questions: Did the men complain of the

inefficiency of their muskets? – No. Did they see what was going on? – No. Could you see what was going on elsewhere, as for instance at Hougoumont? – No. We could see ears of corn cut off one after another; then we heard the bullet. Did you observe wounded men lying close to you, whom you could not leave your ranks to help? – No. Did you receive any supplies of ammunition? – No. Did any staff-officer come to you? – No. Most of the men had never been in action before; unconscious of danger. I have hastened to put this down for fear I should forget the previous evidence of an eye (and leg) witness about Waterloo. Perhaps I may never have another chance of questioning another man who was there.

William Cory

1938

The present political situation is almost comic, diabolically comic, if one has enough detachment to see it that way: the whole of Europe waiting with bated breath for the 'inspired' utterances of a madman! Everything seems to depend on what Hitler will say at Nuremberg this week. All these diplomatic conversations, and 'exchange of views', and sending of notes, and 'attempted conciliations', – all this flurry and nervous chatter in the international henroosts, – because of the lunatic whims of a paranoic little mediocrity of a German housepainter! – The newspapers talk of nothing but the possibility of war. It's all too desperately futile and disgusting to meditate on, our Western civilisation! . . .

David Gascoyne

1939

The King broadcast a speech last night which was badly spoken enough, I should have thought, to finish the Royal Family in this country. It was a great mistake. He should never be allowed to say more than twenty words. His voice sounds like a very spasmodic often interrupted tape machine. It produces an effect of colourless monotony, except that sometimes after a very slow drawn-out passage words come out all jumbled together at the end of a sentence. First of all one tries to listen to what he is saying. Then one forgets this and starts sympathizing with him in his difficulties. Then one wants to smash the radio. Later there were [Arthur] Greenwood and [Archibald] Sinclair. They talked about gallant Poland, our liberties, democracy, etc., in a way which raised very grave doubts in my mind. Greenwood even talked about fighting the last war to end war. Personally, I prefer Chamberlain's line to all this sanctimoniousness, which is that he has done his best to give Hitler everything but feels that now he can give nothing more.

Stephen Spender

1976 [during the filming of *Apocalypse Now*]

I heard there are some real cadavers in body bags in the Kurtz Compound set. I asked the propman about it; he said, 'The script says "a pile of burning bodies"; it doesn't say a pile of burning dummies.'

Eleanor Coppola

1990

A letter from Jilly [Cooper] thanked us for the luncheon party and added that her daily, having done the shopping which included ox's heart for the cats, left a note: 'Your money's in the envelope and your heart's in the freezer.'

Anthony Powell

5 September

1660

Home to dinner, where, (having put away my boy [servant] in the morning) his father brought him again, but I did so clear up my boy's roguery to his father, that he could not speak anything against my putting him away.

Samuel Pepys

1870

Heard that the mob at Paris had rushed into the Senate and proclaimed the downfall of the dynasty, proclaiming a Republic! This was received with acclamation and the proclamation was made from the Hôtel de Ville. Not one voice was raised in favour of the unfortunate Emperor! How ungrateful!

Queen Victoria

1872

I was out early before breakfast this morning bathing from the sands. There was a delicious feeling of freedom in stripping in the open air and running down naked to the sea, where the waves were curling white with foam and the red morning sunshine glowing upon the naked limbs of the bathers.

Rev. Francis Kilvert

1917

Some girls up the road spend a very wet Sunday morning playing leap-frog in their pyjamas around the tennis lawn. It makes me envious. To think I never thought of doing that! and now it is too late [he was dying]. They wore purple pyjamas too. I once hugged myself with pride for undressing in a cave by the sea and bathing in the pouring rain, but that seems tame in comparison.

W. N. P. Barbellion

1976 [during the filming of *Apocalypse Now*]

Late in the afternoon I was standing on the main steps of the temple with Francis [her husband] and Marlon [Brando]. The two of them were talking about Kurtz. Francis asked Marlon to reread *Heart of Darkness*. Now Marlon was saying how his character should be more like Kurtz was in the book. Francis said, 'Yes, that's what I've been trying to tell you. Don't you remember, last spring, before you took the part, when you read *Heart of Darkness* and we talked?'

Marlon said, 'I lied. I never read it.'

Eleanor Coppola

6 September

1831

I have been unwell all the morning. Nota bene, never eat *new* honey. Lay in bed nearly all day, in consequence of that nota bene not having been noted yesterday.

Elizabeth Barrett Browning

1899 [India]

Went to hear a gramophone, which is a wonderful invention. It played many tunes extremely well.

Violet Jacob

1933

Henri de Rothschild has just published a book describing his youth before he got married. He refers to me in rather insulting terms that I might well have deserved but it happens not to be the truth. I met him at Angèle de Varenne's house. I can still hear Angèle saying: 'I like Liane, she's so straight that she doesn't even flutter an eyelash at our little Rothschild.' That wasn't always the case between friends. I never liked to be treacherous; I can't remember a time when I did that – flirted with a friend's lover or husband. I always waited for people to come to me, to love me, to tell me so, to prove it. Sometimes I let myself be won. And often – very often – I couldn't make up my mind: there were many occasions when I refused to give myself. They reproached me for being cold, they said I was made of ice. There were some men – and some women too, yes – who were never able to melt that ice. What I really did was love for Love's sake; and once my head had been won over, my body took great delight in giving itself. There were also a good many times when I was a little intoxicated animal with irresistible appetites . . .

Liane de Pougy

1939

Our first air raid warning at 8.30 this morning. A warbling that gradually insinuates itself as I lay in bed. So dressed and walked on the terrace with L[eonard, her husband]. Sky clear. All cottages shut. Breakfast. All clear. During the interval a raid on Southwark. No news. The Hepworths came on Monday. Rather like a sea voyage. Forced conversation. Boredom. All meaning has run out of everything. Scarcely worth reading papers. The B.B.C. gives any news the day before. Emptiness. Inefficiency. I may as well record these things. My plan is to force my brain to work on Roger [Fry]. But lord this is the worst of all my life's experience. It means feeling only bodily feelings: one gets cold and torpid. Endless interruptions. We have done the curtains. We have carried coals etc. in to the cottage for the 8 Battersea women and children. The expectant mothers are all quarrelling. Some went back yesterday. We took the car to be hooded, met Nessa, were driven to tea at Charleston. Yes, it's an empty meaningless world now. Am I a coward? Physically I expect I am. Going to London tomorrow I expect frightens me. At a pinch enough adrenalin is secreted to keep one calm. But my brain stops. I took up my watch this morning and then put it down. Lost. That kind of thing annoys me. No doubt one can conquer this. But my mind seems to curl up and become undecided. To cure this one had better read a solid book like Tawney. An exercise of the muscles . . . Shall I walk? Yes. It's the gnats and flies that settle on non-combatants. This war has begun in cold blood. One merely feels that the killing machine has to be set in action.

Virginia Woolf

1976

We called on Mr Crann in his tiny cottage, Shepherd's Lodge, and asked him to repair the escutcheon on the south side of our house. The mantling has disintegrated. This old craftsman showed us his workshop, and an infinity of tools with fine handles in maplewood. Told me the names of some of the implements, which I have forgotten. He is a splendid craftsman yet his own taste is execrable. Showed us gargoyles, garden figures, foxes, dwarfs he has carved: to be seen to be believed. In the evening Mr Gentry, the watch-mender in the village, called with the movement of my Louis XV clock. Came bustling in with it in his hand, almost in tears of vexation at what the previous mender had done to it. Put the pin of some important cog in an unorthodox place. Said he ought to be disgraced and struck off the register of horologists. Never seen a man more distraught. His life's training affronted. Then Mr Hayes the builder informed us he was an embalmer in his off time. Fascinating work. Told Peggy he would give her a lesson. It is not done as the Egyptians did it, he assured me (they spent three months to his three hours per client), but only to last a short time, before the corpse can be disposed of. I asked if he gutted the corpse. Oh dear, no, only inject preservatives, he said, and something about removing offensive parts, 'but we are always obliged to restore them' – after treatment, I supposed, but could not ask for further details because the agent to the Beaufort estate came and interrupted.

James Lees-Milne

1997

The morning of Diana's funeral, and my friend David and I joined several thousand people in Hyde Park to watch her cortege pass by. It has been the most extraordinary occasion, the most comprehensive and controlled display of public grief I am ever likely to witness. It was a bright and sparkling day, and the simplicity of the horse-drawn gun carriage contrasted sharply with the glamour of Diana's life. But I am sensing a mood here in the country which I find unsettling, a mood which verges on anarchy. I hope 'the people' have thought about where this will take them; the funeral demonstrated the need for formality and tradition to hold us together in times of tragedy, and yet I'm strongly aware of a potentially destructive element in the emotions on display. Charles, Earl Spencer, Diana's brother, brought the house down at Westminster Abbey with his bold and emotional condemnation of the gross intrusions which plagued his sister's life, in particular her difficult relationship with the media and the Royal Family. As much as I admire him for saying so eloquently what he did, I cannot help feeling that this is not a time for division, unless his intention was revenge and the downfall of the monarchy. If those were his aims, he did very well indeed. If not, then he only achieved personal catharsis and a familial defence of Diana and her sons. There was something ancestral, almost Shakespearean about it. The 'people' applauded as one, and I know what the headlines will be in the morning. The broadsheets will ask serious questions about the future of the monarchy. The tabloids will probably herald the arrival on the scene of the people's choice of a new King Charles – except this one will be a Spencer, not a Windsor.

Deborah Bull

7 September

1875

This morning I went to Bath. Having an hour to spare I went into the Catholic Cathedral. I knelt and prayed for charity, unity, and brotherly love, and the union of Christendom. Surely a Protestant may pray in a Catholic Church and be none the worse.

Rev. Francis Kilvert

1895

I've recently felt death very close. My material life seems to be hanging by a thread, and must very soon break off. I'm getting more and more used to this and beginning to feel – not pleasure, but the interest of expectation, of hope – as I do with the progress of *this* life.

Leo Tolstoy

1922

L[eonard, her husband] put into my hands a very intelligent review of *Ulysses*, in the American *Nation*; which, for the first time, analyses the meaning; and certainly makes it very much more impressive than I judged. Still I think there is virtue and some lasting truth in first impressions; so I don't cancel mine.

Virginia Woolf

1939

I came to London this morning to fix up our small flat so that we can let it furnished at a moment's notice if necessary. Mrs Sparrow [her charlady] helped me pack up our few treasures and our wedding presents – it seemed strange to be sending them to store. She asked me all the questions I have been asking myself: How long will it last? Will they bomb London? What shall I do now? I promised her I will 'let' her with our flat or not let it at all – so she may be sure of work.

I lunched with Grannie Cooper who told me that this morning she put her name down for war work and described herself as 'Eighty but active'. We talked of Poland. Afterwards I walked to the gun shop in Pall Mall and bought a small .25 Colt revolver. The shopkeeper said I may not take possession of it until I get a licence. Then I went to Whitaker's [her butler, gone to war] flat near the Tottenham Court Road and arranged for all his things to be stored. The piano he was buying on the instalment system from Selfridges will have to be returned. On my way home I bought two 'safari' beds made of canvas with slim detachable steel feet. They fold into a neat bundle and are lighter than the old wooden ones. Tomorrow I begin training to be an ambulance driver – in gumboots and gas-mask.

Countess of Ranfurly

1940

An air raid in progress. Planes zooming. No, that one's gone over very quick and loud. Couldn't see if it were English. More planes over the house, going I suppose to London, which is raided every night.

Virginia Woolf

1995

A series of scenes in the Mansion House. De Valera informs Michael Collins he will be part of the team that negotiates the Treaty with England. Collins rails against going, but to no avail. Then, the crucial scene where de Valera confronts Collins about the Treaty he eventually signed.

The first centres round a track on Collins's face, aghast at what has been proposed. Camera tracks down a long table, to reveal the Cabinet, staring at him. Ends with de Valera in the foreground. This is the point at which the story will change, the most worrying one in the script, where the argument with Britain fades and the argument amongst themselves begins. Liam [Neeson] is all directness, straight confrontation. Alan [Rickman] is as intricate as a spider's web. We discuss how Churchill described negotiation with de Valera as 'trying to pick up mercury with a fork'. To which Dev replied, 'Why doesn't he try a spoon?'

Neil Jordan

8 September

1822

'Methinks, as we grow old, our only business here is to adorn the graves of our friends or to dig our own.' [H. Walpole]

Mary Shelley

1937

Marseilles, hotel bedroom. Big yellow flowers on grey wallpaper. Geography of filth. Sticky, muddy corners behind the enormous radiator. Spring mattress, broken light switch . . . That kind of liberty which comes from dubious and shady places.

Albert Camus

1974

Yet again this morning the radio talks [re Vietnam] of 'innocent victims', meaning women and children. Is the implication that the soldiers – those teenage boys who have little choice but to fight – are guilty?

The foetus in repressive society. Suppose a woman were pregnant with what she knew to be, for whatever reason, a homosexual. Has she the right to wilfully miscarry this infant, knowing that in the adult world it would eventually be legally executed? In a repressive society, which is stronger: the horror of abortion or the horror of inversion? If a foetus is a creature with rights, why do we not sing a requiem for a miscarriage?

Ned Rorem

1980 [Leeds]

'Las Vegas,' says my cousin Arnold. 'Then in November it's Mombasa.' We are waiting outside the crematorium at Cottinglye, where his father, Dad's brother Bill, is to be cremated. He's telling me about his retirement, the package holidays he and his wife go on. 'I've lost count of the number of times we've been to Majorca.'

All crematoriums are built on the loggia principle; long open corridors, cloisters even, the walls lined with slips of stone printed with the names of the burned. 'Reunited', 'Loved', and in one case 'He was kind', which is the sort of thing women who don't like sex say of a forbearing husband. Among the names I spot Mr and Mrs Holdsworth, who lived opposite us in the Hallidays during the war and from whose nasturtium border we used to collect caterpillars.

Now the vicar arrives in beige frock and rimless glasses and bounds out of his car to shake our hands.

Two women wait in the sunshine. They are from Mount Pisgah, the chapel Uncle Bill used to go to. 'Well, we still call it Mount Pisgah, only Mount Pisgah's actually a Sikh chapel now.' 'He was a grand feller, your uncle,' one of them says. 'And he had beautiful handwriting.'

The hearse and the attendant cars are grey and low-slung, so that it looks more like the funeral of a Mafia boss than of an ex-tram-driver. As we come out of the chapel cousin Geoff, who always takes the piss, shouts at my Uncle Jim, the last surviving brother, and who's deaf, 'Head of the clan now, Uncle.'

'Aye.' Uncle Jim shouts back. 'There's nobbut me now.'

'Nay, Jim,' somebody says.

Geoff nudges me. 'Give us your autograph.'

The funeral tea is held in the functions room of Waites, at the top of Gledhow Street. Cousin Arnold, who's a retired police photographer, tells me about a visit by the stripper Mary Millington to Blackpool, where he now lives, and how she committed suicide soon afterwards. 'I can't understand why she committed suicide. She had a lovely body.'

I call at Uncle Bill's house. But it's not as I remember it, all chrome and leatherette and the knight in armour holding the fire tongs on the hearth; now just a dull, cream-painted room that could be anywhere.

I take the train back. Through county after county the fields are alight. It's like taking a train through the Thirty Years War.

Alan Bennett

9 September

1937

Today's assignment was the most dangerous of my life – gas escaping from the earth.

The pool of oil under Oklahoma City is amazingly productive. Sometimes 60,000 barrels of oil gush from a single well in one day. This is due to gas pressures so great they have caused spectacular fires here in the city.

Some poor people dig down three feet until they reach a gas pipe and then tap into it by attaching a valve that diverts some of the gas to their homes. Some pipes thus tapped are huge and carry so-called wet gas under pressure suitable only for running engines at oil wells.

The city editor sent me to the east side of town where one such illegal connection has been discovered. The valve had jostled loose, so now gas was escaping at the rate of 100,000 cubic feet per day, according to the fire captain on the scene. It was, in fact, the largest illegal tap ever found here. The hissing of the gas was so loud that we had to shout to be heard. With me was a *Times* photographer who took a shot of the hole in the ground and the disconnected valve. I was afraid the magnesium in his flash bulb might explode the gas and blow up the block.

What does fear feel like? Well, the scalp of my head felt prickly.

Edward Robb Ellis

1939

Yesterday morning while I was waiting for a bus, some soldiers passed down the road singing, 'It's a long way to Tipperary'. An unshaved ragged old tramp wearing the ribbons of several medals so loosely attached to his coat that they were almost falling off, said to me, 'They're singing now, but they won't be singing when they come back. Hearing 'em sing reminds me of when I went to fight in the trenches. We went out singing, but we didn't sing for long.'

There is very little cheering this war. There is no talk of victory. It is a war simply to avoid defeat, and to end the suspense of the last few years with war always hanging over us. The most hopeful thing is this complete lack of desire for a resounding triumph. Get rid of Hitler and then let the Germans do what they like is what the people seem to think.

Stephen Spender

1939

War makes men barbarous because, to take part in it, one must harden oneself against all regret, all appreciation of delicacy and sensitive values. One must live *as if those values did not exist*, and when the war is over one has lost the resilience to return to those values.

Cesare Pavese

1943 [southern Italy]

Landed on 'Red Beach', Paestum [near Salerno], at 7 p.m. Boatloads had been going ashore all day after a dawn shelling from the ships and a short battle for the beach-head. Now an extraordinary false serenity lay on the landward view. A great sweep of bay, thinly pencilled with sand, was backed with distant mountains gathering shadows in their innumerable folds. We saw the twinkle of white houses in orchards and groves, and distant villages clustered tightly on hill-tops. Here and there, motionless columns of smoke denoted the presence of war, but the general impression was one of a splen-did and tranquil evening in the late summer on one of the fabled shores of antiquity.

Norman Lewis

1966

Good press on the Severn Bridge – and my hat. It is almost incredible how much the spotlight is put on one's appearance by TV. Millions of people just talking about the HAT – and about the fact that I bowed instead of curt-seying to the Queen. The *Sun* had a nice photo of me facing the Queen but smiling past her. I was in fact smiling at one of Philip's cracks. When he saw my name as Minister of Transport on the commemorative plaque he said, 'That's pretty cool. It was practically finished before you came along.' Not a bit of it,' I replied, 'It is entirely due to me that it was finished five months ahead of schedule. Anyway I intend to be in on the act.'

Barbara Castle

10 September

1663

Up betimes and to my office, and there sat all the morning making a great contract with Sir W[illiam] Warren for £3,000 worth of masts; but, good God! to see what a man might do were I a knave, the whole business from beginning to end being done by me out of the office, and signed to by them upon the once reading of it. But I hope my pains was such as the king has the best bargain of masts has been bought these 27 years in this office. This day our cook maid (we have no luck in maids now-a-days), which was likely to prove a good servant, though none of the best cooks, fell sick and is gone to her friends, having been with us but 4 days.

Samuel Pepys

1833

He [William IV] hates Louis Philippe and the French with a sort of Jack Tar animosity. The other day he gave a dinner to one of the regiments at Windsor, and as usual he made a parcel of foolish speeches, in one of which, after descanting upon their exploits in Spain against the French, he went on: 'Talking of France, I must say that whether at peace or at war with that country, I shall always consider her as our natural enemy, and whoever may be her King or *ruler*, I shall keep a watchful eye for the purpose of repressing her ambitious encroachments.' If he was not such an ass that nobody does anything but laugh at what he says, this would be very important. Such as he is, it is nothing. 'What can you expect' (as I forget who said) 'from a man with a head like a pineapple?' His head is just of that shape.

Charles Greville

1855 [Balmoral]

Albert said they should go at once and light the bonfire . . . In a few minutes, Albert and all the gentlemen, in every species of attire, sallied forth, followed by all the servants, and gradually by all the population of the village – keepers, gillies, workmen – up to the top of the cairn. We waited, and saw them light it; accompanied by general cheering. The bonfire blazed forth brilliantly, and we could see the numerous figures surrounding it – some dancing, all shouting . . . About three-quarters of an hour after, Albert came down, and said the scene had been wild and exciting beyond everything. The people had been drinking healths in whisky, and were in great ecstasy. The whole house seemed in a wonderful state of excitement. The boys were with difficulty awakened, and when at last this was the case, they begged leave to go up to the top of the cairn.

We remained till a quarter to twelve; and, just as I was undressing, all the people came down under the windows, the pipes playing, the people singing, firing off guns, and cheering, first for me, then for Albert, the Emperor of the French, and the 'downfall of Sebastopol'.

Queen Victoria

1922

Cocteau has sent us a brochure which is entirely about himself. It's the fashion. They open their stomachs and say, 'Look what I've got inside me!' The spectacle is neither clean nor pretty!

Liane de Pougy

1932

Everything is now in shape for the BBC magazine and from various alternatives I chose *Radio Times* for the title.

Lord Reith

1933

After Oxford I think I must try and get a job abroad, even if the prospect is rather frightening. After all the excitement of life needn't end when I go down – it's ridiculous to think of all the thrill being finished when I'm only just twenty-one.

Barbara Pym

1939

I went to Kelvedon on Saturday afternoon in lovely weather in the hope of a peaceful perfect Sunday but it was not to be. There were endless decisions to be made; papers to be stored; fuss and confusion; irritated servants; neglected dogs; plate-room and cellar complications. We packed up all our jewelled toys, the Fabergé bibelots and gold watches, etc., and counted the wine, then we welcomed 150 refugees, all nice East End people, but Honor [his wife] depressed and worn out, and our Sunday not as happy as I had hoped.

On my way I looked in at Bucks and saw several swaggering officers with highly polished belts stuffing themselves with oysters . . . All morning I went about carrying an absurd gasmask in a canvas bag, which I found a bore . . .

'Chips' Channon

1942

I wonder if it's true that all women are born actors. I wonder what I'm *really* like. I know I'm often tired, beaten and afraid, yet someone at the canteen said I radiated confidence. I've a jester's licence at the Centre, and if I stick my bottom lip out and mutter, 'Cor lummy, you've got a blinking nerve,' I can often do more – no, *always* do more – than if I said icily, 'I think that was a perfectly uncalled for remark, and I'd like an apology.' What would I *really* be like if all my nonsense and pretence was taken from me? I have a sneaking feeling I'd be a very scared, ageing woman, with pitifully little. It's an odd thing to reflect: *no* one knows *any*one else, we don't even know ourselves very well.

Nella Last

11 September

1832

Sick of pictures, town, nobility, King, Lords and Commons, I set off by a steamer to Broadstairs. Came in stewed by steam and broiled by sun. I fagged about till sick, and got lodgings for my dears for a short breath of sea air.

Slept at an inn in a small room, fried till morning, got up at half-past five, took a delicious dip and swam exulting like a bull in June, ate a breakfast worthy of an elephant; put off and joined the Ramsgate steamer, and was in town again by half-past four. To-day I am fatigued, and to-morrow I take all my dears down. It is six years since they have changed air but for a day or two. I hope it will do them all good.

B. R. Haydon

1915

In Minsk all was movement; every house, hut and barn was thronging with military and the streets were moving masses of uniformed men and wartime vehicles. Officers were numerous, especially *praporshchiki* [sub-lieutenants], many of whom were walking with Sisters of Mercy at their side; or, rather, may it be said, with ladies who wore the uniform of Sisters. It was strange to look upon some of these women with their painted faces and long gold chains hanging down over the Red Cross on their breast. For many months past, we had been accustomed to the restless, drab existence of field-life, seeing always the dreary colourings of battered earth and darkened skies, and moving always amongst convulsed, apprehensive soldiers, clad in earth-coloured garments; small wonder was it then that we looked on these dandy young officers and on these pink and white, befrilled and becurled women with something akin to awe and perplexity. They, too, were Sisters of Mercy – it was a strange thought! We tried to picture them out there where we had been; passing the long night hours in the open, buffeted by rain and wind; veiled with curtains of thick dust; wearing vermin-infested clothing for days on end; sleeping on benches, floors, under haystacks, on open fields; hunger stricken and thankful beyond measure for dried, black crusts. We looked at our hands; they were rough, reddened, scratched and weatherbeaten; our boots were clumsy, discoloured; and our faces! Ah! surely our faces had suffered the most! The tiny, pocket-mirrors which we carried in our knapsacks could show us only a small part, but we could fill in the rest! We knew without being told, or shown, that our faces were bronzed, freckled, lined by lack of sleep and hardened by the endless effort to endure discomfort and to alleviate pain.

Florence Farmborough

1942

The seat of my office chair, in use for 25 years, is wearing out, my office rug is wearing out, and I am wearing out. As the Chinese say, 'It is later than you think.'

H. L. Mencken

1943 [Naples]

This afternoon we proceeded with our private exploration of the neighbourhood. We are surrounded by a beautiful desolation. All the farms are abandoned, the trees are heavy with apples, and the ripe tomato crop will soon wither. Unhappy animals mooch about looking for water. Two Americans, tired of their packet K rations containing the ham, cheese, biscuits and sweets that seem so desirable to us, chased after a cow that first galloped, then limped, then staggered as they fired innumerable bullets from their pistols into it. Finally they brought it down and hacked off a hindquarter, with which they departed. We took over an empty farmhouse, littered everywhere with the debris of hasty departure: articles of clothing strewn about, unmade beds, a pink-cheeked doll on the floor. Italian soldiers who had walked away from the war were plodding along the railway line in their hundreds on their way to their homes in the south. Their feet were usually in terrible shape, with blood sometimes oozing through the cracked leather of their boots; they were in tremendous spirits, and we listened to the trail of their laughter and song all through the day. I spoke to one of these and gave him a few pieces of cheese salvaged from K ration packs jettisoned by the thousand after the candies they contain had been removed. In return he presented me with a tiny scrap of tinselly material torn from a strip he pulled from his pocket. This was the mantle of a miracle-working Madonna in Pompeii, and by carrying it on my person I would be rendered bullet-proof for at least a year. 'You never know when it might come in handy,' he said, and I agreed.

Norman Lewis

12 September

1940

The Gills [her son's new mother- and father-in-law] left today. Mrs Gill walked round the garden with me, asking me my views on sex – why had I put so much into my books? Some of her friends had been bothered at the idea of Ruth having a mother-in-law who didn't believe in God; but she added that as soon as she saw me she knew it was all right. I never quite know what to say, but explained that I thought sex was rather important, and so one should write about it, simply and straight: also that an attitude of non-attachment about the body was rather important. Not to own people. She asked if I would mind if my sons had sex experience before they were married: I said I thought it was none of my business, but so long as they stuck to kindness and freedom, I would not mind what they did. She said she couldn't think of it like that. But I wonder what Cyril [Mr Gill] feels. She's nice though, but I can't feel she is my own generation.

Naomi Mitchison

1941

Dylan Thomas comes to see me. He wants a job on the B.B.C. He is a fat little man, puffy and pinkish, dressed in very dirty trousers and a loud check coat. I tell him that if he is to be employed by the B.B.C., he must promise not to get drunk. I give him £1, as he is clearly at his wits' end for money. He does not look as if he had been cradled into poetry by wrong. He looks as if he will be washed out of poetry by whisky.

Harold Nicolson

1942

I was going with Mrs Woods to the shop, and taking a short-cut past a street car-park. A plump, marvellously dressed woman was unlocking a gorgeous car door, and our eyes met. She had a flaming crown of red hair, and I knew only one woman with such lovely, vital hair. I put out my hand to find hers outstretched, and I said, 'I'm sure it's Lizzie Turner.' She answered, 'I'm sure it's Nell Lord – I know you by your eyes.' I said, 'And I knew you by your lovely hair' – and it was thirty-three years since we had last met. Mrs Woods said, 'Well, if anyone had told me a thing like that, I'd not have believed it.' Lizzie's life had been like a fairy tale. She married an ambitious man in some way connected with 'textiles'. He had gone to France, where they lived in Lyons, and then on to Madagascar, where he had developed some kind of silk mills. Everything about her breathed luxury, and her tiny, soft plump hands, loaded with emerald rings, spoke of care and freedom from any work.

Emeralds gleamed from her ears and the lace of her dress – she had always said she would wear no jewels but emeralds, and I recalled our laughter.

Her eyes strayed over my white overall, and she said in concern, 'You are not having to *work*, Nell are you?' Mrs Woods said, 'Not having to – choosing to do so,' and we parted. Mrs Woods always says, 'Things *do* happen to you. They don't to *me*.' It gave her quite a thrill to be there at such an odd meeting!

Nella Last

13 September

1786

When you're dealing with water, you can't say: today I'll be in this or that place.

I'm in *Malcesine*, the first place in Venetian territory, on the eastern side of the lake. Now just a bit more about *Torbole*, the harbour where I stayed yesterday.

The inn has no locks on the doors, and the landlord said I could rest easy, even if everything I had with me was diamonds. Then the rooms have no windows, just frames with oil-papers in and yet they're delightful to be in, thirdly no lavatory. So you see one gets pretty close to the state of nature here. When I arrived and asked one of the servants where there was a convenience, he pointed down into the courtyard: *qui abasso! pui servirsi*. I asked him: *dove?* he answered: *per tutto, dove vuol*. [Down there, help yourself . . . where? . . . Anywhere, where you like.] Everything's very happy-go-lucky, but it's all activity and life and all day long the women of the neighbourhood keep up their chattering and shouting, they're always making or doing something, I have yet to see a woman idle.

Johann Wolfgang von Goethe

1930

Folks off to talkies. 'The *Loves* of Robert Burns' – My God! My God! as if he made love so very differently to any one else. Why not 'The Jolly Beggars' of Robert Burns – there's a better talkie for you. But Scotland hasn't any film studios – very few art studios either.

William Soutar

1938

Listened to Hitler's Nuremberg speech on the radio. The call to arms permits a facile eloquence, and it is easier to lead men to combat and stir up their passions than to temper them and urge them to the patient labors of peace. The flattery springs from this: that the affirmation of strength contains a permission of stupidity.

André Gide

1940

A strong feeling of invasion in the air. Roads crowded with army wagons, soldiers. Just back from hard day in London. Raid, unheard by us, started outside Wimbledon. A sudden stagnation. People vanished. Yet some cars went on. We decided to visit lavatory on the hill: shut. So L[eonard, her husband] made use of tree. Pouring. Guns in the distance. Saw a pink brick shelter. That was the only interest of our journey – our talk with the man, woman and child who were living there. They had been bombed at Clapham. Their house unsafe; so they hiked to Wimbledon. Preferred this unfinished gun emplacement to a refugee over-crowded house. They had a roadman's lamp; a saucepan and could boil tea. The nightwatchman wouldn't accept their tea; had his own; someone gave them a bath. In one of the Wimbledon houses there was only a caretaker. Of course they couldn't house us. But she was very nice – gave them a sit down. We all talked. Middle class smartish lady on her way to Epsom regretted she couldn't have the child. But we wouldn't part with her, they said – the man a voluble emotional Celt, the woman placid Saxon. As long as she's all right we don't mind. They sleep on some shavings. Bombs had dropped on the Common. He a housepainter. Very friendly and hospitable. They liked having people in to talk. What will they do? The man thought Hitler would soon be over. The lady in the cocked hat said Never. Twice we left: more guns: came back.

Virginia Woolf

1945

The nine o'clock news announced the discovery of the German blacklist. Among the people to be dealt with when England was invaded were Winston, Vic Oliver, Sybil Thorndike, Rebecca West and me. What a cast!

Noël Coward

1946

Two thoughts:

(1) Do not worry too much about the indiscretion, foolishness or banality of what you write. Leave Time to take care of it all – either to kill it and hide it for ever, or else to change it in its magical way into something strange and rare and not silly at all. This diary, if it is read at all, will make no one blush two hundred years from now. Someone might blush a little in a hundred

years, just as I have squirmed after reading some of Keats's earliest poems this morning.

(2) It becomes more right and acceptable to believe that the other things in the world were made for us to enjoy, if we think that we were made to be enjoyed.

These truisms pounced on me in the very early morning, when I was half in dreamland.

Denton Welch

14 September

1832 [New York]

Sat stitching all the blessed day. At five dressed and went to the Hones, where we were to dine. This is one of the first houses here, so I conclude that I am to consider what I see as a tolerable sample of the ways and manners of being and doing of the *best* society in New York. There were about twenty people, the women in a sort of French demi-toilette with bare necks and long sleeves, hair all frizzed out and thread-net handkerchiefs and capes. The whole of which, to my English eye, appeared a strange marrying of incongruities.

The women here, like those of most warm climates, ripen very early and decay proportionally soon. They are generally speaking, pretty, with good complexions, and an air of freshness, but this I am told is very evanescent. Whereas in England a woman is in the full bloom of health and beauty from twenty to five and thirty, here they scarcely reach the first period without being faded and looking old.

Fanny Kemble

1837

Papa took us to the meeting of the British Scientific Association. [Sir Charles] Wheatstone came up to us in the gallery and was most agreeable and cordial; he told us of his electric conversations which are conducted by subterranean wires between here [Liverpool] and London in a second or two.

Caroline Fox

1865

Trip in steamer. On board a blind man singing to a harmonium played by a woman: 'Became blind at fifteen.' 'Those feel it less who are born blind,' I suggested. 'Perhaps,' he answered, 'but I am glad to have seen the world.'

On deck made friends with a quick bright Boy of seven, whose father sat grave and silent reading letters in a female hand. Boy and I talked oceans of nonsense. Passengers got out at Bournemouth and Yarmouth; then we ran for Lymington by starlight, missed the channel, and stuck in the mud. We had to land by boat, some of the women frightened; one, a smooth fair woman, 'going to Leicester tomorrow', threw her arms around me, which was some compensation. The oars sparkled as they dipped. Landed at the Bath, with wet feet; to Custom House, and home to dinner.

William Allingham

1938

Towards the end of the Banquet came the news, the great world stirring news, that Neville [Chamberlain], on his own initiative, seeing war coming closer and closer, had telegraphed to Hitler that he wanted to see him, and asked him to name an immediate rendezvous. The German Government, surprised and flattered, had instantly accepted and so Neville, at the age of 69, for the first time in his life, gets into an aeroplane tomorrow morning and flies to Berchtesgaden! It is one of the finest, most inspiring acts of all history. The company rose to their feet electrified, as all the world must be, and drank his health. History must be ransacked to find a parallel.

Of course a way out will now be found. Neville by his imagination and practical good sense, has saved the world. I am staggered.

'Chips' Channon

1947

As I was driving home by the Pilgrim's Way above Wrotham Water I came upon a mass of scarlet and red in the corner of a field, that I first mistook for a bright new farm implement. Then as I drew nearer I saw that the mass was soft and not shiny. I then half-explained it to myself as a bundle or folded tent belonging to some very brilliant gypsy. Only when I was almost upon it did I realise that the heap was a man and a woman lying in each other's arms on the stiff dried-up grass. They seemed perfectly still, locked and twisted together intricately – the black legs and arms of the man over the vivid scarlet sausage of the girl's dress. I wondered if they would always remember this Sunday, or whether it would be lost in a vast heap of other clinging, clutching, hugging holidays. Below them the cars rushed by on the arterial road; a man got out of a high old-fashioned Morris, clutched up a handful of yellow flowers and thrust them through the top of the almost shut window to fall on the head of an unheeding child.

Denton Welch

15 September

1907

I forgot to mention that I donned a kilt for the Highland Ball at Glenferness. It was anxious work at first, as it is a garment with no notion of privacy, and delights in giving all present tantalising glimpses of things unseen. However, with careful manipulation and a pair of drawers, I got through the evening tolerably. It is quite comfortable to dance in, but should be a godsend to mosquitoes.

Sir Alan 'Tommy' Lascelles

1922

We have been told that silk will become very expensive this winter, so it's only prudent to lay in a stock. I have ruined myself: white crêpe de chine, black crêpe de chine, white and black satin-backed crêpe, white damask, cyclamen crêpe de chine. Let silk go up, I have nothing to fear. I have enough to dress well for two years.

Liane de Pougy

1927

Last night the unfortunate Isadora Duncan was strangled by her own shawl when it was caught in the back wheel of the car in which she was travelling. The shawl which was so much a part of her dancing has caused her death. Her stage property and slave has taken its revenge on her. Seldom has an artist been so intimately beset by tragedy. Her two small children were killed in a car accident; her husband committed suicide. Now her own life has been ended by this object which was so indispensable to her.

On the evening before the death of her children I was in her box at the Russian ballet. She invited me to luncheon at Neuilly the next day, but I had to refuse because I had an engagement with Hermann Keyserling. The children were supposed to dance for me after the meal. I have always had a feeling that fate intervened and, if I had accepted, the children would not have died.

Count Harry Kessler

1938

Terrible day yesterday: war seemed inevitable. Sick feeling of hopelessness and disgust all day long. Today's news is slightly more reassuring, though Europe remains nearer to disaster than she has been for twenty years.

I suppose we are 'living at an historical moment'. As I write, Chamberlain and Hitler must be having tea together. Charming scene! – This business of heads of governments stepping into aeroplanes and flying off to talk things over with one another may well start a new era in diplomacy.

David Gascoyne

1942 [Jersey]

What a blow has fallen on the island again tonight. In the *Evening Post* there is an Order from a higher authority (Hitler!) saying that all Englishmen, aged 16–70 years, are to be evacuated with their families to Germany. There is no word bad enough to describe the cruelty and beastliness of the Germans. Of course they give no reason whatever for this. Then, to spring this upon us so suddenly; tonight people had orders to leave tomorrow. We have so many friends amongst the English people – it is too dreadful, one can hardly think.

Nan Le Ruez

1964 [Dinner at the Royal Yacht Club]

Charles [Prince of Wales] came to ask me whether I knew Grace [Princess of Monaco] and, on hearing I did, said he particularly wanted to meet her and I promised to fix it.

When Grace eventually did arrive, she sat between Gustaf [King of Sweden] and me and I never had a look in for the first twenty minutes, for they never drew breath talking to each other! Then I had a dance with Grace and finally brought Charles over to sit next to her. They got on like a house on fire, but every time I suggested, in a whisper, that he should ask her to dance he was too shy to do so, and he wouldn't let me help him either. So finally he went away without having asked her.

Earl Mountbatten of Burma

16 September

1852

What makes this such a day for hawks? There are eight or ten in sight from the Cliffs, large and small, one or more with a white rump. I detected the transit of the first by his shadow on the rock, and I look toward the sun for him. Though he is made light beneath to conceal him, his shadow betrays him. A hawk must get out of the wood, must get above it, where he can sail. It is a narrow dodging for him amid the boughs. He cannot be a hawk there, but only perch gloomily. Now I see a large one – perchance an eagle,

I say to myself! – down in the valley, circling and circling, higher and wider. This way he comes. How beautifully does he repose on the air, in the moment when he is directly over you, and you see the form and texture of his wings!

H. D. Thoreau

1932

Very often a thought, like a moth, skims around the flame of complete conscious-ness for some time before it is 'illuminated by acceptance'. We are not wholly unaware of it, but we do not focus on it until it has been on the margin of full consciousness for some time. Yesterday such a thought came into the flame of acceptance – namely, that I cannot hope to live so long as the normally healthy man. A few have lain on their death-bed for 20 years – even granting myself so long, that means I must not look far beyond 50. It is scarcely cred-itable to believe that two-thirds of one's life could be gone so swiftly.

William Soutar

1942

Lovely and sunny, not in keeping with all the happenings. What a day! The evacuation to Germany begins. I went to see if Uncle Gordon had heard anything about himself. It was a shock, as I walked up to the door, to see his small suitcase packed and to hear women's voices saying 'Well, best of luck, Mr Amoore,' and so on. Oh, I thought, he's going. And yes, there he was, just leaving. I couldn't believe it! He has been in Jersey for 40 years. Last night, at 9 o'clock, two Germans, with Constable Crill, arrived to tell him that he must be off by the 4 o'clock boat today. I put his suitcase on my carrier and we walked to the place where a special bus was to pick up all those who were going. Found a good number waiting, so brave, with a smile on their faces as if they were going for a holiday, instead of what I fear, to their deaths perhaps. It is cruel and wicked. Fine boys and girls from our Colleges, waiting there, with blankets on their arms, and their parents with them. One, a typical Englishman, a Mr Fenton, I think, leaning against the wall, with a careless nonchalant air, as if it did not matter at all! Not a sign of what he really felt. As some women were saying to me: 'We must not on any account show the skunks what we feel. We will keep a cheerful face.' How wonderful those English folk are. At last, after an hour's wait, the bus came, and they were all herded in by German soldiers to be driven to the pier. I couldn't help crying a little as the bus went and Uncle waved goodbye. His neighbours took my arm and told me to be brave.

Nan Le Ruez

17 September

1841

At dinner she [Queen Victoria] had the Duke of Wellington next to her (his deaf ear unluckily) and talked to him a good deal. After dinner she spoke to [Prime Minister Sir Robert] Peel, who could not help putting himself into his accustomed attitude of a dancing master giving a lesson. She would like him better if he would keep his legs still. When we went into the drawing room [former prime minister Lord] Melbourne's chair was gone and she had already given orders to the lord-in-waiting to put all the Ministers down to whist, so that there was no possibility of any conversation, and she sat all the evening at her round table. The Queen has no conversation whatever, has never been used to converse with anybody but Melbourne and with him always either on business, or on trifles. She takes no interest in such miscellaneous topics as circulate general society. There was no general conversation. The natural thing would have been to get the Duke of Wellington to narrate some of the events of his life, which are to the last degree interesting, but this never seems to have crossed her mind.

Charles Greville

1907

A peaceful weekend, in which little of interest happened . . . Even if it weren't Harewood, it would always be a most comfortable house to stay in. There are four essentials to comfort – shaving-water that will stay hot for an hour, boot-jacks in every bedroom, grapes for breakfast, and *Ruff's Guide* [*to the Turf*] in the rear [lavatory].

Harewood has them all except, oddly, the last.

Sir Alan 'Tommy' Lascelles

1931 [sailing from Corsica to France]

The 'de luxe' cabin I had to take, since there were no others left, has a divan that will be made up. Deck overcrowded, it is hard to make one's way among the rows of deck-chairs. Mattresses are laid out in the saloons, in the dining-room, in the halls, I think of what a shipwreck, or even a heavy sea, would be like . . .

I should go to sleep at once were it not for these passengers talking in a loud voice outside our porthole. And this until after midnight. And it begins again between one and two. My indignation, especially when faced with such a lack of regard for others, keeps me from sleeping, and the itching [which

a course of autohemotherapy had failed to remedy] starts up again as fero-
cious as ever: like wearing puttees of nettles.

André Gide

1944

What shall I write about? Shall I write about the bright morning with the
sharp bird notes and the delicious spongy cooings of the pigeons on the roof
of this house? Shall I write about the noises of the aeroplanes, the last flower
on the wisteria that I can see mauve and pitiable out of my window? Shall
I write about the war ending? Or my breakfast of porridge, toast and
marmalade and coffee? Or just about autumn. Waking up cold in the morning;
coming back cold through the low blanket of mist by the waterfall last night
– from the pub on Shipbourne Common, where Eric bought me a thim-
bleful of cherry brandy for three shillings, and we heard the loudmouthed
woman holding forth on cubbing before breakfast.

In this house now – in the big part which Eric and I are sleeping in
because Mrs Sloman is away, I have an eighteenth century wooden mantel
in my room, taken from an old house. Then there is a china green basin and
brass locks with drop handles to the doors. The furniture 'limed oak', ugly,
and a chinchilla Persian cat is sleeping and grunting and dribbling on my
bed. Outside the window a tractor is humming. Eric is having a cold bath,
so that the water pipes sing.

Denton Welch

1945

After dinner met two journalists; interviewed by one (all of us) for a National
Press Association article. The other told me I was on a list, published a few
days ago in the *News Chronicle*, of the first people whom the Gestapo intended
to arrest when Nazis invaded England.

Vera Brittain

1986 [during the filming of *Withnail and I*]

A dastardly trick is pulled upon my unsuspecting tonsils during the Drinking
of Lighter Fluid scene. During the camera rehearsal water is the fake fluid,
no doubt matched by the faked gaspings of my acting. Come the take, and
'ACTION' has me upending the little yellow tin down my gullet, and un-
diluted vinegar hits my pipes. I gag, gasp and hope I haven't swallowed
Swarfega, demand, 'GOT ANY MORE?' with demented relish, and then
collapse out of sight and vomit.

'That's the one. Print it,' announces a satisfied [Bruce] Robinson, full of delight at having duped me.

Richard E. Grant

18 September

1859

Dr Bartlett handed me a paper to-day, desiring me to subscribe for a statue to Horace Mann. I declined, and said that I thought a man ought not any more to take up room in the world after he was dead. We shall lose one advantage of a man's dying if we are to have a statue of him forthwith. This is probably meant to be an opposition statue to that of Webster. At this rate they will crowd the streets with them. A man will have to add a clause to his will, 'No statue to be made of me.' It is very offensive to my imagination to see the dying stiffen into statues at this rate. We should wait till their bones begin to crumble – and then avoid too near a likeness to the living.

H. D. Thoreau

1941

The 'Jewish star', black on yellow cloth, at the center in Hebrew-like lettering 'Jew', to be worn on the left breast, large as the palm of a hand, issued to us yesterday for 10 pfennigs, to be worn from tomorrow. The omnibus may *no* longer be used, *only* the front platform of the train. For the time being at least Eva will take over all the shopping, I shall breathe in a little fresh air only under shelter of darkness.

Today we were outside together in daylight for the last time. First cigarette hunt, then on the tram (seat!) to Loschwitz over the suspension bridge, from there along the right bank down by the river toward town as far as the Waldschlösschen. In 21 years we have *never* taken this route. The Elbe, very high, broad, flowing strongly and quietly, a lot of mist, the park gardens behind the high walls autumnal with flowers and falling leaves. A first chestnut fell and burst at our feet. It was like a last day out, a last little bit of freedom before a long (how long?) imprisonment. The same feeling, as we ate in the Löwenbräu in Moritzstrasse.

When one occupant of this house visits another he rings three times. That has been agreed, so that no one catches fright. A simple ring could be the police.

Victor Klemperer

1942

Mrs Crill [wife of the local constable] phoned early to say that her husband got back at 1.45 am and the Germans called for him again before 7 am. He said we could go to Uncle's house to see about his clothes, but later we decided not to touch anything for we know not what other Order is coming out, and we fear to do anything that might bring us into trouble. Anything may annoy the Germans in the state they are in these days. We would rather lose all Uncle's stuff than get into trouble. What are clothes and possessions? It is our lives that matter. We are so afraid of seeing the *Evening Post* because of what may be on; we are in a state of suspense the whole time these days.

10.30 pm The night has come and thank God there was no new Order in the *Evening Post*. How we think of those English families now on board ship on their way to France, open to all dangers. Everyone is in suspense, expecting their turn next, even Jersey folk, wondering if anything is going to happen to us also. We have had many dark days, but none so black as now. Will the dawn come soon?

Nan Le Ruez

1989

Bought Keith Vaughan's *Journal* and collapsed on the bed with it. Sharing his troubles made me aware how lucky I am. I wish now I had got to know him – but when you are young you do not realise your youth is an asset. I never thought I could do anything but bore him – felt tongue-tied, unsophisticated. He mentions he was coming to my exhibition, but never made it. How he would have spent a pleasant afternoon with a group of us.

The last days of the journal are so bleak – the description of the wasps devouring the pears in his garden, flying like bullets; and he, barricaded inside, unable to enjoy a perfect autumn day.

Derek Jarman

19 September

1880

Tennyson – 'A Russian noble, who spoke English well, said one morning to an English guest, "I've shot two peasants this morning" – "Pardon me, you mean pheasants." "No, indeed, two men – they were insolent and I shot them."'

William Allingham

1899 [India]

Took Mrs Gordon out in the buggy. We went out beyond the Towers of Silence and sat under the mango trees for a long time. The moon got up, pale and yellow, over the plain covered with lemon grass and a boy came along and sat on a bank rising out of it; he was just like a faun. At dusk two teams of white bullocks came up out of the fields and trailed slowly over the bank; the grass smelt as only Indian lemon grass can, aromatic and sweet, and the faun got off his rock in front of the huge low moon and followed them slowly home. All disappeared into a dove-coloured horizon as the very last light went.

Violet Jacob

1924

Today my life of poverty, chastity and obedience commences. My mother is purchasing a dog.

Evelyn Waugh

1988

An incredible autumn morning, still and hazy. At seven or thereabouts, before going to the station, I walked the dogs over the Seeds. All the fields are yellow with corn stubble, but in the valley the trees are dark, dark green; in that last cycle before they start to shed their leaves.

I am filled with gloom at the thought of having to go through it all again for yet another year. I am often mindful of that passage in the Moran [Charles McMoran Wilson, 1st Baron] diaries when Churchill is complaining of certain degenerative symptoms – 'Why can't you do something about them?' and Moran tells him, 'You were born with the most wonderful physical endowment. But now you have spent it, every last penny.'

By next autumn I feel that I will be down to my very last reserves of physical, I should say phys*iqu*al, capital. I read a long article in *The Times* on the train, through massive, prolonged, shunting at Tonbridge (even so-called Third World railways can't be this bad, the driver presumably was one of their statutory quota of 'disabled' employees and having an epileptic fit) about *cancer*. I really ought to avoid these blasted A-Doctor-Writes pieces. They're always unsettling. It 'can be undetected – and undetectable for *a long time* before striking'. Really! I thought the whole point was that it grew at colossal speed and, as poor Annie Fleming told Celly, one had to 'run, not walk, to the nearest doctor'?

I have appointed a new secretary, as Peta is leaving to get married. Tedious. Her name is Alison Young. She was not Peta's preferred candidate, but at the interview she showed spirit. I noted that her hair was wet, for some reason, although it was a fine day.

Alan Clark

1990 [Honshu, Japan]

Yesterday I did some sightseeing. We went to Kamakura to the Buddhist temple there which has one of the largest bronze statues of Buddha in the world. It's amazing, this huge thing that dominates the temple – well, the temple isn't there any more, it was blown down by a great tidal wave in the sixteenth century. I was with two of the younger actors, Pete Sullivan and Phil McKee, and the Assistant Director, Cordelia Monsey. I happened to be talking to Cordelia about various things and children, and mentioned that my ex-wife had conceived stillborn twin boys. We were walking up the hill to the temple and as we approached the great Buddha, Peter Sullivan noticed that there was a shrine off to the left. So we went off to the left and were met at the top of the hill by the most extraordinary sight: hundreds of little statues, all covered in baby clothes. I discovered that this was in fact a shrine dedicated to stillborn children and children of abortion, children who had died at birth. The statues had bibs and rattles and little toy windmills and Coca-Cola cans; it was partly obscene but incredibly moving and, given our conversation only five minutes before, the synchronism made the hairs on the back of my neck stand up. I remembered my children and bought some flowers and laid them before a group of these statues.

Brian Cox

20 September

1832 [New York]

At the end of our rehearsal, came home. The weather is sunny, sultry, scorching, suffocating.

By the by, Essex [black servant of a ship's captain] called this morning to fetch away the Captain's claret jug: he asked my father for an order, adding, with some hesitation, 'It must be for the gallery, if you please, sir, for people of colour are not allowed to go to the pit, or any other part of the house.' I believe I turned black myself, I was so indignant.

Fanny Kemble

1938 [Corfu]

We sit for a while over a glass of wine with Spiro [a family friend]. He gives us the gossip of the town. He informs us, with self-importance mixed with a certain shame, that a fire broke out the previous afternoon at a garage. As one of the firemen he had had his first practical experience of fire-fighting. On the whole the affair had been rather a scandal. The brigade had arrived in good time, clinging importantly to the new fire-engine which the

Government had provided, each in his gleaming helmet. Spiro himself had arrived, but riding majestically in his own car, with his helmet on. The garage was well alight. The balconies of the surrounding houses were thronged with sightseers, waiting to see the recently formed Fire Brigade prove itself in its first baptism of fire. All went well. While the hose was being uncoiled the Chief of Police made a short but incisive speech exhorting everyone to stay calm and not to give way to panic. The fire hydrant was unlocked and every-thing placed in position to extinguish the blaze. At this point, however, a disgraceful argument broke out as to who was going to hold the nozzle of the hose. Words became gestures. Gestures became acts. A push here, a scuffle there, and a riot had broken out. A struggling mass of firemen began to fight for possession of the nozzle. At this point the hose bulged and began to emit a creditable jet of water, and what was to be a baptism of fire became a baptism of water for the onlookers. A slowly rotating fountain of water moved across the square. The Minister for the Interior, who had been standing inno-cently on his balcony in heliotrope pyjamas, was all but swept into the street by the force of the jet. Women screamed. The long-averted panic against which the Chief of Police had warned them broke out. The affair ended with a baton charge and a number of arrests. The garage was left to burn itself out. The engine was driven home in disgrace by a civilian. And Spiro tendered his resignation.

Lawrence Durrell

1943

We finally got the jeep to Salerno, but found a battle still going on in the outskirts of the town. German mortar bombs were exploding in the middle of a small square only a hundred yards from Security Headquarters. Here I saw an ugly sight: a British officer interrogating an Italian civilian and repeat-edly hitting him about the head with a chair; treatment which the Italian, his face a mask of blood, suffered with stoicism. At the end of the interro-gation, which had not been considered successful, the officer called in a private of the Hampshires and asked him in a pleasant, conversational sort of manner, 'Would you like to take this man away, and shoot him?' The private's reply was to spit on his hands, and say, 'I don't mind if I do, sir.' The most revolt-ing episode I have seen since joining the forces.

Norman Lewis

1966

We started off from Aberdeen at 10.30 this morning to motor to Balmoral – an absolutely perfect windless autumn day, as we went up the Dee Valley climbing slowly into the mountains. Of course the Grampians are nothing like as beautiful as the west coast. Balmoral was chosen by Prince Albert merely because the weather was drier than in the west. At that time the mountains were almost without trees but now many of them have been beautifully forested. When we arrived we found a typical Scottish baronial house, looking as though it had been built yesterday, with a nice conventional rose garden and by the little church a golf course, which nobody plays except the staff. As soon as we got there I took a little walk with Michael Adeane [Private Secretary to the Queen] by the banks of the Dee and then came back for the Privy Council. As Lord President I had to go and see the Queen first with the papers for the meeting. We chatted for a few moments, then the others came in and lined up beside me and I read aloud the fifty or sixty Titles of the Orders in Council, pausing after every half a dozen for the Queen to say 'Agreed'. When I'd finished, in just two and a half minutes, I concluded with the words, 'So the business of the Council is concluded.' The Privy Council is the best example of pure mumbo-jumbo you can find. It's interesting to reflect that four Ministers, busy men, all had to take a night and a day off and go up there with Godfrey Agnew to stand for two and a half minutes while the list of Titles was read out. It would be simpler for the Queen to come down to Buckingham Palace but it's *lèse-majesté* to suggest it.

Richard Crossman

1979
An interview with a lady called Miss [Sarah] Keays who has been recommended to us as a replacement for Patricia Smallbone when she gets married at Christmas. I thought she was rather good in spite of having a very Tory background, and pretty well decided to engage her. Celia is a bit worried about her because she thinks she is too strong a personality, she will find it very difficult to be as strong a personality as Celia!

Roy Jenkins

21 September

1917
F[elice Bauer] was here, travelled thirty hours to see me; I should have prevented her. As I see it, she is suffering the utmost misery and the guilt is essentially mine. I myself am unable to take hold of myself, am as helpless as I am unfeeling, think of the disturbance of a few of my comforts and, as my only concession, condescend to act my part. In single details she

is wrong, wrong in defending what she calls – or what are really – her rights, but taken all together, she is an innocent person condemned to extreme torture; I am guilty of the wrong for which she is being tortured, and am in addition the torturer. – With her departure (the carriage in which she and Ottla [his sister] are riding goes around the pond, I cut across and am close to her once more) and a headache (the last trace in me of my acting), the day ends.

Franz Kafka

1919

By paying five shillings I have become a member of the Lewes public library. It is an amusing place – full of old ghosts; books half way to decomposition. A general brownness covers them. They are as much alike outwardly as charity schoolchildren. Most have shed their boards years ago, and been recovered in brown paper.

Virginia Woolf

1940 [Berlin]

X came up to my room in the Adlon today, and after we had disconnected my telephone and made sure that no one was listening through the crack of the door to the next room, he told me a weird story. He says the Gestapo is now systematically bumping off the mentally deficient people of the Reich. The Nazis call them 'mercy deaths'. He relates that Pastor Bodelschwingh, who runs a large hospital for various kinds of feeble-minded children at Bethel, was ordered arrested a few days ago because he refused to deliver up some of his more serious mental cases to the secret police. Shortly after this, his hospital is bombed. By the 'British.' Must look into this story.

William L. Shirer

1943 [Naples]

This evening for the first time since the landing we were allowed at last to contribute to the war effort. Someone at Army Headquarters reported suspiciously flashing lights at night in the village of Castello Castelluccia, and someone else remembered the presence of Intelligence personnel in the camp, so we were sent up to make a stealthy Indian approach through the darkness and catch the supposed spy who was presumed to be signalling to the enemy in the hills. We surrounded the village, waited for the light to begin its flashing and then moved in, only to capture a man with a torch on his way to the single outside latrine, used by the entire village.

Norman Lewis

22 September

1832 [New York]

Went into a shop to order a pair of shoes. The shopkeepers in this place with whom I have hitherto had to deal, are either condescendingly familiar, or insolently indifferent in their manner. Your washerwoman sits down before you, while you are standing speaking to her; and a shop-boy bringing things for your inspection, not only sits down, but keeps his hat on in your drawing-room. The worthy man to whom I went for my shoes was so amazingly ungracious, that at first I thought I would go out of the shop; but recollecting that I should probably only go farther and fare worse, I gulped, sat down, and was measured.

All this is bad: it has its origins in a vulgar misapprehension, which confounds ill breeding with independence, and leads people to fancy that they elevate themselves above their condition by discharging its duties and obligations discourteously . . .

Fanny Kemble

1878 [Cévennes]

The bells of Monastier were just knocking nine as I got quit of all my troubles and descended through the common. As long as I was within sight of the windows, a secret shame, and the fear of some laughable defeat, withheld me from tampering with Modestine [his donkey]. She tripped along with a sober daintiness of gait; from time to time she shook her ears or her tail, and she looked so small under the bundle that my heart misgave me. I crossed the ford without difficulty; there was no doubt about the matter, Modestine was docility itself; and once on the other bank, where the road mounts among the pinetrees, I took in my right hand the unhallowed staff and with a quaking spirit, applied it to the donkey. Modestine brisked up her pace for perhaps three steps and then relapsed into her former minuet. Another application had the same effect, and so with another. I am worthy of the name of an Englishman and it goes against my stomach to lay my hand upon a female. I desisted and looked her all over from head to foot. The poor brute's knees were trembling and her breathing was distressed; it was plain that she was pushed to her utmost on the hill. God forbid, thought I, that I should brutalise this innocent creature; let her go at her own pace, and let me patiently follow.

Robert Louis Stevenson

1936

Chips [Channon] is not really a snob in an ordinary way. I suppose everyone has some snobbishness somewhere just like everybody has a few keys somewhere.

What makes Chips so exceptional is that he collects keys for keys' sake. The corridors of his mind are hung with keys which open no doors of his own but are just other people's keys which he collects. There they hang – French keys, English keys, American keys, Italian keys and now a whole housekeeper's truss of Central European keys.

Harold Nicolson

1939

Honor [his wife] came up yesterday and I took her, Brigid and Harold Balfour to luncheon at the Ritz which has become fantastically fashionable; all the great, the gay, the Government; we knew 95% of everyone there. But Ritzes always thrive in wartime, as we are all cookless. Also in wartime the herd instinct rises . . .

'Chips' Channon

1941 [Dresden]

Yesterday shut in all day in glorious weather, in the evening sneaked out for a couple of minutes . . . Even though I went to the grocer's on Wasaplatz on Saturday – as I went back to the wheel after the car accident – the dreadful aversion has not gone. Every step, the thought of every step is desperation. – Lissy Meyerhof writes from Berlin: Passers-by sympathized with the star wearers. She also writes, we should be optimistic, Aryan friends told her, this was the final act. – I too believe it is the fifth act. But some plays in world literature, e.g., Hugo's *Cromwell*, have *six* acts.

On Kreidl's advice, I am now smoking the blackberry tea, which Eva drinks and which I loathe, in my pipe.

Victor Klemperer

23 September

1773 [touring the Western Isles and Hebrides]

As we sailed along Dr Johnson got into one of his fits of railing at the Scots. He owned that they had been a very learned nation for a hundred years, from about 1550 to 1650; but that they afforded the only instance of a people among whom the arts of civil life did not advance in proportion with learning; that they had hardly any trade, any money, or any elegance, before the

Union; that it was strange that, with all the advantages possessed by other nations, they had not any of those conveniences and embellishments which are the fruit of industry, till they came in contact with a civilized people. 'We have taught you, (said he,) and we'll do the same in time to all barbarous nations, – to the Cherokees, – and at last to the Ouran-Outangs;' laughing. . . . – BOSWELL. 'We had wine before the Union.; – JOHNSON. 'No, sir, you had some weak stuff, the refuse of France, which would not make you drunk.' – BOSWELL. 'I assure you, sir, there was a great deal of drunkenness.' – JOHNSON. 'No, sir; there were people who died of dropsies, which they contracted in trying to get drunk.'

James Boswell

1878 [Cévennes]

Blessed be the man who invented goads! Blessed the innkeeper of Bouchet Saint-Nicolas who introduced me to their use! Thenceforward, Modestine [his donkey] was my slave, my chattel, my most obedient, humble servant. A prick and she passed the most inviting stabledoor! A prick and she broke out into a gallant little trotlet that devoured the miles! It was not a remarkable speed when all is said; we took four hours to cover ten miles at the best of it; but what a heavenly change since yesterday! No more wielding of the ugly cudgel, no more flailing with an aching arm; no more broadsword exercise, but a discreet and gentlemanly fence. But what although now and then a drop of blood should appear on Modestine's mouse-coloured, wedge-like rump? I should have preferred it otherwise, indeed, but yesterday's exploits had purged my heart of all humanity. The perverse little devil, if she would not be taken with kindness, must even go with pricking.

Robert Louis Stevenson

1931

Yesterday Fernande Cabanel and her companion Sacha Xanaris, took me into Toulon for the afternoon. On the way Fernande said to me: 'I have some very urgent shopping to do. I'm completely out of something which I have to have. It is making me ill. Yesterday I tried to use some of Sacha's drug but it's too heavy, too strong for me. It upset me dreadfully. Jean Cocteau is here, we'll look him up and he's sure to be able to give me an address.' – 'Fine,' I said. 'Jean is an old friend of mine and I'd like to see him again.' She took me down to the port, near the Arsenal, and led me along a horrible street with reeking gutters which ran parallel with the quay. It was lined on either side with the most frightful shady-looking hotels. She said: 'Oh God – Jean is living in one of these.' We went into a foul slum called Hôtel du Port des Négociants . . . Liou opened the door of a sordid room, letting out a strong whiff of the drug. It was sinister – what an extraordinary pleasure it is! Jean was lying on the floor covered with a disgusting bedspread, behind a horribly filthy bed. His voice was deathly, dull, dry, hoarse. He said: 'What are you doing, Liou? Shut the door. Don't let anyone in. I'm very ill. I backed out onto the narrow landing, but Fernande went in: 'Jean, for pity's sake give me an address. Liane is here with me.' What can he have thought? That I too have started to smoke? He answered almost inaudibly: 'Liou, give her some of my special supply: three francs a gramme. Forgive me, if you knew how ill I am! Lock the door, Liou.'

I got a glimpse of Jean, thin, pale, drawn, a shadow of himself and he was already a shadow. He had a three-day beard and his clothes were in disorder, dirty and crumpled. We went into Liou's room, even more sordid. On the wall a drawing of Jean's, signed and inscribed 'To my dear Liou', and a page of poetry in his handwriting: 'To my dear Liou.' 'How Jean squanders himself,' whispered Fernande while Liou opened a mould-smelling cupboard. Liou: 'Here are 700 grammes, Madame, that will be 2,100 francs.' Fernande: 'That's too much for me. I'm afraid of overdoing it if I have a big supply.' He went back to the cupboard and took out a smaller pot. 'Here are 150 grammes for 450 francs.' – 'That will do,' said Fernande. 'That will keep me going for two months.' She paid and we left.

Liane de Pougy

1944 [Naples]

When I first moved into the hotel I noticed that Don Enrico, enthroned in his wicker armchair in a position in which he could keep under observation every person who entered or left the hotel, occasionally groped in his pocket to touch his testicles on the appearance of a stranger. This, Don Ubaldo explained to me, was a precaution – commonplace in the South, but frequently practised by Northerners, including Mussolini himself – to ward off the evil eye. On two or three occasions in the last week I have noticed women hastily cover their faces with a scarf or a veil at my approach, and scuttle past with averted faces. This, apparently, is how women deal with the problem. Now, this evening, coming into the hotel, I found a row of half a dozen regulars – Don Enrico included – sitting under the palms, and at the sight of me I seemed to notice a sly movement of every left hand towards the right side of the crutch. A disconcerting confirmation of loss of favour.

Norman Lewis

1949

Wrote [*Guardian*] leader on Russia having the atomic bomb which has created a great sensation. Find it quite impossible to get excited about the atomic bomb as such, can't see that it really alters anything.

Malcolm Muggeridge

1949

Mr [Harry] Truman announced today that Russia had set off its first atomic explosion. Public reaction was varied. One Republican remarked: 'Pretty soon he'll be announcing that the Chinese discovered gunpowder.' It reminds me of the dull, dead days of the early 30s when almost anyone could see that a dictator was building up in Europe who would eventually cause war. Those were the days when the people were much more interested in the stock market and the nationwide wave of kidnappings than they were in storm clouds abroad. Today the Brooklyn Dodgers are one-half behind St Louis in the National League and the Yanks and the Boston Red Sox are neck and neck. And the American public is basically probably more interested in this race than in the race of atomic energy.

Drew Pearson

24 September

1870

In the capital of fresh food and early vegetables, it is really ironical to come across Parisians consulting one another in front of the displays of tinned goods in the windows of delicatessen shops or cosmopolitan groceries. Finally they go in, and come out carrying tins of *Boiled Mutton, Boiled Beef,* etc., every possible and impossible variety of preserved meat and vegetable, things that nobody would ever have thought might one day become the food of the rich city of Paris.

The Brothers Goncourt

1937 [Nanking]

In the long hours of crouching in the dugout during the recent bombardment, I turned on Radio Shanghai to take my mind off things with a little music, and they were playing Beethoven's Funeral March, then to make matters worse they announced to their listeners: 'This music is kindly dedicated to you by the Shanghai Funeral Directors.'

John Rabe

1938

Sometimes we may wonder why the relationship of man and woman occupies so large a portion of life and art – but the reason is obvious enough. For the majority of folk, the mutuality of sex is the one relationship which links them to life in vital partnership. Even at its nadir, sex exemplifies the law of gain by reciprocity; even at its blindest, there is acknowledgement of the beauty which is the image of reality. But in true love, sex is the common ground whereon all may find the joy of creative experience.

The other becomes a quintessential knowledge of life's demand for unconditional trust, of life's basic interdependence, so that in the tangible we have a vision of the oneness of things. And with the child, the creative act of faith is come to fullness; in the child, desire and life's need meet, and there both death and life meet and are indistinguishable.

William Soutar

1940

I detect in myself a certain area of claustrophobia. I do not mind being blown up. What I dread is being buried under huge piles of masonry and hearing water drip slowly, smelling the gas creeping towards me and hearing the faint cries of colleagues condemned to a slow and ungainly death. Always as I write this diary the guns boom. One writes that phrase, yet it means nothing. There is the distant drumfire of the outer batteries. There is the nearer crum-crum of the Regent's Park guns. Then there is the drone of aeroplanes and the sharp impertinent notes of some nearer batteries. FF-oopb! they shout. And then in the middle distance there is the rocket sound of the heavy guns in Hyde Park. One gets to love them, these angry London guns. And when they drop into silence, one hears above them, irritating and undeterred, the dentist's drill of the German aeroplanes, seeming always overhead, appearing always to circle round and round, ready always to drop three bombs, flaming, and then . . . crump, crump, crump, somewhere. Is it Bond Street, or Lincoln's Inn Fields? Are Victorian or Georgian buildings slipping down under the crunch of that distant noise? I feel no fear nor anger. Hum and boom. Always I write my nightly diary to that accompaniment.

Harold Nicolson

25 September

1661

Much against my nature and will, yet such is the power of the Devil over me I could not refuse it, to the Theatre, and saw 'The Merry Wives of Windsor,' ill done.

Samuel Pepys

1909

Bad sleeping for a week or two. I waste 2 or 3 hours of every night in useless bed. So I am trying to stay up later. This morning I didn't sleep after 4.30. I got up at 6.15. I went out at 8 to think about my play [*The Honeymoon*], and returned at 10, having done 2 hours' walking in hot sunshine and two hours' thinking. And I was exhausted for the day. I could easily have gone to sleep before lunch.

Arnold Bennett

1939

The PM [Neville Chamberlain] flew back to London yesterday, convened the Cabinet, and had an audience with the King, who has been fitted, like everyone else in London, with a gasmask. There seems to be some hysteria: here all is calm and great beauty. We have our meals alone, the Regent [Paul of Greece], Honor [his wife] and I, and wonder sadly when we will all be together again.

'Chips' Channon

26 September

1818

Had a thorn taken out of the middle of that part of the body which Derham calls a large cushion of flesh by my wife last night.

Rev. Benjamin Newton

1892

Last night, between eleven and twelve, we thought we heard the special [funeral] train taking the Duke of Sutherland on his long, last journey. Some people can see no sentiment or beauty in a railway, simply a monstrosity and a matter of dividends. To my mind there is scarcely a more splendid beast in the world than a large locomotive: if it loses something of mystery through being the work of man, it surely gains in a corresponding degree the pride of possession. I cannot imagine a finer sight than the Express, with two engines, rushing down this incline at the edge of dusk.

The Scotch dote upon funerals and mourning, but I have not seen a scrap of crêpe about the Highland Railway. The unfortunate ending of the Duke's life would probably make little difference in Scotland in the way of dropping him out of favour. It is my opinion that, under a thin veneer of intelligence and gentility, they are all savages, highly descended of course, and the more savage the more hoity-toity, but, making certain slight allowance for circumstances, there are no Class divisions whatever.

Beatrix Potter

1928

I have at last finished D. H. Lawrence's *Lady Chatterley's Lover*. Generally speaking, the lechery scenes are the best.

Arnold Bennett

1938

Today I heard the voice of Adolf Hitler. Some other people and I sat on a balcony in the Black Hotel and listened on the radio to what is being called the Munich Crisis. Hitler spoke in German, of course, his words being translated into English as he spoke. He demanded that Czechoslovakia give Germany the Sudeten area of that country, which is inhabited by a German-speaking minority. Prime Minister Neville Chamberlain has flown from England to Germany to confer with Hitler. He has been called the Mad Dog of Europe, and now I understand why: His demands are extreme and his oratory so menacing that he chills one's blood.

The war scare is a reality here in Oklahoma City. People buy the latest editions of newpapers and talk about diplomacy and war. Young men ask one another how they feel about conscription. Young women tremble lest their men be thrust into battle. I, for one, am a coward and an isolationist. Not only do I not want to go to war, but I don't consider it necessary for the United States to enter the war that seems about to begin.

Edward Robb Ellis

1940 [Berlin]

It burns me up that I cannot mention a raid that is going on during my broadcast. Last night the anti-aircraft guns protecting the *Rundfunk* made such a roar while I was broadcasting that I couldn't hear my own words. The lip microphone we are now forced to use at night prevented the sound of the guns accompanying my words to America, which is a pity. Noticed last night too that instead of having someone talk to New York from the studio below to keep our transmitter modulated for the five minutes before I began to talk, the RRG substituted loud band music. This was done to drown out the sound of the guns.

As soon as I had finished my broadcast at one a.m., the Nazi air-wardens forced me into the air-raid cellar. I tried to read but the light was poor. I became awfully bored. Finally Lord Haw-Haw and his wife suggested we steal out. We dodged past the guards and found an unfrequented underground tunnel, where we proceeded to dispose of a litre of schnapps which 'Lady' Haw-Haw had brought. Haw-Haw can drink as straight as any man, and if you can get over your initial revulsion at his being a traitor, you find him an amusing and intelligent fellow. When the bottle was finished we felt too free to go back to the cellar. Haw-Haw found a secret stairway and we went up to his room, opened the blinds, and watched the fireworks.

Sitting there in the black of the room, I had a long talk with the man. Haw-Haw, whose real name is William Joyce, but who in Germany goes by the name of Froelich (which in German means 'Joyful'), denies that he is a traitor. He argues that he has renounced his British nationality and become a German citizen, and that he is no more a traitor than thousands of British and Americans who renounced their citizenship to become comrades in the Soviet Union, or than those Germans who gave up their nationality after 1848 and fled to the United States. This doesn't satisfy me, but it does him. He kept talking about 'we' and 'us' and I asked him which people he meant.

'We Germans, of course,' he snapped.

William L. Shirer

1943

I hope I shall be remembered as a poet, if for no other reason than that my folks may not be forgotten, nor the fact that they had done so much for me and had received so little in return.

William Soutar

1967 [Bolivia]

A nerve-racking day, which at one point seemed like it would be our last. Early in the morning water was brought up, and right afterward Inti and Willi [guerrillas] went to scout another possible descent into the canyon. However, they returned immediately since there is a road spanning across the entire hill in front of us, with a peasant on horseback traveling along it.

At ten o'clock, 46 soldiers passed right in front of us, carrying knapsacks, and it seemed to take centuries for them to pass by. At noon, another group appeared, this time with 77 men. And to top it all off, a shot was heard just then, which made the soldiers take positions. The officer ordered them to go down the ravine, which appeared to be the one we were in. Finally, however, there was a radio communication and the officer seemed satisfied and resumed the march.

Our refuge has no defense against attack from above, and if we are detected, the possibilities of escape are remote. Later on a soldier passed by, pulling a tired dog behind him, trying to get him to walk. Later still, a peasant went by, guiding another soldier behind him. Later on, the peasant made a return trip, and nothing happened this time. However, the anxiety at the moment the shot was fired was great indeed.

Che Guevara

27 September

1911

Yesterday on the Wenzelsplatz met two girls, kept my eye too long on one while it was just the other, as it proved too late, who wore a plain, soft, brown, wrinkled, ample coat, open a little in front, had a delicate throat and delicate nose, her hair was beautiful in a way already forgotten. – Old man with loosely hanging trousers on the Belvedere. He whistles; when I look at him he stops; if I look away he begins again; finally he whistles even when I look at him. – The beautiful large button, beautifully set low on the sleeve of a girl's dress. The dress worn beautifully too, hovering over American boots. How seldom I succeed in creating something beautiful, and this unnoticed button and its ignorant seamstress succeeded. – The woman talking on the way to the Belvedere, whose lively eyes, independent of the words of the moment, contentedly surveyed her story to its end. The powerful half-turn of the neck of a strong girl.

Franz Kafka

1934

It is very difficult to spend less than £200 a morning when one goes out shopping.

'Chips' Channon

1989

K has been auditioning extras for his film, including a woman who had put down among her special accomplishments 'Flirting with Japanese men'. Had this been a joke it would almost certainly have got her the job, but it turns out to be true. She is irresistibly drawn to the Japanese and has learned the language in order to flirt more effectively. Passing Japanese in the street, she will sometimes murmur (in Japanese), 'I would like to cut your toenails in the warmth of my own home' – apparently a standard come-on in the Land of the Rising Sun.

'And does it work?' asks K. 'Oh yes. Quite often.'

Alan Bennett

1995 [filming in Ireland]

I have managed to squeeze a helicopter from the production for a series of shots that will show the group of ambushers running over the heather towards the heights, then reveal the sweeping valley below, with the convoy snaking through it. The wind is whipping up dangerously, and while waiting for the chopper to arrive I shoot some cover on yesterday's scenes and we have our first serious accident. The shots involve the ambushers taking up position round a statue on the heights above us. One of them falls through the heather, into a hidden chasm, and nobody can get to him. The scene for a while is truly horrible. Screams of panic from above, people trying to climb the inaccessible rocks from below to reach him. We call an emergency helicopter from the military airport nearby and manage to get him out, on to a stretcher, shot with painkillers, as comfortable as he can be. Then, while we are waiting for the emergency chopper to arrive, I begin shooting again. My daughter, Sarah, who is working as a PA and is unused to the callous practicality of a film unit, berates me for being heartless. I try to explain to her that our activity or inactivity down here below won't make the cavalry arrive sooner, so to speak. Mike Roberts smiles wryly, sitting on the dolly, and tells her he fully expects to croak it in mid-shot some day and for the next take to begin while his body's still warm. Then the chopper does arrive, the stuntman is winched up from the heather and we are told by radio that he is fine.

The winds are howling by now and our own chopper has arrived. The pilot, an Irishman with experience in Vietnam, decides to give it a go, though the vortex the winds are creating above the valley makes it extremely dangerous. I go up with them and take them through the shot, bouncing around the skies like a puppet whose strings are about to snap. The shot is spectacular, and the problem as always is trying to get the aircraft low enough, within the margins of safety. Most of these unit helicopter pilots have brief lives and, being up there with him, I can understand why. The extras down below only have so much running in them, particularly after the accident. Leaping over mounds of heather, at full speed, with a helicopter trying to breathe down your neck in a force 9 gale is not the best way to earn your living. After several takes, everyone gives up from exhaustion, and I can feel the film is truly winding itself down.

Neil Jordan

28 September

1940 [SS *The Empress of Britain*. At sea.]

This is Hades. We are clamped down below decks because we are passing enemy territory. The purser told me that the last convoy which came through took a terrible pasting from Italian planes based in Eritrea and Italian Somaliland. For four days we will be in danger. The heat is unbelievable. The swimming pool has been emptied for this perilous period.

At midday, when the bar opens, the rush for it is astonishing. Toby says we're in a floating inebriates' home. The officer commanding troops confided in me today that the lower decks are fast turning into a brothel. He has had to post sentries to try to restore order.

Toby keeps trying to persuade me to go home with her but I am adamant that somehow I will get back to the Middle East. I am reading a lovely book called *Sand, Wind and Stars* [in fact, *Wind, Sand and Stars*], by [Antoine de] St-Exupéry. He tells a delightful story about flying over the Andes and carrying a bowl of goldfish in his plane so as to be sure which way up he was. Quite a lot of people are 'enjoying the voyage'. The officers and crew of this ship are quite remarkable. They have superb discipline, manners and kindness but they have incessant problems – they are often in danger and they must be worried for their own families in England.

Mrs Chitty, a very senior AT, who has just surfaced after being seasick since Suez, is being sent home to recruit shorthand typists for the Middle East. She has kindly promised to recruit me if I return to England!

Countess of Ranfurly

1959

Last night I went to Elsa Lanchester's. Oh the horror of TV! It is so utterly, utterly *inferior*, yet just enough to keep you enslaved, entrapped, on the lower levels of consciousness – for a whole lifetime, if necessary. It is a bondage like that of Tennyson's Lady of Shalott.

Christopher Isherwood

1965

Signing session at Claude Gill [bookshop]. There was quite a crowd to greet me & all went well. Then came the nightmare! On the way to the tube, three young thugs recognised me & pursued us all the way on to the train & began a harangue about a mother dying of cancer: 'Please write a letter to her . . . she is dying.' I said 'We all are' & certainly felt it! Eventually they left, spitting at me. I thought the public transport idea was wrong from the beginning. I should have gone by car.

Kenneth Williams

29 September

1662

(Michaelmas Day.) This day my oaths for drinking of wine and going to plays are out, and so I do resolve to take a liberty to-day, and then to fall to them again. To the King's Theatre, where we saw 'Midsummer's Night's Dream,' which I had never seen before, nor shall ever again, for it is the most insipid ridiculous play that ever I saw in my life. I saw, I confess, some good dancing and some handsome women, which was all my pleasure.

Samuel Pepys

1911

Goethe's diaries. A person who keeps none is in a false position in the face of a diary. When for example he reads in Goethe's dairies: '1/11/1797. All day at home busy with various affairs', then it seems to him that he himself had never done so little in one day.

Franz Kafka

1935

Yesterday I saw the kingfisher again on the river. It flies across and across, very near the surface: it has a bright orange chocolate under side. And it is a tropical bird, sitting weighted on the bank. I have also seen a stoat – brown with a white tipped tail.

Virginia Woolf

1938

In the train the Duce is in a very good humour. We dine together and he speaks with great vivacity on every subject. He criticizes Britain and British policy severely. 'In a country where animals are adored to the point of making cemeteries and hospitals and houses for them, and legacies are bequeathed to parrots, you can be sure that decadence has set in. Besides, other reasons apart, it is also a consequence of the composition of the English people. Four million surplus women. Four million sexually unsatisfied women, artificially creating a host of problems in order to excite or appease their senses. Not being able to embrace one man, they embrace humanity.'

Count Ciano

1938

Yesterday a great rush for provisions began. One lady I heard of has her house quite full of tinned foods of every kind. The only thing I bought was my special brand of China tea: I have got 14 lbs which will last me for a year. I also got last week rather more methylated spirits, rice and matches than usual, but nothing out of the way.

I was guided by my experience in the last war. The fact that I had a gross of matches in the early August of 1914 was of the greatest value. It is one of the things – strange to say – in which there quickly becomes a shortage. I also found then the great value of rice when cooked and mixed with fried onions and a little butter: it really makes a meal for anyone. I ran out of methylated spirits in the last war and had great trouble making my early morning tea before my work – in fact, I was forced to use the Tommy Cookers and the stuff people used for heating their hair tongs, both expensive and unpleasant to use.

Marie Belloc Lowndes

1939

Warsaw has surrendered. Poland is being partitioned by Germany and Russia. I telephoned Jan Smeterlin [Polish pianist] in London. He was so upset he could hardly speak. 'Hold on,' he said. 'I'll put the receiver down on my piano.' He played me a little sad Chopin and then came back on the line – 'That's how I feel,' he said, and hung up.

Firearm Certificate No. 2802 has arrived from the Leicestershire Police. A note was enclosed: 'We had a good laugh over your application – "For use against parachutists".' Now I can collect my revolver and ten rounds of ammunition.

Countess of Ranfurly

1942

More than a thousand English people were due to leave today. We heard that many Jersey people, too, had been warned last night to go today. These were men or women who had served sentences in prison for so-called sabotage, curfew and black-market offences. Some of these had served a month in prison in France, come back home, and are now called to be taken to prison camp in Germany. All day we've been thinking of those hundreds being taken away, and all day Russians have been coming to the house for food – they escape for a few minutes when the Germans' backs are turned.

Nan Le Ruez

1943

There is a quirkiness about a diary which cannot be assessed: something which may seem to the diarist himself to be of real importance may in later days prove a bore; and some little aside or comment which just dropped from his pen, by the way, may prove to be a most penetrating glimpse of a situation, or a revolutionary flash lighting up some strange corner of the spirit. The true diary is one, therefore, in which the diarist is, in the main, communing with himself, conversing openly and without pose, so that trifles will not be absent, nor the intimate little confessions and resolutions which, if voiced at all, must be voiced in such a private confessional as this.

William Soutar

30 September

1832 [Delaware]

The few cottages and farm houses which we passed reminded me of similar dwellings in France and Ireland; yet the peasantry here have not the same excuse for disorder and dilapidation as either the Irish or French. The farms had the same desolate, untidy, untended look: the gates broken, the fences carelessly put up, or ill repaired: the farming utensils sluttishly scattered about a littered yard, where the pigs seemed to preside by undisputed right: house-windows broken, and stuffed with paper or clothes; dishevelled women, and barefooted, anomalous looking human young things; – none of the stirring life and activity which such places present in England and Scotland; above all, none of the enchanting mixture of neatness, order, and rustic elegance and comfort, which render so picturesque the surroundings of a farm, and the various belongings of agricultural labour in my own dear country.

Fanny Kemble

1884

It seems they will not give a child Christian burial at Hatfield unless it has been baptized. I believe it is still a common superstition that a child goes to the wrong place unless baptized. How can anyone believe that the power above us – call it Jehovah, Allah, Trinity, what they will – is a just and merciful father, seeing the end from the beginning, and will yet create a child, a little rosebud, the short-lived pain and joy of its mother's heart, only to consign it after a few days of innocence to eternal torment?

Beatrix Potter

1915

I did expect I should at least hear something to-day but no news came. Again I wandered about but every telegraph boy I saw going in the direction of the Park made me hasten home, and every loud ring at the bell when I was in the house made my heart beat so fast that I felt choked & stifled. From all sides I heard that people had been getting news of casualties during the last few days, and *The Times* obituary list was long with the names of people who had fallen in France & Flanders, chiefly on the 25th & 26th. But in a war like this no news does not necessarily mean good news – quite the reverse. It simply means that in certain parts of the line there has been more confusion than in others. Loos is probably one of those places as the most vigorous part of our attack took place there. It makes me so angry to think that so many people are hearing news of their relations & friends – are even getting them back wounded, but *I* can hear nothing of my one dear soldier. It is impossible he can have come through unharmed; he may be flung unidentified on a pile of forgotten dead, or perhaps dying in some French hospital among strangers who know nothing about him beyond the information on his identity disc.

The Allies' advance seems to be waning somewhat in fury. Well, I wonder if yet *another* day will pass & leave me still in suspense.

Vera Brittain

1938

I was called at 8 a.m.: by my side lay the newspapers – 'Agreement signed at 12.53 in Munich.' So it is peace, and a Chamberlain, respectable gentleman's peace: the whole world rejoices whilst only a few malcontents jeer.

'Chips' Channon

1990 [Labour Party Conference, Blackpool]

Two well-dressed men came up to me at the Conference and said, 'Excuse me, sir, we are from the police. We have to advise you that somebody with a northern accent rang the *Daily Mirror* this morning saying that a contract had been put out to kill you and Ken Livingstone. Do you know where Mr Livingstone is?'

I said, 'I'll see him later, and I'll tell him. Thanks.'

I daresay we are back in the old routine of death threats, with the Gulf crisis.

The layout of the Conference is fantastic – lots of photographs and the slogan, 'Looking to the Future'. The rostrum is quite separate from the platform and everybody has been pushed up on to the second row, except for 'leading figures'. It is now all stage-managed for the telly. It is symbolic of the separation between the leadership and the membership.

Tony Benn

OCTOBER

'I regret, dear Journal, this unworthy, sordid preoccupation with money, but I have worked hard all my life, I am £15,000 overdrawn in London, I am fifty-five years old and I fully intend to end my curious days in as much comfort, peace and luxury as I can get.'

NOËL COWARD

1 October

1909

We dined at the Boeuf à la Mode. A dull, good, nice restaurant. I gave the waiter my usual 10%, which happened to be 70 centimes. He was apparently not content, but politely thanked me. As he carried the plate out with the change on it, he held it the least bit in the world at arm's length, exposing it with scorn to the inspection of the *chasseur* as he passed him. It was a fine, subtle gesture, and pleased me as much as it annoyed me.

Arnold Bennett

1930

Began reading through the *Encyclopædia Britannica* today. Another ten years' project, at least. My odyssey through Chambers' *Twentieth Cent. Dictionary* seems to be within a year of completion – that will make it nine years – one less than my calculated time.

William Soutar

1939

Exactly one month since England's declaration of war. The unimaginable has happened – and, of course, it's utterly different from anything we had pictured. One looks ahead to a war and imagines it as a single, final, absolute event. It is nothing of the kind. War is a condition, like peace, with good days and bad days, moods of optimism and despair. The crisis of August was actually, for us in Santa Monica, worse than this month which has followed the outbreak. I see Frau Frank's face, contorted with hate. I hear Gottfried Reinhardt yelling, Klaus Mann chattering like an enraged monkey. Berthold snorting like a war-horse. The night war was declared, Vernon and I sat listening to our radio at home. It was as though neither of us were really present. The living room seemed absolutely empty – with nothing in it but the announcer's voice. No fear, no despair, no sensation at all. Just hollowness.

Christopher Isherwood

2 October

1784

Rowed up the river as far as the lock, the longest row I ever took. Reflection on the folly of supposing oneself incapable of that which one has never properly attempted.

William Windham

1944 [Palestine]

After a typical cup of Naafi tea – dark with beige-coloured milk – Viola [her pianist] and I wandered in search of the beach. 'Officers' Lido is good,' the proprietor had told us. I haven't got a bathing suit but I thought a pair of fairly opaque lock-knit knickers and a bandana skilfully tied around my chest would do. However when we finally reached the beach it was entirely covered by swarms of all-sized high-legged and incredibly speedy crabs. We took against bathing after this and sat on a marooned raft gazing at the sunset over the sea. Washing in a tin saucer-sized basin requires talent but I have it and made a complete toilet before supper. The club was quite active. Three girls in civilian clothes, six or seven rather nondescript officers. We ate our meal, and then went for a stroll under the moon. It was hot and still. The breeze doesn't rise in the evening here as it does in Cairo. I must say I will always have a very special feeling for Cairo, but I don't think Samson missed much by being eyeless in Gaza. It is remarkably unremarkable.

Joyce Grenfell

1955

Communion. The clocks should have been changed. We remembered to get up late but lunched early by mistake.

Evelyn Waugh

1958

At Cliveden. A young man related a story about Nancy Astor, an occasion when she was worsted by no less a person than Winston Churchill, with whom she was never on very good terms. She said: 'If I'd been your wife, Winston, I'd have put poison in your coffee.' His retort was: 'If I'd been your husband, Nancy, I'd have taken poison.'

Maurice Collis

3 October

1833 [Santa Fe]

I was confined for these two days to my bed by a headache. A good-natured old woman, who attended me, wished me to try many odd remedies. A common practice is to bind an orange leaf or a bit of black plaster to each temple; and a still more general plan is to split a bean into halves, moisten them, and place one on each temple, where they will easily adhere. It is not thought proper ever to remove the beans or plaster, but to allow them to drop off; and sometimes if a man with patches on his head is asked what is the matter, he will answer, 'I had a headache the day before yesterday.' Many of the remedies used by the people of the country are ludicrously strange, but too disgusting to be mentioned. One of the least nasty is to kill and cut open two puppies and bind them on each side of a broken limb. Little hairless dogs are in great request to sleep at the feet of invalids.

Santa Fe is a quiet little town, and is kept clean and in good order. The governor, López, was a common soldier at the time of the revolution, but has now been seventeen years in power. This stability of government is owing to his tyrannical habits, for tyranny seems as yet better adapted to these countries than republicanism. The governor's favorite occupation is hunting Indians; a short time since he slaughtered forty-eight and sold the children at the rate of three or four pounds apiece.

Charles Darwin

1896

At twelve went down to below the terrace, near the ballroom, and we were all photographed by Downey by the new cinematograph process, which makes moving pictures by winding off a reel of film. We were walking up and down.

Queen Victoria

1939

During a conversation which Mr M— had shared lately with a certain Mrs B— (the wife of a K— undertaker), the lady confided that her husband had been advised to take in an enormous stock of timber so that he should be able to cope with the mortality of air-raids; a possible enough eventuality in a town on the Forth. Mr M— commented that this must have entailed a big expenditure; and concluded: 'I suppose it would mean a loss if all that stuff were left on his hands.' 'Oh yes!' innocently answered the good lady: 'It would be a dead loss.'

William Soutar

1951

Francine [Weisweiller] went to Monte Carlo to buy records. The salesman couldn't get over the fact that she was buying classics. 'At your age!' he exclaimed. 'Very few people buy them. M. Matisse buys them from us to paint by. He stops at Beethoven.'

Jean Cocteau

1991

I heard quite a good joke. President Carter, President Nixon and President Jack Kennedy were all in a ship sailing on a cruise when suddenly there was an awful explosion and the order was given to abandon ship and to get to the lifeboats. President Carter cried out, 'Women and children first.' President Nixon cried out, 'Fuck the women and children,' and President Kennedy cried, 'Is there time?'

Woodrow Wyatt

1995

[David] Bowie called from a distant American hotel room to relay the O. J. verdict to me as it was delivered, describing the scene in court etc. Then it was on our TV too, so we were watching it together. I don't know what city he was in – Detroit, I think. Incredible tension, with [Judge] Ito slowly going over all the rules. Then the verdict – and the beautiful sad face of Marcia Clark [prosecuting lawyer], outwitted by shysters. I am now even more convinced (by his reaction at the news) that Simpson was guilty and that he knew he was going to be acquitted. Somehow it was a fix. As David said, 'It's all down to investigative journalism now.'

Brian Eno

4 October

1943

Somewhere a few miles short of Naples proper, the road widened into something like a square, dominated by a vast semi-derelict public building, plastered with notices and with every window blown in. Here several trucks had drawn up and our driver pulled in to the kerb and stopped too. One of the trucks was carrying American Army supplies, and soldiers, immediately joined by several from our truck, were crowding round this and helping themselves to whatever they could lay their hands on. Thereafter, crunching through the broken glass that littered the pavement, each of them carrying a tin of rations, they were streaming into the municipal building.

I followed them and found myself in a vast crowded room with jostling soldiery, with much pushing forward and ribald encouragement on the part of those in the rear, but a calmer and more thoughtful atmosphere by the time one reached the front of the crowd. Here a row of ladies sat at intervals of about a yard with their backs to the wall. These women were dressed in their street clothes, and had the ordinary well-washed respectable shopping and gossiping faces of working-class housewives. By the side of each woman stood a small pile of tins, and it soon became clear it was possible to make love to any one of them in this very public place by adding another tin to the pile. The women kept absolutely still, they said nothing, and their faces were as empty of expression as graven images. They might have been selling fish, except that this place lacked the excitement of a fish market. There was no soliciting, no suggestion, no enticement, not even the discreetest and most accidental display of flesh. The boldest of the soldiers had pushed themselves, tins in hand, to the front, but now, faced with these matter-of-fact family-providers driven here by empty larders, they seemed to flag. Once again reality had betrayed the dream, and the air fell limp. There was some sheepish laughter, jokes that fell flat, and a visible tendency to slip quietly away. One soldier, a little tipsy, and egged on constantly by his friends, finally put down his tin of rations at a woman's side, unbuttoned and lowered himself on her. A perfunctory jogging of the haunches began and came quickly to an end. A moment later he was on his feet buttoning up again. It had been something to get over as soon as possible. He might have been submitting to field punishment rather than an act of love.

Norman Lewis

1977

Came in expecting to cater for twelve and was suddenly swamped by the entire cast of *The Good Woman of Szechuan*, extras and all. In a panic rushed to Sainsbury's, bought fifty chicken pieces, some packets of country stuffing and a few tins of pineapple, combined them all in a couple of roasting tins and rushed down to the oven. A huge success! Ann Jenkins was most impressed. 'The thing about you and me, Joan,' she said, 'is that we are both pros!' I positively glowed with pleasure. I wonder if it would work with pork chops?

Joan Wyndham

5 October

1936

Talking to Henry [Miller], I said I didn't like clowns. I liked madmen. Henry said, 'Madmen are too serious. I like clowns.'

Anaïs Nin

1936

Dine with Bernard Berenson [the art historian] at Lady Horner's house. He is very interesting about London in the 'nineties. He used to dine regularly alone with Oscar Wilde. He said that when alone with him the mask of affectation gradually (but only gradually) dropped off. But in public he posed deliberately. Mrs Berenson says that having met him five nights in succession, he said to her, 'Now you have exhausted my repertoire. I had only five subjects of conversation prepared and have run out. I shall have to give you one of the former ones. Which would you like?' They said they would like the one on evolution. So he gave them the one on evolution. Berenson asks whether there are any conversationalists of my generation. I am bound to say that there are not. Not that I know of. We have no time.

Harold Nicolson

1961

Dinner at the Garrick to celebrate the publication of Harold Acton's second volume of Neapolitan history. Dinner, chosen by John Sutro, excellent; the book unreadable. I sat next to the old Bloomsbury sinologue Arthur Waley who told me that Miss [Ivy] Compton-Burnett's father was a doctor in Hove and that all her rural scenes are entirely imaginary. I reminded him we had met forty years ago at Renishaw (nearly) and that he had then shown a superior knowledge of winter sports to Gaspard Ponsonby. He said: 'Oh, dear. I am sorry.' It is seldom I have heard the voice of Bloomsbury.

Evelyn Waugh

1979

Being a minor poet is like being minor royalty, and no one, as a former lady-in-waiting to Princess Margaret once explained to me, is happy as that.

Stephen Spender

6 October

1826

Went to see Colonel Thornhill's hawks fly. Some part of the amusement is very beautiful particularly the first flight of the hawks when they sweep so beautifully round the company jangling their bells from time to time and throwing themselves into the most elegant positions as they gaze about for their prey. But I do not wonder that the impatience of modern times has renounced this expensive and precarious mode of sporting. The hawks are liable to various misfortunes and are besides addicted to fly away; one of ours was fairly lost for the day and one or two went off without permission but returnd. We killd a crow and and frightend a snipe. There were however ladies and gentlemen enough to make a gallant show on the top of Whitlaw Kipps. The falconer made a fine figure, a handsome and active young fellow with the falcon on his wrist. The Colonel was most courteous and christend a hawk after me which was a compliment. The hawks are not christend till they have merited that distinction. I walkd about six miles and was not fatigued.

Sir Walter Scott

1836

Lord Dudley's place is in this hideous region, one mile on the London side of Basingstoke, our fourth stage, at which we arrived at thirteen minutes to two. Here we dined. Now, I had a great horror of Basingstoke, because when papa and mamma went to Devonshire five years ago, they stopped here at a most horrid inn, and could get nothing to eat but putrid chops; the whole place, too, they described as filthy, abounding with bad smells. So that we rather dreaded dining here; but we were agreeably disappointed. I cannot deny that every street was flanked by two open drains nearly overflowing, nor that the horses marched to their stables through the same passage by which we walked to dinner, and that the only reason we smelt no bad smells might have been that we had no leisure so to do. But when we entered the dining-room, a large apartment, we discovered the following goodly apparitions: at the top a round of beef, at the bottom a fillet of veal, in the centre a ham, chicken, potatoes, bread, and butter; the whole forming a capital cold dinner. Mamma and I, with a very good appetite, fell on the fowl. One of his wings was already gone; we took the other, and stripped him besides of his breast, and a portion of one leg. In about a quarter of an hour we were summoned back to the coach, and left Basingstoke greatly raised in our esteem . . .

Emily Shore (aged 16)

1942

At dinner-time lots more Russians came. When too many come, we can't give them much, but they all had a big handful of boiled pig potatoes each. One of them appeared very ill (we had noticed him lying in the field all morning) and we gave him a cup of hot milk and water.

Another little lad sat on a box in the yard for about three-quarters of an hour eating potatoes and what he could find of bits of raw vegetables we had thrown there for the pigs. Mother asked him his age and he said 15 (on his fingers). Then he began to say 'Kaput, Kaput', trying to show, I think, how many of his family were gone, then the poor little fellow burst into tears. We all wept to see him. Mother put her hand on his shoulder. He showed me an immense hole in his trousers, so we gave him a needle and thread and he mended it and was quite pleased with himself.

Finally, John felt so sorry for him that he gave him a cigarette and a match, and how pleased he was! He stroked John's coat and kissed his hand. As we were leaving, tonight, the same little fellow was working with the squad in Mr Bisson's field. He recognised us and gave us a broad smile. I winked at him, making sure the Todt was not looking. One has to be so careful.

Nan Le Ruez

7 October

1826

The pleasure of the day is not to be measured by the small space it occupies in this journal.

Henry Crabb Robinson

1834

Dr Lardner [notable scientific writer] came into my room and chatted with me for some time; among other things, in speaking of the tour he had made through Scotland and by the lakes, he mentioned his visit to Southey [Poet Laureate] at Keswick. On passing the drawing-room he noticed several ladies apparently in a very cheerful mood; on giving his name, after waiting about five minutes, Southey came to him, the very image of distraction, took his hand, and led him into his study. For a long time he remained silent – at length he told him he believed he must dismiss him; *in fine*, he disclosed to him that within the last five minutes, since he rang the bell at the lawn gate, Mrs Southey had, without previous indication or sympton, gone raving mad, and to that hopeless degree that within an hour he must take her to an asylum. These are the cruel liabilities of our nature, which no human power can cure, but which only resignation and the hope religion offers can alleviate and soothe.

Charles Macready

1967 [Bolivia]

Today marks eleven months since our guerrilla inauguration. The day went by without complications, bucolically, until 12.30 p.m., when an old woman, tending her goats, entered the canyon where we were camped and had to be taken prisoner. The woman gave us no reliable information about the soldiers, simply repeating that she knew nothing, and that it has been quite a while since she has last been there. All she gave us was information about the roads. From what the old woman told us, we gather that we are now about one league from Higueras, one from Jaguey, and about two leagues from Pucara. At 5.30 p.m. Inti, Aniceto and Pablito went to the old woman's house. One of her daughters is bedridden and another is half-dwarf. They gave her 50 pesos and asked her to keep quiet, but held out little hope she would do so, despite her promises.

The 17 of us set out under a waning moon. The march was very tiring, and we left many traces in the canyon where we had been. There were no houses nearby, just a few potato patches irrigated by ditches leading from the stream. At 2:00 a.m. we stopped to rest, since it was now useless to continue. Chino [wounded guerrilla] is becoming a real burden when it is necessary to walk at night.

The army made a strange announcement about the presence of 250 men in Serrano, who are there to cut off the escape of those who are surrounded, 37 in number. They give the area of our refuge as between the Acero and Oro rivers. The item appears to be diversionary.

Altitude = 2,000 meters.

Che Guevara

1970

Went to France again last Friday to go to Jacqueline de Caraman-Chimay's shoot. The guest of honour was the Prince of Wales. At dinner we were at three tables and Mary Soames [daughter of Winston Churchill] was at mine. She makes a tremendous din. Very jolly and kind-hearted, but with all the brashness which, so I have always heard, was characteristic of the home life of the Churchills. Words like bloody, and bugger-off were bandied about loudly, and so excited did she get that at one moment her son Nicholas (who promises to have the same dimensions as his father, and is an equerry to the Prince) came over from his table to tick her off and beg her to be quiet.

Cynthia Gladwyn

8 October

1870

Heavy rain in the night and in the morning the mists had all wept themselves away. In the night the wind had gone round from the cursed East into the blessed West. All evil things have always come from the East, the plague, cholera, and man.

Rev. Francis Kilvert

1924

Walking in Fulham Road yesterday morning I saw in a slatternly chemist's shop a section of window given to 'Yeast is life. Vitamins mean health. X-Yeast Tablets . . . A lightning pick-me-up' guaranteed (or money back) to aid headaches, etc., in 5 minutes, flatulence, etc., in 5 to 10, stomach trouble in 10 to 15, flu cold in 24 hours. I went in and bought some – probably because I used to take yeast and it may have done me a certain amount of good. I didn't know what was in the tablets (beyond yeast). I knew that for many years I had tried all sorts of remedies and that not one of them had succeeded with me. Yet, as usual, I had hope again. I believed again, etc., etc. I took stuff blind again. This indestructible (though often destroyed) faith in quack medicine advertisements is a very interesting and perhaps almost universal trait. I took a tablet. Felt nothing. But about tea time I felt a rather wonderful change in my organism. After tea I took two more tablets – or was it before tea? Anyhow I felt very much better. I took two on going to bed, and have had the best night for many weeks. In fact I slept 5¾ hours, of which 3¼ at a stretch. I felt I could do with more sleep; but I couldn't get it. However, I have much more energy and optimism today.

Arnold Bennett

1941 [Jerusalem]

I feel dreadfully restless. Except for dinner occasionally, I seldom leave Government House and must be on hand always for coded messages which I decipher in the billiard room – often at night. When I can find time I walk round the big garden inside the high wire fence. My work is interesting; I live in great comfort; and yet I am unhappy and long to go away. It seems to be sometimes that there is a curse on Jerusalem – I so seldom meet anyone who is happy here. There is a tense atmosphere, not only over religions but as if the turmoils of centuries are still alive. Perhaps these thoughts stem from my own sadness yet I suspect Jerusalem must remain, for ever, a place of conflict.

Countess of Ranfurly

1946 [Rye]

In the church the great gold pendulum swung slowly and threateningly, as if it were a giant's club foot, swinging to and fro idly in the dusk, while he waited, planning some treachery and death.

Just at the door was a lame woman behind a table heaped with apples, marrows, chrysanthemums, wheat and roses. I could see her surgical boot under the heap of fruits and flowers. She wore glasses too, and perhaps these gave me the notion that she was playing at being a schoolmistress who had ordered all her unruly charges up to the desk for punishment. I imagined her beating the fat bottoms of the marrows, pulling the shaggy gypsy hair of the chrysanthemums, slapping the already tingling cheeks of the apples. But what she said when she really opened her mouth was, 'Thanks, Vera,' (or some such name as that) 'they'll be an enormous help.' Great stress on the 'enormous'.

Now as I write, I wonder if many of us ever think that, while we are talking, moving about our daily business, some stranger may be near us, listening, watching, melting away to write our words down in his little book at home, there to fix them as long as the ink and paper last, or longer still if they are found, printed and scattered broadcast all over the land.

Denton Welch

1950

Read in the papers a great scare story about flying saucers being visitations from another world. As a matter of fact, everything being so peculiar, it is, I suppose, just possible that they might be. I really don't know how the Catholics would get around that.

Noël Coward

1955

A story of Vera Stravinsky's – a very dumb wife is warned by her husband not to say anything during a dinner party. At length the hostess says: 'Shall we have coffee in the library?' The wife inquires innocently: 'Is it still open?'

Christopher Isherwood

1977

I had thought that the making of *Apocalypse Now* was over. I was comfortable being home, starting a Zazen class, meeting once a week with friends to analyze dreams, making fig jam. I could see that Francis was in some deep conflict. We had long conversations about the themes of the film. We talked about opposites, about power and limits, good and evil, peace and violence. I told him about the Zen book which talks about mind and body not being two separate things and not being one thing, but being both two and one.

We talked about how the film was a parallel for the very things that Francis was living out this year. How he had been Willard setting off on his mission to make a film and how he had turned into Kurtz for a while. I thought when he resolved the conflicts within himself, he would see the end of the film clearly. I was busy getting the kids back to school, working on remodeling the house, cooking the fresh vegetables from the garden that all seemed to be ripe at the same time.

Two weeks ago, Francis was as miserable as I have ever seen him. I asked him to tell me about his conflicts, really tell me. He began to cry. He said he was in love with another woman. He said he loved her and he loved me, that we each represented part of himself and he couldn't give up either. I listened to the person I love, in complete anguish and pain. Suddenly I could see the conflict for him was not about peace and violence. The conflict for him would be about romantic ideals and practical reality. A man who loves romance, loves illusion. He's a filmmaker, in the very business of creating illusion. And he loves his wife, he loves his children and fifteen years of that reality. I could see it so clearly. Then, the emotion rose up from my feet like a tide. It hit me in the chest and knocked me backward. I saw myself pick up the vase of flowers and throw it. I heard the words pour out of my mouth. I saw myself go downstairs, and the fragments of white dishes hit the red kitchen walls. I was blind with rage. I was raging at my blindness.

Eleanor Coppola

1979

It is two o'clock in the morning and I feel very tired. But a point of terminology nags at me and I may not rest till I have said something about it.

I have been describing this record of mine, I notice, as a journal, not a diary. What is the difference?

I think that a diary functions at a lower level. It represents – or is thought to represent – a lesser species of literature. It is more gossipy and slapdash, more concerned with jottings, more practical, less obviously intended for other eyes. So we speak of Pepys's Diaries but of Dorothy Wordsworth's Journals and mean, I believe, to denigrate Pepys a little when we make the distinction. Yet who would exchange the former for the latter? Not I, at any rate, though I am fond of both.

I suspect that nowadays at least, there is an element of snobbishness involved in the journal – diary antithesis. Schoolgirls, archetypally, keep diaries; poets, therefore, must write journals. (It is true that Yeats wrote a *diary* but true also that he took the precaution of dignifying it with a fairly resounding title: 'Estrangement'.)

My father, old seaman, was unbothered by such nuances and called his daily notes a 'log'. I shall stick to journal.

Alasdair Maclean

9 October

1762

I packed up my things for Oxford, this afternoon and they were these – 9 Shirts – 9 Stocks – 2 Cravats – 7 Pr of Stockings, 2 White Handkerchiefs – 5 Coloured Handkerchiefs – 2 Night Caps – 1 Towel – 2 Pr of Breeches – besides the things that I wear, wch are 1 Pr of Leather Breeches – 1 White Coat – 1 Buff Waistcoat – 1 Great Coat.

James Woodforde

1911

If I reach my fortieth year then I'll probably marry an old maid with protruding upper teeth left a little exposed by the upper lip. The upper front teeth of Miss K., who was in Paris and London, slant toward each other a little like legs which are quickly crossed at the knees. I'll hardly reach my fortieth birthday, however, the frequent tension over the left half of my skull, for example, speaks against it – it feels like an inner leprosy which, when I only observe it and disregard its unpleasantness makes the same impression on me as the skull cross-sections in textbooks, or as an almost painless dissection of the living body where the knife – a little coolingly, carefully, often stopping and going back, sometimes lying still – splits still thinner the paper-thin integument close to the functioning parts of the brain.

Franz Kafka

1929

'You say you *believe*' (said Count de X., an extreme Catholic, to the good Protestant minister). 'You people believe, but we *know*.'

André Gide

1943

This afternoon another trip along the sea-front at Santa Lucia provided a similar spectacle of the desperate hunt for food. Rocks were piled up here against the sea wall and innumerable children were at work among them. I learned that they were prising limpets off the rocks, all the winkles and sea-snails having long since been exhausted. A pint of limpets sold at the road-side fetched about two lire, and if boiled long enough could be expected to add some faint, fishy flavour to a broth produced from any edible odds and ends. Inexplicably, no boats were allowed out yet to fish. Nothing, absolutely nothing that can be tackled by the human digestive system is wasted in Naples. The butchers' shops that have opened here and there sell nothing we would consider acceptable as meat, but their displays, of scraps of offal are set out with art, and handled with reverence; chickens' heads – from which the beak has been neatly trimmed – cost five lire; a little grey pile of chick-ens' intestines in a brightly polished saucer, five lire; a gizzard, three lire; calves' trotters, two lire apiece; a large piece of windpipe, seven lire. Little queues wait to be served with these delicacies. There is a persistent rumour of a decline in the cat population of the city.

Norman Lewis

10 October

1845 [Ireland]

My next visit was revolting – dirt and filth and discomfort of every kind in and around the dwelling of Michael Doyle and Judy Ryan. They were in the bog, Jane Ryan, literally, not figuratively, nearly naked, her large exposed limbs and chest burned almost black by the sun, was in the field amusing an ugly, dirty enough, but perfectly well dressed baby. She helped me over a wall to the dung yard in front of the cabin which was cleaner than the kitchen floor over which I had to grope in darkness to the fire, carefully holding up my petticoats and stepping so as to avoid what the two fat pigs had been deposit-ing on it. Beside these two beasts on four legs, two others on two, old Mrs Doyle, smoking, and lame James Quinn seemed to be in charge of a lately born infant and a wretched little nursechild both seated in the chimney corner. Energetic measures wanted here.

Elizabeth Grant of Rothiemurchus

1855

I've been in a lazily apathetic, perpetually dissatisfied state for a long time now. Won another 130 roubles at cards. Bought a horse and bridle for 150. What nonsense! My career is literature – to write and write! From tomorrow I'll work all my life or throw up everything – rules, religion, propriety – everything.

Leo Tolstoy

1970

Took part yesterday in a radio programme, 'Speak Easy', to be broadcast this evening. The chairman was Jimmy Savile – an unprepossessing figure with long, bleached-white hair, a necklace of painted shells; gym shoes, white socks and a *very* shabby corduroy suit. But, ignoring the trimmings and looking into his face, you could see that here was an absolutely genuine human being. He gets a lot of money from the B.B.C. and from a column in the *People*, lives in a mini-bus or a caravan (sometimes one, sometimes the other), and devotes his life to good works – particularly at Broadmoor and Rampton. Here is indeed a latter-day saint, dressed up in clothes that render him acceptable to the young multitude. He has great psychological insight. I was saying I wondered why people are uninterested in the old, though they will all be old some day. He said it was 'conscience': the old remind them of their old relatives, who they neglect. He said one of the B.B.C. higher-ups has a mother in Leeds he has not seen for several years. He also said people don't want good health. He recently broke a finger wrestling and still wears a finger-splint when he wants attention and sympathy, though this must not be overdone. People don't want to have to cope with someone really ill, but like sympathizing with someone wearing a finger-splint. With all his fun he devotes his life to the drearier kinds of good works.*

Cecil King

11 October

1852 [Balmoral]

After luncheon, Albert decided to walk through the wood for the last time, to have a last chance, and allowed Vicky and me to go with him. At half-past three o'clock we started, got out at Grant's, and walked up part of *Carrop*, intending to go along the upper path, when a stag was heard to roar, and we all turned into the wood. We crept along, and got into the middle path. Albert soon left us to go lower, and we sat down to wait for him; presently we heard a shot – then complete silence – and, after another pause of some little time, three more shots. This was again succeeded by complete silence. We sent some one to look, who shortly after returned, saying the stag had been twice hit and they were after him. Macdonald next went, and in about five minutes we heard 'Solomon' give tongue, and knew he had the stag at bay. We listened a little while, and then began moving down hoping to arrive in time; but the barking had ceased, and Albert had already killed the stag; and on the road he lay, a little way beyond *Invergelder* – the beauty that we had admired yesterday evening.

Queen Victoria

---

* After Savile's death in 2011, hundreds of allegations of sexual abuse were made against him. He has subsequently been described as Britain's most predatory and prolific sex offender.

1860 [New York, at the time of a visit by the Prince of Wales]

I begin to be weary of this 'sweet young Prince'. The Hope of England threatens to become a bore. In fact, he is a bore of the first order. Everybody has talked of nothing but His Royal Highness for the last week. Reaction is inevitable. It has set in and by Monday next, the remotest allusion to His Royal Highness will act like ipecac. It has been a mild, bland, half-cloudy day. By ten o'clock, people were stationing themselves along the curbstones of Broadway and securing a good place to see the Prince. What a spectacle-loving people we are! Shops were closed and business paralyzed; Wall Street deserted. I spent the morning mostly at the Trinity vestry offices, signing tickets, and so forth. We had to pass on a bushel of applications for admission next Sunday. Lots of Fifth Avenueites sent in letters tendering a private carriage for the conveyance of His Royal Highness to church, with a postscript asking for a 'few' tickets. Corporations of Trinity Church bluster about their rights and insist on reserved pews. I fear we are a city of snobs.

George Templeton Strong

1950

'Are you lost or eternally saved?' This was on a sandwich board being carried out in Regent Street by a young man. I frowned at it, because it isn't really right to ask such intimate questions in public. The young man smiled.

'It's all right,' he said. 'It ain't meant for you.'

J. R. Ackerley

12 October

1923

Mother wrote yesterday, 'I am so cross about your clothes being stolen, and trust you got a ready-made overcoat at once, though I know such a coat would not be at all nice.' To-day I went to try on my new thick suit and overcoat. I asked Morris (the bald, spectacled, and obese little Jewish sartorial expert) whether any of his customers wear corsets. He replied, 'A few conceited young men, sir.' 'The ones with the squeaky voices, I suppose?' said I. He smiled. 'You writers have to know a lot about human nature, I expect, sir.'

Siegfried Sassoon

1939 [Wiltshire]

The kind farmer who lives nearby has lent me his cob for afternoons so that I can teach Whitaker [her husband's valet, about to join his master's Yeomanry] to ride. It is a big, lazy animal with a Roman nose, called Dulcie. Today when

I was saddling her Whitaker announced he did not know which end of her frightened him most. Then our troubles began: Whitaker's legs are so short he could not reach the stirrup to mount, and I found him too heavy for me to give him a 'leg up'. We built a pile of logs quite high and from it Whitaker scrambled into the saddle, only to topple off on the other side. After several attempts we set off with Whitaker perched and petrified in the saddle and me holding the bridle. We walked slowly along the cart track which leads to Salisbury Plain and I had a struggle not to laugh; he looked so funny with his fat face stiff with fear, his hair tousled and his mouth screwed into a button. All went well until we turned to go home, when Dulcie made a tremendous fart, plunged forward and departed at a gallop with Whitaker clutching the saddle. I could not run for laughing. When I reached the farm-yard I found Whitaker seated on the ground and Dulcie grazing. 'I made the trip and then slid down its neck,' he said cheerfully and added. 'I can assure your Ladyship I did not make that horrible rude noise.'

Dan [her husband] brought friends from the Gunnery School to dinner and Whitaker excelled himself – when dinner was ready he announced in his best French: 'Sole a la Shrimpy, Chicken Hellsmere, and Chocolate Manure.'

Countess of Ranfurly

1958

The Great Reaper has been at it again. His latest acquisitions include Chips Channon and the Pope [Pius XII]. As the latter had recently announced that plastic surgery, except for specifically therapeutic reasons, was a sin, I can't feel that the pompous old fool is much loss.

Noël Coward

13 October

1660

To my Lord's [Admiral Sir Edward Montagu] in the morning, where I met with Captain Cuttance, but my Lord not being up I went out to Charing Cross, to see Major-general Harrison [one of the 'judges' who condemned Charles I to death], hanged, drawn, and quartered; which was done there, he looking as cheerful as any man could do in that condition. He was presently cut down, and his head and heart shown to the people, at which there was great shouts of joy. It is said that he said that he was sure to come shortly at the right hand of Christ to judge them that now had judged him; and that his wife do expect his coming again.

Samuel Pepys

1855 [Paris]

A conversation about woman, after a couple of tankards of beer at Binding's. Woman is an evil, stupid animal unless she is educated or civilized to a high degree. She is incapable of dreaming, thinking, or loving. Poetry in a woman is never natural but a product of education. Only the woman of the world is a woman; the rest are females.

Inferiority of the feminine mind to the masculine mind. All the physical beauty, all the strength, and all the development of a woman is concentrated in and as it were directed towards the central and lower parts of the body: the pelvis, the buttocks, the thighs; the beauty of a man is to be found in the upper, nobler parts, the pectoral muscles, the broad shoulders, the high forehead. Venus has a narrow forehead. Dürer's *Three Graces* have flat heads at the back and little shoulders; only their hips are big and beautiful. As regards the inferiority of the feminine mind, consider the self-assurance of a woman, even when she is only a girl, which allows her to be extremely witty with nothing but a little vivacity and a touch of spontaneity. Only man is endowed with the modesty and timidity which woman lacks and which she uses only as weapons.

Woman: the most beautiful and admirable of laying machines.

The Goncourt Brothers

1880

Tennyson – 'I'm seventy-*nine* (this was a joke), but I don't feel the weight of age on my shoulders. I can run up-hill; I can waltz – but when I said this to Fanny Kemble she replied in a ghastly voice, "I hope I shall never see you do it!"'

William Allingham

1910

Thoughts of suicide are growing again, with greater strength than before. But now I nurture them in silence. Today I read in the newspapers about a little girl of fifteen who took an overdose of opium and died quite easily – she just fell asleep. I looked at my big phial – but still lacked the courage.

Life is becoming unbearable. It has been like living under bombardment from Mr Chertkov [Leo Tolstoy's publisher] ever since Lev Nik. [Leo Tolstoy] visited him in June and completely succumbed to his influence. '*Il est despote, il est vrai,*' his mother once said to me.

It all started when this despot took all Lev Nik.'s manuscripts with him to England. Then he took his diaries (which are at the moment in the bank), and which I recovered at the cost of my life. Then he kept Lev Nik. himself with him as long as he could, and slandered me viciously both to my face and behind my back, such as telling my son Lyova that I had spent my entire life murdering my husband.

Eventually he persuaded and helped Lev N. to draft an official renunciation of the copyright, after his death probably (I don't know exactly in what form it was written), thereby stealing the last crust of bread from the mouths of his children and grandchildren who survive him. But the children and I, if I live, will defend his rights.

Monster! What business has he to interfere in our family affairs?

When I suggested to Lev Nik. that it was wicked and unkind of him to give instructions for his copyright to be given after his death to the world, rather than to his own family, he merely kept an obstinate silence, and his general attitude was: 'You are sick, I must endure this in silence, but in my soul I shall hate you.'

Lev Nik. has been infected by Chertkov's vile suggestion that my main motivation was *self-interest*. What 'self-interest' could there possibly be in a sick old woman of 66, who has both a house, and land, and forest, and capital – not to mention my 'Notes', my diaries and my letters, all of which I can publish?

I am hurt by Chertkov's evil *influence*, hurt by all their endless secrets, hurt that Lev Nik.'s 'will' is going to give rise to a lot of anger, arguments, judgements and newspaper gossip over the grave of an old man who enjoyed life to the full while he was alive, but deprived his numerous direct descendants of everything after his death.

Sofia Tolstoy

1915

We dined at Queen's Restaurant, Sloane Square. Just as we had finished and were emerging, there was a bustle and we heard the magic word 'Zeppelin'. We rushed out and found people in dramatic groups, gazing skywards. Some men there said they saw the Zeppelin. Alas, I didn't! But our guns were popping away and shells bursting in the air. I felt excited pleasurably, but not the faintest tremor and I longed and longed for more to happen. Bibs was the only member of the family who had sufficient imagination to be frightened and Letty's fun was spoilt by the thought of the children. My only words were: 'Something for my diary!'

Lady Cynthia Asquith

1943 [Naples]

Now that the mail is operating normally again, a horde of censors are busily slitting open letters to probe for hidden meaning among the trivia of family and business correspondence, and when in doubt they fall back on us.

Unhappily many telephone conversations are being monitored, too, and the typed out 'intercepts' sent to us contain their fair share of absurdity. The prize example received so far was solemnly headed 'Illegal use of telescope'. This referred to a passage in an overheard conversation between two lovers in which the girl had said, 'I can't see you today because my husband will be here, but I'll admire you, as ever, through love's telescope.' Number 3 District adds to these burdens by bombarding us with addenda for the Black Book, which serves as the rag-bag for everybody's paranoia. In one case we had to make an entry for a suspect about which nothing is known but his posses-sion of three teats on his left breast, while another was described as 'having the face of a hypocrite'.

Norman Lewis

14 October

1943

One or two odd points to be noted. During spells of drowsiness I find that I am now gaining a certain amount of satisfaction by speaking out a sentence now and then in a deep voice. Often these have no relation to anything; but many times they are prompted by the imagery that may be passing over my almost-dreaming mind. Some incident takes place, and I ask a question about it as if the folks knew my thoughts. I imagine, if deeply enough drowsed, that someone is in the room; and when I get no answer to my query I open my eyes and realize that I have been half-asleep. This forenoon, however, just after my bed had been made, and while mother was dusting, I suddenly fell into a doze, and heard a vivid account by Jean Soutar of an accident to two soldiers outside Fran's cottage. When Jean had finished, I asked Mops if she had heard how the soldiers were getting on. She was quite mystified – and I had to explain the matter. Last night I must have been talking quite a lot; as the folks said they heard me making noises round about 1.50.

William Soutar

1966

Toured Sunset Boulevard with all its night-clubs and garish signs (the rich man's Blackpool-in-the-sun) before catching the midday plane to New York. We chuckled over the trimmings of the affluent society (first class); book matches printed in gold with our individual names, the Walt Disney film show and earphones for piped music all the time. But the meal, though lavish, was uninspiring. Williams [her Chief Scientific Adviser] called me over to meet Brigadier-General Carlton in the bar, where they had been knocking back endless drinks – the stewardesses turning a blind eye to the legal maximum of two. The General (well lit on a combination of brandy and Benedictine) was beginning to talk wild: 'You got your job by your own efforts? I bet it had something to do with your undies.' Williams hastily headed him off the smut in which they had been indulging. I started to cross-examine him about Vietnam. 'Are you winning?' 'No. The politicians won't let us. I'm just a professional soldier. I just get wounded. I'm going to New York to collect the American Star and to testify to Congress. But the politicians won't listen to me.' Me: 'What do you think should be done?' 'We should take out China now.' 'Nuclear weapons?' 'That's not necessary. Just flatten all her ports and railroads.' 'And when you have "taken her out" what would you do with her?' But that was obviously beyond his political comprehension. He just sat there, a big, flat-faced man with extrovert eyes. He pulled out his daughter's photo to show us. Just before we landed he whipped out an eyebath and bathed his eyes. 'The cameras will be waiting,' he said bashfully.

Barbara Castle

1975

As soon as I got up to give my lecture, I was seized with violent diarrhoea pains – a nightmare situation come true! It seemed to me that I kept on saying confused sentences, though luckily some of the lecture hung together. No one seemed to have noticed. I even pulled myself together sufficiently to do well in answering questions after the talk. Then of course everything delayed my getting to a lavatory. People asking for autographs, the ones too shy to get up in front of the audience asking their little private questions. There was some difficulty in finding a lavatory. Then when the chairman did take me to one, NOT IN USE was written across MEN on the door. We found another and as soon as I got into it an elderly gentleman emerged from one of its stalls and said, 'Didn't I meet you twenty years ago? Now where was it? What did you speak about, etc.' I said, 'Excuse me, I'll speak to you after-wards, outside,' and dashed into the place he had left.

Stephen Spender

15 October

1774

I caught a remarkable large spider in my Wash Place this morning and put him in a small glass decanter and fed him with some bread and intend to keep him . . .

Rev. James Woodforde

1821

Whenever an American requests to see me – (which is *not* unfrequently) I comply – 1stly. because I respect a people who acquired their freedom by firmness without excess – and 2dly. because these transatlantic visits 'few and far between' make me feel as if talking with posterity from the other side of the Styx; – in a century or two new English & Spanish Atlantides will be masters of the old Countries in all probability – as Greece and Europe overcame their Mother Asia in the older or earlier ages as they are called.

Lord Byron

1914

A man is always looking at himself in the mirror if for no other reason than to tie his tie and brush his hair. What does he think of his face? He must have private opinions. But it is usually considered a little out of taste to entertain opinions about one's personal appearance.

As for myself, some mirrors do me down pretty well, others depress me! I am bound to confess I am biased in favour of the friendly mirror. I am not handsome, but I look interesting – I hope distinguished. My eyes are deepset ... but my worst moments are when the barber combs my hair right down over my forehead, or when I see a really handsome man in Hyde Park. Such occasions direct my gaze reflexly, and doubt like a thief in the night forces the back door!

W. N. P. Barbellion

1934

Think about dignity and pride wherein they are good and proper, and wherein they ought to be abandoned to the bigger attribute, generosity. But anyway, never be coy, coquettish, or flirtatious in a physical way. Never egg a man on to be physical. If he wants to leave, say goodbye. This has always been a principle yet why have I abandoned it at times? Anyway, it defeats its own end. From now on I must be mental until I find myself a proper mate. However, may that be soon!

Elizabeth Smart

1941 [POW camp]

Visit of Swiss Red X rep. V. shocked at Camp, 'not fit to live in, particularly P.O.W.'s and even more particularly Officers'. He has been to Poland – Thorn area – and says troops in v. good spirit and better off than we. Considers 1500 should leave at once till Camp is ready – or certainly 1000 insisted on. All rooms should have electric lights. Red X rep. says 1½ million Red X parcels at Geneva.

Whole Camp to be run as a Brigade with the requisite administrative officers. Eric on parcels again. Toby on laundry. Germans promise sheets & towels shortly. Put my name down for dentist.

Camp a sea of mud today. Impossible to keep clean. Dirt in hut is indescribable.

Captain John Mansel

1944

Today is the one hundredth anniversary of the birth of Friedrich Wilhelm Nietzsche. If it is noted anywhere in America it will be on the ground that Nietzsche was a wicked fellow and the inventor of all the devilries of Hitler. I can see little hope for this great Christian country. It has been going downhill steadily throughout my time, and its pace of late has been fast accelerating.

H. L. Mencken

1966

I was interviewed by the local Malta Television Service. The interviewer said, 'Lord Mountbatten, I understand you are here in Malta in connection with making a television serial entitled . . .' Then he pulled a bit of paper out of his pocket and read the title '"The Life and Times of Lord Mountbatten". Is this correct?' I replied, 'Yes.' He then startled me by saying, 'Could you tell me what part you are playing in this serial?'

Earl Mountbatten of Burma

16 October

1783

I went on to Witney. There were uncommon thunder and lightning here last Thursday; but nothing to that which were there on Friday night. About ten the storm was just over the town; and both the bursts of thunder and lightning, or rather sheets of flame, were without intermission. Those that were asleep in the town were waked and many thought the day of judgement was come. Men, women, and children flocked out of their houses, and kneeled down in the streets. With the flames, the grace of God came down also in a manner never known before; and as the impression was general, so it was lasting: It did not pass away with the storm; but the spirit of seriousness, with that of grace and supplication, continued . . .

John Wesley

1942

When we emerged into the Fulham Road this morning there didn't seem to be much of it left – they'd certainly buggered it up! The whole place was a shambles like the last days of Pompeii, with shop windows shattered and their goods destroyed, the road thick with glass and the air with dust. Tulley's has been burnt out and there are two houses down in Limerston Street. People still digging for bodies. Huge crater outside the tobacconist with a burst water main spouting in it. Poor old Redcliffe Road has lost another two houses, three bodies in the wreckage and my skylight broken.

As I approached number 48 there was a huge explosion and the time bomb finally went off behind 37; black smoke hung in the air and everyone ran as big bits of masonry hurtled towards us. The studio looked very dirty with bits of glass everywhere.

Went off to see if Rupert had been hurt but met him half-way – all that was wrong with him was a chill in his stomach, which he'd caught last week from leaping naked out of bed and putting out a fire in his mother's garden by peeing on it. He was wearing his famous black overcoat that he used to impress clients with when he was in advertising. It hangs down to the pavement like a box all round him and has such huge padded shoulders that old ladies in buses turn pale when they lean up against him and half of him collapses.

While he was rather unwillingly patching up my skylight, Madame Arcana came up, pale and ghastly after the night's terrors, and said she hadn't been able to sleep because she had gone to bed in her stays, and when she had finally dozed off she dreamt that Aleister Crowley was trying to rape her, and woke up in a cold sweat just as the time bomb went off.

Joan Wyndham

1943 [Val D'Orcia]

Antonio goes down to Chianciano and returns with the news that at Magione a German captain, as he was driving through a wood, was shot and killed; he was buried yesterday at Chianciano.

In the evening a Moroccan soldier turns up here, an escaped prisoner from Laterina. He can speak only a few words of English and Italian and is very completely lost – travelling north, although he says he wants to get to Rome. We give him food and shelter for the night and point out the road to the south. 'Me ship,' he says. 'Me not swim.' Very slight are his chances of getting home again.

Iris Origo

17 October

1660

This day were executed those murderous Traytors at Charing-Crosse, in sight of the place where they put to death their natural Prince [Charles I], and in the Presence of the King his sonn, whom they also sought to kill: take[n] in the trap they laied for others: The Traytors executed were Scot, Scroope, Cook, Jones. I saw not their execution, but met their quarters mangld and cutt and reaking as they were brought from the Gallows in gaskets on the hurdle.

John Evelyn

1927

I awakened without a kiss, had breakfast alone, dressed without talk; I had nobody to brush, to kiss good-bye; I am having lunch with Mother, and tonight I will sleep alone again. Am I glad to be alone? Was there anything I wanted to do while Hugh [her husband] is away that I cannot do when he is here? No. I miss him deeply, I have no desires, no joy at my independence; and I feel as if I were half alive. This wonderful life I praise so often seems blank and stupid today. I could do without my mirror, without lovely clothes, without sunshine – none of these things are necessary when I am alone. I did a few things to take advantage of my solitude, sleeping on the left side of the bed, which I prefer to the right, and wearing gloves with cold cream. And then, of course, I was glad to have the bathroom to myself. Usually I have to scratch the door and 'miaow' desperately to be allowed in, and even then I often get a shoe or a clothes brush on the head. Also, I slept fifteen minutes longer than usual.

Anaïs Nin

1964

Is my inability to love based on fear of vulnerability & lack of spiritual generosity; or is it the profound belief in the utter hopelessness of human love? I think it is the latter, but it may be the former. I've never once tried. It's almost as if I know it's foredoomed; and yet of course I don't know. One thing is certainly true about me at the present moment: I have no desire for life. Even as I write this, the awful feeling of guilt about such an admission makes me want to erase it. Why on earth commit such a thing to paper? I suppose all diarists are lonely and uncreative people.

Kenneth Williams

18 October

1749

I rode, at the desire of John Bennet, to Rochdale, in Lancashire. As soon as ever we entered the town, we found the streets lined on both sides with multitudes of people, shouting, cursing, blaspheming, and gnashing upon us with their teeth. Perceiving it would not be practicable to preach abroad, I went into a large room, open to the street, and called aloud, 'Let the wicked forsake his way, and the unrighteous man his thoughts.' The word of God prevailed over the fierceness of man. None opposed or interrupted; and there was a very remarkable change in the behaviour of the people, as we afterwards went through the town.

John Wesley

1870

Old James Jones was breaking stones below Pentwyn. He told me how he had once cured his deafness for a time by pouring hot eel oil into his ear, and again by sticking into the ear an 'ellern' (elder) twig, and wearing it there night and day. The effect of the eel oil at first was, he said, to make his head and brains feel full of crawling creatures.

Rev. Francis Kilvert

1873

I visited the county Prison alone and authorized the Governor to introduce gas into the carpenter's and brush shops, the expense not to exceed 10/-, the cost of necessary piping, and the work to be done by the prisoners; also purchase of new carpet for the bedroom of new laundry maid which has been papered and painted since the death of Miss Higgs from typhoid fever.

I saw Butt who has a cold, and Cole who has nearly murdered his wife with a hot poker.

Dearman Birchall

1930

Feeling very depressed with life. Can't make out whether it is mere middle-aged depression or whether it is really that I loathe journalism so much that it covers all my days with a dark cloud of shame. I feel that I have no time to add to my reputation by doing serious work and that my silly work day by day diminishes the reputation I have already acquired. I have become 'famous' as a radio comedian, and shall never be able to live down the impression thus acquired. In fact I feel a pretty feeble creature, just a soppy superficial humorist. I would give my soul to leave the *Standard* but I daren't risk it because of the money. Middle-age for a hedonist like myself is distressing in any case, but with most people it coincides with an increase of power and income. With me I have lost all serious employment, sacrificed my hopes of power, and am up against the anxiety of having not one penny in the world beyond what I earn. Is it this that makes me so perpetually unhappy? I have never been unhappy like this before. Till this year I have, except in rare periods of some definite worry or misery, woken each morning with the zest of being alive. Today each morning comes to me as a renewal of humiliation. It may be that I am overworked. I certainly mind things more than I should if my nerves were in order. I loathe getting fat for instance, and yet at my age [nearly forty-four], I can't expect to be young. Perhaps all this is good for me. Life has been an easy thing for me till this year 1930. And yet I shouldn't mind if I were in a position to fight my difficulties with what is best in me. What depresses me is that I can only live by exposing what is worst in me to the public gaze. I feel a fake: and it is that which humiliates and saddens me.

Harold Nicolson

1937 [Corfu]

Three days of squall and rain. The wind moans on the promontory, and all day long the threshing of sea sound on the white rock outside the house. In the interval as the undertow draws back you hear the dull patient throb of the hand-loom in the magazine, and the cough of the old billy-goat. Trees lean and whirl where the wind pours through the vents and boulder-strewn crevises of [Mount] Pantocrator. The roof has been sprung in several places, but this is the first taste of winter, and it is good that we should be proven wind-and-water tight before the real thunderstorms of December. Theodore [Stephanides, a family friend] has unearthed another charm against accident; it is for fair-weather sailors on moonlit nights. 'It is widely believed that the figure of a woman rising from the sea beside the boat calls out in wild accents "How is it with Alexander [the Great]?" The correct answer for those who do not want their craft overturned by her rage and grief is "He lives and reigns still." I do not know whether this charm will be of any practical assistance to you, but since you say you always run out to the Bay of Fauns at the full moon, it would be better on the whole to memorize it. One can never tell.'

Lawrence Durrell

1973

Wishing to buy another odd pair of trousers I went to what used to be called The Trouser Shop next to the Café Royal in Regent Street. The entrance looked different. A young man dressed in velvet, although in the middle of the day, approached me. Hesitantly I asked if this establishment still sold trousers. His greeting was 'Hullo!' which took me aback. I replied 'Hullo!' Then asked if he had any trousers that would suit me. With bland surprise he said regretfully, 'We can only cater for clients with a waist of less than 36,' and gave me a snide look. 'Besides, all our legs are much flared.' Oh dear, I found myself apologizing for being so old and untrendy. But on reflection, why the hell should a man apologize for no longer being young, as though he was thereby an inferior being?

James Lees-Milne

19 October

1838

Put leeches on my throat, and whilst they were adhering read the romantic play translated by Mrs Sloman, which promises very well.

Charles Macready

1917 [Russian front]

I saw one of our young doctors dressing a wound before the dirt and grime around it had been washed off. I gave way to my wrath and told him that he was asking for serious trouble if he had dressed the wound before first cleansing it. He rudely told me to mind my own business; I told him that it *was* my business to see that our soldiers' wounds were cleaned before bandaging. We exchanged many angry, resentful words. But I knew that I was right; he knew that he was wrong. But he was a doctor! I was only a Sister!

I worked it out before I went to sleep. I knew that I was growing coarse, bad-humoured and fault-finding. At first, I ascribed it to the pressure of warfare, the many hardships and humiliations, the conditions of our every-day life at the Front, when for days we could not undress, or even have a good wash. I decided that there were, indeed, good reasons for my bad temper; yet I began to feel ashamed of myself. Before I became a Red Cross nurse, I had been fully aware that there would be many exasperating moments, but I had been certain that I would overcome them – even welcome them in order to prove the strength of my will. I would often repeat those words of Goethe: *'Es bildet ein Talent sich in der Stille und ein Charakter im Strom der Welt.'* ['Talent is developed in tranquillity, but character is moulded in the tumult of the world.'] I had wanted my character to be strengthened and to come through, as victor, in the struggle. But recently there have been times when the knowledge that I was rude and ill-tempered did not even bother me.

Some of our Sisters and Brothers were not noted for their self-control and when they began to throw nasty, biting words at each other, I would tell myself: 'It is lack of education,' or 'It is the Russian temperament.' And now, I am doing the same thing! And I am English! We English have a reputation here for having our feelings well under control. I really am ashamed of myself and must take myself in hand.

Florence Farmborough

1980 [Goa]

I am approached by a smart, young, white-clad figure, who trudges from a distance across the sands like a survivor from some disastrous desert expedition. He is carrying two bottles. He suggests I need a massage. 'Ah,' he says, 'you very, very old man . . . very tired . . . very much work' . . . He pinches my leg and my upper arm . . . 'very, very old,' he says, shaking his head. I am nettled by this, and, refusing his attentions, walk off into the surf squaring my shoulders. But he has the last laugh as a comber knocks me off my feet. I remember a previous encounter with an itinerant masseur in Agra. When I refused his administrations, he offered, in sequence, his daughter or a copy of *The Reader's Digest*.

Sir Hugh Casson

20 October

1929

There are certain days on which one feels oneself particularly *wide of the mark*; behindhand; in debt; showing a deficit.

Today I see nothing but deficiencies everywhere; what I lack; where I fell short . . .

Take refuge in sleep.

André Gide

1940

The most – what? – impressive, no, that's not it – sight in London on Friday was the queue mostly children with suitcases, outside Warren Street tube. This was about 11.30. We thought they were evacuees waiting for a bus. But there they were, in a much longer line, with women, men, more bags, blankets, sitting still at 3. Lining up for the shelter in the night's raid – which came of course. Thus, if they left the tube at 6 (a bad raid on Thursday) they were back again at 11. So to Tavistock Square. With a sigh of relief saw a heap of ruins. Three houses, I should say, gone. Basement all rubble. Only relics an old basket chair (bought in Fitzroy Square days) and Penman's board To Let. Otherwise bricks and wood splinters. One glass door in the next house hanging. I could just see a piece of my studio wall standing: otherwise rubble where I wrote so many books. Open air where we sat so many nights, gave so many parties. The hotel not touched. So to Meck [Mecklenburgh Square]. All again. Litter, glass, black soft dust, plaster powder. Miss T., and Miss E. in trousers, overalls and turbans, sweeping. I noted the flutter of Miss T.'s hands: the same as Miss Perkins'. Of course friendly and hospitable in the extreme. Jaunty jerky talk. Repetitions. So sorry we hadn't had her card . . . to save you the shock. It's awful . . . Upstairs she propped a leaning bookcase for us. Books all over dining room floor. In my sitting room glass all over Mrs. Hunter's cabinet – and so on. Only the drawing room with windows almost whole. A wind blowing though. I began to hunt out diaries.

Virginia Woolf

1943 [Naples]

A narrow escape today while motor-cycling along the Via Partenope. I was riding towards the Castel Nuovo, through an area badly damaged by bombing, with the sea on the right and the semi-derelict buildings on the left, when I noticed a sudden change ahead from blue sky, sunshine and shadow, to a great opaque whiteness, shutting off the view of the port. The effect was one of a whole district blotted out by a pall of the white smoke sometimes spread from the chimneys of a factory producing lime. On turning a bend, I came upon an apocalyptic scene. A number of buildings including a bank had been pulverized by a terrific explosion that had clearly just taken place. Bodies were scattered all over the street, but here and there among them stood the living as motionless as statues, and all coated in thick white dust. What engraved this scene on the mind and the imagination was that nothing moved, and that the silence was total. Dust drifted down from the sky like a most delicate snowfall. A woman stood like Lot's wife turned to salt beside a cart drawn by two mules. One mule lay apparently dead, the other stood quietly at its side, without so much as twitching an ear. Nearby two men lay in the positions of bodies overcome by the ash at Pompeii, and a third, who had probably been in their company, stood swaying very slightly, his eyes shut. I spoke to him, but he did not reply. There was no blood to be seen anywhere.

This turned out to be one of a series of explosions produced by delayed-action explosive devices constructed by the Germans shortly before their departure, in each case from several hundred mines buried under principal buildings.

Norman Lewis

1985

It's the fortieth anniversary of the UN and I think Mrs Marcos is in town. It's getting so scary in the Philippines. Some papers say the Marcoses are buying up everything in the US, but that could not be true, the papers can lie. Our government must want them out, though. Like the US must have wanted the Shah to fall. But let's see, did we want to lose Vietnam? No, but after everything that's in the papers this week, I guess the Kennedys were just too busy having an affair with Marilyn to worry about Vietnam.

Andy Warhol

21 October

1857

Is not the poet bound to write his own biography? Is there any other work for him but a good journal? We do not wish to know how his imaginary hero, but how he, the actual hero, lived from day to day.

H. D. Thoreau

1880

Looking at the chimney-piece, Tennyson said, 'When I began to read Italian, I wrote down every word that puzzled me on the sides and front of the chimney-piece where I lodged – painted white – and made a kind of dictionary for myself. I went away for two or three days and when I came back it was all washed off. 'Thought it was dirt,' the woman said.

Worse than that – when I was twenty-two I wrote a beautiful poem on Poland, hundreds of lines long, and the housemaid lit the fire with it. I never could recover it.'

William Allingham

1941

The gray busy rainy sky I love, and would like to be out under. But weather, sky, night, sun, wind, rain, or friends are forbidden when there is not money. The invitation of a morning must be ignored for it is a reminder that money must be made – therefore work must be attempted. Actually, there is the empty purse too – a walk, an impulse to use a phone, a bus, buy a newspaper, and these are impossible. I never see autumn anymore without the feeling that I have missed summer – out of doors so forbidden to the poor and the desperate; for us, there is no time, no sun, no daylight, but the endless crouching over a typewriter, trying to keep it from its own will, forcing it in a dozen suggested paths to fortune or at least security.

Dawn Powell

1948

What should I do if I came upon a murder, I sometimes ask myself as Queenie [his dog] and I push our way through the vast tangles of bracken where few other people walk? The common is a likely place for murder, as it is for suicide – the angry lustful man who finds he is not, after all, to be granted the sexual relief that his pick-up has led him to expect. What should I do, I ask myself, if I suddenly smelt something nasty – as I often do – and pushing along came upon a strangled woman? I wouldn't do anything, unless I covered it up with leaves to give the murderer a better chance of escape. I certainly wouldn't report it. I have harboured thoughts of murder myself in my life; I could never help to denounce or catch anyone else.

J. R. Ackerley

1980

I ran into a boy whose job is to go shopping for John [Lennon] and Yoko [Ono], to buy them clothes and things. I asked him if they'd ever made him bring anything back and he said just once. I asked him if they ever *wore* any of the clothes they bought since they don't go out, and he said, 'They're going to make a comeback. They've been wearing them to the studio.' Oh, and the best thing he said was that when he started to work for them he had to sign a paper that said, 'I will not write a book about John Lennon and/or Yoko Ono.' Isn't that great? He said he loves his job. I should find somebody to help me shop – show me where all the good new things are.

Andy Warhol

22 October

1868

Walk to Setley, and find gypsies encamped. Coming back I overtake a little girl carrying with difficulty two bags of sand and just as I am asking how far she is going, up drives Rev. P. F. in his gig, who offers me a lift. I say, 'Help this little girl with her two heavy bags,' upon which his Reverence reddens and drives off. I carry one of the bags.

William Allingham

1871

Coming home in the dusk I turned into the school house to tell the school-master I was going out to-morrow for a few days and that I should not be at school this week. The schoolmaster is learning to play the violin. He produced the instrument and began to play upon it. It had a broken string, and there was something wrong with all the rest, and the noise it made 'fairly raked my bowels' as old Cord used to say at Wadham of Headeach's violon-cello. The schoolmaster however did not appear to notice that anything was wrong. His wife held the book up before him. 'Glory be to Jesus,' sang the schoolmaster, loudly and cheerfully sawing away at the cracked and broken strings, while the violin screeched and shrieked and screamed and groaned and actually seemed to writhe and struggle in his arms like a wild animal in agony. There was something so utterly incongruous in the words and the noise, the heart-rending bowel-raking uproar and screams of the tormented violin, that I smiled. I could not help it. Shriek, shriek, scream, groan, yell, howled the violin, as if a spirit in torment were writhing imprisoned within it, and still the schoolmaster sawed away vigorously, and sung amid the wailing, screeching uproar, 'Glory be to Jesus' in a loud and cheerful voice. It was the most ludicrous thing. I never was so hard put to it not to laugh aloud.

Rev. Francis Kilvert

1913 [The British Museum Reading Room]

I saw it for the first time to-day! Gadzooks!! This is the only fit ejaculation to express my amazement! It's a pagan temple with the Gods in the middle and all around various obscure dark figures prostrating themselves in worship.

W. N. P. Barbellion

1962 [Colorado Springs]

President Kennedy on the screen, perhaps announcing the end of the world; pudding-faced, and reading from a paper like a child, knowing the words, but not always making sense out of the sentences. His appearance was preceded by an ad for some sort of jet-toy – a little boy firing, and triumphantly sang: 'Got it!' (Which was the ad and which was the Presidential broadcast?)

Malcolm Muggeridge

1963

At lunch today I sat next to John Foster. He is pleased about Home [Sir Alec Douglas-Home had become prime minister]. He said he thought it must be the first time that a Prime Minister has two brothers who have been to prison. William Douglas-Home went for honourable reasons; he refused to carry out a command in the war which meant killing people unnecessarily.

Henry D-H was 'drunk in charge'. All this would be a very good response to the accusation that the new PM 'doesn't know how the other half lives'.

Cynthia Gladwyn

1964

I was appointed Minister of Housing on Saturday, October 17th 1964. Now it is only the 22nd but, oh dear, it seems a long, long time. It also seems as though I had really transferred myself completely to this new life as a Cabinet Minister. In a way it's just the same as I had expected and predicted. The room in which I sit is the same in which I saw Nye Bevan for almost the first time when he was Minister of Health, and already I realize the tremendous effort it requires not to be taken over by the Civil Service. My Minister's room is like a padded cell, and in certain ways I am like a person who is suddenly certified a lunatic and put safely into this great vast room, cut off from real life and surrounded by male and female trained nurses and attendants. When I am in a good mood they occasionally allow an ordinary human being to come and visit me; but they make sure that I behave right, and that the other person behaves right; and they know how to handle me. Of course, they don't behave *quite* like nurses because the Civil Service is profoundly deferential – 'Yes, Minister! No, Minister! If you wish it, Minister!' – and combined with this there is a constant preoccupation to ensure that the Minister does what is correct. The Private Secretary's job is to make sure that when the Minister comes into Whitehall he doesn't let the side or himself down and behaves in accordance with the requirements of the institution.

It's also profoundly true that one has only to do absolutely nothing whatsoever in order to be floated forward on the stream. I had forgotten what day it was – indeed, the whole of my life in the last four days has merged into one, curious, single day – when I turned to my Private Secretary, George Moseley, and said, 'Now, you must teach me how to handle all this correspondence.' And he sat opposite me with his owlish eyes and said to me, 'Well, Minister, you see there are three ways of handling it. A letter can either be answered by you personally, in your own handwriting; or we can draft a personal reply for you to sign; or, if the letter is not worth your answering personally, we can draft an official answer.' 'What's an official answer?' I asked. 'Well, it says the Minister has received your letter and then the Department replies. Anyway, we'll draft all three variants,' said Mr Moseley, 'and if you just tell us which you want . . .' 'How do I do that?' I asked. 'Well, you put all your in-tray into your out-tray,' he said, 'and if you put it in without a mark on it then we deal with it and you need never see it again.'

I think I've recorded that literally. I've only to transfer everything that's in my in-tray to my out-tray without a single mark on it to ensure it will be dealt with – all my Private Office is concerned with is to see that the routine runs on, that the Minister's life is conducted in the right way.

Richard Crossman

1978 [Rome]

Dressed in the extraordinary costume of white tie, evening tailcoat, black waistcoat, decorations, which was required for the Papal installation [of John Paul II], I set off for St Peter's just after 9 o'clock. The Mass (in the open air) began at 10 o'clock and went on until 1.15 in steadily improving weather, so that the umbrella I had cautiously taken manifestly became unnecessary by about 11 o'clock. Most of the first hour was taken up by the homage of all the cardinals, and I wished that I had a key to them. Emilio Colombo (next to me) wasn't bad and pointed out about fourteen, but even his knowledge seemed far from perfect. The Duke of Norfolk, in the next row, offered pungent comments about one or two of them. The second hour was taken up by introductory parts of the service and by a half-hour sermon, delivered seated but with great force by the new pope, who has a remarkable linguistic ability. There were passages in French, Spanish, German, English, Serbo-Croat, Polish obviously, Russian, Czech I think, and Portuguese, all thrown in on the Italian base and all rather convincingly done.

Roy Jenkins

23 October

1907

I thank Heaven that at present, though I am damnable, I am in love with nobody, except *myself*.

Katherine Mansfield

1927

To the oculist. Small child sat opposite me, with enormous glasses on, lenses magnified many times. She looked with these large pensive eyes – unnaturally large, like cow's eyes – all over the room, and *me* (feeling very uncomfortable). I felt as if the cow had licked me all over with her large tongue.

Anne Morrow Lindbergh

1943

A tremendous scare this morning following the information given by a captured enemy agent that thousands of delayed-action mines would explode when the city's electricity supply was switched on. This was timed for 2 p.m.

today. An order was given for the whole of Naples to be evacuated, and within minutes army vehicles were tearing up and down the streets broadcasting instructions to the civilian population.

The scene as the great exodus started, and a million and a half people left their houses and crowded into the streets, was like some Biblical calamity. Everyone had to be got away to the safety of the heights of the Vomero, Fontanelle and the Observatory, overlooking the town. This meant that the bedridden, the dying, and all the women in labour had to be coped with in some way or other, not to mention the physically and mentally sick persons in clinics all over the town. The agent had specifically mentioned that 5000 mines had been laid under the enormous building housing the 92nd General Hospital, packed at this time with war casualties, all of whom had to be moved to a place of safety. Our own move took place shortly before midday when streets were beginning to clear of the last of the desperate crowds. I saw men carrying their old parents on their backs, and at one moment a single, small explosion set off a panic with women and children running screaming in all directions, leaving trails of urine.

At the Vomero we took up positions at a spot on the heights where the road had been intentionally widened to assist visitors to appreciate the view, which was splendid indeed. All Naples lay spread out beneath us like an antique map, on which the artist had drawn with almost exaggerated care the many gardens, the castles, the towers and the cupolas. For the first time, awaiting the cataclysm, I appreciated the magnificence of this city, seen at a distance when cleansed of its wartime tegument of grime, and for the first time I realized how un-European, how oriental it was. Nothing moved but a distant floating confetti of doves. A great silence had fallen and we looked down and awaited the moment of devastation. At about four o'clock the order came for everyone to go home.

Norman Lewis

1969

I was asked to one of the Archbishop of Canterbury's press lunches. The faded architectural pomp of the palace is bizarrely at variance with the lower-middle-class lifestyle lived within it. Sherry and orange juice were followed by a utilitarian lunch of stew, apple pie and cream, and cheese.

Archbishop Ramsey is a huge man with no neck, a sweet face and smile and marvellous eyes, all of it arising from a mound of pink and purple. After we'd eaten he held forth, rather apologetically I thought, predicting a further decline of the Church of England, the saving grace being that Christian attitudes were still important in a society even if they were no longer connected with belief. This sounded a pretty grim scenario to me.

Roy Strong

24 October

Near Reilly's Tavern, I saw a pavement artist who had drawn a loaf with the inscription in both French and English: 'This is easy to draw but hard to earn'. A baby's funeral trotted briskly over the Tower Bridge among Pink's jam waggons, carts carrying any goods from lead pencils and matches to bales of cotton and chests of tea.

Walked past great blocks of warehouses and business establishments – a wonderful sight; and everywhere bacon factors, coffee roasters, merchants. On London Bridge, paused to feed the sea-gulls and looked down at the steve-dores. Outside Billingsgate market was a blackboard on an easel – for market prices – but instead some one had drawn an enormously enlarged chalk picture of a cat's rear and tail with anatomical details.

In Aldgate, stopped to inspect a street stall containing popular literature – one brochure entitled *Suspended for Life* to indicate the terrible punishment meted out to – a League footballer. The frontispiece enough to make a lump come into the juveniles' throats! Another stall held domestic utensils with an intimation, 'Anything on this stall *lent* for 1d'. A newsvendor I heard exclaim to a fellow tradesman in the same line, – 'They come and look at your bloody plakaard and then parsse on.'

Loitered at a dirty little Fleet Street bookshop where Paul de Kock's *The Lady with the Three Pairs of Stays* was displayed prominently beside a picture of Oscar Wilde.

In Fleet Street, you exchange the Whitechapel sausage restaurants for Taverns with 'snacks at the bar', and the chestnut roasters, with their buckets of red-hot coals, for Grub Street camp followers, selling *L'Indépendence Belge* or pamphlets entitled, *Why We Went to War*.

In the Strand you may buy war maps, buttonhole flags, etc., etc. I bought a penny stud. One shop was turned into a shooting gallery at three shots a penny where the Inner Temple Barristers in between the case for the defence and the case for the prosecution could come and keep their eye in against the time the Germans come.

Outside Charing Cross Station I saw a good-looking, well-dressed woman in mourning clothes, grinding a barrel organ . . .

W. N. P. Barbellion

According to Roger, nine out of ten of the young men who indulge in prostitution here are in no wise homosexual. They do it moreover without repugnance but solely for the money, which allows them on the other hand to keep a mistress, with whom they are seen everywhere throughout the day. Roger claims to have enjoyed the confidences of a great number of them, in the various establishments where they can be found in the evening, and since he does not go there to 'partake', he boasts of obtaining more sincere confidences than the people they try to flatter; personal confidences, and also about one another. And as I question somewhat the exactness of those statistics, he obstinately maintains his figure: nine out of ten. 'Yes, I am convinced that but one out of ten among them is yielding to a natural inclination.' This would seem to prove at least, if one takes this information to be exact, that even constant practice does not succeed in overcoming a spontaneous taste (as it has often been claimed), does not manage to influence true tendencies. 'Drive out nature and it comes back on the run.'

But I believe also that imperative, irresistible tastes, whether homosexual or heterosexual, are rather rare, and that a great number of people have a mobile taste, *ad libitum*, vacillating, without conviction, without vocation, ready to yield to the occasion, to fashion, to opinion, and indiscriminately seeking sensual pleasure, the only thing that is certain.

André Gide

1944 [ENSA tour in Syria]

Two small signal corps units last night at Homs, and the night before. The first disguised in hive-huts. My background was a wall entirely covered in pin-up girls, mostly stark naked. Princess Elizabeth in pale blue looked rather overdressed among them. Cheese sandwiches and sweet tea to follow the performance and I was shown the works. Last night's groups were housed in small tin huts. The one we used for the show was a round one with a tin roof. Someone had rigged up a light for the piano and a little tin-reflected spot for me.

Three Armenians from the nearby village came to the show – mother and two daughters of about sixteen and ten. They sat in a row on the front bench, dead still, with their hands folded in their laps, their wax white faces entirely without expression and their beetle black eyes on us both without blinking for the whole session.

Afterwards in solemn procession and without smiles they shook us by the hand and filed out in silence. I wonder what they made of it all.

Joyce Grenfell

25 October

1655

After much thought I did this day make known to Eliza [her friend] that I did do the daily journal entry. And most surprised I was that no surprise there was in her. All this time it does seem that she too does make the secret scribbling, yet she shares not this confidence with me. We do promise that one day we will show each to the other the records we do keep, though many there are who would disapprove of such entry-making and would put it with mischief so not to all would we make exposure.

Eliza would have me know that diary-keeping does become the risqué fashion now, among the highborn. Regular accounts do they keep of their duties and days – which is not how my mother does have it. But Eliza does quote her aunt – whom she does set great store by for she has the trusted place in the household of Lady Willoughby – and her aunt does swear that 'tis the noble thing to do to keep the diary.

'Tis her aunt's word that the good Lady each day does write when she does rise, the Bible verses she does read, the prayers she does say, and the viands she does eat. Which does seem a very waste of quire and ink to me. What satisfaction would there be in it for me to note that this very day I did rise, break my fast, and wind yarn for my mother? That I did threaten my brother Balty should he try to wheedle any money from my lover, and did soft-talk my father who does brave the disappointment with his brick-moulding machine.

Yet if my mother should think that the entries be about marriages and births, and deaths and other grave events, and if Lady Willoughby should think that they be about devotions and diet, and if I should think they be about the thoughts I do have – and the wrangles, and the joys – that do make up the day – then only one conclusion should there be. That this diary-keeping can be on anything.

I wonder what content Eliza does put in . . .

'Elizabeth Pepys'

1870

At Maesllwch Castle last week four guns killed seven hundred rabbits in one afternoon.

Rev. Francis Kilvert

1921

My parents were playing cards; I sat apart, a perfect stranger; my father asked me to take a hand, or at least to look on; I made some sort of excuse. What is the meaning of these refusals, oft repeated since my childhood? I could have availed myself of invitations to take part in social, even, to an extent, public life; everything required of me I should have done, if not well at least in middling fashion; even card-playing would probably not have bored me overmuch – yet I refused.

Franz Kafka

26 October

1862

It was Chapuys-Montlaville, the senator, who, after the Emperor had taken a bath at the Prefecture in the course of his tour of the south of France, had the bath-water drawn off and bottled. He decanted it as if it were Jordan water. And this happened in the middle of the nineteenth century – which does not prevent us from laughing at a nation which worships a Grand Lama's excrement. There are two infinities in this world: God up above, and down below, human baseness.

The Goncourt Brothers

1947

Is there anything more pleasant than an autumnal weekend in London? I lazed in bed – revelled in the almost royal splendour of my bedroom, and rose late to arrange my dinner party for the Regent of Iraq and his Minister of Defence. It was a great success. The Regent brought me a coffee set of silver as a present – six cups and a huge salver with palm trees engraved on it. The coffee pot has a spout like a pelican – hideous.

'Chips' Channon

1957

My secret news is that I fear that Old Black Magic has reared itself up again. This is stimulating, disturbing, enjoyable, depressing, gay, tormenting, delightful, silly and sensible. Perhaps I was getting a little smug and too sure of my immunity. It may also be that now that I'm slim as a rail again I'm more attractive not only to myself but to others. I can already see all the old hoops being prepared for me to go through. Ah me!

Noël Coward

1971

During the filming [of *Carry on Matron*] this morning, I had a sausage in a roll and Gerald [Thomas, the director] said, 'Shouldn't eat all that bread . . .

it is fattening . . .' I said, 'You don't want to worry about me! My belly isn't sticking out,' and he said, 'No, but your arse is.'

Kenneth Williams

1981

Stepping across the gate into Sarah's arms. We embrace and kiss. So lovely to touch in legitimate time. We waste no time jumping in the car and heading into the distance.

Accumulated thoughts: I am wondering what it will be like to sleep together, having known each other for four years and been married for almost two. Up the long winding roads the scenery was spectacular. Sitting there with Sarah at my side, the prison far behind and the wonders of the Scottish Highlands all around me I felt stunned with pleasure . . . How can I possibly explain this experience to anyone after fourteen years in prison. Every fibre was open and alert to this vast mountain scenery. Finally we reached our caravan situated high up on the hillside with a wide and full view of the valley. It was getting quite dark though still enough light for us to see our view from the caravan. Sheep were all around us. We looked down the valley to a splattering of cottages and farmhouses. The visual images are overwhelming. The night was spent in a small double bed with me always aware of Sarah next to me. I was restless. It will take some getting used to after fourteen years of sleeping alone . . . It's the first time in years I've slept on a mattress.

Jimmy Boyle

27 October

1846 [New York]

I witnessed this morning, from the steps of Clinton Hall, a scene which is calculated to cause alarm as to future collisions between the citizens of the country, – a trifling incident in the appalling drama which we shall be called to witness, and perhaps bear a part in, during the course of not many years. A negro boy, named George Kirk, a slave from Georgia, secreted himself in a vessel commanded by Captain Cuckley, and was brought to New York. Here he was arrested and confined, at the instance of the captain, who is subjected to severe penalities for the abduction of the slave. The claim of the master to have the fugitive sent back to Georgia was tried before Judge Edwards; N. B. Blunt appearing for the captain, and Mr John Jay and J. L. White for the slave.

The judge's decision set the boy free, for want of evidence to prove his identity; and such a mob, of all colours, from dirty white to shining black, came rushing down Nassau and into Beckman Street as made peaceable people shrink into places of security. Such shouting and jostling, such peals of negro triumph, such uncovering of woolly heads in raising the greasy hats to give effect to the loud huzzas of the sons of Africa, seemed almost to 'fright the neighborhood from its propriety.' A carriage was brought to convey the hero of the day from his place of concealment, but it went away without him. This is all very pretty; but how will it end? How long will the North and the South remain a united people?

Philip Hone

1938

It is possible not to think about women, just as one does not think about death.

Cesare Pavese

1941

The sights – the long tree-lined avenue in Hyde Park at dusk echoing with the noise of soldiers' boots as they come strolling, swinging, whistling, singing, or alone looking for a girl, and the girls plain – most of them – little working girls in short skirts and sweaters with fancy handkerchiefs around their necks. They know they are wanted – they twist and turn as they walk and break into sudden gusts of giggles and cling to each other's arms. The whole length of the avenue is alive with desires. There are satyrs behind every tree. Silhouetted against the half-lights soldiers with their girls sit on the deck-chairs on the grassy stretches that border the avenue. The flicker of a cigarette lighter reveals for a long second – the pose of a head – the movements of hands. Near the park gates the Military Police in their rose-topped caps stand in groups of twos and threes hoping for trouble, longing to exercise summary justice.

In the expensive restaurants at this hour pink, well-scrubbed schoolboys masquerading in Guards uniforms are drinking bad martinis with girl-friends in short fur capes and Fortnum and Mason shoes, who have spent the day driving generals to the War Office or handing cups of tea and back-chat to soldiers in canteens. Grass widows in black with diamond clips or pearls are finding the conversation of Polish officers refreshingly different from that of English husbands. Ugly vivacious A.T.S. [Auxiliary Territorial Service] are ordering *vin rosé* at the Coquille. A film actress (making the best of a patriotic part at present) is just going through the swinging door of the Apéritif with David Niven at her elbow. Ageing Edwardian hostesses whose big houses are now shuttered and silent are taking little naps in their hideouts on the third floor ('so much the safest floor, darling') at Claridges's or the

Dorchester. Cedric (in a yachtsman's jacket) and Nigel are hipping their way through the crowd of pansies in the Ritz bar (they all have the most madly peculiar jobs in the Ministry of Information or the B.B.C.). At the Travellers' Club Harold Nicolson in his fruity voice is embellishing a story as he settles on the leather sofa. Anne-Marie is sitting on the side of her bed at the Ritz making eyes at herself in the mirror and trumpeting down the telephone in Romanian French. It is a world of hotels and bars and little pubs that have become the fashion overnight – of small drinking clubs run by gangsters who make a nice profit out of prostitutes and the dope racket – packed with R.A.F. pilots, Canadian officers, blondes and slot-machines and perhaps a baccarat table in the upstairs rooms.

And along Piccadilly from the Circus to Hyde Park Corner is an incessant parade of prostitutes, and out of the black-out an acquisitive hand on your arm and 'Feeling lonely, dearie?' 'Hello, my sweet,' (in a Noël Coward voice) or '*Chéri.*' In Berkeley Square the railings are down. An old man is making a bonfire of dead leaves beside the little pavilion in the centre of the garden.

Charles Ritchie

1942

Postman brought us a Red Cross message meant for Uncle Gordon, which he asked us to read, then he took it back. I had wondered what happened to Red Cross messages which came for people who have been deported. Evidently, the Germans allow relatives to read them, but not to keep them. Uncle's message came from a lady friend of his . . . I wonder what he would say if he knew we had read it! A young Russian came; poor fellow, he had a leg all swollen and purple and seemed anxious. They know that their German masters have no pity on those who are sick and let them die. I hear that about 13 Russians died at a camp last week, some being taken away in wheelbarrows before they were quite dead. A man who lives close by says he will have to move because he does not want his children to see the Germans beating the poor Russians. To think that such awful things happen in our little island. These are dark days indeed for Jersey.

Nan Le Ruez

28 October

1935

Poetry begins when a simpleton says of the sea: 'It looks like oil!' This is not exactly the best possible description of a flat calm, but he is pleased at discovering the similarity, tickled by the idea of a mysterious connection, and feels he must tell the world what he has noticed. But it would be equally foolish to stop at that. Having started the poem, one must finish it, work up the idea with a wealth of associations and skilfully arrive at an assessment of its value. There you have a typical poem, based on an idea. The typical poem may possibly be remote from reality, consisting up to now (just as we can even live on microbes) of mere odds and ends of similarities (sentiment); constructive thought (logic); and associations caught at random (poetry). A more arbitrary combination would probably be foolish and unbearable.

Cesare Pavese

1937 [Nanking]

Alarm at 9:10 a.m., but a false one. Otherwise an active business day that was quiet until evening when something happened after all: Tsao, my rascal of a cook, was supposed to serve bread and cheese for supper, but had none, got scolded, became angry, and gave notice as of the first. He lost the battle, but saved face. Let him go – I don't care! I won't weaken, I want my cheese!

John Rabe

1943

Neapolitans take their sex lives very seriously indeed. A woman called Lola, whom I met at a dinner-party given by Signora Gentile, arrived at HQ with some denunciation which went into the waste-paper basket as soon as her back was turned. She then asked if I could help her. It turned out she has taken a lover who is a captain in the RASC [Royal Army Service Corps], but as he speaks no single word of Italian, communication can only be carried on by signs, and this gives rise to misunderstanding. Would I agree to inter- pret for them and settle certain basic matters?

Captain Frazer turned out to be a tall handsome man some years Lola's junior . . . She wanted to know all about his marital status and he hers, and they lied to each other to their hearts' content while I kept a straight face and interpreted.

She asked me to mention to him in as tactful a way as possible that comment had been caused among her neighbours because he never called on her during the day. Conjugal visits at midday are *de rigueur* in Naples. This I explained, and Frazer promised to do better.

When the meeting was over we went for a drink, and he confided to me that something was worrying him too. On inspecting her buttocks he had found them covered with hundreds of pinpoint marks, some clearly very small scars. What could they be? I put his mind at rest. These were the marks left by *iniezione reconstituenti*: injections which are given in many of the pharmacies of Naples and which many middle-class women receive daily to keep their sexual powers at their peak. Frequently the needle is not too clean, hence the scars.

She had made him understand by gestures one could only shudderingly imagine that her late husband – although half-starved, and even when in the early stages of tuberculosis from which he died – never failed to have intercourse with her less than six times a night. She also had a habit, which terrified Frazer, of keeping an eye on the bedside clock while he performed. I recommended him to drink – as the locals did – marsala with the yolks of eggs stirred into it, and wear a medal of San Rocco, patron of *coitus reservatus*, which could be had in any religious-supply shop.

Norman Lewis

29 October

1939

Read Aldous Huxley. Good for the soul – not Aldous Huxley, but the relaxation of reading and getting one's mind off the daily track. We are, after all, although bureaucrats, human beings. And no human being can go on for ever chained to a wheel: it's bad for him and he becomes rotten. Must relax, cynically, if you like.

Sir Alexander Cadogan

1941 [POW camp]

Lunch is still, like the washing facilities, typical to my mind of Dickens' description of Oliver Twist conditions. Carrying one's spoon, if in possession of such an invaluable tool, down the High St, queuing up with one's ticket, collecting and carrying away one's little white bowl to sit on a wooden bench at a wooden table and put one's face in it – which is exactly what happens to the unfortunates who haven't got a spoon. Lord, how I laughed watching old Booth, who never stops talking about his pig farm at home, sitting at a table by himself and giving a perfect demonstration of Mr Piglet getting down to it.

Captain John Mansel

1962 [California]

Caught Greyhound bus – cheapest form of travel. Queuing for my bus with poor people, coloured, etc., felt a mounting blissful sense of relief at being with them. Great truth in saying that the poor are blessed. All the manifestations of riches contain misery, implicit if not explicit. Joyousness comes from below. In bus, all windows sealed, glass blue-tinted. Once again the governing

American passion to exclude the world – air, sound, light, food, sensuality. Everything is wrapped, packaged.

Malcolm Muggeridge

30 October

1854

Mme de Caen was looking her best at dinner this evening; I have to take a tight grip on my heart when she is near, but only when she wears full evening dress and shows her arms and shoulders. I become very reasonable next morning when she wears ordinary clothes. She came to look at the paintings in my bedroom this morning and then, without any hesitation, took me through to her dressing-room to see the ones in her own room. I felt secure about my virtue, however, because I found myself thinking of other times when this bedroom and dressing-room housed the exquisite Marcelline who, I suspect, possesses no such breasts and arms, but has a way of pleasing by some quality of her own – her wit perhaps, or the mischief in her eyes, the qualities that make her so impossible to forget.

Eugène Delacroix

1922 [Berlin]

Mussolini has been appointed Prime Minister by the King of Italy. This may turn out to be a black day for Italy and Europe.

Count Harry Kessler

1931

I. D. Stewart along. Gave me a vivid résumé of Chaplin's latest film, *City Lights*. Apart from an occasional desire to leap or dance – there are two experiences which I'd like to enjoy again – a walk over Callerfountain and a Chaplin picture.

William Soutar

1942

One nice Australian sergeant pilot will not come into the canteen again, and tell us tantalizing yarns of bright warm sun, surf-bathing and lovely cheap fruit. He crashed last Monday and was buried today. How hard – or is it philosophical? – we are growing. Beyond a 'Poor lad, I thought he was late', and pity for the wasted lives, no remarks were passed. Things that would have shocked us to our heart's core now receive no more than a passing remark.

Nella Last

1946

Today I retired my old Bible, bought in 1904. During the writing of the two Treatise books I put it to very heavy use, and it is now in tatters, with the binding and many of the leaves loose and some of the leaves torn. It has served me for more than forty years, and I retire it with some regret. Its original cost, I believe, was 50¢. Today I dropped into the Methodist bookstore in Charles Street and bought another Bible of substantially the same print and binding. The price was $1.50. Even God, it appears, begins to profiteer.

H. L. Mencken

31 October

1800

A very fine moonlight night – The moon shone like herrings in the water.

Dorothy Wordsworth

1907

Apropos of the agitation for abolishing the Censor in England, it occurred to me that not even the advocates of freedom seek to justify the free treatment of sexual matters in any other than a high moral-pointing vein. The notion that sexual themes might allowably be treated in the mere aim of amusement does not seem to have occurred to anybody at all.

Arnold Bennett

1937

One stops being a child when one realises that telling one's trouble does not make it better.

Cesare Pavese

1938

Have just been to analysis. At present I have no clear idea of what is happening; today brought out what seemed only a muddled collection of images. Talked about the intermittent bursts of creative enthusiasm I have, which so often fall flat because I feel incapable of fulfilling them. '"La mariée est trop belle", as the proverb says,' Mme Jouve remarked.

Have been thinking it might be useful to put down a few notes about *sex*.

Mme Jouve says I have an exceptional faculty of transformation. I suppose this includes a particular aptitude for sublimating sex urges; because when I read novels about adolescence, confessions of sex experiences, etc., it seems to me I must be undersexed, if anything, so little have I suffered from the usual assault of tormenting carnal desires that most young men appear to have to cope with.

Every now and again, but not so very often, slowly and lazily a somewhat vague sort of sensuality wakes up; my imagination finds itself looking about for something lacking, for an object to which to attach the indefinite desire for tenderness which is the strongest form of manifestation my sensuality generally takes. One could hardly call this being 'enflamed'. (The object looked for, I should add, has become exclusively male). If nothing turns up, I usually find it quite easy to do without till the next time.

David Gascoyne

1939

We now have witnesses' statements regarding deliveries of poison gas to Poland by the English. They will be released at the next good opportunity.

The English radio broadcasts a low, vulgar piece for my birthday. This kind of thing is exclusively the work of the Jews who emigrated from Germany. But then they lost their idiotic struggle against me once already, in Berlin. Let them try again, this time from London. The polemical material from England and France is becoming more idiotic by the day. The *Daily Telegraph* had published a report that we used clandestine radio transmitters to encourage the Poles to resist, by offering them the bait of English aid. This is so moronic that an answer is scarcely worthwhile.

Josef Goebbels

NOVEMBER

'There's an awful lot of writing going on that nobody knows about.'

EDWARD GILDEA, PUBLISHER OF
THE DIARISTS' JOURNAL

1 November

1660

The great chafe I am in, for last night my husband does make to baste me – by reason that I am ill! And does he count the days since we did lie together and demand his dues soon, else he does claim as 'tis his right to put his pintle in some other. Which does bring out the very deep anger in me; and no way to win me to him it is. And will I observe where his pintle does go (and I do have my ways) and the price he should pay if it should find other accommodation.

'Elizabeth Pepys'

1868

Began the second part of 'Little Women.' I can do a chapter a day, and in a month I mean to be done. A little success is so inspiring that I now find my 'Marches' sober, nice people, and as I can launch into the future, my fancy has more play. Girls write to ask who the little women marry, as if that was the only end and aim of a woman's life. I *won't* marry Jo to Laurie to please any one.

Louisa May Alcott

1869

Old Irish airs on violin. I love Ireland: were she only not Catholic! But would she be Ireland otherwise?

William Allingham

1941

Was for the first time subjected to some abuse the day before yesterday. At Chemnitzer Platz a section of Hitler Youth cubs. 'A yid, a yid!' Yelling they run toward the dairy I am just entering, I can still hear them shouting and laughing outside. When I come out, they are lined up. I look calmly at their commander, not a word is spoken. Once I am past, behind me, but not called out loudly, one, two voices: 'A yid!' – A couple of hours later at Lange's nursery, I am fetching sand for Muschel, an older worker: 'You, mate, do you know Herrschmann? – No? – He's a Jew too, porter like me – I just wanted to say: It doesn't matter about the star, we're all human beings, and I know such good Jews.' Such consolation is not very cheering either. But which is the true vox populi?

Today urgent warning card from Sussmann, he must have read something alarming about deportations, I should immediately renew my USA application, he himself would see to it that I got an interim residence permit in Sweden, 'if all conditions for the USA were fulfilled.' I wrote back immediately, every route was now blocked. In fact we heard from several sources that a complete ban on emigration has just been decreed on the German side. Besides a year and a day would pass before the new American conditions were fulfilled. No, we must wait here and see what our fate will be.

Victor Klemperer

1944 [Baghdad]

Yesterday at 4.30 Queen Ali [widow of Ali, formerly King of the Hejaz], her daughter the present Queen, and the Regent's two youngest sisters all came to tea at the Embassy. They are strictly in purdah and arrived veiled; the chancery, that opens on the riverside terraces, was barred for the afternoon and the ambassador kept out of his office. We curtsied all around. The older Queen, about sixty? was in black silk dress and wore her veil unbecomingly thrown over her head, low on the brow and behind the ears, and sat on a sofa in enforced silence and knowing no English – not even joining in when Arabic was spoken. Her little legs were slightly bowed in their sheer sunburn stockings. The Queen was in a bottlegreen and white print with a scalloped crepe de Chine collar of great dullness but her face is enchanting. No make-up. A pity, for she needs the accent of lipstick to balance the importance of her lovely dark eyes in a very pale face. She looked amusing. Understands English but won't speak it. Her eyes had the entirely unsophisticated look of a little girl's. I talked to one Princess about being in purdah – 'veiled' she called it. I said perhaps things would change for them someday. 'Not before I am old,' she said, not with passion but sadly. I asked her what she did all day. 'Garden,' she said, and I said it was fun when it wasn't too hot and what did she grow? 'Oh, not *do* garden, sit in the garden,' she explained. 'If we had not wireless and films our life would be very sad.' Indeed, yes. She and her young sister are about twenty-two and twenty, attractive with lovely figures and neat feet and hands. They are destined to marry one of their already inbred cousins, or not at all. One of their aunts ran off with an Italian waiter in Sicily and was not only cut off for ever by the family but a law was actually passed proving she no longer existed. Later the waiter tired of her – she had no 'dot'. No appeal from her was heard at all and heaven knows what has happened to her. So it takes a lot of thinking before it would be wise for one of them to cut a dash out of the royal circle. We talked in English.

They had an English nurse and governess. Later I sang three songs, including 'Yours' by request of a princess.

Joyce Grenfell

1951

On the way home in the bus where I sat with Matthew [his son], one of his little friends who was seated directly in front of us suddenly turned round, pointed at me with butting finger, and said, 'Spender, is that old, white-haired man with spectacles your daddy?' 'No,' said Matthew with perfect self-possession. When we got off the bus and were at a safe distance from his little friend I asked Matthew why he had said I was not his father. 'Because you aren't,' he exclaimed passionately. 'You aren't like what he said you were.'

Stephen Spender

1977

Worked early, and then climbed into the Moss Bros suit ready for the Palace [to receive knighthood]. The theatre wardrobe has discovered that the correct thing for investitures is black waistcoat and black hat, so that is how I appeared. Much the same drill as thirteen or fourteen years ago when I got the CBE. A grey-haired colonel of the Royal Household briefed us all in amiable military fashion. His eyebrows went up from his nose at about 30 degrees each side and were jet black strips, as if applied with Elastoplast. I was put with some of my fellows in the first waiting room, and my heart sank. I am going to have to talk to complete strangers for the entire morning, I thought. Happily Alexander Gibson, an old friend, arrived, and as he's G and I'm an H we went through the process together, whispering like naughty boys. The Queen Mum officiated. It is remarkable that a lady of 76 or 77 can stand in the same spot for an hour and three quarters and, apparently without being prompted and without a crib, remember a little something significant to say to over a hundred people in the right order. The Guards band played the same music I had heard for the CBE. Selections from Oklahoma came up, and Gilbert and Sullivan, appropriately 'When everybody's somebody, then no one's anybody.' If they'd had some divertimenti by Mozart or Haydn or any of the eighteenth-century occasional musicians, the live muzack we heard would have been bearable. And I think we should have been given a drink. There was a sense of suffering like guardsmen on parade in honour of ceremony.

Peter Hall

1980

Fiddly day. Take M. shopping locally. How difficult and time-consuming it is. By ill-luck we need a broom-head, some bananas, batteries, bulbs, bacon and elastoplast – all from different shops. It takes ages and quickly ruffles the temper. How sheltered are the lives of most married men; and would shopping centres be different if we shopped more often?

Sir Hugh Casson

2 *November*

1860 [New York]

Think I will vote the Republican ticket next Tuesday. One vote is insignificant, but I want to be able to remember that I voted right at this grave crisis. The North must assert its rights, now, and take the consequences.

Think of James J. Roosevelt, United States District Attorney, bringing up certain persons under indictment for piracy as slave-traders to be arraigned the other day, and talking to the Court about the plea the defendants should put in, and saying that 'there had been a great change in public sentiment about the slave trade,' and that 'of course the President would pardon the defendants if they were capitally convicted.' !!! Is Judge Roosevelt more deficient in common sense or in moral sense? If we accede to Southern exactions, we must re-open the slave trade with all its horrors, establish a Slave Code for the territories, and acquiesce in a decision of the United States Supreme Court in the Lemmon case that will entitle every Southerner to bring his slaves into New York and Massachusetts and keep them there. We must confess that our federal government exists chiefly for the sake of nigger-owners. *I can't do that.* Rather let South Carolina and Georgia secede. We will coerce and punish the traitorous seceders if we can; but if we can't, we are well rid of them.

George Templeton Strong

1911

This morning, for the first time in a long time, the joy again of imagining a knife twisted in my heart.

Franz Kafka

1941 [POW camp]

Due to lack of washing facilities in hot water, many have had their head shaved. The result is grotesque to look at, but quite likely wiser. For myself, I am today feeling delightfully clean having last night, just before getting into bed, had a hot tub – I must explain. One stands up in a zinc wash basin which just takes the feet, in 1½" of really hot water, when the feet are in, and by dint of scouring oneself and standing as erect as possible so as not to splash clothes, beds, readers, writers, etc., attains a state of cleanliness which had for weeks seemed unredeemable. Finished off with a powder all over with foot powder and climbing into clean pyjamas, to be followed by a hot drink of Ovaltine, was simply marvellous.

I enjoyed a most rare sensation today, which was jumping clear of traffic – i.e. a lorry on one of the Camp tracks. Having for so long walked dreamily knowing well that barbed wire protected me from vehicles, I was quite staggered by this incident. I wonder what it will feel like to get into a car again.

Captain John Mansel

1951

Theater. A gentleman is pointing out the celebrities in the house to his neighbor. 'Look, there's Jean Marasi! And there's Danielle Darrieux! And there's X, and there's Y! And you see that gentleman with the white hair – that's Paul Valéry.' 'But Paul Valéry's dead!' 'Dead? Look . . . he's moving.'

Jean Cocteau

1961

Ah me! This growing old. This losing of friends and breaking of links with the past. One by one they go – a bit chipped off here, a bit chipped off there. It is an inevitability that one must prepare the heart and mind for. I wonder how long it will be before I make my last exit. Probably quite a while, both Mum and Father had long lives. Unlike Edna St Vincent Millay, I *am* resigned. There is no sense in rebellion. I suppose I should envy the afterlife believers, the genuflectors, the happy-ever-after ones who know beyond a shadow of doubt that we shall all meet again in some celestial vacuum, but I don't. I'd rather face up to finality and get on with life, lonely or not, for as long as it lasts. Those I have really loved are still with me in moments of memory – whole and intact and unchanged. I cannot envisage them in another sphere. I do not even wish to. If I were to see darling Mum again, which phase of her should I choose? The last sad months when she was deaf and nearly blind? The earlier years when she was vital and energetic and frequently maddening? Or the earlier still years when I was tiny and she was my whole world? It's all too complicated. I'll settle, without apprehension, for oblivion. I cannot really feel that oblivion will be disappointing. Life and love and fame and fortune can all be disappointing, but not dear old oblivion. Hurrah for eternity!

Noël Coward

3 November

1935

Miss Bigge to lunch. She said the Prince of Wales's reply to people who spoke to him about his morals was that he did his job and that his private life was his own. This is not so and never can be. It is deplorable and wretched that he carries on as he does. It is common knowledge.

Lord Reith

1950

The Foreign Secretary rang me up at Abbotsbury and asked me to go to argue with the French about conscription. We had already decided to put up our period to two years, but we hoped to persuade the French to do the same before our decision was announced. I had really no option but to agree to go, but made arrangements to be flown as much of the way as possible. Accordingly, at 6 a.m. a car from the Royal Naval Air Station near Yeovil arrived at the Ilchester Arms to pick me up. I managed to wake in time, shave, dress and even had some breakfast, and then saw the car standing in the pouring rain outside, and found to my despair that I could not get out of the hotel. The door seemed to be locked; it was pitch dark inside, and I did not know where the keys were. Everybody else was asleep. Finally in desperation I opened the dining-room window from the top – the bottom would not move – and clambered up and out – all in my best overcoat and black hat. It would have been an amusing sight if anybody but the chauffeur of the car had been there to see it.

It was my first trip in what is called a 'V.I.P.' plane, which was beautifully fitted up with curtains, armchairs, mahogany panelling, etc. We flew off down the coast to Manston. Arriving there I found it was now wholly given over to the Americans, except for the administration. There was a hideous noise of jet Thunderbolts which apparently disturb the citizens of Ramsgate, and no wonder.

Hugh Gaitskell

1950

Sumner [Welles] said the only time he had ever seen Churchill drunk was on the battleship in the North Atlantic when he and Roosevelt were drawing up the North Atlantic pact. At dinner one night, Churchill had had too much to drink and Franklin Roosevelt, Jr, finally led him to the nearest men's room, which happened to be Harry Hopkins's bathroom. Harry had become ill early in the evening and had gone to bed. Churchill, however, was so potted that he missed the bathroom and proceeded to use Harry's bedpost instead. Harry was most irritated but was so sick he couldn't get up. Judging from my own conversation with him, it did not dilute his undying love for Churchill.

Drew Pearson

1954

Notes for talk – people like different books at different times in their lives. It seems odd that such difficult ponderous writers as Walter Scott, Dumas, Victor Hugo are so often pets of our youth when later in life they seem almost over our heads. It must be that, at 12 or 13, our heads need filling – there are few experiences and knowledge to furnish resistance, so the story has a wide screen. The young reader has no experiences of his own to debate the story; he accepts it wholly, is gullible, it blooms in his mind completely. Trollope is certainly a writer for adults.

Dawn Powell

1955

Poor Princess Margaret has made a sorrowful, touching statement that she will *not* marry Peter Townsend. This is a fine slap in the chops for the bloody Press which has been persecuting her for so long. I am really glad that she has at last made the decision, but I do wish there hadn't been such a hideous hulla-baloo about it. Apart from church and royal considerations, it would have been an unsuitable marriage anyway. She cannot know, poor girl, being young and in love, that love dies soon and that a future with two strapping stepsons and a man eighteen years older than herself would not really be very rosy. I am terribly sorry for her. Private sorrow is bad enough but public sorrow is almost unbearable. I am sure she is right to stick by the job. It has all been a silly, mismanaged lash-up and I cannot imagine how the Queen and the Queen Mother and Prince Philip allowed it to get into such a tangle. At least she hasn't betrayed her position and her responsibilities, but that is arid comfort for her with half the world religiously exulting and the other half pouring out a spate of treacly sentimentality. I hope she will not take to religion in a big way and become a frustrated maiden princess. I also hope that they had the sense to hop into bed a couple of times at least, but this I doubt.

Noël Coward

4 November

1774 [Edinburgh]

I went home and saw my wife, then dined with the Colonel at his lodgings, and, as he was to be busy, just drank half a bottle of port; then sallied forth between four and five with an avidity for drinking from the habit of some days before.

I went to Fortune's; found nobody in the house but Captain James Gordon of Ellon. He and I drank five bottles of claret and were most profound politicians. He pressed me to take another; but my stomach was against it. I walked off very gravely though much intoxicated.

Ranged through the streets till, having run hard down the Advocates' Close, which is very steep, I found myself on a sudden bouncing down an almost perpendicular stone stair. I could not stop, but when I came to the bottom of it, fell with a good deal of violence, which sobered me much.

It was amazing that I was not killed or very much hurt; I only bruised my right heel severely. I stopped at Sir George's.

James Boswell

1901 [*Discovery* expedition to Antarctica]

Strange and wonderful sights one sees, and startling expressions of feeling come across the ward-room when an extra roll [of the ship] produces a few extra crashes. It's a strange life, teeming with quiet fun and everyone thoroughly enjoys it all, and one gets to bed dog-tired and sleepy every night to know nothing of rolls or crashes or bangs or anything else till one's tea is brought at 7 in the morning. As for our food it is simply excellent. We have porridge as much as you like with treacle and butter, hot steak and onions or fish cakes or curried stuff – always some hot dish, bread nearly always, fresh baked, or delicious wholemeal scones, butter and marmalade or jam, tea and coffee. That's our breakfast at 8 a.m. and one is too jolly hungry to be late. At 12 we have a hot meat dish with potatoes, also cold meat, bread, butter, cheese and pickles. At 3.30 we have a superb tea with fresh cakes, shortbread, or scones and butter, something different every day. At 7 we have dinner of soup, hot meat and two vegetables. Some good stodgy pudding or fruit, occasionally a savoury, or cheese straws, or then cheese, butter and biscuits. Then coffee, with wine and smokes for those who want them. We don't do badly! and no wonder the weights go up.

Edward Wilson

1914

Endured an hour's torture of indecision to-night asking myself whether I should go over to ask her to be my wife or should I go to the Fabian Society and hear Bernard Shaw. Kept putting off the decision even till after dinner. If I went to the flat, I must shave; to shave required hot water – the landlady had already cleared the table and was rapidly retreating. Something must be done and at once. I called the old thing back impulsively and ordered

shaving water, consoling myself with the reflection that it was still unnecessary to decide; the hot water could be at hand in case the worst happened.
If I decided on matrimony I could shave forthwith. Should I? (After dark I
always shave in the sitting-room because of the better gaslight.)

Drank some coffee and next found myself slowly, mournfully putting on
hat and coat. You can't shave in hat and coat so I concluded I had decided
on Shaw. Slowly undid the front door latch and went off.

W. N. P. Barbellion

1981

The Princess [of Wales] looked sensational, her dress cut straight across revealing the by now famous shoulders, but with a triple choker of pearls fastened
with a diamond clip around her neck in the manner of Queen Alexandra.
She has a clear complexion and lustrous blue eyes. Tonight she seemed a large
girl in a billowing white dress full-skirted to the ground with a broad blue
ribbon at the waist. More petticoats, however, Julia [his wife] observed, were
called for. How can I describe her? Well, after the event I would categorise
her as Eliza Doolittle at the embassy ball. Beautiful, in a way like a young
colt, immensely well-meaning, unformed, a typical product of an upper-class
girls' school. But she has so much to learn, which she will, unless she gets
bored with it and it sours. At the moment she has not learned the royal tech-
nique of asking questions. Nervous, certainly, so I placed myself next to her
and as I promised Edward Adeane [private secretary to the Prince of Wales],
kept an eye on her the whole time. Her accent is really rather awful considering that she is an earl's daughter. Not an upper-class drawl at all but rather
toneless, and dare I say it, a bit common, as though it were the fashion to
learn to talk down. That is what I meant by Eliza at the ball.

Sir Roy Strong

5 November

1911

I want to write, with a constant trembling on my forehead. I sit in my room
in the very headquarters of the uproar of the entire house. I hear all the
doors close, because of their noise only the footsteps of those running between
them are spared me. I hear even the slamming of the oven door in the
kitchen. My father bursts through the doors of my room and passes through
in his dragging dressing gown, the ashes are scraped out of the stove in the
next room, Valli asks, shouting into the indefinite through the anteroom as
though through a Paris street, whether Father's hat has been brushed yet, a

hushing that claims to be friendly to me raises the shout of an answering voice. The house door is unlatched and screeches as though from a catarrhal throat, then opens wider with the brief singing of a woman's voice and closes with a dull manly jerk that sounds most inconsiderate. My father is gone, now begins the more delicate, more distracted, more hopeless noise led by the voices of the two canaries. I had already thought of it before, but with the canaries it comes back to me again, that I might open the door a narrow crack, crawl into the next room like a snake and in that way, on the floor, beg my sisters and their governess for quiet.

Franz Kafka

1928

Heard very good story on Mussolini and Crown Prince [Wilhelm of Germany]. Latter had been to Tripoli and his father asked him what he thought of the natives. He replied, 'I prefer dealing with the black men in white shirts than the white men in black shirts.'

Sir Robert Bruce Lockhart

1935

A specimen day, yesterday: a specimen of the year 1935 when we are on the eve of the Duke of Gloucester's wedding; of a general election; of the Fascist revolution in France; and in the thick of the Abyssinian war; it being mild warm November weather. At 2.30 we went to the BBC and listened to some incomparable twaddle – a soliloquy which the BBC requests me to imitate (a good idea, all the same, if one were free) with all the resources of the BBC behind one: real railway trains; real orchestras; noise, waves, lions and tigers, &c; at 3 we reach [the *Sunday Times* Book Exhibition]: a loudspeaker proclaiming the virtues of literature, the Princess Louise having just declared the show open and said that books are our best friends. There we meet old stringy Rose Macaulay, beating about, like a cat a-hawking odds and ends; home; at 5.15 telephone: the Baroness Nostitz has arrived early; up she comes: a monolithic broad-faced Hindenburg, bulky; can't get in or out of my chair; says Germany is the better for Hitler – so they say; I want to get some young man to lecture on English poetry; has a rather hard, dominating impassive eye: must have been a beauty; statuesque; aristocratic. Then a card: in comes the Indian; stayed till 7.30. Was turned out of a carriage in Bengal. Liberty. Justice. Hatred of the British rule. Still, it's no better than the Italian. *You* are our allies. The British will be kicked out. And now Morgan [E. M. Forster] rings up – May I lunch to discuss the French question. And so we go. Another specimen day.

Virginia Woolf

1939 [trespassing on a canyon stroll with Greta Garbo]

Just as we had finished our stroll and were returning to the wire fence by another path, we met a forest ranger who was cutting some wood. I could hardly believe my luck. What a situation! Of course, he would recognize her at once. Garbo evidently thought so, too, for she pulled down her wide hat brim. I fairly swelled with gallantry. When he asked us what the hell we were doing and took our names, I'd get in front of her and swear she was Miss Smith from Ocean Park, or maybe Mrs Isherwood – and I'd give him my own address to let me know the amount of fine. This, I thought, will really impress her.

The ranger looked us both over, quite pleasantly. Then he said: 'Do you know what I'm doing here?'

'No,' I answered. (This sounded like the build-up for some heavy sarcasm about trespassing.)

'I'm killing two birds with one stone. This ground has to be cleared; so I'm cutting me some firewood for my cabin.'

Christopher Isherwood

1966

Off to Bradford University to receive my honorary doctorate of technology. Harold [Wilson] was in his element during his installation as Chancellor. In his purple velvet and gold-collared gown he looked, as one paper put it, like a medieval merchant prince. I gathered he had laid down strict instructions about the design of his mortar board. Trust him not to miss a trick! He had obviously been appalled at the sight of himself on TV in the floppy medieval cap he had worn at a previous academic occasion. But as always, he disarmed by his total lack of side. When he had conferred my degree on me by a solemn handshake he almost winked and told me afterwards: 'I decided it wouldn't have done for me to tickle your palm.'

Barbara Castle

1980 [Oxford]

Lecture at the University Architectural Society. (I accepted this invitation because I had once been secretary of its equivalent in Cambridge and know the agony of obtaining speakers and/or for that matter audiences.) Sherry with the Society's Officers in Merton, followed by dinner in hall. Oh the gloom of High Table, the black gowns, dark panelling, subdued cross-talk, but perhaps they are all happy enough.

Sir Hugh Casson

6 November

1660

At night my wife and I did fall out about the dogs being put down into the cellar, which I had a mind to have done because of his fouling the house, and I would have my will; and so we went to bed and lay all night in a quarrel. This night I was troubled all night with a dream that my wife was dead, which made me that I slept ill all night.

Samuel Pepys

1834

17 years ago the illustrious author of this work made his entrée into the sublunary world. On which signal anniversary various donations were given & received by the diverse members of the family.

Barclay Fox

1930

[Lord] Beaverbrook told good story of Lloyd George coming back late at night from Criccieth. His car broke down outside Horton Asylum. Knocked up porter. 'Who are you?' 'Oh, I'm the Prime Minister.' 'Come inside. We've seven here already.'

Sir Robert Bruce Lockhart

1935

Ethel Barrymore arrived in New Orleans last night in her private Pullman car and refused to see any reporters or photographers. She is on tour in a play called *The Constant Wife*.

Late this morning in the city room I heard such a hubbub at the city desk that I walked over to see what was happening and found Sue Bryan telling a fascinating story. Sue, an *Item* reporter, is a member of a prominent New Orleans family. She was saying that this morning she waited at the railway station from 7:45 to 10:45 to try to get an interview with Miss Barrymore, but—!

In an excited voice Sue was giving the details to Charlie Campbell, the assistant city editor, with other editors and reporters leaning in to catch her every word. Sue said that at about 10:45 she saw the actress leaving her private railway car and walking toward a taxi.

'Miss Barrymore—' Sue cried, hurrying toward her.

La Barrymore stopped long enough to raise both arms toward heaven in a gesture of supplication. Then—

'I never give interviews!' she screamed at Sue.

Sue now was telling us that Barrymore was drunk, very drunk.

'But, Miss Barrymore! . . . Aw, c'mon, Miss Barrymore!'

'I do *not* give interviews!!'

Sue said her voice was so shrill it frightened pigeons atop the railroad station.

Then the actress added: '—especially to such ignorant young reporters as yourself, you little rat!'

Sue, accustomed to the manners of debutantes, listened in astonishment as Barrymore twice more called her a rat.

'If you call me a rat again,' Sue yelled, 'I'll knock you down!'

'Oh, you will, will you?' screeched the actress. Screwing up her face and reaching out with stiff fingers, she clawed the air close to Sue's eyes.

In the city room Sue told us: 'I actually got scared. She looked like a witch! You can't imagine! Her eyes were sunken in, her hair was black and dishevelled, and her black coat was drawn up around her throat. She was so drunk she hardly could stand up!'

Charlie Campbell told her to go ahead and write the story just as it happened. Staff members cheered and laughed, making so much noise that the publisher, James M. Thomson, shuffled out in his bedroom slippers to ask what all the fuss was about. When he was told, he beckoned Sue into his office. When she came out she mournfully announced that he told her he wouldn't print her story because a friend of his, who knows Miss Barrymore, had called to ask him to treat her well.

'Scoop' Kennedy spoke for all us when he snarled: 'Why, that yellow-livered son-of-a-bitch!'

But the United Press correspondent heard about Sue and asked her to write the yarn for his wire service under her by-line. Great!

Edward Robb Ellis

1938

I spent the whole evening sitting before a mirror to keep myself company.

Cesare Pavese

7 *November*

1850 [Ireland]

A great movement has begun in England at last, against the insolence of Rome. John Bull will never bear such assumption nor such a near view of popery. The Colonel [her husband] thinks it all for the best – that had they gone creeping on as for the last few years, they might have made a progress difficult to check, but having betrayed their designs so soon we can more easily put a stop to them. The spirit of popery is such that the church can never be trusted; they will force us back to modified penal laws and nobody can say that this severity will be undeserved. The movement will open many eyes. Neither national schools, nor national colleges are yet deserted in spite of papal denunciats, and *minds* will surely come very different out of them from what they go in.

Elizabeth Grant of Rothiemurchus

1951

One wonders how a nation's intelligence resists the radio. Moreover, it does not resist. The radio is a faucet of foolishness. The only thing I can bear listening to is the sports reporting. The high-speed precision of the speakers. They are forbidden stupidity. Which exists only in the fact that some men are kicking a ball around a field and the whole world is excited by the fact.

Jean Cocteau

1953 [dining with Lord and Lady Astor]

She [Lady Astor] told of her famous visit to Moscow with Bernard Shaw during the war. The things she said straight out to Stalin were staggering. 'Your régime is no different from the Czars'.' 'Why?' 'Because you dispose of your opposition without trial.' Stalin laughed: 'Of course.' She also spoke of Bernard Shaw's last illness. 'I went to see him the day before he died. I sat by him stroking his head. He was quite clear. Suddenly he said. "That reminds me," and told me this story. "Lord X gave a great party to all the local gentry. As they were about to eat, the butler came in and said to him: 'Excuse me, your lordship, but Mr So & So is in bed with your wife.' At this Lord X, rising in his place, said to the company: 'Go home, go home. There is a man in bed with my wife. The party is cancelled. Off you go.' The guests, much disappointed, for there were quantities of drink, began to disperse. The butler came in again and spoke to his lordship. He got up. 'Don't go, don't go. The man has apologised.'" Those were G.B.S.'s last words.' This story was well received. If it was not Shaw's last words, it might well have been.

Maurice Collis

1992

At 2.20 Frank [Longford] rang. V. [his wife] answered. After a conversation that was obscure to me she said: 'Well, you'd better talk to Tony about it.' Frank began a long rigmarole about his 'being' Widmerpool [odious character in Powell's novel sequence *A Dance to the Music of Time*]. I began to explain that he was not, but he cut me short, saying: 'Authors always say that.' After a bit I began to understand that he *wanted* to 'be' Widmerpool (the fact that Frank does not interest me in the smallest degree as a character in a novel being naturally impossible to explain to him. Indeed a subject so subtle that it is difficult to explain to anyone why certain people are good models, others not). It seemed that some TV programme was being arranged for people who had 'appeared' in novels, and Frank was willing to be included.

Anthony Powell

8 November

1699

There happend this Weeke so thick a Mist and fog; that people lost their way in the streetes, it being so exceedingly intense, as no light of Candle, Torches or Lanterns, yielded any or very little direction: I was my selfe in it, and in extraordinary danger, robberys were committed betwene the very lights which were fixt between Lond: and K[e]nsington on both sides, and whilst Coaches and passengers were travelling: and what was strange, it beginning about 4 in the afternoone was quite gon by 8, without any wind to dissipate it. At the Thames they beate drumms, to direct the Watermen to make the shore, no lights being bright enough to penetrate the fogg.

John Evelyn

1874

Walking with Wm. Splaine, we saw a vast multitude of starlings making an unspeakable jangle. They would settle in a row of trees; then, one tree after another, rising at a signal they looked like a cloud of specks of black snuff or powder struck up from a brush or broom or shaken from a wig; then they would sweep round in whirl-winds – you could see the nearer and farther bow of the rings by the size and blackness; many would be in one phase at once, all narrow black flakes hurling round, then in another; then they would fall upon a field and so on. Splaine wanted a gun: then 'there it would rain meat' he said. I thought they must be full of enthusiasm and delight hearing their cries and stirring and cheering one another.

Gerard Manley Hopkins

1889

Got up late. Tried to write about art, but it's no good. Played patience – a sort of madness. Read. A talk with the children about servants, a letter from

Lyova [his son] and our entire way of life made me think: our life with its slave workers for our convenience, with our servants, seems natural to us . . . We even think, as the children said, 'After all nobody makes him, he became a man-servant of his own accord'; and as the teacher said, 'If a man feels no humiliation at emptying my slops, then I'm not humiliating him'; and we think that we're quite liberal and justified. But this whole position is something so offensive to the nature of man that it would have been impossible not only to establish but even to imagine such a position, had it not been the consequence of a certain, very definite evil which we all know about, and which, we assure ourselves, has long since disappeared. Had it not been for slavery, nothing like this could possibly have been invented.

Leo Tolstoy

1934

I dined alone with the Lindberghs. Charles was more communicative than usual about his personal affairs. He told me that the Western Union had got out a telegram-form with alternative messages of congratulation to him. All one did was to choose No.8, which ran 'Welcome to America's hero'; or No.9, which read 'Greetings to the Lone Eagle' or No.12, which ran 'Lindy does it again'. One paid twenty-five cents to have one's number telegraphed by Western Union in one's home town and then the message corresponding to the number was typed out at the other end and delivered to Lindbergh. In one day he got 52,000 such telegrams, and the next day 63,000. And so on. They had to be delivered in special vans. This was after his pan-American trip.

Since then, of course, they have organised a regular system. All letters of whatsoever nature addressed to them by name are sent down to an office in New York and gone through there. Sometimes there is a great delay, because when the Lindbergh case gets on to the front pages they get about 100,000 letters a day. Many important letters and invitations never reach them. But if the thing were to be done properly they would have to have a trained staff and it would cost them at least £2,000 a year. So they just have office-boys and trust to luck. Of course their nearest and dearest write to them at an accommodation address without their real names. But it must be hell.

Harold Nicolson

1937

In the local cinema, you can buy mint-flavoured lozenges with the words: 'Will you marry me one day?', 'Do you love me?', written on them, together with the replies: 'This evening', 'A lot', etc. You pass them to the girl next to you, who replies in the same way. Lives become linked together by an exchange of mint lozenges.

Albert Camus

1942 [Cairo]

Each morning I breakfast on a balcony overlooking the Nile and gloat over the news: Alexander's soldiers are pressing the Germans back . . . American and British Forces have landed in French North Africa. Surely this must be the beginning of the end of the war in North Africa. . . .

So the days begin – on peaks of optimism. But as the hours wear on and I visit the Cairo hospitals I sink back into chasms of gloom. The price of this news is so terrible: you see it in the leg wards where some of the tallest are the shortest now – poor Richard Wood has lost both his legs; you see it in the long ward where the burn cases lie so still – sometimes even their eyes are bandaged; it glares at you from screened-off beds where people are dying. You put on your gayest frock, paint your face, collect sweets and magazines and determine to be cheerful. Then at the hospital, the smell of rotting flesh meets you in the long dark corridors and you begin thinking again. You owe them so much but there is nothing you can do except try not to talk of things they will never do again. Today when I took down letters in shorthand for those that cannot write I sat with my back to them so they should not see my eyes . . . They all wrote of victory; not one of them mentioned the price.

Countess of Ranfurly

1995

I don't think I have ever seen so many frenetic gestures as those displayed last night by a handful of Booker Prize commentators. Some of the literary hairdos rivalled the grimaces taking place underneath them. The Canadian Mountie TV *Going South* was delightfully restrained and amusing, as usual. To start reading Ford Madox Ford's *Parade's End* for the third time, which I did when the Booker offerings were over, was a genuine, reliable pleasure. The characters deepen and become more subtle with familiarity.

I have turned down a handsome offer to play a slap-up part in a film opposite Jack Lemmon, whom I admire. A number of reasons: (a) it would be unsuitable to push off to the USA for three months in the present circumstances [his wife's illness]; (b) I can't see myself as an old American farmer of the 'Howdy doo, Dad?' variety, (c) I am weary of TV, cinema or theatrical fare set in Old People's Homes. Too near the bare knuckle.

Alec Guinness

9 November

1910

On October 28, at 5 in the morning, Lev Nik. [Tolstoy] slipped out of the house with [Dr] D. P. Makovitsky. His excuse for leaving was that I had been rummaging through his papers the previous night. I had gone into his study for a moment, but I did not touch one paper – indeed there *weren't* any papers on his desk. In his letter to me (written for the entire world) the pretext he gave was our luxurious life and his desire to be alone and to live in a hut, like the peasants. But then why did he have to write telling Sasha [their daughter] to come with her hanger-on, Varvara Mikhailovna?

When I learnt from Sasha and the letter about L. N.'s flight, I jumped into the pond of despair. Sasha and [Tolstoy's secretary, Valentin] Bulgakov got me out, alas! Then nothing passed my lips for the next five days, and on October 31 at 7.30 a.m. I received a telegram from the editors of *Russian Word*: 'Lev Nikolaevich in Astapovo, temperature 40°.' Andrei, Tanya [their children] and I travelled by special train from Tula to Astapovo. They did not let me in to see Lev Nik. They held me by force, they locked the door. They tormented my heart. On November 7, at 6 in the morning, Lev Nik. died. On November 9 he was buried at Yasnaya Polyana.

Sofia Tolstoy

1935

I remember all the times Papa would come home, whip out a picture of a simpering but firm lady in bustle and say (collecting all three of us, alarmed at this unwonted burst of fatherly sentimentality, in his arms): 'Girls, what do you think of her as a stepmother?' Each time it was different.

Dawn Powell

1944

We walked on up the hill and down to Pitt's Cottage again where we had tea in a crowded room, this time with a large party of officers, some in Tartan trews, at one table. They were furtive and repressed, terrified of shaming themselves in each other's eyes. It was painful to watch. It reminded me so much of school. No ease, or grace or enjoyment, only anxiety.

Denton Welch

1960

John Kennedy has been voted President of the USA. This is very exciting to me. To think that, in this kind of world, a man of conscience, integrity, originality & quality *can* win through, against the mud of mediocrity & the fearful political corruption, is inspiring in itself.

Kenneth Williams

10 November

1936

I walked to the House of Commons, as we had been warned not to bring cars. The lobbies were full of hunger marchers come to protest against the new unemployment regulations, the so-called Means Test.

During questions, someone asked, innocuously, about the coming coronation. McGovern [Labour MP for Shettleston, Glasgow] jumped up and shouted, 'Why bother, in view of the gambling at Lloyd's that there will not be one?' There were roars of 'Shame! Shame!' and he called out, 'Yes . . . Mrs Simpson.' This was the first time her name had been used in the House of Commons, although the smoking room and lobbies have long buzzed with it. I was shocked, but the truth is that the monarchy has lost ground in a frightening manner. Prince Charming charms his people no more . . .

Later, I went out into the lobby and found it full to suffocation with marchers, who were being incited by Communists. Many of them wore red shirts and ties. At the door was a queue singing the Red Flag. It really seemed as if trouble must break out. But it didn't, about 8.30 I took the last look at these unfortunate people who have been goaded and misguided by their leaders into walking from Lancashire and South Wales. I went out into the cooler evening air and was amused to see strings of taxis depositing the walkers at St Stephen's. On my way home, I passed the Abbey, which looked beautiful and calm, and flood-lit because it is Armistice eve. Many people, mostly women, were planting little crosses tied to poppies on the lawn surrounding the Abbey, and in the cool light they looked holy, sad and peaceful. As I watched the silent scene, the grey, middle-aged women, thinking of their lost sons, I thought of my warm, gold and pink boy waiting for me at home.

'Chips' Channon

1943

Last week a section member was invited by a female contact to visit the Naples cemetery with her on the coming Sunday afternoon. Informants have to be cultivated in small ways whenever possible, and he was quite prepared to indulge a whim of this kind, in the belief that he would be escorting his friend on a visit to a family tomb, expecting to buy a bunch of chrysanthemums from the stall at the gate. However, hardly were they inside when the lady dragged him behind a tombstone, and then – despite the cold – lay down and pulled up her skirts. He noticed that the cemetery contained a number of other couples in vigorous activity in broad daylight. 'There were more people above ground than under it,' he said. It turned out that the cemetery is the lovers' lane of Naples, and custom is such that one becomes invisible as soon as one passes through the gates. If a visitor runs into anyone he knows neither a sign nor a glance can be exchanged, nor does one recognize any friend encountered on the 133 bus which goes to the cemetery. I have learned that to suggest to a lady a Sunday-afternoon ride on a 133 bus is tantamount to solicitation for immoral purposes.

Norman Lewis

1977

A few days ago I got a vision of a house that I would feel at home in. It was made of eucalyptus, glass and adobe. A contemporary structure in a natural setting. I would have to build it. I walked up by the old water tank today, looking for a site.

Through the years, Francis and I have argued over and over again about our house. He has said all he ever really wanted from me was to make him a home. Once, in a crazy argument in the Philippines, he told me that he would spend a million dollars, if necessary, to find a woman who wanted to make a home, cook and have lots of babies. I could never tell the truth, even to myself, because I thought it would be the end of my marriage. I am not a homemaker. I have always wanted to be a working person. But the kind of work I have done over the years hasn't earned any money, so it looks like I am playing and lazy.

Right now I am feeling a giant relief. I am off the hook. The other woman in Francis's life is not the ultimate homemaker either; she is not dying to step in and take over the mansion.

Eleanor Coppola

11 November

1841 [on the birth of King Edward VII]

A curious point has arisen, interesting to the Guards. It has been the custom for the officer on guard at St James's Palace to be promoted to a majority when a Royal Child is born. The guard is relieved at forty-five minutes after ten. At that hour the new guard marched into the Palace Yard, and at forty-eight minutes after ten the child was born. The question arises which officer is entitled to the promotion. The officer of the fresh guard claims it because the relief marched in before the birth, and the keys were delivered over to him; but the other officer claims it because the sentries had not been changed when the child was actually born, his men were still on guard, and he disputes the fact of the delivery of the keys, arguing that in all probability this had not occurred at the moment of the birth. The case is before Lord Hill for his decision.

It is odd enough that there is a similar case involving civic honours at Chester. The Prince being Earl of Chester by birth, the Mayor of Chester claims a Baronetcy. The old Mayor went out and the new Mayor came into office the same day and about the same hour, and it is doubtful which functionary is entitled to the honour. The ex-Mayor was a Whig banker, and the new one is a Tory linen draper.

Charles Greville

1851

'Says I to myself' should be the motto of my journal.

It is fatal to the writer to be too much possessed by his thought. Things must lie a little remote to be described.

H. D. Thoreau

1872

Heard a story of the mulatto Scotch gentleman who told a wandering Irishman asking help that he ought to go to his own parish. Paddy looked him full in the face; 'I'm thinking your Honour's a long way from your parish too!'

William Allingham

1878

School. Flood falling. So far the second greatest flood of this century. Before breakfast I went down to the bridge to see how the Jenkins family were. Soon after I passed last night the river came down with a sudden rush and wave and filled the road full of water and they had to escape to the trap, carrying their children on their backs, wading through water kneedeep, and leaving 3 feet of water in the house, the house also being surrounded by water and the water running in at front and back. Mr Stokes kindly rode down from the Old Court to see if they were safe, the water was then up to his horse's girths. Many people were flooded out of their houses at Letton and Staunton and spent the night on Bredwardine Bridge watching the flood. A number of cattle and colts were seen to pass under the bridge in the moonlight and it was feared they would be drowned. Some women saw a bullock swept down under the bridge at noon to-day. Mr W. Clarke told me that the Whitney iron railway bridge was carried away last night by the flood and

2 miles of line seriously damaged. No trains can run for 3 months, during which time the gap will be filled by coaches.

Rev. Francis Kilvert

1915 [on hearing of yet another relation killed in action]

Oh why was I born for this time? Before one is thirty to know more dead than living people? Stanway, Clouds, Gosford – all the settings of one's life – given up to ghosts. Really, one hardly knows who is alive and who is dead. One thing is that now at least people will no longer bury their dead as they used. Now they are so many one *must* talk of them naturally and humanly, not banish them by only alluding to them as if it were almost indelicate.

Lady Cynthia Asquith

1918

Twenty-five minutes ago the guns went off, announcing peace. A siren hooted on the river. They are hooting still. A few people ran to look out of windows. The rooks wheeled round, and wore for a moment the symbolic look of creatures performing some ceremony, partly of thanksgiving, partly of valediction over the grave. A very cloudy still day, the smoke toppling over heavenly towards the east; and that too wearing for a moment a look of something floating, waving, drooping. So far neither bells nor flags, but the wailing of sirens and intermittent guns.

Virginia Woolf

1938

H. R. Knickerbocker, foreign correspondent for Hearst, was in Baltimore last night delivering a lecture. I met him later, and for the first time. His appearance rather astonished me. He was born in Texas and is the son of a Protestant preacher, but he looks decidedly Jewish. He has the reddish hair of a blond Jew, along with the faint freckles and pinkish eyes.

He told me that he was well acquainted with Hitler, and used to see him relatively frequently in the days before Hitler came to power. At that time there were rumors that Hitler's iron cross was bogus, and Knickerbocker one day ventured to ask him about it. Hitler said that he had got it in the following manner:

During the war he was a dispatch rider, and one day he was sent across a part of the front that was a kind of No Man's Land. The Germans assumed that there were no Frenchmen in it, but when he had got half way across Hitler heard French voices and on investigation found that there were a number of Frenchmen in a dugout. Hitler approached the only entrance and barked several loud orders, hoping to convince the men within that a considerable German party was above. The trick worked, and in a few minutes Hitler had the Frenchmen coming out one by one, their hands in the air. He was armed only with a pistol, but inasmuch as they came out wholly unarmed, he was able to line them up and march them back to the German lines. It was for this exploit that he received the iron cross.

Knickerbocker said that the story was told to him in the presence of an English correspondent. When it was finished Hitler said politely, 'If these Frenchmen had been either Englishmen or Americans the chances are that I'd not be here.'

Knickerbocker said that Hitler in his private relations is a very amiable fellow, and has a considerable sense of humor. But whenever he gets on public matters he begins to orate. Knickerbocker said that he'll start in an ordinary tone of voice and than in a few minutes he'll be howling like a stump speaker, with his arms sawing the air.

Knickerbocker is also acquainted with Mussolini. He told me that Mussolini hates Hitler violently, and will undoubtedly walk out on him at the first chance.

H. L. Mencken

12 November

1930

Muriel [his wife] and I dined with Sir Herbert Samuel, a rather disappointing party as there was nobody specially interesting. I do not enjoy parties unless there are bigger people than myself present.

Lord Reith

1943 [Cairo]

At seven o'clock this morning the Germans attacked Leros. There is much speculation here as to whether we can hold it.

I lunched with Admiral Kelly who has come from Ankara. There is a story that he and his brother once had a quarrel and shortly afterwards met in Bond Street. They passed each other silently with their noses in the air but one of them came back, tapped the other on the shoulder and said, 'Excuse me, but am I right in thinking that your Father married my Mother?'

Countess of Ranfurly

1975

I settled down to an all-nighter on the Community Land Bill. For the first few hours, I was grateful for the opportunity to catch up with my boxes. By 1 a.m. I began to feel overwhelmed by a desire to sleep. So I lay down on my couch and fell into an exhausted slumber. I was awakened an hour later by the ringing of my telephone. It was my Whip, Jimmie Dunn. Why had I missed the last division? Horrified, I apologized. I just hadn't heard it in these remote recesses. I promised I wouldn't lie down any more. Nor did I. I got up, had a cup of coffee in the tea-room and returned to work on my boxes. At 3 a.m. my work became rather slow. But I soldiered on and managed to see the night through without dozing off any more.

Barbara Castle

13 November

1871

'What a fine day it is. Let us go out and kill something.' The old reproach against the English. The Squire has just gone by with a shooting party.

Rev. Francis Kilvert

1918

We got an authentic version of the armistice terms. To think of our being able to talk like that to the Hun. It leaves one dizzy. The men took it all amazingly calmly. There was hardly any open exultation, but everybody wore an air of complete if somewhat bewildered, satisfaction, as one who rises from a thoroughly good dinner. Small wonder it took some time to assimilate; even now the immensity of what we have done leaves me gasping. That within five months of that nightmare of last spring the Beast should be broken body and soul; that his armies should be in rout, his emasculated fleet in English harbours, the Kaiser in exile, the Crown Prince the jape of Europe, Ludendorff a broken imbecile; that all the wild jingo-hopes we used to toy with in the early days before jingoism died and stank, and hope itself almost withered, should in one thunderclap become stark reality; that, most unbelievable of all, the answer had come to our 'Lord, how long?' of so many endless nights – can you wonder that we were dazed and slow of comprehension?

Other things, too, made revelry difficult; for, at the gathering of this stupendous harvest, too many of the sowers were not there. Even when you win a war, you cannot forget that you have lost your generation.

Sir Alan 'Tommy' Lascelles

1936

I feel a foreboding of impending doom. What can it be – that the throne will totter, or perhaps cease to be, that I shall be ill, or perhaps my baby Paul?

In any case, I am gloomy, though perhaps it is only surfeit combined with constipation. I am too rich, and I dine with kings . . . but I am bored, even sometimes lonely. But my child fills me with such tenderness that I can hardly bear to be away from him . . .

I must take a pull, write a book, become a miser, or perhaps, most important, speak in the House of Commons. I am a good attender and popular, I think, but I cannot just take that small hurdle of speaking constantly. I must. What a Parliament! We saw the death of the late King [George V], the accession of the new. Shall we see yet a third . . . or none? We are faced with an impasse. The country, or much of it, would not accept Queen Wallis, with two live husbands scattered about . . .

'Chips' Channon

14 November

1813

If this had been begun ten years ago, and faithfully kept!! – heigho! there are too many things I wish never to have remembered, as it is. Well, – I have had my share of what are called the pleasures of this life, and have seen more of the European and Asiatic world than I have made a good use of. They say 'virtue is its own reward,' – it certainly should be paid well for its trouble. At five-and-twenty, when the better part of life is over, one should be *something*; – and what am I? nothing but five-and-twenty and the odd months. What have I seen? the same man all over the world, – ay, and woman too.

Lord Byron

1929

We spoke about Lawrence [of Arabia], who is an intimate friend of the [Bernard] Shaws, and his eccentric shyness of publicity. Once Lawrence complained about every move of his being followed by the Press. 'Well, of course, they notice you,' Shaw replied. 'You always hide just in the middle of the limelight.'

Count Harry Kessler

1947 [during a fuel crisis]

How easy it is to say the wrong thing! How easy it is not to recognise one has said the wrong thing!

About three weeks ago I made a speech at a municipal election meeting in Hastings. I was very tired when I got there but it was a good meeting. I tried to keep my speech fairly above party despite the coming election and inevitably referred to fuel economy in the course of it [he was Minister of Fuel and Power]. Then I let fall two fatal sentences:

'It means getting up and going to bed in cold bedrooms. It may mean fewer baths. Personally, I have never had a great many baths myself and I can assure those who are in the habit of having a great many baths that it does not make a great deal of difference to their health if they have fewer. And as far as appearance – most of that is underneath and nobody sees it.'

Of course the first sentence was said in a joking manner and the second was a pure joke, and the audience laughed and took it as such. It is the kind of thing I have said again and again at open air meetings to liven things up. After the meeting one of the local people who was driving me round referred to this, and said he would not be surprised if it was in the headlines the next day. Though he, himself, thought it a joke and took it as such. The press did pick it out though not very flamboyantly. However on Tuesday it so happened that Churchill was making his big speech against the Government and he made great play of these remarks of mine. I was not present at the time but everybody tells me that he was extremely funny at my expense. Since then I have become associated in the public mind with dirt, never having a bath, etc. I am told that at the [Royal] Command Performance no less than three jokes were made about this by music hall comedians, though they all seem to have been in quite a friendly manner.

First of all, I did not worry at all. It seemed inconceivable to me that anybody could believe it was anything but a joke. However, I now consider I really made a mistake. Psychologically it is probably a bad thing for a Minister to be associated in the public mind with not washing. I had a few anonymous letters and some packets of D.D.T. [insecticide] powder sent to me. And two signed letters which reflect different points of view. The first was from a distant connection of some kind, taking me to task for what I said and asking me when I was speaking in public to be more careful of what I said because the name was such an uncommon one. The second was from my old nurse whom I have not seen or heard from for over thirty years, but who always had a very good sense of humour. I was very touched by this.

Hugh Gaitskell

15 November

1879

I admire Zola, but there are things that every one says, and which I cannot resolve to say, or even to write. However, in order that you shall not think they are horrors, I will tell you that the worst is the word *purgé*. I regret to write such a word here. I do not hesitate to use the word *canaille* [scoundrel] and others of the same sort, but as to those little innocent nastinesses they disgust me.

Marie Bashkirtseff

1885

Mr [John Everett] Millais came here in the evening to get papa to photograph next morning. He seemed in good health and high spirits. 'I just want you to photograph that little boy of Effie's. I've got him you know, he's (cocking up his chin at the ceiling), he's like this, with a bowl and soap suds and all that, a pipe, it's called *A Child's World* [later *Bubbles*], he's looking up, and there's a beautiful soap bubble; I can't paint you know, not a bit, (with his head on one side and his eyes twinkling) not a bit! I want just to compare it, I get this little thing (the photo of the picture) and I hold it in my hand and compare it with the life, and I can see where the drawing's wrong.

'How are you getting on with your drawing?' My certes, I was rather alarmed, but he went to another subject in a second. He is a simple person in worldly affairs, he said to papa about the election, 'I suppose we're all obliged to vote aren't we?'

He addressed some most embarrassingly personal remarks to me, but compliments from him would take longer to turn my head than from any other source. If he sees a tolerably comely girl, he cannot keep his tongue still, and I am perfectly certain that when I was a child he used to tease me in order to see me blush.

Beatrix Potter

1972

Dinner last night with the [Oswald] Mosleys. He is very cagey, but evidently very active – comes over from France every fortnight.

Diana Mosley said she was talking to the Duke of Windsor shortly before he died. He was recalling with what relief, when he was a small boy at Court, after the English courtiers and officials had cleared off, the Royals relapsed into German. Edward VII was known to the family as Bertie pronounced *Berrrtie*.

Cecil King

16 November

1837

The Bishop of London said that when the Bishops were first presented to the Queen [Victoria], she received them with all possible dignity, and then retired. She passed through a glass door, and, forgetting its transparency, was seen to run off like a girl, as she is. Mr Quayle, in corroboration of this, told me that lately, asking a maid of honour how she liked her situation, and who of course expressed her delight, she said, 'I do think myself it is good fun playing Queen.' This is just as it should be. If she had not now the high spirits of a healthy girl of 18, we should have less reason to hope she would turn out a sound sensible woman at 30.

Henry Crabb Robinson

1840

There is a chasm of three days in this journal, and gracious Heaven, how has the time been filled! My strength fails me when I attempt to account for it, and yet I feel that it will afford me a sort of melancholy consolation. My heart sinks within me, whenever my thoughts are concentrated on the greatest grief which has ever oppressed it. May the indulgent Father of Mercies sustain me and my bereaved family in this great hour of my affliction, and teach us with resignation to exclaim, 'Father, thy will be done!' My dear, beloved Mary [daughter] left this world of trouble and affliction, and as I firmly and confidently believe, joined her sister angels in heaven, on Friday morning at half past six o'clock. Long and severe as her illness had been, and great as her sufferings, at times she has appeared to be so much better that the blessed rays of hope have shone round her and we have indulged the delusive expectation that the cherished flower would be reanimated and bloom once more in its former loveliness.

Friday was a melancholy day. The body was deposited in its coffin, and placed in the back parlor. After the family had all gone to bed, I obtained the key of the room and taking a lamp went into the chamber of death, seated myself at the side of the cold remains of my darling child, and for half an hour held in imagination delightful converse with the spirit which had of late animated it. The countenance was unchanged, the expression intelligent and lovely as it was wont to be, and that smile, sweet as the smile of a seraph, still hung upon her half-closed lips, and I gazed with fixed eyes upon it, until I almost fancied it moved and spoke to me again. It is strange that I could derive consolation from looking upon the wreck of that which my heart held so dear, and yet it was a half hour of delightful enjoyment. Never shall I desire to have it effaced from my remembrance.

Philip Hone

1952

The explosion of the hydrogen bomb [on Eniwetok Atoll in the Pacific] was announced at five-thirty today just before I went on the air. Public reaction is blasé, rather numb.

Two years ago when I first revealed that the United States was considering a hydrogen bomb, there was a terrific furor. Papers were full of the news. I bumped into the story in a peculiar manner. I was calling on Louis Johnson, then Secretary of Defense, and was shown into an outer waiting room when Dean Acheson walked out.

He and Louis were at loggerheads on most things, especially Formosa, and I asked Louis afterward whether they had had another wrangle over arming China's troops on Formosa. He said no, they were talking about the hydrogen bomb. This was the first intimation that the question of building an H-bomb was even under discussion.

Drew Pearson

17 November

1896

I think one of my pleasantest memories of Esthwaite is sitting on Oatmeal Crag on a Sunday afternoon, where there is a sort of table of rock with a dip, with the lane and fields and oak copse like in a trough below my feet, and all the little tiny fungus people singing and bobbing and dancing in the grass and under the leaves all down below, like the whistling that some people cannot hear of stray mice and bats, and I sitting up above and knowing something about them.

I cannot tell what possesses me with the fancy that they laugh and clap their hands, especially the little ones that grow in troops and rings amongst dead leaves in the woods. I suppose it is the fairy rings, the myriads of fairy fungi that start into life in autumn woods.

I remember I used to half believe and wholly play with fairies when I was a child. What heaven can be more real than to retain the spirit-world of childhood, tempered and balanced by knowledge and common-sense, to fear no longer the terror that flieth by night, yet to feel truly and understand a little, a very little, of the story of life.

Beatrix Potter

1919

Our cold baths have driven away the last signs of our colds. They are really marvellous if you can bear them. As the hour approaches we begin to paw the ground, nothing could rein us in, not the icy house, the pleading of our friends, our aches and pains – we disregard the lot. Undress very quickly, in and out! You emerge merry and brisk, refreshed and ready for anything, rather proud of your heroism . . .

Liane de Pougy

1937

I was sitting at the bar in the Club tonight beside a man on a visit from New York. 'So I took this woman out to dinner,' he said, leaning his two elbows on the bar and looking into his brandy and soda. 'Marvelous-looking woman and from what my brother had told me I thought it was, well, a foregone conclusion.' 'An open and shut proposition,' I suggested. 'Exactly as you say – an open and shut proposition. First of all she ordered three chops straight off like that. That was not all.' He twisted his ragged moustache in an agony of remembrance. 'I picked up the menus – one was table d'hôte. I really shoved the other at her more as a gesture. It was à la carte – everything three times as expensive in it, of course. She chose a dollar apéritif – there were several at forty cents – then right the way through, a three-dollar entrée, lobster mornay, always the most expensive thing in sight, and after dinner several double whiskies in the course of the evening, and I never came near to first base.' He said, 'There must have been something wrong with the woman – physically I mean.'

Charles Ritchie

1943

I looked at my husband tonight, as he sat. In these last two years he has changed so utterly. I feel he has grown a stranger – no, not a stranger, for he has, alas, grown so like his mother. I find myself watching for her mannerisms and reactions. He will grow as eccentric and odd, I fear. Suddenly I thought what a break it had been when he suddenly decided to sleep alone, almost two years ago. He had a bad cold and was restless at the time; and as I prefer – had always longed – to sleep alone, and put on the light to read or write or get up when I felt like it, I was quite suited. Yet it snapped a big link somehow – that last-minute discussion before going to sleep: it's surprising how, when the light goes out, little things could be talked out before going to sleep. Maybe I'm wrong, it may be that it is the way he has aged so rapidly; but tonight I looked at him and could *not* think of *any* kind of intimacy, mental or physical. The boys have gone out of my life. I've no family round me. I felt my whole married life was a dream – so *very* odd!

Nella Last

18 November

1870

Went into the Tump to see young Meredith who has had his jaw locked for six months, a legacy of mumps. He has been to Hereford Infirmary where they kept him two months, gave him chloroform and wrenched his jaws open gradually by a screw lever. But they could not do him any good.

Rev. Francis Kilvert

1962 [Chicago]

In the evening, sat rather gloomily in a bar. Woman perched next to me mentioned that she was fond of opera, looking forward to *Samson and Delilah*. I bring this out in people. Americans, in their happiness, keep together, excluding outsiders. This is why, alone, we can be so lonely in American cities. Strolling, in such a mood, after the meal, I noticed that Lenny Bruce was appearing at a sort of cabaret place; went in, was recognized by a girl at the ticket place, who arranged for me to see the show, though packed out. Bruce dressed in a kind of swami's suit. Act consisted of a monologue, disconnected in theme; a sort of whimpering, spiteful, petulant complaint against the times and man's lot today. Not particularly funny, but the audience laughed in a nervous sort of way when he used an obscene word ('shit', for instance), or at some sally against nuclear war, etc. Occasionally used Yiddish words, which aroused easier laughter. At my table married couple – mother-in-law, she from New Orleans, wife former air hostess, and her husband. Mother-in-law said she'd been married forty years, wonderful husband, wonderful son-in-law, wonderful home. All wonderful. Somehow, from there, got on to the subject of mistresses. Ex-air hostess said American women liked to be wives and mistresses in one. Large assignment, I said.

Malcolm Muggeridge

1977 [Brussels]

I gave a lunch for British Liberals, [Jeremy] Thorpe, [David] Steel and [Lord] Gladwyn. Poor Jeremy was looking appallingly haggard, like Soames Forsyte in the last episode of *The Forsyte Saga*. But this did not affect the flow of his conversation. Even Gladwyn could hardly get a word in, partly because he has got rather deaf, and hardly heard what was going on. David Steel was nice but silent.

Roy Jenkins

19 November

1739

I was greatly troubled in dreams; and about eleven o'clock, waked in an unaccountable consternation, without being able to sleep again. About that time (as I found out in the morning), one who had been designed to be my pupil, but was not, came into the Porter's lodge (where several persons were sitting), with a pistol in his hand. He presented this, as in sport, first at one, and then at another. He then attempted twice or thrice to shoot himself; but it would not go off. Upon his laying it down, one took it up, and blew out the priming. He was very angry, went and got fresh prime, came in again, sat down, beat the flint with his key, about twelve, pulling off his hat and wig, said he would die like a gentleman, and shot himself through the head.

John Wesley

1833

In the evening we proceeded on our road towards Mercedes on the Río Negro. At night we asked permission to sleep at an estancia at which we happened to arrive. It was a very large estate, being ten leagues square, and the owner is one of the greatest landowners in the country. His nephew had charge of it, and with him there was a captain in the Army, who the other day ran away from Buenos Aires.

Considering their station, their conversation was rather amusing. They expressed, as was usual, unbounded astonishment at the globe being round, and could scarcely credit that a hole would, if deep enough, come out on the other side. They had, however, heard of a country where there were six months of light and six of darkness, and where the inhabitants were very tall and thin! They were curious about the price and conditions of horses and cattle in England. Upon finding out we did not catch our animals with the lazo, they cried out, 'Ah, then, you use nothing but the bolas': the idea of an enclosed country was quite new to them. The captain at last said, he had one question to ask me, which he should be very much obliged if I would answer with all truth. I trembled to think how deeply scientific it might be: it was, 'whether the ladies of Buenos Aires were not the handsomest in the world.' I replied, like a renegade, 'Charmingly so.' He added, 'I have one other question: do ladies in any other part of the world wear such large combs?' I solemnly assured him that they did not. They were absolutely delighted. The captain exclaimed, 'Look there! a man who has seen half the world says it is the case; we always thought so, but now we know it.' My excellent judgement in combs and beauty procured me a most hospitable reception; the captain forced me to take his bed, and he would sleep on his recado.

Charles Darwin

1889

A young man took his young woman to a restaurant and asked her what she would have to drink with her dinner. 'I guess I'll have a bottle of champagne.' 'Guess again!' quoth he.

Alice James

1895

Went to the White drawing-room to receive three Chiefs from Bechuanaland, who are Christians. The Chiefs are very tall and very black, but their hair is not woolly. One of the Chiefs is said to be a very remarkable and intelligent man. One of their chief objects in coming was to obtain a permit from the Government to suppress strong drink, which demoralises and kills the poor natives. Alas! everywhere this terrible evil, which has such a fatal effect on the population, seems to follow civilisation!

Queen Victoria

1920

Spent yesterday in Paris. Went in the metro for the first time. It's convenient amusing, cheap, but people are glued up against each other, breathe in each other's faces and travel underground.

Liane de Pougy

1946

Nine-tenths of the people who call me by telephone I don't want to talk to, and three-fourths of the people I have to take to lunch I don't want to see.

H. L. Mencken

20 November

1947 [Wedding of Princess Elizabeth]

I find it difficult to take these things seriously. We had seats in the Abbey and were able to see the Royal personages passing up the aisle fairly well, but I could not get excited. It would, perhaps, have been more fun outside.

Hugh Gaitskell

1974

Growing old is certainly far easier for people like me who have no job from which to retire at a given age. I can't stop doing what I have always done, trying to sort out and shape experience. The journal is a good way to do this at a less intense level than by creating a work of art as highly organized as a poem, for instance, or the sustained effort a novel requires. I find it wonderful to have a receptacle into which to pour vivid momentary insights, and a way of ordering day-to-day experience (as opposed to [Abraham H.] Maslow's 'peak experiences,' which would require poetry). If there is an art to the keeping of a journal intended for publication yet at the same time a very personal record, it may be in what E[lizabeth] Bowen said: 'One must regard oneself impersonally as an instrument.'

May Sarton

1995

In the evening, Princess Di being *Panoramaed*. First time I've ever seen Anthea [his wife] say 'Sh!' very forcefully when I tried to speak over the TV.

Di going on about duty and the nation and the man in the street – all concepts outside the range of any understanding. *Why* should one feel duty? *What* is the Nation'? Who is the man in the street? My sympathy goes out to her for the shitbag scum journos she has to deal with – imagine meeting those vile smarmy ferrets wherever you went. But she has been too carefully tutored – one suspects her sincerity because it is too perfect. Anthea imagining Camilla Parker-Bowles's undoubtedly upcoming programme. Her projected version of Camilla: all jolly and horsy and full of fun – 'Oh well, of course, silly old me. It's all my fault. Should have trusted my instincts, but I thought he wanted to marry a princess-type. HA HA HA! Jolly daft of me. Might've known that love would win in the end or something soppy like that. HA HA HA!'

Brian Eno

21 November

1839

Queen Victoria has announced her intention of marrying Albert in April next. I hope she is not going to make an April fool of herself.

Barclay Fox

1919

Salomon [Reinach, writer and museum curator] dropped in this morning. He brought us the latest volume of the *Chronologie de la guerre*. He is very upset by the behaviour of the Americans who are refusing to ratify the peace treaty and no longer want to belong to the League of Nations. The idea of which – so difficult to put into practice! – came from them. Evidently this young America is lacking in tact.

I distrust Americans. They are a bit childish. When they arrived in Vittel in August 1917, we happened to be there. It was the height of the season. They had been billeted pretty well everywhere and they were scattered all over the park, near the springs and in the restaurants. They received a fraternal welcome. People smiled at them, greeted them, overcharged them in the shops! One evening my husband was walking his little dog round the hotel when a charming Sammy came up to him and drawled: 'That's a very pretty little dog you have there, sir.' Georges smiled, much touched. Thus encouraged, the Sammy went on: 'You have also got a very pretty wife.' At that Georges laughed aloud. They shook hands. The next day Lorenzo Thomson was waiting for us at the springs, introduced himself formally and became my *cavaliere servente*. Eight days later he asked me to divorce Georges and marry him. He might well have said to me what that rogue [Robert] Goldschmidt said when I mentioned my age in order to discourage him. 'I prefer a woman of forty to two women of twenty!'

Liane de Pougy

1938

Today at my very rising I am seized again by anguish upon contemplating the heavy cloud that spreads over Europe, over the entire universe. An anguish that my optimism is not sufficiently egotistical to overcome. Everywhere I see but a promise of death for everything that is still dear to me and for which we live. The threat seems to me so urgent that one would have to be blind not to see it and to continue hoping.

André Gide

1975

When the news of the seven-year persecution of Martin Luther King by the FBI came out yesterday and the day before, I felt rather *sick*. We live in such a dirty world, and as individuals seem more and more helpless to change it. When I am tired, it all becomes overwhelming like a dismal fog that never lifts. Of course, Franco's death the other day had reminded me of the Idealism, the lifting up of so much courage thirty-six years ago in the rallying of youth from all over the world to help the Republic – long, long ago. Then there was still hope and now there is not. Then, before the Nazi camps, we could still believe in the goodness of man. Now man looks more and more like the murderer of all life, animals too – he is the killer of whales and of his own species – the death bringer. Under everything I do there is this sense that there is no foundation anymore. In what do we believe? can we believe? On what to stand firm? There has to be something greater than each individual – greater, yet something that gives him the sense that his life is vital to the whole, that what he does affects the whole, has meaning.

May Sarton

22 November

1876

Now, I have at least a sense of doing good, and some of the pleasant excitement of making nasty people uncomfortable.

John Ruskin

1928

What I want sounds very simple, and yet I can't get it: to have friends; to go out, to cafés or plays or in taxis, or to the Bois; to live, to be intimate with men without falling immediately into complications.

'My dear, don't flirt, and don't let them make love to you.'

But then I cannot be close to them. A little love helps a lot, but then it gets bigger, and, alas, I find myself floating in the usual story.

'Be cynical, be indifferent.'

I am. I cheat. I elude the ultimate surrender, the direct questions, the dangerous places and hours. I give only the little promises, the hand, the glance, which can fill at least an hour and postpone the climax. If I didn't, I wouldn't have any friends. That word in my vocabulary makes every man laugh. I contradict the anodynic effect of it by my softness, my perfume, my femininity.

Evening: My shopping is not real shopping. Ideas buzz into my head like insects, and I go about digging. I choose quickly, always know what I want, never have regrets, buy what makes others say: 'Where on earth did you find this?' I am really watching faces, listening to conversations, evolving theories, building stories.

And yet my novel is terrible. Thirty-five pages of rot. Darling Journal, I am punished for wanting to divorce you. I am really a damn sentimentalist, trying to be clever. I know only myself well. I should mind my own business.

Anaïs Nin

1995

In early evening to a friend's flat where I made my long overdue confession to a holy and illuminating priest. It was a memorable experience which gently sponged away all my recent irascibility, anxieties and spiritual turmoil. Perhaps kneeling at a dining-room table is more relaxing than the upright coffin of an elaborately carved confessional. It would be good to think that from now on I shall spread only sweetness, light and understanding; but I fear I know myself too well. The bad habits of a lifetime, when tackled head on, seem only to bend, not break.

Alec Guinness

23 November

1850 [New York]

Fearful calamity at a public school in Ninth Ward Thursday afternoon, a false alarm of fire, a panic, a stampede downstairs of 1,800 children, and nearly fifty killed on the spot and many more wounded – a massacre of the innocents. The stair banisters gave way, and the children fell into the square well round which the stairs wound, where the heap of killed and wounded lay for hours before help could reach them. The doors opened inwards. The bodies were piled up to the top of the doors; they did not dare to burst them open and had to cut them slowly away with knives.

George Templeton Strong

1874

Restless night, dreaming of my mother, as insane; in prison, restraining her raving when I came near; I listened at the side of a long wall, she becoming loud and wild when she did not see me, speaking of tearing the flesh off her arm; then slowly putting her head out of the window, catching sight of me, and lowering her voice, and speaking rationally as I came to her.

This terrible dream, the consequence of much sad thought restrained, together with overeating at dinner – probably overdrinking also.

John Ruskin

1896

After tea went to the Red drawing-room, where so-called 'animated pictures' were shown off, including the groups taken in September at Balmoral. It is a very wonderful process, representing people, their movements and actions, as if they were alive.

Queen Victoria

1962

Forms of fans. You write a book – it's your book. Someone reads it and is enthusiastic – it's his book. He tells you what's good about it. He isn't trying to flatter you; he's bragging. He's telling you that he knows what's good and he hints that a stupid oaf like you bumbled into writing it by accident and don't know what you've got.

Dawn Powell

24 *November*

1813

I do think the mighty stir made about scribbling and scribes, by themselves and others – a sign of effeminacy, degeneracy, and weakness. Who would write, who had any thing better to do?

Lord Byron

1933

One rarely hears a radio talk or reads an article on Scottish literature nowadays without meeting the Calvinistic bogey. Why has our art been so meagre for 100s of years – *ergo*, because of Calvinism: and that's that. But surely we are over-easily contented with this solution which is but half-a-solution. Must we not go on and admit that there is something very congenial to Calvinism in the Scottish psyche – even our land and climate have something in common with the stern creed of Geneva. One does not turn round and blame a cramping creed in itself but the men who submit to it. If for far too long Scotland has accepted Calvinism – there can be no doubt but that at one time, and for a lengthy period, Calvinism was acceptable.

William Soutar

1935

I keep wondering what I am to do. I should like to retire and live much more simply. There is so much that I want to write, but I don't think that I'll ever do it if I am in a job. Alternatively, I would like some new job if it were distinguished enough, but it doesn't look as if I should ever have one. And I have been such a ghastly mediocrity compared to what I wanted to be and could have been.

Lord Reith

1937 [Nanking]

It's touching how Dr Rosen worries about me. Of all the Germans who have stayed behind, I am his biggest problem child. He is quite rightly afraid that I'll remain here and not want to flee with him and the other Germans and English, etc. on board the *Hulk*. He personally handed me a pass that was issued by Prideaux-Brune, the English consul, and that permits me to board the *Hulk*, which is to be tugged upstream shortly. He has also arranged to pass the house of ex-minister Chang Chun on to me, just in case – no matter whether I can use it or not. In short – he does everything he possibly can! We had a long conversation yesterday afternoon, that is to say, he told me about his life. His grandfather was a friend of Beethoven's. He showed me a letter Beethoven wrote his grandfather. His family has been in diplomatic service for almost a hundred years. His father was once foreign minister, but he will probably stay a legation secretary all his life – a Jewish grandmother in his family has ruined his career. A tragic fate!

John Rabe

1963 [Philadelphia]

The most horrible and incredible catastrophe. On Friday President Kennedy was shot dead in Dallas, Texas, by a young man of twenty-four called Oswald apparently. Oswald himself was shot this morning while he was being transferred from one prison to another. The whole country is in a state of deep shock. Mrs Kennedy, who was with the President in the car when he died, has behaved throughout with dignity, grace and magnificent self-control. I watched her today on television accompanying the President's body from the White House to the Capitol and was moved to tears. The shooting of the suspected murderer by an exhibitionist night-club proprietor is too idiotic to be believed. That the Dallas police should have allowed it to happen is so stupid that the brain reels. Now it will never be satisfactorily proved whether Oswald shot the President or not, and there will be a jungle of rumours. . .

I am now faced with the task of writing a new number – comedy – for Jo[se] Ferrer because 'Long Live the King' had, of course, to be cut immediately as it deals exclusively with assassination. This is a dreadful job. I am genuinely upset over the President's death and the whole atmosphere is quivering. Hardly conducive to writing frivolous lyrics and music. However, I must go on trying. We are giving a performance tonight as there is to be a day of mourning tomorrow and nothing will be open. It is impossible to evade the general feeling of shock. It seems so desolately wasteful that a virile man in the prime of his life, to whom the whole world was looking for leadership and who, incidentally, was doing a gallant job of it, should be wiped out of life by the action of a zany delinquent with Communist tendencies. I feel that I am living through too much history and that my own life is becoming more and more hectic. However, I feel all right so far. Now I have to take charge, write the bloody song, rehearse the company and get on with the job.

Noël Coward

1990

This has been an infamous week because on Thursday morning, Thanksgiving Day, Mrs Thatcher resigned. It was a cause for great celebration by the company. After the performance champagne was brought and we are all feeling a backlash because of it. In a way I think her resignation is a good thing but I'm not sure how good yet, it's early to say. From the point of view of a change of government, I think it would have been better if she had held on a bit longer and then we could have definitely got rid of the Tories. I also think there is a feeling that she was stabbed in the back.

Brian Cox

25 *November*

1762 [London]

I went to Love's and drank tea. I had now been some time in town without female sport. I determined to have nothing to do with whores, as my health was of great consequence to me. I went to a girl with whom I had an intrigue at Edinburgh, but my affection cooling, I had left her. I knew she was come up. I waited on her and tried to obtain my former favours, but in vain. She would by no means listen. I was really unhappy for want of women. I thought it hard to be in such a place without them. I picked up a girl in the Strand; went into a court with intention to enjoy her in armour. But she had none. I toyed with her. She wondered at my size, and said if I ever took a girl's maidenhead, I would make her squeak. I gave her a shilling, and had command enough of myself to go without touching her. I afterwards trembled at the danger I had escaped. I resolved to wait cheerfully till I got some safe girl or was liked by some woman of fashion.

James Boswell

1853

That terrible Dumas, who never leaves his prey, came to hunt me out at midnight with an empty note-book in his hand. God only knows what he intends to do with all the details that I have been fool enough to give him! I quite like him, but we are not of the same clay and we are not striving towards the same goal. His public is not mine; one of us must be crazy. He left the first numbers of his journal with me, they are delightful reading.

Eugène Delacroix

1882

What a blessing I can write in this little book without fearing that anyone will ever read and ridicule the nonsense and half-sense I scribble. That has been the attraction of a 'diary-book' to me – one can talk one's little thinkings out to a highly appreciative audience, dumb but not deaf. And sometimes this is a necessary safety-valve to save one from that most painful operation, watching one's most cherished chicks hatched by unwearied perseverance coolly trodden underfoot. Now my honest desire is to appear commonplace and sensible, so that none of my dear kind family will think it necessary to remark to themselves or to me that I am otherwise than ordinary; to be on the right side of ordinary is the perfection of prudence in a young woman, and will save her from much heartburning and mortification of spirit.

Beatrice Webb

1940 [Berlin]

I have at last got to the bottom of these 'mercy killings.' It's an evil tale.

The Gestapo, with the knowledge and approval of the German government, is systematically putting to death the mentally deficient population of the Reich. How many have been executed probably only Himmler and a handful of Nazi chieftains know. A conservative and trustworthy German tells me he estimates the number at a hundred thousand. I think that figure is too high. But certain it is that the figure runs into the thousands and is going up every day.

William L. Shirer

1943

My experience of Neapolitan gastronomy was expanded by an invitation to a dinner, the main feature of which was a spaghetti-eating competition. Such contests have been a normal feature of social life, latterly revived and raised almost to the level of a cult as a result of the reappearance on the black market of the necessary raw materials.

Present: men of gravity and substance, including an ex-Vice-Questore, a director of the Banco di Roma, and several leading lawyers – but no women. The portions of spaghetti were weighed out on a pair of scales before transfer to each plate. The method of attack was the classic one, said to have been introduced by Fernando IV, and demonstrated by him for the benefit of an ecstatic audience in his box at the Naples Opera. The forkful of spaghetti is lifted high into the air, and allowed to dangle and then drop into the open mouth, the head being held well back. I noticed that the most likely-looking contestants did not attempt to chew the spaghetti, but appeared to hold it in the throat which, when crammed, they emptied with a violent convulsion of the Adam's apple – sometimes going red in the face as they did so. Winner: a 65-year-old doctor who consumed four heaped platefuls weighing 1.4 kilograms, and was acclaimed by hand-clapping and cheers. These he cheerfully acknowledged and then left the room to vomit.

Norman Lewis

1974

I have nightmares about us Americans, weighed down as we are by 'things' and by excessive eating. I read yesterday that Americans eat fifty times the meat the British do, for instance. Overeating makes people lazy in a different way from the apathy induced by too little nourishment, but I feel sure that it takes the edge off perception. Many of us are literally weighed down. Who can imagine hunger who has never experienced it, even for one day?

May Sarton

1975

Princess Margaret and Colin Tennant arrived, HRH in beaming mood, slimmer and wearing quite a weight of make-up, her thin hair heavily back-combed. She addresses rather than speaks to you, but she revels in tough conversation and anecdotes. She is, as we all know, tiresome, spoilt, idle and irritating. She had just come back from Australia, which she hated, and, worse, it rained. Colin said that it would surely be her last visit. The traffic lights were not even cancelled any more and there was no escort for her, and no crowds either. Imagine the effect of that, he said, on someone who had known and expected all of those things. She smokes non-stop. . . . That evening she really looked rather marvellous in floor-length dark turquoise velvet with a string of diamonds close to her neck. How those royals must meditate on the vanishing magic. Colin Tennant said what did one expect of HRH? She had been deliberately brought up as the younger sister, not to be competition, taught only to dance and sing and that was that. She had been the first one to break out of the charmed circle and now it all seems against her. She has no direction, no overriding interest. All she now likes is *la jeunesse dorée* and Young Men.

Roy Strong

26 November

1825

The court met late and sate till *one*. Detained from that hour till four o'clock being engaged in the perplexd affairs of Mr James Stewart of Brugh. This young gentleman is heir to a property of better than £1000 a year in Orkney. His mother married very young and was wife, mother and widow in the course of the first year. Being unfortunately under the direction of a careless perhaps an unfaithful agent she was unlucky enough to embarass her own affairs by money transactions with this person. I was asked to accept the situation of one of his curators and trust to clear out his affairs and hers – at least I will not fail for want of application. I have lent her £300 on a second (and therefore doubtful) security over her house in Newington bought for £1000 and on which £600 is already secured. I have no connection with the family except that of compassion and [may] not be rewarded even by thanks when the young man comes of age. I have known my father often so treated by those whom he had labourd to serve. But if we do not run some hazard in our attempts to do good where is the merit of them? So I will bring through my Orkney Laird if I can.

Sir Walter Scott

1927

How odious are closet sweeps and chapped rough hands and hairs on the dressing table and powder on the edges of the drawers and clothes that slide off hangers and dirty handkerchiefs – and combs.

I hate making a bed from the beginning up: that horrible cold bare look when you have just fastened in the first crisp clean sheet.

Anne Morrow Lindbergh

1943 [Cairo]

The story goes that Randolph Churchill woke his father yesterday morning saying, 'Twinkle, twinkle little star, how I wonder where you are.' Anyhow the Prime Minister suddenly demanded to know why some of our soldiers were not wearing the Desert Star Medal. Churchill had taken trouble over this medal: the yellow on it is for sand, the blue for sea, and so on. Few have yet been issued – hence the dilemma. Now all the ribbon in existence has been made up and any desert soldier who sees Churchill will wear it but will have to return it at the gate on departure for others to wear.

Jimmy Gault, now English aide to General Eisenhower, invited me to dine last night at the Mohammed Ali Club to meet the General and his staff. Being the only outside guest I was placed at dinner next to the General. There were about sixteen people there – all Americans except for Jimmy, Kay Somersby, the General's very nice English secretary [and mistress] who sat on his right, and myself. A superb dinner was served. For the first two courses the General sat with his back turned to me and only spoke to his Secretary and I began to run out of conversation with a shy young American on my left. Opposite me was Elliot Roosevelt who kept putting his arms round the WAC sitting next to him and trying to kiss her with his mouth full of food. (Elliot is the image of his mother!) When the sweet was served and the General had to turn a little in my direction I asked him if he knew Bonner Fellers, the American Attaché we all liked who was here during some of the Desert war. Eisenhower replied tersely: 'Any friend of Bonner Fellers is no friend of mine,' and smartly turned his back on me again to talk to Kay. Soon after dinner I thanked Jimmy, shook hands with everybody and departed.

Early this morning Jimmy Gault telephoned me to say General Eisenhower thought he'd been rude to me last night and would be pleased if I would dine with him tonight. I asked Jimmy to thank the General for his invitation and say I was sorry I have a previous engagement. An awful lie: I have no date tonight.

Countess of Ranfurly

1992

A perk of the place [House of Commons] is a free medical check-up. The doctor (thirty-something, a touch insipid, a specialist in 'occupational medicine') comes in two or three times a week and is available in a small, airless makeshift surgery located off the Cromwell Lobby. He did all the usual tests and I was given the usual verdict. 'A little more exercise probably wouldn't do any harm. Most people put on a stone or so when they come here. You haven't done too badly. Moderation in all things.' My cholesterol is at the upper edge of the range. Why did I lie about my alcohol consumption? I said half a bottle of wine a day and it must be two-thirds. (I assume everyone lies and when you say half a bottle he puts down two-thirds.)

Gyles Brandreth

27 *November*

1858

No, I've let myself go so much that it's impossible. Estate management is a boorish occupation. Today Rezun told lies; I flew into a rage and, following the loathsome custom, said: 'Flog him.' I waited for him to come and see me. I sent someone to stop the flogging, but he didn't get there in time. I'll ask his pardon. I'll never reprimand anyone again before 2 o'clock in the afternoon. I asked his pardon and gave him three roubles, but I suffered agonies.

Leo Tolstoy

1938

Sad, wandering, lonely, absent. Worn-out with wanting what I haven't got (before it was *money* I wanted: now it's *love*: always either one or the other, generally both), what a relief it would be to have something to rest on. But nothing is firm, there is nothing to prevent one falling. The only unfailing relief is sleep, the humiliating abdication of one's consciousness. (Regarded in that sense, sleep becomes a minor form of suicide).

Must now try to begin to work really hard and to forget everything else for a while.

Saw Jean-Pierre again last night and am going to meet him again during the coming week.

David Gascoyne

1964

Lunched at the Golden Egg. Oh, the horror – the cold stuffiness, claustrophobic place of tables, garish lights and mass produced food in steel dishes. And the egg-shaped menu!

But perhaps one could get something out of it [for a novel]. The setting for a breaking-off, or some terrible news or an unwanted declaration of love.

Barbara Pym

28 November

1834

Liszt said to me to-day that God alone deserves to be loved. It may be true, but when one has loved a man it is very difficult to love God. It is so different. Liszt said also that the only keen sympathy he had ever felt was for M. Lamennais, and he added that earthly love would never get possession of him.

He is very lucky, the good little Christian!

I saw Henri [Heine] this morning. He told me that we love with the head and senses and that the heart counts for very little in love. I saw Mme. Allart at two o'clock. She told me that we must use strategem with men and pretend to be angry in order to get them back. Of them all, Sainte-Beuve alone refrained from hurting me with foolish words. I asked him the meaning of love and he answered, 'It means tears; if you weep, you love.'

Yes, dear friend, I love. In vain do I summon anger to my aid. I love, I shall die of it, unless God works a miracle to save me. Perhaps he will give me back my ambition to write or my devotion to religion. I ought to go seek out Sister Martha.

Midnight

I cannot work. Oh, loneliness, loneliness! I can neither write nor pray. Sainte-Beuve says I need distraction. With whom? What do all these people amount to? When they have talked for an hour about things I don't care about, they disappear. They are merely shadows that come and go. I remain alone, alone forever. I want to kill myself. And who has the right to prevent me?

George Sand

1872

I wrote a letter to M. [Arthur Munby, an upper-class poet whom she later married but who never publicly acknowledged their relationship] and all the day & evening I felt more wretched – I wish'd most sincerely that my time was nearly at an end by God's will, for my life seem'd a burden, instead of a joy as it ought to be. I went in the evening to Mrs Smith's to see the letter M. had wrote to Ellen [her sister].

Hannah Cullwick

1967 [at Privy Council, Buckingham Palace]

The queen was entertaining a film star and the racing driver, Graham Hill, to lunch . . . she kept us waiting ten minutes so we stood in the long ante-hall chatting to Sir Peter Agnew, secretary of the Council. Dick [Crossman] is on uproariously good terms with him. Said I, 'No stools today. Dick always disgraces us by falling over them. These Winchester men have no breeding.' 'That's nothing,' said Peter Agnew. And then proceeded to tell us of the time five members of the previous Tory Government had had to be sworn in. Everything was a shambles: 'The worst swearing-in I have ever seen.' The five came streaming in and every one of them flopped on to one knee on the floor! He indicated that they should move nearer the Queen on to the stools and to his astonishment everyone moved towards the stools on his knees! 'It was an incredible sight.' When it came to kissing hands one unfortunate Privy Councillor lunged at the stool in front of the Queen, missed it and knelt there with one leg cocked in the air. He was only saved from toppling right over by clutching the Queen's hand. She looked like thunder. When it was all over, Sir Peter was summoned to see the Queen. 'Here it goes, I thought. Now I'm for it.' But it was about something else. When he apologized to her she giggled. 'Wasn't it funny!' 'I thought you looked very displeased, ma'am.' 'If I hadn't looked like that I should have burst out laughing,' was her reply.

Barbara Castle

29 November

1834 [On tour, in Louth]

Walked with Mr Robertson to the post office and to the theatre, which answers also the double purpose of a Sessions House; it is not the worst I have seen. Went to the theatre – dressed in magistrates' room – 'quite convenient'. When ready to go on the stage Mr Robertson appeared with a face full of dismay; he began to apologise, and I guessed the remainder.

'Bad house?' 'Bad? Sir, there's no one!' 'What? nobody at all?' 'Not a soul, sir – except the Warden's party in the boxes.' 'What the d—l! not one person in the pit or gallery?' 'Oh yes, there are one or two.' 'Are there five?' 'Oh, yes, five.' 'Then go on; we have no right to give ourselves airs, if the public do not choose to come and see us; go on at once!' Mr Robertson was astonished at what he thought my philosophy, being accustomed, as he said, to be 'blown up' by his Stars when the houses were bad. I never acted Virginius better in all my life – good taste and earnestness. Smyth, who was contemporary with me at Rugby and has a living in this neighbourhood, came in and sat with me, and saw the play, with which he was greatly pleased.

Charles Macready

1935

Honor [his wife] is full of energy and glowing health; her accouchement has done wonders for her looks and well-being. She is an angel of good-ness, gentleness and grace: I love her more every day. Our baby boy now smiles and weighs nearly 11 lbs and Honor is content to sit holding him for hours on end while he gurgles. And for me it is an extraordinarily satisfying emotion to meet a white pram in the Park which contains one's own son.

'Chips' Channon

1942

Mr. Churchill was making a speech tonight. In secret, John, Herbert and I heard it. I think the purpose of his speech was to keep the English from getting too elated over the victories lately. He spoke very seriously and again, did not promise anything. He said 1943 would be a stern, terrible year. Felt rather depressed as I listened, but thinking it over, not so much. Mr Churchill never raises false hopes. And he knows his people, how they must always be 'kept up to it.'

Nan Le Ruez

1948

Lunched with Coco Chanel. Not a good word spoken about anyone but very funny.

Noël Coward

1983

Stale air, bad diet. I have barely got the energy even to do yoga.

Alan Clark

30 November

1866

With a sinking heart and trembling knees got out of the train [at Wolverhampton], amidst great cheering, bands playing, troops presenting arms, etc. . . . All along the three or four miles we drove, the town was beautifully decorated, with flags, wreaths of flowers, and endless kind inscriptions. There were also many arches. It seemed so strange being amongst so many, yet feeling so alone, without my beloved husband! Everything so like former great functions, and yet so unlike! I felt much moved, and nearly broke down when I saw the dear name and the following inscription – 'Honour to the memory of Albert the Good,' 'the good Prince,' 'His works follow him,' and so many quotations from Tennyson. There were barriers all along, so that there was no overcrowding, and many Volunteers with bands were stationed at different points.

The Mayor was completely taken by surprise when I knighted him, and seemed quite bewildered, and hardly to understand it when Lord Derby told him. There was some slight delay in the uncovering of the statue but it [the covering sheet] fell well and slowly, amidst shouts and the playing of the dear old Coburg march by the band. How I could bear up, I hardly know, but I remained firm throughout. At the conclusion of the ceremony I walked round the statue followed by the children. I had seen it before at Thornycroft's studio, and it is upon the whole good . . .

We drove back through quite another, and the poorest, part of the town, which took half an hour. There was not a house that had not got its little decoration; and though we passed through some of the most wretched-looking slums, where the people were all in tatters, and many very Irish-looking, they were most loyal and demonstrative. There was not one unkind look or dissatisfied expression; everyone, without exception, being kind and friendly. Great as the enthusiasm used always to be wherever dearest Albert and I appeared, there was something peculiar and touching in the joy and even emotion with which the people greeted their poor widowed Queen!

Queen Victoria

1919

Some sensational American scientist has produced some theory that by conjunction of planets or something the world will end or at any rate become extinct on the 17th December. We can hardly hope that this is true but the weather seems rather hysterical if that is any sign.

Evelyn Waugh

1939

I'm hearing more and more jokes about President Roosevelt. Here's one of them: A man dies and his soul goes to the Pearly Gates. St Peter asks what he did when alive on earth. The man says he was a psychiatrist. St Peter cries: 'Come in! Come in! You're just the man we need. God thinks he's Franklin D. Roosevelt!'

Edward Robb Ellis

1944

And now India! We breakfasted in bed yesterday morning. Then a mooch into Karachi where we bought ourselves nylon toothbrushes, Pears soap (Australian made), and Pond's cold cream.

Driving back in the station wagon from Karangi Creek last night where we did an RAF show – outdoors, about 500 men – exceptionally good audience – the sergeant (too thin) revealed his past to us. He was on the halls with a dressmaking act. It seems he created exclusive models then and there on three living models – a blonde, a brunette and a redhead. He married the redhead. They came on in brassieres and panties and he draped them. He did three numbers, all to music. First there was a black and white picture. One of the girls as an usherette held a tray with accessories, flowers, jewels, gloves, shoes and then the sergeant, in tails, draped. No. 2 was a wedding creation. No. 3 a patriotic number. The orchestra played soft music while he draped the first girl in a US flag and when he stepped back to reveal the completed costume the music burst into 'Stars and Stripes'. Same procedure with a red flag and the Soviet National Anthem and then, on the central model he'd swish around with a Union Jack, whip out a trident, shield and helmet and Lo! Britannia and the finale. He boasted quite simply that he'd stolen the idea of the act from America. He'd seen it done at the World's Fair in Chicago. Dress designing is his forte. Up in Rawalpindi where he is stationed they have their slack periods between ENSA parties and he does 'exclusive designs' as 'Michael' in the dress shop of a lady friend. He likes to study his subject and always attends fittings. He's done a gown for a major-general's wife and is now about to go into the groove over a wedding. 'Solid silver larmy,' he says. 'The bride has a mahvlus figure.'

Joyce Grenfell

DECEMBER

'When all is said and done, leading a good life is better than keeping a good diary.'

SIEGFRIED SASSOON

1 December

1660

This morning, observing some things to be laid up not as they should be by the girl, I took a broom and basted her till she cried extremely, which made me vexed, but before I went out I left her appeased.

Samuel Pepys

1762

On Tuesday I wanted to have a silver-hilted sword, but upon examining my pockets as I walked up the Strand, I found that I had left most of my guineas at home and had not enough to pay for it with me. I determined to make a trial of the civility of my fellow-creatures, and what effect my external appearance and address would have. I accordingly went to the shop of Mr Jefferys, sword-cutter to his Majesty, looked at a number of his swords, and at last picked out a very handsome one at five guineas. 'Mr Jefferys,' said I, 'I have not money here to pay for it. Will you trust me?' 'Upon my word, Sir,' said he, 'you must excuse me. It is a thing we never do to a stranger.' I bowed genteelly and said, 'Indeed, Sir, I believe it is not right.' However, I stood and looked at him, and he looked at me. 'Come, Sir,' cried he, 'I will trust you.' 'Sir,' said I, 'if you had not trusted me, I should not have bought it from you.' He asked my name and place of abode, which I told him. I then chose a belt, put the sword on, told him I would call and pay it tomorrow, and walked off. I called this day and paid him. 'Mr Jefferys,' said I, 'there is your money. You paid me a very great compliment. I am much obliged to you. But pray don't do such a thing again. It is dangerous.' 'Sir,' said he, 'we know our men. I would have trusted you with the value of a hundred pounds.' This I think was a good adventure and much to my honour.

James Boswell

1801

A fine sunny and frosty morning. Mary [Hutchinson, later wife of William Wordsworth] and I walked to Rydale for letters, William was not well and staid at home reading after having lain long in bed. We found a Letter from Coleridge, a short one – he was pretty well. We were overtaken by two soldiers on our return – one of them being very drunk and we wished them to pass us, but they had too much liquor in them to go very fast so we contrived to pass them – they were very merry and very civil. They fought with the mountains with their sticks . . . They never saw such a wild country though one of them was a Scotchman. They were honest looking fellows. The Corporal said he was frightened to see the Road before them. We met Wm at Sara's gate. He went back intending to go round the lake but having attempted to cross the water and not succeeding he came back. The Simpsons Mr and Miss drank tea with us – Wm was very poorly and out of spirits. They stayed supper.

Dorothy Wordsworth

1937

Nimiec has an anecdote, unsavoury if illustrative, which should find a place in the appendix to Harington's *Metamorphoses*; he arrived at a fishing village in Merlera on one of his fishing jaunts, and was housed in a small cottage with an earth lavatory, primitive and so full of flies that he drew the attention of his host to its condition. His host said briskly, 'Flies? Of course there are flies. If you could do as we all do and wait until just before the midday meal you would not find a fly in the lavatory. They all come round to the kitchen.'

Lawrence Durrell

1977

I am sure that the only good diaries are those written by a writer who is constantly coming upon important people in the great world; and by a writer who stays at home, goes nowhere, sees few people and sticks to the common round. Such a writer has time to ruminate and observe his surroundings. He alone can paint a picture of his complete life, little though it may be. Such a person is Francis Kilvert.

James Lees-Milne

1990

This week saw the removal of Mrs Thatcher from Number 10, and apparently, as she left the building, people detected a tear in her eye. But she turned up in the House the following day, sitting in the seat Geoffrey Howe had occupied when he had made his resignation speech, and she listened to John Major. According to the opinion poll, Labour is slipping and the Tories are rising, and I think the media have at last found a candidate they can openly and uncritically support.

Tony Benn

1990 [Muscat]

Last night another huge dinner, given by the distinguished Doctor Omar. In contrast to the previous evening the pleasures of the flesh were much in evidence. Lashings of alcohol – the claret was all '85 and there were some wonderful white Burgundies. Sinuous and scented lovelies shimmered about.

At the end of the meal a belly dancer performed. On and on she went with graceful, but ever more suggestive rhythms. Her stamina was unbeliev-able and never once did she repeat herself. From time to time she 'fixed' particular guests in their places, a special treat.

There was a French Admiral sitting next to me, his face expressionless. I said, it helps one to understand how women can experience ten or eleven orgasms in one night. Myself, three render me *complètement, totalement épuisé*. Ruefully he agreed.

Alan Clark

2 December

1775

When I came home, I found that my wife had been reading this journal and though I had used Greek letters, had understood my visits to ——.

She spoke to me of it with so much reason and spirit that, as I candidly owned my folly, so I was impressed with proper feelings; and, without more argument than that it was disagreeable to so excellent a spouse, resolved firmly to keep clear.

And when I reflected calmly, I thought it lucky that my journal had been read, as it gave an opportunity to check in the beginning what might have produced much mischief. I wondered at my temporary dissipation of thought when I saw the effects of my conduct. I valued and loved my wife with renewed fervour.

James Boswell

1783

After the Company was all gone and we thought everything were agree-able and happy in my house, we were of a sudden alarmed by a great Noise in the kitchen, and on my immediately going out there found my Servant Man Will: Coleman beating about the Maids in a terrible manner and appeared quite frantic and mad. I seized him by the Collar and as soon as he was loose, he ran out into the Yard and jumped into the Pond there in a moment but he was soon taken up by Ben, which frightened us so much that we were obliged to sit up all night. We got him to bed however about

1 o'clock and after some time he was somewhat quiet – but it frightened us so much and Nancy and self did not go to bed till 6 in the morning. Ben and Jack did not go to bed at all. The reason of his being so, was on Lizzy's Account, as he wants to marry her and she will not, and he is very jealous. Am afraid however that it proceeds from a family complaint, his Father having been crazy some time. It is therefore now high time for him to leave me which I shall endeavour to do the first opportunity. It made me very ill almost instantly and made my niece very unhappy as well as ill also.

James Woodforde

1958

Charlie Pannell told me today his delightful story of his visit to Anglesey to speak for Cledwyn Hughes. Throughout his speech he was much struck by an old man who sat there impressively with his head on his stick. Charlie said he couldn't keep his eyes off him, and after the meeting asked Cledwyn who he was. Cledwyn said he was an old, old man well over ninety who had been a friend of Lloyd George.

'Go and talk to him,' said Cledwyn. 'He'd be delighted.'

Charlie moved to the back of the hall and sat down beside the old man.

'Sir,' he said, for he couldn't address him in any other way, 'I understand you knew Lloyd George.'

The old man raised his head slowly and spoke. 'Lloyd George,' he said, 'had a prick like a donkey.'

Charlie was taken aback. 'Ah, well,' he said. 'He was a man of many parts.'

'I know he was,' said the old man. 'And he'll be remembered more for that part than any other.' He gave a deep chuckle.

Tony Benn

1972

In Nottingham for a talk to undergraduates on politics. We stayed with one Owen, the excellent university chaplain. I said it seemed to me that undergraduates, though now legally adults at eighteen, are even less mature than they used to be. Owen said this was indeed so. Ruth thought the university more of a youth club than a seat of learning. Though half the students live in, they mostly go home at weekends to be with their girl-friends!

Cecil King

3 December

1852

Great news stirring in that volcanic Paris. The President has dissolved the Assembly and appealed to the people and the army; he establishes universal suffrage, and has arrested his political opponents. How will it end? Shall we have a Cromwell Junior, or will blood flow there again like water? One learns to give thanks for being born in England.

Caroline Fox

1919

We went for a House run to Nearer Steep Down today. No one could find the way. We stopped a hundred yards too soon; a great white sea mist hung all over the downs and was wet on our bare chests; it seemed to heave and creep up the edges of the slopes. And Mr Einstein has discovered a new theory of the universe!

Evelyn Waugh

1944

The squirrel-faced lift-woman was talking away volubly last night about the English – 'The greatest race on earth,' she said. 'Never has been anything like us – never will be. Look the way we bore the brunt of the war yet we never talk about ourselves – no swank – we just get on with the job.'

The Americans in London are a well-behaved tolerant army of occupation. They are so polite that one almost hears their thoughts and they are thinking, 'These poor, quaint people. They have guts but – backward, reactionary.' And the English with their kindly street directions thinking behind shut faces, 'These people have not got what it takes – no breeding – an inferior race but, damn them, they have the money and the power. We can only dominate them by character, our national asset from which we can always cut and come again.'

The two races and the two arms mingle in street and pub without ever touching except for the collaborating little factory girls who chew gum, wear their hair à la Lana Turner and queue up for movies hand-in-hand with their protectors. The American men are so different with the women. They fondle them in the street, always a hand splaying over breast or buttock. Loose-limbed they amble at the girl-friend's side whispering in her ear, pinching her behind, their two mouths rhythmically moving in unison – so different from the wooden Englishman walking side by side with his girl not seeming to see her except for covert glances and the occasional clumsy touch of his hand on hers.

Charles Ritchie

4 December

In the Stock Exchange today: 'There,' said Conrad, who is pleased to point out celebrities to me, 'is Mr Fleischmann. He is known as Louis XIV – Louis because it is his name; XIV because he is never asked out to dinner except when they would be thirteen without him.' It is his partner, by the way, the melancholy Messel, who has never been known to smile except once when he had the luck to see a child run over by a motor-bus in Threadneedle Street.

Sir Alan 'Tommy' Lascelles

1930

One word of slight snub in the [*Times*] *Lit. Sup.* today makes me determine, first, to alter the whole of *The Waves*; second, to put my back up against the public – one word of slight snub.

Virginia Woolf

1935

I felt the day not a failure because at night perhaps I kept Jon [her small son] from one fear; he said he didn't want me to turn the light out, that he didn't like the dark. I thought in that second of my long fight against fear of the dark, as a child, and tried to think of something nice to say to him. 'Don't you like the dark, Jon? It's like a big blanket over you – like the blanket of leaves and grass over the flowers in the garden we saw this afternoon, so the flowers can sleep all covered up in the dark.'

Jon smiled, relenting: 'I like the dark.' And after I'd gone out and turned off the light and shut the door, I heard him calling out to me, 'I like the dark!' I called back, 'Yes, darling!'

Anne Morrow Lindbergh

1936

The papers are full of the adventures of King Edward VIII who is madly in love with a charming American and wants to marry her. The clergy, severe and cold, have expressed their displeasure. They allege that coronation is a sacrament, that a king's wife must be a queen, and that because Mrs Simpson has been divorced she can't possibly fulfil the conditions. Give way or abdicate. The King does not want to give way; the Duke of York is getting ready to take his place. What a beautiful love story! The people of England are quite crestfallen. They seem to be very fond of their king, who on his side has lent himself to the job's innumerable demands with great good will and much style.

Liane de Pougy

1940

Watch the newsreel with the Führer, who is very pleased with it. The shots of London burning make a particularly profound impression on him. He also takes careful note of the pessimistic opinions from the USA.

Nevertheless, he does not expect the immediate collapse of England and probably rightly. The ruling class there has now lost so much that it is bringing up its last reserves. By which he means not so much the City of London as the Jews, who if we win will be hurled out of Europe, and Churchill, Eden, etc., who see their personal existences as dependent on the outcome of the war. Perhaps they will end up on the scaffold. We can expect little resistance to them from the masses at the moment. The English proletariat lives under such wretched conditions that a few extra privations will not cause it much discomfort. There will be no revolution, anyway, because the opportunity is lacking. England will thus survive through this winter . . . The Führer does not intend to mount any air-raids at Christmas. Churchill, in his madness, will do so, and then the English will be treated to revenge raids that will make their eyes pop.

Josef Goebbels

1941

Thinking over what I have written. What a pack of lies intimate journals are, particularly if one tries too hard to be truthful.

Charles Ritchie

1982 [New York]

One change that has come over public manners was evident at the Falklands homecomings. Combatants (the only airman captured by the Argentinians, for instance), asked what is the first thing they are going to do when they get home, grin cheekily. One says, 'Well, what do you think?' and doubtless others actually do say, 'I'm going to fuck someone silly.' Once upon a time they would have *said*, at any rate, 'Have a nice cup of tea.'

Alan Bennett

5 December

1662

Up, it being a snow and hard frost, and being up I did call up Sarah, who do go away to-day or to-morrow. I paid her her wages, and gave her 10s. myself, and my wife 5s. to give her. For my part I think never servant and mistress parted upon such foolish terms in the world as they do, only for an opinion in my wife that she is ill-natured, in all other things being a good servant. The wench cried, and I was ready to cry too, but to keep peace I am content she should go.

Samuel Pepys

1933

'Besides, it's very simple,' said that excellent lady at that excellent luncheon yesterday . . . 'Besides, it's very simple: if I didn't have servants I couldn't knit any more for the poor.'

André Gide

1944 [Bombay]

We were taken to a flat owned by a very pretty Indian author, style Ivor Novello, and a sibilant friend whose name, appropriately, sounded like Rodent. There we found a collection of pansies that fair shook us.

Soldiers, sailors and one airman. Waving hair, gestures of the 'my dear' sort and soft, gentle, wholly peculiar eyes and voices. Into this set-up arrived three black-haired popsies of extraordinary curve and chocolate-box looks. Just what they were doing there I cannot tell. We sat on a large bed in a big room, with a number of books and some fretwork Victorian furniture and time went sluggishly by. Bruce and I exchanged news and views and raised our eyebrows; Viola was pinned in conversation by an elderly art critic. Liveliness was not the keynote of the evening and at 1.30 we slipped away and drove home through the balmy moonlight.

Joyce Grenfell

1949

Fundamentally, the pleasure of kissing is no more than that of eating. If there were embargoes on eating, as there are on kissing, a whole ideology would come into existence, a *passion* for eating, with standards of chivalry. This ecstasy they talk about – the vision, the dreams evoked by a kiss – is no more than the pleasure of biting into a medlar or a grape fresh from the vine. One can do without it.

Cesare Pavese

6 December

1813

This journal is a relief. When I am tired – as I generally am – out comes this, and down goes every thing. But I can't read it over; – and God knows what contradictions it may contain. If I am sincere with myself (but I fear one lies more to one's self than to any one else), every page should confute, refute, and utterly abjure its predecessor.

Lord Byron

1834

In the evening we reached the island of San Pedro, where we found the *Beagle* at anchor. In doubling the point, two of the officers landed to take a round of angles with the theodolite. A fox (*Canis fulvipes*) of a kind said to be peculiar to the island and very rare in it, and which is a new species, was sitting on the rocks. He was so intently absorbed in watching the work of the officers that I was able, by quietly walking up behind, to knock him on the head with my geological hammer. This fox, more curious or more scientific, but less wise, than the generality of his brethren, is now mounted in the museum of the Zoological Society.

Charles Darwin

1857 [on a Mississippi steamer]

I had no time to tell of my long conversation with the Honourable William Haskell, one of the representatives of Kentucky and his daughter. He was a fine fellow, tall and strong like all these Kentuckians, but so strangely ignorant of the commonest things. He asked me the hours of the House of Commons sittings. I said from seven or eight o'clock a.m. to twelve or one a.m. He turned round and said to his daughter Juliet, 'You know when the lady says seven, that is not the same as seven with us; it is a great deal earlier in the day because the sun sets earlier by some hours,' and I could not make him understand it was the same as seven with them! Miss Juliet was a specimen of a Southern lady. She could not travel alone; she was pale and looked dissipated. She had been brought up in the Great Convent at Washington where fashionable Southerns go for education and where they are worked so hard that (she said) all had complexions like hers after a year of school. I never heard of a worse system of education in my life, and, according to her account, the girls were as bad as the system – intriguing, lying creatures – Miss Juliet told stories of the way in which lovers were got into the convent in disguise, and this before three young men in the coach who very much admired her conversation. She was a horrid animal. She told me her mother was married at thirteen and her sister at fifteen and says it is the custom in the Slave States. So Mrs P. said; she herself was married at fifteen and her husband's first wife was fifteen. Miss Juliet could not walk a mile, says few South state American women can; so say all the ladies here in the boat. Slavery makes all labour dishonourable and walking gets to be thought a labour, an exertion.

Barbara Leigh Smith Bodichon

1995

Button-punching from channel to channel last night I finally alighted on BBC2 sometime after nine o'clock. We thought we were seeing things. And indeed we were. We were confronted by a row of bare bums, bent over and chattering and singing through their anuses. O horribilis! O horribilis! Most horribilis! 'How do they *do* that?' With Latex buttocks and human lips I suppose. Come back, Mary Whitehouse. All is forgiven.

Alec Guinness

7 December

1813

Awoke and up an hour before being called; but dawdled three hours in dressing. When one subtracts from life infancy (which is vegetation), – sleep, eating, and swilling – buttoning and unbuttoning – how much remains of downright existence? The summer of a dormouse.

Lord Byron

1860

Going into a shop to buy some photographs the shopman, who was also a photographer, brought out by the way of temptation various portraits of nude & semi-nude women, which he himself had taken. I enquired what manner of women they were, who were willing to have pictures of their naked bodies taken, and sold to strangers at 2/- each: of course they are virtually prostitutes? 'Not at all, Sir!' cries the worthy photographer, indignant: 'this one' (holding up a stark naked figure) 'is herself an artist, and was a *governess*. No, No – they wouldn't do anything of that: a girl has no need to go on the streets when she can earn *five or six pounds* a week, by this sort of thing & sitting to the Academy!' Nearly £300 a year to be earned by simply sitting in a chair without any clothes on: no wonder such a trade is preferred to the hard and self-accusing life of a prostitute! Nevertheless, one would say on the whole that these delicate gradations of female modesty are somewhat inexplicable to the coarser masculine mind . . .

Arthur F. Munby

1936

Now, we are – without a King? With a Queen? What? The Simpson affair is on the surface. It was on Wednesday 2 December that the Bishop [of Bradford] commented on the King's lack of religion. On Thursday all the papers, *The Times* and *Daily Telegraph* very discreetly mentioned some domestic difficulties; others Mrs Simpson. All London was gay and garrulous – not exactly gay, but excited. We can't have a woman Simpson for Queen, that was the sense of it. She's no more royal that you or me, was what the grocer's young woman said. But today we have developed a strong sense of human sympathy: we are saying hang it all – the age of Victoria is over. Let him marry whom he likes. Harold [Nicolson] is glum as an undertaker, as are the other nobs. They say Royalty is in Peril. The Empire is divided. In fact never has there been such a crisis. Spain, Germany, Russia – all are elbowed out. Parties are forming. The different interests are queueing up behind [Stanley] Baldwin or Churchill. [Oswald] Mosley is taking advantage of the crisis for his ends. In fact we are all talking nineteen to the dozen; and it looks as if this one little insignificant man had moved a pebble which dislodges an avalanche. Things – empires, hierarchies, moralities – will never be the same again.

Virginia Woolf

1943

Start evening classes for the elder refugee children, who have got beyond the elementary school stage: V. teaches them mathematics, physics and science; Signorina G., Italian and history; I, English and Latin. Life is returning to the medieval pattern: as the outside world is more and more cut off, we must learn, not only to produce our own food and spin and weave our own wool – but to provide teaching for the children, nursing for the sick, and shelter for the passer-by.

Iris Origo

8 December

1762

At night I went to Covent Garden and saw *Love in a Village*, a new comic opera, for the first night. I liked it much. I saw it from the gallery, but I was first in the pit. Just before the overture began to be played, two Highland officers came in. The mob in the upper gallery roared out, 'No Scots! No Scots! Out with them!' hissed and pelted them with apples. My heart warmed to my countrymen, my Scotch blood boiled with indignation. I jumped up on the benches, roared out, 'Damn you, you rascals!,' hissed and was in the greatest rage. I am very sure at that time I should have been the most distinguished of heroes. I hated the English; I wished from my soul that the Union was broke and that we might give them another battle of Bannockburn. I went close to the officers and asked them what regiment they were of. They told me Lord John Murray's, and that they were just come from the Havana. 'And this,' said they, 'is the thanks we get – to be hissed when we come home.' If it was French, what could they do worse?

James Boswell

1914 [Red Cross Volunteer on the French front]
I have a little 'charette' [cart] for my soup. It is painted red, and gives a lot of amusement to the wounded. The trains are very long, and my small carriage is useful for cups and basins, bread, soup, coffee, etc. Clemmie Waring designed and sent it to me.

To-day I was giving out my soup on the train and three shells came in in quick succession. One came just over my head and lodged in a haystall on the other side of the platform. The wall of the store has an enormous hole in it, but the thickly packed hay prevented the shrapnel scattering. The station-master was hit, and his watch saved him, but it was crumpled up like a rag. Two men were wounded and one of them died. A whole crowd of refugees came in from Coxide, which is being heavily shelled. There was not a scrap of food for them, so I made soup in great quantities, and distributed it to them in a crowded room whose atmosphere was thick. Ladling out the soup is great fun.

Sarah Macnaughtan

1948
Went to BBC with Kitty to look at a television performance. Very pitiable in quality, but I suppose they will improve it in time, and it will eventually become as popular as wireless.

Malcolm Muggeridge

1969
Saw [portrait painter Pietro] Annigoni again at the [Buckingham] Palace. The portrait [of the Queen] is very advanced, indeed almost finished. For a moment it looked dull and then Hugh uttered the word, 'Varnish.' Annigoni seized a wide brush and dipped it in the water of a flower vase and applied it to the picture as we shrieked, 'Marvellous.'

Roy Strong

1970
I took Ben Nicolson to the opera. Ben is extraordinarily vague but charming. He talked, as he often does, about his parents [Vita Sackville-West and Harold Nicolson]. He adored his father but was never very close to his mother. She was an avowed lesbian long before she married. She used to walk about

London dressed as a man, which she discovered early in life is what she should have been. Ben kept on repeating that Harold was the kindest man in the world, but agreed with me that he had an imp in him and that he enjoyed apologizing to an absurd degree, saying, 'If I go down on my knees, will you forgive me?', and other such expressions of contrition.

Cynthia Gladwyn

9 December

1775
At supper my wife and I had a dispute about some trifle. She did not yield readily enough, and my passion rose to a pitch that I could not quite command. I started up and threw an egg in the fire and some beer after it. My inclination was to break and destroy everything. But I checked it. How curious is it that the thinking principle can speculate in the very instant of anger. My wife soon made up our difference. But I begged of her to be more attentive again.

James Boswell

1826
In gratitude I suppose for the good Burgundy and Champane wt. which I treated them yesterday my bowels allowd me a good night's rest but began their old trade about seven in the morning. So that to keep promise with them I staid at home and sent for Doctor Ross who is to send some Doctor's stuff I suppose.

Sir Walter Scott

1888
Slept sinfully.

Leo Tolstoy

10 December

1860
Coming out of the Odéon after *L'Oncle Million*, I saw Flaubert and [Louis] Bouilhet surrounded by men in cloth caps with whom they were shaking hands; and Bouilhet left us saying that he was going to the café next door. It seems that to keep a play going at the Odéon, one has to supply it with drinks and handshakes.

Flaubert told us that while writing the description of the poisoning of Mme Bovary, he had felt a pain as if he had a copper plate in his stomach, a pain which had made him vomit twice over. He said that one of his most agreeable moments was when, working on the end of his novel, he had been obliged to get up and look for another handkerchief, because he had soaked the one he had! . . . And all that in order to amuse the bourgeois!

The Brothers Goncourt

1936

In the evening we sat listening to the wireless broadcasting the news of the King's abdication. I had the feeling that the affair somehow symbolised the whole horror of life, the struggle between Man's noblest, richest impulses, and the shoddy fabric of Time. Hughie described how he had once visited in Brittany the ruins of an ancient sacrificial Temple, and how there he had first realized what sacrifice meant – the offering up of Youth by Age, a spilling of young blood by withered arms, paying Life as a tribute of Death. I felt that this was true, and an outward manifestation of what goes on in each individual soul.

We drove Hughie back. Blackshirts were selling their papers in the streets, surrounded by a circle of admiring girls. Kit [his wife] keeps saying to me: 'Everything's going to be all right, isn't it?' and I nod without conviction. We went for a walk this morning. It was a perfect winter's morning. I said that most people managed to evolve either a sense of grievance, or illusions; but that I had neither.

Malcolm Muggeridge

1939

An intoxicating day spent with someone I have hardly seen alone since January, i.e. myself. There is no such blissful companionship, no such satisfactory or stimulating friendship. I got up late, wrote many letters, tidied up and telephoned. The war is 100 days old, and a damned bore it is, though no-one seems to talk about it now. It might be somewhere very remote, and I feel that there is a definite danger in such detachment.

'Chips' Channon

1976

This morning I wakened and thought of my Ma. She is dead five years to the day. I rang my bell to get the door opened then went into the yard to do my run. Snow had fallen overnight. I ran round the yard though taking it easy. The hard crispy snow crunched under my feet as I ran. After my exercises I knelt before the bed and said a decade of the rosary for my Ma. It's strange, I'm not the least religious but Ma was so I feel this is the best way to remember her. Only I could possibly know what she gave me throughout my life. I knelt thinking of her and how beautiful she was in standing by me. Also how much she did for my brothers. Doing this is very important for me as I feel as though I'm giving her something in return.

Jimmy Boyle

11 December

1857 [on a Mississippi steamer]

Last night I sat finishing up my sketches at the public table. *Company:* the pretty little Mrs H. and her fair Scotch-looking husband, Mr C. the intellectual-looking Californian gentleman and Mrs B. who has a very beautiful expression and is the most refined woman on the boat. Mr C. is reading a paper and read out loud the announcements of the marriage of a mulatto and a white girl; it excites from all expressions of the utmost disgust and horror. I say, 'It is very uncommon?' *Mr C.:* 'Yes! thank God. Only permitted in Massachusetts and a few states.' 'There seems to be nothing disgusting in it. My brothers went to school with a mulatto and I with a mulatto girl, and I have seen mulattoes in England who were not unlikely to marry with whites.' *All:* 'At school! At school with niggers!' *BLS:* 'Yes.' *All:* 'Horrid idea, how could you?' *BLS:* 'Why your little children all feel it possible to come in close contact with negroes, and they seem to like it; there is no natural antipathy.' *Some:* 'Yes, there is an inborn disgust *which prevents amalgamation.*' (Mark this: only one-half the negroes in the United States are full-blood Africans – the rest [the] product of white men and black women.) *Some:* 'No, it is only the effect of education.' *Mr C.:* 'There is no school or college in the U.S. where negroes could be educated with whites.' *BLS:* 'You are wrong, Sir. At Oberlin men, women and negroes are educated together.' *Mrs B.:* 'Yes, I know that, because Lucy Stone was educated there with people of colour.' *Mr C.:* 'Lucy Stone – she is a Woman's Rights woman, and an atheist. All those people are. Have you heard her speak?' *Mrs B.:* 'Yes, she speaks wonderfully well. She is an elegant orator. I was carried away by her at first. – She said women had a right to vote and all that sort of nonsense.' *Mr C.:* 'Nonsense indeed! Why, women, if that they have not certain rights are exempt from certain duties.' *Mrs B.:* 'Oh, yes, certainly Woman's Rights are great rubbish.' There is evidently a feeling that Abolition and Woman's Rights are supported by the same people and the same arguments, and that both are allied to atheism – and all these slave owners are very religious people.

I wanted the conversation to stick to slavery so I did not answer this argument with the other side which settles that objection. I said instantly, 'Do not you think it right to give any education to the negro race?' *Mrs B.:* 'Oh, yes. Every child should be taught to read the Bible.' *Mrs H.:* 'I do not think they ought to be taught to read. It makes them unhappy, and all the negroes who run away, you will find, are those who have learnt how to read. I would not teach them to read.' *BLS.:* 'But have they not souls and should not they read the Bible?' *Some:* 'Oh, yes, they have souls, but oral instruction is best for them.' *Mrs B.:* 'No, I do think everyone should be able to read the Bible.' *Mrs H.:* 'If you teach them to read they *will* run away.' *Mrs B.* (who lives in Louisville and is evidently very kind to her slaves): 'Well, I say if they will run away, let them.' *Mr and Mrs H.* (who by the bye are bringing south *a woman who leaves a husband and five children behind in Kentucky*): 'Let them run away if they will! Why, every negro would run away if they could – people don't like to lose their servants.' Some said it makes the negroes unhappy to know how to read – what is the use of it to them? They are inferior to the whites and must be so always. *BLS:* 'But you say they improve and are better off every year, and that there is a wonderful difference between the African as he comes from Africa and the African after two or three generations in America. How can you tell where the improvement will stop?' *Mr C.:* 'Yes, they improve, but that is no reason for giving them *much* instruction and us making them discontented – for they *never will be emancipated. We cannot consent to lose our property.*'

Barbara Leigh Smith Bodichon

1936 [France]
At ten o'clock this evening I listened on the BBC to Edward VIII's farewell speech to his peoples and his homeland. He spoke for barely five minutes, but the simplicity, dignity, and genuine humanity of the statement were profoundly moving, like a speech from one of Shakespeare's royal dramas.

Count Harry Kessler

1936
Edward VIII has just abdicated. He has sacrificed his crown for love of a woman. He did not give way; that is royal. He has left everything for the one he loves: he is a marvellous and courageous lover. The story is a larger version of my own. I was rather younger than Mrs Simpson at the time of my marriage to Georges Ghika who was many years younger than I was but who was very serious, basically very serious and didn't often laugh.

Liane de Pougy

1937

It is not true that chastity is sexually alluring, for, if it were, women would be avid for young novices and newly ordained priests, who may be supposed to take their vows seriously. Instead, women go for elderly swine, men with plenty of experience, bald-headed, and bad-tempered.

And you, too. You have never dreamed of nuns, have you?

Cesare Pavese

1969

I was rung up in a panic by the Tate. The Queen Mother was on her way from Clarence House, could I drop everything and come at once. I hopped in a taxi and arrived in time to guide her round three-quarters of it. She loved it for its Englishness and, coming across a warder slumped asleep, tiptoed by, whispering to me, 'We mustn't wake him!'

Roy Strong

1980 [New York]

I am having supper at The Odeon when word goes round the tables that John Lennon has been shot. 'This country of ours,' sighs my waiter. 'May I tell you the specials for this evening?'

The Chinese cooks come and stand at the door of the kitchen as a radio is brought to one of the booths. At another table some diners call instantly for their check, hardly bothering to conceal their appetite for the tragedy (they are, after all, New Yorkers), and take a cab uptown to join what WNEW is already calling 'a vigil'. 'Would you describe the crowd outside the Dakota Apartment as a vigil?' asks Dan, our host. 'I would describe it,' says the woman reporter, whose name is Robin, 'definitely as a vigil.'

In England this will mark New York down yet again as a violent and dangerous place, but I walk back up West Broadway, the street deserted except for a few drunks in doorways ('The slayer thought to be male, white') and feel perfectly safe. Already, though, there are candles burning in windows, and a girl weeps as she waits on this warm, windy night to cross Canal Street – 'Sixty-four degrees here on WNEW, the wind from the south-west', the wind and the warmth making it possible for the male, white slayer to wait however long he had to wait this unseasonable December night for the return of his victim.

Alan Bennett

1992

The *Daily Mail* rang to ask my views on the separation of the Prince and Princess of Wales. I said I had none. They added, 'Constitutionally?' Said I had none on that either. They will have to sort it all out without my help. Actually, I think the Princess has no rights whatever. She was born a lady, came into the world in her right mind, ought to have known what was implied by marrying the heir to the throne, and accordingly put up with whatever befell her. In fact, duty.

Anthony Powell

12 December

1680

This evening looking out of my Chamber Window towards the West, I first saw a Meteor, (or what ever other Phænomenon it was) of an obscure bright Colour (if so I may call it without a solecism) resembling the brightnesse of the Moone when under a thin Clow'd, very much in shape like the blade of a sword, whose point to the starre in appearance, bending Northwards towards London, not seeming at the horizon to be above a yard in bredth, and so pyramidal, the rest of the skie, very serene and cleere; The Moone new, but not appearing, the Weather exceeding sharp, hard frost with some snow falling 2 daies before: What this may Portend (for it was very extraordinarie) God onely knows; but such another Phænomen[on] I remember I saw, which went from North to South, and was much brighter, and larger, but not so Ensiforme in the yeare 1640, about the Triall of the greate Earle of Strafford, præceeding our bloudy Rebellion: I pray God avert his Judgements; we have had of late severall Comets, which though I believe appeare from natural Causes, and of themselves operate not, yet I cannot despise them; They may be warnings from God, as they commonly are forrunners of his Annimadversions.

John Evelyn

1848 [Ireland]

A Sligo steamer bound for Liverpool put into Derry from stress of weather and landed seventy-two corpses. The crew had shut down the hatches on the miserable steerage passengers, all emigrants bound for America, and suffocated half of them. Captain, etc. are in jail. Murder after murder in England. Pope fled to Naples. Emperor of Austria abdicated in favour of his nephew. A thousand emigrants per day still leaving our Irish ports, most of them with money. The runaway farmers have learned the trick of thrashing out their corn by night, leaving the straw neatly cocked, selling off stock and furniture and bolting, with heavy arrears due to the ruined landlords.

Elizabeth Grant of Rothiemurchus

1857 [on a Mississippi steamer]

I find Mrs B. is divorced from her husband as is Miss Sophia Titney. In Kentucky divorce is easy – for adultery, for cruelty, for desertion, for slander, or even public ridicule or intoxication. I believe Mrs B. obtained her divorce on the grounds that her husband had held her up to public ridicule by publishing certain private letters of hers against her wishes. There was a good deal of conversation about her as she was the most interesting woman on board and sang very sweetly. The gentlemen all said she would marry again and that no man would think the divorce any impediment. Mr Collins said a cousin of his had divorced his wife and both married again and the husband to a divorced woman. In California divorce is quite easy. I asked over and over again, 'Do you think easy divorce makes married life happier or unhappier than where divorce is impossible?' They all answered happier except one lady who was a Catholic.

Barbara Leigh Smith Bodichon

1889

One day when my shawls were falling off to the left, my cushions falling out to the right and the duvet off my knees, one of those crises of misery in short which are all in the day's work for an invalid Kath. exclaimed, 'What an awful pity it is that you can't say *damn*.' I agreed with her from my heart. It is an immense loss to have all robust and sustaining expletives refined away from one! At such moments of trial refinement is a feeble reed to lean upon. I wonder, whether, if I had had any education I should have been more, or less, of a fool than I am. It would have deprived me surely of those exquisite moments of mental flatulence which every now and then inflate the cerebral vacuum with a delicious sense of latent possibilities – of stretching oneself to cosmic limits, and who would ever give up the reality of dreams for relative knowledge?

Alice James

1918

B. [formerly a fairly senior Russian Ministry of Foreign Affairs official] gave a very curious account of Rasputin, whom he had known. Rasputin was a perfectly honest son of the soil who, at the age of twelve, was engaged at Court to tend the lamps burning in front of the icons. In that capacity he occasionally entered at night the room of the young grand duchesses, having to light the lamps there, but nothing noteworthy ever arose out of that. It was the ladies of the Court who, when they observed the influence he had, positively sidled up to him and were responsible for his turning into a rake and a glutton. The Empress never had intimate relations with him. She merely showed herself in his company to prove that she was a good Orthodox

Russian, but that was how the gossip started. The Tsar looked on him as 'the voice of the black earth' and saw no need for the Duma as long as Rasputin could echo to him directly the thought of his people. Gradually Rasputin acquired enormous influence and earned a corresponding amount of jealousy and enmity. During the war he was always against the continuation of hostilities, increasing the antipathy of Britain and the party of the grand dukes still more. Britain spent immense sums on efforts to eliminate his influence. In the last analysis, though, he always remained a simple peasant and lamplighter. Everything else is romantic trimmings.

Count Harry Kessler

1978

New York: I wandered about in the brisk cold window-shopping, and gazing at this city of contrasts: such luxury, such elegance, such beautiful modern buildings; and yet such poverty, such cheap unpleasant tat. In my extremely staid hotel there is a bookstall in the lobby at which a blue-rinsed lady presides over gum, candies, magazines and newspapers. I bought a soft porn magazine and saw an article entitled 'Tossing'. It's not, as one would think, about masturbation, but about sexual gratification in which, irrespective of your sex, you have sexual pleasure from another person and then kick them out, denigrate them, or disappoint them, as speedily as possible. According to the article this is the new craze that's sweeping America – 'Tossing'. The sheer indifference to the individual and to human feeling is appalling. But that's typical of this town – as is also an extraordinary multiracial excitement. You walk down a street and see every physical type, every colour, every creed. It's truly a melting pot.

Peter Hall

13 December

1855

This morning it is snowing, and the ground is whitened. The countless flakes, seen against the dark evergreens like a web that is woven in the air, impart a cheerful and busy aspect to nature. It is like a grain that is sown, or like leaves that have come to clothe the bare trees. Now, by 9 o'clock, it comes down in larger flakes, and I apprehend that it will soon stop. It does.

How pleasant a sense of preparedness for the winter, – plenty of wood in the shed and potatoes and apples, etc., in the cellar, and the house banked up! Now it will be a cheerful sight to see the snows descend and hear the blast howl.

Sanborn tells me that he was waked up a few nights ago in Boston, about midnight, by the sound of a flock of geese passing over the city, probably about the same night I heard them here. They go honking over cities where the arts flourish, waking the inhabitants; over State-houses and capitols, where legislatures sit; over harbors where fleets lie at anchor; mistaking the city, perhaps, for a swamp or the edge of a lake, about settling in it, not suspecting that greater geese than they have settled there.

H. D. Thoreau

1940

Five other American correspondents going home from the war, from England, from Germany, from France, sat in the ship's little bar over 'old-fashioneds'. It was a very good way of cushioning your farewell. I joined them. I had one. But alcohol is not always enough. I felt restless, excited. I went up on deck. For a time I stood against the rail watching the lights recede on a Europe in which I had spent fifteen of my adult years, which had given me all of my experience and what little knowledge I had. It had been a long time, but they had been happy years, personally, and for all people in Europe they had had meaning and borne hope until the war came and the Nazi blight and the hatred and the fraud and the political gangsterism and the murder and the massacre and the incredible intolerance and all the suffering and the starving and cold and the thud of a bomb blowing the people in a house to pieces, the thud of all the bombs blasting man's hope and decency.

William L. Shirer

1943

My Cliff's twenty-fifth birthday – I cannot grasp it. These last five years have passed so strangely and unconvincingly that, to me, he feels still my spoilt but loveable boy of twenty, so amazed to find himself a soldier after war broke out. He was such a frail wee baby, only four pounds in weight: a screaming bundle of nerves, who needed such loving, watchful care to rear. How many mothers look back to struggles to rear 'war babies' of twenty-five years ago, and wonder if it was worth it? What effort and endurance, patience and sacrifice goes unheeded into the Pattern, each a grain of sand, no more. I woke suddenly this morning. I felt as though, if I put my hand out, I could gather my baby safe into my arms. If only it *was* that simple. Vera Lynn sang Cliff's song last night, 'I'll see you again', and not even her nostalgic whine could kill its beauty – 'time my life heavy between, but what has been is past forgetting' – I wonder if his thoughts stray home today, whether he thinks of all the gay happy birthdays of so long ago.

Nella Last

14 December

1943 [Cairo]

General Patton of the US Army and his nice Aide, Colonel Codman, have come to stay at General Jumbo's Mess. The General is tall, with a rugged face and manner. He wears battledress with boots and gaiters. It is said that recently when visiting a hospital in North Africa he hit an American soldier and called him a coward. None of us knows the rights and wrongs of this but the American press have made much of the supposed incident and it seems probable that the General has come here to let the story die down.

Yesterday I was asked to take General Patton shopping as he wanted to buy presents for his family in America. On our return for lunch he asked me to find someone to show him the antiquities of Cairo, 'I'll need an expert – someone who knows exactly what he is talking about,' he said. I telephoned Sir Robert Gregg and asked him as a favour to show the General round but unfortunately he was busy. However he kindly arranged for a Professor to meet the General at nine this morning on the terrace at Shepherds Hotel. Jack Wintour, our Aide, would accompany the General, the Professor and Colonel Codman on the tour in one of our cars.

Jack returned to our office after lunch and regaled us, with much laughter, of the expedition. The General arrived very late at Shepherds Hotel and after introductions the General asked the Professor what he was going to show him. 'First we will visit the mosques . . .' began the Professor – but he got no further.

'Now, Professor,' roared the General. 'NO, NO, NO. I don't want to see any of your Goddam mosques. I've seen enough of the darn things in Tunisia to last a lifetime. I guess we'd best go see the Sphinx.' There was an agonising silence and then the Professor announced he knew nothing of the Sphinx. He was angry, but so was the General. 'Waal, Professor, then I guess you'd best go home,' he said and, turning to Jack, said in a loud whisper, 'Should I pay the little old guy off?' Jack, suffocating with laughter, shook his head and turned to the Professor who made a prolonged fart, turned on his heel and departed. Jack hurried the guests into our car and made for Mena where, fortunately, the General wished to go to the lavatory, giving Jack just time to ring our office and tell me to telephone the Professor and grovel – 'Smother him with apologies,' said Jack and rang off.

I rang the Professor who was furious. I could hardly deliver our apologies and for all of twenty minutes he unleashed his opinion of what he thought of the inhabitants of the United States of America. Then he slammed down the telephone. I asked Jack what he had told the General about the Pyramids and the Sphinx. 'While the General was in the lavatory and I'd spoken to you,' said Jack, 'I bought a guide book in the hotel and read out bits to the General and it went fine.'

Countess of Ranfurly

1972

This was the Duchess of Argyll's dance for J. Paul Getty at the Dorchester. We arrived late. Within, it resembled a scene from *The Godfather*. As midnight struck the orchestra played 'You're the Top' and a short procession wound its way across the dance floor propelling a trolley draped in cloths on which sat a cake with eighty red candles.

There was something really macabre about the whole scene, and if a man had jumped out from under the trolley with a machine-gun it wouldn't have surprised me.

Sir Roy Strong

1980

I was in a cab with a black driver during the minutes that were supposed to be silence to remember John [Lennon] and pray for his soul. He had a black station on and they had a ten-minute silence and the disc jockey said, 'We're up there with you, John' and the driver laughed and said. 'Not me, baby, I'm stayin' right down here.'

Andy Warhol

15 December

1852 [New York]

Prospect of a No-Popery riot here. Very numerous and bitter indignation meeting in the Park yesterday, growing out of the arrest of a loafer who undertook to preach Native Americanism and anti-priestcraft in the streets last Sunday and was taken into custody to prevent a riot. He sets up for a Protestant martyr on the strength of his detention, and swears that he will preach in the same place next Sunday; in which case there will be a mob originating with the Irish and German Papishes if he's not arrested, and with the order of United Americans and the godly butcher boys of the Hook and First Avenue if he is.

George Templeton Strong

1922 [visiting his Aunt Lily]

There was one inexplicable anecdote. She had been held up by a crush of prams at Carfax and had asked one obstructive woman to take her pram off the pavement. The woman replied that she had a right to be there. Aunt Lily retorted that she had no right to bring these children into the world for other people to look after and still less to block up the pavement. The woman said she was shopping. Aunt Lily said it was bad for the child to be taken shopping and the only good thing was that it killed some of them off.

I asked her why on earth she said such a thing. 'I was angry,' she answered. I replied, quoting Plato, that anger was an aggravation, not an excuse. She added that she had a lot of leaflets issued by the C.B.C. (Constructive Birth Control): and she was going to drop one into every pram the next time she went into Oxford, wh. would indeed be a good joke: but I don't think she saw it that way.

C. S. Lewis

1926 [Berlin]
Dinner-party at home for the Einsteins.

His wife told me that recently, after numerous admonitions, he at last went to the Foreign Ministry and fetched the two gold medals awarded him by the Royal Society and Royal Astronomical Society. She met him afterwards to go to the cinema. When she asked what the medals looked like, he did not know because he had not yet undone the package. He has no interest in such trifles. She gave me one or two other examples. This year the American Barnard Medal, awarded only every four years to outstanding scientists, has gone to Niels Bohr. The newspapers recalled that last time Einstein was the recipient. He showed her the paper and asked, Is that true? He had completely forgotten. He cannot be induced to wear his *Pour Le Mérite*. At an Academy session not long ago [Walther] Nernst drew his attention to the fact that it was missing: 'I suppose your wife forgot to lay it out for you. Improperly dressed.' To which Einstein retorted, 'She didn't forget. No, she didn't forget; I didn't want to put it on.'

Count Harry Kessler

1987
The Jeffrey Archer party was one for mainly journalists and newspaper people.

Robert Maxwell there. Very friendly on the whole. I asked him why on earth he wanted to own a football club. 'It must be extremely boring mixing with dreary people.'

He admitted that he liked wearing his ridiculous baseball hat in photographs and being an actor. He is a buccaneer and a crook. His energy splashes bogus charm around. He longs to be popular but, however hard he tries, I think he will never succeed in that.

Mary Archer looking very pretty and now far better dressed in expensive, fashionable dresses than she's ever been before. She told Nick Lloyd, an old university friend, when she had lunch with him today that she had now got Jeffrey absolutely under control.

If he makes any false step she can deal with him. And she passed her hand across her throat. She is the one who triumphed in the libel action [in which her husband successfully challenged newspaper reports that he had consorted with a prostitute].

Woodrow Wyatt

1997

The Christmas silly season is on. Off to ITV to record a snippet on the 'twelve Lords a-leaping' of the famous seasonal song. My task was to tell Peter Hayes (political correspondent for Central TV) about the difficulties that would be involved in teaching twelve members of the Upper House to 'leap'. I'm not sure if he actually intends to try this. I think he has one volunteer. Brian Rix, he of the 'Whitehall farces'. Although he is an elderly Lord, and a surprisingly sprightly one at that, I'm not certain he counts. He's a man of the theatre and once a performer, always a performer. Dancing is like riding a bicycle; something you never forget. I suggested that the simplest way to make them all leap was to publish a white paper on the abolition of the Upper House. That would start them jumping.

Deborah Bull

16 December

1899

This morning: first to the dentist, then lesson at Frau Radnitzky's. I'm learning the 'Emperor' Concerto now. When I play Beethoven, I always feel as if my soul were at the dry cleaners, and that the ugly black stains caused by the impurities and nervous traumas of Wagner were being removed.

Alma Mahler-Werfel

1917 [Odessa]

How can I describe all that has happened in these last tragic days? I feel as though I have been caught up in a mighty whirlpool, battered, buffeted, and yet . . . I am still myself, still able to walk, talk, eat and sleep. It is astounding how much a human being can endure without any outward sign of having been broken up into pieces.

It was 12th December. We were hourly expecting orders, but none had arrived. We had little to fear from the war; our Front Line, being half-emptied, was quiet. The Austrian troops were still docile, realising undoubtedly that with the coming of the Bolshevist régime the Russian Regular Army had ceased to exist and the Russian territory lay before them – theirs for the taking! When discussing the insubordination of the so-called fighting-men, the name of [Premier Aleksandr Fyodorovich] Kerensky was continually cropping up; all his great achievements on behalf of his country seemed to have been forgotten – only his lamentable mistakes were remembered. He it was who had insisted on closer comradeship among army ranks and less rigorous army discipline. Alas! that *one* mistake of a great and just man can stamp with indelible blemish his whole character!

When a soldier, conversing with his superior officer, omitted the salute; when he strutted before him with hands in his pockets and a cigarette between his lips, it was easy to guess that chaos must follow. A general, who had been visiting some regiments in our vicinity, had been shot dead by his orderly only the previous morning. It was said that the general called for his high boots; the orderly threw them at him. The general struck the orderly; the orderly shot the general dead. The news spread like lightning. Officers were openly defied by their men and there was no power to support them or protect them. Many were shot. Finally the soldiers, or *tovarishchi* [comrades] as they now call themselves, refused catagorically to take any orders and, leaving their trenches, roamed the countryside at will. Theft and pillage were the order of the day. We heard all this with sinking hearts and we were powerless to act. So far, the Red Cross personnel had always been respected and unharmed, but whispers had reached us of units attacked, doctors shot and nurses assaulted.

Florence Farmborough

1931

William Faulkner, the Southern author who has been visiting New York for six or eight weeks past, has gone home at last, leaving a powerful odor of alcohol behind him. Judging from stories I hear on all sides, he was drunk every night he was here.

Among those who entertained him was Alfred Knopf. The other night Knopf was invited to a dinner somewhere else, with Faulkner as the guest of honor. Knopf took along a couple of copies of Faulkner's books and asked him to autograph them. Faulkner replied about as follows: 'I am sorry, but I don't think I can do it. Too many people are asking for autographs. Yesterday a bell-boy at my hotel wanted one. I believe that it is a mistake for an author to make his signature too common. However, inasmuch as it is you, I think I might very well autograph one of the books.' This extraordinary boorishness to a man who had been hospitable to him struck the whole assemblage dumb. Knopf himself made no reply, and did not mention the books again.

Faulkner's publisher, Harrison Smith, wrote to me a week ago saying that Faulkner would stop off in Baltimore on his way South. Fortunately, he did not do so. The town is full of tales about his incessant boozing. He had a roaring time while he was here, and will go back to Prohibition Mississippi with enough alcohol in his veins to last him a year.

H. L. Mencken

1950

Boy drearily playing tennis. 'I have to do this because my father couldn't afford to when he was my age.'

Taxi driver lost wife – 'Married 26 years and in all those years I never had to raise my voice to her once and she was never short a dime.'

Dawn Powell

17 December

1832 [Tierra de Fuego]

In the afternoon we anchored in the Bay of Good Success. While entering we were saluted in a manner becoming the inhabitants of this savage land. A group of Fuegians, partly concealed by the entangled forest, were perched on a wild point overhanging the sea; and as we passed by, they sprang up and, waving their tattered cloaks, sent forth a loud and sonorous shout.

In the morning the captain sent a party to communicate with the Fuegians and after we had presented them with some scarlet cloth, which they immediately tied round their necks, they became good friends. This was shown by the old man patting our breasts and making a chuckling kind of noise, as people do when feeding chickens. I walked with the old man, and this demonstration of friendship was repeated several times; it was concluded by three hard slaps, which were given me on the breast and back at the same time. He then bared his bosom for me to return the compliment, which being done, he seemed highly pleased. The language of these people, according to our notions, scarcely deserves to be called articulate. Captain Cook has compared it to a man clearing his throat, but certainly no European ever cleared his throat with so many hoarse, guttural, and clicking sounds.

They are excellent mimics: as often as we coughed or yawned or made any odd motion, they immediately imitated us. Some of our party began to squint and look awry; but one of the young Fuegians (whose face was painted black, excepting a white band across his eyes) succeeded in making far more hideous grimaces. They could repeat with perfect correctness each word in any sentence we addressed them, and they remembered such words for some time. Yet we Europeans all know how difficult it is to distinguish apart the sounds in a foreign language. Which of us, for instance, could follow an American Indian through a sentence of more than three words? All savages appear to possess, to an uncommon degree, this power of mimicry. I was told, almost in the same words, of the same ludicrous habit among the Kafirs; the Australians likewise have long been notorious for being able to imitate and describe the gait of any man, so that he may be recognised. How can this faculty be explained? Is it a consequence of the more practiced habits of perception and keener senses, common to all men in a savage state, as compared with those long civilised?

Charles Darwin

1889

I read in the *Nation* last night a notice of Miss [Louisa May] Alcott's *Life and Letters*, where mention is made of Harry's [Henry, her brother] writing a review of *Moods* in the *North American Review* which reminded me of Father's having met Mr Alcott in the street one day and saying to him: 'They are reading *Dumps* at home with great interest.' '*Dumps*?' queried Mr A. 'Yes, *Dumps*, your daughter's novel!' said the pater. The suggestive *Moods* reduced to *Dumps*!

Alice James

1922 [London]

Reached London at ten, after more than eight years' absence.

I left with Rodin on a Friday morning, a week before the war began. I remember our Channel crossing and how Rodin, when we sailed from Folkestone and I asked him whether he wanted anything to eat, replied, '*Non, je n'ai pas faim. Je regarde la nature. La nature me nourrit.*' Then the arrival at Boulogne, with the ultimatum in the papers and my instant firm conviction that war was inevitable and Austria *wanted* it. Thereafter the parting with Rodin at the Gare du Nord in Paris and the arrangement (unreal, to my mind) to meet for tea next Wednesday at Countess Greffule's. By Wednesday I was sitting in Cologne, waiting for war to be declared.

I recalled it all as the train carried me through the sooty, mean London suburbs.

In the late afternoon I walked along the Embankment towards Westminster. The sun shone on the wet streets and heavy clouds scudded low across the sky. The whole city was bathed in a violet and golden light that turned the Thames to glowing copper.

Count Harry Kessler

1931

Two pair of swanky pyjama pants came up to-day – I didn't require the jackets as I always wear a shirt, collar and tie. Why? To prove, of course, that only my lower limbs are asleep. *Nem. con?*

William Soutar

1977

I was complaining to our Peggy this morning that the local clock-mender had not yet come to attend to my gold Louis XV clock, which he has been tinkering with on and off for more than a year, and which has never gone properly since. He has a bad name, Peggy says, and her Gerald says he must never have another of their clocks to mend. Last time he took out the jewels. Now, how often have I heard this remark about the 'jewels' in clocks? Are they really jewels, as we like to suppose, and do all clock-menders systematically 'take them out' and thereby enrich themselves to a vast extent? Or are 'jewels' an old wives' tale? Why should clocks need jewels rather than ordinary pins and screws?

James Lees-Milne

1995

Home for evening, watching *The Beatles Anthology* with Anthea. Interesting to notice how a lot of those quite weak songs have that ring of total authenticity now . . . The Beatles' message was 'Look: we can do anything – and make it work!' So the work becomes cradled within (and assessed in terms of) a process of creative improvisation in which the whole culture is at that moment engaged. And improvisations are very forgiving – entered into in the spirit of 'What's to lose?'

'All You Need is Love', performed for the first global satellite link-up, must have been a great moment. Funny to think that only a few years before that we'd all clustered round the only Catholic TV in the neighbourhood to see the new pope (John XXIII). And my Auntie Rene fell to her knees before the TV.

Brian Eno

18 December

1783

I spent two hours with that great man, Dr Johnson, who is sinking into the grave by a gentle decay.

John Wesley

1937

There is something even sadder than falling short of one's own ideals: to have realised them.

Cesare Pavese

1960

Dined with Edith Sitwell. There were about five people there. Edith sat in her wheelchair looking very pale and tired and ill and really doing all the talking because when she is with a group of people she can listen and talk only on her own wavelength. There was a humiliating atmosphere of everyone being sycophantic, courtiers feeding her with titbits of gossip and malice which would amuse her and draw her out. Whenever there was a silence it was appalling, as though boredom and sterility might seep like the fog outside through a chink in a door or a window. Anecdotes were dragged out of the past and held up for inspection. No one was quite successful in living up to Edith's tone. As a matter of fact she was rather brilliant, although this gave one the feeling that she had to make all the effort and added to the sense of humiliation. She gave one or two amusing examples of her replies to foolish letters. She had a letter from some silly woman saying, 'Dear Dame Edith, As an admirer of your poems I am nevertheless greatly disturbed by a poem containing a line about the mating of tigers. I have a daughter of 19 – at that age where the brook runs into the river – and a son aged 10 who is very restless. I wish to entreat you dear Dame Edith when you write your poetry, to consider the disturbing effect that lines like those about the mating of tigers may have on the young.' Edith wrote back: 'Tell your dirty little brats to read *King Lear.*'

Stephen Spender

19 December

1785

After dinner we saw the learned Pigg at the rampant Horse in St Stephens – there was but a small Company there but soon got larger – We stayed there about an hour – It was wonderful to see the sagacity of the Animal – It was a Boar Pigg, very thin, quite black with a magic Collar on its neck. He would spell out any word or Number from the Letters and figures that were placed before him. Paid for seeing the Pigg 1 shilling.

James Woodforde

1832

The house was very full: the play was *The Wonder*. My dress was not finished till the very last moment – and then, oh, horror! was so small that I could not get into it. It had to be pinned upon me; and thus bebundled, with the dread of cracking my bodice from top to bottom every time I moved, and the utter impossibility of drawing my breath, from the narrow dimensions into which it squeezed me, I went on to play a new part. The consequence was, that I acted infamously, and for the first time in my life was horribly imperfect – out myself, and putting every body else out. Between every scene my unlucky gown had to be pinned together; and in the laughing scene, it took the hint from my admirable performance, and facetiously grinned in an ecstasy of amusement till it was fairly open behind, displaying, I suppose, the lacing of my stays, like so many teeth, to the admiring gaze of the audience; for, as I was perfectly ignorant of the circumstances, with my usual easy nonchalance, I persisted in turning my back to the folk, in spite of all my father's pulls and pushes, which, as I did not comprehend, I did not by any means second either . . .

Fanny Kemble

1914 [Red Cross volunteer on the French front]

Not much to record this week. The days have become more stereotyped, and their variety consists in the number of wounded men who come in. One day we had 280 extra men to feed – a batch of soldiers returning hungry to the trenches, and some refugees. So far we have never refused anyone a cup of soup; or coffee and bread.

I haven't been fit lately; and get fearful bad headaches. I go to the station at 10 a.m. every morning, and work till 1 o'clock. Then to the hospital for lunch. I like the staff there very much. The surgeons are not only skilful, but they are men of education. We all get on well together, in spite of that curious form of temper which war always seems to bring. No one is affable here, except those who have just come out from home, and it is quite common to hear a request made and refused, or granted with, 'Please do not ask again.' Newcomers are looked upon as aliens, and there is a queer sort of jealousy about all the work.

Oddly enough, few persons seem to show at their best at a time when the best should be apparent. No doubt, it is a form of nerves, which is quite pardonable. Nurses and surgeons do not suffer from it. They are accustomed to work and to seeing suffering, but amateur workers are a bit headlong at times. I think the expectation of excitement (which is often frustrated) has a good deal to do with it. Those who 'come out for thrills' often have a long waiting time, and energies unexpended in one direction often show themselves unexpectedly and a little unpleasantly in another.

In my own department I always let Zeal spend itself unchecked, and I find that people who have claimed work or a job ferociously are the first to complain of over-work if left to themselves. Afterwards, if there is any good in them, they settle down into their stride. They are only like young horses, pulling too hard at first and sweating off their strength – jibbing one moment and shying the next – when it comes to "'ammer, 'ammer, 'ammer, 'ammer on the 'ard 'igh road,' one finds who is going to stick and who is not.

Sarah Macnaughtan

1952

I hire a dinner jacket suit to dine at Oxford. My women very excited at the prospect of seeing me once more, a rare sight in such clothes. I explain that they will not have that pleasure, since the suit has to be returned next day. Bunny [his aunt] says, 'When I was in the concert world I often used to think how different evening dress looked on different men. You could always tell the men who were "of the people", they never seemed to carry it well.'

J. R. Ackerley

20 December

1919

After dinner we listened to the Black Syncopated Orchestra. They were amazing – all the semi-religious songs of the negroes. D. [Lloyd George] says it is very significant – their songs about the oppressed people. He says a race who can sing these songs like that will cause trouble one of these days.

Frances Stevenson

1950

'How's your sister? All right?' asked the young lady (a fluffy, blonde, hard-boiled little piece, I always think) in the tobacconist's the other day. Something in her tone of voice seemed to make this question sound like a serious inquiry.

'Yes, thank you. Did you think she wasn't?' I asked.

'Oh no. I didn't think so. But things seem to happen so quickly these days. One day you're all right, and the next you're . . .' she seemed to hesitate.

'Dead?' I supplied, but simultaneously she brought out, 'Not so well.'

The conversation seemed to me worth recording.

J. R. Ackerley

1973

This morning I took my poor old dog, Fop, to the vet to have more teeth out and his anal troubles investigated while under the anaesthetic. I begged the vet, if he found he was beyond recovery from yet another operation, to let him go. I was quite calm. I never said goodbye, nor patted him. I merely took off his lead. The vet, Riley, a nice man, took him in his arms. I just cast one quick glance at Fop's old grey head which was not looking towards me. The vet said, 'I quite understand,' and I left hurriedly. He said he would telephone. During the afternoon A. and I drove to Badminton to collect dead bracken. I thought that because the vet had not telephoned perhaps Fop had come through the operation. Late in the afternoon while I was out he rang. A. said to me, 'The vet had to let him go.' I followed her into the house and said, 'What I must do immediately is to remove all the dog baskets to the attics,' and started to do this before taking off my heavy coat. While carrying his special basket from the library I burst into tears. A. was angelic, comforting and sensible. I recovered quickly, and now merely have the ache of sadness at losing the companion of twelve years, day and night. This house is cheerless without the two dogs, and their departure marks the end of an era, the heyday of Alderly with which they have been so intimately, so essentially associated. *Eheu!* you darling old friends.

James Lees-Milne

21 December

1850

Must not read novels.

Leo Tolstoy

1901 [*Discovery* expedition to Antarctica]

We cast off somewhere about 2 or 3 p.m. and went out amid immense cheering with steamers crowded with visitors; on each side of us and following in our wake, and then as they dropped off at the end of the inlet, the two cruisers *Ringarooma* and *Lizard* were to take us up and escort us to Dunedin.

Happily the crowded steamers had turned and the bands and cheering were no longer to be heard, when one of our R.N. bluejackets fell from the main top and without touching anything in his fall, dashed his head to pieces on the iron roof of the winch house. It was a horrid thud. He was dead instantly and I helped to carry him aft, where we laid him out and covered him up. We signalled the accident to the *Ringarooma* and they took it on to Dunedin. It was a dreadful time for such an accident to happen and some of the men wept like children. It was a horrible lesson too to them, because it was afterwards found that he had taken up a bottle of whisky to drink at the maintop. There was a heavy cloud over the ship the rest of the day.

Edward Wilson

1913

It is amazing how little imagination the clerk-race has sometimes. I wrote to the box-office at Covent Garden for seats for the spring season, on Stock Exchange paper, asking that the tickets might be sent to the Travellers' Club. Yet the letter comes addressed to me as 'Miss'. In acknowledging it, I couldn't help pointing out that if they search all Europe they couldn't find two addresses less likely to shelter a lady.

Sir Alan 'Tommy' Lascelles

1939

Love is the cheapest of religions.

Cesare Pavese

1941

I was in a vile temper with the hopelessness of things at home and in the office. I was feeling in dreadful bad form, inclined to scrap my whole diary. I kicked this volume across the study last thing at night.

Lord Reith

1967

It is finished: except for Cabinet. Harold [Wilson] has had to go to Australia for a funeral, so George [Brown] is in charge and he has kept chopping and changing the time till I've nearly gone mad. Finally he fixed 3pm with six items on the list, only two of them really urgent. I was furious: how was I to get ready for fifty guests at our party tomorrow night? Spent the morning on frantic Christmas food shopping and having my hair done; then sat chafing for two hours in Cabinet while they all talked and talked. Finally I slipped out and sloped off to Hells Corner Farm [her cottage], leaving them to it. Men have no sense of priorities.

Barbara Castle

1972

Mary took me to *Figaro* last night – a splendid performance, perhaps the best I've ever been to. Her other guest, a slender, elegant woman dressed tightly in well-cut black, with a profile reminiscent of Cocteau (whose life I've been reading); her name, Lady Daphne Straight.

My hackles always rise, I hope and believe invisibly, when confronted by consciousness of superiority which isn't *real* superiority – i.e. not such as Shakespeare displays in the Sonnets. And I noticed that, though I was the oldest by ten years, they both tended to walk out of the door first, leave me the back seat in the car and generally treat me rather like an old governess. They prattled away: 'Oh, do you know, Robert wrote to Bobo apologising for being so drunk the other night.' 'Oh, NO! DID he really? How SWEET!' Gossip galore, about the rich or noble, Mrs Heinz of Beans, or Lord Lansdowne. Complaints about how booked up the best chiropodist in London was, so that you 'simply have to devote a whole morning to having your hair and feet done'. Or 'Rosie *will* complain of my drinking habits. She says if I didn't drink red wine at lunch I wouldn't have to have my afternoon kip, but I told her that in that case I'd have to go to bed at seven-thirty because I *must* have my ten hours.'

In our box at the opera my companions took care to break the rules and smoke without going into the passage. 'And they won't let one leave one's glass on the edge of the box!' 'Perhaps they're afraid it might fall into the stalls,' I suggested. 'The class war more likely,' said Lady D. The stalls, I see, are the lower classes! I observed Mary's touchingly old-fashioned belief that the waiters were relishing her glamorous superiority, whereas I could see the cold look of calculation in their eyes as to what tip she was good for, and their annoyance that her bringing her own drink made it less. The same with the market lorry drivers as we wound our way out. They, the aristos, fondly believe these men love seeing expensive cars and women with diamonds among them. What fatuous folly!

Frances Partridge

22 December

1655

This day I did with Eliza meet, though not to market we did go, for still no monies do I have, and greatly does this vex me. From Eliza I should not conceal that little dinner I do get as Mrs Pepys, and so she does quizz me; and feed me. Some pity did I shrink from that she should show, but naught did she give and her sharp words did put the huffe in me for none did I deserve.

Yet does she say that I am the fool, for time enough has there been to learn how to manage the man, yet no sign do I give of how to do it.

She does counsel that I should cease to play the invalid and stay from my bed, that I should put aside my sloth and dress my hair – which truth to tell has no attention since the day I did wed. And that I should don my new gown for when my husband does make his appearance. In her words, this is how the man – and the monies – be managed.

Yet do I say that no effort does my husband make for me and unfair it is that I should do all for him. But Eliza does just cool-say that this is how it be. And she does add that the man has the purse and if it is to be opened, then must the woman please him.

Which is not very loving, but some sense it does have in it and certain it is that I should consult my pillow.

And while we did stroll and have such serious talk, yet did I note more. 'Twas Robin Holmes whom I did see was watching me, and most handsome he is. 'Tis possible that he knows not that I am the wife – and forsooth he does cut a fine figure in his uniform.

And too it does strike me that I be not at my best these past weeks. So do I resolve to get back my looks, and to unfurrow my brow, and think not on the pain that does cut into me.

As I do keep this record here, even more need is there to make it safe from prying eyes. For a great bout there would be if my husband did get to this and all effort should he make to stop me from my diary. And the veriest miserable creature I should be with no journal to keep. 'Tis the greatest comfort that it does provide me, and too do I think to pass these pages on to my daughter, so she should know what I did not. To preserve it, I must take all care to keep it from my husband's eyes and hands. And to think that but a few weeks past, I did seek to have no secrets from my man.

'Elizabeth Pepys'

1825

I wrote six of my close pages yesterd[ay], which is about twenty four pages in print. What is more I think it comes off twangingly. The story is so very interesting in itself that there is no fear of the book answering. Superficial it must be but I do not disown the charge. Better a superficial book which brings well and strikingly together the known and acknowledged facts than a dull boring narrative pausing to see further into a mill stone at every moment than the nature of the mill stone admits. Nothing is so tiresome as walking through some beautiful scene with a minute philosopher, a botanist or pebble gatherer who is eternally calling your attention from the grand features of the natural scenery to look at grasses and chucky stones. Yet in their way they give useful information and so does the minute historian – Gad, I think that will look well in the preface.

Sir Walter Scott

1941

Decrees yesterday – Paul Kreidl brings them up, circular from the Community, signature necessary: (1) *Prohibition on using public telephones.* (Private telephones were taken from us long ago.) (2) *Curfew* for all Jews from the morning of December 24 to January 1, 'since provocative behavior of a Jew in public has caused outrage.' Exempted is only the shopping hour three till four (Saturday twelve till one); so four of the eight days (the Christmas holidays, New Year's Day and Sunday) are days of complete imprisonment. – The one 'outrageous' case is supposed to have been this (reports in agreement and incontestable): A Nazi cow shouts at an elderly gentleman: 'Get down off the sidewalk, Jew!' He refuses, he has a right to be on the sidewalk. He is summoned to the Gestapo 'for questioning' and imprisoned. This was told us by Paul Kreidl whose workmate is a son of the man, who was present at the scene and was likewise summoned to the Gestapo. Kätchen, who worked with the man at Zeiss-Ikon, told exactly the same story.

This month the 200M installment from Georg's blocked account was no longer paid to me. The emigrants have now been expatriated, their assets confiscated. I have insisted that the sum given to me as a gift is my property – it will be no use. I have long been covering everything outside the tax exemption limit from my reserves. They were replenished by Georg's gift. Now there is still 1,000M left. Once that is used up, somewhere about April, I shall have to sell the house. – The Jews say, by April I shall be in the Polish ghetto.

Victor Klemperer

1952

The Movietone News this week had a Christmas feature. A large number of flustered turkeys were driven towards the camera, and the commentator remarked that the Christmas rush was on, or words to that effect. Next they were seen crowded about their feeding trough, making their gobbling turkey fuss, and the commentator observed, with dry humour (again I do not remember his exact words), that it was no use their holding a protest meeting, for they were for it in the morning. Similar facetious jokes followed them wherever they went, hurrying and trampling about in their silly way; for to make them look as silly as possible was no doubt part of the joke and easy to achieve: turkeys, like hens, like all animals, are beautiful in themselves, and have even a kind of dignity when they are leading their own lives, but the fowls, in particular, look foolish when they are being frightened.

These jolly, lip-licking sallies, delivered in the rich, cultivated self-confident voice of one who has no sort of doubt of his own superiority to the animal kingdom, raised no laugh from the considerable audience, I was pleased to note. I took it from the silence that many other people besides myself would have been glad to be spared jeers and jibes at these creatures who, parting unwillingly with their lives, were to afford us pleasure at our Christmas tables. It reminded me of a shop window I noticed in Marylebone High Street, not many weeks ago. A whole calf's head was displayed upon a dish, and the tongue of the dead thing had been dragged out and twisted round into the side of its mouth so that it appeared, idiotically, to be licking its own lips over the taste of its own dead flesh. In order to make it more foolish still, a tomato had been balanced on top of its head. How arrogant people are in their behaviour to the domestic beasts at least. Indeed, yes, we feed upon them, and enjoy their flesh; but does that permit us to make fun of them before they die or after they are dead? If it were possible, without disordering one's whole life, to be a vegetarian, I would be one; nothing could have been more disgusting and degrading than the insensitiveness displayed by these two exhibitions I have described.

J. R. Ackerley

23 December

1858
Came to Moscow with the children. Didn't manage to get another mortgage. Money is needed everywhere. Went bear-hunting. On the 21st – killed one; on the 22nd – was bitten by one. Squandered a pile of money.

Leo Tolstoy

1911
When I look at my whole way of life going in a direction that is foreign and false to all my relatives and acquaintances, the apprehension arises, and my father expresses it, that I shall become a second Uncle Rudolf, the fool of the new generation of the family, the fool somewhat altered to meet the needs of a different period; but from now on I'll be able to feel how my mother (whose opposition to this opinion grows continually weaker in the course of the years) sums up and enforces everything that speaks for me and against Uncle Rudolf, and that enters like a wedge between the conceptions entertained about the two of us.

Franz Kafka

1914 [Red Cross volunteer]
Yesterday I motored into Dunkirk, and did a lot of shopping. By accident our motor-car went back to Furnes without me, and there was not a bed to

be had in Dunkirk! After many vicissitudes I met Captain Whiting, who gave up his room in his own house to me, and slept at the club. I was in clover for once, and nearly wept when I found my boots brushed and hot water at my door. It was so like home again.

I was leaving the station to-day when shelling began again. One shell dropped not far behind the bridge, which I had just crossed, and wrecked a house. Another fell into a boat on the canal and wounded the occupants badly. I went to tell the Belgian Sister not to go down to the station, and I lunched at their house, and then went home till the evening work began. People are always telling one that danger is now over – a hidden gun has been discovered and captured, and there will be no more shelling. Quel blague! [What a joke!] the shelling goes on just the same whether hidden guns are captured or not.

I can't say at present when I shall get home, because no one ever knows what is going to happen. I don't quite know who would take my place at the soup-kitchen if I were to leave.

Sarah Macnaughtan

1946

The presence of my children affects me with deep weariness and depression. I do not see them until luncheon, as I have my breakfast alone in the library, and they are in fact well trained to avoid my part of the house; but I am aware of them from the moment I wake. Luncheon is very painful. Teresa has a mincing habit of speech and a pert, humourless style of wit; Bron is clumsy and dishevelled, sly, without intellectual, aesthetic or spiritual interest; Margaret is pretty and below the age of reason. In the nursery whooping cough rages I believe. At tea I meet the three elder children again and they usurp the drawing-room until it is time to dress for dinner. I used to take some pleasure in inventing legends for them about Basil Bennett, Dr Bedlam and the Sebag-Montefiores. But now they think it ingenious to squeal: 'It isn't true.' I taught them the game of draughts for which they show no aptitude.

Evelyn Waugh

24 December

1868

Ouida [Louise de la Ramée], in green silk, sinister clever face, hair down, small hands and feet, voice like a carving knife. At dinner puns and jokes; Ouida silentish. The ladies go to the drawing-room, upstairs, and when after an interval we follow them we hear, before the door opens, a voice going on inside like a saw, and on entering find Ouida saying in loud harsh tones – 'Women are ungenerous, cruel, pitiless!' Planché, taking refuge on an ottoman with a face expressing humorous alarm, 'God bless my soul! I think they're angels – I adore them – they're the best half of the world.'

Ouida, with severity, – 'I entirely disagree. The woman nearly always leads the man astray,' etc. etc. 'Woman can't be impersonal.'

Ouida departs, after inviting Planché and me to visit her at the Langham Hotel, where she is biding at present with her Mother and an immense Dog. She carries a portrait of the latter round her neck in a locket, which she detached after dinner and handed round for inspection, with the remark, 'This is my hero' (perhaps the hero of one of her books). She asked somebody present, 'Have you read my last book?' – 'Not yet.'

'But you *must* read it, you know!'

She said she had found America 'a mine of wealth' to her, in the payments for her novels.

William Allingham

1905

The Caledonian dinner was a glorious and enjoyable function. I went as Guy Charteris' guest. The C. is a club for Scotchmen, and the enthusiasts turn up in kilts and sporrans. The performance consists in a dinner where one eats haggis, a noisome dish to look at, but not unpleasant to eat, and drinks Athol Brose, a delicious drink, but insidious, composed of whisky, honey, cream and rum. Afterwards we danced – a dangerous game, but full of interest. John Gore and I were knocked backwards into the fireplace.

Sir Alan 'Tommy' Lascelles

1954 [Jamaica]

Oh how nice it would be, just for today and tomorrow, to be a little boy of five instead of an ageing playwright of fifty-five and look forward to all the high jinks with passionate excitement and be given a clockwork train with a full set of rails and a tunnel. However, it is no use repining. As things are, drink will take the place of parlour games and we shall all pull crackers and probably enjoy ourselves enough to warrant at least some of the god-damned fuss.

The news from home is mainly concerned with disaster, floods and gales and houses collapsing. I am very lucky to be here in the warmth and so I will crush down the embittered nausea which the festive season arouses in me and plunge into gaiety with an adolescent whoop.

Noël Coward

1980

Christmas Eve party at the [Sir Claus] Mosers – more literary than musical in membership – but many old friends. Start a promising conversation with handsome stranger who stops in mid-sentence. 'Excuse me,' she says, 'but do you mind if I take off your glasses and clean them?' Take some time to regain confidence after this – or should I take it as a compliment?

Sir Hugh Casson

1987

Christmas Eve. I've got £700,000 in my Abbey National Crazy-High-Interest account. But what's the use: Ash, ash, all is ash. Lay not up for thyself treasures on earth. The cars are all getting streaked and rust-spotted, the books foxed, the furniture dusty. The window panes, all 52,000 of them are *revolting*, so greasily blotched. Translucent only. And there is moth everywhere. My grandfather's great Rothschild coat, bought in Wien in 1906, is terminally degraded . . . The whole thing is out of control.

And why? I know why. Because I'm not rich enough to have servants. We have to do everything ourselves, and we just haven't got the time, and things get neglected. This morning, rummaging up in the archive room I found the old Wages Book for 1960. That was the year James was born, and we bought our first new car, a dear little red Mini. It was the cheapo model with cloth seats, and we saved a further three pounds and ten shillings by hand-painting the registration numbers ourselves. Total cost 'on the road' was £460.

The total wage bill, per week, for the seven servants who worked at the Castle [Saltwood], was thirty-two pounds and five shillings. MacTaggart, a clumsy fellow who had such ugly hands that my mother always made him wear white gloves when he was waiting at table, and who crashed my father's Bentley in circs that will never wholly be explained, in Lee Green, got £12 per week and occupancy of the Lodge.

Everything has decimal points – to the right – or worse. I'm bust, virtually.

Alan Clark

25 December

1860

How different are men and women, e.g. in respect to the adornment of their heads! Do you ever see an old or jammed bonnet on the head of a woman at a public meeting? But look at any assembly of men with their hats on; how large a proportion of the hats will be old, weatherbeaten, and indented, but I think so much the more picturesque and interesting! One farmer rides by my door in a hat which it does me good to see, there is so much character in it, – so much independence to begin with, and then affection for his old friends, etc., etc. I should not wonder if there were lichens on it. Think of painting a hero in a brand-new hat! The chief recommendation of the Kossuth hat is that it looks old to start with, and almost as good as new to end with. Indeed, it is generally conceded that a man does not look the worse for a somewhat dilapidated hat. But go to a lyceum and look at the bonnets and various other headgear of the women and girls, – who, by the way, keep their hats on, it being too dangerous and expensive to take them off! Why every one looks as fragile as a butterfly's wings, having just come out of a bandbox, – as it will go into a bandbox again when the lyceum is over. Men wear their hats for use; women theirs for ornament. I have seen the greatest philosopher in the town with what the traders would call 'a shocking bad hat' on, but the woman whose bonnet does not come up to the mark is at best a 'bluestocking.'

H. D. Thoreau

1870

As I lay awake praying in the early morning I thought I heard a sound of distant bells. It was an intense frost. I sat down in my bath upon a sheet of thick ice which broke in the middle into large pieces whilst sharp points and jagged edges stuck all round the sides of the tub like chevaux de frise, not particularly comforting to the naked thighs and loins, for the keen ice cut like broken glass. The ice water stung and scorched like fire. I had to collect the floating pieces of ice and pile them on a chair before I could use the sponge and then I had to thaw the sponge in my hands for it was a mass of ice. The morning was most brilliant. Walked to the Sunday School and the road sparkled with millions of rainbows, the seven colours gleaming in every glittering point of hoar frost. The Church was very cold in spite of two roaring stove fires.

Rev. Francis Kilvert

1922

Christmas! All the shoes left in my big granite fireplace were collected this morning by their owners. It was fun to have all these curious, greedy, cheerful, delighted, surprised people jostling round my bed.

We ate the truffle yesterday. Exquisite! I had bought a little brown casserole with a tight-fitting lid. When I lifted the lid we were intoxicated by a dizzyingly heady aroma. It smelt of richness, warmth, celebration, elegance, the triumph of gluttony! I had stewed this precious thing from Orangini for two hours over a low heat, shut tightly in with slices of ham, fillet of beef, some good white wine, a vegetable stock and rashers of bacon. My Georges [her husband] ate it slowly, gravely, silently – and went on thanking me for it all day. There's nothing more sincere than the gratitude of a satisfied palate!

Liane de Pougy

1924

I have decided to try and grow a moustache because I cannot afford any new clothes for several years and I want to see some changes in myself. Also if I am to be a schoolmaster it will help to impress the urchins with my age. I look so intolerably young now that I have had to give up regular excessive drinking.

Evelyn Waugh

1941

This must be a specially sad day for many millions of people.

Countess of Ranfurly

1942

My first Christmas in Scotland. I had behaved so well for the last few months, and everyone here thought I was such a nice, quiet intellectual little girl – but not any more!

We were up at the men's Mess, and it was fantastic – colossal buffet, unlimited booze. I decided to break out and go on a jag. I can't remember when I got so drunk or felt so exhilarated, except possibly when I went out with my dad.

I have an awful feeling I called the CO a stinker – it was one of those religious arguments about whether the popes had mistresses.

602, our international squadron, flew over for the party and parked their Spitfires practically in our backyard.

I remember waltzing and eating plum pudding simultaneously, and then being sick in the laurels.

A very nice pongo drove me home and wanted to kiss me but I said No, and he said God, what a swine I am trying to take advantage of a gel when she's tight!

Joan Wyndham

1952

The more hairs fall out, the more antennae grow in.

Journalist: What would you like to see hanging on your Christmas tree?
J. C.: Journalists.

Jean Cocteau

1963

In the evening to Mags [Maggie Smith]. Same as last time. They gave me v. expensive presents & we had the film show & and I left about 11.30. I had to walk all the way home from Kensington to Baker St. All my *loathing* of Christmas and Public Holidays poured over me during the walk home. All those groups of 'merry people', windows open & awful noise of singing, and daft decorations everywhere & drunks and bad driving and just beneath the surface – the extreme rude bestiality. I suppose my worst fault is the instinctive desire to run away from a mess. Instead of trying to do something about it. Run. Get away. No hope of reform, I cry. Away from responsibility for work or people, away from commitment, away from affection, away from trouble – away from the community . . . And all the time these *stinking* performances looming ahead of me.

Kenneth Williams

1995

Great morning excitement as the girls open their gifts. A Barbie horse and carriage for Darla that takes me about two hours to put together. I imagine all over the western hemisphere disgruntled unshaven fathers doing the same thing. And then no pissing batteries (but the Indian shop was open). Anthea and I decided to postpone presents for each other, but nonetheless she bought me some gloves, a key-locator (which goes off every time Darla laughs) and a book by the BMA [British Medical Association] about drugs and medicines, and I bought her a negative-ionizer/room-perfumer, a book about vitamins and minerals, and an electric car-perfumer.

Brian Eno

26 December

1851

I observed this afternoon that when Edmund Hosmer came home from sledding wood and unyoked his oxen, they made a business of stretching and scratching themselves with their horns and rubbing against the posts, and licking themselves in those parts which the yoke had prevented their reaching all day. The human way in which they behaved affected me even pathetically. They were too serious to be glad that their day's work was done; they had not spirits enough left for that. They behaved as a tired woodchopper might. This was to me a new phase in the life of the laboring ox. It is painful to think how they may sometimes be overworked. I saw that even the ox could be weary with toil.

H. D. Thoreau

1911

It is unpleasant to listen to Father talk with incessant insinuations about the good fortune of people today and especially of his children, about the sufferings he had to endure in his youth. No one denies that for years, as a result of insufficient winter clothing, he had open sores on his legs, that he often went hungry, that when he was only ten he had to push a cart through the villages, even in winter and very early in the morning – but, and this is something he will not understand, these facts, taken together with the further fact that I have not gone through all this, by no means lead to the conclusion that I have been happier than he, that he may pride himself on these sores on his legs, which is something he assumes and asserts from the very beginning, that I cannot appreciate his past sufferings, and that, finally, just because I have not gone through the same sufferings I must be endlessly grateful to him. How gladly I would listen if he would talk on about his youth and parents, but to hear all this in a boastful and quarrelsome tone is torment. Over and over again he claps his hands together: 'Who can understand that today! What do the children know! No one has gone through that! Does a child understand that today!'

Franz Kafka

1916

Great adventure! I did a day's nursing at the Winchcomb Hospital from eight to eight. I went in some trepidation, but I hadn't realised the tremendous psychological effect of a uniform. Directly I stepped into the ward I felt an entirely new being – efficient, untiring, and quite unsqueamish – ready to cut off a leg, though generally the mere sight of a hospital makes me feel faint. It's wonderful how right it puts one with the men, too. I feel so shy as a laywoman, but was absolutely at my ease as 'Nurse Asquith'. I loved hearing myself called 'nurse' and would certainly go on with it if I were free. I felt all the disciplined's fear of the Sister and the experienced V.A.D., and most terribly anxious to acquit myself well.

First I was put down to wash an oilskin table. It looked so clean at first, and appeared dirtier and dirtier under my attentions. Then I washed all the lockers, etc., etc. The morning in my memory is a long blur of mops, taps, brooms, and plates. The unpleasant moments are when one can't find anything to do. One can't bear to stand idle and yet one feels a fool when one ostentatiously attacks a quite irreproachable counterpane. My most serious breach of etiquette was that I spoke to a soldier while the doctor was in the ward. We had a meal of cocoa and toast and butter at 9.30, to which I brought a ravenous appetite. It seemed an eternity to 12.30 when we had our lunch.

There really wasn't enough to do. Most of the cases were trench feet –

quite raw, a horrible sight. I assisted at the dressing of them, feverishly obeying curt orders. The men were delightful. Made lots of beds after tea, tidied up lockers, etc., etc. Only got tired in the last hour. Got home at 8.30 feeling excited, and wound up, and very well. Far less tired than after an ordinary London day.

Lady Cynthia Asquith

1936

This was the first occasion on which Jennie, the new maid, gave me my tea. As she went out, I said: 'Leave the door a little open, Jennie.' Whereupon she piped back cheerily, 'Righto, Willie.' So, yet again, it would seem I retain a semblance of youth sufficient enough to elicit a spontaneous Christian-naming even from 17. Yet the grey is in the hair and the Shakespearean frontal already imminent, and the light and shade of maturity gathering on the face – if youth remains, it is on the mouth: tra-la! even yet the edges curl up.

William Soutar

1941 [POW camp]

I can safely say that I have never imagined a more miserable Christmas Day. One as a prisoner is possibly a novelty, but the 2nd is indescribable. Three is no sign of any Christmas feeling and there is nothing to drink – which we did at least have last year. But I am going too fast. We all in our room rose early – Ted and I for 8.30 Communion Service, the remainder to prepare for a Christmas breakfast. Unfortunately, things didn't go quite *planmasig*. There were only 2 padres at the Service and at least 500 chaps turned up. With the natural running out of supplies early on, it was soon evident that we shouldn't be finished by Appell [roll call] and would at the same time miss our Christmas breakfast. In fact only about ¾ of the service was finished. Appell was ages in length due to many being absent and no one knowing who. The little Rittmeister was naturally enough in a bad temper and Ted & I had to sit down after Appell, after the special Christmas breakfast party was over, to what had been left for us – sausage roll and bacon (the treat) now cold, and tea (now cold). I fear I was not feeling seasonably charitable as the day was cold, and the mud deeper than ever. When we went to church in the Dining Hall in the grey light of dawn, you could only see water and mud for miles. In the wash-house it was pitch dark, with scores of officers – and orderlies – falling over one another, feet squelching on the mud-covered concrete floor. 'Peace on earth, goodwill towards men.' 'Comfort and joy, comfort and joy' etc. All very ironical. No Red X Christmas parcels and run out of tobacco. Our hosts have provided not a drop of drink, but have provided extra rations in the form of sauerkraut.

Added to this, if you looked like greeting people, they were apt to warn you of the forceful result and the only apparently permissible greetings were 'A Good Christmas' or 'A Happy Christmas next year'. Tempers were frayed, as it had blown a hurricane and rained all night and the huts had literally rocked. All told a happy start for a festive day.

Captain John Mansel

1945

Marie Teresa and Bron [his children] have arrived; he ingratiating, she covered with little medals and badges, neurotically voluble with the vocabulary of the lower-middle class – 'serviette', 'spare room'. Only on points of theology does she become rational. . . . We managed to collect a number of trashy and costly toys for the stockings. We had a goose for luncheon and a tasteless plum pudding made for us by Mrs Harper, a bottle of champagne. By keeping the children in bed for long periods we managed to have a tolerable day. My only present, a very welcome one, a box of cigars from Auberon. I have seats for both Bath and Bristol pantomimes. The children leave on the 10th. Meanwhile I have my meals in the library.

Evelyn Waugh

27 December

1928 [Paris]

In the evening to a performance of Diaghilev's Ballet at the Opera. Stravinsky's *Rossignol* and *Petruschka*. After the performance I was waiting for Diaghilev in the corridor behind the stage when he appeared in the company of a short, haggard youngster wearing a tattered coat. 'Don't you know who he is?' he asked. 'No,' I replied, 'I really can't call him to mind.' 'But it's Nijinsky!' *Nijinsky!* I was thunderstruck. His face, so often radiant as a young god's, for thousands an imperishable memory, was now grey, hung slackly, and void of expression, only fleetingly lit by a vacuous smile, a momentary gleam as of a flickering flame. Not a word crossed his lips. Diaghilev had hold of him under one arm and, to go down the three flights of stairs, asked me to support him under the other because Nijinsky, who formerly seemed able to leap over roof-tops, now feels his way, uncertainly, anxiously, from step to step. I held him fast, pressed his thin fingers, and tried to encourage him with gentle words. The look he gave me from his great eyes was mindless but infinitely touching, like that of a sick animal.

Slowly, laboriously, we descended the three, seemingly endless flights until we came to his car. He had not spoken a word. Numbly he took his place between two women, apparently in charge of him, and Diaghilev kissed him on the brow. He was driven away. No one knew whether *Petruschka*, once his finest part, had meant anything to him, but Diaghilev said that he was like a child who does not want to leave a theatre. We went to eat in the Restaurant de la Paix but I did not take much part in the talk; I was haunted by this meeting with Nijinsky. A human being who is burned out. Inconceivable, though it is perhaps even less conceivable when a passionate relationship between individuals burns out and only a faint flicker briefly lights the despairing, inert remains.

Count Harry Kessler

1929

The newspapers have related:

that a friend saw me, contrary to my custom, give fifty centimes to a beggar and heard me whisper, as I leaned toward him: 'Yes, but when will you pay them back?'

that a fellow writer (another paper that relates the same absurdity said: an Italian prince), invited to dinner by me, waited in vain for me to call for the bill and was obliged to pay in my stead and to give a tip to the check room, while with clenched teeth, I said: 'I can't help it; I am a miser.'

that, going to cash a check at the bank and seeing people ahead of me at the cashier's window, I said: 'I am André Gide and do not like waiting,' in such a tone that I was served first.

that, caught by the rain at Luna Park, I exclaimed: 'Gosh, it stinks!' assuming a roughneck manner that decidedly did not suit me. Etc.

When I am feeling well, this kind of thing has no effect on me; but as soon as I am weak, such hateful tales rise up within me and I suffer to feel such stupidity and hatred aroused against me. I also fear that such details may cling to my image, since I know so well that falsehood is more readily credited than truth.

André Gide

1953

Met a theatrical agent named Loesser who told me that Maurice Chevalier, for whom he is agent, is worth about $12 million. Chevalier is slightly out of his mind, and is now banned from getting a visa to visit the U.S.A. Winchell takes credit for banning him. What actually caused the trouble between Winchell and Chevalier, and perhaps the visa refusal also, was that some years ago Chevalier was wearing a rather natty, embroidered shirt which Walter admired. Chevalier remarked: 'I'll send you some,' which he promptly did. However when the shirts arrived, Winchell had to pay duty on them which made him so sore that he immediately wrote a column cussing Chevalier out as a skinflint and he has been panning Chevalier ever since. Thus run the motifs of our great opinion-makers.

Drew Pearson

28 December

1801

William, Mary [Hutchinson, later William's wife] and I set off on foot to Keswick. We carried some cold mutton in our pockets, and dined at John Stanley's where they were making Christmas pies.

The son shone but it was coldish. We parted from William and later he joined us opposite Sara's rock. He was busy in composition and sat down upon the wall.

At John Stanley's we roasted apples in the oven.

After we had left there William discovered that he had lost his gloves. He turned back but they were gone.

We were tired and had headaches. We rested often. Once William left his Spenser and Mary turned back for it and found it upon the Bank where we had last rested.

We reached Greta hall at about half past 6 o'clock. After Tea message came inviting William to sup at the Oak. He went. Met a young man (a predestined Marquis). He spoke to him familiarly of the *Lyrical Ballads*. He had seen them everywhere and wondered they did not sell. We all went weary to bed. My bowels very bad.

Dorothy Wordsworth

1868

In answer to a remark of mine of today Carlyle blazed up – 'Write my autobiography? I would as soon think of cutting my throat with my pen knife when I get back home! The Biographers too! If those gentlemen would let me alone I should be much obliged to them. I would say, as Shakespeare would say to Peter Cunningham, "Sweet Friend, for Jesus' sake forbear."'

William Allingham

1914

The year is nearly over. Snow has fallen, and everything is white. It is very cold. I have changed the position of my desk into a corner. Perhaps I shall be able to write far more easily here. Yes, this is a good place for the desk, because I cannot see out of the stupid window. I am quite private. The lamp stands on one corner and *in* the corner. Its rays fall on the yellow and green Indian curtain and on the strip of red embroidery. The forlorn wind scarcely breathes. I love to close my eyes a moment and think of the land outside, white under the mingled snow and moonlight – white trees, white fields – the heaps of stones by the roadside white – snow in the furrows. *Mon Dieu!* How quiet and how patient! If he were to come I could not even hear his footsteps.

Katherine Mansfield

1941

Feeling much better, I do a *Spectator* article on keeping diaries, in which I lay down the rule that one should write down one's diary for one's great-grand-son. I think that is a correct rule. The purely private diary becomes too self-centred and morbid. One should have a remote, but not too remote, audience.

Harold Nicolson

29 December

1832

At half-past five, went to the theatre. I acted only so-so; my father was a leetle *dans les vignes du seigneur* [tipsy]. When the play was over, the folk called for us, and we went on: he made them a neat speech, and I nothing but a cross face and three courtesies. How I hate doing this! 'Tis quite enough to exhibit myself to a gaping crowd, when my profession requires that I should do so in a feigned semblance; but to come bobbing and genuflecting on, as me myself, to be clapped and shouted at, and say, 'Thank ye kindly,' is odious.

Fanny Kemble

1916

A thorough, thorough thaw with the usual effect on the spirits. I am reading the diary of Marie Bashkirtseff for the first time. It makes this one seem sadly insipid and impersonal. No doubt writing it in the form of a journal prevents it being at all an emotional review of one's life, but I'm sure if I exercised discrimination and only described peaks in my life I should never have the energy to write at all. To write about every day automatically is really far less effort.

Lady Cynthia Asquith

1933

Now, in this first lull in the middle of this holiday time, is the moment to write my birthday résumé, which should have been written Wednesday 27th.

I have finished my twenty years a-growing. I have passed out of my teens. I am no longer visibly adolescent. I may now start a-blossoming. So, though I hate to be growing older, I shall say hurray! hurray! Those painful red-nosed years of 'girlhood's hopes and fears' may no longer be pointed at with allowances when I speak.

Elizabeth Smart

1966

We all went to the Chapel of Rest. It's a room, bare, white-washed. Muted organ music from a speaker in the corner. The coffin lid propped up against the wall. It said 'Elsie Mary Orton, aged 62 years'. Betty said, 'They've got her age wrong, see. Your mum was 63. You should tell them about that. Put in a complaint.' I said, 'Why? It doesn't matter now.' 'Well,' said Betty, 'you want it done right, don't you? It's what you pay for.'

Mum quite unrecognisable without her glasses. And they'd scraped her hair back from her forehead. She looked fat, old and dead. They'd made up her face. When I asked about this the mortician said, 'Would you say it wasn't discreet then, sir?' I said, 'No. It seems all right to me.' 'We try to give a life-like impression,' he said. Which seems to be a contradiction in terms somehow. I've never seen a corpse before. How cold they are. I felt Mum's hand. Like marble. One hand was pink, the other white. I suppose that was the disease of which she died. The death certificate said, 'Coronary thrombosis, arterio-sclerosis and hypertension.'

Great argument as we left. The undertaker gave Marilyn a small parcel containing the night-gown Mum was wearing when she died. Nobody wanted it. So the undertaker kept it. Not for himself. 'We pass it on to the old folks,' he said. 'Many are grateful, you know.'

Joe Orton

1975

Afternoon, went to Toledo – left Madrid at three-thirty so by the time we got to Toledo it was almost dark. Last time I was in Toledo, 1935 or 1936, it was a beautiful desolate city with beggars on the steps of the cathedral, a few tourists. It has now been cleared up, a touristic shrine, with arty wrought-iron lamps, brick walls carefully pointed, everywhere evidence of restoration. The cathedral was nearly in darkness, but when we came to the high altar it was a blaze of light; seated in front of it, enthroned, an archbishop, a cardinal or two, bishops, priests, etc., all robed. Then a man pushed forward from the congregation and rearranged the archbishop's mitre – and we realized it was a scene being shot for a film.

Stephen Spender

1977

Out of my window are acres of vineyards, thick patches of yellow mustard blossoms among the rows of bare vines, blue-purple hills, slate sky, flocks of birds that rise in occasional clouds. The big fig tree looks old and small without its leaves. I am in this Victorian house, like a queen alone in her castle. The children are skiing, Francis is in New York receiving an honorary doctorate.

I was thinking about Jackie Kennedy in the White House. How she had to smile and shake hands, go where the Secret Service directed her, be a proper First Lady. Then, after she became a widow, she became visible, the center of international attention. She came into her own, in a way, only after her husband's death. There is part of me that has been waiting for Francis to leave me, or die, so that I can get my life the way I want it. I wonder if I have the guts to get it the way I want it with him in it.

Eleanor Coppola

30 December

1836 [New York]

I went this evening to a party at Mrs. Charles H. Russell's, given in honor of the bride, Mrs William H. Russell. The splendid apartments of this fine house are well adapted to an evening party, and everything was very handsome on this occasion. The home is lighted with gas, and the quantity consumed being greater than common, it gave out suddenly in the midst of a cotillion. 'Darkness overspread the land.' This accident occasioned great merriment to the company, and some embarrassment to the host and hostess, but a fresh supply of gas was obtained, and in a short time the fair dancers were again 'tripping it on the light fantastic toe.'

Gas is a handsome light, in a large room like Mr Russell's, on an occasion of this kind, but liable (I should think) at all times to give the company the slip, and illy calculated for the ordinary uses of a family.

Philip Hone

1968

Reluctantly go back to work. Why does one always feel so muzzy after a holiday?

Barbara Castle

1977

I was looking at the pomegranate tree by the pond. There are still some fat pomegranates hanging on the bare branches. They are cracking open with smiling rows of dark red teeth.

All along I have been talking about Francis's conflicts, mirroring the conflicts of Willard [character in *Apocalypse Now*]. The contradictions of the peace-loving U.S.A. making a bloody war. I've been standing back, as if looking through a wide-angle lens, seeing the big picture. Now I have found myself with a close-up lens, seeing the big picture. It brings into focus *my* contradictions. I am laughing and crying my heart out. How I thought I was the innocent bystander, just recording some snapshots about the making of *Apocalypse*, as if it didn't pertain to me.

I had a belief system that took the world literally. I chose to only see the rational, the literal, and deny the illusion. I believed Francis's words literally. Just like Kay in the last scene of *The Godfather*. All of the evidence tells her that her husband has had people killed, and when she asks him, he says no, and she believes his words. All the evidence through the years, the little presents, notes, things I would find in Francis's pockets after a trip, the pin sent to him in the Philippines that he wore on his hat as a good luck charm. And when I would ask, I would hear, 'Ellie, she is a friend, she has been a big help to me. Please be nice to her. She feels that you resent her because she once had a crush on me. She is no threat to you.' I believed the words, I denied the evidence. I didn't want to see the truth. Now my guts ache, but I feel exhilarated. I am emerging from my tunnel vision. I am in a clearing where I can see more, see the literal and the illusion both at the same time. I am humiliated that my blindness was so obvious, so corny. While I was off taking hip consciousness-raising trips, enlightenment was right there in the 'Dear Abby' column. There is a chapter in Gail Sheehy's book *Passages* on men's life patterns that describes Francis to a T. I'm right there, listed as the 'utilitarian wife,' and there is also the 'adoring young protégée.' My whole personal, gut-wrenching drama is just a common statistic in a $2.50 popular paperback book. It gets me right down out of the clouds.

Eleanor Coppola

31 December

1654

By Gods special Providence we went not to Church, my wife being now so very neere her time: for my little sonne Richard now about 2 yeares old as he was fed with broth in the morning, a square but broad and pointed bone of some part of a ract of Mutton, stuck so fast in the Childs Throate and crosse his Weason, that had certainly choaked him, had not my Wife and I ben at home; for his mayd being alone with him above in the Nurserie, was fallen downe in a swone, when we below (going to prayers) heard an unusual groaning over our head, upon which we went up, and saw them both gasping on the floore, nor had the Wench any power to say what the Child ail'd, or call for any help: At last she sayd, she believed a Crust of bread had choak'd her little Master, and so it almost had, for the eyes and face were s[w]ollen, and clos'd, the Mouth full of froath, and gore, the face black – no Chirurgeon neere: What should we doo?, we cald for drink, power it downe, it returnes againe, the poore babe now neere expiring. I hold its head down, incite it to Vomite, it had no strength, In this dispaire, and my Wife almost as dead as the Child, and neer despaire, that so unknown and sad an accident should take from us so pretty a Child: It pleased God, that on the sudden effort and as it were struggling his last for life, he cast forth a bone . . .

John Evelyn

1661

I suppose myself to be worth about £500 clear in the world, and my goods of my house my own, and what is coming to me from Brampton when my father dies, which God defer. My chiefest thought is now to get a good wife for Tom, there being one offered by the Joyces, a cozen of theirs, worth £200 in ready money. But my greatest trouble is that I have for this last half year been a very great spendthrift in all manner of respects, that I am afeard to cast up my accounts, though I hope I am worth what I say above. But I will cast them up very shortly. I have newly taken a solemn oath about abstaining from plays and wine, which I am resolved to keep according to the letter of the oath which I keep by me.

Samuel Pepys

1870 [Siege of Paris, during the Franco-Prussian war]

In the streets of Paris, death passes death, the undertaker's waggon drives past the hearse. Outside the Madeleine today I saw three coffins, each covered with a soldier's greatcoat with a wreath of immortelles on top.

Out of curiosity I went into Roos's, the English Butcher's shop on the Boulevard Haussmann, where I saw all sorts of weird remains. On the wall, hung in a place of honour, was the skinned trunk of young Pollux, the elephant at the Zoo; and in the midst of nameless meats and unusual horns, a boy was offering some camel's kidneys for sale.

The master-butcher was perorating to a group of women: 'It's forty francs a pound for the fillet and the trunk . . . Yes, forty francs . . . You think that's dear? But I assure you I don't know how I'm going to make anything out of it. I was counting on three thousand pounds of meat and he has only yielded two thousand, three hundred . . . The feet, you want to know the price of the feet? It's twenty francs . . . For the other pieces, it ranges from eight francs to forty . . . But let me recommend the black pudding. As you know, the elephant's blood is the richest there is. His heart weighed twenty-five pounds . . . And there's onion, ladies, in my black pudding.'

I fell back on a couple of larks which I carried off for my lunch tomorrow.

The Brothers Goncourt

1899

This year I have written 335,340 words, grand total. 228 articles and stories (including 4 instalments of a serial of 30,000–7,500 words each) have actually been published.

Also my book of plays – *Polite Farces*.

I have written six or eight short stories not yet published or sold.

Also the greater part of 55,000-word serial – 'Love and Life' for Tillotsons, which begins publication about April next year.

Also the whole draft (80,000 words) of my Staffordshire novel *Anna Tellwright*.

My total earnings were £592 3s. 1d., of which sum I have yet to receive £72 10s.

Arnold Bennett

1931

Of all my years this has been the most unfortunate. Everything has gone wrong. I have lost not only my fortune but much of my reputation. I incurred enmities: the enmity of Beaverbrook; the enmity of the B.B.C. and the Athenaeum Club; the enmity of several stuffies. I left the *Evening Standard*, I failed in my Election [to Parliament, he lost his deposit as a candidate for the New Party]; I failed over *Action*. I have been inexpedient throughout. My connection with Tom [Oswald] Mosley has done me harm. I am thought trashy and a little mad. I have been reckless and arrogant. I have been silly. I must recapture my reputation. I must be cautious and more serious. I must not try to do so much, and must endeavour to do what I do with greater depth and application. I must avoid the superficial.

Yet in spite of all this – what fun life is!

Harold Nicolson

1939

I do not stay to watch the New Year in or the Old Year out. I write this diary at 11.45 and shall not wait. The old year is foul and the new year terrifying. I think, as I go to bed, of Nigel and Ben, Ben and Nigel [his sons]. How stupid life is. Not evil, only stupid. What shall I have to record this time next year?

Harold Nicolson

1941 [POW camp]

The day has been rather uneventful as far as I am concerned, tho' the Scotsmen are making as much of it as they can. Tonight they start their celebrations at 9.00 and continue till after midnight. Special permission has been granted by the Kommandant for lights out to be put back till 1.00 a.m.

A new order came round today saying that as from the 29th no one will be allowed out to the latrines after 10.45 p.m. – back to the delights of the thunderbox!

I found an old stick of plug tobacco in a box tonight. This will last me tomorrow, and will see the New Year in. – And, today brought me my 500th letter.

Well, let 1941 go to hell. It has certainly been eventful for us. Poland and this place have taken 6 months of it – an incredible thought. I say I'll be home in 1942. Is that absurd optimism? Yes, I suppose it is.

1941 – TAKE A RUNNING JUMP AT YOURSELF.

Captain John Mansel

1971

Got a taxi to Gordon & Rona [Jackson]. The house was looking beautiful, with a huge Christmas tree dominating the drawing room, and I suddenly felt so *safe* there. These are the friends to be really cherished, because even the times when we have had disagreements are all informed by a professional awareness of what we are as *actors* – I suppose that is why the only really good permanent relationships that *work* for me are the ones with fellow artists. Gordon played *Valse Ultime* and Rona & he sang it in French & as usual it enchanted me. When I drank a champagne toast with them to 1972 as Big Ben struck, I just adored them both. They've given me a wonderful present – the Oxford Companion to Eng. Lit.!!

Kenneth Williams

1974

I delivered the corrected galley proofs of my diaries to Chatto's and went to Heywood Hill's shop. John Saumarez Smith [bibliophile and managing director of a bookseller's] said, 'I hear you are publishing some diaries next year.' I asked him how he possibly knew. 'Ah,' he said, 'as a shopkeeper I keep my ear to the ground.' He said he hoped the price would not be too high. I told him I had said so to Chatto's in vain, and begged him to tell Norah Smallwood when next he saw her that he thought so too. I think the illustrations should be kept to minimum, and should be of persons rather than buildings.

Oh God! Am I making another dreadful mistake?

James Lees-Milne

1981

We went to Sonny's [Bono] wedding in Aspen. We finally found the beautiful church and we had to stand, the ceremony was already on, and they were singing beautiful songs, and the preacher finally came on and said, 'I pronounce you, Sonny and Cherie' – he said 'Cherie' instead of 'Susie' – and the whole audience gasped and she said, 'My name isn't Cherie, it's Susie,' and the preacher got very upset, he said that he just knew he was going to do that, and then he said a million times, 'Sonny and Susie, Sonny and Susie' till the end of the ceremony. They had lighted candles and Chastity [daughter of Sonny and Cher] was the flower girl, she was kind of tall. And it was really beautiful, it was snowing outside and everybody had candles and Susie was all in white and Sonny was crying. We were invited to the party for Sonny but we went off to one of the halls to a New Year's Eve party instead.

Andy Warhol

1986

Day one of being a Lord. Am enjoying it. The *Times* New Year's Honours List has a large headline, 'Life Peerage Goes to Woodrow Wyatt at head of Varied Field', and I am the first photograph. On the front page they refer to me as the *Times* columnist (there is no mention of *News of the World*).

A telegram from the Duke of Edinburgh: 'Many congratulations on your well deserved honour. Philip.' A letter by hand from Arnold Weinstock, a long one in his own handwriting. Never knew him write such a long one before. Says the main advantage of being a Lord is the free stationery, offset by the disgusting food one is obliged to eat there [the House of Lords].

Charming letter by hand from the editor of the *News of the World* saying he is sure it's entirely due to my column, and can they arrange for the logo at the head of my column to carry a picture of me in robes and coronet, photographed by, of course, Lord [Patrick] Lichfield.

The BBC news ring up with what they describe as a very embarrassing call. They have to disinvite me from appearing on the TV *News at One* because they say their space is being cut. It wasn't of course; it is because of the vendetta conducted against me by Alasdair Milne [BBC Director General] for daring to complain privately and publicly about the lack of impartiality and slipping standards of the BBC.

I point this out in answer to a nice letter I had yesterday from Duke

Hussey [Chairman of the BBC]. I told him I was not asked to any function during the Jubilee celebrations of the BBC though Richard Dimbleby and I were the founder members of *Panorama*; that a few months back I was asked to take part live in celebration shows they put on to talk about being a foreign correspondent for *Panorama* and that ten days or so later I was disinvited as I knew I would be.

I asked Duke Hussey when he has time and inclination to enquire when if ever they are going to take me off the BBC black list. I told him I used to appear quite often on *Any Questions* and after I made an appearance on *Question Time* Robin Day said it was one of the best ever but I was never asked again. Duke Hussey says he is trying to get across the point about the facts being quite separate from the comment and that BBC correspondents have no right to editorialise, nor do commentators, but it is clearly up-hill work.

Bernard Levin sends a letter round by hand addressed to the Baron Wyatt of Wyatt (in the County of Wyatt). 'Good Lord! You may be a peer of the realm to others but you will always be WW to me. Congratulations. Love, Bernard (Mr).'

James [Lord] Hanson apparently sitting in Palm Springs has delivered to me by hand a fax copy of a letter to me of congratulations. His envelope and writing paper has his crest and a little coronet on top. Quite elegant. Should I do the same?

Woodrow Wyatt

Biographies

ACKERLEY, J(OSEPH) R(ANDALL) (1896–1967) As literary editor of *The Listener* from 1935 to 1959, he published and befriended writers such as E. M. Forster and Christopher Isherwood. He wrote elegantly and frankly about aspects of his family life, for instance in *Hindoo Holiday* (1932), which tells of his experiences as private secretary to an Indian maharajah, *My Dog Tulip* (1956), an astonishing record of a relationship with a pet, and *My Father and Myself* (1968), in which he reveals how his father led a double life. His diaries, titled *My Sister and Myself: The Diaries of J. R. Ackerley*, span the years from 1948 to 1957.

ALCOTT, LOUISA MAY (1832–88) Born in Pennsylvania, the daughter of the educationalist Bronson Alcott, who was a friend of Ralph Waldo Emerson and Henry Thoreau. She is best known for her novel *Little Women* which became a bestseller and set her up for life. She kept a secret journal from an early age and maintained it until the year of her death, when she requested that it be destroyed. It was not.

ALLINGHAM, WILLIAM (1824–89) Born in Ireland, he worked first as a customs officer before settling in England in 1863. He was well connected in the literary world and counted among his friends Coventry Patmore, Thomas Carlyle and Tennyson. He is best known for his poetry, most notably 'The Fairies' ('Up the airy mountain') and his diary which appeared in 1907.

ASQUITH, LADY CYNTHIA (1887–1960) The daughter of the eleventh Earl of Wemyss, she married Herbert Asquith, second son of Herbert Henry Asquith, who was prime minister from 1908–16. She was private secretary to Sir J. M. Barrie and inherited most of his fortune. She knew many writers and artists and was an author of note herself. Her works include three volumes of reminiscences, anthologies of ghost and children's stories, novels and biographies. Her *Diaries (1915–18)* were published in 1968.

BARBELLION, W. N. P. (Bruce Frederick Cummings) (1889–1919) By profession a naturalist on the staff of the Natural History Museum in London, he suffered acute ill-health from childhood, and from early manhood knew he was doomed to an incurable and progressive paralysis. Despite this his diaries, first published in 1919 shortly before his death, with the title *The Journal of a Disappointed Man*, are remarkable for their forensic observation and vivid style.

BASHKIRTSEFF, MARIE (1860–84) Born into the nobility in Pultowa, south Russia, she was a painter of promise but succumbed to tuberculosis. She kept a diary in French from her childhood, extracts of which were published posthumously.

BEAUVOIR, SIMONE DE (1908–86) French novelist and feminist, born in Paris. As a student at the Sorbonne she met Jean-Paul Sartre, with whom she had an affair. Together they became leading figures in the Existentialist movement. Her study of women's situation and historical predicament, *The Second Sex*, published in France in 1949, is regarded as a pioneering feminist text. Her novel *Les Mandarins* won the Prix Goncourt in 1954. In 1947, she made a trip to America, travelling coast to coast by train, car and Greyhound bus, the account of which was published with the title *America Day by Day*.

BENN, (ANTHONY WEDGWOOD) TONY (1925–) British politician, the son of Viscount Stansgate. A Labour MP from 1950 to 1960, he was debarred from the House of Commons on succeeding to his father's title. On renouncing it in 1963, he was re-elected to Parliament the same year. An outspoken and eloquent maverick on the left-wing of the Labour party, he has held various positions in opposition and government. His voluminous diaries begin in 1940 and chronicle the century in studied detail.

BENNETT, ALAN (1934–) Born in Yorkshire and educated at Oxford, he is a dramatist and actor. He first appeared on stage at the Edinburgh Festival Fringe in 1960 in *Beyond the Fringe*. He has written for stage and television, including *Forty Years On*, *Habeas Corpus*, *Kafka's Dick*, *An Englishman Abroad* and *The Madness of King George*. *Writing Home* (1994) includes essays and reflections as well as excerpts from his journal.

BENNETT, (ENOCH) ARNOLD (1867–1931) The son of a Staffordshire solicitor, he was destined to follow in his father's footsteps but determined to become a writer and moved to London. A phenomenally successful novelist and playwright and influential reviewer with a prodigious output, his best known books were set in the Potteries of his home region. Begun in 1896, his journal was consciously modelled on that of the Goncourt brothers and covers the years from 1896–1929.

BENSON, A(RTHUR) C(HRISTOPHER) (1862–1925) Son of E. W. Benson, archbishop of Canterbury, he was master of Magdalene College, Cambridge. A prolific author, he wrote many volumes of biography, family reminiscences and criticism and verses, including 'Land of Hope and Glory'. His diary, amounting to some five million words, starts in 1897 and ends in 1925. Extracts were first published in 1926.

BIRCHALL, DEARMAN (1828–97) Born in Leeds and educated at private schools in York and Croydon, he went into the cloth trade in Leeds. He started his own business in 1853, but was only a sleeping partner after he moved to Gloucestershire in 1869. His firm won prizes for cloth at various International Exhibitions. His first wife died two years after their marriage in 1861 and he remarried in 1873. He was then living at Bowden Hall, near Gloucester, where he housed his collection of china, fabrics and paintings.

BODICHON, BARBARA LEIGH SMITH (1827–91) Reformer, feminist, free-thinker, later to endow the founding of Girton College. Bodichon went to the United States on a marriage journey and her journal, 1857–8, is the record of that trip, a critical and vivid portrait of the American South before the Civil War.

BOSWELL, JAMES (1740–95) The eldest son of Alexander Boswell, Lord Auchinleck, a judge who took his title from the name of the family estate in Ayrshire, Scotland. Though he studied law, his passion was for literature and politics, and he wrote many pamphlets and verses. The turning-point in his life came when he met Dr Johnson in London in 1763. Together they made a celebrated tour of the Hebrides in 1773. His life of Johnson, published in 1791, is still reckoned to be the biography against which all others are judged. A philanderer, heavy drinker and hypochondriac, he married his cousin Margaret Montgomerie in 1769. His journals, which are renowned for their self-consciousness and candour, were discovered only at the beginning of the twentieth century.

BOYLE, JIMMY (1944–) Born in the Gorbals, a Glasgow slum, he is a convicted murderer, and a sculptor and author. In his early years he was caught up in gang culture and was sent to Borstal. He later spent two years in jail for assault. He was subsequently twice charged with murder and cleared. Dubbed 'Scotland's Most Violent Man', he was convicted of the murder of Babs Rooney and given a life sentence. In 1973, he became one of the first members of the Barlinnie Prison Special Unit's rehabilitation programme and went on to produce many sculptures. His autobiography, *A Sense of Freedom*, appeared in 1977; *The Pain of Confinement*, his prison diaries, were first published in 1984. In 1999, he published a novel, *Hero of the Underworld*.

BRANDRETH, GYLES (1948–) A former Oxford scholar and President of the Oxford Union, he worked in theatre, television and publishing before becoming a member of parliament and a junior minister in John Major's government. His diaries, 1990–97, which, he said, 'a number of good people, friends and former colleagues, will regard . . . as an act of betrayal,' offer an idiosyncratic insight into modern British politics.

BRECHT, BERTOLT (1898–1956) German playwright and poet, born in Augsburg. He studied medicine and served briefly as a medical orderly. His first two plays – *Trommeln in der Nacht* and *Baal* – won the Kleist prize for drama in 1922. He was a Marxist who believed his plays were social experiments, requiring detachment, not passion. Key works include *The Threepenny Opera*, *Mother Courage* and *The Caucasian Chalk Circle*.

BRITTAIN, VERA MARY (1893–1970) The daughter of a wealthy manufacturer, she was brought up in the north of England and educated at Oxford University. During the First World War, she served as a nurse. Grieving for her fiancé, Roland, who was killed in France, she wrote *Testament of Youth*, a moving account of her childhood and struggle for education.

BROWN, FORD MADOX (1821–93) A painter best known for pictures of historical scenes, he studied at Bruges, Ghent and Antwerp before settling in England in 1845. He was connected with the Pre-Raphaelites and was closely associated with William Morris; he was a founder member of Morris, Marshall, Faulkner and Company, for whom he produced furniture designs and stained glass.

BROWNING, ELIZABETH BARRETT (1806–61) The eldest of 12 children of Edward Barrett, she read Homer in Greek and wrote poetry at the age of eight. A spinal injury when she was 15 meant her spending many years lying on her back. In 1846, she secretly married the poet Robert Browning with whom she had long been in correspondence and they left for Italy where she spent the rest of her life. Her *Sonnets from the Portuguese* appeared in 1850. The Brownings counted among their friends William Thackeray, John Ruskin, Thomas Carlyle, Dante Gabriel Rossetti and many other famous contemporaries.

BULL, DEBORAH (1963–) A principal dancer with The Royal Ballet at Covent Garden in London. Her repertoire is wide-ranging and includes the leading roles in *Swan Lake, The Sleeping Beauty* and *Don Quixote*. She has received particular praise for her notable performances in contemporary works such as William Forsythe's *Steptext* and *in the middle, somewhat elevated*. In 1996 her much-publicised address at the Oxford Union catapulted her into the political arena of the arts world. She has since become a board member of London's South Bank Centre and in 1998 was appointed to the Arts Council of England. She writes regularly for newspapers and magazines and is the author of *The Vitality Plan*.

BURNEY, FANNY (1752–1840) Well connected English novelist who counted among her friends and acquaintances Dr Johnson, Edmund Burke and David Garrick. In 1778 she published anonymously her first novel *Evelina* which, when she was revealed as its author, made her instantly famous. Her diaries, 1768–1840, provide affectionate portraits of her circle and the court of Queen Charlotte.

BYRON, GEORGE GORDON, sixth Baron (1788–1824) Son of 'mad Jack' Byron (1756–91), he was born in London with a club-foot. His hysterical mother took him to Aberdeen where he was abused by a nurse. He became Lord Byron at the age of ten and he and his mother moved south where he continued his education at Harrow. A handsome young man, he had a dissipated time at Cambridge but managed to publish his first collection of poems in 1807. He took up his seat in the House of Lords in 1809 and began to travel extensively. *Childe Harold* was published in 1811 and Byron 'awoke to find himself famous'. He left England in 1816 on the collapse of his marriage and never returned, ceaselessly writing, forming romantic liaisons, living riotously, and becoming involved with political causes, notably in Greece where he predicted, correctly, he would die. He was an inveterate writer of letters and journals many of which were intended for public consumption.

CADOGAN, SIR ALEXANDER GEORGE MONTAGU (1884–1968) The younger son of the fifth Earl Cadogan, he was educated at Eton and Balliol and entered the Diplomatic Service in 1908. He had a distinguished career in the public service, including postings to Peking and the United Nations, and was Chairman of the Governors of the BBC 1952–7. As adviser to three Foreign Secretaries, he had privileged access to the centre of power. His diaries cover the years 1938–45, when he was head of the Foreign Office.

CAMUS, ALBERT (1913–60) Born in Algeria, the setting for much of his work, he was living in occupied France when he wrote *The Myth of Sisyphus* and *The Outsider*, the two works which brought him fame. Other works in which he explored the 'absurd' nature of the human condition are *The Plague*, *The Rebel* and *The Fall*. He won the Nobel Prize for Literature in 1957. In May 1935, when he was 22, he made the first entries in the literary diary which he continued to keep until his death in 1960. The entries were originally made in school exercise books and not intended for publication. In 1954, however, a typewritten copy was made of a number of the notebooks – what Camus called his *cahiers* – and extracts began to appear.

CARRINGTON, DORA DE HOUGHTON (1893–1932) After an 'awful' childhood, which she blamed on her hated mother, she began to show skill in drawing and went to the Slade School of Art where she thrived. A pretty girl, she was described by Lady Ottoline Morrell as looking like 'a wild moorland pony'. A one time lover of fellow artist Mark Gertler, she became acquainted with the Bloomsbury set, befriending Leonard and Virginia Woolf. She formed an odd *menage à trois* with her husband, Ralph Partridge, and Lytton Strachey who, despite being homosexual, was in love with her. He died in January 1932; she shot herself a couple of months later. Extracts from her diaries were published in 1970.

CASSON, SIR HUGH (1901–99) English architect, educated at Cambridge. He was professor of interior design at the Royal College of Art from 1953 to 1975. His books include *Homes by the Million*, *Permanence and Prefabrication* and *Victorian Architecture*. He was president of the Royal Academy from 1976 to 1984.

CASTLE, DAME BARBARA (1911–) British politician, educated at Bradford Girls' Grammar School and St Hilda's College, Oxford. She entered Parliament as Labour MP for Blackburn in 1945, becoming MP for Blackburn East, 1950–5, and winning Blackburn again in 1955, which she represented until her retirement in 1979. She held various ministerial posts and was a prominent member of the Labour Party particularly while it was led by Harold Wilson. Her diaries, which give an insightful account of contemporary politics, were published in two volumes in 1980 and 1984.

CHANNON, SIR HENRY (1897–1958) Nicknamed 'Chips', he arrived in

Europe from America in 1918, aged 21, the only child of a Chicago businessman. Oozing charm, ability and ambition, he rose rapidly in high society. He married Lady Honor Guinness, became a member of parliament and served at the Foreign Office, 1938–41. From the late Twenties he was a ubiquitous figure in London society, his friends including King Edward VIII, the Duke and Duchess of Windsor and Lady Cunard. His diaries, especially those covering the years 1934–52, are wonderfully indiscreet.

CIANO, COUNT GALEAZZO (1903–43) Italian politician. His father, a fascist, was a First World War hero. He married Mussolini's daughter Edda and ran the fascist propaganda office before becoming foreign minister in 1936, from which post he was sacked in 1943, tried and executed on charges of betraying Mussolini, whom he planned to poison. Given to crass behaviour (at the Coronation of Pius XII he scandalised onlookers by strutting down the nave of St Peter's in Rome giving the fascist salute and waving to the crowd), Hitler referred to him as 'that disgusting boy'.

CLARK, ALAN (1928–99) Son of Kenneth Clark, author of *Civilization*. He was Conservative MP for Plymouth (Sutton) 1974–92, Minister of Trade, 1986–92, and Minister of State, Ministry of Defence, 1989–92. His books include *The Donkeys: A History of the BEF in 1915; The Fall of Crete; Barbarossa: The Russo-German Conflict, 1941–45* and *Aces High: the War in the Air over the Western Front*. His diaries cover the period 1983–91 when he was privy to the internal workings of the Thatcher government. He had a well-deserved reputation as a ladies' man.

CLARK, OSSIE (1942–96) Fashion designer, born in Liverpool, the youngest of six children. Academically undistinguished, he had a flair for art and entered Manchester Regional Art College in 1958 at the age of 16. Later he moved to London and the Royal College of Art. Between 1965 and 1974 he was one of the leading fashion designers, fêted by celebrities such as Mick Jagger and was hailed the 'King of the King's Road'. A homosexual, he was sexually promiscuous, addicted to drugs and drink, and given to violence. His diaries begin in 1974 and continue until the day before he died, when he was murdered by his lover, Diego Cogolato.

COCKBURN, HENRY (1779–1854) Scottish judge, educated at the Royal High School in Edinburgh and Edinburgh University. He was called to the Bar in 1800 and seven years later was given an advocate deputyship from which he was dismissed in 1810 on political grounds. Eventually, however, he rose to share the leadership of the Bar and became Solicitor General for Scotland and a judge of the Court of Session. He contributed to the *Edinburgh Review* and is the author of *Memorials of his Time* and *Circuit Journeys*. His journals, published in two volumes in 1874, cover 1831–44.

COCTEAU, JEAN (1889–1963) French all-rounder, associated with the modernist movement. Among those with whom he worked were Picasso, Stravinsky and Diaghilev. His oeuvre is extensive and encompasses novels, poetry, plays and films. He came from a wealthy family and had an early passion for the stage. Notable works include *Le Grand Écart* and *Les Enfants Terribles*.

COLLIS, MAURICE (1889–1973) Born in Ireland and educated in England, he entered the Indian Civil Service and was posted to Burma. After a rather tempestuous career there, he returned to England in 1934 and became a prolific author. In all he published 35 books, the best known being *Siamese White* and *Foreign Mud*. In later life he became an artist and was acquainted with Mervyn Peake, L. S. Lowry, Henry Moore, Stanley Spencer and others. At his death he left 17 volumes of diaries, a selection of which was edited by his daughter.

COPPOLA, ELEANOR In spring 1976 Eleanor Coppola, her film director husband Francis and their three children left California for the Philippines, where *Apocalypse Now* was to be filmed. As the months stretched into years, her diary became an extraordinary record not only of the making of a movie but of the emotional and physical price exacted from all who participated in it.

CORY, WILLIAM (1823–92) Educated at Eton, where he was assistant master for 26 years. He is the author of the 'Eton Boat Song'. An accomplished classical scholar, he wrote verses in Latin and Greek. Perhaps his best known poem is 'Heraclitus'.

COWARD, NOËL (1899–1973) Born in Middlesex the son of a piano sales-man, he was encouraged by his mother to make a career of the theatre. Renowned for his comic talent, he wrote a plethora of popular plays, includ-ing *Hay Fever* (1925), *Private Lives* (1933) and *Blithe Spirit* (1941). He also wrote the screenplay of the hit wartime film, *Brief Encounter* (1944). In the Sixties he had a new lease of life as a cabaret artiste. His diaries, which cover his life from 1941 to 1969, raise name-dropping to a high art.

COX, BRIAN (1946–) Scottish actor and director born in Dundee, where he began his career with Dundee Rep. He won acclaim for his performance of Titus Andronicus for the Royal Shakespeare Company. His first book, *Salem to Moscow – An Actor's Odyssey*, was a personal history covering 30 years in the British theatre and culminating in the fascinating story of directing a production of Arthur Miller's *The Crucible*. His second book, *The Lear Diaries*, records his impression of playing King Lear at the National Theatre in 1990.

CROSSMAN, RICHARD (1907–74) A journalist and politician, as well as a brilliant lecturer and tutor, he worked for the Workers' Educational Association and the *New Statesman* before becoming a Labour MP in 1945. He served in the House of Commons until 1974. Radical and controversial, he was minister of Housing and Local Government and Leader of the House. He failed, however, in his cherished aim of reforming the House of Lords. His extensive diaries appeared in three volumes in the 1970s after an injunction sought by the Attorney-General failed to prevent them appearing.

CULLWICK, HANNAH (1833–1909) The daughter of a housemaid and saddler, she was born in Shifnal, Shropshire. Her working life began at the age of eight when she went to her 'petty place' to learn skills of domestic service. For 18 years, she conducted a clandestine courtship with Arthur Munby, an author and poet who had a lifelong obsession with lower-class women. Her 17 diaries, kept at Munby's request, were designed to keep him informed of every detail of her daily drudgery; when they eventually married in 1873, the diaries ceased. Their relationship was hardly that of equals, Cullwick living in the basement of Munby's house. After four years they separated though they continued to see one another.

DARWIN, CHARLES (1809–82) The author of *The Origin of Species* was born in Shrewsbury, England, and studied medicine at Edinburgh University. He intended originally to go into the church but was diverted by his interest in botany and natural history. He voyaged in the *Beagle* to South America where he had ample opportunity to study the fauna and flora. However, his great breakthrough came in 1859, with the epoch-making work which explained his theory of natural selection.

DELACROIX, FERDINAND VICTOR EUGÈNE (1798–1863) French painter born in Charentin. From boyhood he was enamoured of art and studied under Guérin where he fell under the influence of Géricault, a fellow pupil. His loose drawing and vivid colouring shocked the art establishment and though widely regarded as the greatest French artist of the nineteenth century and the most accomplished colourist of all time, he was generally seen as a rebel. He kept a daily diary from the age of 23 until the year of his death.

DELAFIELD, E. M. The pseudonym of Edmée Elizabeth Monica Dashwood (1890–1943), prolific novelist, journalist, magistrate and upstanding member of the Women's Institute, best known for her satirical novel, *The Diary of a Provincial Lady* and its sequels.

DURRELL, LAWRENCE (1912–90) Novelist, poet and travel writer, best known for *The Alexandria Quartet*. He was born in India but from the mid-1930s onwards he spent his life in and around the Mediterranean, whose islands he adored. Highly sensual, his work is often bracketed with that of his close friend Henry Miller with whom he maintained a voluminous correspondence. Other notable books include *Tunc* and *Nunquam*, the five-part *Avignon Quintet*, *Reflections of a Marine Venus*, *Bitter Lemons* and *Prospero's Cell*, a diary kept when he was living on Corfu.

ELLIS, EDWARD ROBB (1911–) Born in Kewanee, Illinois, he was intent from an early age on becoming a journalist and an author. His newspaper career spanned nearly four decades but his extensive diary, which comprises more than 20 million words, is his true legacy, a one-man history of twentieth-century America. The cast of characters includes Mae West ogling Mr America, Eleanor Roosevelt and Greta Garbo, Paul Robeson,

Grace Kelly and Al Jolson. Only about 1 per cent of the entire diary has been published, under the title *A Diary of the Century*.

ENO, BRIAN (1948–) Rock musician born in Suffolk, England. He joined Roxy Music in 1971 and contributed hugely to their popularity. He has worked with many rock luminaries, including Robert Fripp, Kevin Ayers, Nico, David Bowie and John Cale. He once described himself as a non-musician who just turned dials and switches. He is credited with discovering 'ambient' music. His diary, *A Year with Swollen Appendices*, covers the year 1995.

EVELYN, JOHN (1620–1706) The second son of a wealthy Surrey landowner, he was always a man of substance, though not independently well off until 1699 when he inherited the family estate at Wotton. He went to Balliol College, Oxford, then read law before travelling extensively on the Continent. Throughout his long life he was an eye-witness to many epochal happenings, including the Restoration of Charles II, the Second Dutch War, the Plague and the Great Fire of London. His epitaph described this era as 'an age of extraordinary events, and revelations'. In 1664 he published *Sylva, or a Discourse on Forest Trees*, which was highly influential and made him a celebrity. Of his eight children, only one survived him. His immense *Diary* extends from 1620 in the reign of James I to 1706 in the reign of Queen Anne, a time of enormous transformation.

FARMBOROUGH, FLORENCE (1887–1978) In 1908, at the age of 21, she went to work in Russia as a governess. When war broke out she became a nurse, joined the Red Cross and was sent to the Front. In 1917, when the Russian revolution started, she was ordered to return to Moscow. A year later she came home via Siberia and the United States. Her diary, which she kept in 1914–18, originally ran to some 400,000 words.

FOX, BARCLAY (1817–55) Born in Falmouth, Cornwall. His father was a notable scientist and the family were Quakers. His diary, which he kept from the age of 14 until shortly before he died, is notable not only for its chronicling of provincial life in the mid-nineteenth century but for its portraits of three eminent Victorians: John Sterling, John Stuart Mill and Thomas Carlyle.

FOX, CAROLINE (1819–1871) Born in Cornwall the same day as Queen Victoria, the younger daughter of Robert Were Fox, scientist and inventor, she led a very active social life despite living so far from fashionable society. Of a delicate disposition, she had a Quaker upbringing. Her diaries, written from the age of 17, are crowded with a remarkable gallery of characters, including Tennyson, Wordsworth, Carlyle, John Stuart Mill and many others.

FRANK, ANNE (1929–45) Of German-Jewish stock, she was born in Frankfurt. She fled from the Nazis to Holland in 1933 with her family. After the Nazis invaded Holland they hid in a sealed-off back room in Amsterdam until they were betrayed in 1944. Her diary, the moving story of their concealment, was first published in 1947. She died while imprisoned at

Bergen-Belsen concentration camp three months short of her sixteenth birthday.

GAITSKELL, HUGH (1906–63) British politician, educated at Winchester and New College, Oxford. He joined the Labour Party as an undergraduate and lectured in political economy at University College, London. He was a member of parliament from 1945 to 1963 and Chancellor of the Exchequer, 1950–1. He became party leader in 1955 but lost the 1959 general election.

GASCOYNE, DAVID (1916–) British poet whose first collection, *Roman Balcony*, was published when he was 16. With a generous advance for his first novel he travelled to Paris in 1933 and became interested in the work of the surrealists. Two volumes of journals, covering 1936 to 1939, and giving valuable accounts of the artistic and political movements of the time, have been published.

GIDE, ANDRÉ (1869–1951) French novelist and man-of-letters, born in Paris. An only, lonely child whose father died when he was 11, he was educated privately. Though bisexual he married his cousin in 1892. Key books are *The Immoralist, Strait is the Gate* and *The Counterfeiters*. He wrote over 50 books, including an autobiography and witty, candid and compelling diaries which run from 1889 to 1949. In 1947 he was awarded the Nobel Prize for Literature.

GLADWYN, CYNTHIA (1898–1990) Born in Newcastle-upon-Tyne, she married in 1929 Gladwyn Jebb, who was already a high-flier in the British diplomatic service. Together they shared many foreign postings, including Rome, Paris and New York. In 1960, her husband retired and was granted a peerage. Her diary covers the years 1946–71, the crowning years of her husband's diplomatic career, and a further decade when he attended the House of Lords. Though she hoped it would one day be published she specified that it should not appear until after her death.

GOEBBELS, PAUL JOSEF (1897–1945) German Nazi politician, the son of a Rhenish factory foreman. He was born with a deformed foot and was therefore able to avoid military service. Through scholarships he attended eight universities. Unemployed and directionless, he became an enthusiastic supporter of Hitler and edited the Nazi rag, *Völkische Freiheit*. Ultimately he was head of the ministry of propaganda and popular enlightenment. Vain, rabidly anti-semitic and ruthlessly ambitious, he retained Hitler's confidence to the last. His diaries cover the years 1939 to 1941.

GOETHE, JOHANN WOLFGANG VON (1749–1832) Born in Frankfurt, against his will he trained for the law. Invited to the court of the Duke of Weimar he rose in the government and was raised to the nobility in 1782. In 1791, he was appointed director of Weimar court theatre. He influenced writers as diverse as Thomas Carlyle and George Eliot. All his works are in some sense autobiographical, 'fragments of a great confession'. Key books include *The Sorrows of Young Werther, Elective Affinities*,

Faust and *Italian Journeys*, a journal he kept from September 1786 to June 1787.

GONCOURT, EDMOND DE and JULES DE (1822–96) (1830–70) Originally artists they turned to writing novels, being interested primarily in manners. Their greatest novel is *Madame Gervaisais*. Today, however, they are remembered for the Prix Goncourt, France's most influential literary award, and their journals, a lively, irreverent record of 45 years of their lives and opinions, beginning on the day of Napoleon III's coup d'état in 1851 and ending with Edmond's death in 1896. Flaubert, Zola, Balzac, Baudelaire, Rodin, Degas and George Sand are just a few of the great characters who swim into their orbit.

GRANT, ELIZABETH, OF ROTHIEMURCHUS (1797–1885) Born in Edinburgh, the daughter of a Highland landowner, she spent her formative years in London, holidaying in summer in Scotland. In 1814, the family returned permanently to Edinburgh. She is known chiefly for her diary, *Memoirs of a Highland Lady* and its sequel, *The Highland Lady in Ireland*.

GRANT, RICHARD E. (1957–) Born and brought up in Mbabane, Swaziland. He moved to London in 1982, waitered, repped, toured and fringed until getting a role in a television satire about advertising, *Honest, Decent and True*. This led to his being cast in *Withnail and I* in 1986. His other films include *LA Story, Hudson Hawk, The Player, Dracula, The Age of Innocence, The Portrait of a Lady* and *Twelfth Night*.

GRENFELL, JOYCE (1910–75) Famed for her comic monologues, she was one of the best loved stage performers of her day. Born in London, she made her debut in *The Little Revue* in 1939. She entertained the troops throughout the war as part of ENSA [Entertainments National Services Association], a period lovingly recreated in her journals. Her autobiography, *Joyce Grenfell Requests the Pleasure*, appeared in 1976.

GREVILLE, CHARLES (1794–1865) Politician and clerk to the Privy Council. His diary, which he kept from 1820 to 1860, is an insider's view of politics and power. It includes pen portraits of the Duke of Wellington and Lord Palmerston.

GUEVARA, ERNESTO CHE (1928–67) Argentinian Communist revolutionary leader who graduated in medicine from the University of Buenos Aires and then joined Fidel Castro's revolutionary movement in Mexico. He had a key role in the Cuban revolution and subsequently held a number of government posts. An avid diary keeper, his *Bolivian Diary* tells the story of his painstaking efforts to forge a movement of workers and peasants that could win the battle for land and national sovereignty and open the socialist revolution on the South American continent.

GUINNESS, SIR ALEC (1914–2000) One of the outstanding actors of his generation, he was born in London. He made his first professional appearance in 1933 and went on to become a member of the Old Vic. During the war he served in the Royal Navy. He starred in numerous films, including *Kind Hearts and Coronets*, *The Bridge on the River Kwai* and *Star Wars*. His theatre work includes *The Cocktail Party*, *A Voyage Round My Father* and *Habeas Corpus*. He was George Smiley in a television adaptation of the spy novels by John le Carré. Knighted in 1959, his diary of 'a retiring actor' covers 1995–6.

HALL, PETER (1930–) British theatre, film and opera director. He was appointed successor to Laurence Olivier as director of the National Theatre in 1973. Though he produced many notable performances, his diaries, subtitled 'The Story of a Dramatic Battle', illustrate just how fraught his period in the hot seat was. The diaries start in spring 1972 and finish in January 1980.

HAYDON, B(ENJAMIN) R(OBERT) (1786–1846) English painter, born in Plymouth, best known for his historical themes. He married in 1821 but five of his children died. Dogged by debt and insanity, he shot himself in his studio. His diaries ran to 27 volumes, from which a selection was published posthumously.

HERZBERG, ABEL J. (1893–1989) Born in Amsterdam, he grew up in a non-orthodox but religious home. His father was a broker in uncut diamonds. During the First World War he enrolled as a volunteer in the Dutch army though he did not have Dutch nationality. He qualified as a lawyer and played a prominent role in the Dutch Jewish community. After the occupation of Holland in 1940, Herzberg, his wife and three children were forced to go into hiding, but later returned to Amsterdam where they were arrested. In January 1944 they were taken to Bergen-Belsen but amazingly the whole family survived. His diary was written during their time in the concentration camp. After the war, he wrote many books, most of them taking the theme of the persecution of the Jews.

HILLESUM, ETTY (1914–43) The daughter of a teacher, she was born in Holland, and studied law before turning to psychology. Julius Spier, a psychochirologist, was a formative influence and she became, in turn, his assistant, lover and intellectual partner. She started keeping a diary when she was 27, at a time when Holland was increasingly under the sway of German terror. She reached Auschwitz on 10 September, 1943, the very day her parents were gassed. Her own death was reported by the Red Cross just two months later.

HONE, PHILIP (1780–1851) American businessman and mayor of New York. He kept a diary of over two million words, from 1818 to his death. Though not given to private confession, his diary is a revelatory portrait of a great city.

HOPKINS, GERARD MANLEY (1844–99) English poet and Jesuit priest, born at Stratford, Essex, and educated at Balliol College, Oxford. He wrote poetry from an early age but many of his early efforts were destroyed when he decided to become a Jesuit. His greatest poem, 'The Wreck of the Deutschland', was rejected as too difficult by the Jesuit journal *The Month*. Other well-anthologised poems include 'The Windhover', 'Inversnaid' and 'Spring and Fall'. His journals were published in two volumes in 1959.

ISHERWOOD, CHRISTOPHER (1904–86) Born in Cheshire, England, he was a friend from boyhood of W. H. Auden, with whom he collaborated on several works. Educated at public school and Cambridge, he was much influenced by his experience of living in Berlin in 1929–33. His first novel, *All the Conspirators*, was published in 1928 but it is pallid in comparison to *Mr Norris Changes Trains* (1935) and *Goodbye to Berlin* (1939). The latter was dramatized in 1951 by John van Druten as *I am a Camera* and was later turned into the stage and film musical *Cabaret*. *Christopher and His Kind* (1977) is a frank account of his homosexual adventures as a young man.

JACOB, VIOLET (1863–1946) Scottish poet and novelist, daughter of the eighteenth Laird of Dun. She married an army officer and spent her early married life in India before returning to north-east Scotland. Her diary covers the period 1895 to 1900 when she was in India.

JAMES, ALICE (1848–92) Born into a supremely intelligent and talented family; her brother William was an eminent psychologist, and her brother Henry, the great novelist. Less fortuitously, she was born into mid-nineteenth-century New England, where societal strictures severely limited the experiences and activities of women. The deep frustration bred by this set of circumstances contributed to Alice's decline from an active healthy childhood into chronic invalidism. As Henry James wrote, 'Alice's tragic health was, in a manner, the only solution for her of the practical problem of life.' Her posthumously published diary has become 'a touchstone for feminist analysis of nineteenth-century invalidism and of gender's influence on the family members' lives and careers.'

JARMAN, DEREK (1942–94) English film director and painter born in Middlesex. He first worked in the cinema as a production designer for *The Devils*, directed by Ken Russell. His first feature film was *Sebastiane* in 1976. Other notable films include *Jubilee*, *Caravaggio* and *The Last of England*. Often controversial and innovative, he explored unflinchingly his own homosexuality and the decline of modern Britain.

JENKINS, ROY (1920–) British politician. He was educated at Abersychan Grammar School and Balliol College, Oxford, became a Labour MP in 1948 and a government minister in 1964. In 1981, he stood on behalf of the Social Democratic Party, of which he was a founder member. He became Lord Jenkins of Hillhead in 1987. He is the author of several books, including *Mr Balfour's Poodle*, *Sir Charles Dilke*, *Asquith*, *Truman* and *Baldwin*. His diary runs from 1977 to 1981. 'I found it fairly burdensome,' he wrote in its introduction.

JORDAN, NEIL (1950–) Born in Ireland, he is an award-winning writer and director of internationally acclaimed films, including *The Company of Wolves*, *Mona Lisa* and *The Crying Game*, for which he was awarded an Oscar for best screenplay. His novels include *The Past*, *The Dream of a Beast* and *Sunrise with Sea Monster*. His diary relates the making of the film *Michael Collins*.

KAFKA, FRANZ (1883–1924) Born in Prague, he was a German-speaking Jew. His reputation rests on the posthumous publication of three novels, *The Trial* (1925), *The Castle* (1926) and *Amerika* (1927), and a body of short stories, including *Metamorphosis*. His diaries, published in two volumes, cover the years 1910–23, and detail his misery at having to work in a job he detested, his fractious relationship with his family and his tortured liaison with Felice Bauer, to whom he was twice engaged.

KEMBLE, FANNY (1809–93) Though born into an illustrious stage family, she showed no desire for a theatrical career. But in order to help save her father from bankruptcy she agreed to appear at Covent Garden in 1829. An immediate success, she was to play many of the great female roles, being at home both in comedy and tragedy. From 1849–68 and 1873–8 she lived in America. The author of several autobiographical works, including *Records of a Later Life* (1882).

KESSLER, COUNT HARRY (1868–1937) Born in Paris, the son of a Hamburg banker and an Irish beauty. In the First World War, he was an officer in the German army and later oversaw the withdrawal of more than 100,000 German troops from the Eastern Front. He was both a purveyor of gossip and an intellectual. He kept a diary for 35 years, assuming from the beginning that the events of his time would be worth recording, revealing as they did the German nation in a time of crisis.

KILVERT, REV. (ROBERT) FRANCIS (1840–79) One of six children, he was educated privately, went up to Oxford, was ordained, and for a time acted as curate to his father. For seven years he served as curate to the vicar of Clyro in Radnorshire on the border between England and Wales. It was the happiest time of his life. In August 1879 he married Elizabeth Anne Rowland but he died a month later of peritonitis. His wife inherited his diary and is said to have destroyed two large sections of it for personal reasons. What was left was contained in 22 notebooks, only three of which survive; the rest were destroyed by an elderly niece of Kilvert's who had inherited them from her brother. The diaries were first published in a three-volume edition, 1938–40, edited by William Plomer.

KING, CECIL (1901–87) British newspaperman, educated at Winchester and Christ Church, Oxford. He held a variety of senior managerial positions in the press and paper industry and directorships of many organisations, including the British Film Institute and the Bank of England. His diaries, published in two volumes in the 1970s, span 1965–74.

KLEMPERER, VICTOR (1881–1960) The son of a rabbi, he studied in

Munich, Geneva, Paris and Berlin, where he became a journalist. He taught at the University of Naples, and received the Distinguished Service Medal as a volunteer in the German Army in the First World War. Subsequently, he was a professor of Romance Languages at Dresden Technical College until he was dismissed as a consequence of Nazi laws in 1935. He survived the Holocaust and the war, and taught as an academic in East Germany until his death. His diaries (1933–45), the first volume of which was published in 1998, are a graphic portrayal of life under Nazi rule.

LASCELLES, SIR ALAN 'TOMMY' (1887–1981) A nephew of the fifth Earl of Harewood, he read Greats at Oxford. In the First World War he fought as a cavalry officer in the Bedford Yeomanry, was wounded and awarded the Military Cross. In 1920, he joined the staff of Prince of Wales. From 1931 to 1935 he was Secretary to the Governor General of Canada and Private Secretary to George VI from 1943 to 1952.

LAST, NELLA (1909–1966) A housewife from Barrow, England, she started her diary in September 1939, and continued it for almost 30 years. Writing initially for the Mass Observation, an organisation set up to 'record the voice of the people', she left a detailed record of her life, comprising over two million words.

LE RUEZ, ANNIE MARGARET ('NAN') (1915–) Born on a farm on Jersey, Nan Le Ruez was the second of ten children. She left school at 16 to work on the family farm. She kept a diary 'on and off' throughout her school days, and continued to do so during the German Occupation. At the end of the war she placed the volumes in a Red Cross parcel box, where they remained unopened for fifty years.

LEES-MILNE, JAMES (1908–98) English author and rescuer of decaying country houses, born in Worcestershire and educated at Eton and Oxford. Invalided out of the army in 1941, he spent the war years at the behest of the National Trust trundling up and down the country in his car interviewing the owners of remote and dilapidated country houses, many of which he saved from oblivion. His autobiography, *Another Self*, published in 1970, is a model of self-deprecation. His voluminous diaries are full of well-turned anecdotes.

LEWIS, C(LIVE) S(TAPLES) (1898–1963) Literary scholar, critic and novelist, best known perhaps for his children's books, including *The Lion, the Witch and the Wardrobe*, the first of his seven 'Narnia' stories. *The Allegory of Love* is his most influential critical study. He gained a large audience outside academia for his writings on religion, which include *The Problem of Pain*, *The Screwtape Letters* and *The Four Loves*. He was a member of 'The Inklings', a group of friends at Oxford University, among whom was J. R. R. Tolkien. His diary, *All My Road Before Me*, 1922–1927, which he began when still an undergraduate, gives a vivid account of the odd *ménage* he shared with a woman 26 years his senior.

LEWIS, NORMAN (1918–) British travel and thriller writer born in London. His credentials as a travel writer were established with *A Dragon Apparent*, published in 1951. His experiences of active service as an intelligence officer in Italy during the Second World War form the basis of *Naples '44*; the citizens were so destitute that all the tropical fish in the city's aquarium were devoured and even respectable women were driven to prostitution.

LINDBERGH, ANNE MORROW (1906–2001) Her father was an American ambassador in Mexico where she met aviator Charles Lindbergh in 1927. She learned to fly, operate radios and navigate, and accompanied Charles on his survey flights over North America in 1931 and 1933. She wrote books about flying and her travels. She had five children, one of whom became the famous Lindbergh Baby who, kidnapped in America in 1932, was later found dead.

LOCKHART, SIR ROBERT BRUCE (1887–1970) Diplomat and writer, born in Anstruther on the east coast of Scotland. He took pride – undiplomatically – in having 'no drop of English blood' in his veins. After three years as a rubber planter in Malaysia he went to Russia in 1918 as head of a special mission but when Anglo-Russian relations withered he was imprisoned in the Kremlin for 'espionage'. He worked in journalism and wrote several books, including *My Rod, My Comfort*, a paean to angling. His diaries were published posthumously.

LONGFORD, FRANCIS ANGIER PAKENHAM, 7th Earl of (1905–2001) English politician, prison visitor and author, educated at Eton and New College, Oxford. He lectured in politics at Oxford and was prospective parliamentary Labour candidate there in 1938. He has held many senior positions in government, including Minister of Civil Aviation, First Lord of the Admiralty and Leader of the House of Lords. His numerous books include biographies of St Francis of Assisi, Jesus Christ and Pope John Paul II. *Diary of a Year* appeared in 1982.

LOWNDES, MARIE BELLOC (1868–1947) Novelist and playwright, born in France, the sister of essayist and humorist Hilaire Belloc. After her father's death she moved to London and worked for the *Pall Mall Gazette*. She married Frederick Lowndes.

MACLEAN, ALASDAIR (1926–) Scottish poet, born in Glasgow. He left school at 14, later attending Edinburgh University as a mature student. He worked in the Clydeside shipyards, as a laboratory technician and did National Service. His poetry has been collected in various volumes, including *From the Wilderness* and *Waking the Dead*. His diary, which he published alongside his father's in *Night Falls in Ardnamurchan: The Twilight of a Crofting Family*, is a moving evocation of the passing of a way of life.

MACLEAN, IAN (1898–1973) Father of Alasdair Maclean, he was born in the hamlet of Sanna in western Ardnamurchan, Scotland. He went to sea at 14, adding two years to his age. He served in the Navy during the First World War, then settled in Glasgow, where he suffered severe poverty. He eventually became a deputy harbourmaster. In the early 1950s he retired and moved back to Ardnamurchan to manage the family croft.

MACNAUGHTAN, SARAH (1850–1916) Of Scottish descent, she was the daughter of a JP. She took such care to hide her birth date that it was not even revealed in her obituary in *The Times*. She was of independent means and never married. She wrote novels and was part of the women's suffrage movement. Having trained as a nurse, she served in the Balkans, South Africa and during the First World War. Her diary, 1914–15, dwells on her war experiences.

MACREADY, (WILLIAM) CHARLES (1793–1873) English actor, one of the finest tragedians of his – or any other – time. He made his first appearance at Birmingham as Romeo in 1810, and then toured the provinces. By 1819, he was firmly established as Thomas Kean's main rival. His Lear, Hamlet and Macbeth were especially memorable. He was a man of volcanic temper, and it was not unusual for him to come to blows with his associates. He first performed in America in 1826 and at his final appearance, several years later, a riot ensued and several people were killed. His diary gives a lively picture of the world in which he lived, showing him warts and all.

MAHLER-WERFEL, ALMA (1879–1964) Daughter of the artist Emil Jacob Schindler, she chose to pursue a career in music. Her apparently illegible diaries, 1898–1902, which until recently lay unread in an American university library, open with her in the throes of an affair with Gustav Klimt and close shortly before she was to marry Gustav Mahler. The marriage lasted, but not without turbulence, its strains causing Mahler to consult Freud for psychoanalysis.

MANSEL, JOHN (1909–74) The son of a stockbroker, he was born in London. He attended Winchester College and Liverpool University where he qualified as an architect. He joined the Territorial Army in 1935 and was mobilized in 1939. His diaries describe his five years as a German prisoner-of-war.

MANSFIELD, KATHERINE (1888–1923) A renowned short story writer, born in Wellington, New Zealand, and educated at Queen's College, London. Her personal life was chaotic and brought her much distress, which informed the stories in her first collection, *In a German Pension*, published in 1911, the year she met the critic and editor John Middleton Murry, whom she married in 1918. Through him she was introduced to the Bloomsbury Group but was never totally accepted by it. In her diaries Virginia Woolf revealed a deep dislike of Mansfield. Murry published an expurgated version of her diary in 1927. A fuller version, offering a more painful picture of their often strained relationship, was published in 1976.

MATTHEW, CHRISTOPHER (1939–) Journalist and broadcaster, he was educated at King's School, Canterbury, and Oxford. His fictional *Diary of a*

Somebody consciously echoes the classic *Diary of a Nobody*. Its modern-day Pooter is Simon Crisp, a twittish bachelor whose attempts to charm women are hopelessly (and hilariously) inept.

MENCKEN, H(ENRY) L(OUIS) (1880–1956) Prolific American journalist, critic and lexicographer. He was born in Baltimore and associated with *The Smart Set*, for which he was first literary editor, then co-editor with George Nathan. An iconoclast, he loudly advocated the virtues of American authors. In 1924, he co-founded *The American Nation*. He started his diary in 1930, when he was 50, and made his last entry in 1948.

MITCHISON, NAOMI (1897–1999) Prolific Scottish writer, born in Edinburgh and educated at Oxford. Her brother was the scientist J. B. S. Haldane. She married G. R. Mitchison, a barrister and later Labour MP and life peer. Her early historical novels, including *The Conquered*, *The Bull Calves*, and *The Corn King and the Spring Queen*, are among her best. She also wrote science fiction, biography and memoirs. From the late 1930s onward she spent much of her time on her farm at Carradale, Kintyre. Her friends included E. M. Forster, W. H. Auden and Aldous Huxley. She was an official tribal mother to the Bakgatla of Botswana and a member of the Highlands and Islands Advisory Panel.

MOLE, ADRIAN (1981–) Created by Sue Townsend, Mole is the archetypal teenager trying to cope with the stresses of everyday living while his hormones race around like pinballs. He first appeared in *The Secret Diary of Adrian Mole Aged 13¾*.

MOUNTBATTEN OF BURMA, EARL (LOUIS) (1900–79) British naval commander and statesman, born near Windsor. Educated at Royal Naval colleges Osborne and Dartmouth, he served at sea in the First World War. In the Second World War he commanded the fifth destroyer flotilla and became chief of combined operations. He was appointed the last viceroy of India in 1947. He was murdered by the Irish Republican Army while sailing near his holiday home in County Sligo, Ireland.

MUGGERIDGE, MALCOLM (1903–90) British journalist and broadcaster, born in Croydon. His father was a politician. He joined the *Manchester Guardian* in 1930, though he always chafed at the thought of being merely a journalist and wrote a play, novels and biography. During the war he joined the Intelligence Corps. In 1952, he became editor of *Punch*. He was an early presenter of *Panorama*, a BBC TV current affairs programme, though he had a face that was more suited for radio. Religiously inclined he decided at 60 to renounce drinking, meat-eating, casual love affairs and smoking, though not necessarily in that order. His diaries were published in 1981.

MUNBY, ARTHUR F. (1828–1910) Poet and civil servant, who was heavily involved in the Working Men's College from the outset. He was called to the Bar in 1855. His poems were highly praised by Robert Browning. Throughout his life he was obsessed by the plight of the working woman and he married Hannah Cullwick, a maidservant who refused to become a 'lady'. His marriage was unknown to all the members of his family until the reading of his will. His diaries, published in 1972, show how he kept his two worlds apart, mixing on the one hand with high and artistic society and, on the other, with colliery women, fisher-girls and prostitutes.

MUSIL, ROBERT (ELDER VON) (1880–1942) Born in Austria into a well-to-do family, he grew up as a privileged, protected and lonely child. His experience at a military boarding school gave him the material for his first novel, *Young Törless* (1906). He is best known for the huge and unfinished work *A Man without Qualities* (1930–32). He began writing his diaries when he was 17.

NEWTON, REV. BENJAMIN (1761–1830) Educated at Jesus College, Cambridge, he served in various parishes on the Welsh borders, in Wiltshire, Somerset and Yorkshire. He was also a magistrate and wrote on civil liberty and morals.

NICOLSON, SIR HAROLD (1886–1968) Born in Teheran, the son of a diplomat. He, too, was a diplomat, a politician and, unhappily, a journalist. He was friend and, for a while, follower of Oswald Mosley. He married Vita Sackville-West, who did not attempt to hide from him her affairs with Violet Treyfusis and Virginia Woolf. He was a prolific author, particularly of biographies, his subjects including Verlaine, Swinburne and King George V. His monument, however, is his diaries and letters, 1930–62, published in three volumes, which run to some three million words, many of them highly entertaining.

NIN, ANAÏS (1903–77) Born in Paris, partly of Spanish origin, and lived there until she was 11, when she went to live in the United States. On her marriage to Hugh Guiler, a banker, she returned to Paris where she encountered many artists and writers, including Henry Miller. A voluminous writer, she published novels, criticism and eroticism. Ultimately, her fame rests on her *Journals* which span the years 1931–74.

ORIGO, IRIS (1902–88) Born in England. Her childhood was spent with her grandparents in America, in Ireland with her Anglo-Irish grandparents, and at her mother's villa at Fiesole, outside Florence. An only child, brought up by nurses and governesses, she immersed herself in books. She married Antonio Origo in 1924 and they bought an estate at La Foce in Tuscany, which they worked hard to restore. Her books include *Images and Shadows*, an autobiography, *The Merchant of Prato*, an historical study, and *War in the Val d'Orcia*, a diary which describes the danger of protecting partisans and Allied prisoners-of-war from the Germans.

ORTON, JOE (1933–67) English playwright, born in Leicester. He left school at 16 to train as an actor. His black comedies include *Entertaining Mr Sloane*, *What the Butler Saw* and *Loot*. Infamous to a fault, he was jailed for defacing library books. He was battered to death by a friend, who then committed suicide. His diaries are as acid as his drama.

PARTRIDGE, FRANCES (1900–2002) Born in Bloomsbury, London, one of six children. Friends of the family included Conan Doyle, Henry James and the Stracheys. She was educated at Bedales School and Newham College, Cambridge. She married Ralph Partridge in 1933. She was closely associated with the members of the Bloomsbury group. Her diaries, written without thought of publication, chronicle a long and remarkable life, starting with the death of her husband in 1960.

PAVESE, CESARE (1908–50) Italian novelist and poet, born on a farm in Piedmont. He had a hard upbringing, not least because his father died when he was six. Renowned for the novel *The Moon and the Bonfires*, published in the year in which he committed suicide after a woman with whom he had fallen in love left him. His diaries, covering the troubled years 1935–50, reveal his thoughts on 'This Business of Living'.

PEARSON, ANDREW (1897–69) American journalist, born in Illinois of a Quaker background. His father was a professor of public speaking. In 1919 he did relief work in Serbia and kept a diary. In 1929, the *Baltimore Sun* hired him as its Washington correspondent but he was fired in 1932 for co-writing a book anonymously. He proceeded, however, to turn the book into a column giving an insider's view of politics in the capital. Latterly, he broadcast on radio and television. His diaries open in January 1949 when he was 51, 'an established and respected – though sometimes cussed at – professional'.

PEPYS, ELIZABETH (1640–69) The daughter of a French aristocrat, she married Samuel Pepys when she was only 15. His explanation for this rash behaviour was that Elizabeth was so beautiful, and he was so passionately in love with her, that he was made quite ill. Her 'diary', which opens on 13 October 1655 and closes in November 1669, only recently surfaced in Clapham, South London. So far only a part of it has been 'edited' by the feminist scholar, Dale Spender.

PEPYS, SAMUEL (1633–1703) The son of a tailor, he was educated at St Paul's School, London, and Magdalene College, Cambridge. He married Elizabeth St Michel, who was 15 years old, in 1655. Initially through patronage, he pursued a successful career in the Admiralty. His diary opens on 1 January, 1660, and closes on 31 May 1669, when he erroneously believed that he was going blind. However, he also wrote an interesting diary when he was posted to Tangier in 1683. His career effectively came to an end in 1688 with the 'Glorious Revolution'. He was sent to the Tower in 1699, accused of complicity in the 'Popish Plot' but was soon set free. His diary remained in cipher at Magdalene College until 1825 when the code was broken. An unexpurgated edition was published 1970–83 in 11 volumes.

PLATH, SYLVIA (1932–63) American poet and novelist, born in Boston, Massachusetts. Her father was an entomologist who died when she was eight. She was educated at Smith College, Massachusetts, and Newham

College, Cambridge. In 1956 she married Ted Hughes. Her first collection of poetry was *The Colossus*, published in 1960; it was followed three years later by a novel, *The Bell Jar*. That same year, she committed suicide. Her journals, which cover 1950–62, were published in unexpurgated form in 2000.

POTTER, BEATRIX (1866–1943) English author and illustrator, famed for *The Tale of Peter Rabbit* and its successors. Between the ages of 15 and 30, she kept a secret journal written in code. It was not until more than 20 years after her death that the code was cracked by the patient work of Leslie Linder. When it was published in 1966, under the title *The Journal of Beatrix Potter 1881–1897*, it revealed a remarkable picture of upper-middle-class life in late-Victorian Britain.

POUGY, LIANE DE (1869–1950) Regarded by many as the greatest beauty of her day, she was born Anne-Marie Chassaigne in Brittany, the daughter of an army officer. She ran away to Paris, married, divorced, became a courtesan, and made an unsuccessful bid to become an actress. Her second marriage was to Prince Georges Ghika, a penniless Romanian aristocrat. She began to write her *Blue Notebooks*, so called because of the paper on which they were written not because of licentious content, in 1919, when she and Georges were living in refined retirement.

POWELL, ANTHONY (1905–2000) Fêted as the author of the 12-volume *roman fleuve*, *A Dance to the Music of Time*, he was educated at Eton and Oxford. Before embarking on a career as a novelist, he worked in publishing. As well as novels he wrote a biographical study of John Aubrey and a four-volume autobiography. He began writing a journal in 1982, when he became 'stuck' on a novel, and continued into the Nineties.

POWELL, DAWN (1897–1965) Born in Ohio, Powell ran away from home at the age of 12 and was brought up by an aunt. She graduated from Lake Erie College in 1918 and moved to New York, where she lived and worked for the rest of her life. She married the advertising executive Joseph R. Gousha, and they had one son. She published 15 novels, which at the time of her death were all out of print. However, an article on her by Gore Vidal in the *New York Review of Books* sparked a revival and many of her books are now available. Her voluminous diaries cover the period from 1931 to 1965.

PYM, BARBARA (1913–80) British novelist, educated at St Hilda's College, Oxford. Her father was a Shropshire solicitor. Her work centres mainly on life in the professions, drawing on her experience as an editor of anthropological journals, and on machinations within the Anglican church. In 1963, her publisher rejected *An Unsuitable Attachment* and she consequently suffered a prolonged period of neglect. In 1977, however, David Cecil and Philip Larkin mentioned her in a symposium in the *Times Literary Supplement* on neglected writers and her work gradually came back into print. She was shortlisted for the Booker Prize in 1977 for *Quartet in Autumn*. Her journals and letters appeared in 1984, entitled *A Very Private Eye*.

RABE, JOHN (1882–1949) In 1937, as the Japanese army closed in on Nanking, then the capital of China, all members of the foreign community were ordered to leave. One man, a mild-mannered 55-year-old German, John Rabe, head of the local branch of the Siemens electrical firm and a member of the Nazi Party, refused to go. It is estimated that he saved between 250,000 and 300,000 lives by his efforts. Arrested by the Gestapo on his return to Germany, he survived the war, only to die in obscurity. Every night in Nanking he wrote up his diary, which was published in 1998.

RANFURLY, COUNTESS OF (1914–) 'Since I was about five years old I have kept a diary,' wrote the Countess in the introduction to her wartime diaries, *To War with Whitaker*. When war broke out her husband, Dan Ranfurly, was dispatched to the Middle East with his faithful valet, Whitaker. Defying the War Office, she ran off in pursuit of her husband. Her diaries, covering the six years of the war, include cameo appearances by Churchill and Eisenhower.

REICH, WILHELM (1897–1957) Austrian psychologist who became a practising psychoanalyst while still a student in Vienna, having been preoccupied with sex from a very early age. It was his opinion that regular orgasms for both men and women were the way to better mental health. His seminal work is *The Function of the Orgasm*. He invented the pseudoscientific 'orgone accumulator', which he claimed would improve the user's sex life. He left Germany for Scandinavia in 1933 and emigrated to the USA in 1939, where he established the Orgone Institute. He died in jail after being prosecuted for promoting an illegal treatment.

REITH, LORD, (JOHN) (1889–1971) Born in Stonehaven in the north-east of Scotland, he was educated at Glasgow Academy. After serving an engineering apprenticeship, he entered the field of radio communication. In 1922, he became first general manager of the British Broadcasting Corporation and was its director-general from 1927 to 1938. Thereafter he entered politics. But his career at the BBC is his claim to posterity, for he was largely responsible for defining its didactic tone. He published an autobiography, *Into the Wind*, in 1949. His diaries, which show him to be deeply troubled and vulnerable, were published posthumously.

RITCHIE, CHARLES (1906–) Born in Canada, he was educated there and at Oxford. He joined the Canadian Department of External Affairs and was posted to London in 1939. Until his retirement from the Foreign Service in 1971, he represented Canada in Germany, the United Nations, Washington and London.

ROBINSON, HENRY CRABB (1775–1867) Though a solicitor and a barrister, he is chiefly known for his diaries, reading lists and letters, which give a valuable glimpse of his more illustrious friends, including Wordsworth,

Lamb, Hazlitt, Coleridge and Carlyle, who once said that 'he could talk by the gallon in a minute'. An indefatigable attender of lectures, he was one of the founders of University College London.

ROREM, NED (1923–) American composer, born in Richmond, Indiana. He studied at the Juilliard School in New York. From 1949 to 1958 he was based in Paris, though two of these years, which feature in his 'flamboyantly candid' diaries, were spent in Morocco. His extensive *oeuvre* includes symphonies, instrumental pieces, choral music and, latterly, songs.

RUSKIN, JOHN (1819–1900) English author and art critic. His first love was poetry but after he met the painter J. M. W. Turner, he decided that his first duty was to rescue him from neglect and obscurity. *Modern Painters*, published in 1843, was the result, a book which rather embarrassed Turner. Ruskin's marriage to Effie Chalmers Gray was shortlived and thereafter he championed other painters whom he deemed unloved. Among his other notable works are *The Seven Lamps of Architecture, The Stones of Venice* and *Sesame and Lilies*. He was a vigorous opponent of railways. His diaries run from 1835 to 1889.

SAND, GEORGE, pseudonym of AMANDINE-AURORE-LUCILE DUPIN, BARONNE DUDEVANT (1804–76) French novelist, born in Paris, the illegitimate daughter of Marshal de Saxe. Her father died when she was very young and she lived mainly with her grandmother. She married and had two children, then left her husband and went to Paris, where she had numerous scandalous love affairs. Chopin was her lover for ten years. She was a prolific writer and her complete works comprise over a hundred volumes.

SARTON, (ELEANOR) MAY (1912–95) American poet and novelist, born in Belgium. Her parents were war refugees and she grew up in the United States. From 1937 she taught creative writing at various universities and colleges. In 1958, at the age of 46, she bought a house in 'a village of which I knew absolutely nothing'. Alone in Nelson, in rural New Hampshire, she began a new life in middle age and kept the first of several diaries, *Journal of a Solitude*, published in 1973. 'I suspect the journal as a form,' she once wrote, 'because it is too easy, too quick perhaps.'

SASSOON, SIEGFRIED (1886–1967) Brought up in Kent and Sussex. His mother earmarked him at an early age as a poet. He enjoyed country sports, particularly hunting. He was awarded the Military Cross but discarded it. Sent, 'shell-shocked', to a hospital in Edinburgh, he met Wilfred Owen, whom he helped polish his poetry. Revered as a war poet, he also won acclaim for his autobiographical trilogy, *Memoirs of a Fox-Hunting Man* (1928), *Memoirs of an Infantry Officer* (1930) and *Sherston's Progress* (1936). His diaries cover the years 1915–25.

SCOTT, ROBERT FALCON (1868–1912) English explorer, born near Devonport. He joined the Navy in 1881 and commanded the National Antarctic Expedition, 1900–4. In 1910 he embarked on a second expedition to the Antarctic and reached the South Pole on 17 January 1912 only to discover that they had been beaten to it by the Norwegian expedition commanded by Roald Amundsen. He and his team subsequently perished. Eight months later their bodies and diaries were discovered by a search party. Scott was posthumously knighted.

SCOTT, SIR WALTER (1770–1832) Born in Edinburgh, he was the first international bestselling author. He virtually invented the historical novel, influenced countless authors and is credited with popularising a romantic vision of Scotland which is still potent today. In 1826, at the height of his fame, his printer and his publisher, Ballantyne and Constable, suffered a financial crash, dragging Scott down with them. Determined to pay off his debts – which he managed just before his death – he threw himself even more strenuously into writing. These difficult times are recorded in his diary, his 'Gurnal'. 'I have all my life regretted that I did not keep a regular [journal],' he wrote in his first entry, on 20 November 1825. 'I have myself lost recollection of much that was interesting and I have deprived my family and the public of some curious information by not carrying this resolution into effect.'

SHELLEY, MARY (WOLLSTONECRAFT) (1797–1851) The creator of 'fiction's most famous monster', that created by Dr Frankenstein, was the only daughter of William Godwin and Mary Wollstonecraft, both writers. Her mother died a few days after her birth. In 1814, at the age of 16, she eloped with Percy Bysshe Shelley and they were married in 1816. After his death in 1823, she returned to England, *Frankenstein* having appeared in 1818. Her journal, which she kept during her marriage, is an invaluable record of her life with the great poet.

SHIRER, WILLIAM L. (1904–93) American journalist, author and broadcaster, born in Chicago, Illinois. His father was a lawyer. He was educated in the US and Paris. During the Second World War he was a war correspondent based in Germany. From this experience came his *Berlin Diary: The Journal of a Foreign Correspondent*. He is also the author of the award-winning *Rise and Fall of the Third Reich* and several volumes of autobiography.

SHORE, EMILY (1819–39) Born in Bury St Edmunds, the eldest daughter of a curate. She was a quick learner and wrote fiction, poetry and essays. She died in Madeira, aged 20, of consumption. In homage, her sisters edited a selection from her journal which was published in 1891.

SKINNER, JOHN (1772–1839) A keen antiquarian, he bequeathed to the British Museum 98 manuscript volumes of travels and researches with watercolour drawings. Educated at Trinity College, Oxford, he was ordained as a priest in 1799. His wife and other members of his family died of consumption. He committed suicide.

SMART, ELIZABETH (1913–86) Born in Ottawa, Canada, where she was educated at private schools. She went to London to spend a year at King's College and fell passionately in love with the poet George Barker after reading a collection of his work. Their subsequent relationship produced four children and the bestseller, *By Grand Central Station I Sat Down and Wept*. From her childhood, Smart was an inveterate keeper of diaries, a selection from which, covering the period 1933–41 was first published in 1991.

SOUTAR, WILLIAM (1898–1943) Scottish poet, born in Perth. His parents came of farming stock and his father was a master-joiner. During the First World War Soutar contracted a spinal disease which left him bedridden from 1930 onwards. From then until his death he kept a day-to-day record of his experience and observations. As a poet he specialised in 'bairnrhymes', delightful Scots children's poems of great vigour. His diaries were first published in 1954 under the title *Diaries of a Dying Man*. Reviewing it in the *Observer*, fellow diarist Sir Harold Nicolson greeted it as a 'brave and animating book'.

SPENDER, SIR HAROLD STEPHEN (1909–95) English poet, novelist and critic, friendly with W. H. Auden, Louis MacNeice and Christopher Isherwood. After leaving Oxford he lived for a while in Germany. His first collection of poems appeared in 1930. Shortly thereafter his poem 'The Pylons' appeared, leading to himself and his friends being nicknamed 'Pylon poets'. During the Spanish Civil War he wrote propaganda for the Republican side. In the Second World War he was a member of the National Fire Service. His autobiography, *World Within World*, was published in 1951; his *Journals: 1939–83* were published in 1985.

STEINBECK, JOHN (1902–68) American novelist born in California, which formed the backdrop for much of his early fiction. His best-known novel is *The Grapes of Wrath*, a searing and lyrical account of the struggles of an emigrant farming family from the dustbowl of the West to reach the 'promised land' of California. Other notable works include *Of Mice and Men*, *The Pearl*, *Tortilla Flat* and *East of Eden*. He won the Nobel Prize for Literature in 1962.

STENDHAL, pseudonym of HENRI BEYLE (1783–1842) French novelist brought up in Grenoble. His two masterpieces are *Le Rouge et le noir* and *La Chartreuse de Parme*. The first follows the fortunes of Julien Sorel, a young provincial in Restoration France, the second chronicles the career of Fabrice del Dongo, at a small Italian court at the same time. His *Journal*, published in 1888, covers the years 1801–15.

STEVENSON, FRANCES (1888–1972) After taking a degree in classics at London University, she taught at a girls' boarding school before being employed in 1911 by Lloyd George, then Chancellor of the Exchequer, to coach his daughter, Megan. A year later they began a relationship which ended only with his death in 1945. After Lloyd George's first wife died, they were married in 1943. The diary, which spans three decades, is a unique picture of a British Prime Minister by a woman who was his devoted mistress and confidential secretary.

STEVENSON, ROBERT LOUIS (1850–94) The only child of Thomas Stevenson, engineer, and Margaret Balfour, daughter of a Scots minister, born in Edinburgh. He first tried the law before pursuing a full-time career as a writer. He is probably best known for the novels ostensibly written as adventure stories for boys, *Treasure Island* and *Kidnapped*. Other landmark works include *The Strange Case of Dr Jekyll and Mr Hyde*, *The Master of Ballantrae* and the unfinished *Weir of Hermiston*. One of the world's confirmed itinerants, his only diary is an account of a journey through the Cévennes in September 1878 with a donkey called Modestine.

STOTT, GORDON (1909–99) The youngest son of the Rev. Dr Stott, minister of Cramond, Edinburgh. He was educated at Edinburgh Academy and Edinburgh University, where he studied law. He was called to the Bar in 1936 and was Lord Advocate from 1964 to 1967. He retired in 1984 at the age of 75. His diary covers the period 1961–6.

STRONG, GEORGE TEMPLETON (1820–75) Wall Street lawyer of aristocratic background. His diary was not only remarkable for its length – approximately four million words – but for the 'flavorsome precision' of the writing. While he shared many prejudices of his class, disliking, for instance, the Irish, Jews and socialists, he had a strong sense of civic duty and unusual enthusiams, including chasing fires. His description of the 1863 draft riots is the most stunning account of that nadir in New York's history.

STRONG, SIR ROY (1935–) British aesthete and garden expert, best known for his flamboyant directorship of the National Portrait Gallery and the Victoria and Albert Museum. His diary, which runs from 1967 to 1987, was much influenced by Cecil Beaton's, concerned as it is with a social panorama and not 'the day-to-day technicalities of his professional life'. It includes walk-on parts for David Hockney, Rudolf Nureyev and a 'philistine' Mrs Thatcher.

TAYLER, WILLIAM (1807–92) Born in Grafton, Oxfordshire, England. He entered domestic service, became a footman and began to keep a journal.

THOREAU, H(ENRY) D(AVID) (1817–62) American sage and author, born in Concord, Massachusetts, and educated at Harvard. He took various jobs to supplement his meagre income from writing. He published just two books, *A Week on the Concord and Merrimack River* in 1849, and in 1854 *Walden*, which went largely unnoticed at the time but has since been recognised as a literary classic. It describes his two-year experiment in self-sufficiency when he built a wooden hut on the edge of Walden Pond, Concord. His *Journal*, which runs to 14 volumes, was published in 1906.

TOLSTOY, COUNT LEO (1828–1910) Russian novelist and moralist, born at Yasnaya Polyana, 130 miles from Moscow. Both his parents died young. Dissolute, he abandoned his studies and ran up huge debts. His marriage to Sofia Behrs in 1862 marked a turning point in his life. In 1863, the first of their 13 children was born. He is famed as the author of *War and Peace* and

Anna Karenina. A keen self-improver, he gave up his title, the copyright to his works, alcohol, tobacco, blood sports and eating meat. His family was not in sympathy with his views and after 48 years of marriage he left home for good in 1910, only to die at an obscure railway station.

TOLSTOY, SOFIA (1844–1919) Wife of Leo Tolstoy, whom she married in 1862. Shortly before they married Tolstoy gave his fiancée his bachelor diaries to read and the shock which she – a shy girl of 18 – experienced on learning about his sexual promiscuity was one from which she never truly recovered. Like her husband, she wrote diaries, each having access to what the other wrote. Both, consequently, wrote things they later regretted. 'You're evil, you're a beast,' she once wrote of him. 'She was – and I can see now in what way – the wife I needed' was his opinion of her.

TURNER, THOMAS (1729–93) Born in Groombridge in Kent, he started out as a schoolmaster but became a shopkeeper in East Hoathly in Sussex. He was twice married. He kept a diary – a record of drunkenness, debauchery and retribution – for twelve years between 1754 and 1765, a period overshadowed by the Seven Years War.

VELMANS, EDITH (1925–) Born in Holland, she had a carefree life until the summer of 1942 when it became clear that her family's Jewish background might be fatal. One morning she was sent into hiding with a Christian family in the south of Holland. Her diary, published as *Edith's Book* in 1998, tells the story of how she survived the war, after which she became a psychologist specialising in gerontology and went to live in the United States.

QUEEN VICTORIA (1819–1901) Born at Kensington Palace, she succeeded to the throne on 20 June 1837 at the age of 18 and was crowned the following year on 28 June. She became Empress of India in 1877. In 1840, she married Prince Albert of Saxe-Coburg-Gotha, who took the title of Prince Consort, and who was a major influence on her. When he died in 1861, she was desolate. She remained in retirement for a long time and wore mourning until she died. She kept a diary from the age of 13 until a few days before her death.

WARHOL, ANDY (1926–87) American pop artist and film-maker, famous not least for saying that 'In the future everybody will be world famous for fifteen minutes.' He was a pioneer of 'pop art', including the reproduction of a Campbell soup-can label and posters of film stars such as Marilyn Monroe. In 1968 he was shot and wounded. Each morning for the last ten years of his life he faithfully recorded the events of the previous day.

WAUGH, EVELYN (1903–66) Widely regarded as one of the foremost English novelists of his generation, he was born in London and educated at Lancing and Hertford College, Oxford. After an early sortie into schoolteaching, he produced his first novel, *Decline and Fall*, in 1928. Other notable books include *Scoop*, a newspaper farce, the 'Sword of Honour' trilogy, and *Brideshead Revisited*. He was a dyspeptic wit whose unvarnished self is revealed in his letters and diary, which he kept almost continuously from the age of seven until the year before his death.

WEBB, BEATRICE (1858–1943) Notable as a social reformer and researcher, she married Sidney Webb, who shared her passionate interest in improving conditions for ordinary people. Both were leading lights in the Fabian Society. She wrote two acclaimed autobiographical studies: *My Apprenticeship* and *Our Partnership*. Her exhaustive diaries are a remarkable record of nearly 70 years at the heart of British intellectual and political life.

WELCH, DENTON (1915–48) Born in Shanghai, he spent part of his childhood in China. He trained as an artist, intending to be a painter, but in 1935 he was involved in a bicycle accident from which he never fully recovered. Thereafter he embarked on a literary career. He published *Maiden Voyage*, a volume of autobiography, in 1943, and *In Youth is Pleasure*, a novel, the following year. His journals, comprising over 200,000 words, were kept between 1942 and 1948, and were often written during periods of intense pain.

WESLEY, JOHN (1703–91) English evangelist who founded Methodism, opening the first Methodist chapel in 1739. He preached all around the country and it's estimated that he travelled 250,000 miles and gave 40,000 sermons. Nevertheless, he wrote reams: grammars, abridgements of the classics, collections of psalms, hymns and tunes, his own sermons and journals. In 1751 he married a widow who deserted him 25 years later. His *Journal* describes his journeys and spiritual odyssey.

WILLIAMS, KENNETH (1926–88) Much-loved actor, broadcaster and comedian, best known for his roles in the *Carry On* films. For over 40 years he kept a diary in which he made pen portraits, often poisonous, of his fellow thespians. 'You'll be in my diary!' he would threaten, and not hollowly. As Russell Davies, the editor of his diaries, published five years after his death, observed, 'Williams took against strangers instinctively until proved wrong.'

WILSON, EDWARD (1872–1912) British naturalist and Antarctic explorer, junior surgeon to the National Antarctic Expedition under Robert Falcon Scott, 1901–4. He was chief of scientific staff on the new Antarctic expedition, also under Scott, which reached the South Pole in January 1912. He perished with the rest of the expedition's members on the return journey.

WINDHAM, WILLIAM (1750–1810) British statesman, educated at Eton, and at Glasgow and Oxford universities. He was a friend of Samuel Johnson and Edmund Burke. He was one of the members of parliament charged with the impeachment of Warren Hastings. He helped William Cobbett found the *Political Register* and drew up plans for improving conditions of the military forces. His diary was published in 1866.

WOJNAROWICZ, DAVID (1955–92) Painter, photographer, film-maker, performance artist, AIDS activist, born in Red Bank, New Jersey. His father was a sailor; his mother was very young. His parents divorced and David, his older brother and sister were put in a sinister orphanage. At 12, he contemplated committing suicide. Living on the streets in New York, he dropped out of school and began to study art, hanging out with junkies and bohemians. He is the author of *The Waterfront Journals* and *In the Shadow of the American Dream*. He died of AIDS.

WOODFORDE, REV. JAMES (1740–1803) Born in Somerset, the sixth of seven children; his father was a vicar. He went to Winchester College before being admitted to New College, Oxford, where he began to write his diary. After graduation, he worked in Somerset, most of the time as assistant to his father. He never married, though he proposed to a cousin who, he told his diary, 'proved herself to me a mere Jilt'. In 1774, he found a good living in Norfolk worth £400. He was a man of modest aspirations and even more modest talent. His diary, published in five volumes, 1924–32, is his monument, full of mundane but fascinating detail and evidence of its author's gluttonous habits.

WOOLF, VIRGINIA (1882–1941) Novelist and essayist, born in London, daughter of Sir Leslie Stephen, first editor of the *Dictionary of National Biography*, and wife of Leonard Woolf, a publisher. Her social circle encompassed many of the leading intellectuals of her day, including the Bloomsbury Group. Her novels include *Mrs Dalloway*, *The Waves* and *To the Lighthouse*. Her essay *A Room of One's Own* is a landmark of feminist literature. With James Joyce, of whom she was not a fan, she is regarded as one of the innovators of the modern novel in English. *A Writer's Diary*, edited by her husband, was published in 1958. A five-volume edition of her diaries, edited by Quentin Bell, appeared in 1977–84.

WORDSWORTH, DOROTHY (1771–1855) Sister of William Wordsworth, born in Cockermouth, Cumberland. Throughout the poet's life, she was his constant companion and she was described by Coleridge as Wordsworth's 'exquisite sister'. Her celebrated journals were kept at Alfoxen in the Lake District in 1798, when her brother and Coleridge were composing *Lyrical Ballads*, and at Grasmere from 1800 to 1803, when she and Wordsworth were living at Dove Cottage.

WYATT, WOODROW (1918–97) Politician, journalist and bon viveur, who adored Margaret Thatcher. Most Sunday mornings between 1986 and 1990 he phoned and told her how wonderful she was. He was knighted in 1983 and created a life peer in 1987. His autobiography was called *Confessions of an Optimist*. His column in the *News of the World* was named – without a trace of irony – 'Voice of Reason'.

WYNDHAM, JOAN (1922–) Brought up a strict Catholic and educated at a boarding-school convent, she went to the Royal Academy of Dramatic Art (RADA). She was in the Women's Auxiliary Air Force (WAAF) for five years. After the war she opened Oxford's first Espresso Bar, cooked at pop concerts and dabbled in journalism. Her three part diaries-cum-autobiography are candid, eccentric and irreverent.

Bibliography

Ackerley, J. R., *My Sister and Myself. The Diaries of J.R. Ackerley*, edited by F. King, Hutchinson, London, 1982.

Alcott, Louisa May, *The Journals of Louisa May Alcott*, edited by J. Myerson and D. Shealy, Little Brown and Co., Boston, 1989.

Allingham, William, *William Allingham's Diary*, introduction by G. Grigson, Centaur Press, Fontwell, Sussex, 1967.

Asquith, Lady Cynthia, *The Diaries of Lady Cynthia Asquith 1915–18*, Century, London, 1968.

Barbellion, W. N. P., *The Journal of a Disappointed Man*, Penguin, London, 1948.

Bashkirtseff, Marie, *The Journal of Marie Bashkirtseff*, translated with an introduction by M. Blind, Cassell, London, 1890.

Beauvoir, Simone de, *America Day by Day*, translated by C. Cosman, Victor Gollancz, London, 1998.

Benn, Tony, *The Benn Diaries*, selected and abridged by R. Stone, Hutchinson, London, 1995.

Bennett, Alan, *Writing Home*, Faber & Faber, London, 1994.

Bennett, Arnold, *The Journals of Arnold Bennett*, selected and edited by F. Swinnerton, Penguin, London, 1954.

Birchall, Dearman, *The Diary of a Victorian Squire: Extracts from the Diaries and Letters of Dearman and Emily Birchall*, selected and introduced by D. Verey, Alan Sutton, Gloucester, 1983.

Bodichon, Barbara Leigh Smith, *An American Diary 1857–58*, edited by J. W. Reed, Jr., Routledge & Kegan Paul, London, 1972.

Boswell, James, *Boswell Laird of Auchinleck 1779–82: The Yale Editions of the Private Papers of James Boswell*, edited by J. W. Reed and F. A. Pottle, Edinburgh University Press, Edinburgh, 1993.

— *Boswell's London Journal 1762–63*, edited by F. A. Pottle, Heinemann, London, 1950.

— *Johnson's Journey to the Western Islands of Scotland: The Journal of a Tour to the Hebrides,* edited by R. W. Chapman, Oxford Paperbacks, London, 1970.

— *Boswell: The Ominous Years*, Heinemann, London 1963.

— *Life of Johnson*, Oxford University Press, London, 1969.

Boyle, Jimmy, *The Pain of Confinement: Prison Diaries*, Canongate, Edinburgh, 1984.

Brandreth, Gyles, *Breaking the Code: Westminster Diaries May 1990 to May 1997*, Weidenfeld & Nicolson, London, 1999.

Brecht, Bertolt, *Diaries 1920–22*, Eyre Methuen, London, 1975.

Brett, Simon, ed. *The Faber Book of Diaries*, Faber & Faber, 1987.

Brittain, Vera, *Chronicle of Youth: Vera*

Brittain's War Diary 1913–17, edited by A. Bishop with T. Smart, Book Club Associates, London, 1981.

— *Wartime Chronicle: Vera Brittain's Diary 1939–45*, edited by A. Bishop and Y. A. Bennett, Victor Gollancz, London, 1989.

Brown, Ford Madox, *The Diary of Ford Madox Brown*, edited by V. Surtees, Yale University Press, New Haven and London, 1981.

Browning, Elizabeth Barrett, *The Barretts at Hope End: The Early Diary of Elizabeth Barrett Browning*, edited and with introduction by E. Berridge, John Murray, London, 1974.

Bull, Deborah, *Dancing Away: A Covent Garden Diary*, Methuen, London, 1998.

Byron, Lord, *Selected Letters and Journals*, edited by L. A. Marchand, Picador, London, 1988.

Cadogan, Sir Alexander, *The Diaries of Sir Alexander Cadogan 1838–1945*, edited by D. Dilks, Cassell, London, 1971.

Camus, Albert, *American Journals*, Abacus, London, 1990.

— *Carnets 1935–42*, translation and introduction by P. Thody, Hamish Hamilton, London, 1963.

Carrington, Dora, *Carrington: Letters and Extracts from her Diaries*, selected and with an introduction by D. Garnett, Jonathan Cape, London, 1970.

Casson, Hugh, *Diary*, Macmillan, London, 1981.

Castle, Barbara, *The Castle Diaries 1964–70*, Weidenfeld & Nicolson, London, 1984.

Channon, 'Chips', *Chips: The Diaries of Sir Henry Channon*, edited by R. Rhodes James, Penguin, Harmondsworth, 1984.

Ciano, Count, *Ciano's Diary 1937–38*, translation and notes by A. Mayor with an introduction by M. Muggeridge, Methuen, London, 1952.

Clark, Alan, *Diaries*, Weidenfeld & Nicholson, London, 1993.

Clark, Ossie, *The Ossie Clark Diaries*, edited and introduced by H. Rous, Bloomsbury, London, 1998.

Cockburn, Lord Henry, *Circuit Journeys*, David Douglas, Edinburgh, 1889.

Cocteau, Jean, *Past Tense*, translated by R. Howard, Methuen, London, 1990.

Collis, Maurice, *Maurice Collis Diaries 1949–69*, edited by L. Collis, William Heinemann, London, 1977.

Coppola, Eleanor, *Notes on the Making of 'Apocalypse Now'*, Faber & Faber, London, 1979.

Coward, Noël, *The Noël Coward Diaries*, edited by G. Payn and S. Morley, Papermac, London, 1982.

Cox, Brian, *The Lear Diaries: The Story of the Royal National Theatre's Productions of Shakespeare's Richard II and King Lear*, Methuen, London, 1992.

Crossman, Richard, *The Crossman Diaries 1964–70: Selections from the Diaries of a Cabinet Minister*, edited and introduced by A. Howard, Book Club Associates, London, 1979.

Cullwick, Hannah, *The Diaries of Hannah Cullwick, Victorian Maidservant*, edited and introduced by L. Stanley, Virago, London, 1984.

Darwin, Charles, *The Voyage of the Beagle*, abridged and edited by M. E. Selsam, Harper & Brothers, New York, 1959.

Delacroix, Eugène, *The Journal of Eugène Delacroix: A Selection*, edited with an introduction by H.Wellington, translated from the French by L. Norton, Phaidon, Oxford, 1951.

Delafield, E.M., *The Diary of a Provincial Lady*, Virago, London, 1984.

Durrell, Lawrence, *Prospero's Cell*, Faber & Faber, London, 1945.

Ellis, Edward Robb, *A Diary of the Century: Tales from America's Greatest Diarist*, Kodansha America, New York, 1995.

Eno, Brian, *A Year with Swollen Appendices: Brian Eno's Diary*, Faber & Faber, London, 1996.

Evelyn, John, *The Diary of John Evelyn*, selected and edited by J. Bowle, Oxford University Press, Oxford, 1983.

Farmborough, Florence, *Nurse at the Russian Front: A Diary, 1914–18*, Book Club Associates, London, 1974.

Fox, Barclay, *Barclay Fox's Journal*, edited by R. L. Brett, Bell & Hyman, London, 1979.

Fox, Caroline, *The Journals of Caroline Fox, 1835–71: A Selection*, edited by W. Monk, Elek, London, 1972.

Frank, Anne, *Anne Frank: The Diary of a Young Girl*, edited by O. H. Frank and M. Pressler, translated by S. Massotty, Puffin, London, 1997.

Gaitskell, Hugh, *The Diary of Hugh Gaitskell 1945–56*, edited and introduced by P. M. Williams, Jonathan Cape, London, 1983.

Gascoyne, David, *Collected Journals 1936–42*, Skoob Books Publishing Ltd, London, 1991.

Gide, André, *The Journals of André Gide: Vol. III 1928–39*, translated and annotated by J. O'Brien, Secker & Warburg, London, 1949.

Gladwyn, Cynthia, *The Diaries of Cynthia Gladwyn*, edited by M. Jebb, Constable, London, 1995.

Goebbels, Josef, *The Goebbels Diaries 1939–41*, translated and edited by F. Taylor, Hamish Hamilton, London, 1982.

Goethe, Johann Wolfgang von, *Goethe: The Flight to Italy. Diary and Selected Letters*, new translation by T. J. Reed, Oxford World Classics, Oxford, 1999.

Goncourt, Edmond de and Jules de, *Pages from the Goncourt Journal*, edited, translated and introduced by R. Baldick, Oxford University Press, Oxford, 1978.

Grant, Elizabeth, of Rothiemurchus, *The Highland Lady in Ireland*, Canongate, Edinburgh, 1991.

Grant, Richard E., *With Nails: The Film Diaries of Richard E. Grant*, Picador, London, 1996.

Grenfell, Joyce, *The Time of my Life: Entertaining the Troops – her Wartime Journals*, edited by J. Roose-Evans, Sceptre, London, 1998.

Greville, Charles, *The Greville Diary, Vol. II*, edited by P. Whitwell Wilson, Heinemann, London, 1927.

Guevara, Ernesto Che, *The Bolivian Diary of Ernesto Che Guevara,* edited by Mary-Alice Waters, Pathfinder, New York, 1994.

Guinness, Alec, *My Name Escapes Me: The Diary of a Retiring Actor*, Hamish Hamilton, London, 1996.

Hall, Peter, *Peter Hall's Diaries: The Story of a Dramatic Battle*, edited by J. Goodwin, Hamish Hamilton, London, 1983.

Herzberg, Abel J., *Between Two Streams: A Diary from Bergen-Belsen*, translated from the Dutch by J. Santcross, I. B. Tauris, London, 1997.

Hillesum, Etty, *Etty Hillesum: An Interrupted Life. The Diaries 1941–43* and *Letters from Westerbork*, Henry Holt, New York, 1986. The complete text of *An Interrupted Life* is available from Persephone Books, London.

Hone, Philip, *The Diary of Philip Hone 1828–51* (two volumes), edited by A. Nevins, Dodd, Mead & Co., New York, 1927.

Hopkins, Gerard Manley, *The Journals and Papers of Gerard Manley Hopkins*, edited by H. House, completed by G. Storey, Oxford Univesity Press, London, 1959.

Isherwood, Christopher, *Christopher Isherwood Diaries, Vol One: 1939–60*, edited and introduced by K. Bucknell, Methuen, London, 1966.

Jacob, Violet, *Diaries and Letters from India 1895–1900*, Canongate, Edinburgh, 1990.

James, Alice, *The Diary of Alice James*, edited and with an introduction by L. Edel, Penguin, Harmondsworth, 1982.

Jarman, Derek, *Modern Nature: The Journals of Derek Jarman*, Century, London, 1991.

Jenkins, Roy, *European Diary 1977–81*, Collins, London, 1989.

Johnson, Alexandra, *The Hidden Writer: Diaries and the Creative Life*, Anchor Books, New York, 1998.

Jordan, Neil, *Michael Collins Film Diary and Screenplay*, Vintage, London, 1996.

Kafka, Franz, *The Diaries of Franz Kafka*, (two volumes, 1910–13 and 1914–23), edited by M. Brod, Secker & Warburg, London, 1948 and 1949.

Kemble, Fanny, *Fanny Kemble: The American Journals*, edited by E. Mavor, Weidenfeld & Nicolson, London, 1990.

Kessler, Harry, *The Diaries of a Cosmopolitan Count: Harry Kessler 1918–37*, translated and edited by C. Kessler, Weidenfeld & Nicolson, London, 1971.

Kilvert, Rev. Francis, *Kilvert's Diary 1870–79*, selected and edited by W. Plomer, Penguin, London, 1977.

King, Cecil, *The Cecil King Diary 1965–70*, Jonathan Cape, London, 1971.

— *The Cecil King Diary 1970–74*, Jonathan Cape, London, 1975.

Klemperer, Victor, *I Will Bear Witness: A Diary of the Nazi Years 1933–41*, translated by M. Chalmers, Random House, New York, 1998.

Lascelles, Sir Alan 'Tommy', *End of an Era: Letters and Journals of Sir Alan Lascelles*, edited by D. Hart-Davis, Hamish Hamilton, London, 1986.

Last, Nella, *Nella Last's War: A Mother's Diary 1939–45*, edited by R. Borad and S. Fleming, Falling Wall Press, Bristol, 1981.

Le Ruez, Nan, *Jersey Occupation Diary: Nan Le Ruez, Her Story of the German Occupation 1940–45*, Seaflower Books, St Helier, Jersey, 1994.

Lees-Milne, James, *Ancient as the Hills: Diaries 1973–74*, John Murray, London, 1997.

— *Through Wood and Dale: Diaries 1975–78*, John Murray, London, 1998.

Lewis, C. S., *All My Road Before Me: The Diary of C.S. Lewis 1922–27*, edited by W. Hooper, Fount, London, 1991.

Lewis, Norman, *Naples '44: An Intelligence Officer in the Italian Labyrinth*, Eland, London, 1989.

Lindbergh, Anne Morrow, *Bring Me a Unicorn: Diaries and Letters of Anne Morrow Lindbergh 1922–28*, Chatto & Windus, London, 1972.

— *Locked Rooms and Open Doors: Diaries and Letters of Anne Morrow Lindbergh 1933–35*, Harcourt Brace Jovanovich, New York, 1974.

Lockhart, Sir Robert Bruce, *Diaries of Sir Robert Bruce Lockhart: Vol I 1915–38*, edited by K. Young, Macmillan, London, 1973.

Longford, Lord, *Diary of a Year*, Weidenfeld & Nicolson, London, 1982.

Lowndes, Marie Belloc, *Diaries and Letters of Marie Belloc Lowndes 1911–47*, edited by S. Lowndes, Chatto & Windus, London, 1971.

Maclean, Alasdair, *Night Falls on Ardnamurchan: The Twilight of a Crofting Family*, Victor Gollancz, London, 1984.

Macnaughtan, Sarah Brown, *A Woman's Diary of the War*, Thomas Nelson & Sons, London, 1915.

Macready, Charles, *The Journal of William Charles Macready*, edited by J. C. Trewin, Longman, London, 1967.

Mahler-Werfel, Alma, *Diaries 1898–1902*, selected and translated by A. Beaumont, Faber & Faber, London, 1998.

Mallon, Thomas, *A Book of One's Own: People and their Diaries*, Pan Books, London, 1985.

Mansel, Captain John, *The Mansel Diaries: The Diaries of Captain John Mansel Prisoner-of-War – and Camp Forger – in Germany 1940–45*, edited by E. G. C. Beckwith, T. D., privately published, 1977.

Mansfield, Katherine, *Journal of Katherine Mansfield*, edited by J. Middleton Murry, Constable, London, 1954.

Matthew, Christopher, *Diary of a Somebody*, Hutchinson, London, 1981.

Mencken, H. L., *The Diary of H. L. Mencken*, edited by C. A. Fecher, Alfred A. Knopf, New York, 1989.

Mitchison, Naomi, *Among You Taking Notes: The Wartime Diary of Naomi Mitchison 1939–45*, edited by D. Sheridan, Victor Gollancz, London, 1985.

Mole, Adrian, *The Growing Pains of Adrian Mole*, Sue Townsend, Methuen, London, 1984.

Mountbatten of Burma, Earl, *From Shore to Shore, the Final Years: The Diaries of Earl Mountbatten of Burma, 1953–79*, edited by P. Ziegler, Collins, London, 1989.

Muggeridge, Malcolm, *Like it Was: The Diaries of Malcolm Muggeridge*, selected and edited by J. Bright-Holmes, Collins, London, 1981.

Munby, Arthur F., *Munby Man of Two Worlds: The Life and Diaries of Arthur F. Munby 1828–1910*, John Murray, London, 1972.

Musil, Robert, *Diaries 1899–1941*, translated by P. Payne, edited by Mark Mirsky, Basic Books, New York, 1998.

Nicolson, Harold, *Harold Nicolson Diaries and Letters 1930–39, 1939–45* and *1945–62*, Fontana, London, 1969, 1970, 1971.

— *Vita and Harold: The Letters of Vita Sackville and Harold Nicolson 1910–62*, edited by N. Nicolson. Phoenix, London, 1993.

Nin, Anaïs, *Fire: From a Journal of Love, The Unexpurgated Diary of Anaïs Nin 1934–37*, Peter Owen, London 1996.

— *The Early Diary of Anaïs Nin 1927–31*, Peter Owen, London, 1994.

— *Journals of a Wife: The Early Diary of Anaïs Nin*, Quartet, London, 1986.

Origo, Iris, *War in the Val D'Orcia: An Italian War Diary 1943–44*, David R. Godine, Boston.

Orton, Joe, *The Orton Diaries*, edited by J. Lahr, Methuen, London, 1986.

Partridge, Frances, *Good Company Diaries 1967–70*, Harper Collins, London, 1994.

— *Hanging on Diaries 1960–63*, Collins, London, 1990.

— *Life Regained Diaries 1970–72*, Weidenfeld & Nicolson, London, 1998.

The Past Times Book of Diaries, Past Times, Oxford, 1998.

Pavese, Cesare, *This Business of Living: Diary 1935–50*, edited and translated by A. E. Murch, Peter Owen, London, 1961.

Pearson, Drew, *Diaries 1949–1959*, edited by T. Abell, Jonathan Cape, London, 1974.

Pepys, Elizabeth, *The Diary of Elizabeth Pepys*, edited by D. Spender, Grafton, London, 1991.

Pepys, Samuel, *Everybody's Pepys: The Diary of Samuel Pepys 1660–69*, abridged and edited by O. F. Morshead, G. Bell & Sons, London, 1972.

Plath, Sylvia, *The Journals of Sylvia Plath*, foreword by Ted Hughes, Ted Hughes consulting editor and Frances McCullough, editor, Anchor Books, Doubleday, New York, 1998.

Potter, Beatrix, *The Journal of Beatrix Potter*, transcribed from her code writings by Leslie Linden. Abridged with an introduction by G. Cavaliero, F. Warne, London, 1986.

Pougy, Liane de, *My Blue Notebooks*, Century Publishing, London, 1986.

Powell, Anthony, *Journals 1982–86*, Heinemann, London, 1995.

— *Journals 1987–89*, Heinemann, London, 1996.

— *Journals 1990–92*, Heinemann, London, 1998.

Powell, Dawn, *The Diaries of Dawn Powell 1931–65*, edited with an introduction by T. Page, Steerforth Press, South Royalton, Vermont, 1995.

Pym, Barbara, *A Very Private Eye: The Diaries, Letters and Notebooks of Barbara Pym*, edited by Hazel Holt and Hilary Pym, Macmillan, London, 1984.

Rabe, John, *The Good German of Nanking: The Diaries of John Rabe*, edited by E. Wickert, translated by J. E. Woods, Little, Brown & Co., 1999.

Ranfurly, Countess of, *To War with Whitaker: The Wartime Diaries of the Countess of Ranfurly 1939–45*, Mandarin, London, 1997.

Reich, Wilhelm, *Beyond Psychology: Letters and Journals 1934–39*, edited and with an introduction by M. Boyd Higgins, Farrar, Straus & Giroux, New York, 1994.

Reith, Lord, *The Reith Diaries*, edited by C. Stuart, Collins, London, 1975.

Ritchie, Charles, *The Siren Years: Undiplomatic Diaries 1937–45*, Macmillan, London, 1974.

Robinson, Henry Crabb, *The Diary of Henry Crabb Robinson: An Abridgement*, edited with an introduction by D. Hudson, Oxford University Press, London, 1967.

Rorem, Ned, *Setting the Tone: Essays and a Diary*, Limelight Editions, New York, 1984.

Sand, George, *The Intimate Journal*, edited and translated by M. Jenney Howe, Academy Chicago Publishers, Chicago, 1984.

Sarton, May, *The House by the Sea: A Journal*, The Women's Press, London, 1995.

Sassoon, Siegfried, *Siegfried Sassoon Diaries 1920–22*, edited by R. Hart-Davis, Faber & Faber, London, 1981.

— *Siegfried Sassoon Diaries 1923–25*, edited by R. Hart-Davis, Faber & Faber, London, 1985.

Scott, Captain Robert Falcon, *Scott's Last Journey*, edited by P. King, foreword by B. Bainbridge, Duckworth & Co., 1999.

Scott, Sir Walter, *The Journal of Sir Walter Scott*, edited by W. E. K. Anderson, Canongate, Edinburgh, 1998.

Shelley, Mary, *The Journals of Mary Shelley: Volume II 1822–44*, edited by P. R. Feldman and D. Scott-Kilvert, Clarendon Press, Oxford, 1987.

Shirer, William L., *Berlin Diary 1934–41: The Rise of the Third Reich*, Promotional Reprint Company, London, 1997.

Smart, Elizabeth, *Necessary Secrets: The First Volume of Elizabeth Smart's Journals*, edited by A. Van Wart, Paladin, London, 1992.

Soutar, William, *Diaries of a Dying Man*, edited by A. Scott, Chambers, Edinburgh, 1988.

Spender, Stephen, *Journals 1939–83*, edited by J. Goldsmith, Faber & Faber, London, 1985.

Steinbeck, John, *Journal of a Novel*, Mandarin, London, 1991.

Stendhal, *The Private Diaries of Stendhal*, edited and translated by R. Sage, Victor Gollancz, London, 1955.

Stevenson, Frances, *Lloyd George: A Diary by Frances Stevenson*, edited by A. J. P. Taylor, Hutchinson, London, 1971.

Stevenson, Robert Louis, *The Cévennes Journal: Notes on a Journey through the French Highlands*, Mainstream, Edinburgh, 1978.

Stott, Gordon, *Lord Advocate's Diary 1961–66*, Aberdeen University Press, Aberdeen, 1991.

Strong, George Templeton, *The Diary of George Templeton Strong*, edited by A. Nevins and M. Halsey, Macmillan, New York, 1952.

Strong, Sir Roy, *The Roy Strong Diaries 1967–87*, Weidenfeld & Nicolson, London, 1997.

Thoreau, Henry David, *A Writer's Journal*, selected, edited and introduced by L. Stapleton, Heinemann, London, 1961.

Tolstoy, Sofia, *The Diaries of Sofia Tolstoy*, translated by C. Porter, Jonathan Cape, London, 1985.

Tolstoy, Leo, *Tolstoy's Diaries*, edited and translated by R. F. Christian, Flamingo, London, 1994.

Turner, Thomas, *The Diary of Thomas Turner 1754–65*, edited by D. Vaisey, Oxford University Press, Oxford, 1984.

Velmans, Edith, *Edith's Book*, Viking, London, 1998.

Victoria, Queen, *Queen Victoria in her*

Letters and Journals, selection by C. Hibbert, Penguin, London, 1985.

Warhol, Andy, *The Andy Warhol Diaries*, edited by P. Hackett, Pan, London 1992.

Waugh, Evelyn, *The Diaries of Evelyn Waugh*, edited by M. Davie, Weidenfeld & Nicolson, London, 1976.

Webb, Beatrice, *The Diary of Beatrice Webb Vol I 1873–92: Glitter Around and Darkness Within*, edited by N. and J. MacKenzie, Virago, London, 1986.

— *The Diary of Beatrice Webb Vol II 1892–1905: All the Good Things of Life*, edited by N. and J. MacKenzie, Virago, London, 1986.

Welch, Denton, *The Journals of Denton Welch*, edited by M. De-la-Noy, Penguin, Harmondsworth, 1987.

Wesley, John, *The Journal of John Wesley: A Selection*, edited with an introduction by E. Jay, Oxford University Press, Oxford, 1987.

Williams, Kenneth, *The Kenneth Williams Diaries*, edited by R. Davies, Harper Collins, London, 1993.

Wilson, Edmund, *The Fifties*, edited and introduced by L. Edel, Macmillan, London, 1986.

Wilson, Edward, *Diary of the Discovery Expedition to the Antarctic Regions 1901–04*, edited by A. Savours, Blandford Press, London, 1966.

Wojnarowicz, David, *In the Shadow of the American Dream: The Diaries of David Wojnarowicz*, edited and with an introduction by A. Scholder, Grove Press, New York, 1999.

Woodforde, James, *The Diary of a Country Parson*, (Vol I and Vol V, 1797–1802), edited by J. Beresford, Oxford University Press, London, 1968.

Woolf, Virginia, *A Moment's Liberty: The Shorter Diary*, edited by A. Olivier Bell, introduction by Q. Bell, Hogarth Press, London, 1990.

— *A Writer's Diary*, edited by L. Woolf, Hogarth Press, London, 1975.

Wordsworth, Dorothy, *Journals of Dorothy Wordsworth* (second edition), edited by M. Moorman, Oxford Paperbacks, London, 1976.

Wyatt, Woodrow, *The Journals of Woodrow Wyatt*, (Vols I and II), edited by S. Curtis, Macmillan, London, 1998 and 1999.

Wyndham, Joan, *Love is Blue: A Wartime Diary*, Flamingo, London 1987.

— *Anything Once*, Flamingo, London, 1993.

Permissions Acknowledgements

Various publishers and Estates have generously given permission to use extracts from the following copyright works:

From *My Sister and Myself* by J. R. Ackerley. Copyright by The Estate of J. R. Ackerley 1982. Reprinted by permission of David Higham Associates Ltd. From *The Diaries of Lady Cynthia Asquith* by Lady Cynthia Asquith. Copyright by Michael and Simon Asquith. Reprinted by permission of The Random House Group Ltd. From *America Day by Day* by Simone de Beauvoir, trans. and edited by Carol Cosman. Copyright by Editions Gallimand, 1954, by Regents of the University of California, 1998. Reprinted by permission of The Orion Publishers Group Ltd. and the Regents of the University of California. From *The Benn Diaries* by Tony Benn. Copyright by Tony Benn 1995. Reprinted by permission of Curtis Brown Ltd, London of behalf of Tony Benn. From *Writing Home* by Alan Bennett. Copyright by Forelake Ltd 1994. Reprinted by permission of the publishers, Faber & Faber. Copyright by Alan Bennett 1994 and PFD on behalf of Alan Bennett. From *The Journals of Arnold Bennett* by Arnold Bennett. Reprinted by permission of A.P. Watt Ltd, Literary Agents, on behalf of Madam V.M. Eldin. *From The Pain of Confinement: Prison Diaries* by Jimmy Boyle. Copyright by Jimmy Boyle 1984. Reprinted by permission of the publishers, Canongate Books. From *Breaking the Code* by Gyles Brandreth. Copyright by Gyles Brandreth 1999. Reprinted by permission of The Orion Publishing Group Ltd and Sheil Land Associates Ltd. From *Chronicle of Youth* by Vera Brittain. Diary copyright by The Literary Executors for the Vera Brittain Estate, 1981. Reprinted by permission of Vera Brittain's literary executors, Mark Bostridge and Rebecca Williams. From *Wartime Chronicle* by Vera Brittain. Copyright by The Literary Executors for the Vera Brittain Estate. Reprinted by permission of Vera Brittain's literary executors, Mark Bostridge and Rebecca Williams. From *The Diary of Ford Madox Brown* by Ford Madox Brown. Copyright by Yale University, 1981. Reprinted by permission of the publishers, Yale University Press. From *Dancing Away: A Covent Garden Diary* by Deborah Bull. Copyright by Deborah Bull 1998. Reprinted by permission of the publishers, Methuen. From *American Journals* by Albert Camus, translated by Hugh Levick (Hamish Hamilton, 1989). Copyright by Editions Gallimard 1978. Copyright © by Paragon House,

1988 (first English language edition). Extracts from pp. 63–4, 93, 140 reprinted by permission of Penguin Books Ltd. From *Carnets 1935–1942* by Albert Camus. Copyright by Librairie Gallimard 1962. Extracts from pages pp. 28, 108, 421 reprinted by permission of Penguin Books Ltd. From *Carrington* by Dora Carrington. Copyright by David Garnett and The Sophie Partridge Trust, 1970. Reprinted by permission of the publishers, Jonathan Cape and A.P. Watt on behalf of the Executor of the Estate of David Garnett and Sophie Partridge. From *Diary* by Hugh Casson. Copyright Hugh Casson Ltd. Reprinted by permission of Sir Hugh Casson Ltd. From *The Castle Diaries 1964–1970* by Barbara Castle. Copyright by Barbara Castle 1984. Reprinted by permission of David Higham Associates Ltd. From *Chips: The Diaries of Sir Henry Channon*, edited by Robert Rhodes James. Copyright Paul Channon 1967, introduction and commentary copyright by Robert Rhodes James 1967. Reprinted by permission of The Orion Publishing Group Ltd. From *Ciano's Diary 1937–1938* by Count Ciano. Reprinted by permission of David Higham Associates Ltd. From *Diaries* by Alan Clark. Copyright by Alan Clark 1993. Reprinted by permission of The Orion Publishing Group Ltd and PFD on behalf of the Estate of Alan Clark. From *Past Tense* by Jean Cocteau. Copyright by Editions Gallimard Paris, 1985. English translation © by Harcourt Brace Jovanovich Inc., 1988. Reprinted by permission of the publishers, Methuen. From *Maurice Collis Diaries 1949–1969* by Maurice Collis. Copyright by Louise Collis 1977. Reprinted by permission of Louise Collis. From *Notes: On the Making of Apocalypse Now* by Eleanor Coppola. Copyright by Eleanor Coppola, 1979. Reprinted by permission of the publishers, Faber & Faber and Georges Borchardt, Inc., for the author. From *The Noel Coward Diaries*, edited by Graham Payn and Sheridan Morley. Copyright by Graham Payn 1982. Reprinted by permission of The Orion Publishing Group Ltd. From *The Lear Diaries* by Brian Cox. Copyright by Brian Cox 1992. Reprinted by permission of the publishers, Methuen. From *The Crossman Diaries 1964–1970: Selections from the Diaries of a Cabinet Minister*, edited by Anthony Howard. Copyright by the Estate of R.H.S. Crossman 1979. Extracts from pages 25, 100, 172, 216, and 427 reprinted by permission of Penguin Books Ltd and Henry Holt & Co., LLC. From *The Diaries of Hannah Cullwick* by Hannah Cullwick. Copyright by Liz Stanley 1984. Reprinted by permission of the publishers, Little, Brown & Co. From The Journal *of Eugène Delacroix* by Eugène Delacroix. Copyright by Phaidon Press Ltd., 1951, 1995. Reproduced by permission of the publishers, Phaidon Press Limited. From *Diary of a Provincial Lady* by E.M. Delafield. Copyright by The Estate of E.M. Delafield 1947. Reprinted by permission of the publishers, Little, Brown & Co. and PFD on behalf of the Estate of E.M. Delafield. From *Prospero's Cell* by Lawrence Durrell. Copyright by Lawrence Durrell 1945. Reprinted by permission of the publishers, Faber & Faber and Curtis Brown Ltd. From *A Year with Swollen Appendices* by Brian Eno. Copyright by Brian Eno 1996. Reprinted by permission of the publishers, Faber & Faber. From *Anne Frank: The Diary of a Young Girl* by Anne Frank, edited by Otto H. Frank and Mirjam Pressler, trans. Susan Massotty. Copyright of English translation by Doubleday, 1995. Extract from p. 162 reprinted by permission of Penguin Books Ltd and Doubleday, a division of Random House, Inc. From *Collected Journals 1936–42* by David Gascoyne. Copyright by David Gascoyne, 1978, 1990, 1991. Reprinted by permission of Skoob Books Publishing Ltd. From *The Journals of André Gide*, Vol III 1928–1939 by André Gide. Copyright by Alfred A. Knopf 1949. Reprinted by permission of The Random House Group Ltd and Random House Inc. From *The Diaries of Cynthia Gladwyn* by Cynthia Gladwyn. Copyright by Miles Jebb 1995. Reprinted by permission of the publishers, Constable & Robinson Publishing Ltd. From *The Goebbels Diaries 1939–41* by Josef Goebbels. Copyright by Fred Taylor and Hamish Hamilton 1982. Reprinted by permission of Abner Stein. From *Goethe. The Flight to Italy: Diary and Selected Letters* by Goethe, trans. T.J. Reed. Copyright by T.J. Reed, 1999. Reprinted by permission of Oxford University Press. From *Pages from the Goncourt Journal* by Edmond and Jules de Goncourt. Copyright by Robert Baldick 1962. Reprinted by permission of David Higham Associates Ltd. From *With Nails* by Richard E. Grant. Copyright by Richard E. Grant 1996 and 1998. Reprinted by permission of the publishers, Macmillan. Extracts on pages 40, 52–3, 56–7 and 219 reprinted by permission of The Overlook Press. From *The Time of my Life* by Joyce Grenfell. Copyright by Reginald Grenfell and James Roose-Evans 1989. Reprinted by permission of David Higham Associates Ltd. From *The Bolivian Diary of Ernesto Che Guevara*, edited by Mary-Alice Waters. Copyright by Pathfinder Press, 1994. Reprinted by permission of Pathfinder Press. From *My Name Escapes Me* by Alec Guinness. Copyright by Alec Guinness 1996. Reprinted by permission of Christopher Sinclair-Stevenson. From *Peter Hall's Diaries* by Peter Hall. Copyright by Petard Productions Ltd., 1983. Copyright © Peter Hall. Reprinted by permission of Curtis Brown Ltd, London, on behalf of Peter Hall. From *Between Two Streams* by Abel J. Herzberg. Copyright by the Estate of Abel J. Herzberg, Amsterdam, 1989. Reprinted by permission of I.B. Tauris & Co Ltd. From *An Interrrupted Life: The Diaries of Etty Hillesum 1941–1943* by Etty Hillesum, trans. Arno Pomerans. English translation copyright by Random House, Inc. 1986. Reprinted by permission of Balans BV, Amsterdam, Persephone Books, London and Pantheon Books, a division of Random House, Inc. From *The Journals and Papers of Gerard Manley Hopkins*, edited by Humphry House, completed by Graham Storey. Copyright by The Society of Jesus, 1959. Reprinted by permission of Oxford University Press. From *Christopher*

Isherwood Diaries, Vol One: 1939–1960 by Christopher Isherwood. Copyright by Don Bachardy 1966. Reprinted by permission of The Random House Publishing Group Ltd. From *Modern Nature* by Derek Jarman. Copyright by Derek Jarman. Reprinted by permission of The Random House Group Ltd on behalf of Derek Jarman and The Overlook Press, Woodstock, NY. From *European Diary 1977–1981* by Roy Jenkins. Copyright © Roy Jenkins 1969. Reprinted by permission of PFD on behalf of Roy Jenkins. From *Michael Collins Film Diary and Screenplay* by Neil Jordan. Copyright by Neil Jordan 1996. Reprinted by permission The Random House Group Ltd. From *The Diaries of Franz Kafka*, 2 vols, 1910–1913 by Franz Kafka, trans. Joseph Kresh and edited by Max Brod. Copyright by Schocken Books 1948, renewed 1976. 1914–1923 by Franz Kafka from *The Diaries of Franz Kafka, 1914–1923* by Franz Kafka, trans. Martin Greenberg, edited by Max Brod. Copyright by Schocken Books, 1949, renewed 1977. Reprinted by permission of Schocken Books a division of Random House, Inc. From *Fanny Kemble: The American Journals* by Fanny Kemble. Compilation and original editorial matter copyright © Elizabeth Mavor. Reprinted by permission of Curtis Brown Ltd, London, on behalf of Elizabeth Mavor. From *The Diaries of a Cosmopolitan* by Count Harry Kessler. Copyright by Weidenfeld & Nicolson, Ltd, London. 1971. Reprinted by permission of The Orion Publishing Group, Ltd and Grove/Atlantic, Inc. From *The Cecil King Diary 1965–70* and *The Cecil King Diary 1970–74* by Cecil King. Copyright by Cecil King 1971 and 1975. Reprinted by permission of The Random House Group, Ltd. From *I Will Bear Witness: A Diary of the Nazi Years 1933–1941* by Victor Klemperer, trans. Martin Chalmers. Translation, preface, and notes copyright by Martin Chalmers 1998. Reprinted by permission of The Orion Publishing Group Ltd and Random House, Inc. From *End of an Era: Letters and Journals of Sir Alan Lascelles*, edited by Duff Hart-Davis. Copyright by Lavinia Hankinson and Caroline Erskine 1986. Reprinted by permission of Lavinia Hankinson and Caroline Erskine. From *Jersey Occupation Diary* by Nan Le Ruez. Copyright by Nan Du Feu 1994. Reprinted by permission of Seaflower Books, St Helier Jersey, on behalf of the author Nan Le Ruez. From *Ancient as the Hills* and *Through Wood and Dale* by James Lees-Milne. Copyright by James Lees-Milne 1997 and The Estate of James Lees-Milne 1998. Reprinted by permission of David Higham Associates Ltd. From *All My Road Before Me* by C.S. Lewis. Copyright by C.S. Lewis Pte Ltd, 1991. Reprinted by permission of The C.S. Lewis Company and Harcourt Inc. From *Naples '44* by Norman Lewis. Copyright by Norman Lewis 1978. Published in the UK by Eland Books, and in the USA by Henry Holt and Company INC. Reproduced by permission of the author, c/o Rogers, Coleridge & White Ltd, 20 Powis Mews, London WII IJN. From *Bring Me a Unicorn* by Anne Morrow Lindbergh.

Reprinted by permission of Peter Owen Ltd, London and the Author's Representative, Gunther Stuhlman. From *Journals of a Wife* by Anaïs Nin. Copyright by Rupert Pole as the Trustee for the Anaïs Nin Trust 1983. Reprinted by permission by Peter Owen Ltd, London. From *War in the Val D'Orcia* by Iris Origo. Copyright by Iris Origo 1947. Reprinted by permission of David R. Godine, Publisher, Inc. From *The Orton Diaries* by Joe Orton. Copyright by The Estate of Joe Orton. Reprinted by permission of the publishers, Methuen. From *Hanging On* by Frances Partridge. Copyright by Frances Partridge 1990. Reprinted by permission of the author, c/o Rogers, Coleridge & White Ltd, 20 Powis Mews, London W11 1JN. From *Life Regained* by Frances Partridge. Copyright by Frances Partridge. Reprinted by permission of The Orion Publishing Group Ltd. From *This Business of Living* by Cesare Pavese. Copyright in the translation by Alma E. Murch. Reprinted by permission of Peter Owen Ltd, London. From *The Journals of Sylvia Plath* by Sylvia Plath, consulting editor Ted Hughes, and Frances McCullough, editor. Text of the journals copyright by Ted Hughes, as the Executor of the Estate of Sylvia Plath, 1982. Additional text copyright by Frances McCullough, 1982. Reprinted by permission of Doubleday, a division of Random House, Inc., and Faber & Faber Ltd. From *The Journal of Beatrix Potter 1881–1897*, transcribed from her code writings by Leslie Linder. Copyright by Frederick Warne & Co., 1966, 1989. Reprinted by permission by the publishers, Frederick Warne & Co. From *My Blue Notebooks* by Liane de Pougy. Copyright Liane de Pougy. Reprinted by permission of Librairie Plon, SA. From *Journals 1987–1989* and *Journals 1990–1992* by Anthony Powell. Copyright by Anthony Powell 1996 and 1997. Reprinted by permission of David Higham Associates, Ltd. From *The Diaries of Dawn Powell* by Dawn Powell. Copyright by The Estate of Dawn Powell 1995. Reprinted by permission of the publishers, Steerforth Press of South Royalton, Vermont. From *A Very Private Eye* by Barbara Pym. Copyright by Hilary Walton 1984. Reprinted by permission of the publishers, Macmillan. From *The Good German of Nanking* by John Rabe. Reprinted by permission of the publishers, Little, Brown & Co. From *To War with Whitaker* by The Countess of Ranfurly. Copyright by The Countess of Ranfurly 1994. Reprinted by permission of The Random House Group Ltd and PFD on behalf of Hermione, Countess of Ranfurly. From *The Reith Diaries* edited by Charles Stuart. Copyright by the Trustees of the late Lord Reith of Stonehaven and Charles Stuart 1975. Reprinted by permission of the BBC. From *The Siren Years* by Charles Ritchie. Copyright by Charles Ritchie 1974. Reprinted by permission of the publishers, Macmillan, 1974. From *Setting the Tone* by Ned Rorem. Copyright by Ned Rorem, 1983. Reprinted by permission of Georges Borchardt, Inc., for the author. From *The Intimate Journal* by George Sand. Copyright by Marie Jenney Howe, 1929.

and PFD on behalf of The Estate of Kenneth Williams. From *In the Shadow of the American Dream* by David Wojnarowicz. Edited and with an introduction by Amy Scholder. Copyright by The Estate of David Wojnarowicz 1999. Reprinted by permission of the publishers, Grove/Atlantic Inc. From *A Moment's Liberty* by Virginia Woolf. Copyright by the Estate of Virginia Woolf. Reprinted by permission of The Random House Group Ltd. Excerpts originally published in *The Diary of Virginia Woolf*, Vols I–V. Copyright for all volumes by Quentin Bell and Angelica Garnett: Vol.1 1915–19 – 1977; Vol.2 1920–24 – 1978; Vol.3 1925–30 – 1980; Vol.4 1931–35 – 1982; Vol.5 1936–41 – 1984. Reprinted by permission of Harcourt Inc. From *A Writer's Diary* by Virginia Woolf. Copyright by Leonard Woolf 1954 and renewed by Quentin Bell and Angelica Garnett 1982. Reprinted by permission of The Random House Group Ltd. and Harcourt Inc. From *The Journals of Woodrow Wyatt*, vols 1 and 2 by Woodrow Wyatt. Copyright by the Estate of Woodrow Wyatt. Reprinted by permission of the publishers, Macmillan. From *Love is Blue* by Joan Wyndham. Copyright by Joan Wyndham 1986. Reprinted by permission of The Random House Group Ltd. From *Anything Once* by Joan Wyndham. Copyright by Joan Wyndham 1992. Reprinted by permission of the Peters Fraser & Dunlop Group Ltd. Permission has been sought for several extracts which are not cited above. Every effort was made to chase these permissions before this book went to press.

Index of Diarists

Ackerley, J. R., 13 March 1949, 22 March 1953, 26 May 1955, 27 July 1949, 11 Oct 1950, 21 Oct 1948, 19 Dec 1952, 20 Dec 1950, 22 Dec 1952

Alcott, Louisa May, 14 March 1858, 26 Aug 1868, 1 Nov 1868

Allingham, William, 1 Feb 1867, 18 Feb 1867, 22 June 1866, 28 June 1871, 15 July 1866, 29 July 1873, 5 Aug 1880, 14 Sept 1865, 19 Sept 1880, 13 Oct 1880, 21 Oct 1880, 22 Oct 1868, 1 Nov 1869, 11 Nov 1872, 24 Dec 1868, 28 Dec 1868

Asquith, Lady Cynthia, 6 Jan 1917, 20 Jan 1917, 26 April 1917, 6 May 1915, 14 June 1916, 13 Oct 1915, 11 Nov 1915, 26 Dec 1916, 29 Dec 1916

Barbellion, W. N. P., 15 Feb 1913, 7 March 1914, 30 May 1915, 31 May 1915, 1 June 1917, 27 June 1913, 22 July 1910, 1 Aug 1914, 2 Aug 1914, 2 Aug 1915, 6 Aug 1915, 7 Aug 1915, 12 Aug 1914, 5 Sept 1917, 15 Oct 1914, 22 Oct 1913, 24 Oct 1914, 4 Nov 1914

Bashkirtseff, Marie, 6 July 1874, 16 July 1879, 23 July 1880, 20 Aug 1879, 15 Nov 1879

Beauvoir, Simone de, 31 Jan 1947, 4 Feb 1947, 10 Feb 1947, 16 Feb 1947, 2 April 1947, 3 April 1947, 19 April 1947, 19 May 1947

Benn, Tony, 16 Jan 1979, 18 Jan 1977, 21 Jan 1979 28 Jan 1978, 25 March 1959, 1 April 1985, 13 April 1945, 25 May 1964, 15 June 1982, 22 July 1964, 23 July 1990, 29 July 1981, 15 Aug 1990, 30 Sept 1990, 1 Dec 1990, 2 Dec 1958

Bennett, Alan, 2 Jan 1990, 8 Feb 1983, 3 March 1983, 31 March 1984, 16 April 1989, 20 May 1983, 4 June 1982, 15 June 1982, 2 July 1981, 10 July 1980, 8 Sept 1980, 27 Sept 1989, 4 Dec 1982, 11 Dec 1980

Bennett, Arnold, 11 Jan 1909, 27 Jan 1897, 21 Feb 1904, 26 March 1925, 9 April 1905, 21 April 1904, 4 May 1926, 16 May 1917, 9 June 1917, 25 July 1917, 1 Aug 1897, 2 Sept 1927, 25 Sept 1909, 26 Sept 1928, 1 Oct 1909, 7 Oct 1924, 31 Oct 1907, 31 Dec 1899

Benson, A. C., 4 April 1903, 27 July 1911

Birchall, Dearman, 6 Feb 1881, 15 Feb 1869, 2 March 1886, 13 March 1887, 16 July 1870, 16 Aug 1875, 18 Oct 1873

Bodichon, Barbara Leigh Smith, 21 Jan 1858, 10 Feb 1858, 3 June 1858, 6 Dec 1857, 11 Dec 1857, 12 Dec 1857

Boswell, James, 1 Jan 1763, 2 Jan 1763, 4 Feb 1777, 12 March 1780, 7 April 1779, 11 Aug 1782, 23 Sept 1773, 4 Nov 1774, 25 Nov 1762, 1 Dec 1762, 2 Dec 1775, 8 Dec 1762, 9 Dec 1775

Boyle, Jimmy, 2 Jan 1978, 17 April 1976, 26 June 1976, 23 Aug 1975, 26 Oct 1981, 10 Dec 1976

Brandreth, Gyles, 9 Feb 1991, 12 April 1994, 17 May 1990, 8 June 1992, 26 Nov 1992

Brecht, Bertolt, 10 Feb 1922, 18 June 1920, 19 July 1920, 24 Aug 1920

Brittain, Vera, 8 Jan 1943, 29 March 1943, 30 March 1943, 9 April 1942, 13 April 1945, 28 April 1943, 1 May 1945, 19 May 1941, 26 July 1943, 17 Sept 1945, 30 Sept 1915

Brown, Ford Madox, 13 March 1856, 14 March 1856, 22 Aug 1854

Browning, Elizabeth Barrett, 4 June 1831, 6 Sept 1831

Bull, Deborah, 2 May 1997, 13 May 1997, 10 June 1997, 31 Aug 1997, 1 Sept 1997, 6 Sept 1997, 15 Dec 1997

Burney, Fanny, 27 March 1768, 17 July 1768

Byron, Lord, 5 Jan 1821, 9 Jan 1821, 16 Jan 1814, 2 Feb 1821, 18 Feb 1814, 27 Feb 1814, 15 Oct 1821, 14 Nov 1813, 24 Nov 1813, 6 Dec 1813, 7 Dec 1813